# AN EXEGETICAL SUMMARY OF
# ACTS 15–28

# AN EXEGETICAL SUMMARY OF
# ACTS 15–28

David Abernathy

Robert Stutzman

SIL International®
Dallas, Texas

©2018 by SIL International®

ISBN: 978-1-55671-438-2

Library of Congress Control Number: 2018947310
Printed in the United States of America

All Rights Reserved
No part of this publication may be reproduced, stored in a retrieval system, or transmitted in any form or by any means—electronic, mechanical, photocopy, recording, or otherwise—without the express permission of SIL International®, with the exception of brief excerpts in journal articles or reviews.

Copies of this and other publications of SIL International® may be obtained through distributors such as Amazon, Barnes & Noble, other worldwide distributors and, for select volumes, www.sil.org/resources/publications:

SIL International Publications
7500 West Camp Wisdom Road
Dallas, TX 75236-5629, USA

General inquiry: publications_intl@sil.org
Pending order inquiry: sales_intl@sil.org
www.sil.org/resources/publications

# PREFACE

Exegesis is concerned with the interpretation of a text. Thus, exegesis of the New Testament involves determining the meaning of the Greek text. Translators must be especially careful and thorough in their exegesis of the New Testament in order to accurately communicate its message in the vocabulary, grammar, and literary restraints of another language. Questions occurring to translators as they study the Greek text are answered by summarizing how scholars have interpreted the text. This is information that should be considered by translators as they make their own exegetical decisions regarding the message they will communicate in their translations.

## The Semi-Literal Translation

As a basis for discussion, a semi-literal translation of the Greek text is given so that the reasons for different interpretations can best be seen. When one Greek word is translated into English by several words, these words are joined by hyphens. There are a few times when clarity requires that a string of words joined by hyphens have a separate word, such as "not" (μή), inserted in their midst. In this case, the separate word is surrounded by spaces between the hyphens. When alternate translations of a Greek word are given, these are separated by slashes.

## The Text

Variations in the Greek text are noted under the heading TEXT. The base text for the summary is the text of the fourth revised edition of *The Greek New Testament,* published by the United Bible Societies, which has the same text as the twenty-sixth edition of the *Novum Testamentum Graece* (Nestle-Aland). The versions that follow different variations are listed without evaluating their choices.

## The Lexicon

The meaning of a key word in context is the first question to be answered. Words marked with a raised letter in the semi-literal translation are treated separately under the heading LEXICON. First, the lexicon form of the Greek word is given. Within the parentheses following the Greek word is the location number where, in the author's judgment, this word is defined in the *Greek-English Lexicon of the New Testament Based on Semantic Domains* (Louw and Nida 1988). If the specific reference for the verse is listed in *A Greek-English Lexicon of the New Testament and Other Early Christian Literature* (Danker and Bauer 2000), the outline location and page number is given. Then English equivalents of the Greek word are given to show how it is translated by those commentaries which have translations of the whole Greek text and, after a semicolon, by twelve major versions. "All versions" refers only to those versions used in the lexicon. "All translations" refers to both the versions and the commentaries used in the lexicon. Sometimes further comments are made about the meaning of the word or the significance of a verb's tense, voice, or mood.

**The Questions**

Under the heading QUESTION, a question is asked that comes from examining the Greek text under consideration. Typical questions concern the identity of an implied actor or object of an event word, the antecedent of a pronominal reference, the connection indicated by a relational word, the meaning of a genitive construction, the meaning of figurative language, the function of a rhetorical question, the identification of an ambiguity, and the presence of implied information that is needed to understand the passage correctly. Background information is also considered for a proper understanding of a passage. Although not all implied information and background information is made explicit in a translation, it is important to consider it so that the translation will not be stated in such a way that prevents a reader from arriving at the proper interpretation. The question is answered with a summary of what commentators have said. If there are contrasting differences of opinion, the different interpretations are numbered and the commentaries that support each are listed. Differences that are not treated by many of the commentaries often are not numbered, but are introduced with a contrastive 'Or' at the beginning of the sentence. No attempt has been made to select which interpretation is best.

**The Use of this Book**

This book does not replace the commentaries that it summarizes. Commentaries contain much more information about the meaning of words and passages. They often contain arguments for the interpretations that are taken and they may have important discussions about the discourse features of the text. In addition, they often have information about the historical, geographical, and cultural setting. Translators will want to refer to at least four commentaries as they exegete a passage. However, since no one commentary contains all the answers translators need, this book will be a valuable supplement. It makes more sources of exegetical help available than those to which most translators have access. Even if they had all the books available, few would have the time to search through all of them for the answers.

When many commentaries are studied, it soon becomes apparent that they frequently disagree in their interpretations. That is the reason why so many answers in this book are divided into two or more interpretations. The reader's initial reaction may be that all of these different interpretations complicate exegesis rather than help it. However, before translating a passage, a translator needs to know exactly where there is a problem of interpretation and what the exegetical options are.

**Acknowledgments**

We would like to acknowledge Richard C. Blight for his substantial contribution to the Exegetical Summary series for many years, both as editor of the series and as author of numerous individual volumes.

# ABBREVIATIONS

## COMMENTARIES AND REFERENCE BOOKS

AB    Munck, Johannes. *The Acts of the Apostles*. The Anchor Bible. Revised by William F. Albright and C. S. Mann. Garden City, NY: Doubleday, 1967.

Bar    Barrett, C. K. *The Acts of the Apostles: A Shorter Commentary*. London & New York: T & T Clark, 2002.

BDAG    Danker, Frederick William (Editor), Walter Bauer (Author). *A Greek–English Lexicon of the New Testament and Other Early Christian Literature, 3rd Edition*. Chicago: University of Chicago Press, 2000.

BECNT    Bock, Darrell L. *Acts*. Baker Exegetical Commentary on the New Testament. Grand Rapids: Baker Academic, 2007.

CBC    Packer, J. W. *The Acts of the Apostles*. Cambridge Bible Commentary. Cambridge: Cambridge University Press, 1973.

EBC    Longenecker, Richard N. "The Acts of the Apostles." The Expositor's Bible Commentary, Vol. 9. Grand Rapids: Zondervan, 1981.

LN    Louw, Johannes P., and Eugene A. Nida. *Greek–English Lexicon of the New Testament Based on Semantic Domains*. New York: United Bible Societies, 1988.

NAC    Polhill, John B. *Acts*. The New American Commentary. Nashville: Broadman and Holman, 2001.

NICNT    Bruce, F. F. *The Book of the Acts, Revised Edition*. The New International Commentary on the New Testament. Grand Rapids: Eerdmans, 1988.

PNTC    Peterson, David G. *The Acts of the Apostles*. The Pillar New Testament Commentary. Grand Rapids: Eerdmans, 2009.

TH    Newman, Barclay M., and Eugene Α. Nida. *A Translator's Handbook on the Acts of the Apostles*. London: United Bible Societies, 1972.

TNTC    Marshall, I. Howard. *Acts*. The Tyndale New Testament Commentaries. Grand Rapids: Eerdmans, 1980.

TRT    Carlton, Matthew E. *The Translator's Reference Translation of the Acts of the Apostles*. Dallas: SIL International, 2001.

## GREEK TEXT AND TRANSLATIONS

| | |
|---|---|
| GNT | The Greek New Testament. Edited by B. Aland, K. Aland, J. Karavidopoulos, C. Martini, and B. Metzger. Fourth ed. London, New York: United Bible Societies, 1993. |
| LXX | The Septuagint. The Greek translation of the Jewish Scriptures, translated between 300–200 BC in Alexandria, Egypt. |
| CEV | The Holy Bible, Contemporary English Version. New York: American Bible Society, 1995. |
| ESV | The Holy Bible, English Standard Version. Wheaton: Crossway Bibles, a division of Good News Publishers, 2001. |
| GW | God's Word. Grand Rapids: World Publishing, 1995. |
| KJV | The Holy Bible. Authorized (or King James) Version. 1611. |
| NASB | New American Standard Bible. La Habra, CA: Lockman Foundation, 1995. |
| NCV | New Century Version. Dallas: Word Publishing, 1991. |
| NET | The NET Bible, New English Translation. Version 6r,715, Biblical Studies Press, 2006. |
| NIV | The Holy Bible, New International Version. Grand Rapids: Zondervan, 1995. |
| NLT | The Holy Bible, New Living Translation. Wheaton: Tyndale House, 1996. |
| NRSV | The Holy Bible: New Revised Standard Version. New York: Oxford University Press, 1989. |
| REB | The Revised English Bible. Oxford: Oxford University Press and Cambridge University Press, 1989. |
| TEV | Good News Bible, Today's English Version. Second edition. New York: American Bible Society, 1992. |

## GRAMMATICAL TERMS

| | | | |
|---|---|---|---|
| act. | active | mid. | middle |
| fut. | future | opt. | optative |
| impera. | imperative | pass. | passive |
| imperf. | imperfect | perf. | perfect |
| indic. | indicative | pres. | present |
| infin. | infinitive | subj. | subjunctive |

# EXEGETICAL SUMMARY OF ACTS 15–28

**DISCOURSE UNIT—15:1–35** [BECNT, CBC, NAC, NICNT, PNTC, TNTC; GW, NET]. The topic is the council of Jerusalem [NICNT], the Jerusalem council [PNTC; NET], the assembly at Jerusalem [TNTC], consultation at Jerusalem [BECNT], the great decision [CBC], debate in Jerusalem over acceptance of the Gentiles [NAC], controversy about Moses' teachings [GW].

**DISCOURSE UNIT—15:1–29** [EBC]. The topic is the Jerusalem council.

**DISCOURSE UNIT—15:1–21** [ESV, NCV, NIV, NLT, NRSV, TEV]. The topic is the Jerusalem council [ESV], the council at Jerusalem [NIV, NLT, NRSV], the meeting at Jerusalem [NCV, TEV].

**DISCOURSE UNIT—15:1–12** [NASB]. The topic is the council at Jerusalem.

**DISCOURSE UNIT—15:1–5** [AB, Bar, BECNT, NAC, PNTC]. The topic is dispute in Antioch [Bar], the problem [BECNT], preliminaries to the apostolic council [AB], the criticism from the Circumcision party [NAC], the need for the council [PNTC].

**DISCOURSE UNIT—15:1–4** [EBC]. The topic is the delegation from Syrian Antioch.

**DISCOURSE UNIT—15:1–2** [NICNT]. The topic is Judaizers visit Antioch.

**15:1** Some men **came-down**[a] from Judea and were-teaching the **brothers**,[b] "Unless **you-are-circumcised**[c] according to the **custom**[d] of-Moses, you cannot **be-saved**.[e]"

LEXICON—a. aorist act. participle of κατέρχομαι (LN 15.107) (BDAG 1. p. 531): 'to come down' [AB, Bar, BDAG, BECNT, CBC, LN; ESV, KJV, NASB, NET, NIV, NRSV, REB], 'to move down, to go down, to descend' [LN], 'to come' [CEV, GW, NCV, TEV], 'to arrive' [NLT]. This verb means to move down, irrespective of the gradient [LN]. It means to move in a direction considered the opposite of up but not necessarily with suggestion of a gradient [BDAG].

b. ἀδελφός (LN 11.23): 'brother' [Bar, BECNT; ESV, KJV, NET, NIV, NRSV], 'believer' [GW, NCV], 'fellow believer, a Christian brother' [LN]. The phrase 'the brothers' is also translated 'the Lord's followers' [CEV], 'the believers' [NLT, TEV], 'the brotherhood' [CBC; REB], 'the brethren' [AB; NASB]. This noun denotes a close associate of a group of persons having a well-defined membership. In the NT ἀδελφός 'brother' refers specifically to fellow believers in Christ [LN].

c. aorist pass. subj. of περιτέμνω (LN 53.51) (BDAG a. p. 807): 'to be circumcised' [BDAG, LN; all translations]. This verb means to cut off the foreskin of the male genital organ as a religious rite involving consecration and ethnic identification [LN].

d. ἔθος (LN 41.25) (BDAG 2. p. 277): 'custom' [BDAG, BECNT, LN; ESV, NASB, NET, NIV, NRSV], 'manner' [KJV], 'habit' [LN]. The phrase 'according to the custom of Moses' is also translated 'as Moses had taught' [CEV], 'as Moses taught us' [NCV], 'as Moses' Teachings require' [GW], 'as required by the law of Moses' [NLT], 'as the Law of Moses requires' [TEV], 'in accordance with Mosaic practice' [CBC; REB], 'in accordance with the Mosaic practice' [Bar], 'according to Mosaic law' [AB]. This noun denotes a pattern of behavior more or less fixed by tradition and generally sanctioned by the society [LN]. It denotes a long-established usage or practice common to a group [BDAG].
e. aorist pass. infin. of σῴζω (LN 21.27) (BDAG 2.b. p. 983): 'to be saved' [BDAG, LN; all translations]. This verb means to cause someone to experience divine salvation [LN]. It means to save or preserve from transcendent danger or destruction [BDAG].

QUESTION—Who were the men who came down?
They were Jewish Christians/believers [AB, BECNT, EBC, NAC, TNTC, TRT]. They may be messengers from James (Gal. 2:12) who exceed their authority by insisting on circumcision or they may be false brothers secretly brought in (Gal. 2:4) to spy out Paul and company [BECNT, NICNT].

QUESTION—Who were 'the brothers'?
They were Gentile Christians [AB, TNTC, TRT]. They were uncircumcised believers [Bar]. They were fellow believers [TH].

QUESTION—What is meant by 'according to the custom of Moses'?
It means according to the Mosaic law [AB]. It means, the precepts of the law of Moses [NAC]. 'The custom of Moses' refers to the requirements of the Mosaic Law [TH].

QUESTION—What is meant by 'be saved'?
It means to receive in full the benefits provided by God for his people. Also see 4:12 [Bar].

**15:2** **And after Paul and Barnabas had no small dissension**[a] **and debate**[b] **with them, Paul and Barnabas and some of the others were-appointed**[c] **to-go-up**[d] **to Jerusalem to the apostles and the elders**[e] **about this question.**

LEXICON—a. στάσις (LN 33.448) (BDAG 3. p. 940): 'dissension' [AB, CBC; ESV, KJV, NASB, NRSV, REB], 'trouble' [CEV], 'argument' [NET], 'dispute' [NIV], 'contention' [Bar], 'tension' [BECNT], 'quarrel' [LN], 'policy, strife, discord, disunion' [BDAG], not explicit [GW, TEV]. This noun is also translated as a verb: 'Paul and Barnabas disagreed' [NLT]. The phrase 'Paul and Barnabas had no small dissension' is also translated 'Paul and Barnabas were against this' [NCV]. This noun denotes intense and emotional expressions of different opinions [LN]. It denotes a lack of agreement respecting policy [BDAG].
b. ζήτησις (LN 33.440) (BDAG 3. p. 429): 'debate' [BDAG, BECNT; ESV, NASB, NET, NIV, NRSV], 'discussion' [Bar, BDAG], 'argument' [BDAG; TEV], 'dispute' [LN; GW], 'disputation' [KJV], 'controversy'

[AB, CBC; REB]. This noun is also translated as a verb: 'Paul and Barnabas argued with them' [CEV, NCV], 'Paul and Barnabas…arguing vehemently' [NLT]. This noun denotes an expression of forceful differences of opinion without necessarily having a presumed goal of seeking a solution [LN]. It denotes an engagement in a controversial discussion [BDAG].
- c. aorist act. indic. of τάσσω (LN 37.96) (BDAG 2.a. p. 991): 'to appoint' [Bar, BDAG, LN; NET], 'to designate, to assign, to give a task to' [LN], 'to order' [BDAG], 'to determine' [BDAG; KJV, NASB]. This verb is also translated as a passive verb: 'were appointed' [BECNT; ESV, NIV, NRSV]. The phrase 'Paul and Barnabas and some of the others were appointed to go up' is also translated 'it was decided to send Paul and Barnabas and a few others' [CEV], 'it was decided that Paul and Barnabas and some of the others…should go' [TEV], 'it was decided that Paul and Barnabas and some of the brethren should go up' [AB], 'Paul and Barnabas and some others were sent' [GW], 'the church decided to send Paul, Barnabas, and some others' [NCV], 'the church decided to send Paul and Barnabas' [NLT], 'it was arranged that these two and some others…should go up' [CBC; REB]. This verb means to assign someone to a particular task, function, or role [LN]. This verb means to give instructions as to what must be done [BDAG].
- d. pres. act. infin. of ἀναβαίνω (LN 15.101) (BDAG 1.a.α. p. 58): 'to go up' [AB, Bar, BDAG, BECNT, CBC, LN; ESV, KJV, NASB, NET, NIV, NRSV, REB], 'to come up, to ascend' [LN], 'to go' [TEV], not explicit [CEV, GW, NCV, NLT]. This verb means to move up [LN]. It means to be in motion upward without special focus on making ascent [BDAG].
- e. πρεσβύτερος (LN 53.77) (BDAG 2.b.α. p. 862): 'elder' [BDAG, LN; all translations except CEV, GW], 'presbyter' [BDAG], 'leader' [CEV, GW]. This noun denotes a person of responsibility and authority in matters of socio-religious concerns, both in Jewish and Christian societies [LN]. It denotes an official among the Christians [BDAG].

QUESTION—To whom does 'some of the others' refer to?

They were a number of other responsible members [NICNT].

QUESTION—Who appointed Paul and Barnabas and the others to go up to Jerusalem?

Probably they are the Christians of Antioch [Bar]. The entire congregation at Antioch and its leaders [EBC]. They could be the believers at Antioch or the men from Judea [TRT].

**DISCOURSE UNIT—15:3–21** [CEV]. The topic is the church leaders meet in Jerusalem.

**DISCOURSE UNIT—15:3–5** [NICNT]. The topic is Paul and Barnabas go up to Jerusalem.

**15:3** So, being-sent-on-their-way[a] by the church,[b] they-passed-through[c] both Phoenicia and Samaria, describing-in-detail[d] the conversion[e] of-the Gentiles, and brought great joy to-all the brothers.[f]

LEXICON—a. aorist pass. participle of προπέμπω (LN 15.72) (BDAG 2. p. 873): 'to be sent on their way' [AB, Bar, BECNT, CBC; ESV, NASB, NET, NRSV, REB, TEV], 'to be sent on one's way' [BDAG, LN], 'to be helped on one's way' [LN], 'to be brought on their way' [KJV], 'to be sent' [CEV]. This verb is also translated as an active verb: 'The church sent' [GW, NIV, NLT]. The phrase 'being sent on their way by the church' is also translated 'the church helped them leave on the trip' [NCV]. This verb means to send someone on in the direction in which he has already been moving, with the probable implication of providing help [LN]. It means to assist someone in making a journey [BDAG].

b. ἐκκλησία (LN 11.32) (BDAG 3.b.β. p. 304): 'church' [AB, Bar, BDAG, BECNT, LN; all versions], 'congregation' [BDAG, CBC, LN]. This noun denotes a congregation of Christians, implying interacting membership [LN]. It denotes the totality of Christians living and meeting in a particular locality or larger geographical area, but not necessarily limited to one meeting place [BDAG].

c. imperf. mid./pass. (deponent = act.) of διέρχομαι (LN 15.21) (BDAG 1.b.α. p. 244): 'to pass through' [ESV, KJV, NASB, NET, NRSV], 'to go through' [BDAG; CEV, GW, NCV, TEV], 'to travel through' [AB, Bar, CBC; NIV, REB], 'to come through' [BECNT], 'to travel around through, to journey all through' [LN], not explicit [NLT]. This verb means to travel around through an area, with the implication of both extensive and thorough movement throughout an area [LN]. It means to move within or through an area [BDAG].

d. pres. mid./pass. (deponent = act.) participle of ἐκδιηγέομαι (LN 33.201) (BDAG p. 300): 'to describe in detail' [ESV, NASB], 'to inform, to relate, to tell fully' [LN], 'to tell' [AB, BDAG; CEV, NCV, NIV, NLT], 'to report' [BECNT; NRSV, TEV], 'to declare' [KJV], 'to recount' [Bar]. The phrase 'describing in detail' is also translated 'they were relating at length' [NET], 'they fully related' [LN], 'telling the full story' [CBC; REB], 'told the whole story' [GW]. This verb means to provide detailed information in a systematic manner [LN]. It means to provide detailed information when telling something [BDAG].

e. ἐπιστροφή (LN 41.51) (BDAG 2. p. 382): 'conversion' [AB, Bar, BDAG, BECNT, CBC; ESV, KJV, NASB, NET, NRSV, REB], 'repentance' [LN], 'to change one's ways' [LN]. This noun is also translated as an active verb: 'turned to God' [CEV, GW, NCV, TEV], 'they reported how the Gentiles had turned to God' [LN]. This noun is also translated as a passive verb: 'the Gentiles had been converted' [NIV], 'the Gentiles, too, were being converted' [NLT]. This noun denotes a change in one's manner of life in a particular direction, with the

implication of turning back to God [LN]. It denotes a change of one's way of thinking or believing [BDAG].
- f. ἀδελφός (LN 11.23): 'brother' [Bar; ESV, NET, NIV], 'fellow believer, a Christian brother' [LN]. The phrase 'the brothers' is also translated 'the believers' [GW, NCV, NLT, NRSV, TEV], 'the Lord's followers' [CEV], 'the Christians' [CBC; REB], 'the brethren' [AB, BECNT; KJV, NASB]. This noun denotes a close associate of a group of persons having a well-defined membership. In the NT ἀδελφός 'brother' refers specifically to fellow believers in Christ [LN].

QUESTION—Where was Phoenicia?

The term describes the coastal area of Palestine stretching northward from Carmel and bordering in the south on Samaria [Bar, PNTC].

**15:4** When they came[a] to Jerusalem, they-were-welcomed[b] by the church and the apostles and the elders, and they-reported[c] all that God had done with them.

LEXICON—a. aorist mid. (deponent = act.) participle of παραγίνομαι (LN 15.86) (BDAG 1.a. p. 760): 'to come' [AB, BDAG, BECNT, LN; ESV, KJV, NIV, NRSV], 'to arrive' [BDAG, LN; CEV, GW, NASB, NCV, NET, NLT, TEV], 'to be present' [BDAG], 'to come to be present' [LN], 'to reach' [Bar, CBC; REB]. This verb means to come to be present at a particular place [LN]. It means to be in movement so as to be present at a particular place [BDAG].
- b. aorist pass. indic. of παραδέχομαι (LN 34.53) (BDAG 2. p. 761): 'to be welcomed' [Bar, BECNT, CBC, LN; CEV, ESV, NCV, NIV, NLT, NRSV, REB, TEV], 'to be received' [AB, BDAG, LN; KJV, NASB, NET], 'to be accepted' [BDAG, LN]. This verb is also translated as an active verb: 'the church in Jerusalem, the apostles, and the spiritual leaders welcomed Paul and Barnabas' [GW]. This verb means to accept the presence of a person with friendliness [LN]. It means to accept the presence of someone in a hospitable manner [BDAG].
- c. aorist act. indic. of ἀναγγέλλω (LN 33.197) (BDAG 1. p. 59): 'to report' [Bar, BDAG, CBC; GW, NASB, NET, NIV, NLT, NRSV, REB], 'to announce, to inform' [LN], 'to tell' [AB, LN; CEV, NCV, TEV], 'to declare' [BECNT; ESV, KJV]. This verb means to provide information, with the possible implication of considerable detail [LN]. It means to carry back information [BDAG].

QUESTION—Who does 'the church' refer to here?

'The church' here probably refers to those Christians who did not hold office, as apostles or elders [Bar].

**DISCOURSE UNIT**—**15:5–12** [EBC]. The topic is the nature and course of the debate.

**15:5** But[a] some believers who belonged to the party[b] of-the Pharisees rose-up[c] and said, "It-is-necessary[d] to-circumcise them and to-order-(them)[e] to-keep[f] the law[g] of-Moses."

LEXICON—a. δέ (LN 89.124): 'but' [AB, Bar, BECNT, LN; all versions except NIV], 'on the other hand' [LN], not explicit [CBC; NIV]. This conjunction indicates a contrast [LN].
  b. αἵρεσις (LN 11.50) (BDAG 1.a. p. 28): 'party' [AB, Bar, BDAG, BECNT, CBC; ESV, GW, NIV, REB, TEV], 'sect' [BDAG, LN; KJV, NASB, NLT, NRSV], 'group' [NCV], 'religious party' [LN; NET], 'school' [BDAG]. The phrase 'some believers who belonged to the party of the Pharisees' is also translated 'some Pharisees had become followers of the Lord' [CEV]. This noun denotes a division or group based upon different doctrinal opinions and/or loyalties [LN]. It denotes a group that holds tenets distinctive to it [BDAG].
  c. aorist act. indic. of ἐξανίστημι (LN 17.11) (BDAG 3.a. p. 345): 'to rise up' [ESV, KJV], 'to stand up' [Bar, BDAG, LN; CEV, GW, NASB, NET, NIV, NLT, NRSV, TEV], 'to arise' [BECNT]. The phrase 'rose up' is also translated 'came forward' [AB, CBC; NCV, REB]. This verb means to stand up in a manner distinct from someone else [LN]. It means to come to the fore distinct from others to speak [BDAG].
  d. pres. act. indic. of δεῖ (LN 71.21) (BDAG 1.b. p. 214): 'it is necessary' [Bar, BDAG, BECNT; ESV, NASB, NET, NRSV], 'should do, to have to do' [LN], 'one must do, one has to do' [BDAG]. The phrase 'It is necessary to circumcise' is also translated 'must be circumcised' [AB, CBC; CEV, GW, NCV, NIV, NLT, REB, TEV], 'it was needful to circumcise' [KJV]. This verb means to be something which should be done as the result of compulsion, whether internal (as a matter of duty) or external (law, custom, and circumstances) [LN]. It means to be under necessity of happening, of the compulsion of law or custom [BDAG].
  e. pres. act. infin. of παραγγέλλω (LN 33.327) (BDAG p. 760): 'to order' [LN; ESV, GW, NET, NRSV], 'to command' [Bar, BDAG, BECNT, LN; KJV], 'to direct' [BDAG; NASB], 'to tell' [CBC; CEV, REB, TEV], 'to give orders, to instruct' [BDAG], 'to exhort' [AB]. This verb is also translated as a passive verb: 'to be told' [NCV], 'to be required' [NIV, NLT]. This verb means to announce what must be done [LN]. It means to make an announcement about something that must be done [BDAG].
  f. pres. act. infin. of τηρέω (LN 36.19) (BDAG 3. p. 1002): 'to keep' [AB, BDAG, BECNT, CBC; ESV, KJV, NRSV, REB], 'to observe' [Bar, BDAG; NASB, NET], 'to obey' [LN; CEV, NCV, NIV, TEV], 'to follow' [GW, NLT], 'to keep commandments' [LN], 'to fulfill, to pay attention to' [BDAG]. This verb means to continue to obey orders or commandments [LN]. It means to persist in obedience [BDAG].
  g. νόμος (LN 33.55) (BDAG 2.b. p. 677): 'law' [Bar, BDAG, BECNT, CBC, LN; all versions except GW]. The phrase 'the law of Moses' is also translated 'Moses' Teachings' [GW], 'the Mosaic law' [AB]. This noun

denotes the first five books of the OT called the Torah, often better referred to as 'instruction'. In a number of languages it is not possible to use a singular expression such as 'the Law' since the Torah consisted of five books and included a number of regulations and instructions, so it is necessary in many languages to use 'the laws'. [LN]. It denotes a constitutional or statutory legal system and here it refers specifically to the law that Moses received from God [BDAG].

QUESTION—To whom does 'them' refer?

In this verse 'them' refers to the Gentile Christians in general [AB, CBC, EBC, NAC, PNTC]. It refers to Gentiles/non-Jews [TRT; CEV, GW, NCV, NET, NIV, NLT, REB, TEV].

**DISCOURSE UNIT—15:6–29** [Bar, PNTC]. The topic is council in Jerusalem [Bar], the proceedings of the council [PNTC].

**DISCOURSE UNIT—15:6–21** [AB, BECNT, NAC]. The topic is the negotiations at the apostolic council [AB], the discussion and decision [BECNT], the debate in Jerusalem [NAC].

**DISCOURSE UNIT—15:6** [NICNT]. The topic is the council meets.

**15:6** **The apostles and the elders were-gathered-together**[a] **to-consider**[b] **this matter.**[c]

TEXT—Some manuscripts add 'with the congregation' after πρεσβύτεροι 'elders'. The GNT gave the shorter version an A decision indicating that the text is certain.

LEXICON—a. aorist pass. indic. of συνάγω (LN 15.125) (BDAG 1.b. p. 962): 'to be gathered together' [BECNT, LN; ESV], 'to be called together' [LN], 'to gather' [BDAG]. This verb is also translated as an active verb: 'The apostles and the elders came together' [KJV, NASB], 'The apostles and church/spiritual leaders met' [CEV, GW], 'the apostles and the elders gathered/met together' [Bar; NET, NLT, NRSV, TEV], 'The apostles and the elders gathered/met' [AB; NCV, NIV, REB], 'The apostles and elders held a meeting' [CBC]. This verb means to cause to come together, whether of animate or inanimate objects [LN]. It means to cause persons to come together [BDAG].

b. aorist act. infin. of εἶδον (LN 30.45) (BDAG 3. p. 280): 'to consider' [AB, LN; ESV, GW, KJV, NCV, NIV, NRSV, TEV], 'to look into' [Bar, CBC; NASB, REB], 'to discuss' [CEV], 'to deliberate' [NET], 'to resolve' [NLT], 'to take notice of, to pay attention to, to concern oneself with' [LN], 'to see, to notice, to note' [BDAG], 'to take a look at' [BECNT]. This verb means to take special notice of something, with the implication of concerning oneself [LN]. It means to take special note of something [BDAG].

c. λόγος (LN 33.98) (BDAG 1.a.ε. p. 600): 'matter' [AB, Bar, BDAG, BECNT, CBC; ESV, KJV, NASB, NET, NRSV, REB], 'word' [BDAG, LN], 'statement' [LN; GW], 'question' [LN; NIV, TEV], 'saying, message' [LN], 'problem' [CEV, NCV], 'issue' [NLT]. This noun denotes that which has been stated or said, with primary focus upon the content of the communication [LN]. It denotes the subject under discussion [BDAG].

**DISCOURSE UNIT—15:7–11** [NICNT]. The topic is Peter's speech.

**15:7** And-(after) there had been much debate,[a] Peter stood-up[b] and said to them, "Men, brothers,[c] you know that in the early days God made a choice[d] among you, that by my mouth the Gentiles should hear the word[e] of-the gospel[f] and believe.[g]

LEXICON—a. ζήτησις (LN 33.440) (BDAG 3. p. 429): 'debate' [AB, BDAG, BECNT, CBC; ESV, GW, NASB, NCV, NET, NRSV, REB, TEV], 'discussion' [Bar, BDAG; NIV, NLT], 'argument' [BDAG], 'dispute' [LN; KJV]. This noun is also translated as a verb: 'They had talked it over' [CEV]. This noun denotes an act of expressing forceful differences of opinion without necessarily having a presumed goal of seeking a solution [LN]. It denotes the engagement in a controversial discussion [BDAG].

  b. aorist act. participle of ἀνίστημι (LN 17.6): 'to stand up' [AB, Bar, LN; ESV, GW, NASB, NCV, NET, NRSV, TEV], 'to stand' [NLT], 'to get up' [CEV, NIV], 'to rise up' [BECNT; KJV], 'to rise' [CBC; REB]. This verb means to assume a standing position [LN].

  c. ἀδελφός (LN 11.23) (BDAG 2.a. p. 18): 'brother' [AB, Bar, BDAG, BECNT; ESV, GW, NCV, NET, NIV, NLT, NRSV], 'fellow believer, a Christian brother' [LN], 'fellow member, member, associate' [BDAG]. The noun 'brothers' is also translated 'brethren' [KJV, NASB]. The phrase 'Men, brothers' is also translated 'My friends' [CBC; CEV, REB, TEV]. This noun denotes a close associate of a group of persons having a well-defined membership. In the NT ἀδελφός 'brother' refers specifically to fellow believers in Christ [LN]. It denotes a person viewed as a brother in terms of a close affinity [BDAG].

  d. aorist mid. indic. of ἐκλέγω (LN 30.92) (BDAG 2.c.γ. p. 305): 'to make a choice' [ESV, KJV, NASB, NIV, NRSV], 'to choose' [BECNT, LN; GW, NCV, NET, NLT, TEV], 'to select someone/something for oneself' [BDAG]. The phrase 'God made a choice' is also translated 'God made his choice' [Bar, CBC; REB], 'God decided' [CEV], 'God made the decision' [AB]. This verb means to make a special choice based upon significant preference, often implying a strongly favorable attitude toward what is chosen [LN]. It means to make a choice in accordance with significant preference [BDAG].

  e. λόγος (LN 33.98) (BDAG 1.a.β. p. 600): 'word' [Bar, BDAG, BECNT, LN; ESV, KJV, NASB], 'message' [CBC, LN; NET, NIV, NRSV, REB], 'saying, statement' [LN], not explicit [AB; CEV, GW, NCV, NLT, TEV]. This noun denotes that which has been stated or said, with primary focus upon the content of the communication [LN]. It denotes a communication whereby the mind finds expression [BDAG].

f. εὐαγγέλιον (LN 33.217) (BDAG 1.a.β. p. 402): 'the gospel' [AB, Bar, BECNT, CBC, LN; ESV, KJV, NASB, NET, NIV, REB], 'the good news' [BDAG, LN; CEV, GW, NCV, NLT, NRSV, TEV]. This noun denotes the content of the good news and in the NT it is a reference to the gospel about Jesus [LN]. It denotes God's good news to humans [BDAG].

g. aorist act. infin. of πιστεύω (LN 31.102) (BDAG 2.b. p. 817): 'to believe' [all translations except CEV, NRSV], 'to believe (in), to trust' [BDAG]. This verb is also translated as a noun: 'become believers' [NRSV]. The phrase 'hear the word of the gospel and believe' is also translated 'hear and obey him' [CEV]. This verb means to believe in the good news about Jesus Christ and to become a follower [LN]. It means to entrust oneself to an entity in complete confidence [BDAG].

QUESTION—What is meant by 'in the early days'?

It probably refers to the early days of the Christian movement [Bar]. Peter goes back to the 'days of the beginning' or the start of these events concerning Gentiles. He has gone back as much as a decade in time [BECNT]. Peter speaks of his experiences at Joppa and Caesarea (as one supposes him to mean) as 'in the early days' [CBC]. It refers to Peter's experience in the household of Cornelius, possibly as much as ten years before [NAC]. Peter is referring to the events narrated in chapter 10, which had taken place some ten years before [TH].

**15:8** And God, who-knows[a] the heart, bore-witness[b] to-them, by giving[c] them the Holy Spirit[d] just-as he also did to-us,

LEXICON—a. καρδιογνώστης (LN 28.12) (BDAG p. 509): 'one who knows the heart' [AB, Bar, BDAG, BECNT, LN; ESV, KJV, NASB, NET, NIV, NRSV], 'knower of the heart' [BDAG], 'one who knows what people think' [LN]. The phrase 'God, who knows the heart' is also translated 'He knows what is in everyone's heart' [CEV], 'God, who knows everyone's thoughts' [GW], 'God, who knows the thoughts of everyone' [NCV, TEV], 'God knows people's hearts' [NLT], 'God, who can read human hearts' [REB], 'God, who can read men's minds' [CBC]. This noun denotes one who knows what someone else thinks (literally 'to know what is in the heart') [LN].

b. aorist act. indic. of μαρτυρέω (LN 33.262) (BDAG 1.a.α. p. 618): 'to bear witness' [Bar, BDAG; ESV, KJV], 'to witness' [BECNT, LN], 'to be a witness' [BDAG], 'to testify' [NASB, NET, NRSV], 'to confirm' [AB; NLT]. The phrase 'God...bore witness to them' is also translated 'God...accepted them' [NCV], 'God...showed his approval of them' [CBC], 'God...showed that he accepted them' [NIV], 'God...showed his approval of the Gentiles' [TEV], 'God...showed his approval' [REB], 'God...showed that he approved of people who aren't Jewish' [GW], 'he showed that he had chosen the Gentiles' [CEV]. This verb means to provide information about a person or an event concerning which the

speaker has direct knowledge [LN]. It means to confirm or attest something on the basis of personal knowledge or belief [BDAG].
c. aorist act. participle of δίδωμι (LN 57.71): 'to give' [all translations]. This verb means to give an object, usually implying value [LN].
d. πνεῦμα (LN 12.18) (BDAG 5.c.α. p. 834): 'Spirit' [BDAG, LN; all translations except KJV], 'Spirit of God, Holy Spirit' [LN], 'Ghost' [KJV]. This noun denotes the third person of the Trinity whose titles are 'Spirit, Spirit of God, and Holy Spirit'. In many religious systems the significant difference between the gods and the spirits is that the gods are regarded as supernatural beings which control certain aspects of natural phenomena, while the spirits are supernatural beings, often impersonal, which indwell or inhabit certain places, including rivers, streams, mountains, caves, animals, and people. Spirits are often regarded as being primarily evil, though it may be possible to induce them to be favorable to people. It is extremely difficult to find in some languages a fully satisfactory term to speak of the Spirit of God. If one uses a term which normally identifies local supernatural beings, there is a tendency to read into the term the meaning of an evil or mischievous character. If, however, one uses a term which may identify the spirit of a person, the problems may even be greater, since according to many systems of religious belief, the spirit of an individual does not become active until the individual dies. Therefore, the activity of the Spirit of God would presumably suggest that God himself had died. However, if one uses a term which means 'heart' or 'soul' (and thus the Spirit of God would be literally equivalent to 'the heart of God'), there may be complications since this aspect of human personality is often regarded as not being able to act on its own. The solutions to the problem of 'Spirit' have been varied. In some languages the term for Spirit is essentially equivalent to 'the unseen one', and therefore the Spirit of God is essentially equivalent to 'the invisibleness of God'. In a number of languages the closest equivalent for Spirit is 'breath', and in a number of indigenous religious systems, the 'breath' is regarded as having a kind of independent existence. In other languages the term for Spirit is equivalent to what is often translated as 'the soul,' that is to say, the immaterial part of a person. There is, of course, always the difficulty of employing a term meaning 'soul' or 'life', since it often proves to be impersonal and thus provides no basis for speaking of the Spirit of God as being a person or a personal manifestation of God. In quite a few languages the equivalent of Spirit is literally 'shadow', since the 'shadow' of a person is regarded as the immaterial part of the individual. Moreover, in many systems of religious thought the shadow is regarded as having some significant measure of independent existence. In a few cases the term for Spirit is literally 'wind', but there are frequently difficulties involved in this type of terminology since a term for wind often suggests calamity or evil intent. One meaning of Spirit which must be clearly avoided is that of

'apparition' or 'ghost'. Frequently it is not possible to find a fully satisfactory term for 'Spirit', and therefore in all contexts some characterizing feature is added, for example, either 'of God' or 'holy', in the sense of 'divine'. [LN]. It denotes God's being as controlling influence, with focus on association with humans [BDAG].

QUESTION—What is meant by 'bore witness to them'?
This refers to their fitness for hearing and accepting the Gospel [Bar].

QUESTION—What is meant 'by giving them the Holy Spirit'?
It means 'by causing them to have the Holy Spirit' or 'by causing the Holy Spirit to come upon them' [TH].

**15:9** and he-made- no -distinction[a] between us and them, having-cleansed[b] their hearts[c] by-faith.[d]

LEXICON—a. aorist act. indic. of διακρίνω (LN 30.113) (BDAG 2. p. 231): 'to make a distinction' [Bar, BDAG, BECNT, LN; ESV, NASB, NET, NIV, NLT, NRSV], 'to judge that there is a difference' [LN], 'to differentiate' [BDAG], 'to discriminate' [GW]. The phrase 'he made no distinction between us and them' is also translated 'God treated them in the same way that he treated us' [CEV], 'And put no difference between us and them' [KJV], 'To God, those people are not different from us' [NCV], 'He made no difference between them and us' [CBC; REB], 'He made no difference between us and them' [TEV], 'He has made no difference in any respect between us' [AB]. This verb means to judge that there is a difference or distinction [LN]. It means to conclude that there is a difference [BDAG].

b. aorist act. participle of καθαρίζω (LN 53.28) (BDAG 3.b.α. p. 489): 'to cleanse' [Bar, BECNT, LN; ESV, GW, NASB, NET, NLT, NRSV], 'to purify' [AB, CBC, LN; KJV, NIV, REB], 'to make pure' [CEV, NCV], 'to make clean, to declare clean' [BDAG]. The phrase 'having cleansed their hearts' is also translated 'he forgave their sins' [TEV]. This verb means to cleanse from ritual contamination or impurity [LN]. It means to purify through ritual cleansing [BDAG].

c. καρδία (LN 26.3) (BDAG 1.b.δ. p. 509): 'heart' [BDAG, LN; all translations except GW, TEV], 'inner self, mind' [LN]. The phrase 'having cleansed their hearts by faith' is also translated 'He has cleansed non-Jewish people through faith' [GW], 'he forgave their sins because they believed' [TEV]. This noun denotes a figurative extension of meaning of καρδία 'heart' and denotes the causative source of a person's psychological life in its various aspects, but with special emphasis upon thoughts [LN]. It refers to the heart as the center of moral decisions, the inner life of vices and virtues [BDAG].

d. πίστις (LN 31.102) (BDAG 2.d.α. p. 819): 'faith' [BDAG; all translations except NCV, TEV], 'Christian faith' [LN], 'trust, confidence' [BDAG]. This noun is also translated as a verb: 'they believed' [NCV, TEV]. This noun denotes the belief in the good news about Jesus Christ and becoming a follower [LN]. It denotes a state of believing on the basis of the reliability of the one trusted [BDAG].

QUESTION—Who is referred to by 'us'?

It refers to 'we who are Jews' [TH, TRT; GW].

QUESTION—Who is referred to by 'them'?

It refers to 'they who are Gentiles' [TH, TRT; GW].

QUESTION—What is meant by 'having cleansed their hearts'?

It probably means the forgiveness of sins and inward renewal with a view to future obedience [Bar].

**15:10** Now, therefore, why are-you-putting- God -to-the-test[a] by placing (a)-yoke[b] on the neck of-the disciples that neither our fathers[c] nor we have-been-able[d] to-bear[e]?

LEXICON—a. pres. act. indic. of πειράζω (LN 88.308) (BDAG 2.c. p. 793): 'to put to the test' [Bar, BDAG; ESV, NASB, NET, NRSV, TEV], 'to test' [BECNT; GW, NCV], 'to tempt' [LN; KJV], 'to try to test' [NIV], 'to try' [AB, BDAG], 'to make trial of' [BDAG], 'to trap, to lead into temptation' [LN], 'to challenge' [NLT]. The phrase 'why are you putting God to the test' is also translated 'why are you trying to make God angry' [CEV], 'why do you now try God's patience' [REB], 'why do you now provoke God' [CBC]. This verb means to endeavor or attempt to cause someone to sin [LN]. It means to endeavor to discover the nature or character of something by testing [BDAG].

b. ζυγός (LN 22.27) (BDAG 1. p. 429): 'yoke' [AB, Bar, BDAG, BECNT, CBC; ESV, KJV, NASB, NET, NIV, NLT, NRSV, REB], 'burden' [LN; CEV, GW], 'load' [NCV, TEV]. The idiom 'to put a yoke upon the neck' means to cause difficulty to someone by requiring conformity to rules and regulations [LN]. It denotes a frame used to control working animals or, in the case of humans, to expedite the bearing of burdens [BDAG].

c. πατήρ (LN 10.20): 'father' [AB, Bar, BECNT, CBC; ESV, KJV, NASB, NIV], 'ancestor' [LN; CEV, GW, NCV, NET, NLT, NRSV, TEV], 'forefather' [LN; REB]. This noun denotes a person several preceding generations removed from the reference person [LN].

d. aorist act. indic. of ἰσχύω (LN 74.9) (BDAG 2.b. p. 484): 'to be able' [Bar, BDAG, BECNT, CBC; all versions except CEV, GW], 'to have the strength to' [AB, LN], 'to be able to, to be very capable of' [LN], 'to have power, to be competent' [BDAG], not explicit [CEV]. The phrase 'neither our fathers nor we have been able to bear' is also translated 'neither our ancestors nor we can carry' [GW]. This verb means to have special personal ability to do or experience something [LN]. It means to have requisite personal resources to accomplish something [BDAG].

e. aorist act. infin. of βαστάζω (LN 25.177) (BDAG 2.b.α. p. 171): 'to bear' [AB, Bar, BDAG, BECNT, CBC; ESV, KJV, NASB, NET, NIV, NLT, NRSV, REB], 'to endure' [LN], 'to bear up under' [LN], 'to carry' [BDAG; GW, NCV, TEV], not explicit [CEV]. This verb means to continue to bear up under unusually trying circumstances and difficulties [LN]. It means to sustain a burden and refers to bearing anything burdensome such as legal requirements here [BDAG].

QUESTION—What is meant by the expression 'putting God to the test'?

The expression 'putting God to the test' means to go against the revealed will of God to see if he would bring the deserved punishment [TH].

**15:11** But<sup>a</sup> we-believe<sup>b</sup> that we will-be-saved<sup>c</sup> through<sup>d</sup> the grace<sup>e</sup> of-the Lord Jesus in-(the-same)-way<sup>f</sup> as they-also will."

LEXICON—a. ἀλλά (LN 89.125): 'but' [BECNT, LN; CEV, ESV, KJV, NASB, NCV], 'on the contrary' [Bar, LN; NET, NRSV], 'instead' [LN], 'however' [AB], not explicit [CBC; GW, NIV, NLT, REB, TEV]. This conjunction indicates a more emphatic contrast [LN].

b. pres. act. indic. of πιστεύω (LN 31.85) (BDAG 1.a.γ. p. 816): 'to believe' [BDAG; all translations except CEV, REB], 'to believe in, to have confidence in, to have faith in, to trust' [LN]. This verb is also translated as a noun: 'we are saved by faith in him' [CEV], 'our belief is that we are saved' [REB]. This verb means to believe to the extent of complete trust and reliance [LN]. It means to consider something to be true and therefore worthy of one's trust [BDAG].

c. aorist pass. infin. of σῴζω (LN 21.27) (BDAG 2.b. p. 983): 'to be saved' [LN; all translations except GW], 'to be saved/preserved from eternal death' [BDAG]. This verb is also translated as an active verb: 'the Lord Jesus saves us' [GW]. This verb means to cause someone to experience divine salvation [LN]. It means to save or preserve from transcendent danger or destruction [LN].

d. διά with genitive object (LN 89.76): 'through' [Bar, BECNT, LN; ESV, GW, KJV, NASB, NET, NIV, NRSV], 'by' [AB, CBC, LN; CEV, NCV, NLT, REB, TEV], 'by means of' [LN]. This preposition is a marker of the means by which one event makes another event possible [LN].

e. χάρις (LN 88.66) (BDAG 2.a. p. 1079): 'grace' [BDAG, LN; all translations except CEV, GW], 'kindness' [LN; GW], 'graciousness' [LN], 'favor, gracious care/help, goodwill' [BDAG]. This noun is also translated as a verb: 'our Lord Jesus was kind to us' [CEV]. This noun denotes the kindness shown to someone, with the implication of graciousness on the part of the one showing such kindness [LN]. It denotes a beneficent disposition toward someone. Here it denotes the beneficence or favor of Christ [BDAG].

f. τρόπος (LN 89.83): 'way' [Bar, LN; GW, NASB, NET, NLT, REB], 'manner' [LN]. The phrase 'in the same way as' is also translated 'just as' [AB, BECNT; CEV, ESV, NIV, NRSV, TEV], 'even as' [KJV], not explicit [CBC; NCV]. This noun denotes the manner in which something is done [LN].

QUESTION—How is the phrase 'we believe that we will be saved' to be understood?

This phrase may be understood in one of three ways. 1. We believe and are saved, a present experience. 2. We believe that we shall be saved, a reference to the future. 3. We believe we have been saved, a past fact. Many modern exegetes believe that this context points more naturally to the present tense [TH].

QUESTION—To whom does 'they' refer?

It is most naturally taken to refer to the Gentile believers [Bar; CEV], but 'our fathers' is the nearest antecedent and cannot be excluded as a possibility, though a less likely one [Bar].

**DISCOURSE UNIT—15:12** [NICNT]. The topic is Paul and Barnabas address the council.

**15:12 And all the people kept-silent,[a] and they-listened to-Barnabas and Paul as they related what signs[b] and wonders[c] God had-done[d] through them among the Gentiles.**

LEXICON—a. aorist act. indic. of σιγάω (LN 33.121) (BDAG 1.a. p. 922): 'to keep silent' [BDAG; KJV, NASB, NRSV], 'to keep quiet' [CEV, NET], 'to be silent' [GW, TEV], 'to become quiet' [NCV], 'to become silent' [BECNT; NIV], 'to fall silent' [AB, Bar, CBC; ESV, REB], 'to say nothing, to keep still' [BDAG], 'to keep quiet about, to say nothing about' [LN]. The phrase 'all the people kept silent, and they listened' is also translated 'Everyone listened quietly' [NLT]. This verb means to keep quiet, with the implication of preserving something which is secret [LN]. It means to be silent [BDAG].

b. σημεῖον (LN 33.477) (BDAG 2.a.α. p. 920): 'sign' [AB, Bar, BECNT, CBC, LN; ESV, NASB, NET, NIV, NLT, NRSV, REB], 'miracle' [BDAG; CEV, GW, KJV, NCV, TEV], 'portent' [BDAG]. This noun denotes an event which is regarded as having some special meaning [LN]. It denotes an event that is an indication or confirmation of intervention by transcendent powers [BDAG].

c. τέρας (LN 33.480): 'wonder' [AB, BECNT; all versions except GW, NCV, REB], 'sign' [LN; NCV], 'miracle' [CBC], 'portent' [Bar, LN; REB], 'amazing thing' [GW]. This noun denotes an unusual sign, especially one in the heavens, serving to foretell impending events [LN].

d. aorist act. indic. of ποιέω (LN 90.45): 'to do' [Bar, BECNT, LN; ESV, GW, NASB, NCV, NET, NIV, NLT, NRSV], 'to perform' [LN; TEV], 'to practice, to make' [LN], 'to work' [AB, CBC; KJV, REB]. The phrase 'what signs and wonders God had done through them' is also translated 'God had given them the power to work a lot of miracles and wonders' [CEV]. This verb is a marker of an agent relation with a numerable event [LN].

QUESTION—What is indicated by 'all the people kept silent'?
The silence that followed might indicate the impression made by Peter's speech, but it more likely indicated that it was now possible for the missionaries to the Gentiles to tell about God's action which demonstrated that the Gentiles should receive the gospel as Gentiles. [AB]. The silence of the assembly after Peter spoke implies that the turning point had come [EBC].

QUESTION—What is indicated by God working signs and wonders among the Gentiles?
That God would work miracles in the midst of the Gentiles is another divine indicator for Gentile inclusion [BECNT].

**DISCOURSE UNIT—15:13–35** [NASB]. The topic is James' judgment.

**DISCOURSE UNIT—15:13–21** [EBC, NICNT]. The topic is the summing up by James [EBC], James's summing up [NICNT].

**15:13** After they finished speaking, James replied, "Brothers,[a] listen[b] to-me.

LEXICON—a. ἀδελφός (LN 11.23) (BDAG 2.a. p. 18): 'brother' [AB, Bar, BDAG, BECNT; ESV, GW, NCV, NET, NIV, NLT, NRSV], 'fellow believer, a Christian brother' [LN], 'fellow member, associate' [BDAG]. 'Brothers' is also translated 'Brethren' [KJV, NASB], 'My friends' [CBC; CEV, REB, TEV]. This noun denotes a close associate of a group of persons having a well-defined membership. In the NT ἀδελφός 'brother' refers specifically to fellow believers in Christ [LN]. It denotes a person viewed as a brother in terms of a close affinity [BDAG].

b. aorist act. impera. of ἀκούω (LN 31.56): 'to listen to' [LN; all translations except KJV], 'to accept, to listen and respond, to pay attention and respond, to heed' [LN]. The phrase 'listen to me' is also translated 'hearken unto me' [KJV]. This verb means to believe something and to respond to it on the basis of having heard [LN].

QUESTION—Who was this James?
This James was probably the same James in 12:17 and 21:18 [Bar, BECNT]. Also he was probably the same James in Galatians 1:19, 2:9, 12 [Bar]. He was the Lord's brother [EBC, NAC, NICNT, TH].

**15:14** Simeon has-related[a] how God first visited[b] (the)-Gentiles, to-take[c] from them (a)-people[d] for his name.[e]

LEXICON—a. aorist mid. (deponent = act.) indic. of ἐξηγέομαι (LN 28.41) (BDAG 1. p. 349): 'to relate' [BECNT; ESV, NASB, NRSV], 'to tell' [AB, BDAG, CBC; CEV, NCV, NLT], 'to declare' [KJV], 'to explain' [GW, NET, TEV], 'to describe' [BDAG; NIV, REB], 'to report' [Bar, BDAG], 'to make fully and clearly known' [LN]. This verb means to make something fully known by careful explanation or by clear revelation [LN]. It means to relate in detail [BDAG].

    b. aorist mid. (deponent = act.) indic. of ἐπισκέπτομαι (LN 35.39) (BDAG 3. p. 378): 'to visit' [BECNT; ESV, KJV, NLT], 'to look after' [BDAG, LN], 'to take care of, to see to' [LN], 'to make an appearance to help' [BDAG], 'to be concerned' [NASB, NET], 'to show concern' [GW, NIV], 'to show love' [NCV], 'to show care' [LN; TEV], 'to provide for' [AB]. The phrase 'God first visited the Gentiles' is also translated 'God first came to the Gentiles' [CEV], 'God first looked favorably on the Gentiles' [NRSV], 'it first happened that God took notice of the Gentiles' [CBC], not explicit [Bar; REB]. This verb means to care for or look after, with the implication of continuous responsibility [LN]. It means to exercise oversight in behalf of [BDAG].

    c. aorist act. infin. of λαμβάνω (LN 30.86): 'to take' [AB, Bar; ESV, GW, KJV, NASB, NIV, NLT, NRSV, TEV], 'to select' [LN; NET], 'to choose' [CBC, LN; REB], 'to prefer' [LN], 'to accept' [NCV], 'to receive' [BECNT]. The phrase 'to take from them a people for his name' is also translated 'and made some of them his own people' [CEV]. This verb means to make a choice of one or more possible alternatives [LN].

    d. λαός (LN 11.12) (BDAG 4.b. p. 587): 'people' [BDAG; all translations], 'the people of God' [LN]. This noun denotes the people who belong to God, whether Jews or Christians [LN]. It denotes the people of God [BDAG].

    e. ὄνομα (LN 33.126): 'name' [AB, Bar, BECNT, CBC, LN; ESV, GW, KJV, NASB, NET, NRSV, REB]. The phrase 'to take for them a people for his name' is also translated 'to take from them a people for himself' [NLT], 'taking from the Gentiles a people for himself' [NIV], 'taking from among them a people to belong to him' [TEV], 'accepting from among them a people to be his own' [NCV], 'made some of them his own people' [CEV]. This noun denotes the proper name of a person or object [LN].

QUESTION—What is meant by 'for his name'?

    It means for his possession [EBC, PNTC].

**15:15** **And with-this the words**[a] **of-the prophets agree,**[b] **just-as it-is-written,**

LEXICON—a. λόγος (LN 33.98) (BDAG 1.b. p. 600): 'word' [BDAG, LN; all translations except CEV, GW, NLT], 'saying, message, statement' [LN]. The phrase 'the words of the prophets' is also translated 'what the prophets wrote/said/predicted' [CEV, GW, NLT]. This noun denotes that which has been stated or said, with primary focus upon the content of the communication [LN]. It denotes a communication whereby the mind finds expression and refers to literary or oratorical productions [BDAG].

    b. pres. act. indic. of συμφωνέω (LN 31.15) (BDAG 1.a. p. 961): 'to agree' [AB, Bar, CBC; all versions except NIV, NLT], 'to agree with' [BDAG, LN], not explicit [NLT]. The phrase 'the words of the prophets agree' is also translated 'the words of the prophets fit together' [BECNT]. This verb is also translated as a noun: 'the prophets are in agreement' [NIV].

This verb means to come to an agreement with, often implying a type of joint decision [LN]. It means to fit in with, to match with [BDAG].

QUESTION—What does 'the words of the prophets' refer to?

It refers to the part of the Old Testament scriptures known as 'the Prophets' re: the historical books (Joshua to Kings) and the prophetic books [Bar]. The reference is to the book of the twelve prophets, re: the scroll of the minor prophets as in 7:42, from which the citation from Amos 9:11f comes [TNTC].

QUESTION—What do the words of the prophets agree with?

The teaching of the prophets matches or agrees with the inclusion of the Gentiles. James is stressing fulfillment, for the prophets agree with what Peter has described. This is not an affirmation of analogous fulfillment but a declaration that this is now taking place. God had promised Gentile inclusion; now he is performing it [BECNT].

**15:16** "'After this I-will-return,ᵃ and I-will-rebuildᵇ the tent of-David that has-fallen;ᶜ I-will-rebuild its ruins, and I-will-restoreᵈ it,

LEXICON—a. fut. act. indic. of ἀναστρέφω (LN 15.89) (BDAG 3. p. 73): 'to return' [BDAG, LN; all translations], 'to move back' [LN], 'to come back' [BDAG]. This verb means to move back to a point or area from which one has previously departed, but with more explicit emphasis upon the return [LN]. It means to go back to a locality [BDAG].

b. fut. act. indic. of ἀνοικοδομέω (LN 45.3) (BDAG p. 85): 'to rebuild' [AB, BECNT, CBC, LN; CEV, ESV, NASB, NET, NIV, NRSV, REB], 'to restore' [LN; NLT, TEV], 'to build up again' [Bar, BDAG], 'to build again' [KJV], not explicit [NCV]. The phrase 'I will rebuild the tent of David' is also translated 'I will set up David's fallen tent' [GW]. This verb means to rebuild something which has been destroyed [LN].

c. perf. act. participle of πίπτω (LN 15.119) (BDAG 1.b.β. p. 815): 'to fall' [BDAG, BECNT, LN; ESV, KJV, NASB, NRSV], 'to fall down' [Bar; LN]. This verb is also translated as an adjective: 'David's fallen house/tent' [CEV, GW, NIV], 'a/the fallen tent' [NCV, NET], 'the fallen house/tabernacle' [AB, CBC; NLT, REB], not explicit [TEV]. This verb means to fall from a standing or upright position down to the ground or surface [LN]. It means to move with relative rapidity in a downward direction. Here it refers to something that until recently has been standing upright, especially structures [BDAG].

d. fut. act. indic. of ἀνορθόω (LN 45.4) (BDAG 1. p. 86): 'to restore' [BDAG, LN; ESV, NASB, NET, NIV, NLT], 'to rebuild' [BDAG], 'to build up again' [LN]. The phrase 'I will restore it' is also translated 'I will...set it up again' [CBC; CEV, GW, REB], 'I will raise/set it up' [Bar, BECNT; KJV, NCV, NRSV], 'I will...make it strong again' [TEV], 'I will raise it again' [AB], 'I will build it up again' [LN]. This verb means to build something up again after it has fallen [BDAG, LN].

QUESTION—What does 'the tent of David that has fallen' refer to?
  It is presumably the Davidic royal house which came to an end with the fall of Jerusalem in 587/586 BC [Bar]. It refers to David's kingdom [CBC]. This refers to the 'house' or family of David and thus to the promised Davidic kingdom [PNTC].

**15:17** so-that the remnant of-mankind may-seek[a] the Lord,[b] and all the Gentiles who are-called[c] by my name,[d] says (the)-Lord, who makes[e] these-things **15:18** known[f] from long-ago.[g]'

LEXICON—a. aorist act. subj. of ἐκζητέω (LN 27.35) (BDAG 1. p. 302): 'to seek' [AB, Bar, BECNT, CBC, LN; ESV, KJV, NASB, NET, NIV, NLT, NRSV, REB], 'to search for' [BDAG; GW], 'to seek out' [BDAG], 'to turn to' [CEV], 'to make a careful search, to seek diligently to learn, to make an examination' [LN]. The phrase 'the remnant of mankind may seek the Lord' is also translated 'those people who are left alive may ask the Lord for help' [NCV], 'all the rest of the human race will come to me' [TEV]. This verb means to exert considerable effort and care in learning something [LN]. It means to exert effort to find out or learn something [BDAG].

  b. κύριος (LN 12.9): 'Lord' [LN; all translations except CEV, TEV], 'Ruler, One who commands' [LN], not explicit [CEV, TEV]. This noun denotes a title for God and for Christ. It indicates one who exercises supernatural authority over mankind [LN].

  c. perf. pass. indic. of ἐπικαλέω (LN 11.28) (BDAG 2. p. 373): 'to be called' [AB, BDAG, BECNT; ESV, KJV, NASB, NRSV], 'to be named' [Bar], 'to be given a surname' [BDAG], 'to be one of God's people, to be the people of' [LN], not explicit [CBC; CEV, NCV, REB]. This verb is also translated as an active verb: 'I have called' [NET, NLT, TEV]. The phrase 'who are called by my name' is also translated 'over whom my name is spoken' [GW], 'who bear my name' [NIV]. The idiom 'to have someone's name called upon someone' means to be acknowledged as belonging to the one whose name is called upon such an individual [LN]. It means to address or characterize someone by a special term [BDAG].

  d. ὄνομα (LN 11.28) (BDAG 1.d.β. p. 712): 'name' [AB, Bar, BDAG, BECNT; ESV, GW, KJV, NASB, NIV, NRSV], 'to be one of God's people, to be the people of' [LN], not explicit [CBC; CEV, NCV, NET, NLT, REB, TEV]. The idiom 'to have someone's name called upon someone' means to be acknowledged as belonging to the one whose name is called upon such an individual [LN]. It denotes the proper name of an entity [BDAG].

  e. pres. act. participle of ποιέω (LN 90.45): 'to make' [Bar, BECNT, CBC; ESV, NASB, NCV, NET, NLT, NRSV, TEV], 'to do' [AB, LN; GW, KJV, NIV, REB], 'to perform, to practice' [LN], not explicit [CEV]. This verb is a marker of an agent relation with a numerable event [LN].

- f. γνωστός (LN 28.21): 'known' [LN; all translations except CEV]. The phrase 'known from long ago' is also translated 'I promised it long ago' [CEV]. This adjective pertains to that which is known [LN].
- g. αἰών (LN 67.25) (BDAG 1.a. p. 32): 'long ago' [CBC, LN; CEV, NASB, NET, NLT, NRSV, REB, TEV], 'very long ago' [LN], 'the past, the earliest times' [BDAG]. The phrase 'from long ago' is also translated 'from of old' [AB, Bar, BECNT; ESV], 'from the beginning of the world' [KJV]. The phrase 'known from long ago' is also translated 'have always been known' [GW], 'known for a long time' [NCV], 'known for ages' [NIV]. The idiom ἀπ' αἰῶνος 'from an age' refers to a point of time preceding another point of time, with a very long interval between [LN]. This idiom refers to a long period of time without referring to the beginning or the end. In respect to time it refers to the time gone by, the past, the earlier times [BDAG].

QUESTION—Who does 'the remnant of mankind' refer to?

It refers to the Gentiles [Bar, BECNT, NICNT, PNTC, TH; NET].

QUESTION—What is meant by 'all the Gentiles who are called by my name'?

In biblical language to have God's name called upon someone is to indicate that that person belongs to God [TH].

**15:19** **Therefore my judgment[a] is that we should not trouble[b] those of the Gentiles who are-turning[c] to God,**

LEXICON—a. pres. act. indic. of κρίνω (LN 31.1) (BDAG 3. p. 568): 'to judge' [BDAG, BECNT], 'to think' [BDAG; CEV, NCV], 'to decide' [GW], 'to conclude' [NET], 'to hold' [AB], 'to consider, to look upon' [BDAG], 'to hold a view, to have an opinion, to consider, to regard' [LN]. This verb is also translated as a noun: 'my judgment' [Bar, CBC; ESV, NASB, NIV, NLT, REB], 'my sentence' [KJV], 'my opinion' [LN; TEV]. The phrase 'therefore my judgment is' is also translated 'therefore I have reached the decision' [NRSV]. This verb means to hold a view or have an opinion with regard to something [LN]. It means to make a judgment based on taking various factors into account [BDAG].
- b. pres. act. infin. of παρενοχλέω (LN 22.25) (BDAG p. 775): 'to trouble' [BDAG, BECNT; ESV, GW, KJV, NASB, NRSV, TEV], 'to make trouble' [Bar], 'to cause extra difficulty' [LN; NET], 'to cause difficulty for, to annoy' [BDAG], 'to bother' [NCV], 'to make it difficult' [NIV, NLT], 'to make difficulty' [AB]. The phrase 'we should not trouble' is also translated 'we should impose no irksome restrictions' [CBC; REB], 'I don't think we should place burdens on' [CEV]. This verb means to cause extra difficulty and hardship by continual annoyance [LN]. It means to cause unnecessary trouble [BDAG].
- c. pres. act. participle of ἐπιστρέφω (LN 31.60) (BDAG 4.a. p. 382): 'to turn to' [LN; all translations], 'to turn, to return' [BDAG], 'to come to believe, to come to accept' [LN]. This verb means to change one's belief,

with focus upon that to which one turns [LN]. It means to change one's mind or course of action, for better or worse [BDAG].

QUESTION—What trouble is James referring to?

He is referring to circumcision and the Mosaic law [CBC]. He is referring to forcing them to obey all of the Jewish laws and customs [TRT]. Not troubling the Gentiles means in effect 'stop demanding circumcision' [NICNT]. Gentiles should not be burdened with the law and circumcision [NAC, PNTC]. They should not be burdened with issues of the law [BECNT].

**15:20** but[a] should write to-them to-abstain-from the things-polluted[b] by idols, and from sexual-immorality,[c] and from what has been strangled, and from blood.

LEXICON—a. ἀλλά (LN 89.125): 'but' [AB, Bar, BECNT, CBC, LN; ESV, KJV, NASB, NET, NRSV], 'instead' [LN; GW, NCV, NIV, NLT, REB, TEV], 'on the contrary' [LN], not explicit [CEV]. This conjunction is a marker of more emphatic contrast [LN].

b. ἀλίσγημα (LN 53.37) (BDAG p. 44): 'a thing defiled' [LN], 'pollution' [BDAG, BECNT; KJV], 'defilement' [Bar]. This noun is also translated as a passive verb: 'to be polluted/contaminated/defiled' [CBC; ESV, GW, NASB, NET, NIV, NRSV, REB], 'to be defiled' [LN], not explicit [AB]. The phrase 'the things polluted by idols' is also translated 'anything/food that has been offered to idols' [CEV, NCV], 'food offered to idols' [NLT]. This noun is also translated as an adjective: 'ritually unclean' [TEV]. This noun denotes that which has been ritually defiled [LN].

c. πορνεία (LN 88.271) (BDAG 1. p. 854): 'sexual immorality' [LN; ESV, NET, NIV, NLT, TEV], 'sexual sin' [CEV, GW, NCV], 'sexual impurity' [AB], 'fornication' [Bar, BDAG, CBC, LN; KJV, NASB, NRSV, REB], 'prostitution' [BDAG, LN], 'unchastity' [BDAG, BECNT], 'illicit sex' [LN]. This noun denotes sexual immorality of any kind, often with the implication of prostitution [LN]. It denotes unlawful sexual intercourse [BDAG].

QUESTION—What does the phrase 'the things polluted by idols' refer to?

Most commentators agree that it refers to food that is unclean because it has been offered to idols [TH, TRT]. The term 'polluted' means 'religiously defiled' from the standpoint of the standards of the Christian community [TH]. This refers to meat offered in sacrifice to idols and then eaten in a temple feast or sold in a shop [TNTC]. It refers to eating meat offered in idol temples and then sold in the shops whereby the purchaser partook in idol worship [CBC]. The reference is most likely to participation in pagan temple feasts, not simply to the uncleanness incurred from eating meat bought in the marketplace [PNTC]. It refers to meat offered to idols [NAC].

QUESTION—What does the phrase 'what has been strangled' refer to?

It refers to animals that had been slaughtered in a manner that left the blood in it [Bar, BECNT, NAC, PNTC, TNTC]. Blood was considered sacred to the Jews, and all meat was to be drained of blood before consuming it [AB, BECNT, NAC, NICNT].

**15:21** For from ancient[a] generations[b] Moses has had in-every city those who proclaim[c] him, for he is read every Sabbath in the synagogues.[d]"

LEXICON—a. ἀρχαῖος (LN 67.98) (BDAG 2. p. 137): 'ancient' [BDAG, LN; ESV, NASB, NET], 'for a long time' [LN; NCV], 'for a very long time' [TEV], 'from the beginning' [LN], not explicit [GW]. The phrase 'ancient generations' is also translated 'generations of old' [Bar], 'early generations' [BECNT], 'many generations' [NLT], 'generations past' [CBC; NRSV, REB], 'the earliest times' [AB; NIV], 'many years' [CEV], 'of old time' [KJV]. This adjective pertains to having existed for a long time in the past, with the possible implication of such existence from the beginning of an event or state [LN]. It pertains to what was in former times, long ago [BDAG].

b. γενεά (LN 67.144) (BDAG 3.b. p. 192): 'generation' [Bar, BECNT, CBC; ESV, GW, NASB, NLT, NRSV, REB], 'age' [BDAG, LN], 'epoch' [LN], not explicit [CEV, KJV, NCV, TEV]. The phrase 'ancient generations' is also translated 'ancient times' [NET], 'earliest times' [AB; NIV]. This noun denotes an indefinite period of time, but in close relationship to human existence and in some contexts, a period of time about the length of a generation [LN]. It denotes the time of a generation [BDAG].

c. pres. act. participle of κηρύσσω (LN 33.256) (BDAG 2.b.β. p. 543): 'to proclaim' [Bar; ESV, NET, NRSV], 'to preach' [AB, BECNT, LN; KJV, NASB], 'to proclaim aloud' [BDAG], not explicit [CBC; REB]. This verb is also translated as a passive verb: 'has/have been preached' [CEV, NIV, NLT], 'have been spread' [GW], 'has been taught' [NCV], 'are preached' [TEV]. This verb means to publicly announce religious truths and principles while urging acceptance and compliance [LN]. It means to make public declarations [BDAG].

d. συναγωγή (LN 7.20): 'synagogue' [LN; all translations except CEV], 'Christian assembly place' [LN]. The phrase 'he is read every Sabbath in the synagogues' is also translated 'every Sabbath it is read at our meeting' [CEV]. This noun denotes a building of assembly, associated with religious activity normally a building in which Jewish worship took place and in which the Law was taught [LN].

QUESTION—How is this verse to be understood?

Since Jewish communities are to be found in every city, their scruples are to be respected by Gentile believers [BECNT, EBC, TNTC]. The most obvious link with this verse is verse 20. James implies that there are observant Jews everywhere and that Gentile Christians will know why the requirements of verse 20 are being suggested [PNTC].

**DISCOURSE UNIT—15:22–35** [BECNT; CEV, ESV, NCV, NIV, NLT, NRSV, TEV]. The topic is the reply and messengers [BECNT], a letter to

Gentiles who had faith in the Lord [CEV], the council's letter to Gentile believers [ESV, NIV, NRSV], letter to non-Jewish believers [NCV], the letter for Gentile believers [NLT], the letter to the Gentile believers [TEV].

**DISCOURSE UNIT—15:22-33** [AB]. The topic is the end of the apostolic council and its effect.

**DISCOURSE UNIT—15:22-29** [EBC, NAC, NICNT]. The topic is the decision and letter of the council [EBC], the decision in Jerusalem [NAC], the apostolic letter to Gentile Christians [NICNT].

**15:22** Then it-seemed-(good) to-the apostles and the elders, with (the)-whole church, to choose men from among them and send[a] them to Antioch with Paul and Barnabas. They sent Judas called[b] Barsabbas, and Silas, leading men among the brothers,[c]

> LEXICON—a. aorist act. infin. of πέμπω (LN 15.66) (BDAG 1. p. 794): 'to send' [BDAG, LN; all translations]. This verb means to cause someone to depart for a particular purpose [LN]. It means to dispatch someone, whether human or transcendent being, usually for purposes of communication [BDAG].
> b. pres. pass. participle of καλέω (LN 33.129) (BDAG 1.c. p. 503): 'to be called' [Bar, BDAG, BECNT, LN; ESV, GW, NASB, NET, NIV, NLT, NRSV, TEV], 'to be called by name' [BDAG], 'to be named' [BDAG, LN], 'to be surnamed' [AB; KJV], not explicit [CBC; CEV, NCV, REB]. This verb means to speak of a person or object by means of a proper name [LN]. It means to identify by name or attribute [BDAG].
> c. ἀδελφός (LN 11.23): 'brother' [Bar, BECNT; ESV, NET, NIV, NRSV], 'fellow believer, a Christian brother' [LN]. The phrase 'the brothers' is also translated 'the brethren' [AB; KJV, NASB], 'the believers' [GW, NCV, TEV], 'the Lord's followers' [CEV], 'the church leaders' [NLT]. The phrase 'among the brothers' is also translated 'in the community' [CBC; REB]. This noun denotes a close associate of a group of persons having a well-defined membership. In the NT ἀδελφός 'brother' refers specifically to fellow believers in Christ [LN].

QUESTION—What is meant by 'the whole church'?
> The whole church is clearly the church of Jerusalem, with a handful of delegates from Antioch [Bar].

QUESTION—Who was Judas called Barsabbas?
> He probably was a relative of Joseph Barsabbas [AB].

QUESTION—Who was Silas?
> Silas is almost certainly the Silvanus of Paul's letters [AB, Bar, BECNT, CBC, NAC, NICNT, TNTC]. Silas became the companion of Paul, in succession to Barnabas [PNTC].

**15:23** with the following letter: "The brothers, both the apostles and the elders, to-the brothersª who are of (the)-Gentiles in Antioch and Syria and Cilicia, greetings.

TEXT—Some manuscripts add καί οἱ 'and the' before the first occurrence of ἀδελφοί 'brothers'. This is followed by KJV. The reading without the addition was given a B rating by GNT indicating that the text was almost certain. The textual difference is that in the KJV 'apostles', 'elders', and 'brothers' are three distinct groups, while in the preferred text 'brothers' describes either the apostles and elders (ESV, NRSV, RSV) or their relation to the people to whom they are writing (NCV, NIV, TEV).

LEXICON—a. ἀδελφός (LN 11.23) (BDAG 2.a. p. 18): 'brother' [Bar, BDAG, CBC; ESV, NET, REB, TEV], 'fellow believer, a Christian brother' [LN], 'believer' [NCV, NIV, NLT, NRSV], 'fellow member, associate' [BDAG]. The phrase 'the brothers' is also translated 'the brethren' [AB, BECNT; KJV, NASB], 'followers of the Lord' [CEV], 'brothers and sisters' [GW, NET]. This noun denotes a close associate of a group of persons having a well-defined membership. In the NT ἀδελφός 'brother' refers specifically to fellow believers in Christ [LN]. It denotes a person viewed as a brother in terms of a close affinity [BDAG].

QUESTION—What relationship is 'brothers' describing?

It describes their relationship to the people to whom they are writing [NICNT, PNTC, TH, TRT; NCV, NIV, TEV].

**15:24** Since we-have-heard that some persons have-gone-outª from us and troubledᵇ you with-words, unsettlingᶜ your souls,ᵈ although we-gave- them no -instructions,ᵉ

TEXT—Some manuscripts add the verb ἐξελθόντες 'have gone out'. GNT includes this word in the text in brackets with a C decision, indicating that the Committee had difficulty making the decision. The ESV, NET, NRSV have translated this verb as 'have gone out'. The KJV, NIV translates this verb as 'went out'.

LEXICON—a. aorist act. participle of ἐξέρχομαι (LN 15.40) (BDAG 1.a.α. p. 348): 'to go out' [BDAG; ESV, KJV, NET, NIV, NRSV], 'to come out' [BDAG], 'to go' [TEV], 'to go out of, to depart out of, to leave from within' [LN], 'to come from' [GW], not explicit [AB, Bar, CBC; NASB]. The phrase 'some persons have gone out from us' is also translated 'some of our group have come to you' [NCV], 'some persons from us' [BECNT], 'some people/men from here' [CEV, NLT], 'some of our number' [REB]. This verb means to move out of an enclosed or well defined two or three-dimensional area [LN]. It means to move out of or away from an area [BDAG].

b. aorist act. indic. of ταράσσω (LN 25.244) (BDAG 2. p. 990): 'to trouble' [AB, BECNT; ESV, KJV, NCV, NLT, TEV], 'to disturb' [BDAG, Bar, CBC; NASB, NIV, NRSV, REB], 'to upset' [CEV], 'to confuse' [GW, NET], 'to cause great mental distress' [LN], 'to stir up, to unsettle, to

throw into confusion' [BDAG]. This is a figurative extension of meaning of ταράσσω 'to stir up' and means to cause acute emotional distress or turbulence [LN]. It means to cause inward turmoil and refers to mental confusion caused by false teachings [BDAG].
- c. pres. act. participle of ἀνασκευάζω (LN 25.231) (BDAG p. 71): 'to unsettle' [Bar, BDAG, BECNT, CBC; ESV, NASB, NRSV, REB], 'to distress' [LN], 'to upset' [BDAG, LN; NCV, NET, NLT, TEV], 'to disturb' [GW], 'to trouble' [NIV], 'to subvert' [KJV], not explicit [CEV]. This verb is also translated as a noun: 'brought confusion' [AB]. This verb means to cause someone distress and worry [LN]. It means to cause inward distress [BDAG].
- d. ψυχή (LN 26.4) (BDAG 2.c. p. 1099): 'soul' [Bar, BDAG, BECNT; KJV, NASB], 'mind' [AB, CBC, LN; ESV, NET, NIV, NRSV, REB], 'inner self, thoughts, feelings, heart, being' [LN]. The phrase 'some persons have…troubled you with words, unsettling your souls' is also translated 'some people…have terribly upset you' [CEV], 'some individuals…have confused you with statements that disturb you' [GW], 'some of our group have…said things that trouble and upset you' [NCV], 'some men…have troubled you and upset you with their statements' [NLT], 'some…have troubled you and upset you by what they said' [TEV]. This noun denotes the essence of life in terms of thinking, willing, and feeling [LN]. It denotes the seat and center of the inner human life concerning feelings and emotions [BDAG].
- e. aorist mid. indic. of διαστέλλω (LN 33.323) (BDAG p. 236): 'to give instruction' [Bar, BECNT; ESV, NASB], 'to order' [BDAG, LN; NET], 'to command' [LN], 'to give orders' [BDAG], 'to tell' [NCV], 'to authorize' [GW], 'to give a commandment' [KJV]. This verb is also translated as a passive verb: 'authorized by us' [AB]. This verb is also translated as a noun: 'our authorization' [NIV]. The phrase 'we gave them no instructions' is also translated 'we did not send them' [CEV, NLT], 'with no instructions from us' [NRSV], 'without any instructions from us' [CBC; REB], 'they had not…received any instruction from us' [TEV]. This verb means to state with force and/or authority what others must do [LN]. It means to define or express in no uncertain terms what one must do [BDAG].

QUESTION—What verse does this verse refer back to?

This verse looks back to 15:1; the trouble-makers are emphatically disowned-men to whom we had given no such instruction. [Bar, CBC, TH].

**15:25** it-seemed-(good)[a] to-us, having-come[b] of-one-mind,[c] to choose men to-send[d] to you with our beloved Barnabas and Paul,

LEXICON—a. aorist act. indic. of δοκέω (LN 30.96) (BDAG 2.b.β. p. 255): 'to seem good' [BECNT; ESV, KJV, NASB], 'to seem' [BDAG], 'to choose, to decide, to prefer, to choose as superior' [LN], not explicit [AB, Bar, CBC; all versions except ESV, KJV, NASB]. This verb means to make a choice on the basis of something being better or superior [LN]. It means to appear to one's understanding [BDAG].

b. aorist mid. (deponent = act.) participle of γίνομαι (LN 13.48) (BDAG 7. p. 199): 'to have come' [BECNT; ESV, GW, NLT], 'to become' [LN; NASB], 'to be, to prove to be, to turn out to be' [BDAG], not explicit [Bar; CEV]. The phrase 'having come of one mind' is also translated 'being assembled with one accord' [KJV], 'We have all agreed' [NCV], 'we all agreed' [NIV], 'we have agreed' [AB], 'we have unanimously decided' [NET], 'we have decided/resolved unanimously' [CBC; NRSV, REB], 'we...have all agreed' [TEV]. This verb means to come to acquire or experience a state [LN]. It means to come into a certain state or possess certain characteristics. Here it means to come together in unanimity or reach unanimity [BDAG].

c. ὁμοθυμαδόν (LN 31.23) (BDAG p. 706): 'of one mind' [NASB], 'with one mind, by common consent' [LN], 'unanimously' [CBC, LN; NET, NRSV, REB], 'unanimous' [GW], 'one accord' [BECNT; ESV, KJV], 'complete agreement' [NLT], not explicit [AB, Bar; CEV, NCV, NIV, TEV]. This adjective pertains to mutual consent or agreement [LN]. It means with one mind/purpose/impulse [BDAG].

d. aorist act. infin. of πέμπω (LN 15.66) (BDAG 1. p. 794): 'to send' [BDAG, LN; all translations]. This verb means to cause someone to depart for a particular purpose [LN]. It means to dispatch someone, whether human or transcendent being, usually for purposes of communication [BDAG].

QUESTION—To whom does 'our' refer?

It refers to the writers and the ones written to [TRT].

**15:26** men who have-risked[a] their lives for the name[b] of our Lord Jesus Christ.

LEXICON—a. perf. act. participle of παραδίδωμι (LN 21.7) (BDAG 1.a. p. 761): 'to risk' [AB, LN; CEV, ESV, NASB, NET, NIV, NLT, NRSV, TEV], 'to risk one's life' [LN], 'to hand over, to give (over), to entrust' [BDAG], 'to dedicate' [BECNT; GW], 'to hazard' [KJV], 'to give' [NCV], 'to give up' [REB], 'to devote' [Bar, CBC]. The idiom 'to hand over life' means to expose oneself willingly to a danger or risk [LN]. It means to convey something in which one has a relatively strong personal interest [BDAG].

b. ὄνομα (LN 33.126) (BDAG 1.d.γ.ה. p. 714): 'name' [Bar, BECNT, LN; KJV, NASB, NET, NIV, NLT], 'sake' [AB; ESV, NRSV], not explicit [CEV, NCV, TEV]. The phrase 'for the name of' is also translated 'to the cause of' [CBC; REB]. This noun is also translated as a verb: 'the one named Jesus Christ' [GW]. This noun denotes the proper name of a person or object [LN]. When it refers to God or Christ the word frequently stands alone [BDAG].

QUESTION—What is meant by 'risked their lives for the name'?

Devoting their lives to the name means to preach the name [Bar]. The verb παραδίδωμι means 'give over', so in this context it refers to those willing to lose their lives or dedicate their lives for the sake of the Lord Jesus Christ [BECNT].

**15:27** **We-have- therefore -sent**[a] **Judas and Silas, who themselves will tell**[b] **you the same things by word-(of mouth).**[c]

LEXICON—a. perf. act. indic. of ἀποστέλλω (LN 15.66): 'to send' [LN; all translations]. This verb means to cause someone to depart for a particular purpose [LN].
- b. pres. act. participle of ἀπαγγέλλω (LN 33.198): 'to tell' [AB, BECNT, LN; CEV, ESV, KJV, NCV, NET, NRSV, TEV], 'to report' [Bar; GW, NASB], 'to inform' [LN], 'to confirm' [CBC; NIV, NLT, REB]. This verb means to announce or inform, with possible focus upon the source of information [LN].
- c. λόγος (LN 33.98) (BDAG 1.a.α. p. 599): 'word' [AB, Bar, BDAG, CBC, LN; ESV, NASB, NIV, NRSV, REB], 'saying, message, statement' [LN], not explicit [GW, NCV, NLT]. The phrase 'will tell you the same things by word of mouth' is also translated 'will tell you in person the same things that we are writing' [CEV, TEV], 'will tell you these things themselves in person' [NET], 'who shall also tell [you] the same things by mouth' [KJV], 'will tell you the same things through the spoken word' [BECNT]. This noun denotes that which has been stated or said, with primary focus upon the content of the communication [LN]. It denotes a communication whereby the mind finds expression [BDAG].

QUESTION—What were Judas and Silas supposed to do?

Their task was to convey and expound orally the written message which they took to Antioch [PNTC, TNTC].

**15:28** **For it-seemed-(good)**[a] **to-the Holy Spirit and to-us to-lay-on**[b] **you no greater burden than these essentials:**[c]

LEXICON—a. aorist act. indic. of δοκέω (LN 30.96) (BDAG 2.b.β. p. 255): 'to seem good' [BECNT; ESV, KJV, NASB, NIV, NLT, NRSV], 'to seem best' [NET], 'to choose, to decide, to prefer, to choose as superior' [LN], 'to seem, to be recognized as' [BDAG], not explicit [AB, Bar, CBC; CEV, GW, NCV, REB, TEV]. This verb means to make a choice on the basis of something being better or superior [LN]. It means to appear to one's understanding [BDAG].
- b. pres. pass. infin. of ἐπιτίθημι (LN 90.87) (BDAG 1.a.β. p. 384): 'to lay on' [ESV, NLT], 'to lay upon' [AB, Bar, BDAG, BECNT, CBC; KJV, NASB, REB], 'to subject to' [LN], 'to put upon' [BDAG], 'to put on' [TEV], 'to place on' [CEV, GW, NET], 'to burden' [NIV], 'to impose on' [NRSV]. The phrase 'to lay on you no greater burden' is also translated 'you should not have a heavy load to carry' [NCV]. This verb means to subject someone to a particular experience, normally by the use of force

[LN]. It means to place something on or transfer to (a place or object) [BDAG].

c. ἐπάναγκες (LN 71.39) (BDAG p. 358): 'essential' [CBC; NASB, NRSV, REB], 'necessary' [AB, Bar, BECNT, LN; GW, KJV, NET, TEV], 'indispensable' [LN], not explicit [CEV, NCV]. This adjective is also translated as a noun: 'requirement' [ESV, NIV, NLT]. This adjective pertains to being necessary and indispensable to the occurrence of some event [LN]. It pertains to being essential in connection with something of a necessary nature [BDAG].

QUESTION—What do the words 'For it seemed (good) to the Holy Spirit and to us' stress?

They stress the church's role as the vehicle of the Spirit [NICNT]. The addition of the Holy Spirit in v. 28 is significant. Just as the Spirit had been instrumental in the inclusion of the Gentiles (15:8, 12), so now in the conference the Spirit had led the Jerusalem leaders in considering the conditions for their inclusion [NAC].

**15:29** **that you abstain-from[a] what-has-been-sacrificed-to-idols, and from blood, and from what-has-been-strangled, and from sexual-immorality.[b] If you keep[c] yourselves from these, you-will-do well. Farewell."**

LEXICON—a. pres. mid. infin. of ἀπέχω (LN 13.158) (BDAG 5. p. 103): 'to abstain from' [AB, Bar, BDAG, BECNT, CBC; ESV, KJV, NASB, NET, NIV, NLT, NRSV, REB], 'to keep away from' [BDAG; GW], 'to stay away from' [NCV], 'to restrain from, to not do, to avoid doing' [LN], 'to keep from doing' [LN], 'to refrain from' [BDAG]. The phrase 'you abstain from what has been sacrificed to idols' is also translated 'you should not eat anything offered to idols' [CEV], 'eat no food that has been offered to idols' [TEV]. This verb means to keep on avoiding doing something [LN]. It means to avoid contact with or use of something [BDAG].

b. πορνεία (LN 88.271) (BDAG 1. p. 854): 'sexual immorality' [LN; ESV, NET, NIV, NLT, TEV], 'sexual sin' [CEV, GW, NCV], 'sexual impurity' [AB], 'illicit sex' [LN], 'fornication' [Bar, BDAG, CBC, LN; KJV, NASB, NRSV, REB], 'prostitution' [BDAG, LN], 'unchastity' [BDAG, BECNT]. This noun denotes sexual immorality of any kind, often with the implication of prostitution [LN]. It denotes unlawful sexual intercourse [BDAG].

c. pres. act. participle of διατηρέω (LN 13.153) (BDAG 2. p. 238): 'to keep' [Bar, BECNT, CBC; ESV, KJV, NASB, NET, NRSV, REB], 'to avoid' [LN; GW, NIV], 'to abstain' [AB], 'to keep from doing' [LN], 'to keep free of' [BDAG], 'to stay away' [NCV]. The phrase 'If you keep yourselves from these' is also translated 'If you follow these instructions' [CEV], 'If you do this' [NLT], 'if you take care not to do these things' [TEV]. This verb means to keep oneself from doing something, with the implication of duration [LN]. It means to keep oneself from doing something [BDAG].

QUESTION—What is meant by the phrase 'you will do well'?
It means they perform what is right [BECNT]. It possibly means 'you will prosper' [TH, TNTC, TRT] or 'you will be doing right' [TH, TRT].

**DISCOURSE UNIT—15:30–16:4** [EBC]. The topic is the reception of the council's decision and of the letter.

**DISCOURSE UNIT—15:30–35** [Bar, EBC, NAC, NICNT, PNTC]. The topic is Paul and Barnabas return to Antioch [Bar], at Antioch of Syria [EBC], the decision reported to Antioch [NAC], the church of Antioch receives the apostolic letter [NICNT], the result of the council [PNTC].

**15:30** So when they were-sent-off,[a] they-went-down[b] to Antioch, and having-gathered- the congregation -together,[c] they-delivered the letter.

- LEXICON—a. aorist pass. participle of ἀπολύω (LN 15.43, 15.66) (BDAG 3. p. 117): 'to be sent off' [BECNT, CBC; ESV, NIV, NRSV, TEV], 'to be sent away' [BDAG; NASB], 'to be sent' [BDAG, LN (15.66); GW], 'to let go away' [LN (15.43)], 'to be dismissed' [Bar, BDAG, LN (15.43); KJV, NET], not explicit [NLT]. The phrase 'So when they were sent off' is also translated 'The four men left Jerusalem' [CEV], 'So they left Jerusalem' [NCV], 'So they took their leave' [REB], 'After they had taken their leave' [AB]. This verb means to cause (or permit) a person or persons to leave a particular location [LN (15.43)]. It means to cause someone to depart for a particular purpose [LN (15.66)]. It means to permit or cause someone to leave a particular location [BDAG].
- b. aorist act. indic. of κατέρχομαι (LN 15.107) (BDAG 1. p. 531): 'to go down' [AB, Bar, LN; ESV, NASB, NET, NIV, NRSV], 'to travel down' [CBC; REB], 'to come down' [BDAG, BECNT, LN], 'to move down, to come down, to descend' [LN], 'to go' [CEV, NCV, NLT, TEV], 'to come' [KJV], not explicit [GW]. This verb means to move down, irrespective of the gradient [LN]. It means to move in a direction considered the opposite of up but not necessarily with a suggestion of a gradient [BDAG].
- c. aorist act. participle of συνάγω (LN 15.125) (BDAG 1.b. p. 962): 'to gather together' [Bar, BECNT, LN; ESV, GW, KJV, NASB, NET, NIV, NRSV], 'to gather' [AB; NCV, TEV], 'to call together' [CBC, LN; CEV, REB], 'to gather (in)' [BDAG]. The phrase 'having gathered the congregation together' is also translated 'they called a general meeting of the believers' [NLT]. This verb means to cause to come together, whether of animate or inanimate objects [LN]. It means to cause to come together [BDAG].

QUESTION—To whom does 'they' refer?
It refers to the group mentioned at 15:22 [Bar; CEV].

QUESTION—What does 'the congregation' refer to here?
'The congregation' refers to the whole church at Antioch [Bar, PNTC].

**15:31** And when they had-read-(it), they-rejoiced[a] because of its encouragement.[b]

LEXICON—a. aorist pass. (deponent = act.) indic. of χαίρω (LN 25.125) (BDAG 1. p. 1074): 'to rejoice' [Bar, BDAG, BECNT, CBC, LN; ESV, KJV, NASB, NET, NRSV, REB], 'to be glad' [BDAG, LN; NIV], 'to be pleased' [CEV, GW], 'to be happy' [AB; NCV]. This verb is also translated as a noun: 'there was great joy' [NLT], 'filled with joy' [TEV]. This verb means to enjoy a state of happiness and well-being [LN]. It means to be in a state of happiness and well-being [BDAG].

b. παράκλησις (LN 25.150) (BDAG 3. p. 766): 'encouragement' [CBC, LN; ESV, GW, NASB, NET, REB, TEV], 'comfort' [AB, Bar; BDAG, BECNT], 'consolation' [BDAG; KJV], 'exhortation' [NRSV]. This noun is also translated as a passive verb: 'everyone was…greatly encouraged' [CEV]. This noun is also translated as an adjective: 'encouraging message' [NCV, NIV, NLT]. This noun denotes encouragement or consolation, either by verbal or non-verbal means [LN]. It denotes the lifting of another's spirits [BDAG].

QUESTION—Who is referred to in the phrase 'they rejoiced'?

'They rejoiced' refers to the Antiochenes [Bar].

QUESTION—What does the Greek term παρακλήσει mean?

This term can mean 'comfort' or 'encouragement', but given the past conflict, 'comfort' is slightly better; as the decision is a comfort to them [BECNT]. Here it means 'comfort'; they were relieved that the leading Jewish Christians in Jerusalem had not insisted that they should be circumcised [Bar]. It can mean 'comfort' or 'exhortation'. Either nuance fits this particular context. The letter both comforted them and encouraged them by the conciliatory spirit of its exhortations [NAC].

**15:32** And Judas and Silas, who also were themselves prophets,[a] encouraged[b] and strengthened[c] the brothers[d] with many words.

LEXICON—a. προφήτης (LN 53.79) (BDAG 1.e. p. 891): 'prophet' [BDAG, LN; all translations], 'inspired preacher' [LN]. This noun denotes one who proclaims inspired utterances on behalf of God [LN]. It denotes a person inspired to proclaim or reveal divine will or purpose [BDAG].

b. aorist act. indic. of παρακαλέω (LN 25.150) (BDAG 2. p. 765): 'to encourage' [Bar, BDAG, CBC, LN; all versions except KJV, TEV], 'to console' [LN], 'to appeal to, to urge' [BDAG], 'to exhort' [BDAG, BECNT; KJV], 'to give courage' [TEV], 'to give support' [AB]. This verb means to cause someone to be encouraged or consoled, either by verbal or non-verbal means [LN]. It means to urge strongly [BDAG].

c. aorist act. indic. of ἐπιστηρίζω (LN 74.19) (BDAG p. 381): 'to strengthen' [Bar, BDAG, BECNT, CBC, LN; ESV, GW, NASB, NET, NIV, NLT, NRSV, REB], 'to help' [CEV], 'to confirm' [KJV], 'to make more firm' [LN], 'to make stronger' [NCV], 'to give strength' [AB; TEV]. This verb means to cause someone to become stronger in the sense

of more firm and unchanging in attitude or belief [LN]. It means to cause someone to become stronger or more firm [BDAG].
- d. ἀδελφός (LN 11.23): 'brother' [Bar, LN; ESV, NET, NIV], 'fellow believer' [LN]. The phrase 'the brothers' is also translated 'the brethren' [AB, BECNT; KJV, NASB], 'the Lord's followers' [CEV], 'the believers' [GW, NCV, NLT, NRSV], 'the members' [CBC; REB]. The phrase 'encouraged and strengthened the brothers' is also translated 'giving them courage and strength' [TEV]. This noun denotes a close associate of a group of persons having a well-defined membership. In the NT ἀδελφός 'brother' refers specifically to fellow believers in Christ [LN].

QUESTION—What is significant about the phrase 'Judas and Silas, who were themselves prophets'?

The emphatic description of 'Judas and Silas, who were themselves prophets' is significant in the context. It suggests that prophetic ministry involved explanation and application of apostolic teaching, such as was found in the letter, and not simply prediction, as in the case of Agabus (13:28, 21:10–11), or special guidance, as with the commissioning of Barnabas and Saul for their missionary campaign (13:1–2) [PNTC]. The statement that they 'were also prophets themselves' may imply that they added their prophetic gifts to those of the local 'prophets and teachers' [NICNT]. Prophets in this particular context is primarily not a reference to 'foretelling the future' but to 'speaking on behalf of God' [TH].

QUESTION—What is the word 'also' referring to here?

The word 'also' may be referring to the fact that there were other prophets in the church at Antioch (see Acts 13:1) [TRT].

**15:33** And after they had-spent some time, they-were-sent-off[a] in peace[b] by the brothers to those who had-sent them.

LEXICON—a. aorist pass. indic. of ἀπολύω (LN 15.43) (BDAG 3. p. 117): 'to be sent off' [BECNT; ESV, NCV, NET, NIV, NRSV, TEV], 'to be sent away' [BDAG; NASB], 'to let go away' [LN], 'to be dismissed' [BDAG, CBC, LN], 'to be released' [Bar], 'to be let go' [BDAG; KJV], 'to take leave' [BDAG; REB]. The phrase 'they were sent off' is also translated 'they left' [CEV], 'they parted' [AB]. This verb is also translated as an active verb: 'the congregation/believers sent them' [GW, NLT]. This verb means to cause or permit a person or persons to leave a particular location [LN]. It means to permit or cause someone to leave a particular location [BDAG].
- b. εἰρήνη (LN 22.42) (BDAG 2.a. p. 288): 'peace' [Bar, BDAG, BECNT, LN; all versions except CEV, GW, REB], 'tranquility' [LN], not explicit [GW]. The phrase 'they were sent off in peace' is also translated 'when they left…the followers wished them well' [CEV], 'they took their leave with the good wishes of the brethren' [REB], 'they parted from the brethren on the best of terms' [AB], 'were dismissed with the good wishes of the brethren' [CBC]. This noun denotes a set of favorable

circumstances involving peace and tranquility [LN]. It denotes a state of well-being [BDAG].

**15:34** **[Omitted]**

TEXT—Manuscripts omitting this verse are given an A rating by GNT to indicate the omission was regarded to be certain. Variant readings are "But it seemed good to Silas to remain there." It is followed by the KJV and the NASB, "But it seemed good to Silas that they should remain" and "But it seemed good to Silas that they remain, and Judas journeyed alone." This verse is included in parentheses by the NASB.

**DISCOURSE UNIT—15:35–41** [AB]. The topic is the beginning of Paul's second missionary journey.

**15:35** **But[a] Paul and Barnabas remained[b] in Antioch, teaching and preaching[c] the word[d] of-the Lord,[e] with many others also.**

LEXICON—a. δέ (LN 89.124): 'but' [AB, Bar, BECNT, CBC, LN; CEV, ESV, NASB, NCV, NET, NIV, NRSV, REB], 'on the other hand' [LN], not explicit [GW, KJV, NLT, TEV]. This conjunction indicates a contrast [LN].

b. imperf. act. indic. of διατρίβω (LN 85.61) (BDAG p. 238): 'to remain' [BECNT, LN; ESV, NET, NIV, NRSV], 'to stay' [AB, Bar, CBC, LN; CEV, GW, NASB, NCV, NLT, REB], 'to spend time' [BDAG; TEV]. The phrase 'Paul and Barnabas remained in Antioch' is also translated 'Paul also and Barnabas continued in Antioch' [KJV]. This verb means to remain or stay in a place, with the implication of some type of activity [LN]. It means to remain or stay in a place [BDAG].

c. pres. mid. participle of εὐαγγελίζω (LN 33.215) (BDAG 2.a.β. p. 402): 'to preach' [all translations except GW, NET, NRSV], 'to spread' [GW], 'to proclaim' [NET, NRSV], 'to tell the good news, to announce the gospel' [LN], 'to proclaim the gospel' [BDAG]. This verb means to communicate good news concerning something and in the NT it is a particular reference to the gospel message about Jesus [LN]. It means to proclaim the divine message of salvation [BDAG].

d. λόγος (LN 33.260) (BDAG 1.a.β. p. 599): 'word' [BDAG; all translations except CEV, GW, NCV], 'what is preached, gospel' [LN]. The phrase 'preaching the word of the Lord' is also translated 'preached about the Lord' [CEV]. The phrase 'teaching and preaching the word of the Lord' is also translated 'preached the Good News and taught the people the message of the Lord' [NCV], 'taught people about the Lord's word and spread the Good News' [GW]. This noun denotes the content of what is preached about Christ or about the good news [LN]. It denotes a communication whereby the mind finds expression [BDAG].

e. κύριος (LN 12.9): 'Lord' [LN; all translations], 'Ruler, One who commands' [LN]. This noun denotes a title for God and for Christ. It indicates one who exercises supernatural authority over mankind [LN].

42 ACTS 15:35

QUESTION—What is meant by 'the word of the Lord'?
It means 'the message about the Lord' [TH].

**DISCOURSE UNIT—15:36–21:26** [CBC]. The topic is Paul leads the advance.

**DISCOURSE UNIT—15:36–21:16** [BECNT]. The topic is the second and third missionary journeys: expansion to Greece and consolidation amid opposition.

**DISCOURSE UNIT—15:36–18:23** [Bar, BECNT]. The topic is Paul's mission breaks new ground [Bar], the second missionary journey [BECNT].

**DISCOURSE UNIT—15:36–18:22** [NAC]. The topic is Paul witnesses to the Greek world.

**DISCOURSE UNIT—15:36–18:17** [TNTC]. The topic is Paul's missionary campaign in Macedonia and Achaia.

**DISCOURSE UNIT—15:36–16:10** [CBC]. The topic is Paul leads the advance.

**DISCOURSE UNIT—15:36–16:5** [Bar, NICNT]. The topic is territory of the first journey revisited [Bar], recently planted churches revisited [NICNT].

**DISCOURSE UNIT—15:36–41** [BECNT, EBC, NAC, NICNT, PNTC, TNTC; CEV, ESV, GW, NASB, NCV, NET, NIV, NLT, NRSV, TEV]. The topic is Paul and Barnabas split up [BECNT], Paul and Barnabas separate [ESV, NCV, NLT, NRSV, TEV], Paul and Barnabas go their separate ways [CEV], Paul and Barnabas part company [NET], disagreement and two missionary teams [EBC], parting company with Barnabas [NAC], Paul parts company with Barnabas and takes Silas as his colleague [NICNT], disagreement between Paul and Barnabas [PNTC, NIV], Paul and Barnabas disagree [GW], Paul, Barnabas, Mark and Silas [TNTC], second missionary journey [NASB].

**15:36** **And after some days Paul said to Barnabas, "Let-us- return<sup>a</sup> and -visit<sup>b</sup> the brothers in every city in which we-proclaimed<sup>c</sup> the word of-the Lord, and see how they-are."**

LEXICON—a. aorist act. participle of ἐπιστρέφω (LN 15.90) (BDAG 1.a. p. 382): 'to return' [AB, Bar; ESV, NASB, NET, NRSV], 'to go back' [BDAG, CBC; CEV, GW, NCV, NIV, NLT, REB, TEV], 'to return to, to go back to' [LN], 'to turn around' [BDAG], 'to go again' [KJV], not explicit [BECNT]. This verb means to return to a point or area where one has been before, with probable emphasis on turning about [LN]. It means to return to a point where one has been [BDAG].
  b. aorist mid. (deponent = act.) subj. of ἐπισκέπτομαι (LN 34.50) (BDAG 2. p. 378): 'to visit' [Bar, BDAG, BECNT, LN; all versions except REB], 'to go to see' [CBC, LN], not explicit [AB; REB]. This verb means to go

to see a person on the basis of friendship and with helpful intent [LN]. It means to go to see a person with helpful intent [BDAG].
  c. aorist act. indic. of καταγγέλλω (LN 33.204) (BDAG a. p. 515): 'to proclaim' [Bar, BDAG, BECNT, CBC; ESV, NASB, NET, NRSV, REB], 'to announce' [BDAG, LN], 'to preach' [AB; CEV, KJV, NCV, NIV, NLT, TEV], 'to spread' [GW], 'to proclaim throughout, to speak out about' [LN]. This verb means to announce, with focus upon the extent to which the announcement or proclamation extends [LN]. It means to make known in public, with the implication of broad dissemination [BDAG].
QUESTION—What is the function of this verse?
  This is the beginning of a bridge passage which leads into the account of Paul's missionary campaign (16:6–18:22) [PNTC].
QUESTION—What does the phrase 'see how they are' refer to?
  It refers here mainly to spiritual well-being not physical well-being [TRT].

**15:37** Now Barnabas wanted[a] to-take-with[b] them John called[c] Mark.
LEXICON—a. imperf. mid./pass. (deponent = act.) indic. of βούλομαι (LN 30.56) (BDAG 2.a.β. p. 182): 'to want' [BECNT, CBC; all versions except KJV], 'to wish' [AB, Bar], 'to purpose' [LN], 'to determine' [KJV], 'to plan, to intend' [BDAG, LN]. This verb means to think, with the purpose of planning or deciding on a course of action [LN]. It means to plan on a course of action [BDAG].
  b. aorist act. infin. of συμπαραλαμβάνω (LN 15.169) (BDAG p. 958): 'to take with' [AB, Bar, BECNT, CBC; ESV, KJV, NCV, NIV, NRSV, REB, TEV], 'to take along with' [NASB], 'to take along' [LN; CEV, GW, NLT], 'to bring along with' [LN; NET]. This verb means to take along with, with emphasis upon accompaniment [LN]. It means to take along as adjunct [BDAG].
  c. pres. pass. participle of καλέω (LN 33.129) (BDAG 1.c. p. 503): 'to be called' [Bar, BDAG, BECNT, LN; ESV, NASB, NET, NIV, NRSV], 'to be named' [AB, BDAG, LN], 'to be called by name' [BDAG], not explicit [CBC; GW, NCV, NLT, REB, TEV]. The phrase 'John called Mark' is also translated 'John, whose other name was Mark' [CEV], 'John, whose surname was Mark' [KJV]. This verb means to speak of a person or object by means of a proper name [LN]. It means to identify by name or attribute [BDAG].

**15:38** But[a] Paul thought-best not to-take-with[b] them one who had-withdrawn[c] from them in Pamphylia and had- not -gone-with[d] them to the work.[e]
LEXICON—a. δέ (LN 89.124): 'but' [AB, BECNT, CBC, LN; all versions except GW], 'however' [Bar; GW], 'on the other hand' [LN]. This conjunction indicates a contrast [LN].
  b. pres. act. infin. of συμπαραλαμβάνω (LN 15.169): 'to take with' [AB, Bar, BECNT, CBC; ESV, KJV, NRSV, REB], 'to take along' [LN; GW, NASB, NET], 'to bring along with' [LN], 'to take' [NCV, NIV, TEV].

The phrase 'But Paul thought best not to take with them' is also translated 'But Paul did not want to' [CEV], 'But Paul disagreed strongly' [NLT]. This verb means to take along with, with emphasis upon accompaniment [LN].
  c. aorist act. participle of ἀφίστημι (LN 15.51) (BDAG 2.a. p. 157): 'to withdraw' [BDAG, BECNT; ESV], 'to go away' [BDAG, LN], 'to depart' [LN; KJV], 'to leave' [AB, LN; CEV, NCV, NET, TEV], 'to desert' [CBC; GW, NASB, NIV, NLT, NRSV, REB], 'to part' [Bar]. This verb means to move away from, with emphasis upon separation and possible lack of concern for what has been left [LN]. It means to distance oneself from some person or thing [BDAG].
  d. aorist act. participle of συνέρχομαι (LN 15.148) (BDAG 2. p. 970): 'to go with' [AB, BECNT, LN; ESV, GW, KJV, NASB], 'to come with' [LN], 'to accompany' [Bar, LN; NET, NRSV], 'to travel together with' [BDAG]. The phrase 'had not gone with them to the work' is also translated 'did not continue with them in the work' [NCV], 'had not continued with them in the/their work' [NIV, NLT], 'had stopped working with them' [CEV], 'had not gone on to share in their work' [CBC; REB], 'had not stayed with them to the end of their mission' [TEV]. This verb means to come/go together with one or more other persons [BDAG, LN].
  e. ἔργον (LN 42.42) (BDAG 2. p. 391): 'work' [Bar, BDAG, BECNT, CBC, LN; all versions except CEV, TEV], 'task' [BDAG, LN], 'mission' [TEV], 'ministry' [AB], 'occupation' [BDAG]. This noun is also translated as a verb: 'had stopped working with them' [CEV]. This noun denotes that which one normally does [LN]. It denotes that which one does as a regular activity [BDAG].
QUESTION—What does the phrase 'had not gone with them to the work' suggest?
  It suggests dereliction of duty [Bar].

**15:39** And there occurred[a] (a)-sharp-disagreement, so-that they separated[b] from each-other. Barnabas took[c] Mark with him and sailed-away to Cyprus,
LEXICON—a. aorist mid. (deponent = act.) indic. of γίνομαι (LN 13.107) (BDAG 3.b. p. 197): 'to occur' [LN; NASB], 'to happen, to come to be' [LN], 'to arise' [AB, Bar, BDAG, BECNT; ESV], 'to come about, to develop' [BDAG], not explicit [CBC; CEV, GW, KJV, NCV, NLT, NRSV, REB]. The phrase 'there occurred a sharp disagreement' is also translated 'They had a sharp disagreement' [NET], 'They had such a sharp disagreement' [NIV], 'There was a sharp argument' [TEV]. This verb means to happen, with the implication that what happens is different from a previous state [LN]. It means to come into being as an event or phenomenon from a point of origin [BDAG].
  b. aorist pass. infin. of ἀποχωρίζω (LN 63.30) (BDAG p. 125): 'to be separated' [AB, Bar, BDAG, BECNT; ESV, NASB, NCV, NLT, TEV],

'to be parted' [CBC; GW, NET, NIV, NRSV, REB], 'to separate definitely, to split up' [LN], 'to go one's own way' [LN; CEV]. The phrase 'they separated from each other' is also translated 'they departed asunder one from the other' [KJV]. This verb means to separate more or less definitively one from another [LN].
  c. aorist act. participle of παραλαμβάνω (LN 15.168) (BDAG 1. p. 767): 'to take with' [AB, BDAG, BECNT, CBC; ESV, GW, NASB, NLT, NRSV, REB], 'to take along' [BDAG, LN; NET], 'to bring along' [LN], 'to take to oneself' [BDAG], 'to take' [Bar; CEV, KJV, NCV, NIV, TEV]. This verb means to take or bring someone along with [LN]. It means to take into close association [BDAG].

**15:40** but[a] Paul chose[b] Silas and departed,[c] having-been-commended[d] by the brothers[e] to-the grace[f] of-the Lord.[g]

TEXT—Manuscripts reading κυρίου 'Lord' are given a B rating by GNT indicating that the text is almost certain. Some manuscripts have θεοῦ 'God'. This is followed by CEV, KJV.

LEXICON—a. δέ (LN 89.124): 'but' [AB, BECNT, LN; CEV, ESV, NASB, NCV, NET, NIV, NRSV], 'on the other hand' [LN], not explicit [GW, NLT, REB]. This word is also translated as 'and' [KJV], 'while' [Bar, CBC; TEV]. This conjunction indicates a contrast [LN].
  b. aorist mid. participle of ἐπιλέγω (LN 30.88) (BDAG 2. p. 375): 'to choose' [BDAG, LN; all translations except CEV], 'to select' [BDAG, LN], 'to take' [CEV]. This verb means to choose for a particular purpose [LN].
  c. aorist act. indic. of ἐξέρχομαι (LN 15.40): 'to depart' [BECNT; ESV, KJV], 'to leave' [CEV, GW, NASB, NCV, NIV, NLT, TEV], 'to go out of, to depart out of, to leave from within' [LN], 'to set out' [NET, NRSV], 'to set/go off' [AB, Bar]. The phrase 'Paul chose Silas and departed' is also translated 'Paul chose Silas and started on his journey' [REB], '…Paul chose Silas. He started on his journey' [CBC]. This verb means to move out of an enclosed or well defined two or three-dimensional area [LN].
  d. aorist pass. participle of παραδίδωμι (LN 57.77) (BDAG 2. p. 762): 'to be commended' [BDAG, BECNT, CBC; ESV, NET, NIV, REB, TEV], 'to be committed' [AB, Bar, BDAG; NASB], 'to be recommended' [KJV], 'to be given over' [BDAG, LN], 'to be handed over' [LN]. This verb is also translated as an active verb: 'the believers commending him to the grace of the Lord' [NRSV], 'the followers had placed them in God's care' [CEV], 'the believers entrusted him to the Lord's care' [GW], 'the believers entrusted him to the Lord's gracious care' [NLT], 'The believers…put Paul into the Lord's care' [NCV]. This verb means to hand over to or to convey something to someone, particularly a right or an authority [LN]. It means to entrust for care or preservation [BDAG].

e. ἀδελφός (LN 11.23): 'brother' [Bar, CBC; ESV, NIV, REB], 'fellow believer, Christian brother' [LN]. The phrase 'the brothers' is also translated 'the brethren' [AB, BECNT; KJV, NASB], 'the followers' [CEV], 'the believers' [GW, NCV, NLT, NRSV, TEV], 'the brothers and sisters' [NET]. This noun denotes a close associate of a group of persons having a well-defined membership. In the NT ἀδελφός 'brother' refers specifically to fellow believers in Christ [LN].

f. χάρις (LN 88.66) (BDAG 2.a. p. 1079): 'grace' [AB, Bar, BDAG, BECNT, CBC, LN; ESV, KJV, NASB, NET, NIV, NRSV, REB, TEV], 'favor' [BDAG], 'goodwill' [BDAG], 'kindness' [LN], 'graciousness' [LN], 'gracious care' [BDAG; NLT], 'gracious help' [BDAG]. The phrase 'grace of the Lord' is also translated 'God's care' [CEV], 'the Lord's care' [GW, NCV]. This noun denotes the kindness shown to someone, with the implication of graciousness on the part of the one showing such kindness [LN]. It denotes a beneficent disposition toward someone [BDAG].

g. κύριος (LN 12.9): 'Lord' [Bar, BECNT, CBC, LN; all versions except CEV, KJV], 'God' [AB; KJV], 'Ruler, One who commands' [LN]. The phrase 'grace of the Lord' is also translated 'God's care' [CEV]. This noun denotes a title for God and for Christ. It indicates one who exercises supernatural authority over mankind [LN].

QUESTION—Who had the brothers commended to the grace of the Lord?
1. They commended Paul [AB, Bar, BECNT, CBC, NICNT; ESV, GW, KJV, NASB, NCV, NET, NIV, NLT, NRSV, REB, TEV].
2. They commended Paul and Silas [EBC, PNTC, TNTC, TRT; CEV].

**15:41** And he-was-traveling-through<sup>a</sup> Syria and Cilicia, strengthening<sup>b</sup> the churches.<sup>c</sup>

LEXICON—a. imperf. mid./pass. (deponent = act.) indic. of διέρχομαι (LN 15.21) (BDAG 1.b.α. p. 244): 'to travel through' [AB, CBC; CEV, NASB, REB], 'to travel throughout' [NLT], 'to go through' [BDAG, BECNT; ESV, GW, KJV, NCV, NIV, NRSV, TEV], 'to pass through' [Bar; NET], 'to travel around through, to journey all through' [LN]. This verb means to travel around through an area, with the implication of both extensive and thorough movement throughout an area [LN]. It means to move within or through an area [BDAG].

b. pres. act. participle of ἐπιστηρίζω (LN 74.19) (BDAG p. 381): 'to strengthen' [AB, Bar, BDAG, BECNT, LN; ESV, GW, NASB, NET, NIV, NLT, NRSV, TEV], 'to make more firm' [LN], 'to encourage' [CEV], 'to confirm' [KJV]. This verb is also translated as a noun: 'giving strength' [NCV], 'bringing new strength' [CBC; REB]. This verb means to cause someone to become stronger in the sense of more firm and unchanging in attitude or belief [LN]. It means to cause someone to become stronger or more firm [BDAG].

c. ἐκκλησία (LN 11.32) (BDAG 3.b.β. p. 304): 'church' [AB, Bar, BDAG, BECNT, LN; all versions], 'congregation' [BDAG, CBC, LN]. This noun denotes a congregation of Christians, implying interacting membership [LN]. It denotes the totality of Christians living together and meeting in a particular area, but not necessarily limited to one meeting place [BDAG].

**DISCOURSE UNIT—16:1–13** [NASB]. The topic is the Macedonian vision.

**DISCOURSE UNIT—16:1–5** [AB, BECNT, NAC, PNTC, TNTC; CEV, ESV, GW, NCV, NET, NIV, NRSV, TEV]. The topic is Timothy works with Paul and Silas [CEV], Timothy goes with Paul and Silas [TEV], Timothy goes with Paul [NCV], Timothy joins Paul in Lystra [GW], Timothy joins Paul and Silas in Lystra [BECNT], Timothy joins Paul and Silas [ESV, NET, NIV, NRSV], Paul's visit to the churches from the first journey [AB], Paul's return to Derbe and Lystra [TNTC], revisiting the south Galatian churches [PNTC], revisiting Derbe, Lystra, and Iconium [NAC].

**DISCOURSE UNIT—16:1–4** [EBC, NICNT]. The topic is Paul and Silas in south Galatia; Timothy joins them [NICNT], Paul adds Timothy to the team in Galatia [EBC].

**16:1** **Paul came[a] also to Derbe and to Lystra. A disciple was there, named Timothy, (the)-son of a Jewish woman who was (a)-believer,[b] but (his)-father-(was) a Greek.**
LEXICON—a. aorist act. indic. of καταντάω (LN 15.84) (BDAG 1. p. 523): 'to come to' [AB, BDAG, BECNT, LN; ESV, KJV, NASB, NCV, NET, NIV], 'to go to' [CBC; CEV, NLT, NRSV, REB], 'to travel to' [TEV], 'to reach' [Bar, LN], 'to arrive' [BDAG, LN; GW]. This verb means to move toward and to arrive at a point [LN]. It means to get to a geographical destination [BDAG].

b. πιστός (LN 11.17, 31.103) (BDAG 2. p. 821): 'a believer' [Bar, BECNT, LN (11.17, 31.103); ESV, NASB, NCV, NET, NIV, NRSV], 'a follower' [CEV], 'a Christian' [AB; TEV], 'Christian follower' [LN (11.17, 31.103)], 'a (Christian) believer' [BDAG], 'a Jewish believer' [GW, NLT], 'a Jewish Christian' [CBC; REB]. This adjective is also translated as a verb: 'which was a Jewess, and believed' [KJV]. This adjective pertains to one who is included among the faithful followers of Christ [LN (11.17)]. It pertains to one who believes in Jesus Christ [LN (31.103)]. It pertains to being trusting [BDAG].

QUESTION—Who was Timothy?
Timothy was from either Derbe or Lystra. According to II Timothy 1:5 his mother was Eunice and his grandmother was Lois [AB, TNTC]. He had come to faith in Christ during the previous missionary visit [EBC, NICNT].

**16:2** **He was-well-spoken-of[a] by the brothers[b] at Lystra and Iconium.**
LEXICON—a. imperf. pass. indic. of μαρτυρέω (LN 33.263) (BDAG 2.b. p. 618): 'to be spoken well of' [AB, BDAG, BECNT, CBC, LN; ESV,

NASB, NRSV, REB], 'to be approved of' [BDAG, LN], 'to be well thought of' [NLT]. The phrase 'He was well spoken of by the brothers' is also translated 'The Lord's followers...said good things about Timothy' [CEV], 'The believers...said good things about him' [NCV], 'The believers...spoke well of Timothy' [GW, TEV], 'The brothers...spoke well of him' [NET, NIV], 'was well reported by the brethren' [KJV], 'This disciple had a good reputation with the brothers' [Bar]. This verb means to speak well of a person on the basis of personal experience [LN]. It means to be well spoken of, to be approved [BDAG].
  b. ἀδελφός (LN 11.23): 'brother' [Bar; ESV, NET, NIV], 'fellow believer, a Christian brother' [LN]. The phrase 'the brothers' is also translated 'the brethren' [AB; KJV, NASB], 'the believers' [BECNT; GW, NCV, NLT, NRSV, TEV], 'The Lord's followers' [CEV], 'the Christians' [CBC; REB]. This noun denotes a close associate of a group of persons having a well-defined membership. In the NT ἀδελφός 'brother' refers specifically to fellow believers in Christ [LN].

**16:3** Paul wanted this-man to-go[a] with him, and he- took-(him)[b] and -circumcised[c] him because-of the Jews who were in those places, for they all knew[d] that his father was a Greek.

LEXICON—a. aorist act. infin. of ἐξέρχομαι (LN 15.40): 'to go' [Bar; CEV, GW, NASB], 'to accompany' [BECNT; ESV, NET, NRSV], 'to travel' [AB; NCV], 'to go out of, to depart out of, to leave from within' [LN], 'to go forth' [KJV], 'to join' [NLT]. The phrase 'Paul wanted this man to go with him' is also translated 'Paul wanted to take him along' [NIV], 'Paul wanted to take him with him' [REB], 'Paul wanted to take Timothy along with him' [TEV], 'Paul wanted to have him in his company' [CBC]. This verb means to move out of an enclosed or well defined two or three-dimensional area [LN].
  b. aorist act. participle of λαμβάνω (LN 30.86) (BDAG 1. p. 583): 'to take' [Bar, BDAG, BECNT, CBC; ESV, KJV, NASB, NET, NIV, NRSV, REB, TEV], 'to take hold of, to grasp, to take in hand' [BDAG], 'to choose, to select, to prefer' [LN], not explicit [AB; CEV, GW, NCV, NLT]. This verb means to make a choice of one or more possible alternatives [LN]. It means to get hold of something by laying hands on or grasping something, directly or indirectly [BDAG].
  c. aorist act. indic. of περιτέμνω (LN 53.51) (BDAG a. p. 807): 'to circumcise' [AB, Bar, BDAG, BECNT, CBC, LN; ESV, GW, KJV, NASB, NCV, NET, NIV, TEV]. This verb is also translated as a passive verb: 'to be circumcised' [NLT]. The phrase 'he took him and circumcised him' is also translated 'he...had him circumcised' [NRSV, REB], 'Paul...had him circumcised' [CEV]. This verb means to cut off the foreskin of the male genital organ as a religious rite involving consecration and ethnic identification [LN].

d. pluperfect act. indic. of οἶδα (LN 28.1) (BDAG 1.c. p. 693): 'to know' [BDAG, LN; all translations], 'to know about, to have knowledge of, to be acquainted with' [LN]. This verb means to possess information about [LN]. It means to have information about [BDAG].

QUESTION—Who circumcised Timothy?
1. Paul circumcised Timothy [AB, Bar, BECNT, CBC, EBC, NICNT, PNTC, TNTC].
2. Paul had someone else to circumcise Timothy [NAC; CEV, NLT, NRSV, REB].

QUESTION—Why did Paul circumcise Timothy?

Eunice was a Jewess, but she had been married to a Greek. According to Jewish law the children in such a relationship followed the mother's nationality [AB, BECNT, CBC, NAC, NICNT, TRT]. Timothy was a Jew not a Gentile. Paul circumcised Timothy out of consideration for the Jews of the region, because he wanted the young man to accompany him on his journey [AB, PNTC]. If Paul is going to work in the synagogue, circumcision will ensure Timothy's credibility [BECNT, TRT]. It was absolutely essential that Paul circumcise Timothy to give him good standing in the eyes of the Jews among whom he would be working [NAC, PNTC, TNTC]. It was Timothy's mixed parentage that made Paul decide to circumcise him before taking him along as his colleague [NICNT].

QUESTION—What does the phrase 'all knew that his father was a Greek' mean?

The remark 'all knew that his father was a Greek' must mean that Timothy was uncircumcised [AB].

**16:4** As they-were-traveling-through[a] the cities, they-delivered[b] to-them the rules[c] which they were to-obey[d] that had-been-decided[e] by the apostles and elders[f] who were in Jerusalem.

LEXICON—a. imperf. mid./pass. (deponent = act.) indic. of διαπορεύομαι (LN 15.21) (BDAG 2. p. 235): 'to travel through' [AB], 'to go through' [GW, KJV, NET, TEV], 'to pass through' [Bar, BDAG, BECNT; NASB], 'to travel around through, to journey all through' [LN], 'to travel' [NCV, NIV], 'to go' [CEV, NLT, NRSV]. The phrase 'As they were traveling through' is also translated 'As they went on their way through' [ESV], 'As they made their way' [CBC; REB]. This verb means to travel around through an area, with the implication of both extensive and thorough movement throughout an area [LN]. It means movement from one part or locality to another within a geographical area [BDAG].

b. imperf. act. indic. of παραδίδωμι (LN 33.237) (BDAG 3. p. 763): 'to deliver' [AB, Bar; ESV, KJV, NASB, NIV, NRSV, TEV], 'to give' [NCV], 'to instruct' [LN; NLT], 'to teach' [BDAG, LN], 'to tell' [CEV, GW, 'to pass on' [BDAG, BECNT; NET], 'to hand on' [CBC; REB], 'to hand down' [BDAG]. This verb means to pass on traditional instruction,

often implying over a long period of time [LN]. It means to pass on to another what one knows, of oral or written tradition [BDAG].
- c. δόγμα (LN 33.333) (BDAG 1.a. p. 254): 'rule' [LN; TEV], 'law' [LN], 'ordinance' [BDAG, LN], 'decision' [BDAG, BECNT, CBC; ESV, GW, NCV, NIV, NLT, NRSV, REB], 'command' [BDAG], 'decree' [AB, Bar; KJV, NASB, NET], 'instruction' [CEV]. This noun denotes a formalized rule or set of rules prescribing what people must do [LN]. It denotes formalized sets of rules that are to be observed [BDAG].
- d. pres. act. infin. of φυλάσσω (LN 36.19) (BDAG 5.a. p. 1068): 'to obey' [LN; NCV, NET, NIV, TEV], 'to observe' [BDAG; NASB], 'to follow' [BDAG; CEV, NLT], 'to keep' [KJV], 'to keep commandments' [LN], not explicit [GW]. This verb is also translated as a noun: 'their/for observance' [AB, Bar, BECNT, CBC; ESV, NRSV, REB]. This verb means to continue to obey orders or commandments [LN]. It means to continue to keep a law or commandment from being broken [BDAG].
- e. perf. pass. participle of κρίνω (LN 30.75) (BDAG 4. p. 568): 'to be decided' [Bar, BDAG, LN], 'to be decided upon/on' [NASB, NET, TEV], 'to be taken' [CBC; REB], 'to be reached' [BECNT; ESV, NIV, NRSV], 'to be agreed upon' [AB], 'to be ordained of' [KJV], 'to be made' [NCV, NLT], 'to come to a conclusion, to make up one's mind' [LN], 'to reach a decision' [BDAG]. This verb is also translated as an active verb: 'the apostles and leaders...had decided' [CEV], 'the apostles and spiritual leaders...had made' [GW]. This verb means to come to a conclusion in the process of thinking and thus to be in a position to make a decision [LN]. It means to come to a conclusion after a cognitive process [BDAG].
- f. πρεσβύτερος (LN 53.77) (BDAG 2.b.α. p. 862): 'elder' [BDAG, LN; all translations except CEV, GW], 'presbyter' [BDAG], 'leader' [CEV], 'spiritual leader' [GW]. This noun denotes a person of responsibility and authority in matters of socio-religious concerns, both in Jewish and Christian societies [LN]. It denotes an official among the Christians [BDAG].

QUESTION—Who does 'to them' refer to?

It refers to the believers [Bar, TH; NLT, TEV]. It refers to the churches [TNTC]. It refers to the churches that were in the southern part of the Roman province of Galatia and not a part of Syro-Cilicia [NAC, NICNT, PNTC]. It refers to the Gentile/non-Jewish believers/Christians [TRT; NET].

**DISCOURSE UNIT—16:5** [EBC, NICNT]. The topic is the churches grow in faith and numbers [NICNT], a summary statement [EBC].

**16:5** So the churches[a] were-being-strengthened[b] in-the faith,[c] and they increased[d] in-number daily.

LEXICON—a. ἐκκλησία (LN 11.32) (BDAG 3.b.β. p. 304): 'church' [AB, Bar, BDAG, BECNT, LN; all versions], 'congregation' [CBC, LN]. This noun denotes a congregation of Christians, implying interacting membership

ACTS 16:5

[LN]. It denotes the totality of Christians living together and meeting in a particular area, but not necessarily limited to one meeting place [BDAG].
b. imperf. pass. indic. of στερεόω (LN 74.19) (BDAG 2. p. 943): 'to be strengthened' [AB, BDAG, BECNT, LN; ESV, GW, NASB, NET, NIV, NLT, NRSV], 'to be made stronger' [TEV], 'to be made more firm' [LN], 'to be confirmed' [Bar], 'to be established' [KJV]. This verb is also translated as an active verb: 'grew/became stronger' [CBC; CEV, NCV, REB]. This verb means to cause someone to become stronger in the sense of more firm and unchanging in attitude or belief [LN]. It means to cause to become firmer in such matters as conviction or commitment [BDAG].
c. πίστις (LN 31.102) (BDAG 2.d.α. p. 819): 'faith' [BDAG; all translations], 'Christian faith' [LN], 'trust' [BDAG]. This noun denotes the belief in the good news about Jesus Christ and becoming a follower [LN]. It denotes the state of believing on the basis of the reliability of the one trusted [BDAG].
d. imperf. act. indic. of περισσεύω (LN 59.52) (BDAG 1.a.δ. p. 805): 'to increase' [AB, Bar, CBC; ESV, KJV, NASB, NET, NRSV, REB], 'to abound' [BDAG, LN], 'to grow' [BDAG, BECNT; GW, NCV, NIV, NLT, TEV], 'to be in abundance, to be a lot of, to exist in a large quantity' [LN]. The phrase 'they increased in number daily' is also translated 'each day more people' [CEV]. This verb means to be or exist in abundance, with the implication of being considerably more than what would be expected [LN]. It means to be in abundance [BDAG].

QUESTION—What caused the churches to be strengthened in the faith and to increase in number?

It was from delivering the rules in 16:4. As Luke often notes, such communication serves to strengthen the church or bring joy to the church (Acts 14:28; 15:32, 35, 41), with growth following [BECNT]. Luke makes the important point that resolution of doctrinal and practical issues in the churches promoted the work of the gospel and led to rapid growth (6:7; 9:31) [PNTC]. The strengthening and growth of the churches was the result of Paul's missionary policy and the response of the Jerusalem church to it [EBC]. The churches were strengthened in the faith and grew in number as a result of the message that was given in 16:4 [TRT].

**DISCOURSE UNIT—16:6–18:22** [PNTC]. The topic is the word goes to Europe.

**DISCOURSE UNIT—16:6–40** [NICNT]. The topic is Philippi.

**DISCOURSE UNIT—16:6–10** [AB, Bar, BECNT, EBC, NAC, NICNT, PNTC, TNTC; CEV, ESV, GW, NCV, NET, NIV, NRSV, TEV]. The topic is Paul's vision in Troas [CEV], Paul has a vision [GW], Paul is called out of Asia [NCV], Paul's vision of the Macedonian man [NET], the vision of the Macedonian man [BECNT], Paul's vision of the man of Macedonia [NIV, NRSV], the vision of the Macedonian [AB], in Troas: Paul's vision [TEV], guided by the Spirit to Troas [Bar], the call to Macedonia [TNTC], called to Macedonia [NAC], the call from Macedonia [NICNT], the Macedonian call [ESV], providential direction for the mission [EBC], remarkable guidance [PNTC].

**16:6** And they-went-through[a] the region[b] of Phrygia and Galatia, having-been-forbidden[c] by the Holy Spirit[d] to-speak the word[e] in Asia.

LEXICON—a. aorist act. indic. of διέρχομαι (LN 15.21) (BDAG 1.b.α. p. 244): 'to go through' [BDAG, BECNT; CEV, ESV, GW, KJV, NCV, NET, NRSV], 'to pass through' [Bar; NASB], 'to travel through' [AB, CBC; NLT, REB, TEV], 'to travel around through, to journey all through' [LN], 'to travel throughout' [NIV]. This verb means to travel around through an area, with the implication of both extensive and thorough movement throughout an area [LN]. It means to move within or through an area [BDAG].

b. χώρα (LN 1.79) (BDAG 2.b. p. 1094): 'region' [BDAG, BECNT, CBC, LN; all versions except CEV, NCV, NLT], 'territory' [Bar, LN], 'land' [LN], 'district, place' [BDAG], 'area' [NCV, NLT], 'country' [AB], not explicit [CEV]. This noun denotes a region of the earth, normally in relation to some ethnic group or geographical center, but not necessarily constituting a unit of governmental administration [LN]. It denotes a portion of land area [BDAG].

c. aorist pass. participle of κωλύω (LN 13.146) (BDAG 1.a. p. 580): 'to be forbidden' [Bar, BDAG; ESV, KJV, NASB, NRSV], 'to be prevented' [AB, BDAG, BECNT, CBC; NET, REB], 'to be hindered' [BDAG, LN], 'to be kept' [NIV]. This verb is also translated as an active verb: 'the Holy Spirit had prevented them' [NLT]. The phrase 'having been forbidden by the Holy Spirit to speak' is also translated 'the Holy Spirit would/did not let them preach' [CEV, NCV, TEV], 'the Holy Spirit kept them from speaking' [GW]. This verb means to cause something not to happen [LN]. It means to keep something from happening [BDAG].

d. πνεῦμα (LN 12.18) (BDAG 5.c.α. p. 834): 'Spirit' [BDAG, LN; all translations except KJV], 'Ghost' [KJV]. This noun denotes the third person of the Trinity whose titles are 'Spirit, Spirit of God, and Holy Spirit'. In many religious systems the significant difference between the gods and the spirits is that the gods are regarded as supernatural beings which control certain aspects of natural phenomena, while the spirits are supernatural beings, often impersonal, which indwell or inhabit certain places, including rivers, streams, mountains, caves, animals, and people. Spirits are often regarded as being primarily evil, though it may be possible to induce them to be favorable to people. It is extremely difficult to find in some languages a fully satisfactory term to speak of the Spirit of God. If one uses a term which normally identifies local supernatural beings, there is a tendency to read into the term the meaning of an evil or mischievous character. If, however, one uses a term which may identify the spirit of a person, the problems may even be greater, since according to many systems of religious belief, the spirit of an individual does not become active until the individual dies. Therefore, the activity of the Spirit of God would presumably suggest that God himself had died. However, if one uses a term which means 'heart' or 'soul' (and thus the Spirit of God would be literally equivalent to 'the heart of God'), there may be complications since this aspect of human personality is often regarded as not being able to act on its own. The solutions to the problem of 'Spirit' have been varied. In some languages the term for Spirit is essentially equivalent to 'the unseen one'. and therefore the Spirit of God is essentially equivalent to 'the invisibleness of God'. In a number of languages the closest equivalent for Spirit is 'breath,' and in a number of indigenous religious systems, the 'breath' is regarded as having a kind of independent existence. In other languages the term for Spirit is equivalent to what is often translated as 'the soul,' that is to say, the immaterial part of a person. There is, of course, always the difficulty of employing a term meaning 'soul' or 'life,' since it often proves to be impersonal and thus provides no basis for speaking of the Spirit of God as being a person or a personal manifestation of God. In quite a few languages the equivalent of Spirit is literally 'shadow,' since the 'shadow' of a person is regarded as the immaterial part of the individual. Moreover, in many systems of religious thought the shadow is regarded as having some significant measure of independent existence. In a few cases the term for Spirit is literally 'wind,' but there are frequently difficulties involved in this type of terminology since a term for wind often suggests calamity or evil intent. One meaning of Spirit which must be clearly avoided is that of 'apparition' or 'ghost'. Frequently it is not possible to find a fully satisfactory term for 'Spirit', and therefore in all contexts some characterizing feature is added, for example, either 'of God' or 'holy', in the sense of 'divine'. [LN]. It denotes God's being as controlling influence, with focus on association with humans [BDAG].

e. λόγος (LN 33.260) (BDAG 1.a.β. p. 600): 'word' [AB, Bar, BDAG, BECNT; ESV, GW, KJV, NASB, NIV, NLT, NRSV], 'message' [CBC; NET, REB, TEV], 'Good News' [NCV], 'what is preached, gospel' [LN], not explicit [CEV]. This noun denotes the content of what is preached about Christ or about the good news [LN]. It denotes a communication whereby the mind finds expression [BDAG].

QUESTION—Who does the phrase 'they went through' refer to?
It refers to Paul, Silas and Timothy [Bar, TRT]. It refers to Paul and his friends/companions [CEV, NIV]. It refers to Paul and Silas [GW, NLT]. It refers to Paul and those with him [NCV].

QUESTION—What does 'the region of Phrygia and Galatia' refer to?
It refers to one area 'the Phrygian and Galatian region'. The area called Phrygia lay partly in the Roman province of Asia and partly in the province of Galatia [TNTC]. 'The Phrygian and Galatian area' refers to the part of the

region of Phrygia that was located in Galatia province [TRT]. It refers to the border district which separated the ethnic regions of Phrygia and Galatia [TH].

**16:7** And when they had-come<sup>a</sup> to Mysia, they-were-trying<sup>b</sup> to-go into Bithynia, but the Spirit of-Jesus did- not -allow<sup>c</sup> them.

TEXT—Manuscripts reading τὸ πνεῦμα Ἰησοῦ 'the Spirit of Jesus' are given an A rating by GNT to indicate it was regarded to be certain. A variant reading is τὸ πνεῦμα 'the Spirit' and it is followed by KJV.

LEXICON—a. aorist act. participle of ἔρχομαι (LN 15.81) (BDAG 1.a.β. p. 394): 'to come' [Bar, BDAG, LN; ESV, KJV, NASB, NCV, NET, NIV, NRSV], 'coming' [BECNT, LN; NLT], 'to arrive' [CEV], 'to go' [GW], 'to approach' [CBC; REB], 'to reach' [TEV], 'to go toward' [AB]. This verb means to move toward or up to the reference point of the viewpoint character or event [LN]. It means movement from one point to another, with focus on approach from the narrator's perspective [BDAG].

b. imperf. act. indic. of πειράζω (LN 68.58) (BDAG 1. p. 792): 'to try' [Bar, BDAG, CBC, LN; CEV, GW, NASB, NCV, NIV, REB, TEV] 'to attempt' [AB, BDAG, BECNT, LN; ESV, NET, NRSV], 'to assay' [KJV]. The phrase 'they were trying to go into Bithynia' is also translated 'they headed north for the province of Bithynia' [NLT]. This verb means to attempt to do something, with the implication of not succeeding [LN]. It means to make an effort to do something [BDAG].

c. aorist act. indic. of ἐάω (LN 13.138) (BDAG 1. p. 269): 'to allow' [BECNT, CBC, LN; ESV, GW, NET, NIV, NLT, NRSV, REB, TEV], 'to let' [BDAG, LN; CEV, NCV], 'to permit' [AB, Bar, BDAG, LN; NASB], 'to suffer' [KJV]. This verb means to allow someone to do something [BDAG, LN].

QUESTION—Where was Mysia?

It was in the northern part of the province of Asia. It was bordered on the north by Bithynia, on the south by Lycia, on the east by Galatia, on the west by the sea [Bar, BECNT, EBC, PNTC, TH, TNTC].

QUESTION—Where was Bithynia?

Bithynia lay to the east of Mysian Asia and stretched eastward along the south coast of the Black Sea. During the first century it was a senatorial province [Bar, PNTC, TNTC].

QUESTION—What does 'the Spirit of Jesus' refer to?

'The Spirit of Jesus' refers to the Holy Spirit [Bar, CBC, NAC, PNTC, TH, TNTC, TRT].

**16:8** So, passing-by<sup>a</sup> Mysia, they-went-down<sup>b</sup> to Troas.

LEXICON—a. aorist act. participle of παρέρχομαι (LN 15.28) (BDAG 6. p. 776): 'to pass by' [LN; ESV, GW, KJV, NASB, NCV, NIV, NRSV], 'to pass through' [BECNT; NET, REB], 'to go by' [LN], 'to go through' [BDAG; CEV, NLT], 'to travel through' [AB; TEV], 'to arrive at' [Bar], 'to skirt' [CBC]. This verb means to move past a reference point [LN]. It means to pass through an area [BDAG].

b. aorist act. indic. of καταβαίνω (LN 15.107) (BDAG 1.a.β. p. 514): 'to go down' [BDAG, BECNT, LN; ESV, NET, NIV, NRSV], 'to move down, to descend' [LN], 'to come down' [AB, Bar, BDAG, LN; KJV, NASB], 'to come' [CEV], 'to go' [GW, NCV, TEV]. The phrase 'passing by Mysia, they went down to Troas' is also translated 'they went on through Mysia to the seaport of Troas' [NLT]. The phrase 'they went down to Troas' is also translated 'they…reached the coast at Troas' [CBC; REB]. This verb means to move down, irrespective of the gradient [LN]. It means to move downward [BDAG].

QUESTION—Where was Troas?

Troas was located on the northwestern tip of Asia Minor near ancient Troy. It was about 585 miles from Antioch in Syria [BECNT, CBC].

**16:9** And (a)-vision[a] appeared[b] to-Paul in the night: a man of Macedonia was standing there, urging[c] him and saying, "Come-over to Macedonia and help us."

LEXICON—a. ὅραμα (LN 33.488) (BDAG 1. p. 718): 'vision' [BDAG, LN; all translations], 'something seen, sight' [BDAG]. This noun denotes an event in which something appears vividly and credibly to the mind, although not actually present, but implying the influence of some divine or supernatural power or agency [LN]. It denotes something that is viewed with one's eye [BDAG].

b. aorist pass. indic. of ὁράω (LN 24.1) (BDAG A.1.d. p. 719): 'to appear' [Bar, BDAG, BECNT; ESV, KJV, NASB, NET], 'to be seen' [LN], 'to come' [AB, CBC; REB]. The phrase 'a vision appeared to Paul' is also translated 'Paul had a vision' [CEV, GW, NIV, NLT, NRSV, TEV], 'Paul saw in a vision' [NCV]. This verb means to see [LN]. In the passive voice it means to appear, to become visible [BDAG].

c. pres. act. participle of παρακαλέω (LN 33.168) (BDAG 1.b. p. 764): 'to urge' [ESV, GW, NET], 'to appeal to' [CBC, LN; NASB, REB], 'to plead with' [NLT, NRSV], 'to beg' [AB, Bar; CEV, NCV, NIV, TEV], 'to beseech' [BECNT], 'to ask for earnestly, to request, to plead for' [LN], 'to invite' [BDAG], 'to pray' [KJV]. This verb means to ask for something earnestly and with propriety [LN]. It means to ask to come and be present where the speaker is, and the content of the invitation follows in direct discourse [BDAG].

QUESTION—What is a vision?

In this case the vision occurred at night, so it should probably be thought of as a dream [Bar]. Dreams were a recognized means of divine communication in ancient times (see (9:10, 12; 10:3, 17; 18:9; 22:17) [TNTC].

QUESTION—Where was Macedonia?

Macedonia was a Roman province, located across the Aegean Sea from the province of Asia [TH].

**16:10** And when he-had-seen the vision, immediately we-sought[a] to-go into Macedonia, concluding that God had-called[b] us to-preach-the-gospel[c] to-them.

LEXICON—a. aorist act. indic. of ζητέω (LN 25.9) (BDAG 3.d. p. 428): 'to seek' [Bar, BECNT; ESV, NASB], 'to desire' [BDAG, LN], 'to want to' [LN], 'to strive for, to aim at, to try to obtain, to wish for' [BDAG], 'to endeavor' [KJV]. The phrase 'we sought to go into' is also translated 'we began looking for a way to go to' [CEV], 'we immediately looked for a way to go to' [GW], 'we immediately prepared to leave for' [NCV], 'we attempted immediately to go over to' [NET], 'we got ready at once to leave for' [NIV], 'we decided to leave…at once' [NLT], 'we immediately tried to cross over to' [NRSV], 'we set about getting a passage to' [REB], 'we at once set about getting a passage to' [CBC], 'we got ready to leave for' [TEV], 'we hastened to go at once to' [AB]. This verb means to desire to have or experience something, with the probable implication of making an attempt to realize one's desire [LN]. It means to devote serious effort to realize one's desire or objective [BDAG].

  b. perf. mid. indic. of προσκαλέω (LN 33.312) (BDAG 2.b. p. 881): 'to call' [BDAG; all translations except AB], 'to call to a task' [BDAG, LN], 'to summon' [AB]. This verb means to urgently invite someone to accept responsibilities for a particular task, implying a new relationship to the one who does the calling [LN]. It means to call to a special task or office [BDAG].

  c. aorist mid. infin. of εὐαγγελίζω (LN 33.215) (BDAG 2.a.γ. p. 402): 'to preach the gospel' [AB; ESV, KJV, NASB, NIV], 'to preach the good news' [CEV, NLT, TEV], 'to tell the good news' [LN; NCV], 'to announce the gospel' [LN], 'to proclaim the gospel' [BDAG, BECNT], 'to tell about the Good News' [GW], 'to proclaim the good news' [NET, NRSV]. The phrase 'to preach the gospel to them' is also translated 'to take the good news there' [REB], 'to evangelize them' [Bar], 'to bring them the good news' [CBC]. This verb means to communicate good news concerning something and in the NT it is a particular reference to the gospel message about Jesus [LN]. It means to proclaim the divine message of salvation [BDAG].

QUESTION—What is expressed by the word 'immediately' here?

  It expresses unhesitating obedience to a divine command [Bar].

QUESTION—Who is referred to in the phrase 'we sought'?

  Paul, Timothy and Silas are referred to here [NAC, TNTC] including Luke [AB, BECNT, NICNT, PNTC, TH, TRT].

QUESTION—Who is considered to be the writer/narrator in the phrase 'we sought'?

  Most commentators support the view that Luke introduces his own eyewitness material at this point by using the first-person plural form 'we sought'. This is because it was at Troas that he first became an active participant in the Pauline mission [AB, NICNT, PNTC, TH, TRT].

ACTS 16:11 57

**DISCOURSE UNIT—16:11–40** [AB, Bar, BECNT, EBC, NAC, TNTC; GW]. The topic is Paul and Silas in Philippi [GW], Paul and Silas at Philippi [Bar], Paul in Philippi [AB], in Philippi [BECNT], at Philippi [EBC], Philippi: the first Macedonian church [TNTC], witnessing in Philippi [NAC].

**DISCOURSE UNIT—16:11–34** [PNTC]. The topic is salvation comes to Philippi.

**DISCOURSE UNIT—16:11–15** [CBC, NAC, PNTC; CEV, ESV, NCV, NET, NIV, NRSV, TEV]. The topic is the conversion of Lydia [ESV, NRSV], Lydia's conversion in Philippi [NIV], in Philippi: the conversion of Lydia [TEV], Lydia becomes a follower of the Lord [CEV], Lydia becomes a Christian [NCV], arrival at Philippi [NET], Europe at last [CBC], Lydia and her household [PNTC], founding a church with Lydia [NAC].

**DISCOURSE UNIT—16:11–12** [EBC]. The topic is arrival in the city.

**DISCOURSE UNIT—16:11–12a** [NICNT]. The topic is Troas to Philippi.

**16:11** So setting-sail[a] from Troas, we-ran-(a)-straight-course[b] to Samothrace, and the following-day to Neapolis,

LEXICON—a. aorist pass. participle of ἀνάγω (LN 54.4) (BDAG 4. p. 62): 'to set sail' [Bar, BECNT, LN; ESV, NRSV], 'to put out to sea' [BDAG, LN; NASB, NET, NIV], not explicit [CEV]. The phrase 'So setting sail from Troas' is also translated 'So we took a ship from Troas' [GW], 'Therefore loosing from Troas' [KJV], 'We left Troas' [NCV], 'We sailed from Troas' [CBC; REB], 'We boarded a boat at Troas' [NLT], 'We left by ship from Troas' [TEV], 'When we had sailed from Troas' [AB]. This verb means to begin to go by boat [BDAG, LN].

b. aorist act. indic. of εὐθυδρομέω (LN 54.3) (BDAG p. 406): 'to run a straight course' [BDAG; NASB], 'to sail a straight course' [LN; NET], 'to take a straight course' [NRSV], 'to sail straight to' [LN; GW, NCV], 'to sail straight' [CEV, NIV, NLT, TEV], 'to make a direct voyage' [BECNT; ESV], 'to make a straight run' [Bar, CBC; REB]. The phrase 'we ran a straight course' is also translated 'we came with a straight course' [KJV], 'we set our course straight' [AB], 'we…made a straight run' [Bar]. This verb means to follow a straight course to one's destination or goal [LN].

QUESTION—Where was Samothrace located?

Samothrace is an island in the northeastern part of the Aegean Sea, located about 38 miles from Troas and lying between Troas and Philippi [Bar, BECNT, CBC, EBC, NAC, PNTC, TH].

**DISCOURSE UNIT—16:12b–15** [NICNT]. The topic is the faith of Lydia.

**16:12** and-from-there to Philippi, which is (a)-leading city of-(the)-district of-Macedonia and a Roman colony. We stayed[a] in this city for some days.

TEXT—Manuscripts reading πρώτη[ς] μερίδος τῆς Μακεδονίας πόλις 'a prominent city of the district of Macedonia' are given a D rating by GNT to indicate that choosing it over a variant text was very difficult. A variant reading is πρώτη τῆς μερίδος τῆς Μακεδονίας πόλις 'the prominent city of the district of Macedonia' and it is followed by KJV, NCV, NIV.

LEXICON—a. pres. act. participle of διατρίβω (LN 85.61) (BDAG p. 238): 'to stay' [Bar, CBC, LN; NASB, NCV, NET, NIV, NLT, REB], 'to remain' [BECNT, LN; ESV, NRSV], 'to spend time' [BDAG], 'to abide' [KJV]. The clause 'We stayed in this city for some days' is also translated 'We spent several days in Philippi' [CEV], 'We spent several days there' [TEV], 'We then spent some days in this city' [AB], 'We were in this city for a number of days' [GW]. This verb means to remain or stay in a place [BDAG, LN], with the implication of some type of activity [LN].

QUESTION—Where was Philippi located?

Philippi was located ten miles northwest of Neapolis on a plain bounded by Mount Pangaeus to the north and northeast, with the rivers Strymon and Nestos on either side [EBC].

QUESTION—What does the phrase 'some days' refer to?

The phrase 'some days' should be understood as the days before the Sabbath day [AB]. It probably refers to more than four or five days [TRT].

**DISCOURSE UNIT—16:13–15** [EBC]. The topic is the conversion of Lydia.

**16:13** **And on-the Sabbath day we-went-outside**[a] **the gate to (a)-riverside, where we-supposed there was (a)-place)-of-prayer, and we- sat-down and -spoke to the women who had-come-together.**[b]

LEXICON—a. aorist act. indic. of ἐξέρχομαι (LN 15.40) (BDAG 1.a.α.ℵ. p. 347): 'to go outside' [all translations except GW, KJV, TEV], 'to go out, to come out, to go away' [BDAG], 'to go out of' [LN; GW, KJV, TEV], 'to depart out of, to leave from within' [LN]. This verb means to move out of an enclosed or well-defined two or three-dimensional area [LN]. It means to move out of or away from an area [BDAG].

b. aorist act. participle of συνέρχομαι (LN 15.123) (BDAG 1. p. 969): 'to come together' [BECNT, LN: ESV], 'to gather together, to go together, to meet' [LN], 'to assemble' [AB, BDAG, LN; NASB, NET], 'to gather' [Bar, BDAG, CBC; GW, NCV, NIV, NLT, NRSV, REB, TEV], 'to resort' [KJV]. The phrase 'the women who had come together' is also translated as 'the women who came' [CEV]. This verb means the movement of two or more objects to the same location [LN]. It means to come together with others as a group [BDAG].

QUESTION—What is meant by 'a place of prayer'?

Since there is no mention of men here, it is probable that 'place of prayer' here simply means a place where the women gathered by custom to pray [TNTC]. However, the phrase can be used to mean a synagogue building [BECNT, TNTC].

**DISCOURSE UNIT—16:14–21** [NASB]. The topic is first convert in Europe.

**16:14** A woman named Lydia, from-(the)-city of-Thyatira, (a)-seller-of-purple-cloth, who was a worshiper[a] of God, was-listening.[b] The Lord[c] opened[d] her heart[e] to-pay-attention[f] to-what was-said by Paul.

LEXICON—a. pres. mid. participle of σέβω (LN 53.53) (BDAG 1.b. p. 918): 'to worship' [Bar, BDAG, LN; KJV, NCV, NLT, TEV], 'to venerate' [LN], not explicit [GW]. This verb is also translated as a noun: 'worshiper' [BECNT, CBC; CEV, ESV, NASB, NIV, NRSV, REB]. The phrase 'a worshiper of God' is also translated 'a God-fearing woman' [AB; NET]. This verb means to express in attitude and ritual one's allegiance to and regard for deity [LN]. It means to express in gestures, rites, or ceremonies one's allegiance or devotion to deity [BDAG].

b. imperf. act. indic. of ἀκούω (LN 31.56): 'to listen' [AB, Bar, CBC; GW, NASB, NIV, REB], 'to listen to' [NET, NLT, NRSV], 'to accept, to listen and respond, to pay attention and respond, to heed' [LN], 'to hear' [BECNT; ESV, KJV, TEV], not explicit [CEV]. This verb is also translated as a noun: 'listener' [NCV]. This verb means to believe something and to respond to it on the basis of having heard [LN].

c. κύριος (LN 12.9): 'Lord' [LN; all translations except NCV], 'Ruler, One who commands' [LN]. The phrase 'The Lord opened her heart' is also translated 'he opened her mind' [NCV]. This noun denotes a title for God and for Christ. It indicates one who exercises supernatural authority over mankind [LN].

d. aorist act. indic. of διανοίγω (LN 27.49) (BDAG 1.b. p. 234): 'to open' [BDAG; all translations except CEV, GW], 'to open someone's mind, to cause someone to be open-minded' [LN]. The clause 'The Lord opened her heart to pay attention to what was said by Paul' is also translated 'he made her willing to accept what Paul was saying' [CEV], 'the Lord made her willing to pay attention to what Paul said' [GW]. The idiom 'to open the heart' means to cause someone to be willing to learn and evaluate fairly [LN]. Figuratively 'to open the heart' means to enable someone to perceive [BDAG].

e. καρδία (LN 27.49) (BDAG 1.b.β. p. 509): 'heart' [AB, Bar, BDAG, BECNT, CBC; ESV, KJV, NASB, NET, NIV, NLT, NRSV, REB], 'mind' [NCV, TEV]. The clause 'The Lord opened her heart to pay attention to what was said by Paul' is also translated 'he made her willing to accept what Paul was saying' [CEV], 'the Lord made her willing to pay attention to what Paul said' [GW]. The idiom 'to open the heart' means to cause someone to be willing to learn and evaluate fairly [LN]. The heart denotes the seat of physical, spiritual and mental life and here it is the center and source of inner awareness [BDAG].

f. pres. act. infin. of προσέχω (LN 30.35) (BDAG 2.b. p. 880): 'to pay attention' [BDAG; ESV, GW, NCV, TEV], 'to give heed, follow' [BDAG], 'to pay close attention to, to consider carefully' [LN], 'to give attention' [Bar], 'to listen eagerly' [NRSV], 'to respond' [CBC; NASB, NET, NIV, REB], 'to attend' [KJV], 'to accept' [BECNT; CEV, NLT], not explicit [AB]. This verb means to pay close attention to something [BDAG, LN], with the possible implication of agreement [LN].

QUESTION—Where was Thyatira located?

It was located in the western part of the Roman province of Asia [EBC, TH]. It was located in the district of Lydia in the province of Asia [CBC, NICNT, PNTC, TNTC].

**16:15** **And after she-was-baptized,ᵃ and her householdᵇ as well, she-urged-(us),ᶜ saying, "If you-have-judgedᵈ me to-be faithfulᵉ to-the Lord, come into my house and stay.ᶠ" And she-prevailedᵍ upon us.**

LEXICON—a. aorist pass. indic. of βαπτίζω (LN 53.41) (BDAG 2.c. p. 164): 'to be baptized' [BDAG, LN; all translations], 'to be plunged, to be dipped, to be washed' [BDAG]. This verb means to employ water in a religious ceremony designed to symbolize purification and initiation on the basis of repentance [LN]. It means to use water in a rite for the purpose of renewing or establishing a relationship with God [BDAG].

b. οἶκος (LN 10.8): 'household' [AB, Bar, BECNT, CBC, LN; ESV, KJV, NASB, NET, NIV, NLT, NRSV, REB], 'family' [LN; CEV, GW]. The phrase 'her household' is also translated 'all the people in her house' [NCV], 'the people of her house' [TEV]. This noun denotes the family consisting of those related by blood and marriage, as well as slaves and servants, living in the same house or homestead [LN].

c. aorist act. indic. of παρακαλέω (LN 33.315) (BDAG 1.b. p. 764): 'to urge' [ESV, NASB, NET, NRSV, REB], 'to beg' [CBC; CEV], 'to invite' [AB, BDAG, BECNT, LN; GW, NCV, NIV, TEV], 'to beseech' [KJV], 'to ask' [Bar: NLT], 'to call to one's side' [BDAG]. This verb means to ask a person to accept offered hospitality [LN]. It means to ask to come and be present where the speaker is [BDAG].

d. perf. act. indic. of κρίνω (LN 30.108) (BDAG 3. p. 568): 'to judge' [Bar, BDAG, BECNT, CBC, LN; ESV, KJV, NASB, NRSV], 'to evaluate' [LN], 'to decide' [TEV], 'to think' [BDAG; CEV, NCV], 'to consider' [BDAG; NET, NIV], 'to acknowledge' [AB], 'to look upon' [BDAG]. The phrase 'If you have judged me to be faithful to the Lord' is also translated 'If you're convinced that I believe in the Lord' [GW], 'If you agree that I am a true believer in the Lord' [NLT], 'Now that you have accepted me as a believer in the Lord' [REB]. This verb means to make a judgment based upon the correctness or value of something [LN]. It means to make a judgment based on taking various factors into account [BDAG].

e. πιστός (LN 31.87) (BDAG 2. p. 821): 'faithful' [Bar, BECNT, LN; ESV, KJV, NASB, NRSV], 'trustworthy, dependable, reliable' [LN], 'trusting' [BDAG]. The phrase 'If you have judged me to be faithful to the Lord' is also translated 'If you think I really do have faith in the Lord' [CEV], 'If you're convinced that I believe in the Lord' [GW], 'If you think I am truly a believer in the Lord' [NCV], 'If you have judged me to be a believer in

the Lord' [CBC], 'If you consider me to be a believer in the Lord' [NET], 'If you consider me a believer in the Lord' [NIV], 'If you agree that I am a true believer in the Lord' [NLT], 'Now that you have accepted me as a believer in the Lord' [REB], 'if you have decided that I am a true believer in the Lord' [TEV], 'Since you have acknowledged me as a believer in the Lord' [AB]. This adjective pertains to being trusted [LN]. It pertains to being trusting [BDAG].
- f. pres. act. impera. of μένω (LN 85.55): 'to stay' [LN; all translations except KJV], 'to remain' [LN], 'to abide' [KJV]. This verb means to remain in the same place over a period of time [LN].
- g. aorist mid. (deponent = act.) indic. of παραβιάζομαι (LN 33.299) (BDAG p. 759): 'to prevail' [ESV, NASB, NRSV], 'to urge' [LN; NLT], 'to insist' [CBC; GW, REB], 'to constrain' [Bar; KJV], 'to persuade' [AB; NCV, NET, NIV, TEV], 'to convince' [BECNT], 'to urge strongly, to prevail upon' [BDAG], not explicit [CEV]. This verb means to speak in such a way as to encourage a particular type of behavior or action [LN].

QUESTION—What would be considered as Lydia's household?

A 'household' included everyone that lived in the same house, including family members as well as servants and their children [NICNT, TRT].

**DISCOURSE UNIT—16:16–40** [CBC; CEV, NCV, NET, NIV, NRSV, TEV]. The topic is Paul and Silas are put in jail [CEV], Paul and Silas are thrown into prison [NET], Paul and Silas in jail [NCV], Paul and Silas in prison [NIV, NRSV], in prison at Philippi [TEV], the slave girl and the magistrate [CBC].

**DISCOURSE UNIT—16:16–24** [NAC, PNTC; ESV]. The topic is Paul and Silas in prison [ESV], a fortune teller and her masters [PNTC], healing a possessed girl [NAC].

**DISCOURSE UNIT—16:16–18** [EBC, NICNT]. The topic is the Pythoness [NICNT], the demon-possessed girl [EBC].

**16:16** **It-happened that as we were going to the place-of-prayer, a slave-girl met[a] us who had (a)-spirit of-(divination)[b] and brought her owners much profit[c] by fortune-telling.[d]**

- LEXICON—a. aorist act. infin. of ὑπαντάω (LN 15.78) (BDAG a. p. 1029): 'to meet' [AB, Bar, BDAG, CBC, LN; GW, KJV, NASB, NCV, NET, NLT, NRSV, REB], 'to draw near, to meet up with' [LN]. This verb is also translated as a passive verb: 'to be met' [BECNT; CEV, ESV, NIV, TEV]. This verb means to come near to and to meet, either in a friendly or hostile sense [LN]. It means to meet in a friendly sense [BDAG].
- b. πύθων (LN 12.48, 33.285) (BDAG p. 897): 'spirit of divination' [BDAG, BECNT, LN (12.48); ESV, KJV, NASB, NRSV, REB], 'to be a fortuneteller' [LN (33.285); NLT]. The phrase 'who had a spirit of divination' is also translated 'who had a spirit that enabled her to foretell the future' [NET], 'who had an evil spirit that enabled her to predict the future' [TEV], 'who had an oracular spirit' [Bar], 'who was possessed by

an oracular spirit' [CBC], 'who had a spirit by which she predicted the future' [NIV], 'who was a medium' [AB], 'She had a spirit in her that gave her the power to tell the future' [CEV], 'She was possessed by an evil spirit that told fortunes' [GW], 'She had a special spirit in her...by telling fortunes' [NCV]. This noun denotes a supernatural power of divination known as 'Python' [LN (12.48)]. The idiom 'to have a spirit of python' denotes the act of telling people for pay what would happen to them in the future [LN (33.285)]. It denotes a spirit of divination or prophecy [BDAG].

c. ἐργασία (LN 57.193) (BDAG 4. p. 390): 'profit' [Bar, BDAG, BECNT, CBC, LN; NASB, NET, REB], 'gain' [BDAG; ESV, KJV]. This noun is also translated 'a lot of money' [CEV, GW, NCV, NLT, TEV], 'a great deal of money' [NIV, NRSV]. The phrase 'who had a spirit of divination and brought her owners much profit' is also translated 'Her divinations were very profitable to her owners' [AB]. This noun denotes the act of making a profit from one's business or activity [LN]. It denotes the proceeds of work or activity [BDAG].

d. pres. mid./pass. (deponent = act.) participle of μαντεύομαι (LN 33.284) (BDAG 1. p. 616): 'fortune-telling' [ESV, NASB, NET, NIV, NRSV], 'soothsaying' [BECNT; KJV], 'to tell fortunes' [CBC, LN; GW, NCV, REB, TEV], 'to tell the future' [CEV], 'to give oracles' [Bar], 'to prophesy, to divine, to give an oracle' [BDAG]. This verb is also translated as a noun: 'fortune-teller' [NLT], 'divinations' [AB]. This verb means to function as a more or less professional predictor of future events for the sake of a fee [LN]. It means to practice divination [BDAG].

**16:17** She followed[a] Paul and us, crying-out,[b] "These men are bond-servants[c] of-the Most-High[d] God, who are-proclaiming[e] to-you (the)-way[f] of-salvation.[g]"

TEXT—Manuscripts reading ὑμῖν 'to you' are given a B rating by GNT to indicate it was regarded to be almost certain. A variant reading is ἡμῖν 'to us' and it is followed by KJV.

LEXICON—a. pres. act. participle of κατακολουθέω (LN 15.145) (BDAG p. 518): 'to follow' [BDAG; all translations], 'to follow along behind, to keep on following' [LN]. This verb means to come/go behind or after, with the possible implication of continual and determined action [LN].

b. imperf. act. indic. of κράζω (LN 33.83) (BDAG 2.a. p. 563): 'to cry out' [Bar; ESV, NASB, NET, NRSV], 'to yell' [CEV], 'to shout' [CBC, LN; GW, NCV, NIV, NLT, REB, TEV], 'to scream' [LN], 'to cry' [BDAG, BECNT; KJV], 'to call' [BDAG], 'to call out' [AB, BDAG]. This verb means to shout or cry out, with the possible implication of the unpleasant nature of the sound [LN]. It means to communicate something in a loud voice [BDAG].

c. δοῦλος (LN 87.76) (BDAG 2.b.β. p. 260): 'bondservant' [LN; NASB], 'servant' [AB, BECNT, CBC; all versions except NASB, NRSV] 'slave'

[Bar, BDAG, LN; NRSV]. This noun denotes one who is a slave in the sense of becoming the property of an owner [LN]. It especially refers to the relationship of humans to God. Here it refers to the relationship of the apostles to God [BDAG].

d. ὕψιστος (LN 12.4) (BDAG 2. p. 1045): 'Most High' [AB, Bar, BDAG, BECNT, LN; all versions], 'Supreme' [CBC], 'Highest, Supreme One' [LN]. This adjective is literally 'highest' and is used as a title for God as being the one who is supreme [LN]. It pertains to being the highest in status [BDAG].

e. pres. act. indic. of καταγγέλλω (LN 33.204) (BDAG a. p. 515): 'to proclaim' [Bar, BDAG, BECNT; ESV, NASB, NET, NRSV], 'to preach' [AB], 'to announce' [BDAG, LN; TEV], 'to tell' [CEV, GW, NCV, NIV, NLT], 'to declare' [CBC; REB], 'to show' [KJV], 'to proclaim throughout, to speak out about' [LN]. This verb means to announce, with focus upon the extent to which the announcement or proclamation extends [LN]. It means to make known in public, with the implication of broad dissemination [BDAG].

f. ὁδός (LN 41.16) (BDAG 3.a. p. 691): 'way' [AB, Bar, BDAG, BECNT, CBC; ESV, KJV, NASB, NET, NIV, NRSV, REB], 'way of life, way to live' [LN]. The phrase 'who are proclaiming to you the way of salvation' is also translated 'They are telling you how to be saved' [CEV], 'they have come to tell you how to be saved' [NLT], 'They are telling you how you can be saved' [NCV], 'They're telling you how you can be saved' [GW], 'They announce to you how you can be saved' [TEV]. This noun is a figurative extension of meaning of ὁδός 'road' and denotes a customary manner of life or behavior, with probably some implication of goal or purpose [LN]. It denotes the course of behavior [BDAG].

g. σωτηρία (LN 21.26) (BDAG 2. p. 986): 'salvation' [AB, Bar, BDAG, BECNT, CBC, LN; ESV, KJV, NASB, NET, NRSV, REB]. The phrase 'way of salvation' is also translated 'way to salvation' [BDAG]. This noun is also translated as a passive verb: 'how to be saved' [CEV, NLT], 'how you can be saved' [GW, NCV, TEV], 'the way to be saved' [NIV]. This noun denotes the process of being saved [LN]. It denotes salvation with the focus on transcendent aspects [BDAG].

QUESTION—To whom does 'us' refer?
Here 'us' refers to Silas, Timothy and Luke [TRT].

QUESTION—How might the term 'Most High God' have been understood?
She could have been understood as saying that Paul's God was the highest among many gods, because the expression is not necessarily a reference to Yahweh but simply to a supreme god of one's preference. What the woman is saying could be understood as true, although the fact that she represents many gods makes her testimony less than welcome and potentially misleading [BECNT].

**16:18** And this she-kept-doing[a] for many days. But Paul, having-become-greatly -annoyed,[b] turned[c] and said to-the spirit, "I-command[d] you in (the)-name[e] of-Jesus Christ[f] to-come-out[g] of her." And it-came-out that very hour.

LEXICON—a. imperf. act. indic. of ποιέω (LN 41.7): 'to keep doing' [ESV, GW, NRSV], 'to continue doing' [NASB], 'to continue to do' [NET], 'to behave toward, to deal with, to do to, to act' [LN]. The phrase 'this she kept doing for many days' is also translated 'this she was doing for many days' [BECNT], 'This went on for several days' [CEV], 'this did she many days' [KJV], 'She kept this up for many days' [NCV, NIV], 'She did this day after day' [CBC; REB], 'She did this for many days' [AB, Bar; TEV], 'This went on day after day' [NLT]. This verb means to behave or act in a particular way with respect to someone [LN].

b. aorist pass. participle of διαπονέομαι (LN 88.190) (BDAG p. 235): 'to become annoyed' [ESV, GW, NET], 'to become upset' [CEV, TEV], 'to be annoyed' [BDAG, BECNT; NASB, NRSV], 'to be disturbed' [BDAG], 'to be irked, to be provoked, to become angry' [LN], 'to become troubled' [NIV], 'to become exasperated' [NLT], 'to be grieved' [KJV], not explicit [REB]. The phrase 'Paul having become greatly annoyed' is also translated 'Paul lost patience' [AB], 'This bothered Paul' [NCV], 'Paul could endure/bear it no longer' [Bar, CBC]. This verb means to be strongly irked or provoked at something or someone [LN]. It means to feel burdened as the result of someone's provocative activity [BDAG].

c. aorist act. participle of ἐπιστρέφω (LN 16.13) (BDAG 1.a. p. 382): 'to turn' [Bar, BECNT; all versions except NIV, REB, TEV], 'to turn around' [BDAG, LN; NIV, TEV], 'to turn toward' [LN], 'to go back' [BDAG], 'to turn round' [AB], 'to round' [CBC; REB]. This verb means to turn around to or toward [LN]. It means to return to a point where one has been [BDAG].

d. pres. act. indic. of παραγγέλλω (LN 33.327) (BDAG p. 760): 'to command' [AB, Bar, BDAG, CBC, LN; all versions except CEV, NRSV, TEV], 'to order' [LN; CEV, NRSV, TEV], 'to charge' [BECNT], 'to give orders, to instruct, to direct' [BDAG]. This verb means to announce what must be done [LN]. It means to make an announcement about something that must be done [BDAG].

e. ὄνομα (LN 33.126) (BDAG 1.d.γ.ⅉ. p. 713): 'name' [BDAG, LN; all translations except NCV]. The phrase 'in the name of Jesus Christ' is also translated 'By the power of Jesus Christ' [NCV]. This noun denotes the proper name of a person [LN]. It refers to the name of God or Jesus, meaning 'with the mention of the name' or 'while calling on the name' [BDAG].

f. Χριστός (LN 93.387): 'Christ' [LN; all translations]. This is the Greek translation of the Hebrew and Aramaic word 'Messiah' used as a proper name for Jesus [LN].

g. aorist act. infin. of ἐξέρχομαι (LN 15.40) (BDAG 1.a.β.ב. p. 348): 'to come out' [Bar, BDAG, BECNT, CBC; all versions except CEV], 'to go out' [BDAG], 'to leave' [AB; CEV], 'to go out of, to depart out of, to leave from within' [LN]. This verb means to move out of an enclosed or well defined two or three-dimensional area [LN]. It means to move out of or away from an area. Here it refers to spirits that come or go out of persons [BDAG].

QUESTION—What does the phrase 'this she kept doing for many days' imply?
It implies regular daily contact with her as the missionaries looked for opportunities for teaching and preaching [PNTC].

**DISCOURSE UNIT—16:19-34** [EBC]. The topic is Paul and Silas in prison.

**DISCOURSE UNIT—16:19-24** [NICNT]. The topic is Paul and Silas imprisoned.

**16:19** **But when her owners saw[a] that their hope[b] of profit was gone, they seized[c] Paul and Silas and dragged-(them)[d] into the marketplace before the authorities.[e]**

LEXICON—a. aorist act. participle of εἶδον (LN 32.11): 'to see' [Bar, BECNT, CBC, LN; ESV, KJV, NASB, NCV, NET, NRSV, REB], 'to realize' [CEV, GW, NIV, TEV], 'to discover' [AB], 'to understand, to perceive, to recognize' [LN], not explicit [NLT]. This verb means to come to understand as the result of perception [LN].
  b. ἐλπίς (LN 25.62) (BDAG 1.a. p. 319): 'hope' [Bar, BDAG, BECNT, CBC; all versions except CEV, NCV, TEV], 'expectation' [AB, BDAG], 'the basis for hope, the reason for hope' [LN]. The phrase 'owners saw that their hope of profit was gone' is also translated 'owners realized that they had lost all chances for making more money' [CEV], 'owners realized that their chance of making money was gone' [TEV], 'owners...saw this' [NCV]. This noun denotes that which constitutes the cause or reason for hoping [LN]. It denotes the looking forward to something with the reason for confidence respecting fulfillment [BDAG].
  c. aorist mid. (deponent = act.) participle of ἐπιλαμβάνομαι (LN 37.110) (BDAG 1. p. 374): 'to seize' [AB, Bar, BECNT, CBC, LN; ESV, NASB, NET, NIV, NRSV, REB, TEV], 'to grab' [CEV, GW, NCV, NLT], 'to catch' [BDAG; KJV], 'to arrest' [LN], 'to take hold of, to grasp' [BDAG]. This verb means to take a person into custody for alleged illegal activity [LN]. It means to make the motion of grasping or taking hold of something [BDAG].
  d. aorist act. indic. of ἕλκω (LN 15.178) (BDAG 1. p. 318): 'to drag' [LN; all translations except KJV], 'to lead by force' [LN], 'to draw' [BDAG; KJV]. This verb means to drag or pull by physical force, often implying resistance [LN]. It means to move an object from one area to another in a pulling motion, in the case of a person, it implies that the person is unwilling to move voluntarily [BDAG].

e. ἄρχων (LN 56.29) (BDAG 2.b. p. 140): 'authority' [AB; GW, NASB, NET, NIV, NLT, NRSV, TEV], 'official' [BDAG, LN], 'judge' [LN], 'leader' [BDAG], 'ruler' [Bar, BECNT; ESV, KJV], 'city ruler' [NCV], 'city authority' [CBC; REB]. The phrase 'dragged them into the marketplace before the authorities' is also translated 'dragged them into court' [CEV]. This noun denotes a minor government official serving as a judge [LN]. It denotes one who has administrative authority of gentile officials [BDAG].

**16:20** And when they had-brought[a] them to-the chief-magistrates, they-said, "These men are Jews and they are-disturbing[b] our city.

LEXICON—a. aorist act. participle of προσάγω (LN 15.172) (BDAG 1.a. p. 875): 'to bring' [all translations except CEV, GW, NLT], 'to lead before, to bring into the presence of, to bring to' [LN], 'to bring (forward)' [BDAG], not explicit [CEV, GW, NLT]. This verb means to bring or lead into the presence of someone [LN]. It means to bring into someone's presence [BDAG].

b. pres. act. indic. of ἐκταράσσω (LN 39.44) (BDAG p. 309): 'to disturb' [Bar, BECNT; ESV, NRSV], 'to cause a disturbance' [AB, CBC; REB], 'to upset' [CEV], 'to trouble' [KJV], 'to make/cause trouble' [NCV, TEV], 'to stir up trouble' [GW], 'to throw into confusion' [BDAG; NASB, NET], 'to throw into an uproar' [NIV], 'to stir up against, to start a riot, to cause an uproar' [LN], 'to agitate, to cause trouble to' [BDAG]. The clause 'these men are Jews and they are disturbing our city' is also translated 'The whole city is in an uproar because of these Jews' [NLT]. This verb means to cause people to riot [LN]. It means to cause to be in an uproar [BDAG].

**16:21** They-are-proclaiming[a] customs[b] that are not lawful[c] for-us as Romans to-accept[d] or practice.[e]"

LEXICON—a. pres. act. indic. of καταγγέλλω (LN 33.204) (BDAG a. p. 515): 'to proclaim' [Bar, BDAG; NASB], 'to preach' [AB], 'to announce' [BDAG, LN], 'to advocate' [BECNT, CBC; ESV, GW, NET, NIV, NRSV, REB], 'to teach' [KJV, NCV, NLT, TEV], 'to proclaim throughout, to speak out about' [LN]. The phrase 'They are proclaiming customs' is also translated 'They are telling us to do things' [CEV]. This verb means to announce, with focus upon the extent to which the announcement or proclamation extends [LN]. It means to make known in public, with the implication of broad dissemination [BDAG].

b. ἔθος (LN 41.25) (BDAG 2. p. 277): 'custom' [BDAG, LN; all translations except CEV, NCV, REB], 'practice' [REB], 'habit' [LN]. The phrase 'They are proclaiming customs' is also translated 'They are telling us to do things' [CEV], 'They are teachings things' [NCV]. This noun denotes a pattern of behavior more or less fixed by tradition and generally sanctioned by the society [LN]. It denotes a long established usage or practice common to a group [BDAG].

c. pres. act. indic. of ἔξεστι(ν) (LN 71.32) (BDAG 1.b. p. 348): 'to be lawful' [Bar, BECNT; ESV, KJV, NASB, NET, NRSV], 'to be legal' [AB], 'to be right' [NCV], 'must, ought to' [LN], 'it is right, it is authorized, it is permitted, it is proper' [BDAG], not explicit [GW]. The phrase 'customs that are not lawful for us...to accept or practice' is also translated 'things we Romans are not allowed to do' [CEV], 'customs unlawful for us...to accept or practice' [NIV], 'customs that are illegal for us...to practice' [NLT], 'customs that are against our law' [TEV], 'customs/practices which it is illegal for us...to adopt and follow' [CBC; REB]. This verb means to be obligatory [LN]. It means to be authorized for the doing of something [BDAG].
d. pres. mid./pass. (deponent = act.) infin. of παραδέχομαι (LN 31.52) (BDAG 1. p. 761): 'to accept' [AB, BDAG, BECNT, LN; ESV, GW, NASB, NET, NIV, TEV], 'to receive' [Bar, LN; KJV], 'to adopt' [CBC; NRSV, REB], not explicit [CEV, NCV, NLT]. This verb means to come to believe something to be true and to respond accordingly, with some emphasis upon the source [LN]. It means to acknowledge something to be correct [BDAG].
e. pres. act. infin. of ποιέω (LN 42.7): 'to practice' [Bar, BECNT; ESV, GW, NET, NIV, NLT, TEV], 'to observe' [AB; KJV, NASB, NRSV], 'to do' [LN; CEV, NCV], 'to follow' [CBC; REB], 'to act, to carry out, to accomplish, to perform' [LN]. This verb means to do or perform [LN].

QUESTION—What customs were the owners referring to?

They were referring to Jewish customs [AB, BECNT, NAC, NICNT, PNTC, TNTC, TRT].

**DISCOURSE UNIT—16:22–30** [NASB]. The topic is Paul and Silas imprisoned.

**16:22** The crowd joined-in-attacking[a] them, and the chief-magistrates tore-the garments -off[b] them and gave orders to-beat-(them)-with-rods.

LEXICON—a. aorist act. indic. of συνεφίστημι (LN 39.50) (BDAG p. 970): 'to join in an attack' [Bar, BDAG, BECNT, CBC, LN; all versions except KJV, NASB, NLT], 'to rise up together' [KJV, NASB]. The clause 'The crowd joined in attacking them' is also translated 'A mob quickly formed against Paul and Silas' [NLT], 'The crowd also rose against them' [AB]. This verb means to join in attacking [LN]. It means to join in an uprising [BDAG].
b. aorist act. participle of περιρήγνυμι (LN 19.33) (BDAG p. 804): 'to tear off' [Bar, BDAG, BECNT, CBC, LN; CEV, ESV, GW, NASB, NET, TEV], 'to strip off' [AB, BDAG, LN], 'to rent off' [KJV], 'to tear' [NCV]. The clause 'the chief magistrates tore the garments off them' is also translated 'the magistrates ordered them to be stripped' [NIV], 'the city officials ordered them stripped' [NLT], 'the magistrates had them stripped' [NRSV], 'the magistrates had the prisoners stripped' [REB].

This verb means to tear off or to strip off, as of clothing [LN]. It means to tear off something, especially clothes [BDAG].

QUESTION—Whose clothes were torn off?

The pronouns throughout the sentence seem to refer to Paul and Silas [Bar, EBC, NAC, PNTC, TH, TRT].

**16:23** **And when they had-inflicted- many blows -upon them, they-threw-(them)[a] into prison, ordering[b] the jailer[c] to-guard[d] them securely.[e]**

LEXICON—a. aorist act. indic. of βάλλω (LN 85.34) (BDAG p. 163): 'to throw' [BECNT; ESV, GW, NASB, NET, NRSV], 'to cast' [Bar; KJV], 'to fling' [CBC], 'to put' [AB, LN], 'to cause to be put' [LN]. This verb is also translated as a passive verb: 'were put/thrown/flung' [CEV, NCV, NIV, NLT, REB, TEV]. This verb means to put or place some object or mass in a location, with the possible implication of force in some contexts [LN].

b. aorist act. participle of παραγγέλλω (LN 33.327) (BDAG p. 760): 'to order' [Bar, CBC, LN; ESV, GW, NRSV], 'to command' [BDAG, LN; NASB, NET], 'to charge' [BECNT; KJV], 'to give orders, to instruct, to direct' [BDAG]. This verb is also translated as a passive verb: 'was told/ordered/commanded' [CEV, NCV, NIV, NLT, REB, TEV]. The phrase 'they threw them into prison ordering the jailer' is also translated 'they put them in prison and gave the jailer orders' [AB]. This verb means to announce what must be done [LN]. It means to make an announcement about something that must be done [BDAG].

c. δεσμοφύλαξ (LN 37.124) (BDAG): 'jailer' [BDAG, LN; all translations except Bar], 'prison guard' [LN], 'keeper of a prison' [BDAG], 'gaoler' [Bar]. This noun denotes a person in charge of guarding a jail or prison [LN].

d. pres. act. infin. of τηρέω (LN 37.122) (AB, BDAG 1. p. 1002): 'to guard' [AB, Bar, BDAG, LN; CEV, NASB, NCV, NET, NIV], 'to keep' [BECNT, CBC; ESV, GW, KJV, NRSV, REB], 'to keep watch' [LN], 'to keep watch over' [BDAG]. The phrase 'ordering the jailer to guard them securely' is also translated 'The jailer was ordered to make sure they didn't escape' [NLT], 'the jailer was ordered to lock them up tight' [TEV]. This verb means to continue to hold in custody [LN]. It means to retain in custody [BDAG].

e. ἀσφαλῶς (LN 21.10) (BDAG 1. p. 147): 'securely' [Bar, BDAG, LN; NASB, NET, NRSV], 'safely' [BECNT, LN; ESV, KJV], 'carefully' [AB; CEV, NCV, NIV], 'safe, secure' [LN]. The phrase 'to guard them securely' is also translated 'to keep them under tight security' [GW], 'to keep them under close guard' [CBC; REB], 'to make sure they didn't escape' [NLT], 'to lock them up tight' [TEV]. This adjective pertains to a state of safety and security, and hence free from danger [LN]. It pertains to a manner that ensures continuing detention [BDAG].

QUESTION—What does the idiom 'threw them into prison' mean?

It means that they were put in jail, not that they were literally thrown through the air [TRT].

**16:24** He, having-received[a] this order, put[b] them into the inner prison and fastened[c] their feet in the stocks.[d]

LEXICON—a. aorist act. participle of λαμβάνω (LN 57.125): 'to receive' [AB, Bar, BECNT, LN; ESV, KJV, NASB, NET, NIV, TEV], 'to accept' [LN], not explicit [CEV, GW, NLT, NRSV]. The phrase 'he, having received this order' is also translated 'he heard this order' [NCV], 'in view of these orders' [CBC; REB]. This verb means to receive or accept an object or benefit for which the initiative rests with the giver, but the focus of attention in the transfer is upon the receiver [LN].

b. aorist act. indic. of βάλλω (LN 85.34): 'to put' [AB, Bar, BECNT, CBC, LN; CEV, ESV, GW, NCV, NIV, NLT, NRSV, REB], 'to cause to be put' [LN], 'to throw' [NASB, NET, TEV], 'to thrust' [KJV]. This verb means to put or place some object or mass in a location, with the possible implication of force in some contexts [LN].

c. aorist mid. indic. of ἀσφαλίζω (LN 18.12) (BDAG 1.b. p. 147): 'to fasten' [BDAG, BECNT, LN; ESV, NASB, NET, NIV, NRSV, TEV], 'to tie' [LN], 'to secure' [Bar, BDAG, CBC; REB], 'to chain' [CEV], 'to pin' [NCV], 'to clamp' [NLT], 'to lock' [AB]. The phrase 'fastened their feet in the stocks' is also translated 'made their feet fast in the stocks' [KJV], 'with their feet in leg irons' [GW]. This verb means to fasten something securely [LN]. It means to ensure security by preventive measures [BDAG].

d. ξύλον (LN 6.21) (BDAG 2.b. p. 685): 'stocks' [AB, Bar, BDAG, BECNT, CBC, LN; ESV, KJV, NASB, NET, NIV, NLT, NRSV, REB], 'leg irons' [GW]. The phrase 'fastened their feet in the stocks' is also translated 'fastened their feet between heavy blocks of wood' [TEV], 'chained their feet to heavy blocks of wood' [CEV], 'pinned their feet down between large blocks of wood' [NCV]. This noun denotes an instrument consisting of heavy blocks of wood through which the legs were placed and then securely fastened [LN]. It denotes a device made of wood for confining the extremities of a prisoner [BDAG].

QUESTION—Why were they put into the inner prison?

The magistrates may have feared that such prisoners, who had displayed supernatural powers, needed to be guarded especially carefully [PNTC, TNTC]. The emphasis is placed on the security of the precautions taken, probably to stress the miraculous nature of the deliverance [CBC, NAC].

**DISCOURSE UNIT—16:25–40** [ESV]. The topic is the Philippian jailer converted.

**DISCOURSE UNIT—16:25–34** [NAC, NICNT, PNTC]. The topic is earthquake at midnight: the jailer's conversion [NICNT], a jailer and his household [PNTC], converting a jailer's household [NAC].

**16:25** About[a] midnight Paul and Silas (were)-praying (and)-singing-hymns to-God, and the prisoners were-listening-to[b] them,

LEXICON—a. κατά with accusative object (LN 67.35) (BDAG 2.b. p. 512): 'about' [BDAG, BECNT, CBC, LN; all versions except GW, KJV, NLT],

'around' [GW, NLT], 'toward' [BDAG], 'at' [AB, Bar; KJV]. This preposition is a marker of a point of time which is approximately simultaneous to another point of time [LN]. It is a marker of temporal aspect with indefinite indications of time [BDAG].
- b. imperf. mid./pass. (deponent = act.) indic. of ἐπακροάομαι (LN 24.61) (BDAG p. 358): 'to listen to' [AB, Bar, BDAG, BECNT, LN; ESV, GW, NASB, NET, NIV, NRSV, TEV], 'to listen' [CBC; CEV, NCV, NLT, REB], 'to hear' [KJV]. This verb means to listen to, with the probable implication of one's own interest [LN]. It means to listen to in the sense of overhearing [BDAG].

**16:26** and suddenly there-was<sup>a</sup> (a)-great earthquake, so-that the foundations of-the prison were-shaken.<sup>b</sup> And immediately all the doors were-opened<sup>c</sup> and everyone's chains were-unfastened.<sup>d</sup>

LEXICON—a. aorist mid. (deponent = act.) indic. of γίνομαι (LN 13.107) (BDAG 3.a. p. 197): 'to be' [AB, Bar, BECNT, CBC; ESV, KJV, NCV, NIV, NLT, NRSV, REB, TEV], 'to come' [NASB], 'to occur' [LN; NET], 'to happen, to come to be' [LN], 'to arise, to come about, to develop' [BDAG], not explicit [CEV, GW]. This verb means to happen, with the implication that what happens is different from a previous state [LN]. It means to come into being as an event or phenomenon from a point of origin [BDAG].
- b. aorist pass. infin. of σαλεύω (LN 16.7) (BDAG 1. p. 911): 'to be shaken' [AB, Bar, BDAG, BECNT, CBC, LN; ESV, KJV, NASB, NET, NIV, NLT, NRSV, REB], 'to be made to waver/totter' [BDAG]. This verb is also translated as an active verb: 'shook' [CEV, GW, NCV, TEV]. This verb means to cause something to move back and forth rapidly, often violently [LN]. It means to cause to move to and fro [BDAG].
- c. aorist pass. indic. of ἀνοίγω (LN 79.110) (BDAG 1. p. 84): 'to be opened' [AB, Bar, BECNT; ESV, KJV, NASB, NRSV], 'to open, to make open' [LN]. This verb is also translated as an active verb: 'the doors opened' [CEV, TEV]. This passive verb is also translated as a verb phrase: 'flew/burst/broke open' [CBC; GW, NCV, NET, NIV, NLT, REB]. This verb means to cause something to be open [LN]. It means to move something from a shut or closed position [BDAG].
- d. aorist pass. indic. of ἀνίημι (LN 18.19) (BDAG 1. p. 82): 'to be unfastened' [BDAG, BECNT, CBC, LN; ESV, NASB, NRSV, REB], 'to be loosed' [AB, Bar; KJV], 'to be loosened' [BDAG, LN]. This verb is also translated as a verb phrase: 'fell off/from' [CEV, NLT, TEV], 'came loose' [GW, NET, NIV]. The phrase 'everyone's chains were unfastened' is also translated 'the prisoners were freed from their chains' [NCV]. This verb means to cause something to become loose [LN].

**16:27** When the jailer woke and saw that the prison doors were-opened, he drew<sup>a</sup> his sword and was-about<sup>b</sup> to-kill himself, supposing<sup>c</sup> that the prisoners had-escaped.<sup>d</sup>

LEXICON—a. aorist mid. participle of σπάω (LN 15.212) (BDAG p. 936): 'to draw' [AB, Bar, BDAG, BECNT, CBC, LN; ESV, GW, NASB, NET, NIV, NLT, NRSV, REB], 'to pull, to drag' [LN], 'to pull out' [BDAG; CEV, TEV], 'to draw out' [KJV], 'to get' [NCV]. This verb means to pull or drag, requiring force because of the inertia of the object being dragged [LN]. It means to exert force so as to pull or draw [BDAG].

b. imperf. act. indic. of μέλλω (LN 67.62) (BDAG 1.c.α. p. 627): 'to be about to' [AB, Bar, BDAG, BECNT, LN; all versions except KJV, NLT, REB], not explicit [NLT]. The phrase 'was about to kill himself' is also translated 'would have killed himself' [KJV], 'intending to kill himself' [CBC; REB]. This verb means to occur at a point of time in the future which is subsequent to another event and closely related to it [LN]. It means to take place at a future point of time and so to be subsequent to another event [BDAG].

c. pres. act. participle of νομίζω (LN 31.29) (BDAG 2. p. 675): 'to suppose' [Bar, BECNT, LN; ESV, KJV, NASB, NRSV], 'to think' [BDAG, LN; CEV, GW, NCV, NIV, TEV], 'to assume' [CBC, LN; NET, NLT, REB], 'to believe' [AB, BDAG, LN], 'to presume, to imagine' [LN], 'to consider, to hold' [BDAG]. This verb means to regard something as presumably true, but without particular certainty [LN]. It means to form an idea about something, but with some suggestion of tentativeness or refraining from a definitive statement [BDAG].

d. perf. act. infin. of ἐκφεύγω (LN 15.63) (BDAG 1. p. 312): 'to escape' [LN; all translations except KJV], 'to flee' [KJV], 'to flee out of, to flee from' [LN], 'to run away' [BDAG]. This verb means to flee from or out of [LN]. It means to seek safety in flight [BDAG].

QUESTION—Why was the jailer about to kill himself?

Soldiers who guarded prisons were held responsible for any prisoners that escaped while they were on duty. This jailer would probably have been executed if the prisoners had actually escaped (see Acts 12.18–19 for an example). Rather than be executed in a painful and humiliating way, he preferred to kill himself [AB, Bar, BECNT, CBC, EBC, NAC, TH, TRT].

**16:28** But<sup>a</sup> Paul cried<sup>b</sup> with-(a)-loud voice, saying, "Do not harm yourself, for we-are all here."

LEXICON—a. δέ (LN 89.124): 'but' [LN; all translations]. This conjunction is a marker of contrast [LN].

b. aorist act. indic. of φωνέω (LN 33.77) (BDAG 1.b. p. 1071): 'to cry' [BECNT; ESV, KJV], 'to cry out' [BDAG, LN; NASB], 'to call out' [Bar, BDAG, LN; NET], 'to shout' [AB, CBC, LN; CEV, GW, NCV, NIV, NLT, NRSV, REB, TEV], 'to speak loudly' [BDAG, LN], 'to say with emphasis' [BDAG]. This verb means to speak with considerable

72    ACTS 16:28

volume or loudness [LN]. It means to produce a voiced sound/tone, frequently with reference to intensity of tone [BDAG].

QUESTION—To whom does 'we' refer to?

It refers to all of the prisoners [Bar, BECNT, EBC, NAC, NICNT, TH, TNTC].

**16:29** **And the jailer called-for**[a] **lights**[b] **and rushed-in,**[c] **and trembling-(with-fear)**[d] **he-fell-down-before**[e] **Paul and Silas.**

LEXICON—a. aorist act. participle of αἰτέω (LN 33.163) (BDAG p. 30): 'to call for' [AB, BECNT, CBC; ESV, KJV, NASB, NET, NIV, NLT, NRSV, REB, TEV], 'to ask for' [Bar, BDAG, LN; CEV, GW], 'to demand' [BDAG, LN], 'to plead for' [LN]. The clause 'the jailer called for lights' is also translated 'The jailer told someone to bring a light' [NCV]. This verb means to ask for with urgency, even to the point of demanding [LN]. It means to ask for, with a claim on receipt of an answer [BDAG].

b. φῶς (LN 6.102) (BDAG 2. p. 1073): 'light' [all translations except CEV, GW], 'torch' [BDAG, LN; CEV, GW], 'lamp, lantern' [BDAG]. This noun denotes a stick or bundle of sticks carried about as a light [LN]. It is possible that in Acts 16:29 the meaning of φῶς is a lamp (see 6.104) [LN]. It denotes that which gives/bears light [BDAG].

c. aorist act. indic. of εἰσπηδάω (LN 15.237) (BDAG p. 295): 'to rush in' [BDAG, BECNT, CBC; ESV, NASB, NET, NIV, NRSV, REB, TEV], 'to run inside' [NCV], 'to run into' [LN], 'to run to' [NLT], 'to run in' [AB], 'to rush into' [LN; GW], 'to go into' [CEV], 'to spring in' [Bar; KJV], 'to leap in' [BDAG]. This verb means to run or rush quickly into [LN]. It means a rapid motion forward into [BDAG].

d. ἔντρομος (LN 25.261) (BDAG p. 341): 'trembling' [AB, Bar, BDAG; GW, KJV, NET, NIV, NLT, NRSV, TEV], 'shaking' [CEV]. The word 'trembling' is also translated 'trembling with fear' [BECNT, CBC, LN; ESV, NASB, REB], 'shaking with fear' [NCV], 'extremely fearful' [LN]. This adjective pertains to extreme terror or fear, often accompanied by trembling [LN]. It pertains to being in a quivering condition because of exposure to an overwhelming or threatening circumstance [BDAG].

e. aorist act. indic. of προσπίπτω (LN 17.22) (BDAG 1. p. 884): 'to fall down before' [Bar, BDAG, BECNT, LN; ESV, KJV, NASB, NCV, NLT, NRSV], 'to fall down at the feet of' [NET], 'to fall before' [NIV], 'to prostrate oneself before' [LN], 'to fall at the feet of' [AB, BDAG; TEV], 'to kneel down in front of' [CEV], 'to kneel in front of' [GW]. The phrase 'he fell down before' is also translated 'threw himself down before' [CBC; REB]. This verb means to prostrate oneself before someone, implying supplication [LN]. It means to prostrate oneself before someone [BDAG].

QUESTION—What is meant by the jailer falling down before Paul and Silas?

The jailer intentionally fell/bowed/knelt at Paul and Silas' feet in order to show them respect [BECNT, TRT]. It may have been a gesture of worship. It was certainly an expression of subservience [NAC]. A translation should not sound like he tripped and fell down accidentally [TH, TRT].

**16:30** Then he brought[a] them out and said, "Sirs, what must I do to be-saved?[b]"

LEXICON—a. aorist act. participle of προάγω (LN 15.171) (BDAG 1. p. 864): 'to bring' [Bar, BECNT; ESV, KJV, NASB, NCV, NET, NIV, NLT, NRSV], 'to lead' [AB; CEV, TEV], 'to take' [GW], 'to bring forward, to lead forth' [LN], 'to lead forward, to lead/bring out' [BDAG], 'to escort' [CBC; REB]. This verb means to lead or bring forward or forth [LN]. It means to take or lead from one position to another by taking charge [BDAG].
b. aorist pass. subj. of σῴζω (LN 21.27) (BDAG 2.b. p. 983): 'to be saved' [BDAG, LN; all translations], 'to attain salvation' [BDAG]. This verb means to experience divine salvation [LN].

QUESTION—What does the jailer want to be saved from?
The jailer is asking Paul and Silas about spiritual salvation. Since none of the prisoners escaped, he was in no danger of being executed by the Romans. He had probably heard about the slave girl (see verse 17) and/or heard Paul and Silas singing and praying (verse 25) [EBC, NAC, PNTC, TRT].

**DISCOURSE UNIT—16:31–40** [NASB]. The topic is the jailer converted.

**16:31** And they-said, "Believe[a] in the Lord Jesus, and you will-be-saved, you and your household.[b]"

LEXICON—a. aorist act. impera. of πιστεύω (LN 31.85) (BDAG 2.a.δ. p. 817): 'to believe' [AB, Bar, BECNT; all versions except CEV, REB], 'to have faith' [CEV], 'to believe in, to trust' [BDAG, LN], 'to have confidence in, to have faith in' [LN]. The phrase 'believe in the Lord' is also translated 'put your trust in the Lord' [CBC; REB]. This verb means to believe to the extent of complete trust and reliance [LN]. It means to entrust oneself to an entity in complete confidence with the implication of total commitment to the one who is trusted [BDAG].
b. οἶκος (LN 10.8) (BDAG 2. p. 699): 'household' [AB, Bar, BDAG, BECNT, CBC, LN; ESV, NASB, NET, NIV, NLT, NRSV, REB], 'family' [BDAG, LN; GW, TEV], 'house' [KJV]. The phrase 'your household' is also translated as 'everyone who lives in your home' [CEV], 'all the people in your house' [NCV]. This noun denotes the family consisting of those related by blood and marriage, as well as slaves and servants, living in the same house or homestead [LN].

QUESTION—Is the jailer's belief in the Lord Jesus enough to save himself and his household?
1. Did Paul say that the jailer's belief was sufficient both for him and for his family, or did Paul tell the jailer that if he believed he would be saved, and if his family believed they also would be saved? The first of these alternatives more naturally suits the meaning on the Greek [TH].

2. The jailor's own faith does not cover those in his household. They too have to hear the word, believe and be baptized [TNTC, TRT].

**16:32** **And they-spoke the word<sup>a</sup> of-the Lord<sup>b</sup> to-him and to all who were in his house.<sup>c</sup>**

TEXT—Manuscripts reading τοῦ κυρίου 'of-the Lord' are given a B rating by GNT to indicate it was regarded to be almost certain. Other manuscripts read τοῦ θεοῦ 'of God.' Only AB follows this reading.

LEXICON—a. λόγος (LN 33.260) (BDAG 1.a.β. p. 599): 'word' [BDAG; all translations except CEV, NCV], 'message' [NCV], 'what is preached, gospel' [LN]. The phrase 'they spoke the word of the Lord' is also translated 'Paul and Silas told him and everyone else…about the Lord' [CEV]. This noun denotes the content of what is preached about Christ or about the good news [LN]. It denotes a communication whereby the mind finds expression [BDAG].
  b. κύριος (LN 12.9): 'Lord' [Bar, BECNT, CBC, LN; all versions], 'God' [AB], 'Ruler, One who commands' [LN]. This noun is a title for God and for Christ and refers to one who exercises supernatural authority over mankind [LN].
  c. οἰκία (LN 7.3) (BDAG 1.a. p. 695): 'house' [BDAG, LN; all translations except GW, NLT], 'home' [LN; GW], 'dwelling, residence' [LN], 'household' [NLT]. This noun denotes a building or place where one dwells [LN]. It denotes a structure used as a dwelling [BDAG].

**16:33** **And he took them at that hour of-the night and washed their wounds, and he was-baptized<sup>a</sup> at-once, he and all his household.**

LEXICON—a. aorist pass. indic. of βαπτίζω (LN 53.41) (BDAG 2.c. p. 164): 'to be baptized' [BDAG, LN; all translations], 'to be plunged, to be dipped, to be washed' [BDAG]. This verb means to employ water in a religious ceremony designed to symbolize purification and initiation on the basis of repentance [LN]. It means to use water in a rite for the purpose of renewing or establishing a relationship with God [BDAG].

**16:34** **Then he brought<sup>a</sup> them up into his house and set- food -before- (them).<sup>b</sup> And he-rejoiced<sup>c</sup> along with- his -entire-household that he had-believed in-God.**

LEXICON—a. aorist act. participle of ἀνάγω (LN 15.176) (BDAG 1. p. 61): 'to bring' [Bar, BECNT, CBC; ESV, KJV, NASB, NET, NIV, NLT, NRSV, REB], 'to bring up, to lead up' [BDAG, LN], 'to take' [AB; CEV, GW, NCV, TEV]. This verb means to bring or lead up [LN]. It means to lead or bring from a lower to a higher point [BDAG].
  b. aorist act. indic. of παρατίθημι (LN 57.116) (BDAG 1. p. 772): 'to set before' [AB, BDAG, BECNT; ESV, KJV, NASB, NET, NIV, NLT, NRSV], 'to give food to, to provide with food' [LN]. The phrase 'set food before them' is also translated 'gave them something to eat' [CEV, GW], 'gave them food' [NCV], 'gave them some food to eat' [TEV], 'set out a

meal' [CBC; REB], 'prepared a meal' [Bar]. This verb means to give or to provide for, with the implication of placing something in front of a person, normally food [LN]. It means to place something before someone and frequently it is food [BDAG].
  c. aorist mid. indic. of ἀγαλλιάω (LN 25.133) (BDAG p. 4): 'to rejoice' [AB, Bar, BECNT, CBC; ESV, KJV, NLT, NRSV, REB], 'to be overjoyed' [BDAG, LN], 'to rejoice greatly' [LN; NASB, NET], 'to be extremely joyful' [LN], 'to be glad' [BDAG; CEV], 'to be thrilled' [GW], 'to be very happy' [NCV], 'to be filled with joy' [NIV, TEV], 'to exult' [BDAG]. This verb means to experience a state of great joy and gladness, often involving a verbal expression and appropriate body movement [LN]. It means to be exceedingly joyful [BDAG].
QUESTION—What does the Greek idiom παρέθηκεν τράπεζαν 'he set a table' mean?
  It means he gave them some food to eat [Bar, BECNT, TH, TRT].

**DISCOURSE UNIT—16:35–40** [EBC, NAC, NICNT, PNTC]. The topic is Paul and Silas leave Philippi [NICNT], Paul and Silas leave the city [EBC], leaving Philippi peacefully [PNTC], humbling the city magistrates [NAC].

**16:35** Now when it was day, the magistrates[a] sent[b] the policemen,[c] saying, "Release[d] those men."
LEXICON—a. στρατηγός (LN 37.90) (BDAG 1. p. 948): 'magistrate' [Bar, BECNT, CBC, LN; ESV, KJV, NET, NIV, NRSV, REB], 'chief magistrate' [BDAG; NASB], 'ruler of a city' [LN], 'official' [CEV], 'praetor' [AB, BDAG], 'Roman official/officer/authority' [GW, NCV, TEV], 'city official' [NLT]. This noun denotes the chief legal official of a city [LN]. It denotes the highest official in a Greek-Roman city [BDAG].
  b. aorist act. indic. of ἀποστέλλω (LN 15.66): 'to send' [LN; all translations]. This verb means to cause someone to depart for a particular purpose [LN].
  c. ῥαβδοῦχος (LN 37.89) (BDAG p. 902): 'policeman' [LN; NASB], 'police officer' [BDAG; NET, TEV], 'police' [BECNT; CEV, ESV, NCV, NLT, NRSV], 'constable' [BDAG], 'guard' [GW], 'serjeant' [KJV], 'officer' [CBC; NIV, REB], 'lictor' [AB, Bar]. This noun denotes a person responsible for maintaining law and order by preventing and detecting crime and handing offenders over to legal authorities [LN].
  d. aorist act. impera. of ἀπολύω (LN 37.127) (BDAG 1. p. 117): 'to release' [AB, Bar, BDAG, CBC, LN; GW, NASB, NET, NIV, REB], 'to set free' [BDAG, LN], 'to let go' [BECNT; CEV, ESV, KJV, NLT, NRSV, TEV], 'to let go free' [NCV], 'to pardon' [BDAG]. This verb means to release from control, to set free [LN]. It means to grant acquittal [BDAG].

**16:36** And the jailer reported[a] these words[b] to Paul, saying, "The magistrates have-sent[c] to-release-you(pl). Therefore come-out[d] now and go[e] in peace."

LEXICON—a. aorist act. indic. of ἀπαγγέλλω (LN 33.198) (BDAG 1. p. 95): 'to report' [AB, Bar, BDAG, BECNT, CBC; ESV, GW, NASB, NET, NRSV, REB], 'to tell' [LN; CEV, KJV, NIV, NLT, TEV], 'to inform' [LN], 'to announce' [BDAG], not explicit [NCV]. This verb means to announce or inform, with possible focus upon the source of information [LN]. It means to give an account of something [BDAG].

b. λόγος (LN 33.98) (BDAG 1.a.δ. p. 600): 'word' [AB, Bar, BDAG, BECNT, LN; ESV, NASB, NET], 'message' [CBC, LN; NRSV], 'instruction' [REB], 'saying, statement' [LN], 'order' [GW], not explicit [CEV, KJV, NCV, NIV, NLT, TEV]. This noun denotes that which has been stated or said, with primary focus upon the content of the communication [LN]. It denotes words uttered on various occasions in speeches or instructions given here and there by humans or transcendent beings [BDAG].

c. perf. act. indic. of ἀποστέλλω (LN 15.67): 'to send' [all translations except CEV, NIV, NLT], 'to send a message, to send word' [LN]. The clause 'The magistrates have sent to release you' is also translated 'The officials have ordered me to set you free' [CEV], 'The magistrates have ordered that you and Silas be released' [NIV], 'The city officials have said you and Silas are free to leave' [NLT]. This verb means to send a message, presumably by someone [LN].

d. aorist act. impera. of ἐξέρχομαι (LN 15.40): 'to come out' [ESV, NASB, NET, NRSV], 'to go out' [AB, BECNT], 'to go out of, to depart out of, to leave from within' [LN], 'to depart' [Bar; KJV], 'to leave' [NCV, NIV, TEV], not explicit [CBC; CEV, GW, NLT, REB]. This verb means to move out of an enclosed or well defined two or three-dimensional area [LN].

e. pres. mid./pass. (deponent = act.) impera. of πορεύομαι (LN 15.34) (BDAG 1. p. 853): 'to go' [BDAG, CBC; all versions except CEV, GW], 'to leave' [AB, BECNT, LN; CEV, GW], 'to travel' [Bar, BDAG], 'to proceed' [BDAG], 'to go away' [LN]. This verb means to move away from a reference point [LN]. It means to move over an area, generally with a point of departure or destination specified [BDAG].

QUESTION—To whom does 'to release you' refer?

It refers to Paul and Silas [BECNT, EBC, PNTC, TRT; NIV, NLT, TEV].

QUESTION—What is meant by the phrase 'go in peace'?

1. It means "go quietly away", that is, leave without making any further disturbance [TH].
2. It means "go unmolested", that is, you may leave without any further punishment [TH].
3. It means 'blessings on your journey' [TH].

**16:37** But[a] Paul said to them, "They have-beaten[b] us in-public,[c] uncondemned,[d] men who are Romans, and have-thrown-(us) into prison; and now are-they-sending- us -out[e] secretly? No! But[f] let them come themselves and take- us -out.[g]"

LEXICON—a. δέ (LN 89.124): 'but' [LN; all translations except Bar], not explicit [Bar]. This conjunction is a marker of contrast [LN].
  b. aorist act. participle of δέρω (LN 19.2) (BDAG p. 218): 'to beat' [AB, Bar, BDAG, BECNT, LN; ESV, KJV, NASB, NCV, NIV, NLT, NRSV], 'to whip' [BDAG, LN; TEV], 'to strike' [LN]. This verb is also translated as a passive verb: 'had us beaten' [CEV, GW, NET]. This verb is also translated as a noun: 'a...flogging' [CBC; REB]. This verb means to strike or beat repeatedly [LN].
  c. δημόσιος (LN 28.66) (BDAG 2. p. 223): 'public' [BDAG, CBC, LN; CEV, NASB, NCV, NET, NRSV, REB, TEV], 'open' [LN], 'in the open' [BDAG]. This adjective is also translated as an adverb: 'publicly' [AB, Bar, BECNT; ESV, GW, NIV, NLT], 'openly' [KJV]. This adjective pertains to being able to be known by the public [LN]. It pertains to being able to be known by the general public [BDAG].
  d. ἀκατάκριτος (LN 56.19) (BDAG p. 35): 'uncondemned' [Bar, BDAG, BECNT; ESV, KJV, NRSV], 'without a trial' [AB, LN; CEV, GW, NASB, NCV, NIV, NLT, REB], 'without due process' [BDAG], 'without a proper trial' [NET]. This adjective is also translated as a passive verb: 'were not found guilty' [TEV], 'have not been found guilty' [CBC]. This adjective pertains to not having gone through a judicial hearing, with the implication of not having been condemned [LN]. It pertains to not undergoing a proper legal process [BDAG].
  e. pres. act. indic. of ἐκβάλλω (LN 15.44) (BDAG 2. p. 299): 'to send away' [BDAG, LN; CEV, NASB, NET, TEV], 'to send out' [BDAG], 'to drive out, to expel' [LN], 'to release' [AB, BDAG], 'to bring out' [BDAG], 'to throw out' [ESV, GW], 'to thrust out' [KJV], 'to cast out' [BECNT], 'to put out' [Bar], 'to smuggle out' [CBC; REB], 'to discharge' [NRSV]. The phrase 'are they sending us out' is also translated 'they want to make us go away' [NCV], 'they want to get rid of us' [NIV], 'they want us to leave' [NLT]. This verb means to cause to go out or leave, often, but not always, involving force [LN]. It means to cause to go or remove from a position without force [BDAG].
  f. ἀλλά (LN 89.125) (BDAG 1.a. p. 44): 'but' [BDAG, LN; KJV, NASB], 'rather' [Bar, BDAG], 'on the contrary' [AB, LN], 'instead' [LN], not explicit [BECNT, CBC; all versions except KJV, NASB]. This conjunction is a marker of more emphatic contrast [LN]. It introduces the main point after a question expressed or implied, which has been answered in the negative [BDAG].
  g. aorist act. impera. of ἐξάγω (LN 15.174) (BDAG 1. p. 343): 'to take out' [BECNT; ESV, NRSV], 'to lead out' [AB, Bar, BDAG, LN], 'to let out' [CEV, TEV], 'to bring out' [BDAG; NASB, NCV], 'to escort out' [CBC;

GW, NET, NIV, REB], 'to fetch out' [KJV], 'to bring forth' [LN], 'to release' [NLT]. This verb means to lead or bring out of a structure or area [LN]. It means to conduct from an area [BDAG].

QUESTION—To whom does 'them' refer in the phrase 'Paul said to them'?
It refers to the police officers [CBC, TH, TRT; CEV, NCV, NET, NIV, REB, TEV]. It refers to the guards [GW]. It refers to the rod-bearers/attendants/soldiers [TRT].

QUESTION—What is significant about the phrase 'men who are Romans'?
It was against Roman law for a Roman citizen to be punished or put in jail without a proper trial and conviction. The Roman government strongly protected the rights of Roman citizens. If Paul were to complain to higher Roman authorities about what had happened to him and Silas, the magistrates could lose their jobs and be severely punished [AB, Bar, CBC, EBC, NAC, NICNT, PNTC, TNTC, TRT].

QUESTION—Why was it important that the magistrates release Paul and Silas themselves?
Paul's caning had been a public shame for him. This would not be a good result for others in Philippi who also might be subject to persecution for their faith [BECNT, EBC, PNTC, TNTC].

**16:38** The policemen reported these words to-the magistrates, and they-were-afraid[a] when they heard[b] that they-were Roman citizens.

LEXICON—a. aorist pass. indic. of φοβέω (LN 25.252) (BDAG 1.a. p. 1061): 'to be afraid' [Bar, BDAG, BECNT, LN; CEV, ESV, GW, NASB, NCV, NRSV, TEV], 'to be frightened' [NET], 'to be alarmed' [AB, CBC; NIV, NLT, REB], 'to fear' [LN; KJV]. This verb means to be in a state of fearing [LN]. It means to be in an apprehensive state [BDAG].

b. aorist act. participle of ἀκούω (LN 33.212): 'to hear' [LN; all translations except CEV, NLT], 'to learn' [NLT], 'to receive news' [LN], not explicit [CEV]. This verb means to receive information about something, normally by word of mouth [LN].

QUESTION—To whom does the 'they' in 'they were afraid' and 'they heard' refer?
The 'they' in both cases refers to the magistrates [TRT]. The 'they' in both cases refers to the Roman officials/officers [GW, NCV]. The 'they' in both cases refers to the city officials [NLT]. The officials were afraid [CEV].

QUESTION—To whom does the 'they' in 'they were' refer?
It refers to Paul and Silas [TRT; CEV, GW, NCV, NET, NIV, NLT, TEV].

QUESTION—What were the magistrates afraid of?
They were afraid that Paul would have them punished for illegally beating and jailing them [TRT]. They were justifiably afraid, since severe penalties were often placed upon persons who violated the rights of Roman citizens [BECNT, EBC, NAC, NICNT, PNTC, TH, TNTC].

**16:39** So they came[a] and apologized[b] to them. And they took-(them)-out and asked-(them)[c] to-leave[d] the city.

LEXICON—a. aorist act. participle of ἔρχομαι (LN 15.81): 'to come' [LN; all translations except GW, TEV], 'to go' [GW, TEV], 'coming' [LN]. This verb means to move toward or up to the reference point of the viewpoint character or event [LN].
- b. aorist act. indic. of παρακαλέω (LN 33.168) (BDAG 4. p. 765): 'to apologize' [AB, CBC; CEV, ESV, GW, NET, NLT, NRSV, REB, TEV], 'to appeal to' [LN; NASB], 'to appease' [BECNT; NIV], 'to beseech' [KJV], 'to placate' [Bar], 'to ask for (earnestly), to request, to plead for' [LN], 'to comfort, to encourage, to cheer up' [BDAG]. The phrase 'they came and apologized to them' is also translated as 'the officials came and reassured them' [BDAG], 'they came and told Paul and Silas they were sorry' [NCV]. This verb means to ask for something earnestly and with propriety [LN]. It means to instill someone with courage or cheer [BDAG].
- c. imperf. act. indic. of ἐρωτάω (LN 33.161) (BDAG 2. p. 395): 'to ask' [AB, Bar, BDAG, BECNT; CEV, ESV, GW, NCV, NET, NRSV, TEV], 'to request' [BDAG, CBC, LN; NIV, REB], 'to beg' [NASB, NLT], 'to ask for' [LN], 'to desire' [KJV]. This verb means to ask for, usually with the implication of an underlying question [LN]. It means to ask for something [BDAG].
- d. aorist act. infin. of ἀπέρχομαι (LN 15.37): 'to leave' [AB, Bar, BECNT, LN; all versions except KJV, REB], 'to depart' [LN; KJV], 'to go away' [CBC, LN; REB]. This verb means motion away from a reference point with emphasis upon the departure, but without implications as to any resulting state of separation or rupture [LN].

QUESTION—To whom does 'they' refer in this verse?
It refers to the magistrates [BECNT, EBC, NAC, NICNT, PNTC, TRT]. It refers to the officials [GW].

**16:40** So they went-out of the prison and went to Lydia('s house). And when they had-seen[a] the brothers,[b] they-encouraged[c] them and departed.

LEXICON—a. aorist act. participle of εἶδον (LN 34.50) (BDAG 5. p. 280): 'to see' [AB, Bar, BECNT; CEV, ESV, KJV, NASB, NCV, NET, NRSV], 'to visit' [BDAG, LN], 'to go to see' [LN], 'to meet' [CBC; GW, NIV, NLT, REB, TEV]. This verb means to go to see a person on the basis of friendship and with helpful intent [LN]. It means to show an interest in [BDAG].
- b. ἀδελφός (LN 11.23): 'brother' [Bar; ESV, NET, NIV], 'fellow believer, a Christian brother' [LN]. The phrase 'the brothers' is also translated 'the brethren' [AB, BECNT; KJV, NASB], 'the believers' [GW, NCV, NLT, TEV], 'the Lord's followers' [CEV], 'the brothers and sisters' [NRSV], 'fellow-Christians' [CBC; REB]. This noun denotes a close associate of a

group of persons having a well-defined membership. In the NT ἀδελφός 'brother' refers specifically to fellow believers in Christ [LN].
c. aorist act. indic. of παρακαλέω (LN 25.150) (BDAG 2. p. 765): 'to encourage' [AB, Bar, BDAG, LN; all versions except KJV, REB, TEV], 'to exhort' [BDAG, BECNT], 'to console' [LN], 'to appeal to, to urge' [BDAG], 'to comfort' [KJV]. This verb is also translated as a noun: 'encouragement' [CBC; REB, TEV]. This verb means to cause someone to be encouraged or consoled, either by verbal or non-verbal means [LN]. It means to urge strongly [BDAG].

QUESTION—To whom does 'they' refer in this verse?
It refers to Paul and Silas [EBC, NAC, PNTC, TRT; CEV, GW, NIV, NLT, TEV].

**DISCOURSE UNIT—17:1–34** [NICNT]. The topic is Thessalonica to Athens.

**DISCOURSE UNIT—17:1–15** [Bar, CBC, NAC, PNTC, TNTC]. The topic is from Philippi to Athens [Bar], to Athens: on the way [CBC], Thessalonica and Beroea [TNTC], establishing churches in Thessalonica and Berea [NAC], the word in Thessalonica and Berea [PNTC].

**DISCOURSE UNIT—17:1–10a** [GW]. The topic is Paul and Silas in Thessalonica.

**DISCOURSE UNIT—17:1–9** [AB, BECNT, EBC, NAC, PNTC; CEV, ESV, NASB, NCV, NET, NIV, NLT, NRSV, TEV]. The topic is Paul and Silas in Thessalonica [ESV, NCV], Paul and Silas at Thessalonica [NET], Paul at Thessalonica [NASB], Paul in Thessalonica [AB], Paul preaches in Thessalonica [NLT], trouble in Thessalonica [CEV], the uproar in Thessalonica [NRSV], in Thessalonica [BECNT; NIV, TEV] at Thessalonica [EBC], acceptance and rejection in Thessalonica [NAC], the gospel provokes jealousy and turmoil [PNTC].

**DISCOURSE UNIT—17:1–4** [NICNT]. The topic is arrival at Thessalonica.

**17:1** Now when they had-passed-through[a] Amphipolis and Apollonia, they-came to Thessalonica, where there-was (a)-synagogue[b] of-the Jews.

LEXICON—a. aorist act. participle of διοδεύω (LN 15.21) (BDAG 1. p. 250): 'to pass through' [BECNT; ESV, KJV, NIV, NRSV], 'to travel through' [BDAG; CEV, GW, NASB, NCV, NET, NLT], 'to travel on through' [TEV], 'to travel around through, to journey all through' [LN], 'to travel' [AB, CBC; REB], 'to go' [BDAG]. The phrase 'they had passed through' is also translated 'they followed the road through' [Bar]. This verb means to travel around through an area, with the implication of both extensive and thorough movement throughout an area [LN].
b. συναγωγή (LN 7.20) (BDAG 2.a. p. 963): 'synagogue' [BDAG, LN; all translations except CEV], 'Christian assembly place' [LN], 'Jewish meeting place' [CEV]. This noun denotes a building of assembly, associated with religious activity. Normally a building in which Jewish

worship took place and in which the Law was taught [LN]. It denotes a place of assembly for the Jews [BDAG].

QUESTION—To whom does 'they' refer?

It refers to Paul and Silas [Bar, BECNT; GW, NCV, NLT, NRSV, TEV]. It refers to Paul, Silas and Timothy [NICNT]. It refers to Paul and his friends [CEV].

QUESTION—Where was Amphipolis located?

It was located 33 miles south-southwest of Philippi [BECNT, EBC, NAC].

QUESTION—Where was Apollonia located?

It was located 27 miles west-southwest of Amphipolis [BECNT, EBC].

QUESTION—Where was Thessalonica located?

It was located 35 miles west of Apollonia and 70 miles southwest of Philippi. It was the capital city of the second district of Macedonia [BECNT, CBC, EBC, PNTC] and also served as capital of the whole region and home of the proconsul from 148 BC [BECNT, EBC, PNTC].

**17:2** **And according-to Paul's custom,[a] he-went[b] to them, and on three Sabbath days he-(reasoned)[c] with-them from the Scriptures,**

LEXICON—a. εἴωθα (LN 41.26) (BDAG p. 295): 'custom' [AB, Bar, BECNT; ESV, NASB, NIV, NLT, NRSV], 'habit' [TEV], 'practice' [CBC; REB], 'to be in the habit of, to carry out a custom, to maintain a tradition' [LN]. The phrase 'according to Paul's custom' is also translated 'as usual' [CEV, GW], 'as his manner was' [KJV], 'as he always did' [NCV], 'as he customarily did' [NET]. This noun denotes the act of carrying out a custom or tradition [LN]. It denotes the act of maintaining a custom or tradition [BDAG].

b. aorist act. indic. of εἰσέρχομαι (LN 15.93): 'to go' [AB, CBC; CEV, NASB, NET, NLT, REB, TEV], 'to go into' [LN; GW, NCV, NIV], 'to go in' [Bar, BECNT; ESV, KJV, NRSV], 'to move into, to come into, to enter' [LN]. This verb means to move into a space, either two-dimensional or three-dimensional [LN].

c. aorist mid. (deponent = act. ) indic. of διαλέγομαι (LN 33.446) (BDAG 1. p. 232): 'to reason' [ESV, KJV, NASB, NIV, NLT], 'to address' [NET], 'to argue' [Bar, BDAG, BECNT, CBC, LN; NRSV, REB], 'to dispute' [LN], 'to converse' [AB, BDAG], 'to discuss' [BDAG]. The clause 'he reasoned with them' is also translated 'he spoke to the people' [CEV], 'he talked with the Jews' [NCV]. This verb is also translated as a noun: 'he had discussions about Scripture' [GW], 'he held discussions with the people' [TEV]. This verb means to argue about differences of opinion [LN]. It means to engage in speech interchange [BDAG].

**17:3** **explaining[a] and proving[b] that it-was-necessary-(for)[c] the Christ[d] to-suffer[e] and to-rise[f] from (the)-dead, and saying, "This Jesus, whom I am-proclaiming[g] to-you, is the Christ."**

LEXICON—a. pres. act. participle of διανοίγω (LN 33.142) (BDAG 2. p. 234): 'to explain' [AB, BDAG, BECNT, LN; all versions except CEV, KJV,

REB], 'to open up, to make evident' [LN], 'to interpret' [BDAG], 'to expound' [Bar, CBC; REB], 'to open' [KJV], not explicit [CEV]. This verb means to explain something which has been previously hidden or obscure [LN].

b. pres. mid. participle of παρατίθημι (LN 72.4) (BDAG 2.b. p. 772): 'to prove' [BECNT, LN; ESV, NCV, NIV, NLT, NRSV, TEV], 'to show' [CBC; CEV, GW, REB], 'to allege' [KJV], 'to show to be true, to present evidence of truth' [LN], 'to give evidence' [NASB], 'to demonstrate' [BDAG; NET], 'to expound' [AB], 'to point out' [BDAG], 'to submit' [Bar]. This verb means to establish evidence to show that something is true [LN]. It means to set forth in teaching [BDAG].

c. imperf. act. indic. of δεῖ (LN 71.34) (BDAG 2.c. p. 214): 'to be necessary' [Bar, BECNT, LN; ESV, NRSV]. The phrase 'it was necessary for the Christ to suffer' is also translated 'the Christ had to suffer' [NASB, NET, NIV], 'the Christ must die' [NCV], 'that Christ must needs have suffered' [KJV], 'the Messiah had to suffer' [CBC; CEV, GW, REB, TEV], 'the Messiah must suffer' [NLT], 'the Messiah was bound to suffer' [AB]. This verb means to be that which must necessarily take place, often with the implication of inevitability [LN]. It means to indicate that something that happened should by all means have happened [BDAG].

d. Χριστός (LN 53.82) (BDAG 1. p. 1091): 'Christ' [Bar, BECNT, LN; ESV, KJV, NASB, NCV, NET, NIV], 'Messiah' [AB, CBC, LN; CEV, GW, NLT, NRSV, REB, TEV], 'the Anointed One' [BDAG]. This noun, which means one who has been anointed, denotes Jesus as the Messiah [LN]. This refers to the fulfiller of the Israelite expectation of a deliverer [BDAG].

e. aorist act. infin. of πάσχω (LN 24.78) (BDAG 3.a.α. p. 785): 'to suffer' [BDAG, LN; all translations except NCV], 'to endure' [BDAG], 'to be in pain' [LN]. The phrase 'it was necessary for the Christ to suffer' is also translated 'the Christ must die' [NCV]. This verb means to suffer pain [LN].

f. aorist act. infin. of ἀνίστημι (LN 23.93) (BDAG 7. p. 83): 'to rise' [all translations except GW], 'to come back to life' [LN; GW], 'to live again, to be resurrected' [LN], 'to rise up, to come back from the dead' [BDAG]. This verb means to come back to life after having once died [LN]. It means to come back to life from the dead [BDAG].

g. pres. act. indic. of καταγγέλλω (LN 33.204) (BDAG b. p. 515): 'to proclaim' [Bar, BDAG, BECNT, CBC; ESV, NASB, NET, NIV, NRSV, REB], 'to announce' [BDAG, LN; TEV], 'to proclaim throughout, to speak out about' [LN], 'to talk/tell about' [GW, NCV, NLT], 'to preach about' [CEV], 'to tell' [AB], 'to preach' [KJV]. This verb means to announce, with focus upon the extent to which the announcement or proclamation extends [LN]. It means to make known in public, with the implication of broad dissemination [BDAG].

**17:4** And some of them were-persuaded[a] and joined[b] Paul and Silas, as did (a)-large number of-the worshipping[c] Greeks and not (a)-few of-the leading[d] women.

TEXT—Manuscripts reading γυναικῶν τε τῶν πρώτων 'of the leading women' are given an A rating by GNT to indicate it was regarded to be certain. This phrase may also be translated 'of the wives of the leading men'. A variant reading is γυναῖκες δε τῶν πρώτων which would be translated 'of the wives of the leading men'. GW translates this way, though it is unclear if that is because of the textual variant or because it is how they interpret the UBS text.

LEXICON—a. aorist pass. indic. of πείθω (LN 33.301) (BDAG 3.a. p. 792): 'to be persuaded' [BDAG, BECNT, LN; ESV, GW, NASB, NET, NIV, NLT, NRSV], 'to be convinced' [AB, CBC, LN; NCV, REB, TEV]. This verb is also translated as an active verb: 'some of them believed' [Bar; CEV, KJV]. This verb means to convince someone to believe something and to act on the basis of what is recommended [LN]. It means to be won over as the result of persuasion [BDAG].

  b. aorist pass. indic. of προσκληρόω (LN 34.22) (BDAG p. 881): 'to join' [AB, BDAG, BECNT, CBC, LN; all versions except CEV, KJV], 'to join oneself to, to become a part of' [LN], 'to be in close association, to be attached to' [BDAG], 'to consort' [KJV]. The phrase 'some of them...joined Paul and Silas' is also translated 'they became followers with Paul and Silas' [CEV], 'some of them...accepted their lot with Paul and Silas' [Bar]. This verb means to begin an association with someone, whether temporary or permanent [LN].

  c. pres. mid. participle of σέβω (LN 53.53) (BDAG 1.b. p. 918): 'to worship' [BDAG, BECNT, LN; NCV, TEV], 'to venerate' [LN], not explicit [CEV, GW]. This verb is also translated as an adjective: 'devout' [ESV, KJV, NRSV], 'God-fearing' [AB, Bar, CBC; NASB, NET, NIV, NLT, REB]. This verb means to express in attitude and ritual one's allegiance to and regard for deity [LN]. It means to express in gestures, rites, or ceremonies one's allegiance or devotion to deity [BDAG].

  d. πρῶτος (LN 87.45) (BDAG 2.a.β. p. 894): 'leading' [Bar, BECNT; ESV, NASB, NRSV, TEV], 'important' [LN; CEV, NCV], 'prominent' [AB, LN; GW, NET, NIV, NLT], 'great' [LN], 'foremost' [BDAG, LN], 'influential' [CBC; REB], 'chief' [KJV], 'first, most important, most prominent' [BDAG]. This adjective pertains to being of high rank, with the implication of special prominence and status [LN]. It pertains to prominence of persons [BDAG].

QUESTION—To whom does 'them' refer?

  It refers to some of the Jews [Bar, BECNT, CBC, EBC, NAC, NICNT, PNTC, TNTC; GW, NCV, NIV, NLT].

QUESTION—What is meant by the term 'joined' here?

  The term joined must not be understood in the technical sense of joining an association but in the more informal meaning of "counted themselves one with Paul and Silas," "took the part of Paul and Silas," or "identified themselves as being companions of Paul and Silas" [TH]. It means that they formed a separate group and met apart from the synagogue [TNTC]. It may suggest that they are meeting separately from the Jews [BECNT].

**DISCOURSE UNIT—17:5–9** [NICNT]. The topic is trouble in Thessalonica.

**17:5** But[a] the Jews were-jealous,[b] and taking[c] some wicked[d] men from the market place, they formed-(a)-mob, set- the city -in-an-uproar,[e] and attacked[f] the house of-Jason, seeking[g] to-bring them out to the crowd.

LEXICON—a. δέ (LN 89.124): 'but' [LN; all translations except Bar; CEV, GW, REB], 'on the other hand' [LN], 'then' [GW], not explicit [Bar; CEV, REB]. This conjunction indicates a contrast [LN].

b. aorist act. participle of ζηλόω (LN 88.163) (BDAG 2. p. 427): 'to be jealous' [AB, BECNT, LN; CEV, ESV, NIV, NLT, TEV], 'to be envious' [LN], 'to be filled with jealousy/envy' [BDAG], 'to become jealous' [Bar; GW, NASB, NCV, NET, NRSV]. The phrase 'the Jews were jealous' is also translated 'the Jews...moved with envy' [KJV], 'the Jews in their jealousy' [CBC; REB]. This verb means to experience strong envy and resentment against someone [LN]. It means to have intense negative feelings over another's achievements or success [BDAG].

c. aorist mid. participle of προσλαμβάνω (LN 15.127, 15.167) (BDAG 5. p. 883): 'to take' [AB, Bar, BECNT; ESV, GW, KJV], 'to get' [CEV, NCV], 'to gather' [NLT, TEV], 'to gather together' [LN (15.127); NET], 'to recruit' [CBC; REB], 'to form a group' [LN (15.127)], 'to take along' [BDAG, LN (15.167); NASB], 'to bring along' [LN (15.167)], 'to round up' [NIV], not explicit [NRSV]. This verb means to gather together to oneself a group of persons [LN (15.127)]. It means to take or bring along in addition to oneself [LN (15.167)]. It means to take or bring along with oneself [BDAG].

d. πονηρός (LN 88.110) (BDAG 1.a.α. p. 851): 'wicked' [BDAG, BECNT, LN; ESV, NASB], 'evil' [Bar, LN; NCV], 'immoral' [LN], 'worthless' [AB, BDAG; CEV, NET, TEV], 'low-class' [GW], 'low' [CBC], 'lewd' [KJV], 'bad' [BDAG; NIV], 'base, vicious, degenerate' [BDAG]. The phrase 'some wicked men' is also translated 'some troublemakers' [NLT], 'some ruffians' [NRSV, REB]. This adjective pertains to being morally corrupt and evil [LN]. It pertains to being morally or socially worthless [BDAG].

e. imperf. act. indic. of θορυβέω (LN 39.44) (BDAG 1. p. 458): 'to set in an uproar' [Bar, BECNT; ESV, NASB, NET, NRSV, TEV], 'to set on an uproar' [KJV], 'to put in an uproar' [REB], 'to have in an uproar' [CBC], 'to throw into an uproar' [AB], 'to start a riot' [LN; CEV, GW, NCV, NIV, NLT], 'to stir up against, to cause an uproar' [LN], 'to throw into disorder' [BDAG]. This verb means to cause people to riot against [LN].

f. aorist act. participle of ἐφίστημι (LN 39.47) (BDAG 3. p. 418): 'to attack' [AB, BDAG, BECNT, LN; ESV, GW, NASB, NET, NLT, NRSV,

ACTS 17:5

TEV], 'to assault' [LN; KJV]. The clause 'they…attacked the house of Jason' is also translated 'they gathered at the house of Jason' [Bar], 'they rushed to Jason's house' [NIV], 'they mobbed Jason's house' [CBC], 'they…made for Jason's house' [REB], 'they ran to Jason's house' [NCV], 'they went straight to Jason's home' [CEV]. This verb means to use sudden physical force against someone as the outgrowth of a hostile attitude [LN]. It means to come near with the intention of harming [BDAG].

g. imperf. act. indic. of ζητέω (LN 68.60): 'to seek' [AB, Bar, BECNT; ESV, KJV, NASB], 'to seek to do, to try' [LN]. The phrase 'seeking to bring them out to the crowd' is also translated 'They wanted to drag Paul and Silas out to the mob' [CEV], 'wanting to bring them out to the people' [NCV], 'trying to find Paul and Silas to bring them out to the assembly' [NET], 'searching for Paul and Silas so they could drag them out to the crowd' [NLT], 'searching for Paul and Silas to bring them out to the assembly' [NRSV], 'in order to bring them out to the crowd' [GW, NIV], 'with the intention of bringing Paul and Silas before the town assembly' [CBC; REB], 'in an attempt to find Paul and Silas and bring them out to the people' [TEV]. This verb means to seek to do something, but without success [LN].

QUESTION—Why were the Jews jealous?

They were jealous because so many people were becoming believers [AB, EBC, NAC, NICNT, TRT]. They were afraid that they were losing control of the synagogue and their appeal to religious non-Jews [Bar].

QUESTION—To whom does 'they' refer?

It refers to the wicked men from the market place and the Jews who formed them into a mob [TH, TRT].

QUESTION—In what way did they attack Jason's house?

Probably the best way to say it is "they broke down the doors of the house," since this was apparently what happened in their attempt to find Paul and Silas and to bring them out to the people [TH, TRT].

QUESTION— Who was Jason?

If this is the same Jason who is mentioned in Romans 16.21, he is one of Paul's relatives [TRT].

QUESTION—To whom does 'them' refer?

It refers to Paul and Silas [AB, Bar, BECNT, CBC, EBC, NAC, PNTC, TRT; CEV, GW, NCV, NET, NIV, NLT, NRSV, REB, TEV].

QUESTION—To whom does 'the crowd' refer?

It may refer to the mob that had gathered or 'the town assembly,' by which is meant the citizens assembled for judicial purposes [TH, TRT]. It refers to the popular assembly, which in a free city had juridical functions [PNTC].

**17:6** When they did- not -find[a] them, they-dragged[b] Jason and some of the brothers[c] before the city-authorities,[d] shouting,[e] "These-men who have- upset[f] the world[g] have-come[h] here also,

LEXICON—a. aorist act. participle of εὑρίσκω (LN 27.27): 'to find' [LN; all translations except ESV, NRSV], 'to be able to find' [ESV, NRSV], 'to learn the whereabouts of something, to discover, to come upon, to happen to find' [LN]. This verb means to learn the location of something, either by intentional searching or by unexpected discovery [LN].

b. imperf. act. indic. of σύρω (LN 15.178) (BDAG p. 978): 'to drag' [BDAG, LN; all translations except KJV], 'to draw' [BDAG; KJV], 'to lead by force' [LN], 'to pull, to drag away' [BDAG]. This verb means to drag or pull by physical force, often implying resistance [LN].

c. ἀδελφός (LN 11.23): 'brother' [Bar, BECNT; ESV, NET, NIV], 'fellow believer, (Christian) brother' [LN]. The phrase 'some of the brothers' is also translated 'some brethren/believers' [NASB, NRSV], 'some of the brethren' [AB], 'certain brethren' [KJV], 'some of the Lord's followers' [CEV], 'some other believers' [GW, NCV, TEV], 'some of the other believers' [NLT], 'some members of the congregation' [CBC; REB]. This noun denotes a close associate of a group of persons having a well-defined membership. In the NT ἀδελφός 'brother' refers specifically to fellow believers in Christ [LN].

d. πολιτάρχης (LN 37.93) (BDAG p. 845): 'city authority' [BECNT; CEV, ESV, NASB, NRSV, TEV], 'city official' [BDAG, LN; GW, NET, NIV], 'city council' [NLT]. The phrase 'the city authorities' is also translated 'the rulers/leaders of the city' [KJV, NCV], 'the magistrates/politarchs' [AB, Bar, CBC; REB]. This noun denotes a public official responsible for administrative matters within a town or city and a member of the ruling council of such a political unit [LN]. It denotes a magistrate who formed part of a town or city council [BDAG].

e. pres. act. participle of βοάω (LN 33.81) (BDAG 1.a. p. 180): 'to shout' [AB, Bar, BDAG, CBC, LN; all versions except KJV NCV, NET], 'to cry' [BECNT; KJV], 'to cry out' [BDAG, LN], 'to yell' [NCV], 'to scream' [LN; NET], 'to call' [BDAG]. This verb means to cry or shout with unusually loud volume [LN]. It means to use one's voice at a high volume and refers to emotionally charged cries [BDAG].

f. aorist act. participle of ἀναστατόω (LN 39.41) (BDAG p. 72): 'to upset' [BDAG; CEV, NASB], 'to make/cause trouble' [CBC; GW, NCV, NIV, NLT, REB, TEV], 'to stir up trouble' [AB; NET], 'to disturb, to trouble' [BDAG], 'to incite to revolt, to cause to rebel' [LN]. The clause 'These men who have upset the world' is also translated 'These men who have turned the world upside down' [BECNT; ESV], 'These that have turned the world upside down' [KJV], 'These people who have been turning the world upside down' [NRSV], 'These men who have led the whole world into revolt' [Bar]. This verb means to cause people to rebel against or to reject authority [LN]. It means to upset the stability of a person or group [BDAG].

g. οἰκουμένη (LN 9.22) (BDAG 2.b. p. 699): 'world' [all translations except CEV, TEV], 'people, all mankind' [LN], 'the Roman empire' [BDAG]. The clause 'These men who have upset the world' is also translated 'Paul and Silas have been upsetting things everywhere' [CEV], 'These men have caused trouble everywhere' [TEV]. This is a figurative extension of meaning of οἰκουμένη 'inhabited earth', and of γῆ 'earth', and denotes all people who dwell on the earth [LN]. It denotes the world as administrative unit and refers to its inhabitants [BDAG].

h. pres. act. indic. of πάρειμι (LN 15.86) (BDAG 1.a. p. 773): 'to come' [LN; all translations except GW, NLT], 'to arrive, to come to be present' [LN], 'to be present' [BDAG], not explicit [GW, NLT]. This verb means to come to be present at a particular place [LN].

QUESTION—Was Jason a Christian?

Considered solely upon the basis of the Greek text of this verse, one would conclude that Jason was not one of the "brothers." However, when other passages are taken into the consideration, there is sufficient evidence to indicate that Luke may have intended Jason to have been included among the "brothers." For example, 1:14 mentions the women, and…Mary the mother of Jesus, with the evident indication that Mary is not to be excluded from among the women. Again, the expression 'the believers and the widows' in 9:41 does not imply that the widows were not believers. One may also argue, from the casual way in which Luke has introduced Jason, that he probably should be considered as one of the believers. Otherwise, one would have expected that Luke would have indicated clearly Jason's relationship to the believing community [TH]. It is probably implied that Jason was a Christian [Bar]. He was probably a Diaspora Jew who became one of Paul's first converts at Thessalonica [EBC].

QUESTION—What were Paul and Silas accused of?

They were accused of disrupting civil peace and were now bringing this practice to Thessalonica [BECNT]. They were accused of causing trouble all over the world [NAC], which probably means throughout the Roman empire [PNTC].

QUESTION—To what does the word 'world' refer?

It refers to the civilized world (more specifically the Roman empire) and is used here in an exaggerated sense [TH].

**17:7** and Jason has-received[a] them, and they are- all -acting[b] against the decrees of-Caesar, saying that there is another king, Jesus."

LEXICON—a. perf. mid./pass. (deponent = act.) indic. of ὑποδέχομαι (LN 34.53) (BDAG p. 1037): 'to receive' [BDAG, BECNT, LN; ESV, KJV], 'to welcome' [BDAG, LN; CEV, NASB, NIV, NLT], 'to accept, to have as a guest' [LN], 'to welcome as a guest' [GW, NET], 'to receive as a guest' [AB], 'to entertain as a guest' [BDAG; NRSV], 'to harbour' [CBC;

REB], 'to keep' [NCV, TEV], 'to take in' [Bar]. This verb means to accept the presence of a person with friendliness [LN]. It means to receive hospitably [BDAG].
- b. pres. act. indic. of πράσσω (LN 42.8) (BDAG 2. p. 860): 'to act' [AB, Bar, BDAG, BECNT; ESV, NASB, NET, NRSV], 'to do' [LN; KJV, NCV], 'to carry out, to perform' [LN], 'to behave' [BDAG]. The clause 'they are all acting against the decrees of Caesar' is also translated 'All of them break the laws of the Roman Emperor' [CEV], 'They are all breaking the laws of the Emperor' [TEV], 'All of them oppose the emperor's decrees' [GW], 'They are all defying Caesar's decrees' [NIV], 'They are all guilty of treason against Caesar' [NLT], 'They all flout the emperor's laws' [CBC], 'All of them flout the emperor's laws' [REB]. This verb means to carry out some activity (with possible focus upon the procedures involved) [LN]. It means to engage in activity or behave in a certain way [BDAG].

QUESTION—What Roman emperor is referred to in this verse?

It refers to Claudius, who ruled from A.D. 41 to 54 [EBC, TH, TRT].

QUESTION—What were the Christians accused of?

They are accused of saying that someone else other than Claudius was king, and his name was Jesus [AB, BECNT, NAC, PNTC, TH, TNTC, TRT]. Jason was accused of harboring the troublemakers [NAC, NICNT].

**17:8** And they-stirred-up[a] the crowd[b] and the city-authorities[c] who heard[d] these-things.

LEXICON—a. aorist act. indic. of ταράσσω (LN 39.44) (BDAG 2. p. 990): 'to stir up' [AB, BDAG; NASB], 'to trouble' [KJV], 'to alarm' [REB], 'to cause confusion' [NET], 'to cause a commotion' [CBC], 'to throw in an uproar' [TEV], 'to disturb' [Bar, BDAG], 'to unsettle, to throw into confusion' [BDAG], 'to stir up against, to start a riot, to cause an uproar' [LN]. This verb is also translated as a passive verb: 'to be disturbed' [BECNT; ESV, NRSV], 'to be upset' [CEV, GW], 'to become upset' [NCV], 'to be thrown into turmoil' [NIV, NLT]. This verb means to cause people to riot against [LN]. It means to cause inward turmoil [BDAG].
- b. ὄχλος (LN 11.1): 'crowd' [AB, Bar, LN; GW, NASB, NET, NIV, TEV], 'multitude' [LN], 'mob' [CBC; REB], 'people' [BECNT; CEV, ESV, KJV, NCV, NLT, NRSV]. This noun denotes a casual non-membership group of people, fairly large in size and assembled for whatever purpose [LN].
- c. πολιτάρχης (LN 37.93) (BDAG p. 845): 'city authority' [BECNT; ESV, NASB, TEV], 'city official' [BDAG, LN; NET, NIV, NRSV], 'city council' [NLT], 'official' [CEV, GW], 'ruler' [KJV], 'leader' [NCV], 'magistrate' [CBC; REB], 'politarch' [AB, Bar]. This noun denotes a public official responsible for administrative matters within a town or city and a member of the ruling council of such a political unit [LN]. It denotes a magistrate who formed part of a town or city council [BDAG].

d. pres. act. participle of ἀκούω (LN 33.212): 'to hear' [AB, BECNT, LN; all versions except NLT, REB, TEV], 'to listen' [Bar], 'to receive news' [LN]. The clause 'they stirred up the crowd and the city authorities who heard these things' is also translated 'The people of the city, as well as the city council, were thrown into turmoil by these reports' [NLT], 'These words alarmed the mob and the magistrates' [REB], 'These words caused a great commotion in the mob, which affected the magistrates' [CBC], 'With these words they threw the crowd and the city authorities in an uproar' [TEV]. This verb means to receive information about something, normally by word of mouth [LN].

**17:9** **And when they had-taken[a] bond-money[b] from Jason and the rest, they-let- them -go.[c]**

LEXICON—a. aorist act. participle of λαμβάνω (LN 57.65) (BDAG 10.c. p. 585): 'to take' [AB, Bar, BECNT; ESV, KJV, NRSV, REB], 'to receive' [BDAG; NASB, NET], 'to receive (interest), to collect (taxes)' [LN], 'to get, to obtain' [BDAG], not explicit [CBC]. The clause 'they had taken bond money from Jason and the rest' is also translated 'they made Jason and the other followers pay bail' [CEV], 'they had made Jason and the others post bond' [GW, NIV], 'They made Jason and the others put up a sum of money' [NCV], 'the officials forced Jason and the other believers to post bond' [NLT], 'The authorities made Jason and the others pay the required amount of money' [TEV]. This verb means to collect what is due (normally in terms of taxes and interest), with the possible implication of extortion [LN].

b. ἱκανός (LN 57.169) (BDAG 1. p. 472): 'bond' [LN; GW, NIV, NLT] 'bail' [LN; CEV, NET, NRSV], 'pledge' [NASB], 'security' [AB, Bar; KJV, REB], 'security for peace' [BECNT], 'sum of money' [NCV], 'the amount of money required for release' [LN], 'sufficient, adequate, large enough' [BDAG]. This adjective is also translated 'the required amount of money' [TEV], 'money as security' [ESV]. This adjective is also translated as a verb: 'to bind over' [CBC]. This adjective refers to the amount of money required to release someone who has been held in custody [LN]. It refers to being sufficient in degree [BDAG].

c. aorist act. indic. of ἀπολύω (LN 37.127): 'to let go' [BECNT, CBC; CEV, ESV, GW, KJV, NIV, NRSV, REB, TEV], 'to let go free' [NCV], 'to release' [AB, LN; NASB, NET, NLT], 'to set free' [LN], 'to dismiss' [Bar]. This verb means to release from control, to set free (highly generic meaning applicable to a wide variety of circumstances, including confinement, political domination, sin, sickness) [LN].

QUESTION—What was the bond money for?

The bond money refers to the security or money which was given to the city officials and which would have been forfeited by Jason had the offense been repeated [NAC, TH]. The city officials/leaders made Jason and the other Christians pay bond money in order to make them responsible for making sure that there would be no more trouble [BECNT, EBC, NICNT, PNTC, TRT]. If there was any more trouble, Jason and his companions would lose their bond money and be put in jail again [TRT].

QUESTION—To whom does 'they' refer?

It refers to the authorities/officials/magistrates/politarchs [AB, BECNT, EBC, NAC, NICNT, PNTC, TH, TNTC, TRT; NET, NLT, REB, TEV].

**DISCOURSE UNIT—17:10–15** [AB, BECNT, EBC, NAC, NICNT, PNTC; CEV, ESV, NASB, NCV, NET, NIV, NLT, NRSV, TEV]. The topic is Paul and Silas in Berea [ESV, NLT], Paul and Silas in Beroea [NRSV], Paul and Silas at Berea [NET], Paul and Silas go to Berea [NCV], Paul at Berea [NASB], Paul in Berea [AB], people in Berea welcome the message [CEV], at Berea [EBC], in Berea [NIV, TEV], in Beroea [BECNT], witness in Berea [NAC], the gospel provokes an eager searching of the scriptures [PNTC], Beroea [NICNT].

**DISCOURSE UNIT—17:10b–14** [GW]. The topic is Paul and Silas in Berea.

**17:10** **The brothers[a] immediately sent- Paul and Silas -away[b] by night to Berea, and when they arrived[c] they went into the Jewish synagogue.**

LEXICON—a. ἀδελφός (LN 11.23): 'brother' [Bar, BECNT; ESV, NET, NIV], 'fellow believer, (Christian) brother' [LN]. The phrase 'the brothers' is also translated 'the believers' [GW, NCV, NLT, NRSV, TEV], 'the brethren' [AB; KJV, NASB], 'the Lord's followers' [CEV], 'the members of the congregation' [CBC; REB]. This noun denotes a close associate of a group of persons having a well-defined membership. In the NT ἀδελφός 'brother' refers specifically to fellow believers in Christ [LN].

b. aorist act. indic. of ἐκπέμπω (LN 15.68) (BDAG p. 307): 'to send away' [AB, BECNT; ESV, KJV, NASB, NIV], 'to send' [LN; CEV, GW, NCV, NLT, TEV], 'to send out' [BDAG, LN], 'to send forth' [LN], 'to send off' [Bar, CBC; NET, NRSV, REB]. This verb means to send out or away from, presumably for some purpose [LN]. It means to cause someone to go away (for a purpose) [BDAG].

c. aorist mid. (deponent = act.) participle of παραγίνομαι (LN 15.86) (BDAG 1.a. p. 760): 'to arrive' [BDAG, LN; all translations except KJV, NCV], 'to come' [BDAG, LN], 'to draw near, to be present' [BDAG], 'to come to be present' [LN], 'to come (thither)' [KJV], not explicit [NCV]. This verb means to come to be present at a particular place [LN]. It means to be in movement so as to be present at a particular place [BDAG].

QUESTION—To whom does 'the brothers' refer?

It refers to the entire Christian community of Thessalonica and not merely to the ones who had been released [AB, Bar, TH, TRT].

QUESTION—Why did the brothers send Paul and Silas to Berea at night?

They sent them to Berea most likely because of the fear of further mob violence [TNTC]. They sent Paul to Berea at night, possibly indicating a hasty exit [BECNT, NAC] and concern for safety [BECNT].

QUESTION—Where was Berea located?
Berea was located 45 to 60 miles west of Thessalonica and south of the Ignatian Way [Bar, BECNT, EBC, NAC, NICNT, PNTC, TH, TRT].
QUESTION—Why did Paul and Silas go into the synagogue in Berea?
They went into the synagogue to proclaim the Good News of salvation in Jesus Christ [EBC].

**17:11** **Now these were more-noble-minded-than**[a] **those in Thessalonica; they received**[b] **the word**[c] **with all eagerness,**[d] **examining**[e] **the Scriptures daily to see if these-things were so.**

LEXICON—a. εὐγενής (LN 27.48) (BDAG 2. p. 404): 'more noble-minded than' [NASB], 'more noble than' [BECNT; ESV, KJV], 'more noble character than' [NIV], 'more open-minded than' [GW, NET, NLT, TEV], 'more fair-minded than' [REB], 'more receptive than' [NRSV], 'more courteous than' [AB], 'more liberal than' [Bar], 'more civil than' [CBC], 'more willing to listen than' [NCV], 'much nicer than' [CEV], 'willingness to learn' [LN], 'to be open-minded, to be noble-minded' [BDAG, LN]. This adjective pertains to a person who has a willingness to learn and evaluate something fairly [LN]. It pertains to having the type of attitude ordinarily associated with well-bred persons [BDAG].

b. aorist mid. (deponent = act.) indic. of δέχομαι (LN 31.51) (BDAG 5. p. 221): 'to receive' [AB, Bar, BECNT, CBC; ESV, GW, KJV, NASB, NET, NIV, REB], 'to accept' [BDAG, LN; CEV], 'to receive readily, to believe' [LN], 'to be receptive of, to be open to, to approve' [BDAG], 'to welcome' [NRSV], 'to listen' [TEV]. The clause 'they received the word with all eagerness' is also translated 'The Bereans were eager to hear what Paul and Silas said' [NCV], 'they listened eagerly to Paul's message' [NLT]. This verb means to readily receive information and to regard it as true [LN]. It means to indicate approval or conviction by accepting [BDAG].

c. λόγος (LN 33.260) (BDAG 1.a.β. p. 599): 'word' [AB, Bar, BDAG, BECNT; ESV, KJV, NASB], 'message' [CBC; CEV, GW, NET, NIV, NLT, NRSV, REB, TEV], 'what is preached, gospel' [LN]. The clause 'they received the word with all eagerness' is also translated 'The Bereans were eager to hear what Paul and Silas said' [NCV]. This noun denotes the content of what is preached about Christ or about the good news [LN]. It denotes a communication whereby the mind finds expression [BDAG].

d. προθυμία (LN 25.68) (BDAG p. 870): 'eagerness' [Bar, BECNT, CBC, LN; ESV, NASB, NIV, REB, TEV], 'desire' [LN], 'readiness' [BDAG; KJV], 'willingness, goodwill' [BDAG], 'interest' [AB]. The clause 'they received the word with all eagerness' is also translated 'they gladly accepted the message' [CEV]. This noun is also translated as a verb: 'They were very willing to receive God's message' [GW], 'The Bereans were eager to hear what Paul and Silas said' [NCV]. This noun is also translated as an adverb: 'they eagerly received the message' [NET], 'they

listened eagerly to Paul's message' [NLT], 'they welcomed the message very eagerly' [NRSV]. This noun denotes the eagerness to engage in some activity or event [LN]. It denotes exceptional interest in being of service [BDAG].
- e. pres. act. participle of ἀνακρίνω (LN 27.44) (BDAG 1. p. 66): 'to examine' [AB, BDAG, BECNT; ESV, GW, NASB, NET, NIV, NRSV], 'to study' [CBC; CEV, NCV, REB, TEV], 'to examine carefully, to investigate, to study thoroughly' [LN], 'to question' [BDAG], 'to search' [Bar; KJV, NLT]. This verb means to try to learn the nature or truth of something by the process of careful study, evaluation and judgment [LN]. It means to engage in careful study of a question [BDAG].

QUESTION—To whom does 'these' refer?

It refers to the people of Berea [BECNT, EBC, NAC, PNTC, TRT; CEV, GW, NIV, NLT].

QUESTION—What is meant by the phrase 'more noble minded than'?

In the present context the reference is to the attitude of the Bereans toward the Christian message and is best understood in the sense of "receptive" [TH]. It means that the Berean Jews did not allow any prejudice to prevent them from giving Paul a fair hearing [Bar, PNTC]. The Bereans noble character was demonstrated in two ways. First, they received the message with great eagerness, responding enthusiastically because they realized its relevance to their own lives. Second, they examined the scriptures every day to see if what Paul said was true [PNTC].

QUESTION—To what does the phrase 'these things' refer?

'These things' that they examined most likely include Christ's suffering, his being raised, and his kingship [BECNT].

**17:12** **Therefore many of them believed,[a] with not (a)-few Greek women of high-standing[b] as well as men.**

LEXICON—a. aorist act. indic. of πιστεύω (LN 31.102) (BDAG 2.b. p. 817 ): 'to believe' [AB, BECNT; all versions except CEV, GW, REB], 'to believe (in), to trust' [BDAG]. This verb is also translated as a noun: 'became believers' [Bar, CBC; GW, REB]. The clause 'many of them believed' is also translated 'Many of them put their faith in the Lord' [CEV]. This verb means to believe in the good news about Jesus Christ and to become a follower [LN]. It means to entrust oneself to an entity in complete confidence [BDAG].
- b. εὐσχήμων (LN 87.33) (BDAG 2. p. 414): 'high standing' [BECNT; ESV, NRSV], 'high social standing' [TEV], 'good standing' [Bar], 'prominent' [GW, NASB, NET, NIV, NLT], 'important' [CEV, NCV], 'honourable' [KJV], 'esteemed, honored' [LN], 'most respected' [AB], 'of standing' [CBC; REB], 'of high standing/repute, noble' [BDAG]. This adjective pertains to having special prestige or honor [LN]. It pertains to being considered especially worthy of public admiration [BDAG].

QUESTION—To whom does the phrase 'many of them' refer?
1. It refers to the Jews [Bar, NICNT, TH; NIV, NLT] or the so called "devout people" who accepted Jewish beliefs about God but who had not become proselytes [TH].
2. It is possible to understand "many of them" believed as a general expression made more specific by the additional phrases many Greek women and many Greek men [TH].

**17:13 But when the Jews from Thessalonica learned<sup>a</sup> that the word of-God was-proclaimed by Paul in Berea also, they-came<sup>b</sup> there-too, agitating<sup>c</sup> and stirring-up the crowds.**

LEXICON—a. aorist act. indic. of γινώσκω (LN 27.2): 'to learn' [AB, BECNT, CBC, LN; ESV, NCV, NIV, NLT, NRSV, REB], 'to find out' [LN; GW, NASB], 'to hear' [CEV, NET, TEV], 'to know' [Bar]. The phrase 'when the Jews...learned' is also translated 'when the Jews...had knowledge' [KJV]. This verb means to acquire information by whatever means, but often with the implication of personal involvement or experience [LN].
  b. aorist act. indic. of ἔρχομαι (LN 15.81): 'to come' [AB, Bar, BECNT, CBC, LN; ESV, KJV, NASB, NCV, NET, NRSV, TEV], 'to go' [CEV, GW, NIV, NLT]. The phrase 'they came there too' is also translated 'they followed him there' [REB]. This verb means to move toward or up to the reference point of the viewpoint character or event [LN].
  c. pres. act. participle of σαλεύω (LN 39.44) (BDAG 2. p. 911): 'to agitate' [ESV, NASB, NIV], 'to stir up against, to start a riot, to cause an uproar' [LN], 'to disturb, to shake' [BDAG], 'to stir up' [Bar, BECNT; KJV, NRSV], 'to stir up a riot' [AB], 'to cause trouble' [CEV], 'to stir up trouble' [CBC; NLT, REB], 'to upset' [GW, NCV], 'to incite' [NET], 'to excite' [TEV]. This verb means to cause people to riot against [LN]. It means to disturb inwardly [BDAG].

**17:14 Then the brothers immediately sent- Paul -out to-go<sup>a</sup> as-far-as the sea, and Silas and Timothy remained<sup>b</sup> there.**

LEXICON—a. pres. mid./pass. (deponent = act.) infin. of πορεύομαι (LN 15.18) (BDAG 1. p. 853): 'to go' [AB, BDAG, CBC; KJV, NASB], 'to travel' [Bar, LN], 'to journey, to be on one's way' [LN], 'to proceed' [BDAG]. The phrase 'the brothers immediately sent Paul out to go' is also translated 'the brothers immediately sent Paul off on his way' [BECNT; ESV], not explicit [all versions except KJV, NASB]. This verb means to move a considerable distance, either with a single destination or from one destination to another in a series [LN]. It means to move over an area, generally with a point of departure or destination specified [BDAG].
  b. aorist act. indic. of ὑπομένω (LN 85.57) (BDAG 1. p. 1039): 'to remain' [Bar, BDAG, BECNT; ESV, NASB, NET], 'to stay' [AB; CEV, GW, NCV, NIV, TEV], 'to abide' [KJV], 'to stay behind' [BDAG, CBC, LN; REB], 'to remain behind' [NLT, NRSV], 'to remain longer than' [LN].

This verb means to stay longer in a place than one is expected to [LN]. It means to stay in a place beyond an expected point of time [BDAG].

QUESTION—To whom does 'the brothers' refer?

It refers to the Christian community [Bar].

QUESTION—To what does the phrase 'the sea' refer?

The phrase 'the sea' refers to the Aegean sea [TH].

**DISCOURSE UNIT—17:15–34** [GW]. The topic is Paul in Athens.

**17:15** Now those who escorted<sup>a</sup> Paul brought-(him)<sup>b</sup> as-far-as Athens, and after receiving<sup>c</sup> (a)-command for Silas and Timothy to come to him as soon-as-possible, they-departed.<sup>d</sup>

LEXICON—a. pres. act. participle of καθίστημι (LN 15.175) (BDAG 1. p. 492): 'to escort' [BECNT; GW, NASB, NIV, NLT], 'to conduct' [ESV, KJV, NRSV], 'to lead' [NCV], 'to take' [AB, BDAG; TEV], 'to bring' [BDAG], 'to bring down, to lead down' [LN], 'to accompany' [Bar; NET], not explicit [CEV]. This verb is also translated as a noun: 'Paul's escort' [CBC; REB]. This verb means to lead or to bring down [LN]. It means to take someone somewhere [BDAG].

b. aorist act. indic. of ἄγω (LN 15.165) (BDAG 1.b. p. 16): 'to bring' [Bar, BECNT, CBC, LN; ESV, KJV, NASB, NIV, NRSV, REB], 'to lead' [LN], 'to take' [GW], 'to bring/take along' [BDAG], 'to escort' [NET]. The phrase 'those…brought him' is also translated 'The people…went with him' [NCV], 'Those…went with him' [AB; NLT], 'The men…went with him' [TEV], 'Some men went with Paul' [CEV]. This verb means to direct or guide the movement of an object, without special regard to point of departure or goal [LN]. It means to direct the movement of an object from one position to another [BDAG].

c. aorist act. participle of λαμβάνω (LN 57.125): 'to receive' [BECNT, LN; ESV, KJV, NASB, NET, NRSV], 'to accept' [LN], not explicit [AB, Bar, CBC; CEV, GW, NCV, NIV, NLT, REB, TEV]. This verb means to receive or accept an object or benefit for which the initiative rests with the giver, but the focus of attention in the transfer is upon the receiver [LN].

d. imperf. act. indic. of ἔξειμι (LN 15.40) (BDAG I. p. 347): 'to depart' [BECNT; ESV, KJV], 'to leave' [Bar; GW, NASB, NET, NIV, NRSV], 'to go out of, to depart out of, to leave from within' [LN], 'to come away' [CBC; REB], not explicit [AB; CEV, NCV, NLT, TEV]. This verb means to move out of an enclosed or well defined two or three-dimensional area [LN]. It means to depart from an area [BDAG].

**DISCOURSE UNIT—17:16–34** [Bar, BECNT, CBC, EBC, NAC, PNTC, TNTC; CEV, NCV, NET, NIV, NLT, NRSV, TEV]. The topic is Paul in Athens [CEV, NRSV], Paul at Athens [Bar; NET], Paul preaches in Athens [NCV, NLT], Athens: the Areopagus address [TNTC], in Athens [BECNT; NIV, TEV], at Athens [EBC], to Athens: in the city [CBC], witnessing to the Athenian intellectuals [NAC], the word in Athens [PNTC].

**DISCOURSE UNIT—17:16-21** [AB, EBC, NAC, NICNT, PNTC; ESV, NASB]. The topic is Paul in Athens [AB; ESV], Paul at Athens [NASB], the Athenians' curiosity [NAC], inauguration of a ministry [EBC], responding to idolatry [PNTC], Athens [NICNT].

**17:16** Now while Paul was-waiting[a] for them at Athens, his spirit[b] was-being-provoked[c] within him as he was-observing-(that)[d] the city was full-of-idols.[e]

LEXICON—a. pres. mid./pass. (deponent = act.) participle of ἐκδέχομαι (LN 85.60) (BDAG p. 300): 'to wait' [BDAG, LN; all translations], 'to wait for' [LN], 'to expect' [BDAG]. This verb means to remain in a place and/or state, with expectancy concerning a future event [LN]. It means to remain in a place or state and await an event or the arrival of someone [BDAG].

b. πνεῦμα (LN 26.9) (BDAG 3.b. p. 833): 'spirit' [Bar, BDAG, BECNT, LN; ESV, KJV, NASB, NET], 'spiritual nature, inner being' [LN]. The phrase 'his spirit was being provoked' is also translated 'he was upset' [CEV], 'he was troubled' [NCV], 'he was deeply troubled' [NLT], 'he was deeply distressed' [NRSV], 'he was greatly distressed' [NIV], 'he was greatly upset' [TEV], 'he was outraged' [REB], 'he was exasperated' [CBC], 'he became filled with indignation' [AB], 'This upset him' [GW]. This noun denotes the non-material, psychological faculty which is potentially sensitive and responsive to God [LN]. It denotes a part of human personality as the source and seat of insight, feeling and will, generally as the representative part of human inner life [BDAG].

c. imperf. pass. indic. of παροξύνω (LN 88.189) (BDAG p. 780): 'to be provoked' [BECNT, LN; ESV, NASB], 'to be stirred' [KJV], 'to be upset' [LN; CEV, GW], 'to be greatly upset' [NET, TEV], 'to be troubled' [NCV], 'to be deeply troubled' [NLT], 'to be greatly distressed' [NIV], 'to be deeply distressed' [NRSV], 'to be outraged' [REB], 'to be vexed' [Bar], 'to be exasperated' [CBC], 'to become irritated, to become angry' [BDAG], 'to become filled with indignation' [AB]. This verb means to be provoked or upset at someone or something involving severe emotional concern [LN].

d. pres. act. participle of θεωρέω (LN 24.14) (BDAG 1. p. 454): 'to observe' [BDAG, LN; NASB], 'to see' [BDAG; all translations except NASB, TEV], 'to notice' [TEV], 'to be a spectator of, to look at' [BDAG, LN], 'to perceive' [BDAG]. This verb means to observe something with continuity and attention, often with the implication that what is observed is something unusual [LN]. It means to observe something with sustained attention [BDAG].

e. κατείδωλος (LN 6.98) (BDAG p. 530): 'full of idols' [BDAG, BECNT, CBC, LN; ESV, NASB, NCV, NET, NIV, NRSV, REB, TEV], 'full of cult-images' [BDAG], 'overgrown with idols' [Bar]. The phrase 'the city was full of idols' is also translated 'all the idols in the city' [CEV], 'the city had statues of false gods everywhere' [GW], 'the city wholly given to idolatry' [KJV], 'all the idols…everywhere in the city' [NLT], 'how idolatrous the city was' [AB]. This adjective pertains to numerous idols [LN].

QUESTION—Where was Athens?

The city of Athens was located five miles inland from the port of Piraeus which is on the Saronic Gulf. It is situated on a narrow plain between Mount Parnes to the north, Mount Pentelicus to the east and Mount Hymettus to the southeast [EBC].

QUESTION—To what does the phrase 'his spirit was being provoked within him' refer?

The phrase could refer either to Paul's anger, to his grief, or to his desire to win the Athenians over to the Christian message [TH]. Paul was probably grieved by what he saw, and somewhat angry, but at the same time he was deeply concerned that the people of Athens were worshiping false gods instead of the true God [TRT].

**17:17** **So he-reasoned[a] in the synagogue[b] with-the Jews and the worshipping[c] Gentiles, and in the marketplace every day with those who happened-to-be-there.**

LEXICON—a. imperf. mid./pass. (deponent = act.) indic. of διαλέγομαι (LN 33.446) (BDAG 1. p. 232): 'to reason' [ESV, NASB, NIV, NLT], 'to argue' [AB, BDAG, BECNT, CBC, LN; NRSV, REB], 'to dispute' [Bar, LN; KJV], 'to converse, to discuss' [BDAG], 'to address' [NET], 'to talk with' [NCV], 'to speak to' [CEV]. The phrase 'he reasoned in the synagogue' is also translated 'He held discussions in the synagogue' [GW, TEV]. This verb means to argue about differences of opinion [LN]. It means to engage in speech interchange [BDAG].

b. συναγωγή (LN 7.20) (BDAG 2.a. p. 963): 'synagogue' [BDAG, LN; all translations except CEV], 'Christian assembly place' [LN], 'Jewish meeting place' [CEV]. This noun denotes a building of assembly, associated with religious activity. Normally a building in which Jewish worship took place and in which the Law was taught [LN]. It denotes a place of assembly for the Jews [BDAG].

c. pres. mid. participle of σέβω (LN 53.53) (BDAG 1.b. p. 918): 'to worship' [BDAG, LN; CEV, NCV, TEV], 'to venerate' [LN], not explicit [GW]. This verb is also translated as an adjective: 'devout' [Bar, BECNT; ESV, KJV, NRSV], 'God-fearing' [AB; NASB, NET, NIV, NLT]. This verb is also translated as a noun: 'worshipper' [CBC; REB]. This verb means to express in attitude and ritual one's allegiance to and regard for deity [LN]. It means to express in gestures, rites, or ceremonies one's allegiance or devotion to deity [BDAG].

QUESTION—What is the function of μὲν οὖν 'so'?

It introduces a new scene, possibly tying together Luke's introduction (17:16) with his source material (17:17ff).

ACTS 17:18

**17:18** And also some of-the Epicurean[a] and Stoic[b] philosophers[c] were-conversing[d] with-him. And some said, "What does this babbler[e] wish[f] to-say?" Others-(said), "He-seems to-be (a)-proclaimer[g] of-foreign[h] divinities[i]"—because he-was-preaching[j] Jesus and the resurrection.[k]

LEXICON—a. Ἐπικούρειος (LN 11.96) (BDAG p. 374): 'Epicurean' [BDAG, LN; all translations], 'a follower of Epicurus' [LN]. This noun denotes the philosophical system of the Greek philosopher Epicurus, who taught that the world is a series of fortuitous combinations of atoms and that the highest good is pleasure [LN].

b. Στοϊκός (LN 11.97) (BDAG p. 946): 'Stoic' [BDAG, LN; all translations], 'one who adheres to Stoic philosophy' [LN]. This adjective pertains to the philosophical system of the Greek philosopher Zeno, who taught that people should be free from excessive joy or grief and submit without complaint to necessity [LN].

c. φιλόσοφος (LN 32.39) (BDAG p. 1059): 'philosopher' [BDAG, LN; all translations except CEV, TEV], 'scholar' [LN], 'teacher' [TEV], not explicit [CEV]. This noun denotes a person of professional or semi-professional status regarded as having particular capacity or competence in understanding the meaning or significance of human experience [LN].

d. imperf. act. indic. of συμβάλλω (LN 33.439) (BDAG 1. p. 956): 'to converse' [BDAG; ESV, NASB, NET], 'to debate' [LN; NRSV, TEV], 'to discuss forcefully' [LN], 'to confer' [BDAG], 'to argue' [Bar; CEV, NCV], 'to dispute' [NIV], 'to encounter' [KJV], 'to confront' [AB], 'to join issue' [CBC; REB], 'to meet' [BECNT]. This verb is also translated as a noun: 'had discussions' [GW], 'had a debate' [NLT]. This verb means to express differences of opinion in a forceful way, involving alternative opportunities for presenting contrasting viewpoints [LN]. It means to engage in mutual pondering of a matter [BDAG].

e. σπερμολόγος (LN 27.19, 33.381) (BDAG 937): 'babbler' [ESV, KJV, NIV, NLT, NRSV], 'charlatan' [CBC, LN (27.19); REB], 'ignorant show-off' [LN (27.19); TEV], 'foolish babbler' [LN (33.381); NET], 'idle babbler' [BECNT; NASB], 'know-it-all' [CEV], 'scrapmonger, scavenger' [BDAG], 'babbling fool' [GW], 'phrase merchant' [AB], 'third rate journalist' [Bar]. The clause 'What does this babbler wish to say?' is also translated 'What is he trying to say?' [NCV]. This adjective is a figurative extension of meaning of a term based on the practice of birds in picking up seeds, one who acquires bits and pieces of relatively extraneous information and proceeds to pass them on with pretense and show [LN (27.19)]. It is a figurative expression, literally 'one who picks up seed,' originally a reference to birds picking up seed, but figuratively applied to a person who is an information scavenger, one who is not able to say anything worthwhile in view of his miscellaneous collection of tidbits of information [LN (33.381)].

f. pres. act. opt. of θέλω (LN 25.1) (BDAG 2. p. 448): 'to wish' [BDAG, LN; ESV, NASB], 'to desire' [LN], 'to want' [Bar, BDAG, LN; NET,

NRSV], 'to will, to be ready' [BDAG], not explicit [BECNT; KJV]. The phrase 'wish to say' is also translated 'trying to say' [AB, CBC; CEV, GW, NCV, NIV, NLT, REB, TEV]. This verb means to desire to have or experience something [LN]. It means to have something in mind for oneself of purpose, resolve [BDAG].

g. καταγγελεύς (LN 33.205) (BDAG p. 515): 'proclaimer' [BDAG, LN; NASB, NET, NRSV], 'preacher' [AB, Bar, BDAG, BECNT; ESV], 'herald, announcer' [LN], 'propagandist' [CBC; REB], 'setter forth' [KJV]. This noun is also translated as a verb: 'Paul must be preaching' [CEV], 'He seems to be preaching' [NLT], 'He seems to be speaking' [GW], 'He seems to be telling' [NCV], 'He seems to be talking' [TEV], 'He seems to be advocating' [NIV]. This noun denotes one who proclaims [LN].

h. ξένος (LN 28.34) (BDAG 1.a.α. p. 684): 'foreign' [all translations except KJV, NASB, NCV], 'strange' [BDAG; KJV, NASB], 'unknown, unheard of, unfamiliar, surprising' [LN]. The phrase 'of foreign divinities' is also translated 'some other gods' [NCV]. This adjective pertains to not being previously known and hence unheard of and unfamiliar [LN]. It pertains to being unfamiliar because of something being unknown [BDAG].

i. δαιμόνιον (LN 12.26) (BDAG 1. p. 210): 'divinity' [BECNT; ESV, NRSV], 'deity' [AB, CBC; NASB, REB], 'god' [Bar, LN; CEV, GW, KJV, NCV, NET, NIV, NLT, TEV], 'lesser god' [LN], 'semi-divine being, a divinity, spirit, (higher) power' [BDAG]. This noun denotes a supernatural being of somewhat lesser status than θεός 'god' [LN]. It denotes a transcendent incorporeal being with status between humans and deities [BDAG].

j. imperf. mid. indic. of εὐαγγελίζω (LN 33.215) (BDAG 2.a.β. p. 402): 'to preach' [AB, Bar, CBC; ESV, KJV, NASB, NIV, REB, TEV], 'to proclaim' [BECNT; NET], 'to tell' [GW, NCV, NLT, NRSV], 'to tell the good news, to announce the gospel' [LN], 'to proclaim the gospel' [BDAG]. The clause 'he was preaching Jesus' is also translated 'he talks about Jesus' [CEV]. This verb means to communicate good news concerning something and in the NT it is a particular reference to the gospel message about Jesus [LN]. It means to proclaim the divine message of salvation. Here it denotes the object of the proclamation, the Christ [BDAG].

k. ἀνάστασις (LN 23.93) (BDAG 2.a. p. 71, 2.b. p. 71, 3. p. 71): 'resurrection' [AB, Bar, BDAG (2.a. p. 71, 2.b. p. 71), BECNT, LN; ESV, KJV, NASB, NET, NIV, NLT, NRSV, TEV], 'Resurrection' [BDAG (3. p. 71), CBC; REB]. The clause 'he was preaching...the resurrection' is also translated 'he talks...about people rising from death' [CEV], 'Paul was...saying that people would come back to life' [GW], 'Paul was telling them about Jesus and his rising from the dead' [NCV]. This noun denotes resurrection from the dead [BDAG (2.a. p. 71), LN] and refers to Jesus' resurrection [BDAG (2.a. p. 71)] or to the future resurrection linked with Judgment Day [BDAG (2.b. p. 71)]. It denotes a deity within a polytheistic system. The Athenians assumed that Paul was a proclaimer of 'new divinities'. From their perspective the term suggests a divinity named Resurrection [BDAG (3. p. 71)].

QUESTION—What did the Epicureans believe?

The Epicureans followed the teachings of a man named Epicurus (342–270 B.C.) [AB, BECNT, CBC, EBC, NICNT, TNTC, TRT] who had taught that the main goal/purpose in life was happiness. As a result, they were very materialistic, pursuing anything that caused physical and mental pleasure and avoiding anything that caused pain or fear [AB, EBC, NICNT, TNTC, TRT]. They believed that the gods were not interested in mankind [CBC, EBC, NAC, PNTC, TNTC, TRT].

QUESTION—What did the Stoics believe?

The Stoics followed the teaching of a man named Zeno (332–260 B.C.) [AB, BECNT, EBC, TNTC, TRT] who had taught that mankind should live in harmony with nature, suppress his desires (that is, be self-controlled), develop his ability to reason/think and be independent/self-sufficient. The way to find happiness was to let fate/nature take its course (that is, let things happen the way they happen) [EBC, NICNT, TRT]. Stoics were very proud [EBC, TNTC, TRT]. They had a pantheistic conception of God as the world soul [EBC, NICNT, PNTC, TNTC]. They believed that the human race was one, proceeding from a single point of origin, that there was a divine being, and that it was man's duty to live in accordance with this indwelling god [Bar, PNTC].

QUESTION—What does the word 'babbler' mean?

The word referred to a bird picking up scraps in the gutter and came to be used of worthless loafers and also of person who had acquired mere scraps of learning [TNTC]. It means 'one who picks up and retails scraps of knowledge' [Bar]. This word literally refers to birds that pick up seeds and so it often means 'scavenger' or 'scrapmonger'. The word has the connotation of a person who picks up bits of information and then passes them off as if he knows what he is talking about [BECNT, CBC, EBC, NAC, PNTC].

QUESTION—How is the phrase 'Jesus and the resurrection' to be understood?

This phrase is understood in one of two ways:
1. Paul was preaching about Jesus and the resurrection (probably not only about the resurrection of Jesus, but the doctrine of the resurrection in general) [TH].
2. Paul's hearers thought he was speaking about two deities, Jesus (the male deity) and Resurrection (the female deity). In light of the fact that there were a number of religions in which the male deity was brought back to life by the female deity [TH], it is possible that Paul's hearers understood him to be speaking of two gods, Jesus and Resurrection [AB, Bar, PNTC, TH, TNTC, TRT].

**17:19** And they took[a] him and brought-(him) to the Areopagus, saying, "Can-we[b] know what this- new teaching -(is) that you are-presenting[c]?

LEXICON—a. aorist mid. (deponent = act.) participle of ἐπιλαμβάνομαι (LN 18.2) (BDAG 1. p. 374): 'to take' [CBC; ESV, KJV, NASB, NET, NIV, NLT, NRSV, TEV], 'to take hold of' [AB, BDAG, BECNT, LN], 'to get hold of' [Bar], 'to grasp' [BDAG, LN], 'to get' [NCV], not explicit [CEV, GW, REB]. This verb means to take hold of or grasp, with focus upon the goal of the motion [LN]. It means to make the motion of grasping or taking hold of something [BDAG].

b. pres. mid./pass. (deponent = act.) indic. of δύναμαι (LN 74.5): 'can' [LN], 'to be able to' [BECNT, LN], 'may' [AB, Bar, CBC; ESV, KJV, NASB, NET, NIV, NRSV, REB]. The phrase 'Can we know what this new teaching is' is also translated 'Tell us what your new teaching is' [CEV], 'Could you tell us these new ideas' [GW], 'Please explain to us this new idea' [NCV], 'Come and tell us about this new teaching' [NLT], 'We would like to know what this new teaching is' [TEV]. This verb means to be able to do or to experience something [LN].

c. pres. pass. participle of λαλέω (LN 33.70) (BDAG 2.b. p. 582): 'to present' [BECNT; ESV, NIV, NRSV], 'to proclaim' [NASB, NET], 'to teach' [GW, NCV], 'to speak' [Bar, BDAG, LN; KJV], 'to talk' [BDAG, LN; TEV], 'to say, to tell' [LN], 'to commend' [AB], 'to propound' [CBC; REB], not explicit [CEV, NLT]. This verb means to speak or talk, with the possible implication of more informal usage [LN]. It means to utter words [BDAG].

QUESTION—What is the function of the particle τέ 'and'?

The transitional particle τέ is important, since it marks the beginning of the next episode, resulting from what Paul had been saying to various persons [TH].

QUESTION—What does the word ἐπιλαμβάνομαι 'took' imply here?

In this context 'took' does not imply the use of force. It implies that they invited Paul to come with them. The council of Athens wanted information from Paul. They were not putting him on trial [TH, TRT]. The word may imply an arrest, with or without violence, or a friendly approach. The intention was probably to bring Paul to the Areios Pagos court (not necessarily for a formal trial) [Bar]. Paul was brought before the Court more for an inquiry than to answer for some offence [CBC]. Paul was brought before the Areopagus simply to have an opportunity of expounding his teaching before experts [NICNT].

QUESTION—To what does the Areopagus refer?

It refers to Ares/Mars Hill and to the main council/court of the city of Athens that met on that hill. There were twelve judges on this council. However, many other people would come to listen to their discussions with people like Paul [TH, TNTC, TRT]. The Areopagus was both a court and a hill, due to the fact that the court traditionally met on that hill. The term 'Areopagus' means 'hill of Ares' [NAC, NICNT].

**17:20** For you-bring<sup>a</sup> some strange-(things)<sup>b</sup> to our ears. Therefore, we-wish<sup>c</sup> to-know what these-things mean." **17:21** Now all the Athenians and the foreigners who lived there would spend their time in nothing except telling or hearing something new.

LEXICON—a. pres. act. indic. of εἰσφέρω (LN 33.92) (BDAG 2. p. 295): 'to bring' [Bar, BECNT; ESV, KJV, NASB, NET, NIV], 'to bring to the attention of, to speak about to' [LN], 'to bring in' [BDAG], 'to introduce' [CBC; REB], not explicit [NRSV]. The clause 'you bring some strange things to our ears' is also translated 'We have heard you say some strange things' [CEV], 'Some of the things you say sound strange to us' [GW], 'Some of the things we hear you say sound strange to us' [TEV], 'what we have heard from you seems strange to us' [AB], 'You are saying some rather strange things' [NLT], 'The things you are saying are new to us' [NCV]. The idiom 'to bring into the ears' means to bring something to the attention of people by means of speech, but probably not in a formal or open manner [LN]. It means to cause someone to enter into a certain event or condition [BDAG].
  b. pres. act. participle of ξενίζω (LN 25.206) (BDAG 2. p. 684): 'to astonish, to surprise' [BDAG], 'to be surprised' [LN]. This verb is also translated as an adjective: 'strange' [all translations except NCV, NET], 'surprising' [NET], 'new' [NCV]. This verb means to experience a sudden feeling of unexpected wonder [LN]. It means to cause a strong psychological reaction through introduction of something new or strange [BDAG].
  c. pres. mid./pass. (deponent = act.) indic. of βούλομαι (LN 25.3) (BDAG 2.a.β. p. 182): 'to wish' [AB, BECNT; ESV], 'to want' [LN; CEV, NASB, NCV, NET, NIV, NLT], 'to desire' [LN], 'to will' [BDAG, LN], 'to intend, to plan' [BDAG]. The phrase 'we wish to know' is also translated 'we would/should like to know' [Bar, CBC; GW, NRSV, REB, TEV], 'we would know' [KJV]. This verb means to desire to have or experience something, with the implication of some reasoned planning or will to accomplish the goal [LN]. It means to plan on a course of action [BDAG].

**DISCOURSE UNIT—17:22–34** [AB; ESV, NASB]. The topic is Paul addresses the Areopagus [ESV], Paul's speech in Athens [AB], sermon on Mars hill [NASB].

**DISCOURSE UNIT—17:22–31** [EBC, NAC, NICNT, PNTC]. The topic is Paul's testimony before the Areopagus [NAC], Paul's address before the council of Ares [EBC], Paul's areopagitica [NICNT], establishing God's claim on all people [PNTC].

**17:22** So Paul, standing in (the)-midst[a] of-the Areopagus, said: "Men of Athens, I-perceive[b] that in every-way you-(are) very-religious.[c]

LEXICON—a. μέσος (LN 83.10) (BDAG 1.b. p. 635): 'the midst' [Bar; ESV, KJV, NASB], 'the middle' [AB, BECNT; GW], 'in the midst' [LN], 'in the middle' [BDAG, LN], 'middle' [BDAG], 'in front' [CEV, NRSV, TEV], 'before' [CBC; NCV, NET, NLT, REB], not explicit [NIV]. This adjective pertains to a position in the middle of an area, either an object in the midst of other objects or an area in the middle of a larger area [LN]. It pertains to a middle position spatially or temporally [BDAG].

b. pres. act. indic. of θεωρέω (LN 32.11) (BDAG 2.a. p. 454): 'to perceive' [BDAG, BECNT, LN; ESV, KJV], 'to observe' [BDAG; NASB], 'to see' [Bar, CBC, LN; CEV, GW, NCV, NET, NIV, NRSV, REB, TEV], 'to notice' [BDAG; NLT], 'to find' [AB, BDAG], 'to understand, to recognize' [LN]. This verb means to come to understand as the result of perception [LN]. It means to come to the understanding of something especially on the basis of what one has seen and heard [BDAG].

c. δεισιδαίμων (LN 53.3) (BDAG p. 216): 'religious' [BDAG, BECNT, LN; all versions except KJV, REB], 'devout' [BDAG], 'superstitious' [KJV]. The clause 'I perceive that in every way you are very religious' is also translated 'I find that you are rather given to religious observances' [AB], 'I see that you make a great display of piety' [Bar], 'I see that in everything that concerns religion you are uncommonly scrupulous' [CBC; REB]. This adjective pertains to being religious [LN].

QUESTION—What did Paul mean by the clause 'I perceive that in every way you are very religious'?

Paul was complimenting the people of Athens for being very religious, probably as a way of getting their attention [TNTC, TRT].

**17:23** For as I was passing-through[a] and observed[b] the objects-of- your -worship,[c] I-found[d] also an-altar with this inscription, 'To-(the)-unknown god.' Therefore what you-worship[e] as unknown, this I proclaim[f] to-you.

LEXICON—a. pres. mid./pass. (deponent = act.) participle of διέρχομαι (LN 15.21) (BDAG 1.a. p. 244): 'to pass through' [NASB], 'to go through' [CEV, GW, NCV, NRSV], 'to walk through' [TEV], 'to go around' [CBC; NET, REB], 'to walk around' [AB; NIV], 'to walk along' [NLT], 'to pass along' [BECNT; ESV], 'to pass by' [Bar; KJV], 'to travel around through, to journey all through' [LN], 'to move within or through an area' [BDAG]. This verb means to travel around through an area, with the implication of both extensive and thorough movement throughout an area [LN]. It means to travel or move about from place to place through an area [BDAG].

b. pres. act. participle of ἀναθεωρέω (LN 24.47) (BDAG 1. p. 63): 'to observe' [BECNT, LN; ESV], 'to observe closely' [NET], 'to examine' [NASB], 'to notice' [LN], 'to look at' [AB, Bar, CBC; CEV, REB, TEV], 'to look carefully at' [BDAG; NIV, NRSV], 'to look closely at' [GW], 'to

behold' [KJV], 'to see' [NCV, NLT]. This verb means to observe closely and give serious consideration to, suggesting the possibility of something unusual [LN]. It means to examine something carefully [BDAG].
c. σέβασμα (LN 53.54, 53.55) (BDAG p. 917): 'object of worship' [BECNT, CBC, LN (53.55); ESV, NASB, NET, NIV, NRSV, REB], 'object and instrument of worship' [Bar], 'devotional object' [BDAG], 'sanctuary' [LN (53.54)]. The phrase 'the objects of your worship' is also translated 'the things/objects you worship' [CEV, GW, NCV], 'the places where you worship' [TEV], 'your devotions' [KJV], 'your many shrines' [NLT], 'your shrines' [AB]. This noun denotes an object which is worshiped [LN]. It denotes something that relates to devotional activity [BDAG]. It denotes a place of worship [LN (53.54)].
d. aorist act. indic. of εὑρίσκω (LN 27.27) (BDAG 1.b. p. 411): 'to find' [BDAG, BECNT, LN; all versions except GW, NLT, REB], 'to learn the whereabouts of something, to discover, to happen to find' [LN], 'to come upon' [AB, LN], 'to notice' [CBC; GW, REB], 'to see' [Bar], not explicit [NLT]. This verb means to learn the location of something, either by intentional searching or by unexpected discovery [LN]. It means to come upon something accidentally without seeking [BDAG].
e. pres. act. indic. of εὐσεβέω (LN 53.53) (BDAG a. p. 413): 'to worship' [BDAG, LN; all translations except AB], 'to venerate' [LN], 'to honor' [AB], 'to show exceptional devotion to' [BDAG]. This verb means to express in attitude and ritual one's allegiance to and regard for deity [LN]. It means to show uncommon reverence or respect for divine beings [BDAG].
f. pres. act. indic. of καταγγέλλω (LN 33.204) (BDAG a. p. 515): 'to proclaim' [Bar, BDAG, BECNT, CBC; ESV, NASB, NET, NIV, NRSV, REB, TEV], 'to preach' [AB], 'to announce' [BDAG, LN], 'to declare' [KJV], 'to proclaim throughout, to speak out about' [LN], 'to tell' [CEV, GW, NCV, NLT]. This verb means to announce, with focus upon the extent to which the announcement or proclamation extends [LN]. It means to make known in public with the implication of broad dissemination [BDAG].

**17:24** The God who made[a] the world[b] and everything in it, being Lord[c] of-heaven[d] and earth, does not live in temples made by-man,
LEXICON—a. aorist act. participle of ποιέω (LN 42.29) (BDAG 1.b. p. 839): 'to make' [BDAG LN; all translations except CBC; REB], 'to fashion' [LN], 'to create' [BDAG, CBC; REB]. This verb means to produce something new, with the implication of using materials already in existence [LN]. It means to produce something material and refers to divine activity, specifically of God's creative activity [BDAG].
b. κόσμος (LN 1.1) (BDAG 3. p. 561): 'world' [BDAG; all translations except GW], 'universe' [LN; GW], 'cosmos' [LN], 'the (orderly)

universe' [BDAG]. This noun denotes the universe as an ordered structure [LN]. It denotes the sum total of everything here and now [BDAG].
   c. κύριος (LN 12.9) (BDAG 2.b.α. p. 578): 'Lord' [BDAG, LN; all translations], 'Ruler, One who commands' [LN], 'master' [BDAG]. This noun denotes one who exercises supernatural authority over mankind, a title for God and for Christ [LN]. It denotes one who is in a position of authority, and is used as a designation for God [BDAG].
   d. οὐρανός (LN 1.5) (BDAG 1.a.α. p. 737): 'heaven' [BDAG; all translations except NCV], 'sky' [LN; NCV]. This noun denotes space above the earth, including the vault arching high over the earth from one horizon to another, as well as the sun, moon, and stars [LN]. It denotes the portion or portions of the universe generally distinguished from planet earth [BDAG].

**17:25** nor is- he -served- by human hands, -(as though)[a] he needed anything, since he himself gives[b] to-all (people) life and breath and all things.

LEXICON—a. pres. pass. indic. of θεραπεύω (LN 35.19) (BDAG 1. p. 453): 'to be served' [AB, Bar, BDAG, BECNT, LN; ESV, GW, NASB, NET, NIV, NRSV], 'to be worshipped' [KJV], 'to help' [LN]. This verb is also translated as a noun: 'he accepts service' [CBC; REB]. The phrase 'nor is he served by human hands as though he needed anything' is also translated 'Nor does he need anything that we can supply by working for him' [TEV], 'He doesn't need help from anyone' [CEV], 'He does not need any help from them; he has everything he needs' [NCV], 'human hands can't serve his needs–for he has no needs' [NLT]. This verb means to render assistance or help by performing certain duties, often of a humble or menial nature [LN]. It means to render service or homage [BDAG].
   b. pres. act. participle of δίδωμι (LN 57.71): 'to give' [AB, Bar, BECNT, LN; all translations except CBC; REB], 'giving' [LN]. This verb is also translated as a noun: 'giver' [CBC; REB]. This verb means to give an object, usually implying value [LN].

**17:26** And he-made[a] from one (man) every nation[b] of-mankind[c] to-live on all (the)-face[d] of-the earth,[e] having-determined[f] allotted[g] periods and the boundaries of their dwelling-place.

TEXT—Manuscripts reading ἐξ ἑνὸς 'from one' are given a B rating by GNT to indicate it was regarded to be almost certain. A variant reading is ἐξ ἑνὸς αἵματος 'of one blood' and it is followed by KJV.

LEXICON—a. aorist act. indic. of ποιέω (LN 13.9) (BDAG 2.h.α. p. 840): 'to make' [AB, Bar, BECNT, LN; all versions except NLT, REB, TEV], 'to create' [CBC; NLT, REB, TEV], 'to cause to be, to make to be, to result in, to bring upon' [LN], 'to bring about' [BDAG, LN], 'to do, to cause, to accomplish, to prepare' [BDAG]. This verb means to cause a state to be

[LN]. It means to undertake or do something that brings about an event, state, or condition [BDAG].
b. ἔθνος (LN 11.55) (BDAG 1. p. 276): 'nation' [AB, BDAG, BECNT, LN; all versions except NCV, TEV], 'people' [BDAG, LN], 'race' [Bar, CBC; TEV], not explicit [NCV]. This noun denotes the largest unit into which the people of the world are divided on the basis of their constituting a socio-political community [LN]. It denotes a body of persons united by kinship, culture, and common traditions [BDAG].
c. ἄνθρωπος (LN 9.1): 'mankind' [LN; ESV, NASB], 'humanity' [GW], 'men' [Bar, BECNT, CBC; KJV, NIV, REB], 'people' [LN; TEV], 'person, human being, individual' [LN], 'persons' [LN], not explicit [AB; CEV, NLT, NRSV]. This noun is also translated 'all the different people' [NCV], 'the human race' [NET]. This noun denotes a human being [LN].
d. πρόσωπον (LN 79.93) (BDAG 3. p. 888): 'face' [Bar, BDAG, BECNT, LN; ESV, KJV, NASB], 'surface' [AB, BDAG, CBC, LN; REB], not explicit [CEV]. The phrase 'on all the face of the earth' is also translated 'all over the earth' [GW], 'everywhere in the world' [NCV], 'the entire/whole earth' [NET, NIV, NRSV, TEV], not explicit [NLT]. This noun denotes the two-dimensional surface of an object [LN]. It denotes the outer surface of something [BDAG].
e. γῆ (LN 1.39) (BDAG 1.b. p. 196): 'earth' [BDAG, LN; all translations except NCV], 'world' [LN; NCV]. This noun denotes the surface of the earth as the dwelling place of mankind, in contrast with the heavens above and the world below [LN]. It denotes the surface of the earth as the habitation of humanity [BDAG].
f. aorist act. participle of ὁρίζω (LN 30.83) (BDAG 2.a.α. p. 723): 'to determine' [BDAG, BECNT, LN; ESV, KJV, NASB, NET, NIV, REB], 'to decide' [LN; CEV, NCV, NLT], 'to fix' [AB, BDAG, CBC; TEV], 'to appoint' [Bar, BDAG], 'to resolve' [LN], 'to set' [BDAG], not explicit [GW, NRSV]. This is a figurative extension of meaning of ὁρίζω 'to set limits on' and it means to come to a definite decision or firm resolve [LN]. It means to make a determination about an entity [BDAG].
g. perf. pass. participle of προστάσσω (LN 62.9) (BDAG p. 885): 'to be allotted' [BECNT; ESV], 'to be appointed' [KJV, NASB], 'to be set' [NET, NIV], 'to be foreordained' [Bar], 'to be prescribed, to be arranged for' [LN], 'to be determined' [BDAG], not explicit [AB, CBC; CEV, GW, NCV, NLT, REB, TEV]. This verb is also translated as an active verb: 'he allotted the times' [NRSV]. This verb means to arrange in a prescribed manner [LN]. It means to issue an official directive or make a determination [BDAG].

QUESTION—What is meant by the phrase 'having determined allotted periods'?

There are two possibilities.

1. It refers to the periods of time that people would live and die [TRT]. It possibly refers to divinely appointed periods for nations to flourish

[NICNT, TNTC]. It refers to historical epochs [NAC]. It refers to their appointed times in history [PNTC].
2. It refers to the seasons of the year [Bar, NAC, NICNT, PNTC, TNTC; GW].

QUESTION—What is meant by the phrase 'the boundaries of their dwelling place'?
There are two possibilities.
1. It refers to the national boundaries [NAC, TNTC].
2. It refers to the natural boundaries between the land and the sea [NAC, NICNT, TNTC]. It refers to the different zones of the earth [Bar].

**17:27** **that they should seek[a] God, if perhaps they-might-grope[b] for-him and find-(him),[c] though he is not far from each one of-us,**

TEXT—Manuscripts reading ζητεῖν τὸν θεόν 'to seek God' are given an A rating by GNT to indicate it was regarded to be certain. A variant reading is ζητεῖν τὸν κύριον 'to seek the Lord' and it is followed by KJV.

LEXICON—a. pres. act. infin. of ζητέω (LN 27.41) (BDAG 1.b. p. 428): 'to seek' [AB, Bar, BDAG, BECNT, CBC; ESV, KJV, NASB, NIV, NLT, REB], 'to look for' [BDAG, LN; CEV, GW, NCV, TEV], 'to search for' [NET, NRSV], 'to try to learn where something is, to try to find' [LN]. This verb means to try to learn the location of something, often by movement from place to place in the process of searching [LN]. It means to try to find what one desires somehow to bring into relation with oneself or to obtain without knowing where it is to be found [BDAG].
b. aorist act. opt. of ψηλαφάω (LN 27.40) (BDAG 2. p. 1098): 'to grope for' [BDAG, LN; NASB, NET, NRSV], 'to grope after' [Bar; REB], 'to feel around for' [BDAG, LN; TEV], 'to search for' [NCV], 'to try to find' [LN], 'to reach out' [CEV], 'to reach for' [GW], 'to reach out for' [NIV], 'to touch' [CBC]. The phrase 'they might grope for him' is also translated 'they might feel their way toward him' [AB; ESV], 'the nations…to feel their way toward him' [NLT], 'they might feel after him' [BECNT; KJV]. This is a figurative extension of meaning of ψηλαφάω 'to touch, to feel' and means to make an effort, despite difficulties, to come to know something, when the chances of success in such an enterprise are not particularly great [LN]. It means to look for something in uncertain fashion [BDAG].
c. aorist act. opt. of εὑρίσκω (LN 27.1) (BDAG 2. p. 412): 'to find' [BDAG, all translations], 'to discover' [BDAG, LN], 'to learn, to find out' [LN]. This verb means to learn something previously not known, frequently involving an element of surprise [LN]. It means to discover intellectually through reflection, observation, examination, or investigation [BDAG].

**17:28** **for[a] "'In him we-live[b] and move[c] and exist;[d]' as even some of your own poets have-said, 'For we- also -are his offspring.[e]'**

LEXICON—a. γάρ (LN 89.23): 'for' [AB, Bar, BECNT, CBC, LN; ESV, KJV, NASB, NET, NIV, NLT, NRSV, REB], 'because' [LN], 'and' [CEV], not

explicit [GW, NCV, TEV]. This conjunction is a marker of cause or reason between events, though in some contexts the relation is often remote or tenuous [LN].
   b. pres. act. indic. of ζάω (LN 23.88) (BDAG 1.c. p. 425): 'to live' [BDAG, LN; all translations], 'to be alive' [LN]. This verb means to be alive physically and refers to living in God [BDAG].
   c. pres. pass. indic. of κινέω (LN 15.1) (BDAG 3. p. 545): 'to move' [BDAG, LN; all translations except NCV, NET], 'to move around' [BDAG], 'to move about' [NET], 'to come, to go' [LN], 'to walk' [NCV]. This verb means to make a change of location in space [LN]. It means to be in motion [BDAG].
   d. pres. act. indic. of εἰμί (LN 13.69) (BDAG 3.c. p. 284): 'to exist' [AB, CBC, LN; GW, NASB, NET, NLT, REB, TEV], 'to be' [Bar, BDAG, LN; CEV, NCV]. This verb is also translated as a noun: 'have our being' [BECNT; ESV, KJV, NIV, NRSV]. This verb means to exist, in an absolute sense [LN]. It means to be in reference to location, persons, condition, or time and refers to humankind having its basis of existence in God [BDAG].
   e. γένος (LN 10.32) (BDAG 1. p. 194): 'offspring' [AB, BECNT, CBC, LN; ESV, KJV, NET, NIV, NLT, NRSV, REB], 'descendant' [BDAG, LN], 'children' [CEV, GW, NASB, NCV, TEV], 'family' [Bar]. This noun denotes a non-immediate descendant (possibly involving a gap of several generations), either male or female [LN]. It denotes ancestral stock [BDAG].
QUESTION—What is the function of the conjunction 'for'?
   It shows that this verse is intended to supply the basis for the statement in v. 27 that God is not far from each one of us [Bar].
QUESTION—What is meant by the phrase 'we also are his offspring'?
   It means that everyone was created/made by God [NAC, TH, TRT]. It does not mean that everyone is part God or that everyone is saved from eternal punishment [TRT].

**17:29** Being then God's offspring, we-ought not to-think[a] that the divine (being) is like gold or silver or stone, an-image-formed[b] by-(the)-skill and thought of-man.
LEXICON—a. pres. act. infin. of νομίζω (LN 31.29) (BDAG 2. p. 675): 'to think' [BDAG, BECNT, LN; all versions except REB, TEV], 'to believe' [AB, BDAG, LN], 'to suppose' [Bar, CBC, LN; REB, TEV], 'to presume, to assume, to imagine' [LN], 'to hold, to consider' [BDAG]. This verb means to regard something as presumably true, but without particular certainty [LN]. It means to form an idea about something but with some suggestion of tentativeness or refraining from a definitive statement [BDAG].
   b. χάραγμα (LN 6.96) (BDAG 2. p. 1077): 'image' [BDAG, CBC, LN; ESV, GW, NASB, NET, NIV, NRSV, REB, TEV], 'likeness' [LN], 'idol'

[CEV, NLT], 'object' [Bar], 'thing formed' [BDAG], 'representation' [BECNT], not explicit [AB; KJV, NCV]. This noun denotes an object (not necessarily three-dimensional) which has been formed to resemble a person, god, animal, etc. [LN]. It denotes an object fashioned by artistic skill involving alteration of a medium [BDAG].

**17:30** Therefore God having-overlooked[a] the times[b] of-ignorance,[c] he- now -commands[d] all people everywhere to-repent,[e]

LEXICON—a. aorist act. participle of ὑπεροράω (LN 30.49) (BDAG 2. p. 1034): 'to overlook' [Bar, BDAG, BECNT, CBC, LN; all versions except CEV, KJV, NCV], 'to forgive' [CEV], 'to purposely pay no attention to, to disregard' [LN], 'to ignore' [NCV], 'to wink at' [KJV]. The phrase 'God having overlooked the times of ignorance' is also translated 'After having borne with these ignorant past ages' [AB]. This verb means to intentionally not regard or be concerned about certain objects or events [LN]. It means to indulgently take no notice of [BDAG].

b. χρόνος (LN 67.78) (BDAG 1. p. 1092): 'time' [Bar, BDAG, BECNT, CBC, LN; ESV, GW, KJV, NASB, NET, NRSV, TEV], 'period of time' [BDAG, LN], 'earlier time' [NLT], 'age' [REB], 'past age' [AB]. The phrase 'the times of ignorance' is also translated 'In the past, people did not understand' [NCV]. The phrase 'God having overlooked the times of ignorance' is also translated 'In the past, God forgave all this' [CEV], 'In the past God overlooked such ignorance' [NIV]. This noun denotes an indefinite unit of time (the actual extent of time being determined by the context) [LN]. It denotes an indefinite period of time during which some activity or event takes place [BDAG].

c. ἄγνοια (LN 28.13) (BDAG 2.b. p. 13): 'ignorance' [Bar, BDAG, BECNT, CBC, LN; ESV, KJV, NASB, NET, NIV, NLT, REB], 'human ignorance' [NRSV], 'unawareness, lack of discernment' [BDAG]. This noun is also translated as a verb: 'to not understand' [NCV], 'to not know' [CEV, GW, TEV]. This noun is also translated as an adjective: 'ignorant past ages' [AB]. This noun denotes not having information about [LN]. It denotes the lack of information that may result in reprehensible conduct [BDAG].

d. pres. act. indic. of παραγγέλλω (LN 33.327) (BDAG p. 760): 'to command' [Bar, BDAG, BECNT, CBC, LN; all versions except CEV, NASB, NCV], 'to order' [LN], 'to give orders, to instruct, to direct' [BDAG], 'to declare' [NASB], 'to proclaim' [AB], 'to say' [CEV], 'to tell' [NCV]. This verb means to announce what must be done [LN]. It means to make an announcement about something that must be done [BDAG].

e. pres. act. infin. of μετανοέω (LN 41.52) (BDAG 2. p. 640): 'to repent' [AB, Bar, BDAG, BECNT, CBC, LN; ESV, KJV, NASB, NET, NIV, NRSV, REB], 'to change one's way' [LN], 'to be converted' [BDAG]. This verb is also translated 'turn to him' [CEV, GW], 'change their hearts and lives' [NCV], 'repent of their sins and turn to him' [NLT], 'turn away from their evil ways' [TEV]. This verb means to change one's way of life as the result of a complete change of thought and attitude with regard to sin and righteousness [LN]. It means to feel remorse [BDAG].

QUESTION—What is meant by the phrase 'God having overlooked'?
It means that God did not punish men as they deserved [TH].

QUESTION—What is meant by the phrase 'the times of ignorance'?
It refers to the time before men came to know God's will in Jesus Christ [TH], men remained ignorant of his true nature [CBC]. The Athenians did not know or worship the one true God [NAC].

**17:31** because he-has-fixed[a] (a)-day in which he will judge[b] the world in righteousness[c] by (a)-man whom he-has-appointed;[d] having-given[e] proof[f] to-all-(by) raising[g] him from (the)-dead."

TEXT—Manuscripts reading ἐν ἀνδρί 'by a man' are given an A rating by GNT to indicate it was regarded to be certain. A variant reading is ἐν ἀνδρὶ Ἰησοῦ 'by a man Jesus' and it is followed by CEV.

LEXICON—a. aorist act. indic. of ἵστημι (LN 76.21) (BDAG 6.a. p. 482): 'to fix' [BECNT, CBC; ESV, NASB, NRSV, REB, TEV], 'to set' [Bar; CEV, GW, NCV, NET, NIV, NLT], 'to appoint' [AB; KJV], 'to set/fix a time' [BDAG], 'to establish, to authorize, to put into force' [LN]. This verb means to establish as validated and in force [LN].

b. pres. act. infin. of κρίνω (LN 56.20) (BDAG 5.b.α. p. 568): 'to judge' [BDAG; all translations], 'to decide a legal question, to make a legal decision, to arrive at a verdict, to try a case' [LN], 'to decide, to hale before a court, to condemn' [BDAG]. This verb means to decide a question of legal right or wrong, and thus determine the innocence or guilt of the accused and assign appropriate punishment or retribution [LN]. It means to engage in a judicial process. Here it refers to the divine tribunal occupied by God or Christ [BDAG].

c. δικαιοσύνη (LN 88.13) (BDAG 1.a. p. 247): 'righteousness' [Bar, BECNT, LN; ESV, KJV, NASB, NET, NRSV], 'fairness' [BDAG; CEV, NCV], 'justice' [BDAG; GW, NIV, NLT, TEV], 'equitableness' [BDAG], 'doing what God requires, doing what is right' [LN]. This noun is also translated as an adverb: 'justly' [AB, CBC; REB]. This noun denotes the act of doing what God requires [LN]. It denotes the quality, state or practice of judicial responsibility with focus on fairness [BDAG].

d. aorist act. indic. of ὁρίζω (LN 37.96) (BDAG 2.b. p. 723): 'to appoint' [Bar, BDAG, BECNT, LN; ESV, GW, NASB, NIV, NLT, NRSV], 'to designate' [BDAG, LN; NET, REB], 'to choose' [CEV, NCV, TEV], 'to ordain' [AB; KJV], 'to assign, to give a task to' [LN], 'to determine, to fix, to set' [BDAG]. This verb is also translated as a noun: 'his choosing' [CBC]. This verb means to assign someone to a particular task, function, or role [LN]. It means to make a determination about a person [BDAG].

e. aorist act. participle of παρέχω (LN 90.91) (BDAG 2.a. p. 776): 'to give' [BECNT, CBC, LN; CEV, ESV, GW, KJV, NIV, NRSV, REB, TEV], 'to provide' [Bar; NET], 'to furnish' [NASB], 'to cause to, to cause to experience' [LN], 'to grant, to show' [BDAG], not explicit [AB; NCV, NLT]. This verb means to cause someone to experience something, with the possible implication of a duration [LN]. It means to cause to experience something [BDAG].

f. πίστις (LN 31.43) (BDAG 1.c. p. 818): 'proof' [Bar, BDAG, LN; CEV, GW, NASB, NET, NIV, TEV], 'assurance' [BECNT, CBC; ESV, KJV, NRSV, REB], 'pledge' [BDAG], 'what can be fully believed, that which is worthy of belief, believable evidence' [LN]. This noun is also translated as a verb: 'to prove' [NCV, NLT]. The phrase 'having given proof to all by raising him from the dead' is also translated 'whom he has accredited by raising him from the dead' [AB]. This noun denotes that which is completely believable [LN]. It denotes a token offered as a guarantee of something promised [BDAG].

g. aorist act. participle of ἀνίστημι (LN 23.94) (BDAG 2. p. 83): 'to raise' [BDAG; all translations except GW], 'to raise up' [BDAG], 'to raise to life, to make live again' [LN]. The phrase 'raising him from the dead' is also translated 'bringing that man back to life' [GW]. This verb means to cause someone to live again after having once died [LN]. It means to raise up by bringing back to life [BDAG].

**DISCOURSE UNIT—17:32–34** [EBC, NAC, NICNT, PNTC]. The topic is the mixed response [NAC], the response to Paul's address [EBC], the Athenians' reaction [NICNT], founding a church [PNTC].

**17:32** Now when they heard-(of)[a] (the)-resurrection of-(the)-dead, some mocked.[b] But others said, "We-will-hear you again about this."

LEXICON—a. aorist act. participle of ἀκούω (LN 33.212) (BDAG 1.c. p. 38): 'to hear' [BDAG, LN; all translations], 'to receive news' [LN]. This verb means to receive information about something, normally by word of mouth [LN]. It means to have or exercise the faculty of hearing [BDAG].

b. imperf. act. indic. of χλευάζω (LN 33.408) (BDAG 1. p. 1085): 'to mock' [AB, Bar, BDAG, BECNT; ESV, KJV], 'to scoff' [BDAG, CBC, LN; NET, NRSV, REB], 'to jeer, to joke at' [LN], 'to sneer' [BDAG; NASB, NIV], 'to laugh' [CEV, NCV, NLT], 'to joke' [GW], 'to make fun' [TEV]. This verb means to make fun of someone by joking or jesting [LN]. It means to engage in mockery [BDAG].

QUESTION—Why did some of them mock Paul?

The idea of a resurrection from the dead was foreign to Greek thought [AB, NAC, NICNT, TH, TNTC]. The individual soul might be immortal, but Greeks were unwilling to think of a resurrection of the body [AB, TNTC, TRT]. To the majority of Athenians the resurrection of Jesus from the dead was the height of folly [EBC].

**17:33** So Paul went-out[a] from their midst.[b]

LEXICON—a. aorist act. indic. of ἐξέρχομαι (LN 15.40): 'to go out' [Bar, BECNT; ESV, NASB], 'to go away' [NCV], 'to leave' [AB, CBC; CEV, GW, NET, NIV, NRSV, REB, TEV], 'to depart' [KJV]. 'to go out of, to depart out of, to leave from within' [LN], not explicit [NLT]. This verb means to move out of an enclosed or well defined two or three-dimensional area [LN].

b. μέσος (LN 83.10) (BDAG 2.b. p. 635): 'midst' [Bar, LN; ESV, NASB], 'middle' [LN], 'among' [BDAG, BECNT; KJV], not explicit [NLT]. The phrase 'went out from their midst' is also translated 'left the council meeting' [CEV], 'left the court' [GW], 'left the Council' [NIV], 'left the assembly' [CBC; REB], 'left the Areopagus' [NET], 'left them' [AB; NRSV], 'left the meeting' [TEV], 'went away from them' [NCV]. This adjective describes a position in the middle of an area [LN]. It pertains to a position within a group, without focus on mediate position [BDAG].

**17:34** But some men joined[a] him and believed,[b] among whom also were Dionysius the Areopagite and (a)-woman named Damaris and others with them.

LEXICON—a. aorist pass. participle of κολλάω (LN 34.22) (BDAG 2.b.α. p. 556): 'to join' [AB, BDAG, BECNT, CBC, LN; all versions except CEV], 'to join oneself to, to become a part of' [LN], 'to associate with' [BDAG], 'to cleave to' [KJV], 'to adhere to' [Bar]. The phrase 'some men joined him' is also translated 'some of the men…went with Paul' [CEV], 'A few men became followers of Paul' [NIV]. This verb means to begin an association with someone, whether temporary or permanent [LN]. It means to be closely associated with someone [BDAG].

b. aorist act. indic. of πιστεύω (LN 31.102) (BDAG 2.b. p. 817): 'to believe' [AB, Bar, BECNT; ESV, KJV, NASB, NCV, NET, NIV, TEV], 'to believe (in), to trust' [BDAG]. The phrase 'some men…believed' is also translated 'some of the men put their faith in the Lord' [CEV]. This verb is also translated as a noun: 'became believers' [CBC; GW, NLT, NRSV, REB]. This verb means to believe in the good news about Jesus Christ and to become a follower [LN]. It means to entrust oneself to an entity in complete confidence [BDAG].

QUESTION—Who was Dionysius?

He was a member of the Areopagus council [BECNT, CBC, EBC, NAC, NICNT, PNTC, TH, TNTC, TRT; CEV, GW, NCV, NET, NIV, NLT, REB, TEV].

**DISCOURSE UNIT—18:1–23** [Bar, CBC]. The topic is Paul at Corinth, with return to Palestine [Bar], Corinth and home [CBC].

**DISCOURSE UNIT—18:1–22** [NASB]. The topic is Paul at Corinth.

**DISCOURSE UNIT—18:1–17** [AB, BECNT, NAC, NICNT, PNTC, TNTC; CEV, ESV, GW, NIV, NLT, NRSV, TEV]. The topic is Paul in Corinth [AB;

CEV, ESV, GW, NRSV], in Corinth [BECNT; NIV, TEV], Corinth [NICNT, TNTC], Paul meets Priscilla and Aquila in Corinth [NLT], establishing a church in Corinth [NAC], the word in Corinth [PNTC].

**DISCOURSE UNIT—18:1–11** [NAC; NCV, NET]. The topic is Paul in Corinth [NCV], Paul at Corinth [NET], the mission to Corinth [NAC].

**DISCOURSE UNIT—18:1–4** [EBC, NICNT, PNTC]. The topic is arrival at Corinth [EBC], Paul arrives in Corinth [NICNT], Jews together in Corinth [PNTC].

**18:1** **After this he/Paul left$^a$ Athens and went$^b$ to Corinth.**

LEXICON—a. aorist pass. participle of χωρίζω (LN 15.49) (BDAG 2.b. p. 1095): 'to leave' [BDAG, LN; all translations except KJV, NET], 'to depart' [LN; KJV, NET], 'to be taken away' [BDAG]. This verb means to separate from, as the result of motion away from [LN]. It means to separate by departing from someone [BDAG].

b. aorist act. indic. of ἔρχομαι (LN 15.81): 'to go' [CBC; all versions except KJV], 'to come' [AB, Bar, BECNT, LN; KJV]. This verb means to move toward or up to the reference point of the viewpoint character or event [LN].

QUESTION—To what does the word 'this' refer?
It refers to the end of the Athenian episode [Bar].

QUESTION—Where was Corinth?
Corinth was about 50 miles (80 kilometers) to the west of the city of Athens. Both cities were located in Achaia/Greece Province [BECNT, NAC, TRT]. Corinth was the capital city of the province of Achaia [AB, NICNT, PNTC, TNTC, TRT].

**18:2** **And he found$^a$ a Jew named Aquila, a native of-Pontus, having-come recently from Italy with his wife Priscilla, because Claudius had-commanded$^b$ all the Jews to-leave$^c$ Rome. He-went-to-see$^d$ them,**

LEXICON—a. aorist act. participle of εὑρίσκω (LN 27.27) (BDAG 1.b. p. 411): 'to find' [Bar, BDAG, BECNT, LN; ESV, KJV, NASB, NET, NRSV], 'to meet' [AB; CEV, GW, NCV, NIV, REB, TEV], 'to become acquainted' [NLT], 'to come upon' [BDAG, LN], 'to learn the whereabouts of something, to discover, to happen to find' [LN], 'to fall in with' [CBC]. This verb means to learn the location of something, either by intentional searching or by unexpected discovery [LN]. It means to come upon something accidentally without seeking [BDAG].

b. perf. act. infin. of διατάσσω (LN 33.325) (BDAG 2. p. 238): 'to command' [BECNT, LN; ESV, KJV, NASB, NCV], 'to order' [BDAG, LN; CEV, GW, NET, NIV, NRSV, TEV], 'to instruct, to tell' [LN]. The phrase 'Claudius had commanded all the Jews to leave' is also translated 'Claudius...deported all Jews' [NLT], 'Claudius had issued an edict that all Jews should leave' [CBC; REB], 'Claudius had issued an edict that all the Jews should leave' [Bar], 'Claudius had issued a decree that all Jews

were to leave' [AB]. This verb means to give detailed instructions as to what must be done [BDAG, LN].
c. pres. pass. infin. of χωρίζω (LN 15.49) (BDAG 2.b. p. 1095): 'to leave' [BDAG, LN; all translations except KJV, NET, NLT], 'to depart' [LN; KJV, NET], 'to be taken away' [BDAG]. This infinitive is also translated as an active finite verb: 'They had left Italy' [NLT]. This verb means to separate from, as the result of motion away from [LN]. It means to separate by departing from someone [BDAG].
d. aorist act. indic. of προσέρχομαι (LN 15.77) (BDAG 1.a p. 878): 'to go to see' [BECNT; CEV, ESV, NIV, NRSV, TEV], 'to go to visit' [GW, NCV], 'to come to' [BDAG; KJV, NASB], 'to go to' [AB, BDAG], 'to approach' [Bar, BDAG, CBC, LN; NET, REB], 'to move toward, to come near to' [LN], not explicit [NLT]. This verb means to move toward a reference point, with a possible implication in certain contexts of a reciprocal relationship between the person approaching and the one who is approached [LN]. It means to move towards [BDAG].

QUESTION—What was Pontus?

Pontus was a Roman province [NAC, TH]. It was a region in northern Asia Minor on the south shore of the Black Sea [EBC]. It was a region in Asia Minor that had been united with Bithynia to form a Roman province [PNTC].

QUESTION—Why had Claudius commanded all the Jews to leave Rome?

He expelled all the Jews from Rome because they were constantly rioting at the instigation of Chrestus [Bar, BECNT, CBC, EBC, NAC, NICNT, PNTC, TNTC].

QUESTION—Why did Paul approach Aquila and Priscilla?

It is not known for sure, possibly because they were Jews or because they were Christians or because he had the hope of earning a living at his trade [Bar]. Paul and these two make an immediate connection because they share the same trade [BECNT, NICNT] and because they are fellow Jews and fellow Christians [NAC].

**18:3** **and because he-was (of-the)-same-trade[a] he-stayed[b] with them and worked, for they-were tentmakers by-trade.**

TEXT—Manuscripts reading ἠργάζετο 'worked' are given a B rating by GNT to indicate it was regarded to be certain. A variant reading is ἠργάζοντο 'they were working' and it is followed by CEV, GW, NASB, NRSV.

LEXICON—a. ὁμότεχνος (LN 42.52) (BDAG p. 709): 'of the same trade' [Bar, BECNT, CBC, LN; ESV, NASB, NRSV, REB], 'of the same craft' [AB, LN; KJV], 'involved in the same occupation, having the same kind of work' [LN], 'practicing the same trade' [BDAG], not explicit [CEV, GW, NCV, NIV, NLT, TEV]. The phrase 'he was of the same trade' is also translated 'he worked at the same trade' [NET]. This adjective pertains to joint activity in some occupation or craft [LN].

b. imperf. act. indic. of μένω (LN 85.55) (BDAG 1.a.α. p. 631): 'to stay' [AB, Bar, BDAG, BECNT, LN; all versions except KJV, NLT, REB], 'to remain' [BDAG, LN], 'to abide' [KJV], 'to live with' [NLT]. The phrase 'he stayed with them' is also translated 'he made his home with them' [CBC; REB]. This verb means to remain in the same place over a period of time [LN].

**18:4** And he-reasoned[a] in the synagogue[b] every Sabbath, and (tried) to-persuade[c] Jews and Greeks.

LEXICON—a. imperf. mid./pass. (deponent = act.) indic. of διαλέγομαι (LN 33.446) (BDAG 1. p. 232): 'to reason' [ESV, KJV, NASB, NIV], 'to discuss' [BDAG; GW], 'to argue' [Bar, BDAG, BECNT, LN; NRSV], 'to dispute' [LN], 'to converse' [BDAG], 'to speak to' [CEV], 'to talk with' [NCV], 'to address' [NET], not explicit [NLT]. This verb is also translated as a noun: 'held discussions' [AB, CBC; REB, TEV]. This verb means to argue about differences of opinion [LN]. It means to engage in speech interchange [BDAG].
b. συναγωγή (LN 7.20) (BDAG 2.a. p. 963): 'synagogue' [BDAG, LN; all translations except CEV], 'Christian assembly place' [LN], 'Jewish meeting place' [CEV]. This noun denotes a building of assembly, associated with religious activity. Normally it was a building in which Jewish worship took place and in which the Law was taught [LN]. It denotes a place of assembly for the Jews [BDAG].
c. imperf. act. indic. of πείθω (LN 33.301) (BDAG 1.a. p. 791): 'to persuade' [Bar, BECNT, LN; ESV, KJV, NASB, NCV, NET, NIV], 'to convince' [AB, BDAG, CBC, LN; NLT, NRSV, REB, TEV], 'to win over' [CEV, GW]. This verb means to convince someone to believe something and to act on the basis of what is recommended [LN]. It means to cause to come to a particular point of view or course of action [BDAG].

QUESTION—What was Paul trying to persuade the Jews and Greeks to do?
He was trying to persuade them to believe in Jesus [BECNT, NAC, TRT].

**DISCOURSE UNIT—18:5–11** [EBC, NICNT]. The topic is an eighteen-month ministry [EBC], Paul spends eighteen months in Corinth [NICNT].

**DISCOURSE UNIT—18:5–8** [PNTC]. The topic is a new centre for ministry.

**18:5** When Silas and Timothy came-down[a] from Macedonia, Paul was-occupied-with[b] the word,[c] testifying[d] to-the Jews that the Christ[e] was Jesus.

TEXT—Manuscripts reading τῷ λόγῳ 'the word' are given a B rating by GNT to indicate it was regarded to be certain. A variant reading is πνεύματι 'spirit' and it is followed by the KJV.

LEXICON—a. aorist act. indic. of κατέρχομαι (LN 15.107) (BDAG 1. p. 531): 'to come down' [AB, Bar, BDAG, CBC, LN; NASB, NLT, REB], 'to move down, to go down, to descend' [LN], 'to arrive' [BECNT; ESV, GW, NET, NRSV, TEV], 'to come' [CEV, KJV, NCV, NIV]. This verb means to move down, irrespective of the gradient [LN]. It means to move

in a direction considered the opposite of up but not necessarily with suggestion of a gradient [BDAG].
  b. imperf. pass. indic. of συνέχω (LN 68.19) (BDAG 6. p. 971): 'to be occupied with' [BDAG; ESV, NRSV], 'to be absorbed in' [AB, BDAG], 'to be wholly absorbed with' [NET], 'to continue to give oneself to, to continue to apply oneself to' [LN], 'to devote oneself completely to' [NASB], 'to devote oneself exclusively to' [NIV], 'to devote oneself entirely to' [CBC; REB], 'to be devoted to' [BECNT], 'to be constrained' [Bar]. The phrase 'Paul was occupied with the word' is also translated 'he spent all his time preaching' [CEV], 'Paul spent all his time preaching the word' [NLT], 'Paul gave his whole time to preaching the message' [TEV], 'Paul spent all his time telling people the Good News' [NCV], 'Paul devoted all his time to teaching' [GW], 'Paul was pressed in the spirit' [KJV]. This verb means to continue with close attention and devotion [LN]. It means to occupy someone's attention intensely [BDAG].
  c. λόγος (LN 33.260) (BDAG 1.a.β. p. 600): 'word' [AB, Bar, BDAG; ESV, NASB, NET, NLT, NRSV], 'what is preached, gospel' [LN], 'word of God' [GW], 'Good News' [NCV], 'message' [TEV], not explicit [BECNT, CBC; CEV, KJV, NIV, REB]. This noun denotes the content of what is preached about Christ or about the good news [LN]. It denotes a communication whereby the mind finds expression [BDAG].
  d. pres. mid./pass. (deponent = act.) participle of διαμαρτύρομαι (LN 33.223) (BDAG 1. p. 233): 'to testify' [AB, Bar, BECNT, LN; ESV, KJV, NASB, NET, NIV, NLT, NRSV, TEV], 'to declare, to assert' [LN], 'to testify of, to bear witness to' [BDAG], 'to assure' [GW], 'to affirm' [CBC], 'to show' [NCV], 'to maintain' [REB], 'to preach' [CEV]. This verb means to make a serious declaration on the basis of presumed personal knowledge [LN]. It means to make a solemn declaration about the truth of something [BDAG].
  e. Χριστός (LN 53.82) (BDAG 1. p. 1091): 'Christ' [Bar, BDAG, BECNT, LN; ESV, KJV, NASB, NCV, NET, NIV], 'Messiah' [AB, BDAG, CBC, LN; CEV, GW, NLT, NRSV, REB, TEV], 'Anointed One' [BDAG]. Literally 'one who has been anointed' this is a title for Jesus as the Messiah [LN]. It denotes the fulfiller of Israelite expectation of a deliverer [BDAG]. This title occurs in verses 3:31, 36; 9:22; 17:3; 18:5, 28; 26:23.

QUESTION—When did Paul begin to be occupied with the word?

Paul stopped making tents and devoted himself to the word after Silas and Timothy arrived from Macedonia [AB, BECNT, EBC, NAC, NICNT, PNTC, TH, TRT]. It is possible that Silas and Timothy brought gifts of money which freed Paul from the need to work to support himself in Corinth. Then he could do missionary work throughout the week and not just on the Sabbath [AB, EBC, NAC, NICNT, PNTC, TNTC, TRT]. Silas and Timothy could earn enough for three so there was no need for Paul to spend time in tent making [Bar, PNTC].

**18:6** But (when)-they opposed[a] and reviled[b] (him), he shook-out[c] his garments and said to them, "Your- blood[d] -(be) on your own heads![e] I-(am) clean.[f] From now-(on) I-will-go to the Gentiles."

LEXICON—a. pres. mid. participle of ἀντιτάσσω (LN 39.1) (BDAG p. 90): 'to oppose' [Bar, BDAG, BECNT, CBC, LN; all versions except CEV, NASB, NCV], 'to resist' [BDAG; NASB], 'to be hostile toward, to show hostility' [LN], 'to turn against' [CEV]. The phrase 'when they opposed...him' is also translated 'they would not accept Paul's teaching' [NCV]. The phrase 'when they opposed and reviled him' is also translated 'When they blasphemously rebuffed him' [AB]. This verb means to oppose someone, involving not only a psychological attitude but also a corresponding behavior [LN].

b. pres. act. participle of βλασφημέω (LN 33.400) (BDAG a. p. 178): 'to revile' [BDAG, BECNT, LN; ESV, NET, NRSV], 'to blaspheme' [Bar, LN; KJV, NASB], 'to defame' [LN], 'to slander, to defame' [BDAG], 'to insult' [CEV, GW, NLT]. This verb is also translated as an adjective: 'became abusive' [NIV]. This verb is also translated as a noun: 'resorted to abuse' [CBC; REB]. This verb is also translated: 'said some evil things' [NCV], 'said evil things' [TEV]. The phrase 'when they opposed and reviled him' is also translated 'When they blasphemously rebuffed him' [AB]. This verb means to speak against someone in such a way as to harm or injure his or her reputation (occurring in relation to persons as well as to divine beings) [LN]. It means to speak in a disrespectful way that demeans, denigrates, maligns in relation to humans [BDAG].

c. aorist mid. participle of ἐκτινάσσω (LN 16.8) (BDAG 2. p. 310): 'to shake out' [Bar, BECNT, CBC, LN; ESV, NASB, NET, NIV, REB], 'to shake from' [LN; CEV, GW, NLT, NRSV, TEV], 'to shake off' [LN; NCV], 'to shake out clothes' [BDAG], 'to shake' [AB; KJV]. This verb means to shake something out or off, in order to get rid of an object or a substance [LN]. It means to agitate something with forceful jerky motions [BDAG].

d. αἷμα (LN 23.107) (BDAG 2.a. p. 26): 'blood' [AB, Bar, BDAG, BECNT, CBC; ESV, KJV, NASB, NET, NIV, NLT, NRSV, REB], 'death, violent death' [LN]. The phrase 'Your blood be on your own heads' is also translated 'Whatever happens to you will be your own fault' [CEV], 'You're responsible for your own death' [GW], 'If you are not saved, it will be your own fault' [NCV], 'If you are lost, you yourselves must take the blame for it' [TEV]. This noun denotes the death of a person, generally as a result of violence or execution [LN]. It is a figurative use of 'blood' as constituting the life of an individual [BDAG].

e. κεφαλή (LN 37.102) (BDAG 1.a. p. 542): 'head' [AB, Bar, BDAG, BECNT, CBC; ESV, KJV, NASB, NET, NIV, NLT, NRSV, REB], 'upon someone's head, responsibility' [LN]. The phrase 'Your blood be on your own heads' is also translated 'Whatever happens to you will be your own fault' [CEV], 'You're responsible for your own death' [GW], 'If you are

not saved, it will be your own fault' [NCV], 'If you are lost, you yourselves must take the blame for it' [TEV]. The idiom 'on your own heads' means to accept responsibility for some action, often with the implication of blame [LN]. The idiom 'on your own heads' means you are responsible for your own destruction [BDAG].
    f. καθαρός (LN 53.29) (BDAG 3.a. p. 489): 'clean' [Bar, LN; KJV, NASB], 'pure' [BDAG, LN], 'free' [BDAG], 'innocent' [BECNT; ESV, GW, NLT, NRSV], 'guiltless' [NET], 'not to blame' [CEV], 'without blame' [AB]. The phrase 'I am clean' is also translated 'I have done all I can do' [NCV], 'I am clear of my responsibility' [NIV], 'I am not responsible' [TEV], 'My conscience is clear' [CBC; REB]. This adjective pertains to being ritually clean or pure [LN]. It pertains to being free from moral guilt [BDAG].

QUESTION—What were they reviling against"
They were reviling against either Paul or to the subject of his message, Jesus [BECNT].

QUESTION—What is meant by the phrase 'he shook out his garments'?
It was a sign that he was breaking off fellowship with them [Bar, BECNT, PNTC, TNTC]. This kind of action was performed by Jews against Gentiles. In this instance it was to indicate that in the sight of the missionaries those who rejected the gospel were no better than the Gentiles, cut off from the true people of God [TNTC]. It was a sign of rejection [CBC]. It was an act symbolizing repudiation of the Jews' opposition, exemption from further responsibility for them and protest against what Paul considered the Jews' blasphemy [EBC].

QUESTION—What is meant by the idiom 'Your blood be on your own heads'?
This expression means that those who reject the Gospel will be responsible for the loss they suffer [Bar, BECNT, TH].

**18:7** And he left[a] there and went[b] into the house of-a-man named Titius Justus, a worshiper[c] of God. His house was next door to the synagogue.

TEXT—Manuscripts reading Τιτίου Ἰούστου 'Titius Justus' are given a C rating by GNT to indicate that choosing it over a variant text was difficult. A variant reading is Ἰούστου 'Justus' and it is followed by KJV.

LEXICON—a. aorist act. participle of μεταβαίνω (LN 15.2) (BDAG 1.a.α. p. 638): 'to leave' [CBC; all versions except CEV, KJV], 'to depart' [LN; KJV], 'to move from one place to another, to change one's location' [LN], 'to go/pass over' [BDAG], 'to go/move away' [AB, Bar], 'to go out' [BECNT], not explicit [CEV]. This verb means to effect a change of location in space, with the implication that the two locations are significantly different [LN]. It means that a person transfers from one place to another [BDAG].
    b. aorist act. indic. of εἰσέρχομαι (LN 15.93): 'to go' [BECNT, CBC; all versions except CEV, KJV, NCV], 'to come' [AB], 'to move into, to come into, to go into' [LN], 'to enter' [Bar, LN; KJV], 'to move' [CEV,

NCV]. This verb means to move into a space, either two-dimensional or three-dimensional [LN].
c. pres. mid. participle of σέβω (LN 53.53) (BDAG 1.b. p. 918): 'to worship' [BDAG, LN; CEV, KJV, NCV, NET, NLT, TEV], 'to venerate' [LN], 'to reverence' [Bar], not explicit [GW]. This verb is also translated as a noun: 'worshiper' [BECNT, CBC; ESV, NASB, NIV, NRSV, REB]. This verb is also translated as an adjective: 'god-fearing' [AB]. This verb means to express in attitude and ritual one's allegiance to and regard for deity [LN]. It means to express in gestures, rites, or ceremonies one's allegiance or devotion to deity [BDAG].

**18:8** Crispus, the leader-of-the-synagogue,[a] believed[b] in-the Lord,[c] together with his entire household.[d] And many of-the Corinthians hearing (Paul) believed and were-baptized.[e]

LEXICON—a. ἀρχισυνάγωγος (LN 53.93) (BDAG p. 139): 'leader of the synagogue' [AB; NASB, NLT, TEV], 'president of a/the synagogue' [BDAG, LN; NET, REB], 'leader of a synagogue' [BDAG, LN], 'leader of that synagogue' [NCV], 'synagogue leader' [GW], 'ruler of the synagogue' [BECNT; ESV], 'synagogue ruler' [NIV], 'chief ruler of the synagogue' [KJV], 'official of the synagogue' [NRSV], 'leader of the meeting place' [CEV], 'Archisynagogue' [Bar]. This noun is also translated 'who held office in the synagogue' [CBC]. This noun denotes one who is the head of and who directs the affairs of a synagogue [LN]. It denotes an official whose duty it was especially to take care of the physical arrangements for the worship services [BDAG].
b. aorist act. indic. of πιστεύω (LN 31.102) (BDAG 2.a.α. p. 817): 'to believe' [AB, BECNT; all versions except CEV, NRSV, REB], 'to believe (in), to trust' [BDAG]. This verb is also translated as a noun: 'became a believer' [Bar, CBC; NRSV, REB]. The phrase 'Crispus,…believed in the Lord, together with his entire household' is also translated 'He and everyone in his family put their faith in the Lord' [CEV]. This verb means to believe in the good news about Jesus Christ and to become a follower [LN]. It means to entrust oneself to an entity in complete confidence [BDAG].
c. κύριος (LN 12.9): 'Lord' [LN; all translations], 'Ruler, One who commands' [LN]. This noun denotes a title for God and for Christ. It indicates one who exercises supernatural authority over mankind [LN].
d. οἶκος (LN 10.8) (BDAG 2. p. 699): 'household' [AB, Bar, BDAG, BECNT, CBC, LN; ESV, NASB, NET, NIV, NLT, NRSV, REB], 'family' [BDAG, LN; CEV, GW, TEV], 'house' [KJV]. The phrase 'entire household' is also translated 'all the people living in his house' [NCV]. This noun denotes the family consisting of those related by blood and marriage, as well as slaves and servants, living in the same house or homestead [LN].

e. imperf. pass. indic. of βαπτίζω (LN 53.41) (BDAG 2.c. p. 164): 'to be baptized' [BDAG, LN; all translations], 'to be plunged, to be dipped, to be washed' [BDAG]. This verb means to employ water in a religious ceremony designed to symbolize purification and initiation on the basis of repentance [LN]. It means to use water in a rite for the purpose of renewing or establishing a relationship with God [BDAG].

QUESTION—To whom does 'the Lord' refer?
It refers to Jesus [BECNT, TRT].

**DISCOURSE UNIT—18:9–11** [PNTC]. The topic is an encouraging vision.

**18:9** And the Lord said to-Paul one night in (a)-vision,[a] "Do- not -be-afraid, but go on speaking and do- not -be-silent,

LEXICON—a. ὄραμα (LN 33.488) (BDAG 2. p. 718): 'vision' [BDAG, LN; all translations]. This noun denotes an event in which something appears vividly and credibly to the mind, although not actually present, but implying the influence of some divine or supernatural power or agency [LN]. It denotes the act by which the recipient of a vision is granted a vision, or the state of being in which the person receives a vision [BDAG].

QUESTION—To whom does 'the Lord' refer?
It refers to Jesus [BECNT, EBC, NICNT, PNTC, TNTC]. It refers to God or his angel [NAC].

**18:10** for I am with you, and no-one will-attack[a] you to-harm[b] you, for I have many in this city who are my people."

LEXICON—a. fut. mid. indic. of ἐπιτίθημι (LN 39.47) (BDAG 2. p. 384): 'to attack' [BDAG, BECNT, LN; ESV, GW, NASB, NIV, NLT], 'to assault' [LN; NET], 'to lay a hand on' [BDAG; NRSV], 'to set on' [KJV], 'to set upon' [Bar], 'to make an attempt upon' [AB], not explicit [CBC; CEV, NCV, TEV]. This verb is also translated as a noun: 'no attack' [REB]. This verb means to use sudden physical force against someone as the outgrowth of a hostile attitude [LN]. It means to set upon [BDAG].

b. aorist act. infin. of κακόω (LN 20.12) (BDAG 1. p. 502): 'to harm' [BDAG, LN; all translations except CEV, KJV, NCV], 'to hurt' [LN; KJV, NCV], 'to injure' [LN], 'to mistreat' [BDAG]. This verb is also translated as a passive verb: 'to be harmed' [CEV]. This verb means to cause harm or injury to someone or something [LN]. It means to cause harm to [BDAG].

QUESTION—To whom does the phrase 'my people' refer?
It refers to the believers [TH], his followers [TRT], those who will become believers [PNTC].

**18:11** And he-stayed[a] (a)-year and six months, teaching the word[b] of-God among them.

LEXICON—a. aorist act. indic. of καθίζω (LN 85.63) (BDAG 4. p. 492): 'to stay' [AB, Bar, BDAG, LN; CEV, ESV, NCV, NET, NIV, NLT, NRSV,

TEV], 'to settle' [BDAG, LN; NASB, REB], 'to settle down' [CBC], 'to reside' [BDAG, LN], 'to remain, to inhabit, to be' [BECNT, LN], 'to live' [BDAG; GW]. The phrase 'he stayed' is also translated 'he continued (there)' [KJV]. This verb means to remain for some time in a place, often with the implication of a settled situation [LN]. It means to remain in a place [BDAG].
  b. λόγος (LN 33.260) (BDAG 1.a. β. p. 599): 'word' [AB, Bar, BDAG, BECNT, CBC; all translations except CEV], 'message' [CEV], 'what is preached, gospel' [LN]. This noun denotes the content of what is preached about Christ or about the good news [LN]. It denotes a communication whereby the mind finds expression [BDAG].
QUESTION—What is meant by 'the word of God'?
  It means the gospel and all it entails [BECNT]. It means the content of the Christian message [Bar]. It is the message about Jesus [EBC].

**DISCOURSE UNIT—18:12–17** [EBC, NAC, NICNT, PNTC; NCV, NET]. The topic is Paul is brought before Gallio [NCV], Paul before the proconsul Gallio [NET], Paul before Gallio [NICNT], before the proconsul Gallio [EBC], the accusation before Gallio [NAC], Jews and Christians in public dispute [PNTC].

**18:12** **But when Gallio was proconsul[a] of-Achaia, the Jews- rose-up[b] with-one-accord[c] -(against) Paul and brought him before the judgment-seat,[d]**
LEXICON—a. ἀνθύπατος (LN 37.82) (BDAG p. 82): 'proconsul' [AB, Bar, BDAG, BECNT, CBC, LN; ESV, NASB, NET, NIV, NRSV, REB], 'governor' [CEV, GW, NCV, NLT, TEV], 'deputy' [KJV], 'important official' [LN]. This noun denotes an official ruling over a province traditionally under the control of the Roman senate [LN]. It denotes the head of the government in a senatorial province [BDAG].
  b. aorist act. indic. of κατεφίστημι (LN 39.47) (BDAG p. 532): 'to rise up' [BDAG; NASB, NLT], 'to rise against' [AB], 'to attack' [LN; GW, NET], 'to assault' [LN], 'to seize' [TEV], 'to grab' [CEV], 'to set upon' [Bar, CBC]. The phrase 'the Jews rose up with one accord against Paul' is also translated 'the Jews made a united attack on Paul' [ESV], 'the Jews made insurrection with one accord against Paul' [KJV], 'some of the Jews came together against Paul' [NCV], 'the Jews made a united/concerted attack on/upon Paul' [BECNT; NIV, NRSV, REB]. This verb means to use sudden physical force against someone as the outgrowth of a hostile attitude [LN]. It means to rise up against someone [BDAG].
  c. ὁμοθυμαδόν (LN 31.23) (BDAG p. 706): 'with one accord' [Bar; KJV, NASB], 'with one mind' [BDAG, LN], 'by common consent, unanimously' [LN], 'with one purpose/impulse' [BDAG], 'united' [BECNT; ESV, NIV, NRSV], 'together' [NCV, NET, NLT], 'concerted' [REB]. The phrase 'the Jews rose up with one accord' is also translated 'some of the Jewish leaders got together' [CEV], 'the Jews had one thought in mind' [GW], 'Jews there got together' [TEV], 'all the Jews

rose' [AB], 'the Jews set upon Paul in a body' [CBC]. This adjective pertains to mutual consent or agreement [LN].

d. βῆμα (LN 7.63) (BDAG 3. p. 175): 'judgment seat' [LN; KJV, NASB, NET], 'judgment place' [LN], 'tribunal' [BDAG, BECNT; ESV, NRSV], 'court' [CBC; CEV, GW, NCV, NIV, REB, TEV], 'court of justice' [AB], 'place of judgement' [Bar], 'governor' [NLT]. This noun denotes a raised platform mounted by steps and usually furnished with a seat, used by officials in addressing an assembly, often on judicial matters [LN]. It denotes a dais or platform that required steps to ascend [BDAG].

QUESTION—Who was Gallio?

He was the son of the orator Seneca the Elder [BECNT, EBC, NICNT, PNTC]. Gallio was a brother of the philosopher Seneca [AB, Bar, BECNT, CBC, EBC, NICNT, PNTC]. He held office as proconsul in either A.D. 50–51 or 52–53 [AB]. Gallio assumed the governorship of Greece around A.D. 51 [TH]. Gallio was the proconsul/governor of Achaia/Greece Province A.D. 51–52 [BECNT, CBC, TRT]. Gallio became proconsul in A.D. 50 or 51 and held the office for two years [Bar].

QUESTION—What was Achaia?

Achaia was a Roman province that included the most important part of Greece [TH].

**18:13** saying, "This-man persuades[a] people to-worship[b] God contrary to the law.[c]"

LEXICON—a. pres. act. indic. of ἀναπείθω (LN 33.302) (BDAG p. 70): 'to persuade' [AB, Bar, BECNT, LN; ESV, GW, KJV, NASB, NET, NIV, NLT, NRSV], 'to incite' [LN], 'to induce' [BDAG, CBC; REB]. The phrase 'This man persuades people to worship' is also translated 'This man…is trying to persuade people to worship' [TEV], 'This man is trying to make our people worship' [CEV], 'This man is teaching people to worship' [NCV]. This verb means to persuade, with the possible implication of resistance and/or for wrong motives or results [LN]. It means to move someone to do something by persuasion [BDAG].

b. pres. mid. infin. of σέβω (LN 53.53) (BDAG 1.b. p. 918): 'to worship' [BDAG, LN; all translations], 'to venerate' [LN]. This verb means to express in attitude and ritual one's allegiance to and regard for deity [LN]. It means to express in gestures, rites, or ceremonies one's allegiance or devotion to deity [BDAG].

c. νόμος (LN 33.56) (BDAG 2.b. p. 678): 'law' [Bar, BDAG, BECNT, CBC; all versions except CEV, GW], 'Law' [AB; CEV], 'holy writings, Scriptures, sacred writings' [LN], 'Moses' Teachings' [GW]. This noun denotes the sacred writings of the OT [LN]. It denotes the constitutional or statutory legal system and specifically the law that Moses received from God and is the standard according to which membership in the people of Israel is determined [BDAG].

QUESTION—What is meant by 'the law'?
It can either refer to Roman law or Jewish law or both [AB, TRT]. If it is understood to be the Jewish law, then the question was whether the governor could be expected to enforce their own domestic laws. A better charge for the Jews would be to accuse Paul of teaching people to worship God in a way that was against the Roman law [TNTC]. The charge preferred against Paul was that of propagating a religion and on that basis forming a society not permitted by Roman law [NICNT].

**18:14** But when Paul was-about to-open<sup>a</sup> his mouth, Gallio said to the Jews, "If it-were a matter of wrongdoing<sup>b</sup> or vicious crime, O Jews, I would have (a valid)-reason to put-up-with- your -(complaint).<sup>c</sup>

LEXICON—a. pres. act. infin. of ἀνοίγω (LN 33.29) (BDAG 5.a. p. 84): 'to open' [Bar, BDAG, BECNT; ESV, KJV, NASB], 'to address, to start speaking, to begin to speak, to utter' [LN], not explicit [CEV]. The phrase 'Paul was about to open his mouth' is also translated 'Paul was about to answer/speak' [AB; GW, NET, NIV, NRSV, TEV], 'Paul was just about to speak' [CBC; REB], 'Paul was about to say something' [NCV], 'Paul started to make his defense' [NLT]. The idiom 'to open the mouth' means to begin to speak in a somewhat formal and systematic manner [LN]. It means to cause to function and refers to the mouth [BDAG].
  b. ἀδίκημα (LN 88.23) (BDAG 1. p. 20): 'wrongdoing' [BECNT; ESV, NLT], 'unrighteous act' [LN], 'crime' [AB, BDAG, CBC, LN; CEV, NCV, NET, NRSV, REB], 'a wrong' [BDAG; KJV, NASB, TEV], 'misdeed' [BDAG], 'misdemeanor' [GW, NIV], 'injury' [Bar]. This noun denotes what is done in an unrighteous or unjust manner [LN]. It denotes a violation of norms of justice [BDAG].
  c. aorist mid. indic. of ἀνέχω (LN 56.10) (BDAG 3. p. 78): 'to put up with' [GW, NASB], 'to bear with' [BECNT; KJV], 'to be patient with' [TEV], 'to be forbearing with' [Bar], 'to accept a complaint in court, to admit a complaint to judgment' [LN], 'to accept a complaint' [BDAG; ESV, NET, NRSV], 'to accept a case' [NLT]. The phrase 'I would have a valid reason to put up with your complaint' is also translated 'it would be reasonable for me to listen to you' [NIV], 'I should,...,have given you Jews a patient hearing' [CBC; REB], 'I would deal with your complaint as reason would demand' [AB], 'I would have to listen to you' [CEV], 'I would listen to you' [NCV]. The idiom 'to accept in accordance with a charge' means to accept a complaint against someone for a legal review [LN].

**18:15** But<sup>a</sup> since it-is a matter of questions about words and names and your own law,<sup>b</sup> see-(to it)<sup>c</sup> yourselves. I refuse to-be (a)-judge of-these-things."

LEXICON—a. δέ (LN 89.136): 'but' [Bar, BECNT, CBC; all versions], 'however' [AB], 'on the one hand...but on the other hand' [LN]. This conjunction is a marker of sets of items in contrast with one another [LN].

b. νόμος (LN 33.55) (BDAG 2.b. p. 677): 'law' [AB, Bar, BDAG, BECNT; all versions except GW, NLT, REB], 'the Law' [LN], 'Jewish law' [CBC; NLT, REB], 'teaching' [GW]. This noun denotes the first five books of the OT called the Torah [LN]. It denotes the constitutional or statutory legal system and specifically to the law that Moses received from God and is the standard according to which membership in the people of Israel is determined [BDAG].
c. aorist act. impera. of ὁράω (LN 30.45) (BDAG B.3. p. 720): 'to see to' [Bar, BDAG, BECNT, CBC; ESV, NRSV], 'to look to' [KJV], 'to look after' [NASB], 'to take care of' [CEV, GW, NLT], 'to take notice of, to consider, to pay attention to, to concern oneself with' [LN], 'to deal with' [AB], 'to look, to take care' [BDAG]. The phrase 'see to it yourselves' is also translated 'solve this problem yourselves' [NCV], 'settle it yourselves' [NET, REB], 'settle the matter yourselves' [NIV], 'you yourselves must settle it' [TEV]. This verb means to take special notice of something, with the implication of concerning oneself [LN]. It means to accept responsibility for causing something to happen [BDAG].

QUESTION—What law is meant here?
It refers to the Jewish law [Bar, CBC, TNTC, TRT; NLT, REB], it refers to the Jews' own law [PNTC].

**18:16** And he-drove- them -away<sup>a</sup> from the judgment-seat.

LEXICON—a. aorist act. indic. of ἀπελαύνω (LN 15.56) (BDAG p. 101): 'to drive away' [AB, BDAG, LN; NASB], 'to drive out' [TEV], 'to drive' [Bar, BECNT; ESV, KJV], 'to force to leave' [LN], 'to force out' [GW], 'to force away' [NET], 'to throw out' [NLT], 'to send out' [CEV], 'to make leave' [NCV], 'to eject' [CBC; NIV], 'to dismiss' [NRSV, REB]. This verb means to cause to move away from a point by threat or by force [LN].

QUESTION—What does this sentence indicate?
It indicates that Gallio did not want to listen to their complaints any further [TNTC]. It indicates that the plaintiffs did not have a case worth being heard by a proconsul [EBC]. Gallio drove them off because he believed there was no charge to be answered under Roman law and because he had no time for Jewish theological debates [PNTC]. The charge against Paul was plainly a disagreement about Jewish religious terminology that the Jews must settle themselves. So Gallio made them leave his tribunal [NAC, NICNT].

**18:17** And they all seized[a] Sosthenes, the leader-of-the-synagogue, and beat-(him) in-front-of the judgment-seat. But Gallio was- not -concerned[b] about any of-these-things.

TEXT—Manuscripts reading πάντες 'all' are given a B rating by GNT to indicate it was regarded to be almost certain. A variant reading is πάντες τοὺς Ἑλληνιστὰς 'the Greeks' and it is followed by KJV.

LEXICON—a. aorist mid. (deponent = act.) participle of ἐπιλαμβάνομαι (LN 18.2) (BDAG 1. p. 374): 'to seize' [AB, BECNT; ESV, NET, NRSV], 'to grab' [CEV, NCV, NLT, TEV], 'to take hold of' [Bar, BDAG, LN; NASB], 'to grasp' [BDAG, LN], 'to take' [GW, KJV], 'to catch' [BDAG], 'to turn on' [NIV], 'to attack' [REB]. The phrase 'they all seized Sosthenes' is also translated 'there was a general attack on Sosthenes' [CBC]. This verb means to take hold of or grasp, with focus upon the goal of the motion [LN]. It means to make the motion of grasping or taking hold of something [BDAG].

b. imperf. act. indic. of μέλει (LN 25.223) (BDAG 1.d. p. 627): 'to be concerned' [NASB, NET], 'to be of concern, to be anxious about' [LN], 'to show concern' [BECNT; NIV], 'to care' [KJV], 'to pay attention' [ESV, NLT, NRSV], 'to take notice' [AB], 'it is a care/concern' [BDAG]. The clause 'Gallio was not concerned about any of these things' is also translated 'none of this mattered to Gallio' [CEV], 'none of these things troubled Gallio' [Bar], 'Gallio couldn't have cared less' [GW], 'this/that did not bother Gallio' [NCV, TEV], 'all this left Gallio quite unconcerned' [CBC; REB]. This verb means to be particularly concerned about something, with the implication of some apprehension [LN].

QUESTION—To whom does 'they' refer?

It may refer to the Jews or the Gentiles [Bar, NAC, TH]. Most major manuscripts do not have 'the Greeks', which would mean that 'the Jews' who had just spoken to Gallio are the ones who beat Sosthenes [TRT].

QUESTION—Why did the people beat Sosthenes?

The people beat him possibly because he was not successful in presenting the Jews' case, or possibly because he was starting to become a Christian himself [TRT]. If the Jews beat Sosthenes, then it was because he mismanaged the case against Paul [Bar, PNTC]. If the Greeks beat Sosthenes, then it was because the Jews were often unpopular. For the moment the Jews were out of favor and it would be safe to attack one of them [Bar].

QUESTION—Why wasn't Gallio concerned?

He apparently thought that public order was not threatened and that it wouldn't do any harm if some angry people vented their wrath on a Jew [Bar, PNTC].

**DISCOURSE UNIT—18:18–19:20** [NICNT]. The topic is Ephesus.

**DISCOURSE UNIT—18:18–28** [NIV]. The topic is Priscilla, Aquila and Apollos.

**DISCOURSE UNIT—18:18–23** [AB, BECNT, EBC; CEV, ESV, GW, NCV, NET, NLT, NRSV, TEV]. The topic is Paul returns to Antioch [ESV, NCV], Paul returns to Antioch in Syria [CEV, NET, NLT], Paul's return trip to Antioch [GW], Paul's return to Antioch [NRSV], the return to Antioch [TEV], Paul's return to Palestine-Syria [EBC], Paul in Corinth, Ephesus, and Jerusalem [AB], back to Antioch and through the region [BECNT].

**DISCOURSE UNIT—18:18–22** [NAC, PNTC]. The topic is returning to Antioch [NAC], completion of the second missionary journey [PNTC].

**DISCOURSE UNIT—18:18–21** [NICNT, TNTC]. The topic is Paul's departure from Corinth [TNTC], hasty visit to Ephesus [NICNT].

**18:18** After this, Paul stayed[a] many days longer and then took-leave-of[b] the brothers[c] and set sail for Syria, and with him Priscilla and Aquila. In Cenchrea he had his hair cut, for he-was-keeping (a)-vow.[d]

LEXICON—a. aorist act. participle of προσμένω (LN 85.59) (BDAG 2. p. 883): 'to stay' [AB, BECNT; CEV, ESV, GW, NCV, NET, NIV, NLT, NRSV], 'to remain' [LN; NASB], 'to stay on' [Bar, CBC, LN; REB, TEV], 'to remain longer' [BDAG], 'to tarry' [KJV]. This verb means to stay or remain in a place beyond some point of time [LN]. It means to stay on at a place beyond some point of time [BDAG].
  b. aorist mid. participle of ἀποτάσσω (LN 15.55) (BDAG 1. p. 123): 'to take leave of' [AB, BDAG, BECNT, CBC, LN; ESV, NASB, REB], 'to say goodbye' [LN; NLT], 'to say farewell to' [BDAG; NET, NRSV], 'to leave' [GW, NCV, NIV, TEV]. The phrase 'took leave of' is also translated 'took his leave' [Bar]; KJV]. The phrase 'Paul...took leave of the brothers' is also translated 'he told them good-by' [CEV]. This verb means to say goodbye and to leave [LN]. It means to express a formal farewell [BDAG].
  c. ἀδελφός 'brother' [ESV, NET, NIV], 'fellow believer, (Christian) brother' [LN], not explicit [Bar; GW]. The phrase 'the brothers' is also translated 'the brethren' [AB, BECNT; KJV, NASB], 'the Lord's followers' [CEV], 'the believers' [NCV, NRSV, TEV], 'the brotherhood' [CBC], 'the brothers and sisters' [NLT], 'the congregation' [REB]. This noun denotes a close associate of a group of persons having a well-defined membership. In the NT ἀδελφός 'brother' refers specifically to fellow believers in Christ [LN].
  d. εὐχή (LN 33.469) (BDAG 2. p. 416): 'vow' [Bar, BDAG, BECNT, CBC, LN; all versions except CEV, NCV], 'promise' [CEV, NCV], 'Nazirite vow' [AB]. This noun denotes a promise to God that one will do something, with the implication that failure to act accordingly will result in divine sanctions against the person in question [LN]. It denotes a solemn promise with the understanding that one is subject to penalty for failure to discharge the obligation [BDAG].

QUESTION—What kind of vow did Paul keep?
  It is not certain what kind of vow this was. There are 4 popular views.
  1. It may have been a Nazirite vow [BECNT, CBC, EBC, NAC].
  2. It may have been a vow of thanksgiving for preservation as God promised in verse 10 [BECNT, NICNT].
  3. Sailors sometimes shaved after surviving a tough journey [BECNT].
  4. A private vow is more likely than a Nazirite vow [BECNT, NICNT].

QUESTION—Where was Cenchrea?
Cenchrea was the seaport of Corinth. It was located about 7 miles east of Corinth [BECNT, PNTC, TH, TRT].

**18:19** **And they-came[a] to Ephesus, and he-left[b] them there, but he himself entered the synagogue and reasoned-with the Jews.**
TEXT—Manuscripts reading κατήντησαν 'they came' are given a B rating by GNT to indicate it was regarded to be almost certain. A variant reading is κατήντησεν 'he arrived' and it is followed by KJV.
LEXICON—a. aorist act. indic. of καταντάω (LN 15.84) (BDAG 1. p. 523): 'to come' [AB, BECNT; ESV, KJV, NASB], 'to arrive' [BDAG, LN; CEV, GW, NIV, TEV], 'to reach' [Bar, BDAG, CBC, LN; NET, NRSV], 'to come to' [BDAG, LN], 'to go' [NCV], 'to put in' [REB]. The phrase 'they came to Ephesus' is also translated 'They stopped first at...Ephesus' [NLT]. This verb means to move toward and to arrive at a point [LN]. It means to get to a geographical destination [BDAG].
  b. aorist act. indic. of καταλείπω (LN 85.65) (BDAG 1.a.α. p. 520): 'to leave' [AB, Bar, BECNT, LN; all versions except NET, NLT, REB], 'to part' [CBC; REB], 'to leave behind' [BDAG, LN; NET, NLT]. This verb means to cause or permit something to remain in a place and to go away with or without implying purpose [LN]. It means to cause to be left in a place and refers to leaving one or more people [BDAG].
QUESTION—Where was Ephesus?
Ephesus was located near the mouth of the Cayster River. It was the capital of the Roman province of Asia and one of the most important commercial centers [Bar, BECNT, EBC, NICNT, TH, TNTC, TRT] and it was on the main trade route east from Rome [BECNT, NICNT].
QUESTION—To whom does 'them' refer?
It refers to Priscilla and Aquila [AB, CBC, EBC, NAC, NICNT, PNTC, TH, TNTC, TRT; CEV, GW, NCV, NET, NIV, TEV].

**18:20** **(When)-they asked-(him) to-stay[a] for (a)-longer period, he-did- not - consent.[b]**
LEXICON—a. aorist act. infin. of μένω (LN 85.55) (BDAG 1.a.α. p. 631): 'to stay' [BDAG, LN; all translations except KJV, NIV], 'to remain' [BDAG, LN], 'to tarry' [KJV]. The phrase 'they asked him to stay for a longer period' is also translated 'they asked him to spend more time' [NIV]. This verb means to remain in the same place over a period of time [LN].
  b. aorist act. indic. of ἐπινεύω (LN 33.279) (BDAG p. 376): 'to consent' [Bar, LN; KJV, NASB, NET, TEV], 'to agree' [LN], 'to give consent (by a nod)' [BDAG]. The phrase 'he did not consent' is also translated 'he declined' [BECNT, CBC; ESV, NIV, NLT, NRSV, REB], 'he refused' [AB; CEV, GW, NCV]. This verb means to indicate one's approval or agreement, sometimes only by nodding [LN].
QUESTION—To whom does 'they' refer?
It refers to the Jews [TRT]. It refers to the Ephesian Jews [AB, NAC].

**18:21** But[a] taking-leave-of them he said, "I-will-return[b] to you again (if) God wills,[c]" and he-set-sail from Ephesus.

TEXT—Manuscripts that do not add the phrase 'I must by all means keep this feast that cometh in Jerusalem' after εἰπών 'he said' are given an A rating by GNT to indicate it was regarded to be certain. A variant reading adds 'I must by all means keep this feast that cometh in Jerusalem' after εἰπών 'he said' and it is followed by KJV.

LEXICON—a. ἀλλά (LN 89.125): 'but' [Bar, BECNT, CBC, LN; ESV, KJV, NASB, NCV, NET, NIV, NRSV], 'instead' [LN; TEV], 'on the contrary' [LN], 'however' [NLT], not explicit [AB; CEV, GW, REB]. This conjunction indicates a more emphatic contrast [LN].

b. fut. act. indic. of ἀνακάμπτω (LN 15.89) (BDAG 1.a. p. 65): 'to return' [AB, BDAG, BECNT, LN; ESV, KJV, NASB, NRSV], 'to come back' [Bar, CBC; CEV, GW, NCV, NET, NIV, NLT, REB, TEV], 'to move back' [LN]. This verb means to move back to a point or area from which one has previously departed, but with more explicit emphasis upon the return [LN]. It means to go back to a point or area from which an entity has departed [BDAG].

c. pres. act. participle of θέλω (LN 30.58) (BDAG 2. p. 448): 'to will' [AB, BDAG, BECNT; ESV, KJV, NASB, NET, NRSV], 'to want' [BDAG; GW, NCV], 'to purpose' [LN], 'to wish' [BDAG]. The phrase 'if God wills' is also translated 'If God lets me' [CEV]. This verb is also translated as a noun: 'God's will' [CBC; NIV, REB], 'the will of God' [TEV]. This verb is also translated as an adjective: 'God willing' [Bar; NLT]. This verb means to purpose, generally based upon a preference and desire [LN]. It means to have something in mind for oneself of purpose, resolve [BDAG].

**DISCOURSE UNIT—18:22–23** [NICNT, TNTC]. The topic is Paul's journey to Caesarea and Antioch [TNTC], brief visit to Judaea and Syria [NICNT].

**18:22** When he had-landed[a] at Caesarea, he went-up[b] and greeted[c] the church, and then went-down[d] to Antioch.

LEXICON—a. aorist act. participle of κατέρχομαι (LN 54.15) (BDAG 2. p. 531): 'to land' [AB, Bar, BECNT, CBC; ESV, KJV, NASB, NCV, NIV, NRSV, REB], 'to arrive' [BDAG; GW, NET, TEV], 'to arrive at land, to put in at' [LN], 'to arrive at a place, to put in' [BDAG], not explicit [CEV, NLT]. This verb means to go by ship toward the shore [LN]. This verb means to arrive at a place and here it means to arrive at a harbor [BDAG].

b. aorist act. participle of ἀναβαίνω (LN 15.101) (BDAG 1.a.α. p. 58): 'to go up' [AB, Bar, BDAG, BECNT, CBC, LN; ESV, KJV, NASB, NET, NIV, NLT, NRSV, REB], 'to ascend' [BDAG, LN], 'to come up' [LN], 'to go' [GW, NCV, TEV], not explicit [CEV]. This verb means to move up [LN]. It means to be in motion upward [BDAG].

c. aorist mid. (deponent = act.) participle of ἀσπάζομαι (LN 33.20) (BDAG 1.b. p. 144): 'to greet' [AB, Bar, BDAG, BECNT, LN; all versions except

KJV, NCV, NLT], 'to salute' [KJV], 'to welcome' [BDAG], 'to send greetings' [LN], 'to give greetings' [NCV], 'to visit' [NLT], 'to pay respects' [CBC]. This verb means to employ certain set phrases as a part of the process of greeting, whether communicated directly or indirectly [LN]. It means to engage in hospitable recognition of another through short friendly visits [BDAG].
- d. aorist act. indic. of καταβαίνω (LN 15.107) (BDAG 1.a.β. p. 514): 'to go down' [AB, BDAG, BECNT, CBC, LN; ESV, KJV, NASB, NET, NIV, NRSV, REB], 'to come down' [Bar, BDAG, LN], 'to move down, to descend' [LN], 'to go' [CEV, NCV, TEV], 'to go back' [GW, NLT]. This verb means to move down, irrespective of the gradient [LN]. It means to move downward [BDAG].

QUESTION—Where was the church that Paul greeted?

It was the church in Jerusalem [EBC, NAC, NICNT, PNTC, TH, TNTC, TRT; GW, NCV, NET, NLT, NRSV, TEV].

**DISCOURSE UNIT—18:23–20:38** [PNTC]. The topic is the word in Ephesus: the climax of Paul's mission as a free man.

**DISCOURSE UNIT—18:23–28** [NAC, PNTC; NASB]. The topic is third missionary journey [NASB], Apollos in Ephesus [NAC], Priscilla, Aquila and Apollos in Ephesus [PNTC].

**18:23** **After spending some time there, he-departed**[a] **and went- from one place to the next -through**[b] **the Galatian region**[c] **and Phrygia, strengthening**[d] **all the disciples.**

LEXICON—a. aorist act. indic. of ἐξέρχομαι (LN 15.40): 'to depart' [BECNT; ESV, KJV, NRSV], 'to leave' [Bar; CEV, NASB, NCV, NET, TEV], 'to set out' [AB, CBC; NIV, REB], 'to go out of, to depart out of, to leave from within' [LN], not explicit [GW, NLT]. This verb means to move out of an enclosed or well defined two or three-dimensional area [LN].
- b. pres. mid./pass. (deponent = act.) participle of διέρχομαι (LN 15.21) (BDAG 1.b.α. p. 244): 'to go through' [BDAG, BECNT; ESV, GW, NCV, NET, NRSV, TEV], 'to go over' [KJV], 'to pass through' [Bar; NASB], 'to travel around through, to journey all through' [LN], 'to journey through' [AB], 'to travel throughout' [NIV], 'to go back through' [NLT], not explicit [CEV, REB]. The phrase 'went from one place to the next through' is also translated 'made a journey through' [CBC]. This verb means to travel around through an area, with the implication of both extensive and thorough movement throughout an area [LN]. It means to move through an area [BDAG].
- c. χώρα (LN 1.79) (BDAG 2.b. p. 1094): 'region' [BDAG, BECNT, LN; ESV, GW, NASB, NCV, NET, NIV, NRSV, TEV], 'place' [BDAG; CEV], 'country' [AB, CBC; KJV, REB], 'territory' [Bar, LN], 'land' [LN], 'district' [BDAG], not explicit [NLT]. This noun denotes a region or regions of the earth, normally in relation to some ethnic group or

geographical center, but not necessarily constituting a unit of governmental administration [LN]. It denotes a portion of land area [BDAG].

d. pres. act. participle of ἐπιστηρίζω (LN 74.19) (BDAG p. 381): 'to strengthen' [AB, Bar, BDAG, BECNT, LN; all versions except CEV, NCV, REB], 'to make more firm' [LN]. The phrase 'strengthening all the disciples' is also translated 'helped the followers...to become stronger' [CEV], 'giving strength to all the followers' [NCV], 'bringing new strength to all the converts/disciples' [CBC; REB]. This verb means to cause someone to become stronger in the sense of more firm and unchanging in attitude or belief [LN]. It means to cause someone to become stronger or more firm [BDAG].

QUESTION—Where was the Galatian region and Phrygia?

The Galatian region and Phrygia is possibly the area in south Galatia evangelized in Acts 13–14 [TNTC]. Also see 16:6.

QUESTION—In what way did Paul strengthen the disciples?

He strengthened them spiritually not physically [TRT]. He helped them to become stronger in their faith [Bar; CEV, GW].

**DISCOURSE UNIT—18:24–19:22** [CBC]. The topic is Ephesus: steady progress.

**DISCOURSE UNIT—18:24–19:7** [Bar]. The topic is Apollos and the twelve disciples.

**DISCOURSE UNIT—18:24–28** [AB, BECNT, EBC, NICNT, TNTC; CEV, ESV, GW, NCV, NET, NLT, NRSV, TEV]. The topic is the arrival of Apollos [TNTC], Apollos speaks boldly in Ephesus [ESV], Apollos tells others about Jesus [GW], Apollos begins his ministry [NET], ministry of Apollos [NRSV], Apollos in Ephesus and Corinth [NCV, TEV], Apollos at Ephesus and Corinth [EBC], Apollos in Ephesus [CEV], Apollos instructed at Ephesus [NLT], events in Ephesus before Paul's arrival [AB], backdrop to Ephesus: Apollos [BECNT], Apollos [NICNT].

**18:24** Now a Jew named Apollos, an-Alexandrian by-birth, came to Ephesus. He was an eloquent[a] man, competent[b] in the Scriptures.

LEXICON—a. λόγιος (LN 27.20, 33.32) (BDAG 2. p. 598): 'eloquent' [Bar, BECNT, CBC, LN (33.32); ESV, GW, KJV, NASB, NET, NLT, NRSV, REB, TEV], 'learned' [AB, BDAG, LN (27.20); NIV], 'cultured' [BDAG, LN (27.20)]. The phrase 'He was an eloquent man' is also translated 'He was a very good speaker' [CEV], 'He...was a good speaker' [NCV]. This adjective pertains to one who has learned a great deal of the intellectual heritage of a culture [LN (27.20)]. It pertains to attractive and convincing speech [LN (33.32)].

b. δυνατός (LN 74.4) (BDAG 1.b.α. p. 264): 'competent' [BDAG, LN; ESV], 'particularly capable, expert' [LN], 'mighty' [KJV, NASB], 'powerful' [Bar, CBC; REB], 'well versed' [BECNT; NET, NRSV], 'well read' [AB]. The phrase 'competent in the Scriptures' is also translated 'knew a lot about the Scriptures' [CEV], 'knew how to use the Scriptures in a powerful way' [GW], 'knew the Scriptures well' [NCV, NLT], 'with a thorough knowledge of the Scriptures' [NIV], 'had a thorough knowledge of the Scriptures' [TEV]. This adjective pertains to having special competence in performing some function [LN]. It pertains to being capable or competent [BDAG].

QUESTION—Who was Apollos?

He was a native of Alexandria, he was a Jew, was an educated man and had a thorough knowledge of the Jewish Scriptures [EBC, NICNT, PNTC].

**18:25** He had-been instructed[a] in the way[b] of-the Lord. And being-fervent[c] in-spirit, he-spoke and taught accurately the-things concerning Jesus, though he knew[d] only the baptism of-John.

TEXT—Manuscripts reading τοῦ Ἰησοῦ 'Jesus' are given an A rating by GNT to indicate it was regarded to be certain. A variant reading is τοῦ κυρίου 'the Lord' and it is followed by KJV.

LEXICON—a. perf. pass. participle of κατηχέω (LN 33.225) (BDAG 2.a. p. 534): 'to be instructed' [AB, Bar, BDAG, CBC, LN; all versions except CEV, NCV, NLT], 'to be taught' [BDAG, LN; NCV, NLT], not explicit [CEV]. This verb is also translated as an active verb: 'he was instructing' [BECNT]. This verb means to teach in a systematic or detailed manner [LN].

b. ὁδός (LN 41.35) (BDAG 3.c. p. 692): 'way' [all translations except CEV, NRSV, TEV], 'Way' [LN; CEV, NRSV, TEV], 'Christian way of life' [LN], 'teaching' [BDAG]. This noun denotes behavior in accordance with Christian principles and practices [LN]. It denotes the whole way of life from a moral and spiritual viewpoint [BDAG].

c. pres. act. participle of ζέω (LN 25.73) (BDAG p. 426): 'to be fervent' [Bar, BECNT; ESV, KJV, NASB], 'to show enthusiasm' [LN; NET], 'to commit oneself completely to' [LN], 'to be enthusiastic' [BDAG; GW, NLT], 'to be excited' [BDAG; NCV], 'to be on fire' [BDAG], 'to be full of spiritual fervour' [CBC; REB], 'to speak with great excitement' [CEV], 'to speak with great fervor' [NIV], 'to speak with burning enthusiasm' [NRSV]. This verb is also translated as a noun: 'great enthusiasm' [TEV]. This verb is also translated as an adjective: 'ardent spirit' [AB]. The idiom literally 'to boil in the spirit' means to show great eagerness toward something [LN]. It means to be stirred up emotionally [BDAG].

d. pres. mid./pass. (deponent = act.) participle of ἐπίσταμαι (LN 28.3) (BDAG 2. p. 380): 'to know' [BDAG, LN; all translations except NASB], 'to be acquainted with' [BDAG; NASB]. This verb means to possess information about, with the implication of an understanding of the significance of such information [LN]. It means to acquire information about something [BDAG].

QUESTION—What 'spirit' is referred to here?
Most Bible scholars think it refers to Apollos's spirit [EBC, TRT]. Some think it refers to the Holy Spirit and some think it means both [TRT]. 'Fervent in spirit' is the more likely reading here [BECNT].

**18:26** **He began to-speak-boldly**[a] **in the synagogue, and when Priscilla and Aquila heard him, they took**[b] **him and explained to-him the way of-God more-accurately.**
LEXICON—a. pres. mid./pass. (deponent = act.) infin. of παρρησιάζομαι (LN 33.90) (BDAG 1. p. 782): 'to speak boldly' [AB, Bar, BECNT, CBC, LN; ESV, GW, KJV, NIV, NRSV, REB, TEV], 'to speak out boldly' [NASB], 'to speak very boldly' [NCV], 'to speak openly' [BDAG, LN], 'to speak bravely' [CEV], 'to speak freely/fearlessly' [BDAG], 'to speak out fearlessly' [NET], 'to preach boldly' [NLT]. This verb means to speak openly about something and with complete confidence [LN]. It means to express oneself freely [BDAG].
b. aorist mid. indic. of προσλαμβάνω (LN 15.180) (BDAG 3. p. 883): 'to take' [AB, Bar, BECNT; CEV, ESV, GW, KJV, NCV, TEV], 'to lead aside' [LN], 'to take aside' [BDAG, LN; NASB, NET, NLT, NRSV], 'to take in hand' [CBC; REB]. The phrase 'they took him' is also translated 'they invited him' [NIV]. This verb means to take or lead off to oneself [BDAG, LN].

**18:27** **And when he wanted to-go to Achaia, the brothers**[a] **encouraged**[b] **(him) and wrote to-the disciples to-welcome him. When he arrived,**[c] **he-greatly -helped**[d] **those who had-believed**[e] **through grace,**[f]
LEXICON—a. ἀδελφός (LN 11.23): 'brother' [Bar; ESV, NET, NIV], 'fellow believer, (Christian) brother' [LN]. The phrase 'the brothers' is also translated 'the brethren' [AB, BECNT; KJV, NASB], 'the believers' [GW, NCV, NRSV, TEV], 'the Lord's followers' [CEV], 'the brotherhood' [CBC], 'the congregation' [REB], 'the brothers and sisters' [NLT]. This noun denotes a close associate of a group of persons having a well-defined membership. In the NT ἀδελφός 'brother' refers specifically to fellow believers in Christ [LN].
b. aorist mid. participle of προτρέπω (LN 33.300) (BDAG p. 889): 'to encourage' [AB, Bar, BDAG, BECNT; CEV, ESV, GW, NASB, NET, NIV, NLT, NRSV], 'to urge' [BDAG, LN], 'to exhort' [KJV], 'to impel, to persuade' [BDAG], 'to help' [NCV, TEV]. The phrase 'the brothers encouraged him' is also translated 'the brotherhood/congregation gave him their support' [CBC; REB]. This verb means to urge a particular course of action [LN]. It means to promote a particular course of action [BDAG].
c. aorist mid. (deponent = act.) participle of παραγίνομαι (LN 15.86) (BDAG 1.a. p. 760): 'to arrive' [AB, Bar, BDAG, BECNT, LN; all versions except KJV, NRSV, REB], 'to come' [BDAG, LN; KJV], 'to come to be present' [LN], 'to be present, to draw near' [LN]. This verb is

also translated as a noun: 'his arrival' [CBC; NRSV, REB]. This verb means to come to be present at a particular place [LN]. It means to be in movement so as to be present at a particular place [BDAG].
d. aorist mid. indic. of συμβάλλω (LN 35.1) (BDAG 6. p. 956): 'to help' [BDAG, BECNT, LN; ESV, GW, KJV, NASB, NCV, NRSV], 'to assist' [NET], 'to support' [Bar], 'to be of assistance' [BDAG], 'to be of benefit' [NLT], 'to be helpful' [CBC; REB], 'to be a help' [CEV, NIV, TEV], 'to be of help' [AB]. This verb means to assist in supplying what may be needed [LN]. It means to be of assistance [BDAG].
e. perf. act. participle of πιστεύω (LN 31.102) (BDAG 2.b. p. 817): 'to believe' [AB, BECNT; ESV, KJV, NASB, NCV, NET, NIV, NLT], 'to believe (in), to trust' [BDAG]. The phrase 'those who had believed' is also translated 'everyone who had put their faith in the Lord' [CEV]. This verb is also translated as a noun: 'the believers' [GW], 'become believers' [Bar, CBC; NRSV, REB, TEV]. This verb means to believe in the good news about Jesus Christ and to become a follower [LN]. It means to entrust oneself to an entity in complete confidence [BDAG].
f. χάρις (LN 88.66) (BDAG 3.b. p. 1080): 'grace' [Bar, BECNT, LN; ESV, KJV, NASB, NET, NIV, NRSV], 'graciousness' [AB, LN], 'kindness' [LN], 'favor, gracious deed, gracious gift, benefaction' [BDAG], 'God's kindness' [CEV, GW], 'God's grace' [CBC; NCV, NLT, REB, TEV]. This noun refers to the kindness shown to someone, with the implication of graciousness on the part of the one showing such kindness [LN]. It denotes the practical application of goodwill on the part of God and Christ [BDAG].

QUESTION—Who were the brothers?
They were the believers in Ephesus [CBC, EBC, NAC, PNTC, TH, TNTC, TRT; GW, NLT, TEV].
QUESTION—Whom did the brothers encourage?
1. They encouraged Apollos [Bar, EBC, PNTC, TRT; ESV, GW, NASB, NCV, NET, NIV, NLT, NRSV, REB, TEV].
2. They encouraged the believers in Achaia [CEV, KJV].

**18:28** for[a] he- powerfully -refuted[b] the Jews in-public, showing by the Scriptures that the Christ was Jesus.
LEXICON—a. γάρ (LN 89.23): 'for' [AB, Bar, BECNT, CBC, LN; ESV, KJV, NASB, NET, NIV, NRSV, REB, TEV], 'because' [LN], not explicit [CEV, GW, NCV, NLT]. This conjunction is a marker of cause or reason between events, though in some contexts the relation is often remote or tenuous [LN].
b. imperf. mid./pass. (deponent = act.) indic. of διακατελέγχομαι (LN 33.443) (BDAG p. 229): 'to refute' [AB, LN; ESV, NASB, NET, NIV, NLT, NRSV], 'to argue' [NCV], 'to debate' [Bar], 'to defeat in debate' [LN; TEV], 'to confute' [BECNT, CBC, LN; REB], 'to overwhelm in argument' [LN], 'to convince' [KJV], not explicit [GW]. The phrase 'he

powerfully refuted the Jews in public' is also translated 'He got into fierce arguments with the Jewish people' [CEV]. This verb means to refute completely in a debate [LN].

QUESTION—What scriptures are referred to here?

Apollos would have used scriptures from the Old Testament [EBC, NAC].

**DISCOURSE UNIT—19:1–41** [BECNT]. The topic is in Ephesus.

**DISCOURSE UNIT–19:1–22** [GW, NIV]. The topic is Paul in Ephesus [GW, NIV].

**DISCOURSE UNIT—19:1–10** [CEV, ESV, NASB, NCV, NRSV, TEV]. The topic is Paul in Ephesus [CEV, ESV, NCV, NRSV, TEV], Paul at Ephesus [NASB].

**DISCOURSE UNIT—19:1–7** [AB, EBC, NAC, NICNT, PNTC, TNTC; NET, NLT]. The topic is disciples of John the Baptist at Ephesus [NET], twelve disciples of John the Baptist become Christians [PNTC], the twelve disciples at Ephesus [TNTC], Paul and the twelve disciples of Ephesus [NICNT], Paul's witness to the disciples of John [NAC], Paul's third missionary journey [NLT], Christians baptized with John's baptism [AB], twelve men without the Spirit [EBC].

**19:1** And it-happened[a] that while Apollos was at Corinth, Paul passed-through[b] the inland country and came to Ephesus. There he found[c] some disciples.

LEXICON—a. aorist mid. (deponent = act.) indic. of γίνομαι (LN 13.107) (BDAG 4.e. p. 198): 'to happen' [AB, BDAG, LN; ESV, NASB], 'to occur, to come to be' [LN], 'to turn out, to take place' [BDAG], not explicit [all translations except AB; ESV, KJV, NASB]. The phrase 'And it happened' is also translated 'And it came to pass' [KJV]. This verb means to happen, with the implication that what happens is different from a previous state [LN]. It means to occur as a process or result [BDAG].

b. aorist act. participle of διέρχομαι (LN 15.17) (BDAG 1.a. p. 244): 'to pass through' [Bar, BECNT; ESV, KJV, NASB, NRSV], 'to go through' [BDAG; NET], 'to travel through' [AB, CBC; GW, NLT, REB, TEV], 'to travel across' [CEV], 'to move on to, to go on to' [LN], not explicit [NCV]. The phrase 'Paul passed through the inland country' is also translated 'Paul took the road through the interior' [NIV]. This verb means to complete movement in a particular direction [BDAG]. It means to move within or through an area [BDAG].

c. aorist act. infin. of εὑρίσκω (LN 27.27) (BDAG 1.b. p. 411): 'to find' [Bar, BDAG, BECNT, CBC, LN; all versions except CEV, GW], 'to come upon' [BDAG, LN], 'to learn the whereabouts of something, to discover, to happen to find' [LN], 'to meet' [AB; CEV, GW]. This verb means to learn the location of something, either by intentional searching or by unexpected discovery [LN]. It means to come upon something accidentally without seeking [BDAG].

QUESTION—What is meant by the 'inland country'?

It may refer literally to hill country or to the hinterland [Bar]. It refers to the overland route from Phrygia [CBC].

QUESTION—What is meant by the word 'found'?

It means that he met up with some disciples [PNTC, TH; CEV, GW].

QUESTION—Who were the disciples here?

1. The disciples referred to here are considered Christian believers and not merely disciples of John the Baptist [NAC, TH]. The word 'disciples' here is used for Christians, not for disciples of John the Baptist or others [AB]. They were disciples of Jesus [NICNT].
2. These men were not Christians since they had not received the gift of the Spirit [BECNT, TNTC]. Luke is not saying that the men were disciples but is describing how they *appeared* to Paul [TNTC]. The disciples whom Paul met in Ephesus had been baptized by John, but they didn't understand the purpose of his mission. They needed to understand where Jesus fit into the picture to be baptized in his name and to receive the Holy Spirit [PNTC].

**19:2** And he-said to them, "Did you-receive[a] (the)-Holy Spirit[b] when you believed?[c]" And they (said)-to him, "No, we- have not even -heard[d] whether there-is (a)-Holy Spirit."

LEXICON—a. aorist act. indic. of λαμβάνω (LN 57.125): 'to receive' [LN; all translations except CEV], 'to accept' [LN]. This verb is also translated as a passive verb: 'were you given' [CEV]. This verb means to receive or accept an object or benefit for which the initiative rests with the giver, but the focus of attention in the transfer is upon the receiver [LN].

b. πνεῦμα (LN 12.18) (BDAG 5.c.β. p. 834): 'Spirit' [BDAG, LN; all translations except KJV], 'Ghost' [KJV]. This noun denotes the third person of the Trinity whose titles are 'Spirit, Spirit of God, and Holy Spirit'. In many religious systems the significant difference between the gods and the spirits is that the gods are regarded as supernatural beings which control certain aspects of natural phenomena, while the spirits are supernatural beings, often impersonal, which indwell or inhabit certain places, including rivers, streams, mountains, caves, animals, and people. Spirits are often regarded as being primarily evil, though it may be possible to induce them to be favorable to people. It is extremely difficult to find in some languages a fully satisfactory term to speak of the Spirit of God. If one uses a term which normally identifies local supernatural beings, there is a tendency to read into the term the meaning of an evil or mischievous character. If, however, one uses a term which may identify the spirit of a person, the problems may even be greater, since according to many systems of religious belief, the spirit of an individual does not become active until the individual dies. Therefore, the activity of the

Spirit of God would presumably suggest that God himself had died. However, if one uses a term which means 'heart' or 'soul' (and thus the Spirit of God would be literally equivalent to 'the heart of God'), there may be complications since this aspect of human personality is often regarded as not being able to act on its own. The solutions to the problem of 'Spirit' have been varied. In some languages the term for Spirit is essentially equivalent to 'the unseen one', and therefore the Spirit of God is essentially equivalent to 'the invisibleness of God', In a number of languages the closest equivalent for Spirit is 'breath', and in a number of indigenous religious systems, the 'breath' is regarded as having a kind of independent existence. In other languages the term for Spirit is equivalent to what is often translated as 'the soul', that is to say, the immaterial part of a person. There is, of course, always the difficulty of employing a term meaning 'soul' or 'life', since it often proves to be impersonal and thus provides no basis for speaking of the Spirit of God as being a person or a personal manifestation of God. In quite a few languages the equivalent of Spirit is literally 'shadow', since the 'shadow' of a person is regarded as the immaterial part of the individual. Moreover, in many systems of religious thought the shadow is regarded as having some significant measure of independent existence. In a few cases the term for Spirit is literally 'wind', but there are frequently difficulties involved in this type of terminology since a term for wind often suggests calamity or evil intent. One meaning of Spirit which must be clearly avoided is that of 'apparition' or 'ghost'. Frequently it is not possible to find a fully satisfactory term for 'Spirit', and therefore in all contexts some characterizing feature is added, for example, either 'of God' or 'holy', in the sense of 'divine'. [LN]. It denotes God's being as controlling influence, with focus on association with humans [BDAG].

c. aorist act. participle of πιστεύω (LN 31.102) (BDAG 2.b. p. 817): 'to believe' [AB, BECNT; ESV, KJV, NASB, NCV, NET, NIV, NLT], 'to believe (in), to trust' [BDAG]. The phrase 'when you believed' is also translated 'when you put your faith in Jesus' [CEV]. This verb is also translated as a noun: 'became believers' [Bar, CBC; GW, NRSV, REB, TEV]. This verb means to believe in the good news about Jesus Christ and to become a follower [LN]. It means to entrust oneself to an entity in complete confidence [BDAG].

d. aorist act. indic. of ἀκούω (LN 33.212): 'to hear' [LN; all translations except REB], 'to receive news' [LN]. The phrase 'we have not even heard' is also translated 'we were not even told' [REB]. This verb means to receive information about something, normally by word of mouth [LN].

QUESTION—Were the disciples in 19:1 Christians?

The answer that they gave Paul in 19:2 showed that they definitely were not Christians [PNTC]. They are at best nominal Christians and at worst simply disciples of John [BECNT].

**19:3** And he-said, "Into what then were-you-baptized?ᵃ" And they-said, "Into John's baptism."

LEXICON—a. aorist pass. indic. of βαπτίζω (LN 53.41) (BDAG 2.a. p. 164): 'to be baptized' [AB, Bar, BDAG, BECNT, LN; CEV, ESV, KJV, NASB, NET, NRSV], 'to be plunged, to be dipped, to be washed' [BDAG]. The phrase 'Into what then were you baptized?' is also translated 'What kind of baptism did you have/receive?' [GW, NCV, TEV], 'Then what baptism did you receive/experience?' [NIV, NLT], 'Then what baptism were you given?' [CBC; REB]. This verb means to employ water in a religious ceremony designed to symbolize purification and initiation on the basis of repentance [LN]. It means to use water in a rite for the purpose of dedicatory cleansing associated with the ministry of John the Baptist [BDAG].

QUESTION—What is referred to by 'John's baptism'?

'John's baptism' refers to the baptism that John taught people about. It does not refer to a time that John was baptized. And it does not necessarily mean that John baptized them, someone else may have done that [TRT].

**19:4** And Paul said, "John baptized-(with) (the)-baptism of-repentance,ᵃ telling people to believeᵇ in the-one who was-comingᶜ after him, that is, in Jesus." **19:5** On hearing-(this), they-were-baptized in the nameᵈ of-the Lordᵉ Jesus.

LEXICON—a. μετάνοια (LN 41.52) (BDAG p. 640): 'repentance' [BDAG, LN; all translations except CEV, NCV, TEV], 'conversion' [BDAG]. The phrase 'John baptized with the baptism of repentance' is also translated 'The baptism of John was for those who turned from their sins' [TEV], 'John baptized people so that they would turn to God' [CEV]. The phrase 'of repentance' is also translated 'of changed hearts and lives' [NCV]. This noun denotes a complete change of thought and attitude with regard to sin and righteousness [LN].

b. aorist act. subj. of πιστεύω (LN 31.102) (BDAG 2.a.β. p. 817): 'to believe' [all translations except CBC; CEV, REB], 'to believe (in), to trust' [BDAG], 'to put one's faith in' [CEV], 'to put one's trust in' [CBC; REB]. This verb means to believe in the good news about Jesus Christ and to become a follower [LN]. It means to entrust oneself to an entity in complete confidence [BDAG].

c. pres. mid./pass. (deponent = act.) participle of ἔρχομαι (LN 15.81): 'coming' [Bar, LN; CEV, GW, NASB, NIV, TEV], 'to come' [AB, BECNT, CBC, LN; ESV, KJV, NCV, NET, NLT, NRSV, REB]. This verb means to move toward or up to the reference point of the viewpoint character or event [LN].

d. ὄνομα (LN 33.126) (BDAG 1.d.γ.ב. p. 713): 'name' [BDAG, LN; all translations]. This noun denotes the proper name of a person [LN]. Through baptism those who are baptized become the possession of and come under the dedicated protection of the one whose name they bear. [BDAG].

e. κύριος (LN 12.9) (BDAG 2.b.γ.ℶ. p. 578): 'Lord' [BDAG, LN; all translations], 'Ruler, One who commands' [LN], 'master' [BDAG]. This noun denotes a title for God and for Christ. It indicates one who exercises supernatural authority over mankind [LN]. It denotes one who is in position of authority [BDAG].

QUESTION—To whom does 'they were baptized' refer?

It refers to the disciples in 19:1 [BECNT, TH].

**19:6** And when Paul had-laid- his hands -on[a] them, the Holy Spirit came on[b] them, and they-began-speaking in tongues[c] and prophesying.[d] **19:7** There were about twelve men in all.

LEXICON—a. aorist act. participle of ἐπιτίθημι (LN 85.51) (BDAG 1.a.α. p. 384): 'to lay on' [AB, CBC, LN; ESV, NCV, NLT, NRSV, REB], 'to place on' [LN; CEV, GW, NET, NIV, TEV], 'to put on' [LN], 'to lay upon' [Bar, BDAG, BECNT; KJV, NASB], 'to put upon' [BDAG]. This verb means to place something on something [LN]. It means to place something on or transfer to (a place or object) [BDAG].

b. ἐπί with accusative object (LN 90.57): 'on' [BECNT, LN; ESV, KJV, NASB, NIV, NLT], 'upon' [AB, Bar, CBC; NCV, NET, NRSV, REB, TEV], 'to' [LN; GW], 'at' [LN]. The clause 'the Holy Spirit came on them' is also translated 'The Holy Spirit was given to them' [CEV]. This preposition is a marker of the experiencer, often with the implication of an action by a superior force or agency [LN].

c. γλῶσσα (LN 33.3) (BDAG 3. p. 201): 'tongue' [AB, Bar, BDAG, BECNT, LN; ESV, KJV, NASB, NET, NIV, NRSV], 'ecstatic language, ecstatic speech' [BDAG, LN], 'unknown language' [CEV], 'other language' [GW], 'different language' [NCV], 'tongue of ecstasy' [CBC; REB], 'other tongue' [NLT], 'strange tongue' [TEV]. This noun denotes an utterance having the form of language but requiring an inspired interpreter for an understanding of the content [LN]. It denotes an utterance outside the normal patterns of intelligible speech and therefore requiring special interpretation [BDAG].

d. imperf. act. indic. of προφητεύω (LN 33.459) (BDAG 1. p. 890): 'to prophesy' [BDAG, LN; all translations except GW, TEV], 'to make inspired utterances' [LN]. This verb is also translated 'to speak what God had revealed' [GW], 'proclaimed God's message' [TEV]. This verb means to speak under the influence of divine inspiration, with or without reference to future events [LN]. It means to proclaim an inspired revelation [BDAG].

QUESTION—Why did Paul lay his hands on them?

The laying on of hands should be understood as a special act of fellowship, incorporating the people concerned into the fellowship of the church [TNTC]. In the context, it expresses prayer for the recipients, while welcoming them into the fellowship of Christ [PNTC].

138  ACTS 19:8

**DISCOURSE UNIT—19:8–22** [TNTC; NLT]. The topic is Paul ministers in Ephesus [NLT], Paul's work in Ephesus [TNTC].

**DISCOURSE UNIT—19:8–20** [AB, Bar, PNTC]. The topic is Paul's successful ministry at Ephesus [Bar], Paul's preaching in Ephesus and his defeat of the magicians [AB], teaching and mighty works in Asia [PNTC].

**DISCOURSE UNIT—19:8–12** [EBC, NAC]. The topic is a summary of the apostle's ministry [EBC], Paul's preaching in Ephesus [NAC].

**DISCOURSE UNIT—19:8–10** [NICNT, PNTC; NET]. The topic is Paul continues to minister at Ephesus [NET], from synagogue to lecture hall [PNTC], the lecture hall of Tyrannus [NICNT].

**19:8** And he entered[a] the synagogue[b] and for three months spoke-boldly,[c] reasoning[d] and persuading[e] them about the kingdom of-God.

LEXICON—a. aorist act. participle of εἰσέρχομαι (LN 15.93): 'to enter' [BECNT, LN; ESV, NASB, NET, NIV, NRSV], 'to go into' [Bar, LN; GW, KJV, NCV, TEV], 'to move into, to come into' [LN], 'to go to' [AB; CEV, NLT]. The phrase 'he entered the synagogue' is also translated 'he attended the synagogue' [CBC; REB]. This verb means to move into a space, either two-dimensional or three-dimensional [LN].

b. συναγωγή (LN 7.20) (BDAG 2.a p. 963): 'synagogue' [BDAG, LN; all translations except CEV], 'Jewish meeting place' [CEV], 'Christian assembly place' [LN]. This noun denotes a building of assembly, associated with religious activity. Normally a building in which Jewish worship took place and in which the Law was taught [LN]. It denotes a place of assembly for the Jews [BDAG].

c. imperf. mid./pass. (deponent = act.) indic. of παρρησιάζομαι (LN 33.90) (BDAG 1. p. 782): 'to speak boldly' [LN; all translations except CEV, NET, NLT], 'to speak openly' [BDAG, LN], 'to speak fearlessly' [BDAG; NET], 'to speak freely' [BDAG], 'to talk bravely' [CEV], 'to preach boldly' [NLT]. This verb means to speak openly about something and with complete confidence [LN]. It means to express oneself freely [BDAG].

d. pres. mid./pass. (deponent = act.) participle of διαλέγομαι (LN 33.446) (BDAG 1. p. 232): 'to reason' [ESV, NASB], 'to argue' [Bar, BDAG, BECNT, LN; NIV, NLT, NRSV], 'to dispute' [LN; KJV], 'to converse' [AB, BDAG], 'to discuss' [BDAG], 'to address' [NET], not explicit [CEV, NCV]. This verb is also translated as a noun: 'he had discussions' [GW], 'holding discussions' [TEV], 'persuasive argument' [REB], 'using argument' [CBC]. This verb means to argue about differences of opinion [LN]. It means to engage in speech interchange especially of instructional discourse that frequently includes exchange of opinions [BDAG].

e. pres. act. participle of πείθω (LN 33.301) (BDAG 1.a. p. 791): 'to persuade' [Bar, BECNT, LN; ESV, KJV, NASB, NCV], 'to convince' [BDAG, LN; GW, NET, TEV], 'to try to explain' [AB], not explicit

[CEV]. This verb is also translated as an adverb: 'arguing persuasively' [NIV, NLT], 'argued persuasively' [NRSV]. This verb is also translated as an adjective: 'persuasive argument' [REB]. This verb is also translated as a noun: 'using…persuasion' [CBC]. This verb means to convince someone to believe something and to act on the basis of what is recommended [LN]. It means to cause to come to a particular point of view or course of action [BDAG].

QUESTION—To whom does 'he' refer?

It refers to Paul [TH, TRT; CEV, GW, NCV, NET, NIV, NLT, TEV].

QUESTION—What is meant by 'for three months'?

It means he went to the synagogue regularly, that is, each day or at least every Sabbath day [TRT]. It means that Paul's activity was regularly repeated during this period of three months, not that he was continually in the synagogue arguing with the people this entire period of time [TH].

**19:9** But$^a$ when some became-stubborn$^b$ and refused-to-believe,$^c$ speaking-evil-of$^d$ the Way$^e$ before the people, he-withdrew$^f$ from them and took the disciples (with him), reasoning daily in the school$^g$ of-Tyrannus.

LEXICON—a. δέ (LN 89.124): 'but' [LN; all translations except NRSV, REB], 'on the other hand' [LN], not explicit [NRSV, REB]. This conjunction is a marker of contrast [LN].

b. imperf. pass. indic. of σκληρύνω (LN 88.225) (BDAG b. p. 930): 'to become stubborn' [ESV, GW, NCV, NLT], 'to be stubborn' [LN; CEV, NET, TEV], 'to be obstinate' [LN], 'to become obstinate' [NIV], 'to be hardened' [AB, BDAG; KJV], 'to become hardened' [BDAG; NASB], 'to grow hard' [Bar], 'to be obdurate' [CBC; REB]. This verb is also translated as an active verb: 'some hardened themselves' [BECNT]. This verb is also translated as an adverb: 'some stubbornly refused' [NRSV]. This verb means to be stubborn, in the sense of refusing to believe [LN]. It means to cause to be unyielding in resisting information [BDAG].

c. imperf. act. indic. of ἀπειθέω (LN 31.107) (BDAG p. 99): 'to refuse to believe' [LN; CEV, GW, NCV, NET, NIV, NRSV], 'to continue in unbelief' [ESV], 'to disbelieve' [Bar, BECNT], 'to not believe' [KJV], 'to refuse to be a believer, to reject the Christian message' [LN], 'to disobey' [BDAG], 'to be disobedient' [BDAG], 'to become disobedient' [NASB]. The phrase 'refused to believe' is also translated 'rejecting his message' [NLT], 'would not believe' [AB, CBC; REB, TEV]. This verb means to refuse to believe the Christian message [LN].

d. pres. act. participle of κακολογέω (LN 33.399) (BDAG p. 500): 'to speak evil of' [AB, Bar, BDAG, BECNT, CBC; ESV, KJV, NASB, NRSV, REB], 'to say terrible/evil things about' [CEV, NCV, TEV], 'to speak against' [NLT], 'to revile' [LN; NET], 'to insult' [BDAG], 'to denounce' [LN], 'to malign' [NIV]. The phrase 'speaking evil of' is also translated 'had nothing good to say…about' [GW]. This verb means to insult in a particularly strong and unjustified manner [LN].

e. ὁδός (LN 41.35) (BDAG 3.c. p. 692): 'Way' [Bar, BECNT, LN; ESV, KJV, NASB, NET, NIV, NLT, NRSV], 'way' [AB, BDAG], 'Christian way of life' [LN], 'teaching' [BDAG]. The phrase 'the Way' is also translated 'God's Way' [CEV], 'the way of Christ' [GW], 'the Way of Jesus' [NCV], 'the Way of the Lord' [TEV], 'the new way' [CBC; REB]. This noun is a figurative extension of ὁδός 'road, way' and it denotes behavior in accordance with Christian principles and practices [LN]. It denotes the whole way of life from a moral and spiritual viewpoint [BDAG].
f. aorist act. participle of ἀφίστημι (LN 15.51) (BDAG 2.a. p. 157): 'to withdraw' [BDAG, BECNT; ESV, NASB, REB], 'to go away' [BDAG, LN], 'to depart' [LN; KJV], 'to leave' [AB, CBC, LN; CEV, GW, NCV, NET, NIV, NLT, NRSV, TEV], 'to separate' [Bar]. This verb means to move away from, with emphasis upon separation and possible lack of concern for what has been left [LN]. It means to distance oneself from some person or thing [BDAG].
g. σχολή (LN 7.14) (BDAG p. 982): 'school' [AB, Bar, LN; KJV, NASB, NCV], 'hall' [BECNT; ESV], 'lecture hall' [BDAG, CBC, LN; CEV, GW, NET, NIV, NLT, NRSV, REB, TEV]. This noun denotes a building where teachers and students met for study and discussion [LN].

QUESTION—What was the 'school of Tyrannus'?

It was probably a lecture room or school building [BECNT, TNTC]. This was probably the hall of a local philosopher, Tyrannus, or one rented out to travelling philosophers by a landlord of that name [EBC].

QUESTION—Who was Tyrannus?

He was possibly the owner of the building or the teacher at the school [BECNT, NICNT, PNTC, TNTC].

**19:10** This continued[a] for two years, so-that all who lived[b] in Asia heard the word[c] of-the Lord, both Jews and Greeks.

LEXICON—a. aorist mid. (deponent = act.) indic. of γίνομαι (LN 13.107): 'to continue' [AB, BECNT; ESV, GW, KJV, NRSV], 'to take place' [NASB], 'to happen, to occur, to come to be' [LN], 'to last' [Bar], not explicit [CEV, NCV]. The phrase 'This continued' is also translated 'This went on' [CBC; NET, NIV, NLT, REB, TEV]. This verb means to happen, with the implication that what happens is different from a previous state [LN].
b. pres. act. participle of κατοικέω (LN 85.69) (BDAG 2. p. 534): 'to live' [AB, Bar, LN; GW, NASB, NET, NIV, TEV], 'to dwell' [LN; KJV], 'to reside' [LN], 'to inhabit' [BDAG], not explicit [CBC; CEV, NCV, NLT, REB]. The phrase 'all who lived in Asia' is also translated 'all the residents of Asia' [BECNT; ESV, NRSV]. This verb means to live or dwell in a place in an established or settled manner [LN]. It means to make something a habitation or dwelling by being there [BDAG].

c. λόγος (LN 33.260) (BDAG 1.a.β. p. 599): 'word' [AB, Bar, BDAG, BECNT, CBC; all translations except CEV], 'message' [CEV], 'what is preached, gospel' [LN]. This noun denotes the content of what is preached about Christ or about the good news [LN]. It denotes a communication whereby the mind finds expression [BDAG].

QUESTION—What does 'this' refer to?

It refers to Paul's ministry in Ephesus [EBC, TNTC]. It refers to the pattern where Paul works in the morning and preaches in the afternoon [BECNT]. It refers to Paul's ministry in the school of Tyrannus [NAC, NICNT, PNTC].

**DISCOURSE UNIT—19:11–41** [NASB]. The topic is miracles at Ephesus.

**DISCOURSE UNIT—19:11–22** [NCV]. The topic is the sons of Sceva.

**DISCOURSE UNIT—19:11–20** [PNTC; CEV, ESV, NET, NRSV, TEV]. The topic is the sons of Sceva [CEV, ESV, NRSV, TEV], the seven sons of Sceva [NET], miracles and their impact [PNTC].

**DISCOURSE UNIT—19:11–19** [NICNT]. The topic is conflict with the magicians.

**19:11** **And God was doing extraordinary miracles**[a] **by**[b] **the hands**[c] **of-Paul,**

LEXICON—a. δύναμις (LN 76.7) (BDAG 3. p. 263): 'miracle' [BDAG, BECNT, CBC, LN; all versions], 'powerful deed' [AB], 'mighty deed' [LN], 'work of power' [Bar], 'deed of power, wonder' [BDAG]. This noun denotes a deed manifesting great power, with the implication of some supernatural force [LN]. It denotes a deed that exhibits ability to function powerfully [BDAG].

b. διά with genitive object (LN 89.76) (BDAG 3.a. p. 224): 'by' [AB, Bar, BDAG, BECNT, LN; ESV, KJV, NASB, NET], 'by means of' [LN], 'through' [BDAG, CBC, LN; GW, NIV, NRSV, REB, TEV], 'via' [BDAG], not explicit [CEV, NCV, NLT]. This preposition indicates the means by which one event makes another event possible [LN]. It indicates the means or instrument whereby something is accomplished or effected [BDAG].

c. χείρ (LN 9.17) (BDAG 2.a. p. 1082): 'the hands (of)' [AB, Bar, BDAG, BECNT; ESV, KJV, NASB, NET], 'person, agent' [LN], not explicit [CBC; CEV, GW, NCV, NIV, NLT, NRSV, REB, TEV]. This is a figurative extension of meaning of χείρ 'hand' and it denotes a human as an agent in some activity [LN]. It denotes an acting agent [BDAG].

**19:12** **so-that even handkerchiefs**[a] **or aprons**[b] **that had touched his skin were carried-away**[c] **to the sick, and the diseases left**[d] **them and the evil**[e] **spirits went-out**[f] **(of them).**

LEXICON—a. σουδάριον (LN 6.159) (BDAG p. 934): 'handkerchief' [BECNT, CBC, LN; all versions], 'towel, napkin' [LN], 'face cloth' [BDAG, LN], 'scarf' [AB], 'sweatband' [Bar]. This noun denotes a small piece of cloth used as a towel, napkin, or face cloth [LN]. It denotes a face cloth for wiping perspiration [BDAG].

b. σιμικίνθιον (LN 6.179) (BDAG p. 923): 'apron' [BDAG, BECNT, LN; all versions except NCV, REB], 'cloth' [NCV], 'scarf' [CBC; REB], 'garment' [AB], 'sweatcloth' [Bar]. This noun denotes an apron, normally worn by workmen [BDAG, LN].

c. pres. pass. infin. of ἀποφέρω (LN 15.202) (BDAG 2. p. 124): 'to be carried away' [BECNT, LN; ESV], 'to be carried' [Bar, CBC; NASB, REB], 'to be taken away' [LN], 'to be taken' [BDAG; NIV, TEV], 'to be brought' [BDAG; KJV, NET, NRSV], 'to be placed' [NLT]. This verb is also translated as an active verb: 'they carried them' [CEV], 'People would take handkerchiefs and aprons' [GW], 'Some people took handkerchiefs and cloths' [NCV], 'they…took scarves or garments' [AB]. This verb means to carry something away from a point [LN]. It means to bring from one point to another [BDAG].

d. pres. pass. infin. of ἀπαλλάσσω (LN 13.40) (BDAG 2. p. 96): 'to leave' [Bar, BDAG, BECNT; ESV, NASB, NET, NRSV], 'to cease, to stop' [LN], 'to depart' [BDAG, LN; KJV], 'to vanish' [AB]. The phrase 'the diseases left them' is also translated 'All of the sick people were healed' [CEV], 'the sick were healed' [NCV], 'Their sicknesses would be cured' [GW], 'their illnesses were cured' [NIV], 'they were healed of their diseases' [NLT], 'they were cured of their diseases' [REB], 'they were rid of their diseases' [CBC], 'their diseases were driven away' [TEV]. This verb means to cease as of a state, with a significant element of change of state involved [LN]. It means to go away [BDAG].

e. πονηρός (BDAG 1.a.α. p. 851): 'evil' [BDAG; all translations], 'wicked, bad, base, worthless, vicious, degenerate' [BDAG]. This adjective pertains to humans or transcendent beings who are morally or socially worthless [BDAG].

f. pres. mid./pass. (deponent = act.) infin. of ἐκπορεύομαι (LN 15.40) (BDAG 1.a. p. 308): 'to go out' [Bar; CEV, KJV, NASB, NET, TEV], 'to come out' [BECNT, CBC; ESV, NRSV, REB], 'to go' [BDAG], 'to go out of, to depart out of, to leave from within' [LN], 'to leave' [AB; GW, NCV, NIV], 'to be expelled' [NLT]. This verb means to move out of an enclosed or well defined two or three-dimensional area [LN]. It means to be in motion from one area to another [BDAG].

**DISCOURSE UNIT—19:13–20** [NAC]. The topic is Paul's encounter with false religion in Ephesus.

**DISCOURSE UNIT—19:13–19** [EBC]. The topic is the seven sons of Sceva.

**DISCOURSE UNIT—19:13–16** [NAC]. The topic is Jewish exorcists.

**19:13** Then some of-the Jewish exorcists,[a] who went-from-place-to-place,[b] undertook[c] to-invoke[d] the name of-the Lord Jesus over[e] those who had evil spirits, saying, "I-adjure[f] you-(by) the Jesus whom Paul proclaims.[g]"

LEXICON—a. ἐξορκιστής (LN 53.103) (BDAG p. 351): 'exorcist' [AB, Bar, BDAG, BECNT, CBC, LN; ESV, KJV, NASB, NET, NRSV, REB], 'one casting/driving/forcing out evil spirits' [LN; GW, NLT, NIV, TEV], 'one making evil spirits go out of people' [NCV]. The phrase 'Jewish exorcists' is also translated 'Jewish men' [CEV]. This noun denotes one who drives out evil spirits, usually by invoking supernatural persons or powers or by the use of magic formulas [LN]. It denotes one who drives out evil spirits by invocation of transcendent entities [BDAG].
  b. pres. mid./pass. (deponent = act.) participle of περιέρχομαι (LN 15.23) (BDAG 1. p. 800): 'to go from place to place' [NASB], 'to travel from place to place' [GW], 'to travel from town to town' [NLT], 'to travel about, to wander about' [LN], 'to go about' [BDAG], 'to go around' [CEV, NIV], 'to travel around' [NCV, TEV]. This verb is also translated as an adjective: 'itinerant' [Bar, BECNT; ESV, NET, NRSV, REB], 'wandering' [AB], 'strolling' [CBC], 'vagabond' [KJV]. This verb means to move about from place to place, with significant changes in direction [LN]. It means to go about in various directions [BDAG].
  c. aorist act. indic. of ἐπιχειρέω (LN 68.59) (BDAG p. 386): 'to undertake' [BECNT, LN; ESV], 'to attempt' [NASB], 'to try' [AB, BDAG, CBC, LN; GW, NCV, NET, NIV, NLT, NRSV, REB, TEV], 'to set about' [Bar], 'to endeavor' [BDAG], not explicit [CEV]. The phrase 'undertook to invoke the name of the Lord Jesus' is also translated 'took upon them to call…the name of the Lord Jesus' [KJV]. This verb means to undertake to do something, but not necessarily without success [LN]. It means to set one's hand to [BDAG].
  d. pres. act. infin. of ὀνομάζω (LN 33.133) (BDAG 2. p. 714): 'to invoke' [AB; ESV, NET, NIV], 'to pronounce a name, to call out a name' [LN], 'to name a name, to use a name/word' [BDAG]. The phrase 'to invoke the name' is also translated 'to call the name' [KJV], 'to pronounce the name' [BECNT], 'to name the name' [Bar; NASB], 'to use the name' [CBC; CEV, GW, NCV, NLT, NRSV, REB, TEV]. This verb means to utter a name in a ritual context [LN]. It means to pronounce a name or a word [BDAG].
  e. ἐπί with accusative object (LN 90.57) (BDAG 1.c.γ. p. 363): 'over' [AB, Bar, BECNT; ESV, KJV, NASB, NET, NIV, NRSV], 'on' [CBC, LN; REB] 'to' [LN], 'at' [BDAG, LN], 'by, near' [BDAG], not explicit [CEV, GW, NCV, NLT, TEV]. This preposition is a marker of the experiencer, often with the implication of an action by a superior force or agency [LN]. It is a marker of location or surface, answering the question 'where?' [BDAG].
  f. pres. act. indic. of ὁρκίζω (LN 33.467) (BDAG p. 723): 'to adjure' [Bar, BDAG, BECNT, CBC; ESV, KJV, NASB, NRSV, REB], 'to implore'

[BDAG], 'to command' [NIV, NLT, TEV], 'to order' [GW, NCV], 'to conjure' [AB], 'to sternly warn' [NET], 'to put under oath, to insist that one take an oath, to require that one swear' [LN], not explicit [CEV]. This verb means to demand that a person take an oath as to the truth of what is said or as to the certainty that one will carry out the request or command [LN]. It means to give a command to someone under oath [BDAG].
  g. pres. act. indic. of κηρύσσω (LN 33.256) (BDAG 2.b.β. p. 544): 'to proclaim' [CBC; ESV, NRSV, REB], 'to preach' [AB, Bar, BECNT, LN; CEV, KJV, NASB, NET, NIV, NLT, TEV], 'to proclaim aloud' [BDAG], 'to talk about' [GW, NCV]. This verb means to publicly announce religious truths and principles while urging acceptance and compliance [LN]. It means to make public declarations [BDAG].

**19:14** Seven sons of (a)-Jewish chief-priest[a] named Sceva were-doing this.
LEXICON—a. ἀρχιερεύς (LN 53.88): 'chief priest' [Bar, BECNT, CBC, LN; GW, NASB, NIV, REB], 'high priest' [AB; CEV, ESV, NET, NRSV, TEV], 'leading priest' [NCV, NLT]. The phrase 'a Jewish chief priest' is also translated 'a Jew, and chief of the priests' [KJV]. This noun denotes a principal priest, in view of belonging to one of the high priestly families [LN].
QUESTION—Who was Sceva?
  Nothing is known of him. Perhaps he came from an important priestly family [CBC].

**19:15** And the evil spirit answered them, "I-know[a] Jesus, and I-know-about[b] Paul, but who are-you(pl)?"
  LEXICON—a. pres. act. indic. of γινώσκω (LN 28.1) (BDAG 6.a.β. p. 200): 'to know' [AB, Bar, BDAG, BECNT, LN; all versions except NASB, NET, REB], 'to recognize' [NASB, REB], 'to know about' [LN; NET], 'to acknowledge' [CBC], 'to have knowledge of, to be acquainted with' [LN]. This verb means to possess information about [LN]. It means to have come to the knowledge of someone [BDAG].
  b. pres. mid./pass. (deponent = act.) indic. of ἐπίσταμαι (LN 28.3) (BDAG 2. p. 380): 'to know about' [CBC; NASB, NCV, NIV, TEV], 'to know' [BDAG, LN; KJV, NLT, NRSV, REB], 'to be acquainted with' [Bar, BDAG, BECNT; GW, NET], 'to recognize' [ESV], 'to hear of/about' [AB; CEV]. This verb means to possess information about, with the implication of an understanding of the significance of such information [LN]. This verb means to acquire information about something [BDAG].

**19:16** And the man, in whom was the evil spirit, leaped[a] on them and subdued[b] all of them and overpowered[c] them, so-that they fled out-of that house naked and wounded.
  LEXICON—a. aorist mid. (deponent = act.) participle of ἐφάλλομαι (LN 15.239) (BDAG p. 417): 'to leap' [AB, Bar, BECNT; ESV, KJV, NASB, NLT, NRSV], 'to jump' [CEV, NCV, NET, NIV], 'to jump on' [LN], 'to

leap upon' [BDAG, LN]. The phrase 'the man...leaped on them' is also translated 'the man...flew at them' [CBC; REB]. The phrase 'the man...leaped on them and subdued all of them' is also translated 'The man...attacked them' [GW, TEV]. This verb means to leap or jump onto a place or object [LN].

b. aorist act. participle of κατακυριεύω (LN 39.55) (BDAG 1. p. 519): 'to subdue' [BDAG; NASB], 'to master' [BECNT; ESV, NRSV], 'to become master, to gain dominion over' [BDAG], 'to overpower' [AB, Bar, CBC, LN; NIV, NLT, REB], 'to overcome' [KJV], not explicit [NCV]. The phrase 'the man...subdued all of them' is also translated 'the man...beat them all into submission' [NET]. The phrase 'the man...subdued all of them and overpowered them' is also translated 'the man...beat them up' [CEV]. The phrase 'the man...leaped on them and subdued all of them' is also translated 'the man...attacked them' [GW, TEV]. This verb means to subject someone or something to a superior force [LN]. It means to bring into subjection [BDAG].

c. aorist act. indic. of ἰσχύω (LN 79.64) (BDAG 3. p. 484): 'to overpower' [BECNT; ESV, NASB, NRSV, TEV], 'to master' [Bar], 'to be strong enough to, to be able to, to have the strength to' [LN], 'to have power, to be mighty' [BDAG], 'to prevail against' [KJV, NET], 'to gain the advantage over' [AB], not explicit [NCV]. The phrase 'the man...subdued all of them and overpowered them' is also translated 'the man...beat them up' [CEV]. The phrase 'the man...overpowered them so that they fled' is also translated 'He gave them such a beating that they ran' [NIV], 'He beat them up so badly that they ran' [GW], 'the man attacked them with such violence that they fled' [NLT], 'the man...handled them with such violence that they ran' [CBC; REB]. This verb means to be physically strong enough for some purpose [LN]. It means to be in control [BDAG].

**DISCOURSE UNIT—19:17-20** [NAC]. The topic is overcoming magic.

**19:17** And this became known[a] to-all who lived in Ephesus, both Jews and Greeks. And fear[b] fell[c] upon them all, and the name of the Lord Jesus was-being-exalted.[d]

LEXICON—a. γνωστός (LN 28.21) (BDAG 1.a. p. 204): 'known' [AB, Bar, BDAG, BECNT, CBC, LN; ESV, KJV, NASB, NET, NIV, NRSV]. The phrase 'this became known to all...both Jews and Greeks' is also translated 'the Jews and Gentiles heard about this' [CEV], 'All the Jews and Greeks...heard about this' [GW], 'All the Jews and Gentiles...heard about this' [TEV], 'All the people...–Jews and Greeks–learned about this' [NCV], 'The story of what happened spread quickly...to Jews and Greeks' [NLT], 'Everybody..., Jew and Gentile alike, got to know of it' [REB]. This adjective pertains to that which is known [LN]. It pertains to being familiar or known [BDAG].

b. φόβος (LN 25.251) (BDAG 2.a.α. p. 1062): 'fear' [AB, Bar, BDAG, BECNT, LN; ESV, KJV, NASB, NCV, NET, NIV, NLT, TEV], 'alarm, fright' [BDAG]. The phrase 'fear fell upon them all' is also translated 'they were so frightened' [CEV], 'all of them were filled with awe' [GW], 'everyone was awestruck' [NRSV], 'all were awestruck' [REB], 'they were all awestruck' [CBC]. This noun denotes a state of severe distress, aroused by intense concern for impending pain, danger, evil, etc., or possibly by the illusion of such circumstances [LN]. It denotes the product of an intimidating/alarming force [BDAG].

c. aorist act. indic. of ἐπιπίπτω (LN 13.122) (BDAG 2. p. 377): 'to fall' [AB, Bar, BECNT; ESV, KJV, NASB], 'to fall upon' [LN], 'to befall' [BDAG], 'to come over' [NET], 'to descend' [NLT]. The phrase 'fear fell upon them all' is also translated 'they were so frightened' [CEV], 'all of them were filled with awe' [GW], 'All the people...were filled with fear' [NCV], 'they were all filled with fear' [TEV], 'they were all seized with fear' [NIV], 'everyone was awestruck' [NRSV], 'all were awestruck' [REB], 'they were all awestruck' [CBC]. This verb means to happen suddenly to, with the connotation of something bad and adverse [LN]. It means to happen to [BDAG].

d. imperf. pass. indic. of μεγαλύνω (LN 33.358) (BDAG 2. p. 623): 'to be exalted' [BDAG], 'to be magnified' [Bar, BDAG; KJV, NASB], 'to be praised' [AB; NET, NRSV], 'to be glorified' [BDAG], 'to be extolled' [BECNT; ESV], 'to be held in high honor' [NIV], 'to be greatly honored' [NLT], 'to be given greater honor' [TEV], not explicit [CBC; REB]. This passive verb is also translated as an active verb: 'they praised the name of the Lord' [CEV], 'All of them...began to speak very highly about it' [GW], 'All the people...gave great honor to the Lord' [NCV]. This verb means to praise a person in terms of that individual's greatness [LN]. It means to cause to be held in greater esteem through praise or deeds [BDAG].

**19:18** Also many of-those who had-believed[a] came,[b] confessing[c] and disclosing[d] their practices.[e]

LEXICON—a. perf. act. participle of πιστεύω (LN 31.102) (BDAG 2.b. p. 818): 'to believe' [AB, Bar; KJV, NASB, NET, NIV], 'to believe (in), to trust' [BDAG]. This verb is also translated as a noun: 'believers' [BECNT; ESV, GW, NCV, TEV], 'became believers' [NLT, NRSV], 'had become believers' [CBC; REB], 'followers' [CEV]. This verb means to believe in the good news about Jesus Christ and to become a follower [LN]. It means to entrust oneself to an entity in complete confidence [BDAG].

b. imperf. mid./pass. (deponent = act.) indic. of ἔρχομαι (LN 15.81): 'to come' [AB, Bar, BECNT, CBC, LN; ESV, KJV, NET, NIV, REB, TEV], not explicit [CEV, GW, NCV, NLT, NRSV]. The imperfect tense of this verb is translated 'to keep coming' [NASB]. This verb means to move toward or up to the reference point of the viewpoint character or event [LN].

c. pres. mid. participle of ἐξομολογέω (LN 33.275) (BDAG 2. p. 351): 'to confess' [BDAG, LN; all translations except CEV, GW, TW], 'to admit' [BDAG, LN; GW, TEV]. The phrase 'came confessing and disclosing their practices' is also translated 'started telling everyone about the evil things they had been doing' [CEV]. This verb means to acknowledge a fact publicly, often in reference to previous bad behavior [LN]. It means to make an admission of wrong-doing/sin [BDAG].

d. pres. act. participle of ἀναγγέλλω (LN 33.197) (BDAG 2. p. 59): 'to disclose' [Bar, BDAG; NASB, NRSV], 'to announce' [BDAG, LN], 'to tell' [AB, LN; GW, NCV], 'to inform' [LN], 'to divulge' [BECNT; ESV], 'to show' [KJV], 'to make known' [NET], 'to reveal' [TEV], not explicit [CBC; NIV, NLT, REB]. The phrase 'came confessing and disclosing their practices' is also translated 'started telling everyone about the evil things they had been doing' [CEV]. This verb means to provide information [BDAG, LN], with the possible implication of considerable detail [LN].

e. πρᾶξις (LN 42.8) (BDAG 4.b. p. 860): 'practice' [ESV, NASB, NRSV], 'deed' [BDAG, LN; KJV, NET, NIV], 'act, action' [BDAG], 'sinful practice' [NLT], 'magical practice' [Bar], 'magic/magical spell' [AB, BECNT, CBC; GW, REB]. The phrase 'their practices' is also translated 'the evil things they had been doing' [CEV], 'the evil things they had done' [NCV], 'what they had done' [TEV]. This noun denotes the act of carrying out some activity (with possible focus upon the procedures involved) [LN]. It denotes the performance of some deed and here it refers to an evil or disgraceful deed [BDAG].

QUESTION—What is meant by 'their practices'?
In this context the term πρᾶξις means 'magic spells' or 'magical acts' [BECNT]. Many Bible scholars think that in this context 'their (evil) deeds' refers to 'practicing magic' [TRT]. Some think it means that they announced the secrets of their magic and in that way made their magic spells powerless [BECNT, NICNT, TRT]. Ephesus was known as the city of the magicians. It was not strange that among the newly converted Christians there should be many who as pagans used magical arts [AB, NAC].

**19:19** And (a)-number of-those who had-practiced[a] magic[b] (arts) brought-their books -together[c] and burned-(them) in-the-sight-of[d] everyone. And they-counted the value of-them and found it came to fifty-thousand-(pieces) of silver.

LEXICON—a. aorist act. participle of πράσσω (LN 42.8) (BDAG 1.a. p. 860): 'to practice' [all translations except GW, KJV, NCV], 'to do' [LN], 'to carry out, to perform' [LN], 'to accomplish' [BDAG], 'to use' [KJV, NCV]. The phrase 'a number of those who had practiced magic arts' is also translated 'Many of those who were involved in the occult' [GW]. This verb means to carry out some activity (with possible focus upon the

procedures involved) [LN]. It means to bring about or accomplish something through activity [BDAG].
  b. περίεργος (LN 53.99) (BDAG 2. p. 800): 'magic' [AB, Bar, BECNT, CBC, LN; ESV, NASB, NCV, NET, NRSV, REB, TEV], 'sorcery' [NIV, NLT], 'witchcraft' [LN; CEV], 'occult' [GW], 'curious arts' [KJV]. This adjective pertains to the use of magic based on superstition [LN]. It pertains to undue or misdirected curiosity as in the practice of magic [BDAG].
  c. aorist act. participle of συμφέρω (LN 15.125) (BDAG 1. p. 960): 'to bring together' [BDAG, BECNT; ESV, KJV, NASB, NIV, TEV], 'to gather together' [Bar, LN], 'to collect' [AB, CBC; NET, NRSV, REB], 'to bring' [CEV, NCV, NLT], 'to gather' [GW]. This verb means to cause to come together, whether of animate or inanimate objects [LN]. It means to bring together into a heap [BDAG].
  d. ἐνώπιον with genitive object (LN 83.33) (BDAG 2.a. p. 342): 'in the sight of' [AB, BDAG, BECNT; ESV, NASB], 'in front of' [LN; GW], 'in the presence of' [Bar, BDAG; NET], 'before' [LN; KJV, NCV], 'among' [BDAG]. The phrase 'in the sight of everyone' is also translated 'in public' [CEV, TEV], 'publicly' [CBC; NIV, NRSV, REB], 'at a public bonfire' [NLT]. This preposition pertains to a position in front of an object, whether animate or inanimate, which is regarded as having a spatial orientation of front and back [LN]. It pertains to being present or in view [BDAG].
QUESTION—What does the phrase 'their books' refer to?
  They were books that told how to do magic/sorcery/witchcraft [BECNT, CBC, NICNT, PNTC, TH, TRT].

**DISCOURSE UNIT—19:20** [NICNT]. The topic is further progress report.

**19:20** So the word of-the Lord continued to increase[a] and prevail[b] mightily.
TEXT—Manuscripts reading τοῦ κυρίου ὁ λόγος 'the word of the Lord' are given a B rating by GNT to indicate it was regarded to be almost certain. A variant reading is τοῦ θεοῦ ὁ λόγος 'the word of God' and it is followed by KJV.
LEXICON—a. imperf. act. indic. of αὐξάνω (LN 59.62) (BDAG 2.b. p. 151): 'to increase' [BDAG, LN; ESV], 'to grow' [Bar, BECNT, LN; KJV, NASB, NRSV], 'to grow in power' [NET], 'to spread' [LN; CEV, GW, NCV, TEV], 'to spread widely' [CBC; NIV, NLT, REB], 'to extend' [LN], 'to prosper' [AB]. This verb means to increase in the extent of or in the instances of an activity or state [LN]. It means to become greater [BDAG].
  b. imperf. act. indic. of ἰσχύω (LN 79.64) (BDAG 3. p. 484): 'to prevail' [Bar; ESV, KJV, NASB, NET, NRSV], 'to be strong enough to, to be able to, to have the strength to' [LN], 'to have power, to be mighty' [BDAG], 'to become more powerful' [CEV], 'to become strong' [BECNT], 'to gain

strength' [GW], 'to gain power' [AB], 'to grow in power' [NIV], 'to grow stronger' [TEV], 'to grow' [NCV], 'to spread effectively' [CBC; REB]. This verb is also translated 'had a powerful effect' [NLT]. This verb means to be physically strong enough for some purpose [LN]. It means to be in control [BDAG].

**DISCOURSE UNIT—19:21–20:6** [NICNT]. The topic is he prepares to leave Ephesus for Macedonia and Achaia.

**DISCOURSE UNIT—19:21–41** [CEV, ESV, NET, NRSV, TEV]. The topic is a riot at Ephesus [ESV, NET], the riot in Ephesus [CEV, NRSV, TEV].

**DISCOURSE UNIT—19:21–40** [AB, Bar, PNTC]. The topic is riot at Ephesus [Bar], the demonstration of the silversmiths [AB], provoking the idolaters [PNTC].

**DISCOURSE UNIT—19:21–22** [NAC, NICNT]. The topic is Paul makes plans for the future [NICNT], Paul's determination to go to Jerusalem [NAC].

**19:21** Now after these-things were-finished,[a] Paul resolved[b] in the spirit to-go to Jerusalem after he had-passed-through[c] Macedonia and Achaia, saying, "After I have-been there, I must also see Rome."

LEXICON—a. aorist pass. indic. of πληρόω (LN 68.26) (BDAG 5. p. 829): 'to be finished' [BDAG, LN; NASB], 'to be completed' [BDAG, LN], 'to be accomplished' [NRSV], 'to be done' [Bar], 'to be ended' [KJV], not explicit [AB, BECNT, CBC; ESV, NCV, NLT, REB]. This verb is also translated 'had taken place' [NET], 'had happened' [CEV, GW, NIV, TEV]. This verb means to finish an activity after having done everything involved [LN]. It means to bring to completion an activity in which one has been involved from its beginning [BDAG].

b. aorist mid. indic. of τίθημι (LN 30.76) (BDAG 1.b.ε. p. 1003): 'to resolve' [BECNT; ESV, NET, NRSV], 'to purpose' [KJV, NASB], 'to decide' [LN; CEV, GW, NCV, NIV], 'to make up one's mind' [AB, CBC, LN; REB, TEV], 'to have (in mind)' [BDAG]. The phrase 'Paul resolved in the spirit' is also translated 'Paul felt compelled by the Spirit' [NLT], 'Paul formed the intention' [Bar]. The idiom 'to place in the spirit or mind' means to engage in the process of deciding [LN]. It means to contrive something in one's mind [BDAG].

c. aorist act. participle of διέρχομαι (LN 15.21) (BDAG 1.b.α. p. 244): 'to pass through' [Bar, BECNT; ESV, KJV, NASB, NET, NIV], 'to travel through' [GW, TEV], 'to travel around through, to journey all through' [LN], 'to go through' [BDAG; NCV, NRSV], 'to go over to' [NLT], 'to visit' [CBC; CEV, REB], not explicit [AB]. This verb means to travel around through an area, with the implication of both extensive and thorough movement throughout an area [LN]. It means movement through something [BDAG].

QUESTION—What does the phrase 'these things' refer to?
'These things' may refer back either to the events described in verses 13–19 [TH, TRT], or it may refer back to the two years of verse 10. The former possibility is more probable, since two years is apparently too far removed to be the antecedent [TH].

QUESTION—What 'spirit' is referred to here?
1. It refers to his own spirit [Bar; KJV, NASB]. The Greek word for 'spirit' occurs here but there is no reference to the Holy Spirit. The word 'spirit,' in the sense of human spirit, is needed with the verb to express the thought of intention [Bar].
2. It refers to the Holy Spirit [EBC, PNTC; ESV, NLT, NRSV]. The Holy Spirit is referred to in 20:22 [EBC, PNTC] and in 21:4 and both references relate to Paul's travel plans [EBC]. This seems to be supported by the use of the verb δεῖ 'must', which in Luke's writings usually connotes the divine will [EBC, PNTC]. By the combination of ἐν τῷ πνεύματι and δεῖ, Luke appears to be making the point in 19:21 that this mission was under the direction of the Spirit [EBC].

**19:22** **And having-sent[a] into Macedonia two of his helpers, Timothy and Erastus, he himself stayed[b] in Asia for (a)-while.**
LEXICON—a. aorist act. participle of ἀποστέλλω (LN 15.66): 'to send' [LN; all translations]. This verb means to cause someone to depart for a particular purpose [LN].
b. aorist act. indic. of ἐπέχω (LN 85.59) (BDAG 3. p. 362): 'to stay' [AB, BDAG, BECNT, CBC; all versions except CEV, NET, TEV], 'to stay on' [LN; CEV, NET], 'to remain' [LN], 'to stop' [BDAG]. The phrase 'he...stayed in Asia for a while' is also translated 'he spent more time in...Asia' [TEV], 'He...extended his stay in Asia' [Bar]. This verb means to stay or remain in a place beyond some point of time [LN]. It means to remain at a place for a period of time [BDAG].

**DISCOURSE UNIT—19:23–41** [CBC, EBC, NAC, NICNT, TNTC; GW, NCV, NIV, NLT]. The topic is a riot in Ephesus [GW], the riot in Ephesus [NIV, NLT], the riot at Ephesus [EBC, NICNT], Ephesus: the riot [CBC], trouble in Ephesus [NCV], the reaction of paganism in Ephesus [TNTC], opposition to Paul by the craftsmen of Ephesus [NAC].

**DISCOURSE UNIT—19:23–27** [NAC]. The topic is instigation of a riot by Demetrius.

**19:23** **About that time there-occurred[a] no little disturbance concerning the Way.[b]**
LEXICON—a. aorist mid. (deponent = act.) indic. of γίνομαι (LN 91.5) (BDAG 3.b. p. 197): 'to occur' [NASB], 'to take place' [NET], 'to develop' [NLT], 'there was' [LN; CEV, NCV, TEV], 'and it happened that' [LN], 'to arise' [AB, Bar, BDAG, BECNT, CBC; ESV, KJV, NIV, REB], 'to break out' [GW, NRSV], 'to come about, to develop' [BDAG].

This verb is a marker of new information, either concerning participants in an episode or concerning the episode itself [LN]. It means to come into being as an event or phenomenon from a point of origin [BDAG].
b. ὁδός (LN 41.35) (BDAG 3.c. p. 692): 'Way' [Bar, BECNT, LN; ESV, NASB, NET, NIV, NLT, NRSV], 'Christian way of life' [LN], 'way' [AB, BDAG; KJV], 'teaching' [BDAG]. The phrase 'the Way' is also translated 'the Lord's Way' [CEV], 'the way/Way of Christ' [GW, NCV], 'the Way of the Lord' [TEV], 'the Christian movement' [CBC; REB]. This noun is a figurative extension of ὁδός 'road, way' and it denotes behavior in accordance with Christian principles and practices [LN]. It denotes the whole way of life from a moral and spiritual viewpoint [BDAG].

**19:24** For a-man named Demetrius, (a)-silversmith, who made silver shrines of-Artemis, brought no little business to-the craftsmen. **19:25** These he gathered-together,ᵃ with the workmen in similar trades, and said, "Men, you-know that our prosperityᵇ comes from this business.
LEXICON—a. aorist act. participle of συναθροίζω (LN 15.131) (BDAG 1. p. 964): 'to gather together' [BECNT, LN; ESV, NASB, NET, NRSV], 'to bring together' [BDAG; CEV], 'to call together' [AB, LN; KJV, NIV, NLT, TEV], 'to gather' [Bar, BDAG], 'to cause to come together' [LN]. The phrase 'These he gathered together' is also translated 'He called a meeting of his workers' [GW], 'He called a meeting of them' [REB], 'He called a meeting of these men' [CBC], 'Demetrius had a meeting with them' [NCV]. This verb means to cause to gather together [LN]. It means to cause to gather together as a group [BDAG].
b. εὐπορία (LN 57.32) (BDAG p. 410): 'prosperity' [Bar, BDAG, LN; NASB, NET, REB, TEV], 'wealth' [BECNT; ESV, KJV, NLT, NRSV], 'high standard of living' [CBC]. The phrase 'our prosperity comes from this business' is also translated 'we make a good living at this' [CEV], 'we make a lot of money from our business' [NCV], 'we're earning a good income from this business' [GW], 'we earn a good living by this work' [AB], 'we receive a good income from this business' [NIV]. This noun denotes the result of having acquired wealth [LN].
QUESTION—Who was Artemis?
Artemis, the major goddess in Ephesus, was known as a goddess of fertility and as 'mistress of the wild beasts,' a daughter of Zeus and Leto, and a sister of Apollo [BECNT]. The Roman name for the Greek 'Artemis' is Diana [CBC].

**19:26** And you-seeᵃ and hearᵇ that not only in-Ephesus, but-(in)ᶜ almost all of-Asia this Paul has-persuadedᵈ and turned-awayᵉ (a)-great many people, saying that gods made with hands are not gods.ᶠ
LEXICON—a. pres. act. indic. of θεωρέω (LN 24.14) (BDAG 1. p. 454): 'to see' [BDAG; all translations except NCV], 'to observe' [LN], 'to look at' [BDAG, LN; NCV], 'to perceive' [BDAG]. This verb means to observe

something with continuity and attention, often with the implication that what is observed is something unusual [LN]. It means to observe something with sustained attention [BDAG].
- b. pres. act. indic. of ἀκούω (LN 33.212): 'to hear' [LN; all translations except NCV], 'to receive news' [LN], not explicit [NCV]. This verb means to receive information about something, normally by word of mouth [LN].
- c. ἀλλά (LN 89.125): 'but' [LN; all translations except NCV, NIV, TEV], 'instead, on the contrary' [LN], not explicit [NCV, NIV, TEV]. This conjunction is a marker of more emphatic contrast [LN].
- d. aorist act. participle of πείθω (LN 33.301) (BDAG 1.a. p. 791): 'to persuade' [AB, Bar, BECNT, LN; ESV, KJV, NASB, NET, NLT, NRSV], 'to convince' [BDAG, LN; NCV, NIV, TEV]. The phrase 'Paul has persuaded and turned away a great many people' is also translated 'Paul is upsetting a lot of people' [CEV], 'Paul...has perverted crowds of people' [CBC; REB], 'He has won over a large crowd' [GW]. This verb means to convince someone to believe something and to act on the basis of what is recommended [LN]. It means to cause to come to a particular point of view or course of action [BDAG].
- e. aorist act. indic. of μεθίστημι (LN 31.73) (BDAG 2. p. 625): 'to turn away' [BDAG, BECNT, LN; ESV, KJV, NASB, NCV, NET], 'to draw away' [NRSV], 'to mislead' [BDAG, LN], 'to lead astray' [AB, Bar; NIV], not explicit [NLT, TEV]. The phrase 'Paul has persuaded and turned away a great many people' is also translated 'Paul is upsetting a lot of people' [CEV], 'Paul...has perverted crowds of people' [CBC; REB], 'He has won over a large crowd' [GW]. This verb is a figurative extension of meaning of μεθίστημι 'to cause to move' and it means to cause a complete change in someone's beliefs, normally in the unfavorable sense of causing someone to turn away from a previous belief and hence to be misled [LN]. It means to bring to a different point of view [BDAG].
- f. θεός (LN 12.22) (BDAG 1. p. 450): 'god' [BDAG, LN; all translations]. This noun denotes any one of many different supernatural beings regarded as having authority or control over some aspect of the universe or human activity [LN]. It denotes a transcendent being who exercises extraordinary control in human affairs [BDAG].

**19:27** And there is-danger not only that this trade of ours may come into disrepute,[a] but also that the temple of-the great[b] goddess Artemis may be-considered[c] as nothing,[d] and that she may even be-deposed[e] from her magnificence,[f] she whom all Asia and the world worship.[g]"

LEXICON—a. ἀπελεγμός (LN 33.416) (BDAG p. 101): 'disrepute' [Bar, BECNT; ESV, NASB, NET, NRSV], 'serious criticism, reproach' [LN], 'refutation, exposure, discredit' [BDAG], 'nought' [KJV]. This noun is also translated as an active verb: 'people will discredit' [GW]. This noun is also translated as a passive verb: 'will be discredited' [AB, CBC; REB].

The phrase 'this trade of ours may come into disrepute' is also translated 'this business of ours will get a bad name' [TEV], 'Everyone will start saying terrible things about our business' [CEV], 'our business/trade will lose its good name' [NCV, NIV], 'the loss of public respect for our business' [NLT]. This noun denotes serious and strong criticism based upon presumed evidence [LN]. It denotes criticism relating to questionable conduct [BDAG].

b. μέγας (LN 87.22) (BDAG 4.a. p. 624): 'great' [BDAG, LN; all translations except CEV], 'important' [LN], not explicit [CEV]. This adjective pertains to being great in terms of status [LN]. It pertains to being relatively superior in importance and refers to rational entities of God and other deities [BDAG].

c. aorist pass. infin. of λογίζομαι (LN 31.1) (BDAG 1.b. p. 597): 'to be considered' [BDAG, LN], 'to be regarded' [LN; NASB, NET], 'to be reckoned' [Bar, BECNT], 'to hold a view, to have an opinion' [LN], 'to evaluate, to estimate, to look upon as' [BDAG], 'to be counted' [ESV]. The phrase 'the temple...may be considered as nothing' is also translated 'They will stop respecting the temple' [CEV], 'people will think that the temple...is nothing' [GW], 'People will begin to think that the temple...is not important' [NCV], 'the temple...should be despised' [KJV], 'the temple...will come to mean nothing' [TEV], 'the sanctuary...will cease to command respect' [CBC], 'the shrine...will be despised' [AB], 'the temple...will be discredited' [NIV], 'the temple...will lose its influence' [NLT], 'the temple...will be scorned' [NRSV], 'the sanctuary...will cease to command respect' [REB]. This verb means to hold a view or have an opinion with regard to something [LN].

d. οὐδείς (LN 92.23) (BDAG 2.b.β. p. 735): 'nothing' [Bar, BECNT, LN; ESV, GW, NET, TEV], 'worthless' [BDAG; NASB], 'not important' [NCV], 'meaningless, invalid' [BDAG]. The phrase 'the temple...may be considered as nothing' is also translated 'the shrine...will be despised' [AB], 'the temple...will be discredited' [NIV], 'They will stop respecting the temple' [CEV], 'the temple...will lose its influence' [NLT], 'the temple...should be despised' [KJV], 'the sanctuary...will cease to command respect' [CBC; REB], 'the temple...will be scorned' [NRSV]. This adjective pertains to a negative reference to an entity, event, or state [LN].

e. pres. pass. infin. of καθαιρέω (LN 13.38) (BDAG 2.b. p. 488): 'to be deposed' [AB, BECNT; ESV], 'to be dethroned' [NASB], 'to be destroyed' [BDAG; KJV, NCV, TEV], 'to be robbed' [GW, NIV, NLT], 'to be deprived' [NRSV], 'to be cast/brought down' [Bar, CBC; REB], 'to be done away with, to be removed, to be eliminated' [LN], 'to be torn down, to be overpowered' [BDAG]. This verb is also translated as a noun: 'suffer the loss' [NET]. The phrase 'she may even be deposed from her magnificence' is also translated 'Our great goddess will be forgotten'

[CEV]. This verb means to cause a state to cease [LN]. It means figuratively to destroy by tearing down [BDAG].
   f. μεγαλειότης (LN 87.21) (BDAG 1. p. 622): 'magnificence' [BECNT; ESV, KJV, NASB], 'greatness' [Bar, LN; NCV, NET, TEV], 'majesty' [BDAG; NRSV], 'prominence, importance' [LN], 'esteem, grandeur, sublimity' [BDAG], 'glory' [GW], not explicit [CEV]. This noun is also translated 'divine majesty/pre-eminence' [CBC; NIV, REB], 'great prestige' [NLT], 'place of high honor' [AB]. This noun denotes a state of greatness or importance [LN]. It denotes the quality or state of being foremost in esteem [BDAG].
   g. pres. mid. indic. of σέβω (LN 53.53) (BDAG 1.b. p. 918): 'to worship' [BDAG, LN; all translations except AB], 'to honor' [AB], 'to venerate' [LN]. This verb means to express in attitude and ritual one's allegiance to and regard for deity [LN]. It means to express in gestures, rites, or ceremonies one's allegiance or devotion to deity [BDAG].

**DISCOURSE UNIT—19:28–34** [NAC]. The topic is uproar in the theater.

**19:28** When they heard this they became full of-anger[a] and began crying-out,[b] saying, "Great[c] (is)-Artemis of-(the)-Ephesians!"
LEXICON—a. θυμός (LN 88.178) (BDAG 2. p. 461): 'anger' [BDAG, LN; NLT], 'fury' [CBC, LN], 'wrath' [BDAG; KJV], 'rage' [AB, Bar, BDAG, BECNT, LN; NASB], 'indignation' [BDAG]. This noun is also translated as an adjective: 'they were enraged' [ESV, NRSV, REB], 'they were furious' [NIV], 'they got angry' [CEV], 'they became very angry' [NCV], 'they became furious/enraged' [GW, NET, TEV]. This noun denotes a state of intense anger, with the implication of passionate outbursts [LN]. It denotes a state of intense displeasure [BDAG].
   b. imperf. act. indic. of κράζω (LN 33.83): 'to cry out' [BECNT; ESV, KJV, NASB], 'to shout' [AB, Bar, CBC, LN; all versions except ESV, KJV, NASB], 'to scream' [LN]. This verb means to shout or cry out, with the possible implication of the unpleasant nature of the sound [LN].
   c. μέγας (LN 87.22): 'great' [LN; all translations], 'important' [LN]. This adjective pertains to being great in terms of status [LN].
QUESTION—To whom does 'they' refer?
   It refers to the craftsmen [Bar, EBC, NAC, NICNT, PNTC, TNTC, TRT]. It refers to the people in the city [BECNT].

**19:29** So the city was-filled[a] with-confusion,[b] and they-rushed[c] together into the theater,[d] dragging[e] with them Gaius and Aristarchus, Macedonians who were Paul's travelling-companions.
LEXICON—a. aorist pass. indic. of πίμπλημι (LN 59.38) (BDAG 1.a.α. p. 813): 'to be filled' [AB, Bar, BDAG, BECNT; ESV, KJV, NASB, NET, NLT, NRSV], 'to be filled completely, to be filled up' [LN]. The phrase 'the city was filled with confusion' is also translated 'the whole city was in a riot' [CEV], 'the whole city was in confusion' [CBC], 'the whole city

was in an uproar' [NIV, REB], 'the confusion spread throughout the city' [GW], 'The uproar spread throughout the whole city' [TEV], 'The whole city became confused' [NCV]. This verb means to cause something to be completely full [BDAG, LN].

b. σύγχυσις (LN 39.43) (BDAG p. 954): 'confusion' [AB, Bar, BDAG, BECNT, CBC; ESV, GW, KJV, NASB, NLT, NRSV], 'tumult' [BDAG], 'uproar' [LN; NET, NIV, REB, TEV], 'revolt' [LN], 'riot' [CEV]. This noun is also translated as an adjective: 'confused' [NCV]. This noun denotes disorderly mob revolt, with special implications of uproar and disturbance [LN].

c. aorist act. indic. of ὁρμάω (LN 15.222) (BDAG p. 724): 'to rush' [AB, Bar, BDAG, BECNT, LN; all versions except NCV, REB], 'to run' [LN; NCV]. This verb is also translated as a noun: 'concerted rush' [CBC; REB]. This verb means a fast movement from one place to another [LN]. It means to make a rapid movement from one place to another [BDAG].

d. θέατρον (LN 7.54) (BDAG 1. p. 446): 'theater [BDAG, LN; all translations except CEV, NLT], 'amphitheater' [NLT]. The phrase 'they rushed together into the theater is also translated 'everyone in the crowd rushed to the place where the town meetings were held' [CEV]. This noun denotes a rather large, normally semicircular open structure capable of seating several thousand people and often used for public assemblies [LN]. It denotes a place for public assemblies [BDAG].

e. aorist act. participle of συναρπάζω (LN 18.5) (BDAG p. 966): 'to drag' [AB, BECNT; ESV, NASB, NET, NLT, NRSV], 'to grab' [CEV, GW, NCV, TEV], 'to seize' [Bar, BDAG, CBC, LN; NIV], 'to catch' [KJV], 'to take off with' [LN], 'to hustle along' [REB]. This verb means to seize or snatch by force and to take away with [LN]. It means to take hold of forcibly [BDAG].

QUESTION—What was the 'theater' used for?

It was the regular meeting place of the civic assembly which was held three times a month. It had seating for nearly 25,000 people [NICNT, PNTC]. Civic festivals and plays were also held here [PNTC].

**19:30** And (when) Paul wanted[a] to-go into the assembly,[b] the disciples would- not -let[c] him.

LEXICON—a. pres. mid./pass. (deponent = act.) participle of βούλομαι (LN 30.56) (BDAG 2.a.β. p. 182): 'to want' [AB, CBC; CEV, GW, NASB, NCV, NET, NIV, NLT, REB, TEV], 'to wish' [Bar; ESV, NRSV], 'to desire' [BECNT], 'to purpose' [LN], 'to plan, to intend' [BDAG, LN], 'to will' [BDAG]. The phrase 'Paul wanted to go into the assembly' is also translated 'Paul would have entered in unto the people' [KJV]. This verb means to think, with the purpose of planning or deciding on a course of action [LN]. It means to plan on a course of action [BDAG].

b. δῆμος (LN 11.78) (BDAG 2. p. 223): 'assembly' [AB, CBC, LN; NASB, REB], 'gathering' [LN], 'popular assembly' [BDAG], 'public assembly'

[NET], 'crowd' [BECNT; ESV, GW, NCV, NIV, NRSV, TEV], 'people' [Bar; CEV, KJV], not explicit [NLT]. This noun denotes a group of citizens assembled for socio-political activities [LN]. It denotes, in a Hellenistic city, a convocation of citizens called together for the purpose of transacting official business [BDAG].
   c. imperf. act. indic. of ἐάω (LN 13.138) (BDAG 1. p. 269): 'to let' [BDAG, BECNT, CBC, LN; all versions except KJV], 'to allow' [AB, LN], 'to permit' [Bar, BDAG, LN], 'to suffer' [KJV]. This verb means to allow someone to do something [BDAG, LN].

QUESTION—Why did Paul want to go into the assembly?
   Paul probably had hopes of reasoning with them [TH]. He believed that because of his Roman citizenship and his earlier successful appearances before government officials, he could quiet the mob, free his companions, and turn the whole affair to the advantage of the gospel [EBC].

**19:31** And also some of-the Asiarchs,[a] who were friends of his, sent[b] to him and were-urging-(him)[c] not to-venture[d] into the theater.

LEXICON—a. Ἀσιάρχης (LN 37.81) (BDAG p. 143): 'Asiarch' [AB, Bar, BDAG, BECNT; ESV, NASB], 'provincial authority' [LN; NET, TEV], 'local official' [LN; CEV], 'official' [GW]. This noun is also translated 'chief of Asia' [KJV], 'leader of Asia' [NCV], 'official of the province' [NIV, NLT], 'dignitary of the province' [CBC; REB], 'official of the province of Asia' [NRSV]. This noun denotes a high-ranking official in Asia Minor (in an area which is now Turkey) [LN].
   b. aorist act. participle of πέμπω (LN 15.67) (BDAG 1. p. 794): 'to send' [BDAG; all translations], 'to send a message, to send word' [LN]. This verb means to send a message, presumably by someone [LN]. It means to dispatch someone, whether human or transcendent being, usually for purposes of communication [BDAG].
   c. imperf. act. indic. of παρακαλέω (LN 33.168) (BDAG 3. p. 765): 'to urge' [BECNT, CBC; ESV, GW, NET, NRSV, REB], 'to repeatedly urge' [NASB], 'to ask for (earnestly)' [LN], 'to request' [BDAG, LN], 'to plead for, to appeal to' [LN], 'to implore, to entreat' [BDAG], 'to beg' [Bar; NCV, NIV, NLT, TEV], 'to warn' [CEV], 'to ask' [AB], 'to desire' [KJV]. This verb means to ask for something earnestly and with propriety [LN]. It means to make a strong request for something [BDAG].
   d. aorist act. infin. of δίδωμι (LN 21.7) (BDAG 11. p. 243): 'to venture' [BECNT, CBC; ESV, NASB, NET, NIV, NRSV, REB], 'to go' [AB, Bar, BDAG; CEV, NCV], 'to venture somewhere' [BDAG], 'to adventure' [KJV], 'to risk' [LN; GW], 'to risk one's life' [LN; NLT]. The phrase 'were urging him not to venture' is also translated 'begging him not to show himself' [TEV]. The idiom literally 'to hand over life' means to expose oneself willingly to a danger or risk [LN]. It means to cause (oneself) to go [BDAG].

QUESTION—To whom does the term 'Asiarchs' refer?
It refers to people who were among the most outstanding individuals in the Roman province of Asia. The cities of Asia had formed a league, the main purpose of which was to foster the religion of the Roman Emperor and of the goddess Roma, and it was the duty of these men to encourage these functions [AB, EBC, TH]. These provincial authorities were usually elected from the wealthiest and most influential families of the province [AB, EBC, PNTC, TH]. It refers to members of a religious and political grouping of cities in Asia, and they belonged to the aristocracy [TNTC]. They were civic rulers or leading men of Ephesus from the upper class rather than merely cultic figures. They proposed motions to the civic council and distributed undertakings to them in line with the needs for the city's administration [BECNT]. They were representatives of the Asian cities who formed a council to maintain political links with Rome and especially to uphold the cult of Emperor worship [CBC].

**19:32** **Now some shouted-out one thing, some another, for the assembly was-in-confusion<sup>a</sup> and the majority did- not -know why they-had-come-together.<sup>b</sup>**

LEXICON—a. perf. pass. participle of συγχέω (LN 25.221): 'to be in confusion' [CBC; ESV, NASB, NET, NIV, NLT, NRSV], 'to be in chaos' [BECNT], 'to experience consternation, to be confounded' [LN], 'to be confused' [Bar; CEV, GW, KJV, NCV], 'to be in an uproar' [REB, TEV]. This verb is also translated as an adjective: 'confused assembly' [AB]. This verb means to cause such astonishment as to bewilder and dismay [LN].

b. pluperfect act. indic. of συνέρχομαι (LN 15.123) (BDAG 1. p. 969): 'to come together' [Bar, BECNT, LN; ESV, GW, KJV, NASB, NCV, NRSV, TEV], 'to gather together, to go together, to meet' [LN], 'to meet together' [NET], 'to assemble' [BDAG, LN], 'to gather' [BDAG]. This verb is also translated as a passive verb: 'they were gathered' [AB]. The phrase 'the majority did not know why they had come together' is also translated 'most of them/the-people did not even know why they were there' [CEV, NIV, NLT], 'most of them did not know what they had all come for' [CBC; REB]. This verb means the movement of two or more objects to the same location [LN]. It means to come together with others as a group [BDAG].

**19:33** **Some of the crowd<sup>a</sup> prompted<sup>b</sup> Alexander, whom the Jews had-put-forward.<sup>c</sup> And Alexander, having-motioned<sup>d</sup> with his hand, wanted to-make-a-defense<sup>e</sup> to-the assembly.**

TEXT—Manuscripts reading συνεβίβασαν Ἀλέξανδρον 'prompted Alexander' are given a B rating by GNT to indicate it was regarded to be almost certain. A variant reading is προεβίβασαν Ἀλέξανδρον 'drew Alexander out (of the multitude)' and it is followed by KJV.

LEXICON—a. ὄχλος (LN 11.1): 'crowd' [AB, Bar, BECNT, CBC, LN; ESV, NASB, NET, NIV, NLT, NRSV, REB], 'multitude' [LN; KJV], 'people' [GW, NCV, TEV], 'Jewish leaders' [CEV]. This noun denotes a casual non-membership group of people, fairly large in size and assembled for whatever purpose [LN].
   b. aorist act. indic. of συμβιβάζω (LN 30.82, 33.298) (BDAG 4. p. 957): 'to prompt' [BECNT; ESV], 'to instruct' [Bar, BDAG, LN (33.298)], 'to advise' [BDAG, LN (33.298)], 'to teach' [BDAG], 'to conclude' [LN (30.82); GW, NASB, NET, TEV]. The phrase 'Some of the crowed prompted Alexander' is also translated 'Several of the Jewish leaders…started telling him what to say' [CEV], 'some of them told him what to do' [NCV], 'some of the crowd shouted instructions to him' [NIV], 'The Jews…told him to explain the situation' [NLT], 'Some of the crowd gave instructions to Alexander' [NRSV], 'some of the crowd explained the trouble to Alexander' [CBC; REB], 'Members of the crowd explained the matter to Alexander' [AB], 'they drew Alexander out' [KJV]. This verb means to advise by giving instructions [BDAG, LN].
   c. aorist act. participle of προβάλλω (LN 15.171) (BDAG 1. p. 865): 'to put forward' [Bar, BDAG, BECNT; ESV, KJV, NASB], 'to push forward' [AB; NLT, NRSV], 'to push to the front' [CBC; CEV, GW, NET, NIV, REB], 'to put in front' [NCV], 'to make go to the front' [TEV], 'to bring forward, to lead forth' [LN]. This verb means to lead or bring forward or forth [LN]. It means to cause to come forward [BDAG].
   d. aorist act. participle of κατασείω (LN 33.478) (BDAG 1. p. 526): 'to motion' [BECNT, CBC; all versions except KJV, NCV, NET], 'to beckon' [KJV], 'to make a sign, to give a signal' [LN], 'to shake' [BDAG], 'to wave' [BDAG; NCV], 'to gesture' [NET], 'to make a gesture' [AB, Bar]. This verb means to communicate by means of a sign or signal [LN]. It means to make rapid motions [BDAG].
   e. pres. mid./pass. (deponent = act.) infin. of ἀπολογέομαι (LN 33.435) (BDAG p. 117): 'to make a defense' [Bar, BECNT, CBC; ESV, KJV, NASB, NET, NIV, NRSV, REB], 'to defend oneself' [BDAG, LN; GW]. The phrase 'Alexander,…,wanting to make a defense' is also translated 'He…tried to explain what was going on' [CEV], 'he tried to make a speech of defense' [TEV], 'Alexander…tried to offer a plea' [AB], 'Alexander waved his hand so he could explain things' [NCV], 'He…tried to speak' [NLT]. This verb means to speak on behalf of oneself or of others against accusations presumed to be false [LN]. It means to speak in one's own defense against charges presumed to be false [BDAG].

QUESTION—Why did the Jews push Alexander, one of their own, forward to make a defense?

   Possibly because they were not always differentiated from the Christians, who had provoked the mob, or because they were known to be opposed to idolatry and were generally unpopular [Bar]. Possibly the Jews pushed him to the front to explain that they had nothing to do with Paul or the Christians

[CBC, EBC, NAC, NICNT, TNTC]. Perhaps the Jews intended that their representative should make clear the difference between themselves and the Christians. Jews were known to be opposed to idolatry and were unpopular in the Roman empire [PNTC].

**19:34** But when they recognized[a] that he-was (a)-Jew, for about two hours they all cried-out[b] with one voice, "Great[c] (is)-Artemis of-(the)-Ephesians!"
LEXICON—a. aorist act. participle of ἐπιγινώσκω (LN 27.61) (BDAG 1.b. p. 369): 'to recognize' [Bar, BECNT, CBC, LN; ESV, GW, NASB, NET, NRSV, REB, TEV], 'to realize' [AB; NIV, NLT], 'to know' [BDAG; KJV]. The phrase 'when they recognized' is also translated 'when the-crowd/they saw' [CEV, NCV]. This verb means to identify newly acquired information with what had been previously learned or known [LN]. It means to have knowledge of something or someone [BDAG].
  b. pres. act. participle of κράζω (LN 33.83) (BDAG 2.a. p. 563): 'to cry out' [BECNT; ESV, KJV], 'to shout' [LN; all translations except BECNT; ESV, KJV, REB], 'to scream' [LN], 'to call, to call out, to cry' [BDAG]. The phrase 'they all cried out with one voice' is also translated 'one shout arose from them all' [REB]. This verb means to shout or cry out, with the possible implication of the unpleasant nature of the sound [LN]. It means to communicate something in a loud voice [BDAG].
  c. μέγας (LN 87.22) (BDAG 4.a. p. 624): 'great' [BDAG, LN; all translations], 'important' [LN]. This adjective pertains to being great in terms of status [LN]. It pertains to being relatively superior in importance and refers to rational entities of God and other deities [BDAG].
QUESTION—To whom does 'they' refer?
  It refers to the crowd in 19:33 [TH]. It refers to the Ephesians/Gentiles/non-Jews in the crowd [TRT].
QUESTION—Why didn't the Ephesians want to listen to Alexander?
  The reason the Ephesians would not listen to Alexander is probably that they saw no difference between the Jews and Christians, because both refused to worship Artemis [EBC, TRT]. Alexander probably wanted to tell the crowd/Ephesians that Paul was an enemy of the Jews too [TRT].

**DISCOURSE UNIT—19:35–41** [NAC]. The topic is pacification by the city clerk.

**19:35** And when the town-clerk[a] had-quieted[b] the crowd, he said, "Men of Ephesus, who is-there who does- not -know that the city of-(the)-Ephesians is guardian-of-the-temple[c] of-the great Artemis and of-the-(image) which fell-from-the-sky?
LEXICON—a. γραμματεύς (LN 37.94) (BDAG 1. p. 206): 'town clerk' [Bar, BECNT, CBC, LN; ESV, KJV, NASB, NRSV, REB], 'city clerk' [GW, NCV, NIV, TEV], 'city secretary' [NET], 'city scribe' [AB], 'town official' [CEV], 'town secretary' [LN], 'secretary (of state), clerk' [BDAG], 'mayor' [NLT]. This noun denotes a city official with

responsibility for the records of a town or city and apparently certain responsibilities for maintaining law and order [LN]. It denotes a chief executive officer of a governmental entity [BDAG].
   b. aorist act. participle of καταστέλλω (LN 37.31) (BDAG p. 527): 'to quiet' [AB, BDAG, BECNT, CBC; ESV, GW, NASB, NET, NIV, NLT, NRSV, REB], 'to restrain' [BDAG], 'to calm' [TEV], 'to still' [Bar], 'to subject to, to bring under control' [LN], 'to appease' [KJV]. The phrase 'the town clerk had quieted the crowd' is also translated 'a town official made the crowd be quiet' [CEV], 'the city clerk made the crowd be quiet' [NCV]. This verb means to bring something under the firm control of someone [LN].
   c. νεωκόρος (LN 53.95) (BDAG p. 670): 'guardian of the temple' [NASB, NIV, NLT], 'temple keeper' [BECNT, LN; ESV, NRSV], 'temple warden' [Bar, CBC; REB], 'keeper of the temple' [GW, NET, TEV], 'honorary temple keeper' [BDAG], 'guardian' [AB]. This noun is also translated as a verb: 'the city that keeps the temple' [NCV]. The phrase 'the city of the Ephesians is guardian of the temple' is also translated 'our city is the center for worshipping the great goddess Artemis' [CEV], 'the city of the Ephesians is a worshipper of the great goddess Diana' [KJV]. This noun denotes one who had responsibility to tend to and to guard a temple. In Acts 19:35 νεωκόρος is used in a somewhat figurative sense, since it is the city of Ephesus itself which is regarded as being the keeper of the temple [LN]. It denotes one who is responsible for the maintenance and security of a temple [BDAG].

QUESTION—What were the responsibilities of the town clerk?
   The town clerk is a keeper of records, registrar and accountant for temple funds. He is the highest civic official in the city, operating much like a powerful city manager [BECNT]. He serves as the liaison to Roman authorities [BECNT, NAC, NICNT]. He presides over both the council of city magistrates and the public assembly [NAC].

QUESTION—What is referred to by the phrase 'of the image which fell from the sky'?
   It refers to a stone, perhaps a fragment of a meteorite, which fell from heaven and which the people of Ephesus looked upon as being the sacred representation of their goddess Artemis [TH]. The Ephesians believed that their chief god Zeus threw the stone image of Artemis down to them. Artemis was a goddess who served under Zeus. Most Bible scholars think the Ephesians were worshiping a meteorite that had the shape of a woman with many breasts [TRT]. This will have been a meteorite and regarded as a divinely sent image [TNTC].

**19:36** Seeing then that these-things are undeniable,[a] you ought[b] to-be quiet[c] and do nothing rash.[d]
   LEXICON—a. ἀναντίρρητος (LN 33.458) (BDAG p. 69): 'undeniable' [BDAG; NASB, NIV, NLT], 'cannot be denied' [LN; ESV, NRSV],

'cannot be contradicted' [BECNT], 'cannot be spoken against' [KJV], 'without opposition, without objection' [LN], 'indisputable' [AB, LN; NET], 'beyond dispute' [CBC; REB], 'not to be contradicted' [BDAG], 'not open to contradiction' [Bar]. This adjective is also translated as a verb: 'No one can deny this' [CEV, GW], 'Nobody can deny these things' [TEV], 'no one can say this is not true' [NCV]. This adjective pertains to what cannot be spoken against or objected to [LN].
b. pres. act. participle of δεῖ (LN 71.34) (BDAG 2.a. p. 214): 'ought' [BECNT; ESV, KJV, NASB, NIV, NRSV], 'should' [AB; CEV, NCV, NLT], 'must' [Bar, LN; NET, TEV], 'have to' [GW], 'to be necessary' [LN]. The phrase 'you ought to be quiet' is also translated 'your proper course is to keep quiet/calm' [CBC; REB]. This verb means to be that which must necessarily take place, often with the implication of inevitability [LN]. It means to be something that should happen because of being fitting [BDAG].
c. perf. pass. participle of καταστέλλω (LN 37.31) (BDAG p. 527): 'to be quiet' [BDAG, BECNT; ESV, GW, KJV, NCV, NIV, NRSV], 'to keep quiet' [CBC; NET], 'to remain quiet' [Bar], 'to keep calm' [NASB, REB], 'to stay calm' [NLT], 'to remain calm' [AB], 'to be restrained' [BDAG], 'to be subject to, to bring under control' [LN]. This verb is also translated as an active verb: 'you should/must calm down' [CEV, TEV]. This verb means to bring something under the firm control of someone [LN].
d. προπετής (LN 88.98) (BDAG p. 873): 'rash' [AB, Bar, BDAG, BECNT, CBC; ESV, NASB, NIV, NLT, NRSV, REB], 'foolish' [CEV, GW], 'reckless' [BDAG, LN; NET, TEV], 'impetuous' [LN], 'thoughtless' [BDAG]. This adjective is also translated as an adverb: 'rashly' [KJV]. The phrase 'do nothing rash' is also translated 'Stop and think before you do anything' [NCV]. This adjective pertains to impetuous and reckless behavior [LN]. It pertains to being impetuous [BDAG].

**19:37** **For you- (have) -brought[a] these men-(here) who are neither temple-robbers[b] nor blaspheming[c] our goddess.**
TEXT—Manuscripts reading ἡμῶν 'our' are given a B rating by GNT to indicate it was regarded to be almost certain. A variant reading is ὑμῶν 'your' and it is followed by KJV.
LEXICON—a. aorist act. indic. of ἄγω (LN 15.165): 'to bring' [LN; all translations], 'to lead' [LN]. This verb means to direct or guide the movement of an object, without special regard to point of departure or goal [LN].
b. ἱερόσυλος (LN 57.242) (BDAG 1. p. 471): 'temple robber' [LN; NET, NRSV], 'robber of temples' [NASB], 'robber of churches' [KJV], 'sacrilegious' [BECNT; ESV]. This adjective is also translated as a verb: 'they have not robbed temples' [TEV], 'men...who have not robbed temples' [CEV], 'men...don't rob temples' [GW], 'they have not....stolen anything' [NCV], 'they have stolen nothing' [NLT], 'they have neither

robbed temples' [NIV], 'they have neither desecrated the temple' [AB]. This adjective is also translated as a noun: 'men…have committed no sacrilege' [CBC; REB], 'who are neither guilty of temple profanation' [Bar]. This adjective pertains to one who robs temples [LN]. It pertains to a temple robber [BDAG].
   c. pres. act. participle of βλασφημέω (LN 33.400) (BDAG b.α. p. 178): 'to blaspheme' [AB, LN; NIV], 'to revile, to defame' [BDAG, LN], 'to speak against' [CEV], 'to insult' [GW], 'to slander, to speak irreverently/impiously/disrespectfully of or about' [BDAG], 'to say anything evil against' [NCV], 'to speak against' [NLT], 'to say evil things about' [TEV]. This verb is also translated as a noun: 'blasphemer' [Bar, BECNT; ESV, KJV, NASB, NET, NRSV], 'uttered no blasphemy' [CBC; REB]. This verb means to speak against someone in such a way as to harm or injure his or her reputation, occurring in relation to persons as well as to divine beings [LN]. It means to speak in a disrespectful way that demeans, denigrates, maligns in relation to transcendent or associated entities [BDAG].

QUESTION—To whom does 'these men' refer?
   It refers to Gaius and Aristarchus in 19:29 [TH].

**19:38** If therefore Demetrius and the craftsmen with him have (a)-complaint[a] against anyone, the courts are-in-session,[b] and there-are proconsuls.[c] Let-them-bring-charges-against[d] one-another.

LEXICON—a. λόγος (LN 56.7) (BDAG 1.a.ε. p. 600): 'complaint' [BECNT; ESV, NASB, NET, NRSV], 'legal complaint' [GW], 'case' [AB, CBC; CEV, NLT, REB], 'charge' [LN; NCV], 'accusation' [LN; TEV], 'declaration of wrongdoing' [LN], 'suit' [Bar], 'grievance' [NIV], 'word' [BDAG], 'matter' [KJV]. This noun denotes a formal declaration of charges against someone in court [LN]. It denotes a communication whereby the mind finds expression [BDAG].
   b. pres. pass. indic. of ἄγω (LN 42.1) (BDAG 4. p. 17): 'to be in session' [NASB, NLT], 'to be open' [BECNT; ESV, KJV, NET, NIV, NRSV], 'to be held' [Bar, CBC], 'to carry on, to function, to be operative' [LN], 'to spend, to observe' [BDAG], 'to hold court' [GW], not explicit [CEV, NCV, REB, TEV]. The phrase 'the courts are in session' is also translated 'there are court sittings' [AB]. This verb means to be actively performing some function [LN]. It means to make use of time for a specific purpose [BDAG].
   c. ἀνθύπατος (LN 37.82) (BDAG p. 82): 'proconsul' [AB, Bar, BDAG, BECNT, CBC, LN; ESV, NASB, NET, NIV, NRSV, REB], 'judge' [CEV, NCV], 'official' [GW, NLT], 'deputy' [KJV], 'important official' [LN], 'authority' [TEV]. This noun denotes an official ruling over a province traditionally under the control of the Roman senate [LN]. It denotes the head of the government in a senatorial province [BDAG].

d. pres. act. impera. of ἐγκαλέω (LN 33.427) (BDAG p. 273): 'to bring charges against' [BECNT; ESV, GW, NASB, NET, NRSV], 'to bring actions against' [AB], 'to accuse' [Bar, BDAG, LN], 'to bring charges' [LN], 'to bring charges and countercharges' [CBC; REB], 'to press charges' [NIV], 'to make formal charges' [NLT], not explicit [NCV]. The phrase 'Let them bring charges against one another' is also translated 'Let them take their complaints there' [CEV], 'let them implead one another' [KJV], 'charges can be made there' [TEV]. This verb means to bring serious charges or accusations against someone, with the possible connotation of a legal or court context [LN]. It means to bring charges against [BDAG].

**19:39** **But if you-seek[a] anything further, it-shall-be-settled[b] in the lawful[c] assembly.**

TEXT—Manuscripts reading τι περαιτέρω 'anything further' are given a B rating by GNT to indicate it was regarded to be almost certain. A variant reading is περὶ ἑτέρων 'anything about other matters' and it is followed by KJV, NLT.

LEXICON—a. pres. act. indic. of ἐπιζητέω (LN 25.9) (BDAG 1.b. p. 371): 'to seek' [AB, Bar, BECNT; ESV], 'to seek after' [BDAG], 'to want' [GW, NASB, NCV, NET, NIV, NRSV, TEV], 'to desire' [LN], 'to want to' [LN], 'to want to do' [CEV], 'to inquire' [KJV], not explicit [CBC; NLT, REB]. This verb means to desire to have or experience something, with the probable implication of making an attempt to realize one's desire [LN]. It means to inquire, want to know [BDAG].

b. fut. pass. indic. of ἐπιλύω (LN 30.81) (BDAG 2. p. 375): 'to be settled' [AB, BDAG, BECNT, LN; ESV, NASB, NET, NIV, NLT, NRSV, TEV], 'to be determined' [KJV], 'to be decided' [BDAG; NCV], 'to be dealt with' [Bar, CBC; REB], 'to be resolved' [BDAG, LN], 'to come to a decision' [LN], not explicit [CEV]. This verb is also translated as an active verb: 'you must settle the matter' [GW]. This verb means to come to a conclusion concerning a presumably difficult or complex matter [LN]. It means to come to a conclusion about a difficult matter [BDAG].

c. ἔννομος (LN 33.336) (BDAG p. 337): 'lawful' [AB, Bar, BDAG; KJV, NASB], 'legal' [BDAG, LN; GW, NET, NIV, NLT, TEV], 'statutory' [CBC; REB], 'in accordance with law' [LN], 'regular' [BECNT; ESV, NCV, NRSV], not explicit [CEV]. This adjective pertains to being in accordance with law [BDAG, LN].

QUESTION—What does 'the lawful assembly' refer to?

It refers to the official public gatherings of the citizens of Ephesus; it would have been presided over by the city clerk. The Roman government allowed certain cities to have freedom of government, so long as they were obedient to the Roman authority [TH].

**19:40** For we- really -are-in-danger[a] of being-charged-with[b] an-uprising[c] in connection with today. There is no real reason[d] (for it) and there is no account[e] that we can give concerning this commotion.[f]"

LEXICON—a. pres. act. indic. of κινδυνεύω (LN 21.6) (BDAG p. 544): 'to be in danger' [AB, BDAG; ESV, KJV, NASB, NET, NIV, NLT, NRSV], 'to run a risk' [Bar, BDAG, CBC, LN; GW, REB], 'to risk' [BECNT], not explicit [CEV, NCV]. The phrase 'we really are in danger of being charged' is also translated 'there is the danger that we will be accused' [TEV]. This verb means to expose oneself to danger [LN].

b. pres. pass. infin. of ἐγκαλέω (LN 33.427) (BDAG p. 273): 'to be charged' [BECNT, CBC; ESV, NET, NIV, NLT, NRSV, REB], 'to be accused' [AB, Bar, BDAG, LN; CEV, GW, NASB, TEV], 'to bring charges' [LN], 'to be called in question' [KJV], not explicit [NCV]. This verb means to bring serious charges or accusations against someone, with the possible connotation of a legal or court context [LN]. It means to bring charges against [BDAG].

c. στάσις (LN 39.34) (BDAG 2. p. 940): 'uprising' [BDAG] 'riot' [Bar, BDAG, CBC; CEV, NASB, REB, TEV], 'revolt, rebellion' [BDAG, LN], 'uproar' [KJV], 'insurrection' [LN]. This noun is also translated as a verb: 'to riot' [AB, BECNT; ESV, GW, NCV, NET, NIV, NLT, NRSV]. This noun denotes the action of rising up in open defiance of authority, with the presumed intention to overthrow it or to act in complete opposition to its demands [LN]. It denotes the movement toward a (new) state of affairs [BDAG].

d. αἴτιος (LN 89.15) (BDAG 1.b. p. 31): 'reason' [AB, BDAG, LN; GW, NCV, NIV], 'cause' [Bar, BDAG, LN; KJV, NASB, NLT], 'justification' [CBC; REB], 'excuse' [CEV, TEV], 'source' [LN], not explicit [BECNT; ESV, NET, NRSV]. This adjective pertains to the reason or cause for an event or state [LN]. It pertains to being the cause of something [BDAG].

e. λόγος (LN 89.18) (BDAG 2.a. p. 600): 'account' [KJV], 'cause' [BECNT; ESV, NET, NRSV], 'reason' [Bar, LN; CEV, TEV], 'explanation' [CBC; REB], 'computation, reckoning' [BDAG], not explicit [NLT]. This noun is also translated as a verb: 'to account' [AB; NASB, NIV], 'to explain' [GW, NCV]. This noun denotes a reason, with the implication of some verbal formulation [LN]. This noun denotes a formal accounting especially of one's actions [BDAG].

f. συστροφή (LN 39.43) (BDAG 1. p. 979): 'commotion' [BDAG, BECNT; ESV, NIV, NLT, NRSV], 'uproar' [CBC, LN; CEV, TEV], 'revolt' [LN], 'turmoil' [REB], 'disorderly gathering' [BDAG; NASB, NET], 'seditious gathering' [BDAG], 'mob' [GW], 'crowd' [AB], 'concourse' [KJV], 'meeting' [Bar; NCV]. This noun denotes a disorderly mob revolt, with special implications of uproar and disturbance [LN]. It denotes a tumultuous gathering of people [BDAG].

QUESTION—What was the town clerk afraid would happen?
He was afraid that the right of self-government may be taken away from the city if there is a riot which they cannot explain or defend to the Roman authorities [AB, BECNT, PNTC, TH, TRT].

**19:41** **And when he had-said these-things, he-dismissed**[a] **the assembly.**
LEXICON—a. aorist act. indic. of ἀπολύω (LN 15.43) (BDAG 3. p. 117): 'to dismiss' [BDAG, LN; all translations except CEV, NCV], 'to let go away' [LN], 'to let go, to send away' [BDAG]. The phrase 'he dismissed the assembly' is also translated 'he told the people to leave' [CEV], 'he told the people to go home' [NCV]. This verb means to cause or permit a person or persons to leave a particular location [BDAG, LN].

**DISCOURSE UNIT—20:1–21:16** [NAC]. The topic is Paul's journey to Jerusalem.

**DISCOURSE UNIT—20:1–16** [AB, Bar, BECNT, CBC, TNTC]. The topic is Paul's journey from Ephesus to Miletus [TNTC], from Macedonia and Greece back to Miletus [BECNT], from Ephesus to Greece and back to Miletus [CBC], back to Palestine, through Macedonia, Greece, and Troas [Bar], the beginning of Paul's slow journey to Rome [AB].

**DISCOURSE UNIT—20:1–12** [PNTC; NASB, NET]. The topic is Paul in Macedonia and Greece [NASB], Paul travels through Macedonia and Greece [NET], encouraging the churches in Macedonia, Greece, and Troas [PNTC].

**DISCOURSE UNIT—20:1–6** [EBC, NAC, NICNT; CEV, ESV, NCV, NIV, NLT, NRSV, TEV]. The topic is Paul in Macedonia and Greece [ESV, NCV], Paul goes through Macedonia and Greece [CEV], Paul goes to Macedonia and Greece [NLT, NRSV], Paul visits Macedonia and Greece [NICNT], through Macedonia and Greece [NIV], to Macedonia and Achaia [TEV], a return visit to Macedonia and Achaia [EBC], final ministry in Macedonia and Achaia [NAC].

**20:1** **After the uproar**[a] **had-ceased,**[b] **Paul sent-for**[c] **the disciples, and after encouraging-(them),**[d] **he said-goodbye and departed**[e] **to-go to Macedonia.**
LEXICON—a. θόρυβος (LN 14.79) (BDAG 3.b. p. 458): 'uproar' [AB, Bar, BDAG, BECNT; ESV, GW, KJV, NASB, NIV, NLT, NRSV, TEV], 'riot' [CEV], 'clamor, noise' [LN], 'turmoil, excitement' [BDAG], 'trouble' [NCV], 'disturbance' [CBC; NET, REB]. This noun denotes a noise or clamor marked by confusion [LN]. It denotes a state or condition of varying degrees of commotion and refers to the noise and confusion of excited crowds [BDAG].
   b. aorist mid. infin. of παύω (LN 68.34) (BDAG 2. p. 790): 'to cease' [Bar, BDAG, BECNT, CBC, LN; ESV, KJV, NASB, NRSV], 'to stop' [BDAG, LN; NCV], 'to end' [NET, NIV], 'to die down' [AB; TEV]. The phrase 'After the uproar had ceased' is also translated 'When the riot/uproar/disturbance was over' [CEV, GW, NLT, REB]. This verb

means to cease from an activity in which one is engaged [LN]. It means to cease doing something and refers to an uproar [BDAG].
  c. aorist mid. participle of μεταπέμπω (LN 15.73) (BDAG p. 641): 'to send for' [BDAG, LN; all translations except KJV, TEV], 'to summon' [BDAG, LN], 'to call unto' [KJV], 'to call together' [TEV]. This verb means to send someone to obtain something or someone [LN].
  d. aorist act. participle of παρακαλέω (LN 25.150) (BDAG 2. p. 765): 'to encourage' [AB, BDAG, CBC, LN; all versions except KJV, NASB, TEV], 'to exhort' [BDAG, BECNT; NASB], 'to appeal to, to urge' [BDAG], 'to console' [LN], 'to embrace' [KJV]. This verb is also translated as a noun: 'encouragement' [TEV], 'gave them an exhortation' [Bar]. This verb means to cause someone to be encouraged or consoled, either by verbal or non-verbal means [LN]. It means to urge strongly [BDAG].
  e. aorist act. indic. of ἐξέρχομαι (LN 15.40) (BDAG 1.a.α.ℸ. p. 348): 'to depart' [ESV, KJV], 'to leave' [CEV, GW, NCV, NET, NLT, NRSV, TEV], 'to set out' [AB, Bar, CBC; NIV, REB], 'to take leave' [BECNT; NASB], 'to go out of, to depart out of, to leave from within' [LN], 'to go out, to come out, to go away' [BDAG]. This verb means to move out of an enclosed or well defined two or three-dimensional area [LN]. It means to move out of or away from an area of humans [BDAG].

**20:2** **When he had-gone-through**[a] **those regions**[b] **and had-encouraged**[c] **them with-many word(s), he-came**[d] **to Greece.**

LEXICON—a. aorist act. participle of διέρχομαι (LN 15.21) (BDAG 1.a. p. 244): 'to go through' [BDAG, BECNT; ESV, GW, NASB, NET, NRSV, TEV], 'to travel through' [AB, CBC; NIV, REB], 'to pass through' [Bar; NLT], 'to travel around through, to journey all through' [LN], 'to go over' [KJV], 'to travel from place to place' [CEV]. The phrase 'When he had gone through' is also translated 'on his way through' [NCV]. This verb means to travel around through an area, with the implication of both extensive and thorough movement throughout an area [LN]. It means to move within or through an area [BDAG].
  b. μέρος (LN 1.79) (BDAG 1.b.γ. p. 633): 'region' [AB, LN; ESV, GW, NET, NRSV, REB, TEV], 'district' [NASB], 'territory, land' [LN], 'area' [NIV], 'town' [NLT], 'place' [NCV], 'part' [Bar, BDAG, BECNT, CBC; KJV]. The phrase 'he had gone through those regions' is also translated 'he traveled from place to place' [CEV]. This noun denotes a region or regions of the earth, normally in relation to some ethnic group or geographical center, but not necessarily constituting a unit of governmental administration [LN].
  c. aorist act. participle of παρακαλέω (LN 25.150) (BDAG 2. p. 765): 'to encourage' [BDAG, BECNT, LN; CEV, GW, NLT, REB, TEV], 'to console' [LN], 'to exhort' [AB, Bar, BDAG], 'to appeal to, to urge' [BDAG]. This verb is also translated as a noun: 'encouragement' [CBC;

ESV, NET, NIV, NRSV], 'exhortation' [KJV, NASB]. The phrase 'he...had encouraged them with many words' is also translated 'He said many things to strengthen the followers' [NCV]. This verb means to cause someone to be encouraged or consoled, either by verbal or non-verbal means [LN]. It means to urge strongly [BDAG].
   d. aorist act. indic. of ἔρχομαι (LN 15.81): 'to come' [AB, Bar, BECNT, CBC, LN; ESV, KJV, NASB, NET, NRSV, TEV], 'to go' [CEV, GW, NCV], 'to travel' [NLT], 'to arrive' [NIV], 'to reach' [REB]. This verb means to move toward or up to the reference point of the viewpoint character or event [LN].
QUESTION—What does the phrase 'those regions' refer to?
   'Those regions' refers back to the territory of Macedonia in 20:1 [Bar, BECNT, TH] and would probably have included the communities of Philippi, Thessalonica, and Berea [BECNT, TH].
QUESTION—To whom does 'them' refer?
   It refers to the believers in 'those regions' [BECNT, TH, TRT].

**DISCOURSE UNIT—20:3–12** [GW]. The topic is Paul in Troas.

**20:3** And there he spent three months, and when (a)-plot[a] was-made[b] against-him by the Jews as he was-about[c] to-set-sail[d] for Syria, he decided to-return[e] through Macedonia.
LEXICON—a. ἐπιβουλή (LN 30.71) (BDAG p. 368): 'plot' [AB, Bar, BDAG, BECNT, CBC, LN; ESV, NASB, NET, NIV, NLT, NRSV, REB], 'plan, scheme' [LN]. This noun is also translated as a verb: 'leaders plotted against him' [CEV], 'the Jews were plotting to kill him' [GW], 'Jews plotting against him' [TEV]. The phrase 'a plot was made against him by the Jews' is also translated 'the Jews laid wait for him' [KJV], 'some Jews were planning something against him' [NCV]. This noun denotes a plan for treacherous activity against someone [LN]. It denotes a secret plan to do something evil or cause harm [BDAG].
   b. aorist mid. (deponent = act.) participle of γίνομαι (LN 13.80) (BDAG 7. p. 199): 'to be made' [Bar, BECNT; ESV, NRSV], 'to be formed' [AB, LN; NASB], 'to be laid' [CBC; REB], 'to come to exist' [LN], 'to be, to prove to be, to turn out to be' [BDAG], not explicit [CEV, GW, KJV, NCV, NLT, TEV]. This passive verb is also translated as active: 'the Jews had-made/made a plot' [NET, NIV]. This verb means to come into existence [LN]. It means to come into a certain state or possess certain characteristics [BDAG].
   c. pres. act. participle of μέλλω (LN 67.62) (BDAG 1.c.γ. p. 628): 'to be about to' [Bar, BDAG, BECNT, LN; CEV, ESV, KJV, NASB, NIV, NRSV], 'to be going to' [GW], 'to be intending to' [NET], 'to intend to' [AB]. The phrase 'he was about to set sail for Syria' is also translated 'He was ready to sail for Syria' [NCV], 'He was preparing to sail...to Syria' [NLT], 'He was getting ready to go to Syria' [TEV], 'he...was on the point of embarking for Syria' [CBC; REB]. This verb means to occur at a

point of time in the future which is subsequent to another event [BDAG, LN] and closely related to it [LN]. Here it denotes an intended action [BDAG].
  d. pres. pass. infin. of ἀνάγω (LN 54.4) (BDAG 4. p. 62): 'to set sail' [BECNT, LN; ESV, NASB, NRSV], 'to sail' [AB; CEV, KJV, NCV, NET, NIV, NLT], 'to put out to sea' [BDAG, LN], 'to embark' [CBC; REB], 'to go' [TEV], 'to leave' [Bar]. The phrase 'to set sail for Syria' is also translated 'to board a ship for Syria' [GW]. This verb means to begin to go by boat [BDAG, LN].
  e. pres. act. infin. of ὑποστρέφω (LN 15.88) (BDAG p. 1041): 'to return' [AB, Bar, BDAG, BECNT, CBC, LN; CEV, ESV, KJV, NASB, NET, NLT, NRSV, REB], 'to go back' [LN; GW, NCV, NIV, TEV], 'to come back' [LN], 'to turn back' [BDAG]. This verb means to move back to a point from which one has previously departed [LN].

**20:4** And he was-accompanied[a] by Sopater (the)-Berean, (the son)-of-Pyrrhus; and of-(the)-Thessalonians, Aristarchus and Secundus; and Gaius of-Derbe, and Timothy; and (the)-Asians, Tychicus and Trophimus.

TEXT—Some manuscripts add ἄχρι τῆς Ἀσίας 'as far as Asia' after 'accompanied' and this reading is followed by KJV. Manuscripts that do not add this phrase are given a B rating by GNT to indicate it was regarded to be almost certain.

TEXT—Manuscripts reading Πύρρου '(the son) of Pyrrhus' are given a B rating by GNT to indicate it was regarded to be almost certain. A variant reading that does not have this is followed by KJV.

LEXICON—a. imperf. mid./pass. (deponent = act.) indic. of συνέπομαι (LN 15.157) (BDAG p. 969): 'to be accompanied' [BDAG, CBC, LN; NASB, NET, NIV, NRSV, REB], 'to be followed' [LN], 'to be associated with' [Bar]. This passive verb is also translated as active: 'accompanied Paul/him' [BECNT; ESV, GW, KJV], 'went with him' [NCV, TEV], 'travelling with him' [NLT]. The phrase 'he was accompanied' is also translated 'with him were' [CEV], 'with him went' [AB]. This verb means to accompany someone, with explicit marking of association [LN].

QUESTION—What does the word 'accompanied' mean here?
  These men are probably traveling with Paul to Jerusalem as representatives of the churches in Macedonia and Achaia Provinces which had collected money to help the Christians in Jerusalem who were suffering from a famine [BECNT, NAC, PNTC, TRT]. Some of them go ahead to Troas, probably by sea, while Paul and some of the others join them there [BECNT].

**20:5** And these had-gone-ahead[a] and were-waiting[b] for-us at Troas,

LEXICON—a. aorist act. participle of προέρχομαι (LN 15.141) (BDAG 3. p. 868): 'to go ahead' [AB, BECNT, CBC; GW, NRSV, REB, TEV], 'to go on ahead' [Bar, BDAG; CEV, ESV, NASB, NCV, NET, NIV, NLT], 'to come/go prior to, to come/go beforehand, to precede' [LN], 'to go before' [BDAG; KJV], 'to come before, to go on before' [BDAG]. This verb

means to come/go prior to some other event, normally one involving a similar type of movement [LN]. It means to precede so as to be ahead [BDAG].
b. imperf. act, indic. of μένω (LN 85.60) (BDAG 3.a. p. 631): 'to wait' [all translations except KJV], 'to await, to wait for' [BDAG, LN], 'to tarry' [KJV]. This verb means to remain in a place and/or state, with expectancy concerning a future event [LN]. It means to wait for someone who is arriving [BDAG].

QUESTION—To whom does 'these' refer?
1. It may refer here to all seven of the men mentioned in verse 4 [TRT].
2. It may only refer to Tychicus and Trophimus [NAC, TNTC, TRT].

QUESTION—To whom does 'us' refer?
1. It may refer only to Luke and Paul [CBC, TH].
2. It may refer to an indefinite number of Christians from Philippi, among whom was included the author himself [TH].
3. It may be that only Tychicus and Trophimus went on ahead, since they were from Asia and were known by the churches there, and so 'us' would refer to the other persons listed as well as Luke [TH].
4. It may refer to Paul, Luke, Silas and Timothy [EBC].

**20:6** **but we sailed-away from Philippi after the days of-the Unleavened-Bread,**[a] **and in five days we-came to them at Troas, where we-stayed**[b] **seven days.**

LEXICON—a. ἄζυμος (LN 51.6) (BDAG 2. p. 23): 'Unleavened Bread' [BECNT; ESV, NASB, NET, NRSV], 'unleavened bread' [AB; KJV], 'festival of unleavened bread' [BDAG], 'Festival of Thin Bread' [CEV], 'Festival of Unleavened Bread' [GW, TEV], 'Feast of Unleavened Bread' [NCV, NIV], 'Unleavened Loaves' [Bar], 'Passover festival' [LN], 'Passover' [CBC, LN; NLT, REB]. This adjective describes the Jewish festival commemorating the deliverance of Jews from Egypt [LN].
b. aorist act. indic. of διατρίβω (LN 85.61) (BDAG p. 238): 'to stay' [LN; all translations except CBC; KJV, REB, TEV], 'to remain' [LN], 'to abide' [KJV], 'to spend time' [BDAG]. The phrase 'where we stayed seven days' is also translated 'where we spent a week' [CBC; REB, TEV]. This verb means to remain or stay in a place [BDAG, LN], with the implication of some type of activity [LN].

QUESTION—To whom does 'we sailed away' refer?
It refers to Paul and Luke [CBC, NICNT]. It refers to Paul, Luke, Silas and Timothy [EBC].

**DISCOURSE UNIT—20:7–21:16** [NICNT]. The topic is the journey to Jerusalem.

**DISCOURSE UNIT—20:7–16** [ESV]. The topic is Eutychus raised from the dead.

**DISCOURSE UNIT—20:7–12** [EBC, NAC, NICNT; CEV, NCV, NIV, NLT, NRSV, TEV]. The topic is Paul's last visit to Troas [CEV, NCV, TEV], Paul's final visit to Troas [NLT], Paul's farewell visit to Troas [NRSV], Paul at Troas [NICNT], Eutychus raised from the dead at Troas [NIV], the raising of Eutychus [EBC], restoration of Eutychus [NAC].

**20:7** On-the first-(day) of-the week, when we were-gathered-together[a] to-break[b] bread, Paul talked with-them, intending to-depart on-the next-day, and he prolonged[c] his message until midnight.

LEXICON—a. perf. pass. participle of συνάγω (LN 15.125) (BDAG 1.b. p. 962): 'to be gathered together' [BECNT, LN; ESV, NASB], 'to be gathered (in)' [BDAG], 'to be called together' [LN], 'to be assembled' [AB]. This passive verb is also translated as active: 'we gathered' [NLT, REB], 'we gathered together' [TEV], 'we had gathered' [Bar], 'we met' [CEV, GW, NET, NRSV], 'we all met together' [NCV], 'the disciples came together' [KJV], 'we came together' [NIV]. This verb is also translated as a noun: 'our assembly' [CBC]. This verb means to cause to come together, whether of animate or inanimate objects [LN]. It means to cause to come together of persons [BDAG].

b. aorist act. infin. of κλάω (LN 23.20) (BDAG p. 546): 'to break' [BDAG; all translations except NLT, TEV], 'to eat a meal, to have a meal' [LN]. The phrase 'to break bread' is also translated 'to share in the Lord's Supper' [NLT], 'for the fellowship meal' [TEV]. The idiom 'to break bread' means to eat a meal, without reference to any particular time of the day or to the type of food involved [LN]. This verb as used in the New Testament refers exclusively to breaking bread [BDAG].

c. imperf. act. indic. of παρατείνω (LN 67.120, 68.21) (BDAG p. 771): 'to prolong' [Bar, BDAG, BECNT, LN (67.120, 68.21); ESV, NASB], 'to extend' [BDAG; NET], 'to stretch out' [LN (68.21)], 'to keep on' [LN (68.21); NCV, NIV, TEV], 'to go on' [AB, CBC; REB], 'to continue' [KJV, NRSV], not explicit [CEV]. The phrase 'he prolonged his message until midnight' is also translated 'he kept talking until midnight' [GW, NLT]. This verb means to extend a period of time [LN (67.120)]. It means to cause an event to continue beyond an expected period of time [LN (68.21)].

QUESTION—What does 'the first day of the week' refer to?

1. This meeting would have taken place in the evening; and according to the Jewish calculation the first day of the week would have begun on Saturday evening and continued until Sunday at sunset [CBC, NAC, TH; REB, TEV].
2. The evening of the first day must have been Sunday night, since Luke seems to follow the Roman method of reckoning the beginning of the week [BECNT, NICNT, PNTC; GW].

QUESTION—What does the phrase 'to break bread' refer to?
It refers to the initiating of an ordinary meal [PNTC]. The breaking of the bread was probably a fellowship meal [Bar, BECNT, NICNT] in the course of which the Eucharist was celebrated [NICNT]. It refers to celebrating the Lord's Supper [EBC].

**20:8** (There)-were many lamps in the upper-room[a] where we-were gathered.
LEXICON—a. ὑπερῷον (LN 7.27) (BDAG p. 1034): 'upper room' [AB, Bar, CBC; ESV, NASB], 'upstairs room' [LN; CEV, GW, NET, NIV, NLT, REB, TEV], 'upper story' [BDAG], 'room upstairs' [BDAG; NCV, NRSV], 'upper chamber' [BECNT; KJV]. This noun denotes a room on the level above the ground floor (second story in American usage and first story in most other languages) [LN].
QUESTION—Why did Luke mention that there were many lamps in the upper room?
An explanation is that they emitted an odor which helped to cause Eutychus to fall asleep [EBC, NAC, NICNT, PNTC, TNTC].

**20:9** And a young-man named Eutychus, sitting on the window-(sill), sank[a] into (a)-deep sleep as Paul talked[b] still longer. And being-overcome[c] by sleep, he-fell down from the third-story and was-picked-up dead.
LEXICON—a. pres. pass. participle of καταφέρω (LN 23.68) (BDAG 3. p. 529): 'to sink' [BECNT; ESV, NASB, NET, NIV, NRSV], 'to fall' [NCV], 'to be fallen' [KJV], 'to be overcome' [Bar], 'to get sleepier, to become more and more sleepy' [LN]. The phrase 'sank into a deep sleep' is also translated 'got very sleepy' [CEV], 'became very drowsy' [AB; NLT], 'was gradually falling asleep' [GW], 'grew more and more sleepy/drowsy' [CBC; REB], 'got sleepier and sleepier' [TEV]. The idiom 'to be carried away by sleep' means to become increasingly more sleepy [LN]. It means to get into a state of being [BDAG].
b. pres. mid./pass. (deponent = act.) participle of διαλέγομαι (LN 33.26) (BDAG 1. p. 232): 'to talk' [AB, BECNT, CBC; ESV, GW, NASB, NCV, NIV, NRSV, REB, TEV], 'to speak' [CEV, NET, NLT], 'to preach' [KJV], 'to address, to make a speech' [LN], 'to converse, to discuss, to argue' [BDAG], 'to discourse' [Bar]. This verb means to speak in a somewhat formal setting and probably implying a more formal use of language [LN]. It means to engage in speech interchange [BDAG].
c. aorist pass. participle of καταφέρω (LN 23.71) (BDAG 3. p. 529): 'to be overcome' [AB, Bar, BECNT, CBC; ESV, GW, NASB, NRSV, REB], 'to be sound asleep, to be completely asleep' [LN], 'to be brought into' [BDAG]. The phrase 'being overcome by sleep' is also translated 'sunk down with sleep' [KJV], 'went sound asleep' [NCV, TEV], 'fell sound asleep' [NLT], 'went to sleep' [CEV], 'fast/sound asleep' [NET, NIV]. The idiom 'to be carried away from sleep' means to be in a state of deep sleep [LN]. It means to get into a state of being [BDAG].

QUESTION—How old was Eutychus?
According to the classification of one ancient Greek writer, the word used in this verse would normally describe a man who was from 23 to 28 years old [TH]. This young man was probably around 14–25 years old [TRT]. However, the Greek word used in verse 12 suggests an even younger age, possibly 8–14 years old [BECNT, TH, TNTC, TRT]. Most Bible scholars think he was in his mid to late teens [TRT].

**20:10** But Paul went-down$^a$ and fell-upon$^b$ him, and having-embraced-(him),$^c$ he-said, "Do- not -be-troubled,$^d$ for his life is in him."

LEXICON—a. aorist act. participle of καταβαίνω (LN 15.107) (BDAG 1.a.α. p. 514): 'to go down' [BDAG, LN; all translations except GW], 'to come down' [BDAG, LN], 'to move down, to descend' [LN], 'to climb down' [BDAG], not explicit [GW]. This verb means to move down, irrespective of the gradient [LN]. It means to move downward with the indication of the place from which one comes or goes down [BDAG].

b. aorist act. indic. of ἐπιπίπτω (LN 19.43) (BDAG 1.b. p. 377): 'to fall upon' [NASB], 'to fall on' [Bar, BDAG; KJV], 'to press against, to push against' [LN], 'to press' [BDAG], 'to bend over' [BECNT; CEV, ESV, NLT, NRSV], 'to kneel down' [NCV], not explicit [GW]. The phrase 'Paul…fell upon him' is also translated 'Paul…threw himself on the young man' [NET, NIV], 'Paul…threw himself on him' [TEV], 'Paul…threw himself upon him' [AB, CBC; REB]. This verb means to press or push against [LN]. It means to cause pressure by pushing against or falling on [BDAG].

c. aorist act. participle of συμπεριλαμβάνω (LN 34.65) (BDAG p. 959): 'to embrace' [Bar, BDAG, BECNT, LN; KJV, NASB], 'to hug' [LN; TEV]. The phrase 'Paul…having embraced him' is also translated 'Paul…taking him in his arms' [ESV], 'Paul…took him into/in his arms' [GW, NLT, NRSV], 'He took him in his arms' [CEV], 'he had put his arms around him' [AB], 'Paul…clasped him in his arms' [REB], 'Paul…seizing him in his arms' [CBC], 'Paul…put his arms around him' [NCV, NET, NIV]. This verb means to embrace, as an expression of great concern for someone [LN]. It means to throw one's arms around [BDAG].

d. pres. pass. impera. of θορυβέω (LN 25.234) (BDAG 2. p. 458): 'to be troubled' [LN; KJV, NASB], 'to be distressed' [LN; NET], 'to be upset' [LN], 'to be disturbed, to be agitated' [BDAG], 'to be alarmed' [AB, BECNT; ESV, NIV, NRSV], 'to be worried' [CEV, GW, NCV, NLT, TEV]. This passive verb is also translated as active: 'Do not distress yourselves' [REB]. The phrase 'Do not be troubled' is also translated 'Stop this commotion' [CBC], 'Stop making a disturbance' [Bar]. This verb means to be emotionally upset by a concern or anxiety [LN]. It means to cause emotional disturbance [BDAG].

**20:11** And when he had-gone-up[a] and had-broken[b] the bread and eaten, he talked (with them) (a)-long while, until daybreak, and so he-departed.[c]

LEXICON—a. aorist act. participle of ἀναβαίνω (LN 15.101) (BDAG 1.a.α. p. 58): 'to go up' [Bar, BECNT, LN; ESV, KJV], 'to come up, to ascend' [LN]. The phrase 'he had gone up' is also translated 'he had gone back up' [NASB], 'Paul had gone back upstairs' [CEV], 'Paul went back upstairs' [NET], 'he went back upstairs' [TEV], 'Paul went upstairs' [NCV, NRSV], 'Eutychus went upstairs' [GW], 'he...went upstairs' [AB, CBC; NIV, REB], 'they all went back upstairs' [NLT]. This verb means to move up [LN]. It means to be in motion upward of living beings [BDAG].

  b. aorist act. participle of κλάω (LN 23.20) (BDAG p. 546): 'to break' [BDAG; all translations except NLT], 'to eat a meal, to have a meal' [LN]. The phrase 'he...had broken the bread and eaten' is also translated 'they all...shared in the Lord's Supper' [NLT]. The idiom 'to break bread' means to eat a meal, without reference to any particular time of the day or to the type of food involved [LN].

  c. aorist act. indic. of ἐξέρχομαι (LN 15.40): 'to depart' [BECNT, CBC; ESV, KJV, REB], 'to leave' [AB, Bar; all versions except ESV, KJV, REB], 'to go out of, to depart out of, to leave from within' [LN]. This verb means to move out of an enclosed or well defined two or three-dimensional area [LN].

QUESTION—To whom does 'he' refer?

1. It refers to Paul [Bar, BECNT, EBC, NAC, NICNT, PNTC, TH, TRT; CEV, ESV, NCV, NET, NRSV].
2. It refers to Eutychus [GW].

**20:12** And they-took- the young-man -away[a] alive,[b] and were- greatly -comforted.[c]

LEXICON—a. aorist act. indic. of ἄγω (LN 15.165) (BDAG 1.a. p. 16): 'to take away' [BECNT, CBC; ESV, NASB, NRSV], 'to lead' [BDAG], 'to bring' [BDAG, LN; KJV], 'to lead off, to lead away' [BDAG]. The phrase 'took the young man away' is also translated 'took the young-man/boy home' [CEV, GW, NCV, NET, NIV, REB, TEV], 'took up the boy' [Bar]. This active verb is also translated as passive: 'the young man was taken home' [NLT], 'The boy was brought (up)' [AB]. This verb means to direct or guide the movement of an object, without special regard to point of departure or goal [LN]. It means to direct the movement of an object from one position to another [BDAG].

  b. pres. act. participle of ζάω (LN 23.93) (BDAG 1.a.β. p. 425): 'alive' [all translations except NLT], 'to live, to become alive again' [BDAG], 'to come back to life, to live again, to be resurrected' [LN]. The phrase 'they took the young man away alive' is also translated 'the young man was taken home unhurt' [NLT]. This verb means to come back to life after

having once died [LN]. It means to be alive physically in regard to dead persons who return to life [BDAG].
c. aorist pass. indic. of παρακαλέω (LN 25.150) (BDAG 4. p. 765): 'to be comforted' [Bar, BDAG, BECNT, CBC; ESV, KJV, NASB, NCV, NET, NIV, NRSV, TEV], 'to be encouraged' [BDAG, LN], 'to be consoled' [LN], 'to be cheered up' [BDAG], 'to be relieved' [GW, NLT, REB]. The phrase 'they…were greatly comforted' is also translated 'the followers…were very happy' [CEV]. This verb is also translated as a noun: 'this was a great comfort' [AB]. This verb means to cause someone to be encouraged or consoled, either by verbal or non-verbal means [LN]. It means to instill someone with courage or cheer [BDAG].

QUESTION—To whom does 'they' refer?
The Greek text does not say exactly who took the young man home. It may have been the young man's relatives or the believers who had been at the meeting [TH, TRT].

QUESTION—What is the function of the phrase παρεκλήθησαν οὐ μετρίως 'they were comforted not moderately' (translated: 'were greatly comforted)?
This phrase is a litotes [BECNT, PNTC, TRT], that is, a negative phrase that has a positive meaning. It is used to increase the prominence of this phrase and means "greatly/very comforted" [TRT].

**DISCOURSE UNIT—20:13–38** [PNTC; NET, NIV, NLT]. The topic is the voyage to Miletus [NET], Paul's farewell to the Ephesian elders [NIV], saying farewell to the Ephesian elders [PNTC], Paul meets the Ephesian elders [NLT].

**DISCOURSE UNIT—20:13–17** [PNTC]. The topic is gathering.

**DISCOURSE UNIT—20:13–16** [EBC, NAC, NICNT; CEV, GW, NASB, NCV, NRSV, TEV]. The topic is Troas to Miletus [NASB], the voyage from Troas to Miletus [CEV, NRSV], the trip from Troas to Miletus [NCV], from Troas to Miletus [EBC, NICNT; TEV], Paul's trip to Miletus [GW], voyage to Miletus [NAC].

**20:13** And we(excl), going-ahead[a] to the ship, set-sail[b] for Assos, intending to-take- Paul -aboard[c] there, for so he-had arranged-(it),[d] intending himself to-go-by-land.

LEXICON—a. aorist act. participle of προέρχομαι (LN 15.141) (BDAG 3. p. 868): 'to go ahead' [AB, BECNT, CBC; ESV, GW, NASB, NRSV], 'to go on ahead' [Bar, BDAG; CEV, NCV, NET, NIV, REB, TEV], 'to go before' [BDAG; KJV], 'to come/go prior to, to come/go beforehand, to precede' [LN], 'to come before, to go on before' [BDAG], not explicit [NLT]. This verb means to come/go prior to some other event, normally one involving a similar type of movement [LN]. It means to precede so as to be ahead [BDAG].
b. aorist pass. indic. of ἀνάγω (LN 54.4) (BDAG 4. p. 62): 'to set sail' [Bar, BECNT, LN; ESV, NASB, NRSV], 'to put out to sea' [BDAG, LN; NET], 'to sail' [AB, CBC; GW, KJV, NCV, NIV, TEV], 'to travel'

[NLT], 'to embark' [REB], not explicit [CEV]. This verb means to begin to go by boat [BDAG, LN].
c. pres. act. infin. of ἀναλαμβάνω (LN 15.100) (BDAG 4. p. 67): 'to take aboard' [BECNT, CBC, LN; CEV, ESV, NET, NIV, REB, TEV], 'to take on board' [AB; NASB, NRSV], 'to receive aboard' [LN], 'to take along' [BDAG], 'to pick up' [GW], 'to take up' [Bar], 'to take in' [KJV], not explicit [NCV, NLT]. This verb means to cause or permit someone to move up onto an object, used especially in relation to boats, but with the possible associated meaning of welcoming or receiving [LN]. It means to take someone along on a journey [BDAG].
d. perf. mid. participle of διατάσσω (LN 62.8) (BDAG 1. p. 237): 'to arrange' [BECNT; ESV, NASB, NET, NLT], 'to arrange for' [LN], 'to plan' [LN; NCV], 'to make arrangements' [BDAG, CBC; GW, NIV, NRSV, REB], 'to decide' [AB], 'to appoint' [KJV], not explicit [CEV, TEV]. The phrase 'for so he had arranged it' is also translated 'for so he had given orders' [Bar]. This verb means to arrange matters in a particular manner [LN]. It means to put into a proper order or relationship [LN].

QUESTION—To whom does 'we' refer?

It refers to all of the companions of Paul [CBC, EBC, NICNT] along with the author of the book [BECNT, NAC, PNTC, TH, TNTC].

**20:14** And when he-met[a] us at Assos, we took- him -on-board and came to Mitylene.

LEXICON—a. imperf. act. indic. of συμβάλλω (LN 15.79) (BDAG 4. p. 956): 'to meet' [BDAG, LN; all translations except AB; NLT], 'to fall in with' [BDAG], 'to join up with' [LN], 'to join' [AB; NLT]. This verb means to meet and join up with, with either friendly or hostile intent [LN]. It means to come together at a point [BDAG].

QUESTION—Where is Assos?

Assos was a port city about twenty miles southwest of Troas [BECNT, EBC].

QUESTION—Where is Mitylene?

Mitylene was the main town on the island of Lesbos [Bar, BECNT, CBC, EBC, NAC, NICNT, PNTC, TH, TNTC, TRT] about 44 miles south of Assos [BECNT, PNTC].

**20:15** And- sailing-away[a] -from-there we-arrived[b] the following-(day) opposite Chios; the next-(day) we-crossed-over[c] to Samos; and the day after that we-came[d] to Miletus.

LEXICON—a. aorist act. participle of ἀποπλέω (LN 54.7) (BDAG p. 119): 'to sail away' [BDAG, LN], 'to sail from' [LN], 'to sail on' [AB], 'to sail' [Bar, BECNT, CBC; ESV, GW, KJV, NASB, NCV, NRSV, REB, TEV], 'to set sail' [NET, NIV], not explicit [CEV, NLT]. This verb means to sail away from a point [LN].
b. aorist act. indic. of καταντάω (LN 15.84) (BDAG 1. p. 523): 'to arrive' [BDAG, CBC, LN; NASB, NET, NIV, NRSV, REB, TEV], 'to come to'

[BDAG, LN; CEV, NCV], 'to reach' [BDAG, LN], 'to come' [Bar, BECNT; ESV, KJV]. The phrase 'we arrived the following day opposite Chios' is also translated 'we approached the island of Chios' [GW], 'we sailed past the island of Kios' [NLT]. The phrase 'we arrived…opposite Chios' is also translated 'we…were opposite Chios' [AB]. This verb means to move toward and to arrive at a point [LN]. It means to get to a geographical destination [BDAG].
   c. aorist act. indic. of παραβάλλω (LN 54.12) (BDAG 4. p. 758): 'to cross over' [NASB, NIV], 'to cross' [NLT], 'to approach' [BDAG, LN; NET], 'to arrive at' [LN; KJV], 'to sail to' [LN; NCV], 'to come to' [TEV], 'to reach' [Bar; CEV]. The phrase 'we crossed over to Samos' is also translated 'we touched at Samos' [BECNT; ESV, NRSV], 'we made Samos' [CBC; REB], 'we…approached Samos' [AB], 'we went by the island of Samos' [GW]. This verb is a technical, nautical term and means to sail up to or near [LN]. This verb means to come near to someone or something [BDAG].
   d. aorist act. indic. of ἔρχομαι (LN 15.81): 'to come' [AB, Bar, BECNT, LN; KJV, NASB, NRSV], 'to go' [ESV], 'to arrive' [GW, NET, NIV, NLT], 'to reach' [CBC; NCV, REB, TEV], 'to sail' [CEV]. This verb means to move toward or up to the reference point of the viewpoint character or event [LN].
QUESTION—Where was Chios?
   Chios is one of the larger Aegean islands off the coast of Asia [TH]. The island of Chios lies at the end of a long peninsula which juts out between Smyrna on the north and Ephesus on the south [TNTC].
QUESTION—Where was Samos?
   Samos was one of the larger Aegean islands. It was located slightly south of Ephesus [TH, TNTC].
QUESTION—Where was Miletus?
   Miletus was a town located about 30 miles south of Ephesus [BECNT, EBC, TH, TNTC]. It was located on the south shore of the Latonian gulf at the mouth of the river Maeander [NAC].

**20:16** For Paul had-decided[a] to-sail-past Ephesus so-that he would not have to-spend-time[b] in Asia, for he-was-hurrying[c] to be in Jerusalem, if possible, on the day of-Pentecost.
LEXICON—a. pluperfect act. indic. of κρίνω (LN 30.75) (BDAG 4. p. 568): 'to decide' [BDAG, LN; all translations except Bar; KJV], 'to determine' [KJV], 'to choose' [Bar], 'to come to a conclusion, to make up one's mind' [LN], 'to reach a decision, to propose, to intend' [BDAG]. This verb means to come to a conclusion in the process of thinking and thus to be in a position to make a decision [LN]. It means to come to a conclusion after a cognitive process [BDAG].
   b. aorist act. infin. of χρονοτριβέω (LN 67.79) (BDAG p. 1092): 'to spend time' [Bar, BDAG, BECNT, CBC, LN; ESV, GW, NASB, NET, NIV,

NRSV, REB], 'to lose time' [BDAG]. The phrase 'to spend time' is also translated 'to spend too much time' [CEV], 'to spend any more time' [NLT], 'spend the time' [KJV], 'lose any time' [TEV]. The phrase 'he would not have to spend time in Asia' is also translated 'he did not want to stay too long in...Asia' [NCV], 'he might not be delayed in...Asia' [AB]. This verb means to experience a duration of time [BDAG, LN].
c. imperf. act. indic. of σπεύδω (LN 25.74, 68.79) (BDAG 1.a. p. 937): 'to hurry' [BDAG; NASB, NCV, NET, NLT], 'to hasten' [BDAG, BECNT; ESV, KJV], 'to hasten to, to hurry to, to do quickly' [LN (68.79)], 'to be eager' [CBC, LN (25.74); NRSV, REB], 'to be in a hurry' [AB; CEV, GW, NIV, TEV]. The phrase 'he was hurrying' is also translated 'he was making haste' [Bar]. This verb means to be eager to do something, with the implication of readiness to expend energy and effort [LN (25.74)]. It means to do something hurriedly, with the implication of associated energy [LN (68.79)]. It means to be in a hurry [BDAG].

QUESTION—What is indicated by the pluperfect verb κεκρίκει 'had decided'? The verb points to a resolved decision to avoid Ephesus [BECNT, PNTC].

**DISCOURSE UNIT—20:17–38** [AB, Bar, BECNT, CBC, EBC, TNTC; CEV, ESV, GW, NASB, NCV, NRSV, TEV]. The topic is Paul speaks to the Ephesian elders [ESV, NRSV], Paul meets with the spiritual leaders from Ephesus [GW], Paul says good-by to the church leaders of Ephesus [CEV], Paul's farewell speech to the elders of Ephesus [TEV], Paul's farewell address to the Ephesian elders [EBC], Paul's farewell address at Miletus [AB, TNTC], Paul's speech at Miletus [Bar], the farewell speech to the Ephesian elders at Miletus [BECNT], the address at Miletus to the elders of Ephesus [CBC], farewell to Ephesus [NASB], the elders from Ephesus [NCV].

**DISCOURSE UNIT—20:17–35** [NAC]. The topic is farewell address to the Ephesian elders.

**DISCOURSE UNIT—20:17** [NICNT]. The topic is Paul sends for the elders of the Ephesian church.

**20:17** From Miletus he sent[a] to Ephesus and called[b] the elders[c] of the church[d] (to come to him).

LEXICON—a. aorist act. participle of πέμπω (LN 15.67) (BDAG 1. p. 794): 'to send' [Bar, BDAG, BECNT, CBC; ESV, KJV, NASB, NCV, NIV, REB], 'to send a message' [LN; CEV, NET, NLT, NRSV, TEV], 'to send word' [AB, LN], 'to send a messenger' [GW]. This verb means to send a message, presumably by someone [LN]. It means to dispatch someone, whether human or transcendent being, usually for purposes of communication [BDAG].
b. aorist mid. indic. of μετακαλέω (LN 33.311) (BDAG p. 639): 'to call' [BECNT; ESV, GW, KJV, NASB, NCV], 'to summon' [Bar, BDAG, CBC, LN; REB], 'to ask' [NLT, NRSV, TEV], 'to tell to come' [LN], 'to call to oneself' [BDAG], not explicit [AB; CEV, NIV]. The phrase 'called

the elders of the church' is also translated 'telling the elders of the church' [NET]. This verb means to summon someone, with considerable insistence and authority [LN].

c. πρεσβύτερος (LN 53.77) (BDAG 2.b.α. p. 862): 'elder' [LN; all translations except CEV, GW]. This noun is also translated 'church leader' [CEV], 'spiritual leader' [GW]. This noun denotes a person of responsibility and authority in matters of socio-religious concerns, both in Jewish and Christian societies [LN]. It denotes an official among the Christians [BDAG].

d. ἐκκλησία (LN 11.32) (BDAG 3.b.β. p. 304): 'church' [BDAG, LN; all translations except CBC; CEV], 'congregation' [BDAG, CBC, LN], not explicit [CEV]. This noun denotes a congregation of Christians, implying interacting membership [LN]. It denotes the totality of Christians living together and meeting in a particular area, but not necessarily limited to one meeting place [BDAG].

QUESTION—Who were the elders?
Elders were older men who were the leaders of the local church [TRT]. The elders were responsible for shepherding the church and guiding it [BECNT].

**DISCOURSE UNIT—20:18–35** [NICNT]. The topic is Paul bids farewell to the Ephesian church.

**DISCOURSE UNIT—20:18–21** [PNTC]. The topic is recalling the past.

**20:18** And when they-came[a] to him, he-said to-them, "You yourselves know[b] I-was[c] with you the whole time from (the)-first day that I-set-foot[d] in Asia,

LEXICON—a. aorist mid. (deponent = act.) indic. of παραγίνομαι (LN 15.86) (BDAG 1.a. p. 760): 'to come' [AB, BDAG, BECNT, LN; ESV, KJV, NASB, NCV, NRSV], 'to arrive' [BDAG, LN; NET, NIV, NLT, TEV], 'to come to be present' [LN], 'to draw near, to be present' [BDAG]. The phrase 'when they came to him' is also translated 'when they got there' [CEV], 'when they were with him' [GW], 'when they joined him' [CBC; REB], 'when they reached him' [Bar]. This verb means to come to be present at a particular place [LN]. It means to be in movement so as to be present at a particular place [BDAG].

b. pres. mid./pass. (deponent = act.) indic. of ἐπίσταμαι (LN 28.3) (BDAG 2. p. 380): 'to know' [BDAG, LN; all translations], 'to be acquainted with' [BDAG]. This verb means to possess information about, with the implication of an understanding of the significance of such information [LN]. It means to acquire information about something [BDAG].

c. aorist mid. (deponent = act.) indic. of γίνομαι (LN 85.6) (BDAG 9.c. p. 199): 'to be (in a place)' [Bar, CBC, LN; CEV, KJV, NASB, NCV, NET, NIV, TEV], 'to belong to' [BDAG], not explicit [AB; NLT]. The phrase 'I was with you' is also translated 'I lived among you' [BECNT; ESV, NRSV], 'I spent all my time with you' [GW], 'I spent my whole time with

you' [REB]. This verb means to be in a place, with the possible implication of having come to be in such a place [LN]. It means to be closely related to someone or something [BDAG].
  d. aorist act. indic. of ἐπιβαίνω (LN 15.83) (BDAG 2. p. 367): 'to set foot' [Bar, BECNT, CBC; ESV, NASB, NET, NLT, NRSV, REB], 'to come' [AB; CEV, KJV, NCV, NIV], 'to arrive' [LN; GW, TEV], 'to set foot in' [BDAG], 'to come to' [LN]. This verb means to move to or on to, generally with the implication of having arrived [LN]. It means to move to an area and be there [BDAG].

**20:19** serving[a] the Lord[b] with all humility[c] and with tears and with trials[d] that happened to-me through[e] the plots[f] of-the Jews:
LEXICON—a. pres. act. participle of δουλεύω (LN 35.27) (BDAG 2.a.β. p. 259): 'to serve' [BDAG, LN; all translations except NLT, TEV], 'to obey, to perform the duties of a slave' [BDAG]. The phrase 'serving the Lord' is also translated 'I have done the Lord's work' [NLT], 'I did my work as the Lord's servant' [TEV]. This verb means to serve, normally in a humble manner and in response to the demands or commands of others [LN]. It means to act or conduct oneself as one in total service to transcendent beings, especially in expressions relating to God or Jesus Christ as recipients of undivided allegiance [BDAG].
  b. κύριος (LN 12.9): 'Lord' [LN; all translations], 'Ruler, One who commands' [LN]. This noun denotes a title for God and for Christ. It indicates one who exercises supernatural authority over mankind [LN].
  c. ταπεινοφροσύνη (LN 88.53) (BDAG p. 989): 'humility' [AB, BDAG, BECNT, CBC, LN; ESV, KJV, NASB, NET, NIV, NRSV, REB, TEV], 'humble attitude, without arrogance' [LN], 'modesty' [BDAG], 'humble-mindedness' [Bar]. This noun is also translated as a verb: 'I...was humble' [CEV]. This noun is also translated as an adverb: 'I humbly served' [GW], 'I have done the Lord's work humbly' [NLT], 'I...served the Lord unselfishly' [NCV]. This noun denotes the quality of humility [LN].
  d. πειρασμός (LN 27.46) (BDAG 2.b. p. 793): 'trial' [AB, BECNT, CBC; ESV, NASB, NET, NLT, NRSV, REB], 'test, examination' [LN], 'temptation' [BDAG; KJV], 'wrong, enticement' [BDAG], 'trouble' [CEV], 'affliction' [Bar], 'difficult times' [GW], 'hard times' [TEV]. This noun is also translated as a passive verb: 'was tested' [NIV]. The phrase 'trials that happened to me through the plots of the Jews' is also translated 'The Jews made plans against me, which troubled me very much' [NCV]. This noun denotes the act of learning the nature or character of someone or something by submitting such to thorough and extensive testing [LN]. It denotes an attempt to make one do something [BDAG].
  e. ἐν (LN 89.76): 'through' [Bar, BECNT, CBC, LN; ESV, NASB, NRSV, REB], 'by' [KJV, NIV], 'by means of' [LN], 'because of' [NET, TEV], 'from' [AB; NLT], not explicit [CEV, GW, NCV]. This preposition

indicates the means by which one event makes another event possible [LN].

f. ἐπιβουλή (LN 30.71) (BDAG p. 368): 'plot' [Bar, BDAG, BECNT, LN; ESV, NASB, NET, NIV, NLT, NRSV, TEV], 'plan, scheme' [LN], 'intrigue' [REB], 'persecution' [AB], 'machination' [CBC], 'the lying in wait' [KJV]. This noun is also translated as a verb: 'plotted' [CEV, GW], 'made plans' [NCV]. This noun denotes a plan for treacherous activity against someone [LN]. It denotes a secret plan to do something evil or cause harm [BDAG].

QUESTION—Should 'tears' be taken along 'with all humility' as an expression of Paul's inner attitude, or should it be taken with 'trials' as an expression of the difficulties that were brought upon Paul because of the plots of the Jews?

1. 'Tears' should be taken with 'humility' [GW, NCV, NIV, NLT, NRSV, TEV].
2. 'Tears should be taken with 'trials' [CEV].

**20:20** how I-did- not -shrink[a] from declaring[b] to-you anything that was-profitable,[c] and teaching[d] you in-public and from-house-to-house,

LEXICON—a. aorist mid. indic. of ὑποστέλλω (LN 13.160) (BDAG 2.c. p. 1041): 'to shrink' [AB, BECNT; ESV, NASB, NRSV], 'to hold back' [CEV, NCV, NET, TEV], 'to shrink back' [NLT], 'to keep back' [Bar, CBC; KJV, REB], 'to avoid' [LN; GW], 'to shrink from' [LN], 'to hold back from' [LN], 'to be timid about, to keep silent about' [BDAG], 'to hesitate' [NIV]. This verb means to hold oneself back from doing something, with the implication of some fearful concern [LN]. It means to be hesitant in regard to something [BDAG].

b. aorist act. infin. of ἀναγγέλλω (LN 33.197) (BDAG 2. p. 59): 'to declare' [Bar, BECNT; ESV, NASB], 'to tell' [LN; CEV, GW, NLT], 'to show' [KJV], 'to announce' [BDAG, LN], to inform' [LN], 'to proclaim' [BDAG; NET], 'to disclose, to teach' [BDAG], 'to preach' [AB; NCV, NIV, TEV], 'to deliver' [CBC; REB]. The clause 'I did not shrink from declaring to you anything that was profitable' is also translated 'I did not shrink from doing anything helpful' [NRSV]. This verb means to provide information, with the possible implication of considerable detail [LN]. It means to provide information [BDAG].

c. pres. act. participle of συμφέρω (LN 65.44) (BDAG 2.b.α. p. 960): 'to be profitable' [Bar, BDAG, BECNT; ESV, KJV, NASB], 'to help' [BDAG; CEV, GW, NCV], 'to be helpful' [NET, NIV], 'to be of help' [TEV], 'to be advantageous, to be better off, to be to someone's advantage' [LN], 'to be useful, to confer a benefit' [BDAG], not explicit [NRSV]. The phrase 'anything that was profitable' is also translated 'what you needed to hear' [NLT], 'that was for your good' [CBC; REB], 'all that is good' [AB]. This verb means to be of an advantage to someone [LN]. It means to be advantageous [BDAG].

d. aorist act. infin. of διδάσκω (LN 33.224): 'to teach' [LN; all translations except AB; NLT], 'teaching' [LN], 'to tell' [AB; NLT]. This verb means to provide instruction in a formal or informal setting [LN].

QUESTION—What does the phrase 'I did not shrink' mean in this context?
It could have the sense of 'shrink back' in fear, but the context suggests no withholding of the truth [PNTC].

**20:21** **testifying<sup>a</sup> both to-Jews and Greeks of repentance<sup>b</sup> toward God and faith<sup>c</sup> in our Lord Jesus.**

TEXT—Manuscripts reading κύριον ἡμῶν Ἰησοῦν 'our Lord Jesus' are given a B rating by GNT to indicate it was regarded to be almost certain. A variant reading adds Χριστός 'Christ' after 'Jesus' and it is followed by ESV, KJV, NASB.

LEXICON—a. pres. mid./pass. (deponent=act.) participle of διαμαρτύρομαι (LN 33.223) (BDAG 1. p. 233): 'to testify' [Bar, BECNT, LN; ESV, KJV, NASB, NET, NRSV], 'to declare' [LN; NIV], 'to assert' [LN], 'to testify of' [BDAG], 'to bear witness to' [AB, BDAG], 'to tell' [CEV], 'to warn' [GW, NCV]. The phrase 'testifying both to Jews and Greeks' is also translated 'I have had one message for Jews and Greeks' [NLT], 'with Jews and Gentiles alike I insisted' [CBC; REB], 'to Jews and Gentiles alike I gave solemn warning' [TEV]. This verb means to make a serious declaration on the basis of presumed personal knowledge [LN]. It means to make a solemn declaration about the truth of something [BDAG].

b. μετάνοια (LN 41.52) (BDAG p. 640): 'repentance' [AB, Bar, BDAG, BECNT, CBC, LN; ESV, KJV, NASB, NET, NIV, NRSV, REB], 'conversion' [BDAG]. The phrase 'testifying both to Jews and Greeks of repentance toward God' is also translated 'I told Jews and Gentiles to turn to God' [CEV], 'I warned Jews and Greeks to change the way they think and act' [GW], 'I warned both Jews and Greeks to change their lives and turn to God' [NCV], 'I have had one message for Jews and Greeks...the necessity of repenting from sin and turning to God' [NLT], 'To Jews and Gentiles alike I gave solemn warning that they should turn from their sins to God' [TEV]. This noun denotes a complete change of thought and attitude with regard to sin and righteousness [LN].

c. πίστις (LN 31.102) (BDAG 2.b.β. p. 819): 'faith' [Bar, BDAG, BECNT; all versions except GW, NCV, TEV], 'trust' [BDAG, CBC], 'confidence' [BDAG], 'Christian faith' [LN]. This noun is also translated as a verb: 'believe in our Lord' [AB; GW, NCV, TEV]. This noun denotes the belief in the good news about Jesus Christ and becoming a follower [LN]. It denotes the state of believing on the basis of the reliability of the one trusted and here it refers to faith in Christ [BDAG].

**DISCOURSE UNIT—20:22–35** [PNTC]. The topic is facing the future.

**20:22** And now, behold,[a] I am-going[b] to Jerusalem, bound[c] by-the Spirit,[d] not knowing[e] what will-happen[f] to-me there,

LEXICON—a. ἰδού (LN 91.13) (BDAG 1.b.δ. p. 468): 'behold' [Bar, BDAG; ESV, KJV, NASB], 'look' [BDAG, BECNT, LN], 'listen, pay attention' [LN], 'listen carefully' [AB], 'see' [BDAG], not explicit [CEV, GW, NCV, NET, NIV, NLT, NRSV, TEV]. This is also translated 'as you see' [CBC; REB]. This particle functions as a prompter of attention, also serving to emphasize the statement which follows [LN]. It is a prompter of attention [BDAG].

b. pres. mid./pass. (deponent = act.) indic. of πορεύομαι (LN 15.18) (BDAG 1. p. 853): 'to go' [Bar, BDAG, BECNT; all versions except NASB, NRSV], 'to travel' [AB, BDAG, LN], 'to proceed' [BDAG], 'to journey' [LN], 'to be on one's way' [CBC, LN; NASB, NRSV]. This verb means to move a considerable distance, either with a single destination or from one destination to another in a series [LN]. It means to move over an area generally with a point of departure or destination specified [BDAG].

c. perf. pass. participle of δέω (LN 37.33) (BDAG 1.b. p. 221): 'to be bound' [Bar, BDAG, BECNT; KJV, NASB, NLT], 'to be constrained' [CBC; ESV, REB], 'to be tied' [BDAG], 'to be compelled' [AB, LN; NET, NIV], 'to be forced' [LN], not explicit [GW]. The phrase 'bound by the Spirit' is also translated 'I must obey God's Spirit' [CEV], 'I must obey the Holy Spirit' [NCV], 'as a captive to the Spirit' [NRSV], 'in obedience to the Holy Spirit' [TEV]. This verb means to compel someone to act in a particular manner [LN]. It means to confine a person or thing by various kinds of restraints [BDAG].

d. πνεῦμα (LN 12.18, 26.9) (BDAG 5.d.α. p. 835): 'Spirit' [AB, Bar, BDAG, BECNT, CBC, LN (12.18); ESV, NET, NIV, NLT, NRSV, REB], 'God's Spirit' [CEV], 'Spirit of God' [LN (12.18)], 'Holy Spirit' [LN (12.18); NCV, TEV], 'spirit' [BDAG, LN (26.9); KJV, NASB], not explicit [GW]. This noun denotes a title for the third person of the Trinity [LN (12.18)]. This noun denotes the non-material, psychological faculty which is potentially sensitive and responsive to God [LN (26.9)]. It denotes God's being as controlling influence, with focus on association with humans [BDAG].

e. perf. act. participle of οἶδα (LN 28.1): 'to know' [LN; all translations], 'to know about, to have knowledge of, to be acquainted with' [LN]. This verb means to possess information about [LN].

f. fut. act. participle of συναντάω (LN 13.120) (BDAG 2. p. 965): 'to happen' [AB, BDAG; CEV, ESV, GW, NASB, NCV, NET, NIV, NRSV, TEV], 'to come upon, to happen to' [LN], 'to befall' [Bar, CBC; KJV, REB]. The phrase 'not knowing what will happen to me' is also translated 'I don't know what awaits me' [NLT], 'not knowing what shall meet me' [BECNT]. This verb means to happen, with the implication of that which one meets up with [LN].

QUESTION—What is meant by 'bound by the Spirit'?
It is a figurative expression about divine constraint [Bar, BECNT].
QUESTION—To whom does the 'Spirit' refer?
1. It refers to the Holy Spirit [AB, Bar, BECNT, CBC, EBC, NAC, NICNT, PNTC, TH, TNTC; CEV, NCV, TEV].
2. It refers to Paul's spirit [KJV, NASB].

**20:23** except[a] that the Holy Spirit[b] testifies[c] to-me in-every city, saying that bonds[d] and tribulations[e] await me.

LEXICON—a. πλήν (LN 89.130) (BDAG 1.d. p. 826): 'except' [AB, BECNT, CBC, LN; ESV, NASB, NET, NLT, NRSV, REB], 'but, nevertheless' [LN], 'only' [Bar], 'however' [GW], 'save' [KJV], 'except that' [BDAG], not explicit [CEV]. The phrase 'except that' is also translated 'I know only that' [NCV], 'I only know that' [NIV, TEV]. This conjunction indicates a contrast, implying the validity of something irrespective of other considerations [LN]. It is a marker of something that is contrastingly added for consideration [BDAG].

b. πνεῦμα (LN 12.18) (BDAG 5.c.α. p. 834): 'Spirit' [BDAG, LN; all translations except KJV], 'Ghost' [KJV]. This noun denotes the third person of the Trinity whose titles are 'Spirit, Spirit of God, and Holy Spirit'. In many religious systems the significant difference between the gods and the spirits is that the gods are regarded as supernatural beings which control certain aspects of natural phenomena, while the spirits are supernatural beings, often impersonal, which indwell or inhabit certain places, including rivers, streams, mountains, caves, animals, and people. Spirits are often regarded as being primarily evil, though it may be possible to induce them to be favorable to people. It is extremely difficult to find in some languages a fully satisfactory term to speak of the Spirit of God. If one uses a term which normally identifies local supernatural beings, there is a tendency to read into the term the meaning of an evil or mischievous character. If, however, one uses a term which may identify the spirit of a person, the problems may even be greater, since according to many systems of religious belief, the spirit of an individual does not become active until the individual dies. Therefore, the activity of the Spirit of God would presumably suggest that God himself had died. However, if one uses a term which means 'heart' or 'soul' (and thus the Spirit of God would be literally equivalent to 'the heart of God'), there may be complications since this aspect of human personality is often regarded as not being able to act on its own. The solutions to the problem of 'Spirit' have been varied. In some languages the term for Spirit is essentially equivalent to 'the unseen one,' and therefore the Spirit of God is essentially equivalent to 'the invisibleness of God'. In a number of languages the closest equivalent for Spirit is 'breath', and in a number of indigenous religious systems, the 'breath' is regarded as having a kind of independent existence. In other languages the term for Spirit is equivalent to what is often translated as 'the soul', that is to say, the immaterial part of a person. There is, of course, always the difficulty of employing a term meaning 'soul' or 'life', since it often proves to be impersonal and thus provides no basis for speaking of the Spirit of God as being a person or a personal manifestation of God. In quite a few languages the equivalent of Spirit is literally 'shadow', since the 'shadow' of a person is regarded as the immaterial part of the individual. Moreover, in many systems of religious thought the shadow is regarded as having some significant measure of independent existence. In a few cases the term for Spirit is literally 'wind', but there are frequently difficulties involved in this type of terminology since a term for wind often suggests calamity or evil intent. One meaning of Spirit which must be clearly avoided is that of 'apparition' or 'ghost'. Frequently it is not possible to find a fully satisfactory term for 'Spirit', and therefore in all contexts some characterizing feature is added, for example, either 'of God' or 'holy', in the sense of 'divine', [LN]. It denotes God's being as controlling influence, with focus on association with humans [BDAG].

c. pres. mid./pass. (deponent=act.) indic. of διαμαρτύρομαι (LN 33.223, 33.425) (BDAG 1. p. 233): 'to testify' [Bar, BECNT, LN (33.223); ESV, NASB, NRSV], 'to declare, to assert' [LN (33.223)], 'to testify' [BDAG], 'to bear witness to' [AB, BDAG], 'to warn' [LN (33.425); GW, NET, NIV, TEV], 'to tell' [NCV, NLT], 'to witness' [KJV], 'to assure' [CBC; REB]. The phrase 'the Holy Spirit testifies to me' is also translated 'I am told by the Holy Spirit' [CEV]. This verb means to make a serious declaration on the basis of presumed personal knowledge [LN (33.223)]. It means to admonish or instruct with regard to some future happening or action, with the implication of personal knowledge or experience [LN (33.425)]. It means to make a solemn declaration about the truth of something [BDAG].

d. δεσμός (LN 37.115) (BDAG 1.a. p. 219): 'bond' [Bar, BDAG; KJV, NASB], 'fetter' [BDAG], 'chain' [AB], 'imprisonment' [BECNT, CBC, LN; ESV, GW, NET, NRSV, REB], 'jail' [NCV, NLT], 'prison' [NIV, TEV]. The phrase 'that bonds...await me' is also translated 'I will be put in jail' [CEV]. This noun is a figurative extension of meaning of δεσμός 'bonds' and denotes the state of being in prison [LN]. It denotes that which serves as a means of restraint by tying or fastening [BDAG].

e. θλῖψις (LN 22.2) (BDAG 1. p. 457): 'tribulation' [AB, BDAG], 'oppression' [BDAG], 'affliction' [Bar, BDAG, BECNT; ESV, KJV, NASB], 'suffering' [LN; GW, NLT], 'trouble' [NCV, TEV], 'persecution' [LN; NET, NRSV], 'hardship' [CBC; NIV, REB], 'trouble and suffering' [LN]. The phrase 'that...tribulations await me' is also translated 'I...will be in trouble' [CEV]. This noun denotes trouble involving direct suffering [LN]. It denotes trouble that inflicts distress [BDAG].

**20:24** But[a] I do- not -account (my) life of any value (nor as precious) to-myself, so-that[b] I may finish[c] my course[d] and the ministry[e] which I-received[f] from the Lord Jesus, to-testify to the gospel[g] of-the grace[h] of-God.

LEXICON—a. ἀλλά (LN 89.125): 'but' [Bar, BECNT, LN; all versions except NCV, NIV, REB], 'however' [NIV], 'instead, on the contrary' [LN], 'yet' [AB], not explicit [CBC; NCV, REB]. This conjunction is a marker of more emphatic contrast [LN].

b. ὡς (LN 89.61) (BDAG 9.a. and b. p. 1106): 'so that' [Bar, LN; KJV, NASB, NET], 'then' [LN], 'in order to' [BDAG, LN], 'with a view to' [BDAG], 'if only' [AB, BECNT; ESV, NIV, NRSV, REB, TEV], not explicit [CBC; CEV, GW, NCV, NLT]. This conjunction is a marker of purpose, with the implication that what has preceded serves as a means [LN]. It is a final particle expressing intention/purpose [BDAG].

c. aorist act. infin. of τελειόω (LN 68.22) (BDAG 1. p. 996): 'to finish' [Bar, BDAG, CBC, LN; all versions except NCV, TEV], 'to accomplish' [BDAG, BECNT, LN], 'to complete' [AB, LN; NCV, TEV], 'to end' [LN], 'to bring to an end' [BDAG]. This verb means to bring an activity to a successful finish [LN]. It means to complete an activity [BDAG].

d. δρόμος (LN 42.26) (BDAG 2. p. 261): 'course' [Bar, BECNT; ESV, KJV, NASB, NRSV], 'task' [LN; NET], 'mission' [BDAG, LN; NCV, TEV], 'course of life' [BDAG], 'race' [CBC; GW, NIV, REB], 'allotted span' [AB], not explicit [CEV, NLT]. This noun is a figurative extension of meaning of δρόμος 'race' and denotes a task or function involving continuity, serious effort, and possibly obligation [LN]. It denotes carrying out of an obligation or task [BDAG].

e. διακονία (LN 35.21) (BDAG 3. p. 230): 'ministry' [AB, Bar, BECNT, LN; ESV, KJV, NASB, NET, NRSV], 'task' [CBC, LN; NIV, REB], 'work' [CEV, NCV, NLT, TEV], 'service, office' [BDAG], 'mission' [GW]. This noun denotes the role or position of serving [LN]. It denotes functioning in the interest of a larger public [BDAG].

f. aorist act. indic. of λαμβάνω (LN 57.125) (BDAG 10.c. p. 585): 'to receive' [AB, Bar, BDAG, BECNT, LN; ESV, GW, KJV, NASB, NET, NRSV], 'to accept' [LN], 'to get, to obtain' [BDAG]. The phrase 'I received from the Lord Jesus' is also translated 'the Lord Jesus gave me' [CEV, NCV, TEV], 'the Lord Jesus has given me' [NIV]. The phrase 'the ministry which I received from the Lord Jesus' is also translated 'the work assigned me by the Lord Jesus' [NLT], 'the task which the Lord Jesus assigned to me' [CBC; REB]. This verb means to receive or accept an object or benefit for which the initiative rests with the giver, but the focus of attention in the transfer is upon the receiver [LN]. It means to be a receiver [BDAG].

g. εὐαγγέλιον (LN 33.217) (BDAG 1.b.β.ℵ. p. 403): 'the gospel' [AB, Bar, BECNT, CBC, LN; ESV, KJV, NASB, NIV, REB], 'the good news' [BDAG, LN; CEV, GW, NCV, NET, NLT, NRSV, TEV]. This noun denotes the content of the good news (in the NT it is a reference to the

gospel about Jesus) [LN]. It denotes God's good news to humans [BDAG].
  h. χάρις (LN 88.66) (BDAG 3.b. p. 1080): 'grace' [LN; all translations except CEV, GW], 'kindness' [LN; CEV, GW], 'graciousness' [LN], '(a sign of) favor, gracious deed/gift, benefaction' [BDAG]. This noun denotes the act of showing kindness to someone, with the implication of graciousness on the part of the one showing such kindness [LN]. It denotes the practical application of goodwill on the part of God and Christ [BDAG].

QUESTION—What is meant by 'finish my course'?
  It is a metaphor in this context that refers to Paul's ministry/work [TRT].

**20:25** And now, behold, I know that all of you, among whom I-went-about[a] proclaiming[b] the kingdom, will no-longer see my face.

LEXICON—a. aorist act. indic. of διέρχομαι (LN 15.21) (BDAG 1.a. p. 244): 'to go about' [Bar, CBC; ESV, NASB, NIV, NRSV, REB, TEV], 'to go around' [NET], 'to travel around through, to journey all through' [LN], 'to go (through)' [BDAG], 'to go from place to place' [CEV], 'to go' [BECNT; KJV], 'to travel' [AB], not explicit [GW, NCV, NLT]. This verb means to travel around through an area, with the implication of both extensive and thorough movement throughout an area [LN]. It means to travel or move about from place to place [BDAG].
  b. pres. act. participle of κηρύσσω (LN 33.256) (BDAG 2.b.β. p. 543): 'to proclaim' [Bar, CBC; ESV, NET, NRSV, REB], 'to proclaim aloud' [BDAG], 'to preach' [AB, BECNT, LN; CEV, KJV, NASB, NCV, NIV, NLT, TEV], 'to tell' [GW]. This verb means to publicly announce religious truths and principles while urging acceptance and compliance [LN]. It means to make public declarations [BDAG].

QUESTION—What is the function of the phrase 'And now'?
  This phrase clearly marks a shift in viewpoint and content [TH].

**20:26** Therefore, I-testify to-you this day that I-am innocent[a] of the blood[b] of-all (of you),

LEXICON—a. καθαρός (LN 88.316) (BDAG 3.a. p. 489): 'innocent' [LN; ESV, NASB, NET, NIV], 'guiltless' [LN], 'pure' [BDAG; KJV], 'free' [AB, BDAG], 'clear' [Bar], 'clean' [BECNT], 'not responsible' [CEV, GW, NCV, NRSV, TEV], 'not at fault' [NLT], not explicit [CBC; REB]. This adjective pertains to not being guilty of wrongdoing [LN]. It pertains to being free from moral guilt [BDAG].
  b. αἷμα (LN 23.107) (BDAG 2.a. p. 26): 'blood' [AB, Bar, BDAG; ESV, KJV, NASB, NET, NIV, NRSV], 'life-blood' [BDAG], 'bloodguilt' [BECNT], 'death, violent death' [LN], '(eternal) death' [NLT], '(spiritual) death' [GW], not explicit [CBC; CEV, NCV, REB, TEV]. This noun is a figurative extension of meaning of αἷμα 'blood' and denotes the death of a person, generally as the result of violence or execution [LN]. It denotes blood as constituting the life of an individual [BDAG].

QUESTION—What is meant by the phrase 'I am innocent of the blood of all of you'?

It means that Paul is not responsible for any man's (eternal) death through neglecting to preach the gospel to all and to deliver it in all its fullness [Bar]. He is 'clean' or 'pure' with respect to any guilt regarding people's lives [BECNT]. Paul had preached the full gospel, the whole will of God. He had called people to repentance. Now the responsibility rested with them [NAC].

**20:27** for[a] I-did- not -shrink-from[b] declaring[c] to-you the whole purpose[d] of-God.

LEXICON—a. γάρ (LN 89.23): 'for' [LN; all translations except CEV, GW, NCV, REB], 'because' [LN; NCV], not explicit [CEV, GW, REB]. This conjunction is a marker of cause or reason between events, though in some contexts the relation is often remote or tenuous [LN].

b. aorist mid. indic. of ὑποστέλλω (LN 13.160, 68.53) (BDAG 2.b. p. 1041): 'to shrink from' [AB, BDAG, BECNT, LN (13.160); ESV, NASB, NLT, NRSV], 'to hold back from' [LN (13.160); NET, TEV], 'to avoid' [BDAG, LN (13.160); GW], 'to keep back' [Bar, CBC], 'to cease, to stop, to give up doing' [LN (68.53)], 'to hesitate' [NIV], 'to shun' [KJV], not explicit [CEV, NCV, REB]. This verb means to hold oneself back from doing something, with the implication of some fearful concern [LN (13.160)]. It means to cease doing something of presumed positive value because of adverse circumstances or fear [LN (68.53)].

c. aorist act. infin. of ἀναγγέλλω (LN 33.197) (BDAG 2. p. 59): 'to declare' [BECNT; ESV, KJV, NASB, NLT, NRSV], 'to announce' [BDAG, LN; NET, TEV], 'to inform' [LN], 'to tell' [LN; CEV, GW, NCV], 'to proclaim' [Bar, BDAG; NIV], 'to disclose' [BDAG, CBC; REB], 'to teach' [BDAG], 'to preach' [AB]. This verb means to provide information, with the possible implication of considerable detail [LN]. It means to provide information [BDAG].

d. βουλή (LN 30.57) (BDAG 2.b. p. 182): 'purpose' [CBC, LN; NASB, NET, NRSV, REB, TEV], 'plan' [LN; GW], 'will' [AB; NIV], 'intention' [LN], 'resolution, decision' [BDAG], 'counsel' [Bar, BECNT; ESV, KJV]. The phrase 'declaring to you the whole purpose of God' is also translated 'declaring all that God wants you to know' [NLT], 'told you everything God wants you to know' [CEV, NCV]. This noun denotes that which has been purposed and planned [LN]. It denotes that which one decides and here it refers to the divine will [BDAG].

QUESTION—What is meant by the phrase 'the whole purpose of God'?

Here it must refer to God's plan for the redemption of all mankind [Bar]. It refers to the whole plan of God for humanity and the created order revealed in the Scriptures and fulfilled in Jesus Christ [PNTC].

**20:28** Pay-(careful)-attention[a] to-yourselves and to-all the flock,[b] in which the Holy Spirit has-made[c] you overseers,[d] to-shepherd[e] the church[f] of-God, which he-purchased[g] with his-own blood.[h]

TEXT—Manuscripts reading τὴν ἐκκλησίαν τοῦ θεοῦ 'the church of God' are given a C rating by GNT to indicate that choosing it over a variant text was difficult. A variant reading is τὴν ἐκκλησίαν τοῦ τὸν κύριον 'the church of the Lord' and it is followed by REB.

LEXICON—a. pres. act. impera. of προσέχω (LN 27.59) (BDAG 1. p. 879): 'to pay attention' [ESV, GW], 'to be on guard' [NASB], 'to look after' [CEV], 'to take heed' [BECNT; KJV], 'to be careful' [NCV], 'to watch out' [NET], 'to keep watch' [NIV, NRSV, TEV], 'to guard' [NLT], 'to keep guard/watch' [CBC; REB], 'to pay attention to, to keep on the lookout for, to be alert for, to be on one's guard against' [LN], 'to be concerned about, to care for, to take care' [BDAG], 'to look' [AB], 'to take thought' [Bar]. This verb means to be in a continuous state of readiness to learn of any future danger, need, or error, and to respond appropriately [LN]. It means to be in a state of alert [BDAG].

b. ποίμνιον (LN 11.31) (BDAG 2.b. p. 843): 'flock' [BDAG; all translations except CEV, NCV, NLT], 'everyone' [CEV], 'people' [NCV], 'God's people' [NLT], 'people who are like a flock' [LN]. This noun is a figurative extension of meaning of ποίμνιον 'flock' and denotes the followers of Christ constituting a well-defined membership group [LN]. It denotes a defined group of persons under a leader and here it refers to the Christian community [BDAG].

c. aorist mid. indic. of τίθημι (LN 37.96) (BDAG 5.b. p. 1004): 'to make' [AB, BDAG, BECNT; ESV, KJV, NASB, NET, NIV, NRSV], 'to appoint' [Bar, LN; NLT], 'to designate, to assign, to give a task to' [LN], 'to consign' [BDAG]. The phrase 'the flock in which the Holy Spirit has made you overseers' is also translated 'everyone the Holy Spirit has placed in your care' [CEV], 'the flock which the Holy Spirit has placed in your care' [TEV], 'the entire flock in which the Holy Spirit has placed you as bishops' [GW], 'the people the Holy Spirit has given to you to care for' [NCV], 'the flock of which the Holy Spirit has given you charge' [CBC; REB]. This verb means to assign someone to a particular task, function, or role [LN]. It means to cause to undergo a change in experience/condition [BDAG].

d. ἐπίσκοπος (LN 53.71) (BDAG 2. p. 379): 'overseer' [AB, BDAG, BECNT; ESV, KJV, NASB, NET, NIV, NRSV], 'supervisor' [BDAG], 'elder' [NLT], 'church leader' [LN], 'bishop' [Bar; GW]. The phrase 'the flock in which the Holy Spirit has made you overseers' is also translated 'everyone the Holy Spirit has placed in your care' [CEV], 'the people the Holy Spirit has given to you to care for' [NCV], 'the flock of which the Holy Spirit has given you charge' [CBC; REB], 'the flock which the Holy Spirit has placed in your care' [TEV]. This noun denotes one who serves as a leader in a church [LN].

e. pres. act. infin. of ποιμαίνω (LN 36.2) (BDAG 2.a.β. p. 842): 'to shepherd' [Bar, BDAG, BECNT; NASB, NET, NLT, NRSV], 'to care for' [ESV], 'to guide and to help, to guide and take care of' [LN], 'to feed' [KJV], 'to guard' [AB]. This verb is also translated 'be like shepherds' [CEV, NCV], 'be shepherds' [GW, NIV, TEV]. This verb is also translated as a noun: 'shepherds' [CBC; REB]. This verb is a figurative extension of meaning of ποιμαίνω 'to shepherd' and means to lead, with the implication of providing for [LN]. It means to watch out for other people [BDAG].

f. ἐκκλησία (LN 11.32) (BDAG 3.c.α. p. 304): 'church' [LN; all translations], '(universal) church' [BDAG]. This noun denotes a congregation of Christians, implying interacting membership [LN]. It denotes the global community of Christians [BDAG].

g. aorist mid. indic. of περιποιέω (LN 57.61) (BDAG 2. p. 804): 'to purchase' [KJV, NASB, NLT], 'to acquire' [Bar, BDAG, LN; GW], 'to buy' [CEV, NCV, NIV], 'to achieve, to win' [LN], 'to obtain' [BDAG, BECNT; ESV, NET, NRSV], 'to gain for oneself' [BDAG], 'to win for oneself' [AB, CBC; REB], 'to make one's own' [TEV]. This verb means to acquire possession of something, with the probable component of considerable effort [LN]. It means to gain possession of something [LN].

h. αἷμα (LN 23.107) (BDAG 2.b. p. 27): 'blood' [BDAG; all translations except NCV], 'life blood' [BDAG], 'death' [LN; NCV], 'violent death' [LN]. This noun is a figurative extension of meaning of αἷμα 'blood' and denotes the death of a person, generally as the result of violence or execution [LN]. It is a figurative extension of αἷμα and denotes the blood and life as an expiatory sacrifice, especially of the blood of Jesus [BDAG].

QUESTION—What is meant by the phrase 'Pay careful attention to yourselves'?

The phrase is used here as an idiom that means you should be concerned about your spiritual wellbeing, not that you should look at each other [TH, TRT]. It means they should maintain the quality and integrity of their own Christian life [Bar].

QUESTION—To whom does the phrase 'with his own blood' refer?

It refers to the blood of his own son. [AB, Bar, BECNT, CBC, EBC, NAC, NICNT, PNTC, TNTC; CEV, NCV, NET, NRSV, TEV].

**20:29** I know that after my departure[a] savage[b] wolves[c] will-come-in among you, not sparing[d] the flock;

LEXICON—a. ἄφιξις (LN 15.37) (BDAG p. 157): 'departure' [AB, Bar, BDAG, BECNT; ESV, NASB], 'departing' [KJV]. The phrase 'after my departure' is also translated 'after/when I am gone' [CBC; CEV, NET, REB]. This noun is also translated as a verb: 'I leave' [GW, NCV, NIV, NLT, TEV], 'I have gone' [NRSV]. This noun denotes the motion away

from a reference point with emphasis upon the departure, but without implications as to any resulting state of separation or rupture [LN].
  b. βαρύς (LN 20.7) (BDAG 4. p. 168): 'savage' [AB, BDAG, CBC; NASB, NIV, NRSV, REB], 'fierce' [BDAG, BECNT, LN; CEV, ESV, GW, NET, TEV], 'cruel' [BDAG, LN], 'vicious' [LN; NLT], 'fearsome' [Bar], 'grievous' [KJV], 'wild' [NCV]. This adjective describes one who is vicious and cruel [LN]. It pertains to being of unbearable temperament [BDAG].
  c. λύκος (LN 88.121) (BDAG 2. p. 604): 'wolf' [BDAG; all translations], 'vicious person, fierce wolf, fierce person' [LN]. This noun is a figurative extension of meaning of λύκος 'wolf' and denotes a person who is particularly vicious and dangerous [LN]. It denotes a fierce or vicious person [BDAG].
  d. pres. mid./pass. (deponent = act.) participle of φείδομαι (LN 22.28) (BDAG 1. p. 1051): 'to spare' [BDAG, LN; all translations except CEV, NCV], 'to prevent trouble happening to someone' [LN], not explicit [CEV, NCV]. This verb means to cause someone not to be troubled [LN]. It means to save from loss or discomfort [BDAG].
QUESTION—To whom does the phrase 'savage wolves' refer?
It refers to outsiders who will come and try to indoctrinate the church to their false teaching [TH, TNTC]. They may be Jewish or Gentile teachers who make their way into the church and propagate false doctrine within it [Bar].

**20:30 and from among your own selves will-arise[a] men speaking- perverse -(things), to-draw-away[b] the disciples after them.**
LEXICON—a. fut. mid. indic. of ἀνίστημι (LN 13.81): 'to arise' [AB, BECNT, LN; ESV, KJV, NASB, NET, NIV, REB], 'to come into existence, to appear' [LN], 'to come forward' [CBC; GW], 'to rise up' [Bar; NCV, NLT], 'to come' [NRSV], not explicit [CEV, TEV]. This verb means to come into existence, with the implication of assuming a place or position [LN].
  b. pres. act. infin. of ἀποσπάω (LN 31.74) (BDAG 2.a. p. 120): 'to draw away' [Bar, BDAG, BECNT, LN; ESV, KJV, NASB, NET, NIV], 'to lead away' [LN; NCV, TEV], 'to lure away to' [LN], 'to attract, to proselyte' [BDAG], 'to win over' [AB; CEV], 'to lure' [GW], 'to draw' [NLT], 'to entice' [NRSV]. The phrase 'to draw away the disciples after them' is also translated 'to induce/get the disciples to break away and follow them' [CBC; REB]. This verb is a figurative extension of meaning of ἀποσπάω 'to pull out, to drag' and means to cause a change of belief so as to correspond more with the beliefs of the person or factor causing the change [LN].

**20:31 Therefore be-alert,[a] remembering that for (a)-three-year-period I-did- not -cease[b] night and day to-admonish[c] everyone with tears.**
LEXICON—a. pres. act. impera. of γρηγορέω (LN 27.56) (BDAG 2. p. 208): 'to be alert' [BECNT, LN; ESV, GW, NET, NRSV], 'to be on the alert'

[BDAG, CBC; NASB, REB], 'to be watchful, to be vigilant' [LN], 'to be careful' [NCV], 'to watch' [KJV]. The phrase 'be alert' is also translated 'be on your guard' [AB; CEV, NIV], 'Watch out!' [NLT], 'Watch' [Bar; TEV]. This verb is a figurative extension of meaning of γρηγορέω 'to stay awake' and means to be in continuous readiness and alertness to learn [LN]. It means to be in constant readiness [BDAG].
- b. aorist mid. indic. of παύω (LN 68.34) (BDAG 2. p. 790): 'to cease' [AB, Bar, BDAG, BECNT, CBC, LN; ESV, KJV, NASB, NRSV, REB], 'to stop' [LN; NCV, NET, NIV], 'to stop (oneself)' [BDAG], not explicit [GW, NLT, TEV]. The phrase 'I did not cease…to admonish everyone' is also translated 'I kept warning you' [CEV]. This verb means to cease from an activity in which one is engaged [LN]. It means to cease doing something [BDAG].
- c. pres. act. participle of νουθετέω (LN 33.424) (BDAG p. 679): 'to admonish' [Bar, BDAG, BECNT; ESV, NASB], 'to warn' [AB, BDAG, LN; CEV, KJV, NCV, NET, NIV, NRSV, REB], 'to teach' [TEV], 'to instruct' [BDAG; GW], 'to counsel' [CBC], not explicit [NLT]. This verb means to advise someone concerning the dangerous consequences of some happening or action [LN]. It means to counsel about avoidance or cessation of an improper course of conduct [BDAG].

QUESTION—What is meant by the phrase 'night and day' here?

This phrase is a hyperbole/exaggeration [TNTC, TRT].

**20:32** And now I-commend[a] you to-God and to-the word[b] of his grace, which is-able[c] to-build[d] (you up) and to-give you the inheritance[e] among all those who are-sanctified.[f]

LEXICON—a. pres. mid. indic. of παρατίθημι (LN 35.47) (BDAG 3.b. p. 772): 'to commend' [BDAG, BECNT, CBC; ESV, KJV, NASB, NRSV, REB, TEV], 'to give over' [BDAG], 'to entrust' [BDAG; GW, NET, NLT], 'to commit' [AB, Bar; NIV], 'to entrust oneself to, to commit oneself to the care of' [LN], 'to put in the care of' [NCV]. The phrase 'I commend you to God' is also translated 'I now place you in God's care' [CEV]. This verb means to entrust oneself to the care of someone [LN]. It means to entrust for safekeeping and here it means to entrust someone to the care or protection of someone [BDAG].
- b. λόγος (LN 33.260) (BDAG 1.a.β. p. 600): 'word' [AB, Bar, BDAG, BECNT, CBC; ESV, KJV, NASB, NIV, REB], 'message' [CEV, GW, NCV, NET, NLT, NRSV, TEV], 'what is preached, gospel' [LN]. This noun denotes the content of what is preached about Christ or about the good news [LN]. It denotes a communication whereby the mind finds expression [BDAG].
- c. pres. mid./pass. (deponent=act.) participle of δύναμαι (LN 74.5): 'to be able' [AB, Bar, BECNT; ESV, KJV, NASB, NCV, NET, NLT, NRSV, TEV], 'to be able to' [LN], 'can' [LN; CEV, GW, NIV]. The phrase 'which is able to build you up' is also translated 'which has power to

build you up' [CBC; REB]. This verb means to be able to do or to experience something [LN].
  d. aorist act. infin. of οἰκοδομέω (LN 74.15) (BDAG 3. p. 696): 'to build up' [BDAG, LN; all translations except CEV, GW, NCV], 'to strengthen, to make more able' [BDAG, LN]. The phrase 'which is able to build you up' is also translated 'This/That message can help you' [CEV, GW], 'It is able to give you strength' [NCV]. This verb means to increase the potential of someone or something, with focus upon the process involved [LN]. It means to help improve ability to function in living responsibly and effectively [BDAG].
  e. κληρονομία (LN 57.140) (BDAG 3. p. 548): 'inheritance' [AB, Bar, BECNT, LN; ESV, GW, KJV, NASB, NET, NIV, NLT, NRSV], 'transcendent salvation' [BDAG], 'blessings' [NCV, TEV], 'heritage' [CBC; REB]. The phrase 'to give you the inheritance' is also translated 'give you what belongs to you' [CEV]. This noun denotes that which is received from a deceased person [LN].
  f. perf. pass. participle of ἁγιάζω (LN 53.44) (BDAG 2. p. 10): 'to be sanctified' [AB, Bar, BDAG, BECNT; ESV, KJV, NASB, NET, NIV, NRSV], 'to be dedicated' [BDAG, CBC], 'to be consecrated' [BDAG, LN], 'to be dedicated to God' [LN]. The phrase 'those who are sanctified' is also translated 'those he has set apart' [NLT], 'those whom God has made his own' [REB], 'all his people' [TEV], 'God's people' [CEV], 'God's/his holy people' [GW, NCV]. This verb means to dedicate to the service of and to loyalty to deity [LN]. It means to include a person in the inner circle of what is holy, in both cultic and moral associations of the word [BDAG].
QUESTION—What is the function of the phrase 'And now'?
  It introduces the final part of Paul's speech [TH].
QUESTION—What is meant by the phrase 'word of his grace'?
  It possibly refers to Paul's own message which he preached about the grace of God [TH].
QUESTION—To what does 'the inheritance' refer?
  In this context it refers to the transcendent salvation that stands as the center of the gospel rooted in grace [BECNT].

**20:33** **I coveted[a] no one's silver[b] or gold or clothing.**
LEXICON—a. aorist act. indic. of ἐπιθυμέω (LN 25.20) (BDAG 1. p. 371): 'to covet' [BECNT, LN; ESV, KJV, NASB, NIV, NLT, NRSV], 'to lust' [LN], 'to desire' [Bar, BDAG; NET], 'to long for' [BDAG], 'to want' [CBC; CEV, GW, NCV, REB, TEV], 'to ask (for)' [AB]. This verb means to strongly desire to have what belongs to someone else and/or to engage in an activity which is morally wrong [LN]. It means to have a strong desire to do or secure something [BDAG].
  b. ἀργύριον (LN 6.69) (BDAG 2.a. p. 128): 'silver' [all translations except CBC; CEV, NCV, REB], 'money' [CBC, LN; CEV, NCV, REB], 'silver

money' [BDAG]. The idiom 'silver and gold' denotes a generic expression for currency [LN]. It denotes silver money besides gold [BDAG].

**20:34** You- yourselves -know[a] that these hands ministered[b] to my needs and to those who were with me.

LEXICON—a. pres. act. indic. of γινώσκω (LN 28.1) (BDAG 6.c. p. 200): 'to know' [BDAG, LN; all translations], 'to have come to know' [BDAG], 'to know about, to have knowledge of, to be acquainted with' [LN]. This verb means to possess information about [LN]. It means to have come to the knowledge of [BDAG].

b. aorist act. indic. of ὑπηρετέω (LN 35.32) (BDAG p. 1035): 'to minister' [Bar, BECNT; ESV, KJV, NASB], 'to provide for' [LN; NET], 'to provide' [TEV], 'to supply' [NIV, NLT], 'to support' [LN; GW, NRSV], 'to serve, to be helpful' [BDAG]. The phrase 'these hands ministered to my needs' is also translated 'I have worked with my own hands to make a living for myself' [CEV], 'I always worked to take care of my own needs' [NCV], 'these hands of mine earned enough for the needs of myself' [CBC; REB], 'these hands have earned what was needful for me' [AB]. This verb means to provide continuous and possibly prolonged assistance and help by supplying the needs of someone [LN]. It means to render service [BDAG].

**20:35** In all-things I-showed[a] you that by working-hard in-this-way (we) must help[b] the weak and remember the words of-the Lord Jesus, that he-himself -said, 'It-is more blessed[c] to-give than to-receive.'"

LEXICON—a. aorist act. indic. of ὑποδείκνυμι (LN 28.47) (BDAG 2. p. 1037): 'to show' [BDAG, LN; all translations except GW, NLT, NRSV], 'to make known, to demonstrate' [LN], 'to give direction, to prove, to set forth' [BDAG]. The phrase 'I showed you' is also translated 'I have given you an example' [GW, NRSV], 'I have been a constant example' [NLT]. This verb means to make known the character or significance of something by visual, auditory, gestural, or linguistic means [LN]. It means to give instruction or moral direction [BDAG].

b. pres. mid. infin. of ἀντιλαμβάνω (LN 35.1) (BDAG 1. p. 89): 'to help' [LN; all translations except KJV, NRSV], 'to support' [KJV, NRSV], 'to take part, to come to the aid of' [BDAG]. This verb means to assist in supplying what may be needed [LN]. It means to take someone's part by assisting [BDAG].

c. μακάριος (LN 25.119) (BDAG 2.b.γ. p. 611): 'blessed' [AB, Bar, BDAG, BECNT; ESV, KJV, NASB, NCV, NET, NIV, NLT, NRSV], 'happy' [BDAG, LN], 'fortunate, privileged' [BDAG], 'satisfied' [GW]. This adjective is also translated as a noun: 'blessings' [CEV], 'happiness' [CBC; REB, TEV]. This adjective pertains to being happy, with the implication of enjoying favorable circumstances [LN]. It pertains to being especially favored [BDAG].

QUESTION—To whom does 'the weak' refer?
It can refer to the sick [TH, TRT] and it can include people who have any kind of need, including those who are poor, old or spiritually weak [TRT].

QUESTION—What is meant by the phrase 'It is more blessed to give than to receive'?
This phrase does not mean that those who benefit from the generosity of others are less blessed than those who give. The principle is rather, it is better for a person who can do so to give to help others rather than to amass further wealth for himself [PNTC, TNTC]. Paul applied this rule to the specific problem of avarice among church leaders. The minister is to be a servant, a giver and not a taker. The one who leads the flock of God should focus on the needs of others, be more concerned with giving than with receiving [NAC].

**DISCOURSE UNIT—20:36–38** [NAC, NICNT, PNTC]. The topic is departing [PNTC], an affectionate parting [NICNT], final leave-taking [NAC].

**20:36** **And when he had-said these-things, he knelt-down[a] and prayed with them all.**

LEXICON—a. aorist act. participle of τίθημι (LN 17.19) (BDAG 1.b.γ. p. 1003): 'to kneel down' [LN; all translations except NLT], 'to kneel' [LN; NLT], 'to show deference to' [BDAG]. This verb means to kneel down before, with the implication of an act of reverence or of supplication [LN].

QUESTION—What is indicated by Paul kneeling to pray?
The usual posture for prayer was standing [TNTC], but on solemn occasions kneeling was practiced [BECNT, TNTC].

**20:37** **And there-was much weeping[a] on the part of-all; they embraced[b] Paul and kissed[c] him,**

LEXICON—a. κλαυθμός (LN 25.138) (BDAG p. 546): 'weeping' [AB, BDAG, LN; ESV, NRSV], 'crying' [BDAG, LN], 'lamentation' [Bar], 'tears' [BECNT]. This noun is also translated 'loud cries of sorrow' [CBC; REB]. This noun is also translated as a verb: 'to weep' [KJV, NASB, NET, NIV], 'to cry' [CEV, GW, NCV, NLT, TEV]. This noun denotes the act of weeping or wailing, with emphasis upon the noise accompanying the weeping [LN].
  b. aorist act. participle of ἐπιπίπτω (LN 34.64) (BDAG 1.b. p. 377): 'to embrace' [AB, BECNT, LN; ESV, NASB, NIV, NLT, NRSV], 'to hug' [LN; CEV, NET, TEV], 'to fall on' [Bar, BDAG; KJV], 'to press' [BDAG]. The phrase 'they embraced Paul' is also translated 'they put their arms around Paul/him' [GW, NCV], 'they folded Paul in their arms' [CBC; REB]. The idiom 'to fall on the neck' means to show special affection for by throwing one's arms around a person [LN]. It means to cause pressure by pushing against or falling on [BDAG].
  c. imperf. act. indic. of καταφιλέω (LN 34.62) (BDAG p. 529): 'to kiss' [BDAG, LN; all translations]. This verb means to kiss, either as an

expression of greeting or as a sign of special affection and appreciation [LN].

**20:38** grieving[a] most-of-all because of the word which he-had-spoken, that they would not see[b] his face again. And they-accompanied[c] him to the ship.
LEXICON—a. pres. pass. participle of ὀδυνάω (LN 25.236) (BDAG 2. p. 692): 'to be grieving' [Bar; NASB, NRSV], 'to be grieved' [NIV], 'to be very much distressed, to be terribly worried' [LN], 'to be pained' [BDAG], 'to be distressed' [AB, CBC, BDAG; REB], 'to be sorrowful' [ESV], 'to be sorrowing' [BECNT; KJV], 'to be sad' [CEV, NLT, TEV], 'to be saddened' [NET], 'to be hurt' [GW], not explicit [NCV]. This verb means to experience great distress or anxiety [LN]. It means to experience mental and spiritual pain [BDAG].
    b. pres. act. infin. of θεωρέω (LN 24.14) (BDAG 1. p. 454): 'to see' [BDAG; all translations], 'to observe, to be a spectator of, to look at' [BDAG, LN]. This verb means to observe something with continuity and attention, often with the implication that what is observed is something unusual [LN]. It means to observe something with sustained attention [BDAG].
    c. imperf. act. indic. of προπέμπω (LN 15.155) (BDAG 1. p. 873): 'to accompany' [BDAG, LN; ESV, KJV, NASB, NET, NIV], 'to escort' [BDAG, CBC, LN; NLT, REB], 'to go with' [AB; CEV, NCV, TEV], 'to take' [GW], 'to bring' [BECNT; NRSV], 'to see off' [Bar]. This verb means to accompany a person for a short distance at the beginning of a journey [LN]. It means to conduct someone who has a destination in mind [BDAG].

**DISCOURSE UNIT—21:1–28:31** [TNTC]. The topic is Paul's arrest and imprisonment.

**DISCOURSE UNIT—21:1–22:29** [Bar]. The topic is Paul returns to Jerusalem.

**DISCOURSE UNIT—21:1–40** [NCV]. The topic is Paul's journey to Jerusalem.

**DISCOURSE UNIT—21:1–26** [CBC]. The topic is to Jerusalem.

**DISCOURSE UNIT—21:1–16** [BECNT, EBC, NAC, PNTC, TNTC; CEV, ESV, NCV, NIV, NRSV, TEV]. The topic is Paul's journey to Jerusalem [BECNT, TNTC; NRSV], on to Jerusalem [EBC; NIV], the voyage to Jerusalem [NAC], following the way of Jesus [PNTC], Paul goes to Jerusalem [CEV, ESV, NCV, TEV].

**DISCOURSE UNIT—21:1–14** [AB, Bar; NASB, NLT]. The topic is from Miletus to Caesarea [AB], journey to Jerusalem [Bar], Paul's journey to Jerusalem [NLT], Paul sails from Miletus [NASB].

**DISCOURSE UNIT—21:1–6** [NAC, NICNT, PNTC; GW]. The topic is warning at Tyre [NAC], Miletus to Tyre [NICNT], from Miletus to Tyre [PNTC], Paul in Tyre [GW].

**21:1** And it-happened-(that) we having-parted[a] from them (we)-set-sail,[b] having-run-(a)-straight-course[c] we-came to Cos, and on-the next-(day) to Rhodes and-from-there to Patara. **21:2** And having-found (a)-ship crossing-over[d] to Phoenicia having-gone-aboard[e] we-set-sail.

LEXICON—a. aorist pass. participle of ἀποσπάω (LN 15.54) (BDAG 2.b. p. 120): 'to part' [CBC; ESV, NASB, NRSV], 'to tear oneself away from' [AB, BECNT; NET, NIV, REB], 'to say goodbye' [CEV, NCV, TEV], 'to say farewell' [NLT], 'to leave' [LN; GW], 'to separate from (someone)' [Bar], 'to go off, to withdraw' [LN], 'to be gotten from (someone)' [KJV]. This verb means to draw oneself away from, suggesting that the movement was not sudden [LN]. It means to draw away from a place or point of view [BDAG].

  b. aorist pass. infin. of ἀνάγω (LN 54.5) (BDAG 4. p. 62): 'to set sail' [AB, Bar, BECNT, CBC, LN; ESV, NASB, NRSV], 'to sail' [CEV, GW, NCV, NLT, TEV], 'to put out to sea' [BDAG, LN; NET, NIV], 'to put to sea' [REB], 'to launch' [KJV]. This verb means to begin to go by boat [BDAG, LN].

  c. aorist act. participle of εὐθυδρομέω (LN 54.3) (BDAG p. 406): 'run a straight course' [BDAG; NASB], 'to make a straight course' [Bar, BECNT], 'to make a straight run' [CBC; REB], 'to come by a straight course' [ESV, NRSV], 'to come with a straight course' [KJV], 'to sail a straight course' [LN; NET], 'to sail straight to' [LN; CEV, GW, NCV, NIV, NLT], 'to sail straight across' [TEV], 'to come straight ahead' [AB]. This verb means to follow a straight course to one's destination or goal [LN].

  d. pres. act. participle of διαπεράω (LN 15.31) (BDAG p. 235): 'to cross over (to)' [BDAG, LN; NASB, NET, NIV], 'to cross (to)' [Bar, BECNT; ESV], 'to go over' [LN], 'to go (to)' [CEV, GW, NCV, REB], 'to sail to' [NLT], 'to follow (unto)' [KJV]. The phrase 'crossing over' is also translated 'bound for' [AB, CBC; NRSV, REB]. This verb means to move from one side to another of some geographical object (for example, a body of water, chasm, valley, etc.) [LN]. It means to move across the area between two sides of a geographical object [BDAG].

  e. aorist act. participle of ἐπιβαίνω (LN 15.97) (BDAG 1. p. 367): 'to go aboard' [AB, BECNT, CBC; ESV, GW, KJV, NASB, NCV, NET, NRSV, TEV], 'to go on board' [NIV, NRSV], 'to get on board' [CEV], 'to board' [BDAG; NLT], 'to embark' [Bar, LN], 'to go onto, to mount' [LN], 'to go up/upon' [BDAG]. This verb means to move up onto some object [LN]. It means to move up onto something [BDAG].

QUESTION—What is the function of Ὡς δὲ ἐγένετο 'and it happened that'?

  It is transitional, beginning a new phase in the story by introducing a subordinate clause [TH]. It is translated 'when' [AB, Bar, BECNT, CBC;

ESV, GW, NASB, NRSV], 'after' [CEV, NCV, NET, NIV, NLT], 'it came to pass' [KJV].

QUESTION—What is implied in the verb phrase 'we having parted'?

It suggests that the parting was not an easy one, something that they were not eager to do [AB, Bar, BECNT, EBC, NICNT, TNTC; NET, NIV, REB]. Their leaving was emotionally difficult [BECNT]. It simply means to part from someone [TH].

**21:3** **And having-come-in-sight-of**[a] **Cyprus and leaving it on-(the)-left**[b] **we-sailed to Syria and landed**[c] **at Tyre, since the ship was to-unload**[d] **the cargo there.**

LEXICON—a. aorist act. participle of ἀναφαίνω (LN 24.23) (BDAG p. 75): 'to come in sight of' [BECNT, CBC; ESV, NASB, NRSV, REB], 'to come within sight of' [CEV], 'to come to be seen, to appear, to come into view' [LN], 'to light up, to cause to appear' [BDAG]. The phrase 'having come in sight of Cyprus' is also translated 'we could see Cyprus' [GW, TEV], 'we sighted Cyprus' [AB; NET, NLT], 'after sighting Cyprus' [NIV], 'sailed near...seeing it' [NCV], 'having raised Cyprus' [Bar], 'having discovered Cyprus' [KJV]. This verb means to come to a point of being visible, with focus upon the process of becoming seen [LN].

b. εὐώνυμος (LN 82.7) (BDAG p. 417): 'left' [AB, Bar, BDAG, BECNT, LN; ESV, GW, NASB, NLT, NRSV], 'left hand' [KJV], 'left side' [LN], 'port side' [NET], 'port beam' [CBC], 'port' [REB]. The phrase 'on the left' is also translated 'south of it' [CEV, NIV, TEV], '(seeing it) to the north' [NCV]. This adjective describes being to the left of some point of reference [LN]. It is a point of reference opposite of 'right' [BDAG].

c. aorist act. indic. of κατέρχομαι (LN 54.15) (BDAG 2. p. 531): 'to land' [Bar, BECNT; ESV, GW, KJV, NASB, NIV, NCV, NRSV], 'to put in' [CBC, LN; NET, REB], 'to touch (at)' [AB], 'to sail on (to)' [CEV], 'to stop (at)' [NCV], 'to go ashore (at)' [TEV], 'to arrive at land' [LN]. This verb, which is a technical, nautical term, means to go by ship toward the shore [LN].

d. pres. mid. or pass. (deponent = act.) participle of ἀποφορτίζομαι (LN 15.209) (BDAG p. 125): 'to unload' [BDAG, LN; all translations except Bar; KJV], 'to unlade' [KJV], 'to discharge cargo' [Bar, LN]. This verb means to cause a load to be carried off [LN].

QUESTION—What is the time reference for the present tense participle ἀποφορτίζομαι 'to unload'?

It is used to refer to a future event [TH; all translations].

**21:4** **And having-sought-out**[a] **the disciples,**[b] **we-stayed there seven days, who were-saying to-Paul through**[c] **the Spirit not to-go-up**[d] **to Jerusalem.**

LEXICON—a. aorist act. participle of ἀνευρίσκω (LN 27.28) (BDAG p. 78): 'to seek out' [Bar, BECNT; ESV, NIV, REB], 'to search for' [BDAG; GW], 'to find' [AB; KJV, NCV, NLT, TEV], 'to go and find' [CBC], 'to look up' [CEV, NASB, NRSV], 'to locate' [NET], 'to look for' [BDAG],

'to find by searching, to look for and find' [LN]. This verb means to learn the location of something by intentional searching [LN].
  b. μαθητής (LN 36.38): 'disciple' [LN; all translations except CEV, NCV, NLT, TEV], 'the Lord's follower' [CEV], 'follower' [LN; NCV], 'believer' [TEV], '(local) believer' [NLT]. This noun denotes a person who is a disciple or follower of someone [LN].
  c. διά with genitive object (LN 90.4) (BDAG 4.b.β. p. 225): 'through' [AB, Bar, BDAG, BECNT, LN; ESV, KJV, NASB, NCV, NET, NIV, NLT, NRSV], 'by' [BDAG, CBC, LN; REB], 'by the power of' [TEV]. The phrase 'who were saying to Paul through the Spirit' is also translated 'the Spirit had the disciples tell Paul' [GW], 'the Holy Spirit had told them to warn Paul' [CEV]. This preposition indicates an intermediate agent, with implicit or explicit causative agent [LN]. It indicates personal agency [BDAG].
  d. pres. act. infin. of ἐπιβαίνω (LN 15.97) (BDAG 1. p. 367): 'to go up (to)' [KJV], 'to go on (to)' [BECNT; CEV, ESV, NIV, NLT, NRSV], 'to go (to)' [Bar; GW, NCV, TEV], 'to travel on (to)' [AB], 'to set foot in' [NASB, NET], 'to embark, to go onto' [LN], 'to mount' [BDAG, LN], 'to go up/upon, to board' [BDAG]. The phrase 'not to go up to' is also translated 'to abandon his visit to' [CBC; REB]. This verb means to move up onto some object [LN]. It means to move up onto something [BDAG].

QUESTION—What does it mean that it was 'through the Spirit' that they were telling him not to go to Jerusalem?
  1. The Holy Spirit was letting him know that there would be suffering and danger [Bar, BECNT, NICNT, PNTC, TNTC], but this does not mean that in his resolve to go to Jerusalem Paul was being disobedient [Bar, NICNT, PNTC, TNTC]. The warning from his friends not to go to Jerusalem arose from their human concern [Bar, BECNT, NAC, PNTC, TNTC], not from the Holy Spirit [Bar, PNTC]. There was some degree of inspiration in what they were saying [Bar]. It was the Holy Spirit who was driving Paul to Jerusalem [NAC].
  2. The Holy Spirit was telling Paul not to go to Jerusalem [CEV, GW].

**21:5** And so-it-was when our days were-ended,[a] having-left[b] we-went-our-way,[c] everyone accompanying[d] us with (their) wives and children as-far-as outside[e] the city and bowing[f] the knees on the beach, having-prayed, **21:6** we-said-goodbye[g] to-one-another and went-aboard the ship, and they returned to their own-homes.

LEXICON—a. aorist act. infin. of ἐξαρτίζω (LN 67.71) (BDAG 1. p. 346): 'to be ended' [BECNT, CBC; ESV, NASB, NRSV, REB], 'to complete' [AB, Bar, BDAG], 'to accomplish' [KJV], 'to be over' [CEV, NET, TEV], 'to be up' [GW], 'to end, to bring to an end' [LN], 'to finish' [BDAG]. The phrase 'when our days were ended' is also translated 'at the end of the week' [NLT], 'when we finished our visit' [NCV], 'when it was time to leave' [NIV]. This verb means to cause a duration to come to an end [LN]. It means to bring something to an end [BDAG].

b. aorist act. participle of ἐξέρχομαι (LN 15.40): 'to leave' [Bar, CBC; NASB, NCV, NET, NIV, NRSV, REB, TEV], 'to go out' [AB], 'to depart' [BECNT; ESV, KJV], 'to go out of, to depart out of, to leave from within' [LN], not explicit [CEV, GW, NLT]. This verb means to move out of an enclosed or well defined two or three-dimensional area [LN].

c. imperf. mid. or pass. (deponent = act.) indic. of πορεύομαι (LN 15.10): 'to go one's way' [KJV], 'to go on one's way' [NET, NRSV], 'to go on a journey' [BECNT; ESV], 'to start on a journey' [NASB], 'to set out on a journey' [Bar], 'to continue a journey' [CBC; REB], 'to continue a trip' [NCV], 'to proceed on one's journey' [NRSV], 'to continue on one's way' [NIV], 'to start on one's way' [CEV, GW], 'to set off' [AB], 'to go, to move' [LN]. The phrase 'having left we went our way' is also translated 'when we returned to the ship' [NLT]. This verb means to move from one place to another, with the possible implication of continuity and distance [LN].

d. pres. act. participle of προπέμπω (LN 15.155) (BDAG 1. p. 873): 'to accompany' [BDAG, LN; ESV, GW, NET, NIV], 'to go with' [AB], 'to walk with' [CEV], 'to come with' [NCV, NLT, TEV], 'to see someone off' [Bar], 'to bring someone on their way' [BECNT; KJV], 'to escort' [BDAG, CBC, LN; NASB, NRSV, REB]. This verb means to accompany a person for a short distance at the beginning of a journey [LN]. It means to conduct someone who has a destination in mind [BDAG].

e. ἔξω with genitive object (LN 83.20) (BDAG 2.b. p. 354): 'outside' [Bar, BECNT, LN; ESV, NCV, NET, NRSV], 'apart from' [LN], 'out' [BDAG]. The phrase 'as far as outside the city' is also translated 'out of the city' [AB, CBC; GW, KJV, NASB, NIV, REB, TEV], 'from the town' [CEV], 'left the city' [NLT]. This preposition denotes a position not contained within a particular area [LN]. It denotes a position outside an area or limits, as result of an action [BDAG].

f. aorist act. participle of τίθημι (LN 17.19) (BDAG 1.b.γ. p. 1003): 'to kneel down' [AB, BECNT, CBC, LN; ESV, KJV, NASB, NET, NRSV, REB], 'to kneel' [Bar, LN; CEV, GW, NCV, NIV, NLT, TEV], 'to show deference to' [BDAG]. This verb means to kneel down before, with the implication of an act of reverence or of supplication [LN].

g. aorist mid. (deponent = act.) indic. of ἀπασπάζομαι (LN 33.21) (BDAG p. 98): 'to say goodbye to' [AB; CEV, GW, NCV, NIV, TEV], 'to bid goodbye to' [CBC, LN; REB], 'to say farewell to' [Bar, BDAG; ESV, NASB, NET, NRSV], 'to say one's farewells' [NLT], 'to bid farewell to' [BECNT], 'to take leave of' [BDAG, LN; KJV]. This verb means to say goodbye [LN].

**DISCOURSE UNIT—21:7–16** [PNTC]. The topic is from Tyre to Jerusalem.

**DISCOURSE UNIT—21:7–14** [NAC; GW]. The topic is warning of Agabus [NAC], Paul in Caesarea [GW].

**DISCOURSE UNIT—21:7–9** [NICNT]. The topic is Tyre to Caesarea.

**21:7** **And we having-finished<sup>a</sup> the voyage from Tyre we-reached Ptolemais and having-greeted<sup>b</sup> the brothers we-stayed with them one day.**

LEXICON—a. aorist act. participle of διανύω (LN 68.25) (BDAG 1. p. 234): 'to finish' [BECNT, LN; ESV, KJV, NASB, NRSV], 'to conclude' [AB], 'to complete' [BDAG, LN], 'to make (the passage)' [CBC; REB], 'to continue' [Bar; NCV, NET, NIV, TEV], not explicit [NLT]. The phrase 'having completed the voyage' is also translated 'we sailed' [CEV], 'our sea travel ended when we sailed' [GW]. This verb means to complete an activity, normally involving movement [LN]. It means to carry out an activity [BDAG].

b. aorist mid. (deponent = act.) participle of ἀσπάζομαι (LN 33.20) (BDAG 1.b. p. 144): 'to greet' [BDAG; all translations except KJV], 'to salute' [KJV], 'to send greetings' [LN], 'to welcome' [BDAG]. This verb means to employ certain set phrases as a part of the process of greeting, whether communicated directly or indirectly [LN]. It means to engage in hospitable recognition of another [BDAG].

QUESTION—Did they finish the voyage and then go on to Caesarea by land, or did they continue the voyage to Caesarea by ship?

They completed the voyage from Tyre to Ptolemais, and then continued on to Caesarea by ship as well [BECNT, CBC, EBC, NAC]. They completed the voyage from Tyre to Ptolemais, but may have continued on to Caesarea by land [NICNT]. It is not known if he went by ship or by land [AB]. If this verb means he completed his voyage, he would have gone on to Caesarea by land, but if it means that the voyage was continued, then it could mean that he might have gone on to Caesarea by ship. However, it would have been difficult to travel the forty miles to Caesarea by land and arrive the following day, as is indicated in v.8 [TH].

**21:8** **And on-the next-day having-left we-came to Caesarea and going-into the house of-Philip the evangelist,<sup>a</sup> being-(one) of the seven, we-stayed with him.** **21:9** **And (he) had four unmarried<sup>b</sup> daughters (who) would-prophesy.<sup>c</sup>**

LEXICON—a. εὐαγγελιστής (LN 53.76) (BDAG p. 403): 'evangelist' [BDAG, LN; all translations except CEV, GW, NCV], 'preacher' [CEV, NCV], 'missionary' [GW], 'proclaimer of the gospel' [BDAG]. This noun denotes one who announces the gospel [LN].

b. παρθένος (LN 9.39) (BDAG a. p. 777): 'unmarried' [BECNT, CBC; all versions except KJV, NASB], 'virgin' [AB, Bar, BDAG, LN; KJV, NASB], 'young woman' [LN], 'chaste person' [BDAG]. This noun denotes a female person beyond puberty but not yet married and a virgin (though in some contexts virginity is not a focal component of meaning) [LN]. It denotes one who has never engaged in sexual intercourse [BDAG].

c. pres. act. participle of προφητεύω (LN 33.459) (BDAG 1. p. 890): 'to prophesy' [Bar, BDAG, BECNT, LN; CEV, ESV, KJV, NET, NIV], 'to make inspired utterances' [LN]. This participle is also translated as a phrase: 'who possessed the gift of prophecy' [CBC; REB], 'who had the gift of prophesy/prophesying' [NCV, NLT, NRSV], 'who had the ability to speak what God had revealed' [GW], 'who proclaimed God's message' [TEV]. It is also translated as a noun: 'prophetesses' [NASB], 'ecstatics' [AB]. This verb means to speak under the influence of divine inspiration, with or without reference to future events [LN]. It means to proclaim an inspired revelation [BDAG].

QUESTION—What does it mean that Philip was an evangelist?

This is a reference to the missionary activity he had carried out in Samaria and the coastal plain of Judea [NICNT]. It means he preached the good news [CBC]. It describes his gift, but also distinguishes him from the apostle named Philip [PNTC, TNTC]. He may have founded the church in Caesarea [TNTC].

QUESTION—What does it mean that he was one of 'the seven'?

This is a reference to Acts 6 where men were appointed to help the apostles distribute food [BECNT, EBC, NICNT, PNTC, TNTC, TRT; CEV, GW, NLT]. He was not the Philip who was an apostle [Bar, BECNT, EBC, TNTC].

**DISCOURSE UNIT—21:10–14** [NICNT]. The topic is Agabus reappears.

**21:10** And as-(we)-were-staying many days a-certain prophet from Judea Agabus by-name, came-down **21:11** and coming to us and taking Paul's belt, having-bound[a] his-own feet and hands he-said, "The Holy Spirit says this, 'In-this-way[b] the Jews in Jerusalem will-bind the man whose belt this is, and they-will-hand-(him)-over[c] into (the)-hands of-(the)-Gentiles.'"

LEXICON—a. aorist act. participle of δέω (LN 18.13) (BDAG 1.b. p. 221): 'to bind' [AB, Bar, BDAG, BECNT, CBC; ESV, KJV, NASB, NLT, NRSV, REB], 'to tie' [BDAG, LN; GW, NCV, NET, NIV], 'to tie up' [LN; CEV, TEV], 'to tie together' [LN]. This verb means to tie objects together [LN]. It means to confine a person or thing by various kinds of restraints [BDAG].

b. οὕτως (LN 61.9): 'in this way' [LN; NASB, NIV, TEV], 'so' [AB, LN; KJV, NLT], 'thus' [Bar, BECNT, CBC, LN; ESV, REB], 'this is how' [GW, NCV], 'this is the way' [NET, NRSV], not explicit [CEV]. This adverb describes that which precedes [LN].

c. fut. act. indic. of παραδίδωμι (LN 37.12) (BDAG 1.b. p. 762): 'to hand over' [AB, BDAG, CBC, LN; CEV, GW, NET, NIV, NRSV, REB, TEV], 'to deliver' [Bar, BDAG, BECNT; ESV, KJV, NASB], 'to give over' [NCV], 'to turn over' [NLT], 'to deliver to the control of' [LN], 'to give (over), 'to turn over, to give up' [BDAG]. This verb means to hand someone over into the control of others [LN]. It means to convey something in which one has a relatively strong personal interest [BDAG].

QUESTION—Why is Agabus' travel to Caesarea described as 'coming down' in this passage, and a proposed trip to Jerusalem in v.12 and v.15 as 'going up'?

Caesarea is on the coast, and is at a lower elevation than Jerusalem [TRT].

QUESTION—What area is meant by 'Judea' here?
Since Caesarea is located in the Roman province of Judea, this use of 'Judea' is in a more restricted sense of the Jewish territory, since Caesarea was considered a Gentile area [Bar, NAC, NICNT, PNTC, TH]. He is referring to the mountainous area of Judea, and possibly to Jerusalem [AB]. It is possible that Luke is equating 'Judea' with Jerusalem [TH]. Agabus came to Caesarea from Jerusalem [EBC].

**21:12 And when we-heard these-things, we and the-people-there were-begging[a] (him) not to-go-up[b] to Jerusalem. 21:13 Then Paul answered, "What are-you-doing, weeping[c] and breaking[d] my heart? For I am prepared[e] not only to-be-bound but also to-die in Jerusalem for the name of-the Lord Jesus."**

LEXICON—a. imperf. act. indic. of παρακαλέω (LN 33.168) (BDAG 3. p. 765): 'to beg' [AB, Bar, BECNT; CEV, GW, NASB, NCV, NET, NLT, TEV], 'to beg and implore' [CBC; REB], 'to plead' [NIV], 'to urge' [ESV, NRSV], 'to beseech' [KJV], 'to ask for (earnestly), to plead for, to appeal to' [LN], 'to request' [LN, BDAG], 'to implore, to entreat' [BDAG]. This verb means to ask for something earnestly and with propriety [LN]. It means to make a strong request for something [BDAG].
  b. pres. act. infin. of ἀναβαίνω (LN 15.101) (BDAG 1.a.a. p. 58): 'to go up' [AB, Bar, BDAG, BECNT, LN; ESV, KJV, NASB, NET, NIV, NRSV], 'to go' [CEV, GW, NCV, TEV], 'to go on' [NLT], 'to come up' [LN], 'to ascend' [BDAG, LN]. The phrase 'not to go up' is also translated 'to abandon his visit' [CBC; REB]. This verb means to move up [LN]. It means to be in motion upward [BDAG].
  c. pres. act. participle of κλαίω (LN 25.138) (BDAG 1. p. 545): 'to weep' [AB, Bar, BDAG, BECNT, LN; ESV, KJV, NASB, NET, NIV, NLT, NRSV], 'to cry' [BDAG; CEV, GW, NCV, TEV], 'to wail, to lament' [LN]. The phrase 'what are you doing, weeping' is also translated 'why all these tears' [CBC; REB]. This verb means to weep or wail, with emphasis upon the noise accompanying the weeping [LN].
  d. pres. act. participle of συνθρύπτω (LN 25.282) (BDAG p. 972): 'to break in pieces' [BDAG]. The phrase συνθρύπτοντές μου τὴν καρδίαν 'breaking my heart' [Bar, BDAG, BECNT, LN; all versions except NCV, REB], is also translated '(attempts to) make me fainthearted' [AB], '(trying to) weaken my resolution' [CBC; REB], 'making me so sad' [NCV]. It means to cause great sorrow and grief [LN]. The idiom συνθρύπτω τὴν καρδίαν means to break someone's heart, to make grieve [LN].
  e. ἑτοίμως (LN 77.2) (BDAG p. 401): 'ready' [BDAG, LN; all translations except CEV], 'willing' [BDAG; CEV], 'prepared' [LN]. This adverb describes a state of readiness [LN].

QUESTION—Who is included in the 'we' of v.12?
It is the author and Paul's other traveling companions [Bar, EBC, NAC].

QUESTION—Was breaking Paul's heart a matter of causing him sorrow or of weakening his resolve?
1. It mean to weaken his resolve [AB, Bar, CBC, NICNT, PNTC; REB].
2. It means to cause him sadness or sorrow [BECNT, NAC, TNTC; NCV]. They are pressing his emotions [BECNT, TNTC].

**21:14** And he not being-persuaded[a] we-became-silent[b] (after)-having-said, "The will[c] of-the Lord be-(done)."

LEXICON—a. pres. pass. participle of πείθω (LN 33.301) (BDAG 3.a. p. 792): 'to be persuaded' [Bar, BDAG, BECNT, CBC, LN; ESV, GW, KJV, NASB, NET, NRSV], 'to be dissuaded' [AB; NIV, REB], 'to be convinced' [LN]. The phrase 'he not being persuaded' is also translated 'we could not persuade him' [NCV, NLT], 'we could not convince him' [TEV], 'we could not get Paul to change his mind' [CEV]. This verb means to convince someone to believe something and to act on the basis of what is recommended [LN]. It means to be won over as the result of persuasion [BDAG].
b. aorist act. indic. of ἡσυχάζω (LN 33.119) (BDAG p. 440): 'to remain silent' [BDAG; NRSV], 'to be quiet' [BDAG], 'to fall silent' [Bar; NASB], 'to say no more' [NET], 'to cease' [AB, BECNT; ESV, KJV], 'to give up' [CBC; CEV, NIV, NLT, REB, TEV], 'to drop the issue' [GW], 'to stop begging' [NCV], 'to say nothing, to remain quiet' [LN]. This verb means to maintain a state of silence, with a possible focus upon the attitude involved [LN]. It means to refrain from saying something [BDAG].
c. θέλημα (LN 30.59) (BDAG 1.a. p. 447): 'will' [LN; all translations except CEV, NCV], 'intent, purpose, plan' [LN], 'what is willed' [BDAG]. The phrase 'the will of the Lord be done' is also translated 'Lord, please make us willing to do what you want' [CEV], 'we pray that what the Lord wants will be done' [NCV]. This noun denotes that which is purposed, intended, or willed [LN]. It is what one wishes to happen [BDAG].

QUESTION—Does the statement 'the Lord's will be done' express resignation or strong resolution by Paul's friends?
It shows acceptance of Paul's plan, and that the will of God will ultimately be done [Bar, BECNT, NAC]. It indicates acquiescence on their part that such suffering would prove to be the will of God for Paul [PNTC]. It is strong resolution, not just resignation; they are praying that things will turn out exactly the way the Lord wants it to [TH].

**DISCOURSE UNIT—21:15–36** [GW]. The topic is Paul in Jerusalem.

**DISCOURSE UNIT—21:15–26** [AB, Bar; NASB]. The topic is Paul in the church of Jerusalem [AB], Paul and the church of Jerusalem [Bar], Paul at Jerusalem [NASB].

**DISCOURSE UNIT—21:15–25** [NLT]. The topic is Paul arrives at Jerusalem.

**DISCOURSE UNIT—21:15–16** [NAC, NICNT]. The topic is arrival in Jerusalem [NAC], arrival at Jerusalem [NICNT].

**21:15** And after these days having-made-preparations[a] we-were-going-up to Jerusalem; **21:16** and also-(some) of-the disciples from Caesarea went with us, bringing-(us) to-a-certain Mnason (a)-Cypriot (an) early[b] disciple with whom we-might-lodge.[c]

LEXICON—a. aorist mid. (deponent = act.) participle of ἐπισκευάζομαι (LN 77.8) (BDAG p. 378): 'to get ready' [AB, BDAG, CBC; CEV, ESV, GW, NASB, NCV, NET, NRSV], 'to get things ready' [TEV], 'to make ready' [BECNT, LN], 'to pack up' [Bar], 'to pack one's things' [NLT], 'to pack one's baggage' [REB], 'to be ready, to become ready, to prepare' [LN], 'to take up carriages' [KJV]. The phrase 'having made preparations we were going up' is also translated 'we started on our way' [NIV]. This verb means to be or to become ready for some purpose [LN]. It means to prepare for some activity or objective [BDAG].
  b. ἀρχαῖος (LN 67.98) (BDAG p. 137): 'early' [Bar; ESV, NIV, NLT, NRSV], 'from/since the early days' [AB, CBC; REB, TEV], 'from the earliest times' [NET], 'from the beginning' [LN; CEV], 'one of the first' [GW, NCV], 'of long standing' [BDAG; NASB], 'original' [BECNT], 'for a long time, ancient' [LN], 'old' [BDAG; KJV]. This adjective describes having existed for a long time in the past, with the possible implication of such existence from the beginning of an event or state [LN]. It describes what has existed from the beginning or for a long time, with connotation of present existence [BDAG].
  c. aorist pass. subj. of ξενίζω (LN 34.57) (BDAG 1. p. 683): 'to lodge' [Bar, BECNT, CBC; ESV, KJV, NASB], 'to stay as a guest' [AB], 'to stay' [CEV, GW, NCV, NET, NIV, NRSV, TEV], 'to spend the night' [REB], 'to be received as a guest, to be entertained' [BDAG], 'to be shown hospitality, to be a stranger received as a guest' [LN], not explicit [NLT]. This verb means to receive and show hospitality to a stranger, that is, someone who is not regarded as a member of the extended family or a close friend [LN]. It means to show hospitality [BDAG].

QUESTION—What does it mean that they 'made preparations'?
  They likely went by horseback and had to prepare the animals [Bar, BECNT, NAC, NICNT, PNTC, TNTC].
QUESTION— What does it mean that Mnason was an 'early disciple'?
  He had been a believer since the very beginning [NICNT], since the early days of the Christian movement [AB, Bar, EBC, NAC, PNTC].
QUESTION—Where was Mnason's house?
  He was probably living in Jerusalem [AB, BECNT, CBC, EBC, NAC, PNTC, TNTC]. Mnason was probably living somewhere between Caesarea and Jerusalem [Bar].

**DISCOURSE UNIT—21:17–28:31** [BECNT]. The topic is the arrest: the message is defended and reaches Rome.

**DISCOURSE UNIT—21:17–26:32** [NAC]. The topic is Paul witnesses before Gentiles, kings, and the people of Israel.

**DISCOURSE UNIT—21:17–23:35** [BECNT, NAC]. The topic is in Jerusalem [BECNT], witness before the Jews [NAC].

**DISCOURSE UNIT—21:17–23:30** [NICNT]. The topic is Paul at Jerusalem.

**DISCOURSE UNIT—21:17–23:22** [EBC]. The topic is various events and Paul's defenses at Jerusalem.

**DISCOURSE UNIT—21:17–40** [Bar, PNTC; NASB]. The topic is riot at Jerusalem [Bar], captured in Jerusalem [PNTC], Paul visits James [NASB].

**DISCOURSE UNIT—21:17–36** [TNTC]. The topic is Paul's arrest in Jerusalem.

**DISCOURSE UNIT—21:17–26** [BECNT, EBC, NAC, NICNT, PNTC; CEV, ESV, NIV, NRSV, TEV]. The topic is Paul and James [BECNT], arrival at Jerusalem [EBC], Paul's arrival at Jerusalem [NIV], the concern of the Jerusalem elders [NAC], meeting with James and the elders [NICNT], a well-meaning proposal [PNTC], Paul visits James [CEV, ESV, TEV], Paul visits James in Jerusalem [NRSV].

**21:17** And we having-come to Jerusalem, the brothers[a] received[b] us gladly.[c] **21:18** And on-the following-(day) Paul went-in with us to James, and all the elders[d] were-present.

LEXICON—a. ἀδελφός (LN 11.23): 'fellow believer, (Christian) brother' [LN]. This plural noun is translated 'brothers' [Bar, BECNT; ESV, NET, NRSV], 'brothers and sisters' [NIV, NLT], 'brotherhood' [CBC], 'brethren' [AB; KJV, NASB], 'believers' [GW, NCV, TEV], 'the Lord's followers' [CEV], 'congregation' [REB]. This noun denotes a close associate of a group of persons having a well-defined membership (in the NT ἀδελφός refers specifically to fellow believers in Christ) [LN].

b. aorist mid. (deponent = act.) indic. of ἀποδέχομαι (LN 34.53) (BDAG 1. p. 109): 'to receive' [AB, BECNT, LN; ESV, KJV, NASB, NIV], 'to welcome' [Bar, BDAG, CBC, LN; CEV, GW, NET, NLT, NRSV, REB, TEV], '(were glad) to see (us)' [NCV], 'to accept, to have as a guest' [LN]. This verb means to accept the presence of a person with friendliness [LN]. It means to receive someone favorably [BDAG].

c. ἀσμένως (LN 25.128) (BDAG p. 144): 'gladly' [Bar, BDAG, BECNT, CBC, LN; CEV, ESV, KJV, NASB, NET, REB], 'warmly' [GW, NIV, NLT, NRSV, TEV], 'joyfully' [AB], 'happily' [LN]. The phrase 'received us gladly' is also translated 'were glad to see us' [NCV]. This adverb describes experiencing happiness, implying ready and willing acceptance [LN].

d. πρεσβύτερος (LN 53.77) (BDAG 2.b.α. p. 862): 'elder' [BDAG, LN; all translations except CEV, GW, NLT, TEV], 'church elder' [TEV], 'elder(s) of the Jerusalem church' [NLT], 'church leader' [CEV], 'spiritual leader' [GW], 'presbyter' [BDAG]. This noun denotes a person of responsibility and authority in matters of socio-religious concerns, both in Jewish and Christian societies [LN]. It denotes an official [BDAG].

QUESTION—Who is the James mentioned here?

He was the brother of Jesus [Bar, NAC, NICNT], and the leader of the church in Jerusalem [Bar, BECNT, CBC, EBC, NAC, NICNT, TNTC].

**21:19** And having-greeted$^a$ them he-was-explaining$^b$ one by-one$^c$ the-things God had-done among the Gentiles through$^d$ his ministry.$^e$

LEXICON—a. aorist mid. (deponent = act.) participle of ἀσπάζομαι (LN 33.20) (BDAG 1.a. p. 144): 'to greet' [BDAG, LN; all translations except KJV], 'to salute' [KJV], 'to send greetings' [LN], 'to welcome' [BDAG]. This verb means to employ certain set phrases as a part of the process of greeting, whether communicated directly or indirectly [LN]. It means to engage in hospitable recognition of another [BDAG].

b. imperf. mid. or pass. (deponent = act.) indic. of ἐξηγέομαι (LN 33.201) (BDAG 1. p. 349): 'to explain' [NET], 'to tell' [BDAG; CEV, NCV], 'to report' [BDAG; NIV], 'to describe' [BDAG, CBC; REB], 'to relate' [Bar, BECNT, LN; ESV, GW, NASB, NRSV], 'to give an account' [NLT], 'to give a report' [TEV], 'to declare' [KJV], 'to recount' [AB], 'to inform, to tell fully' [LN]. This verb means to provide detailed information in a systematic manner [LN]. It means to relate in detail [BDAG].

c. ἕκαστος (LN 59.27) (BDAG b. p. 298 ): 'each one, every one' [BDAG], 'each' [LN]. The phrase καθ' ἓν ἕκαστον 'one by one' [BECNT; ESV, NASB, NRSV] is also translated 'in detail' [AB, Bar, CBC; NET, NIV, REB], 'detailed (account)' [NLT], 'complete (report)' [TEV], 'everything' [GW, NCV], 'particularly' [KJV], not explicit [CEV]. This adjective describes each one of a totality in a distributive sense [LN]. It describes one of an aggregate in a distributive sense [BDAG].

d. διά with genitive object (LN 89.76): 'through' [LN; all translations except CEV, KJV, REB], 'by' [LN; KJV], 'by means of' [LN; REB], not explicit [CEV]. This preposition indicates the means by which one event makes another event possible [LN].

e. διακονία (LN 35.21) (BDAG 3. p. 230): 'ministry' [LN; all translations except CEV, GW, NCV, TEV], 'work' [GW, TEV], 'service' [BDAG], 'task' [LN], 'office' [BDAG], not explicit [NCV]. The phrase 'through his ministry' is also translated 'how God had used him to help the Gentiles' [CEV]. This noun denotes the role or position of serving [LN]. It is functioning in the interest of a larger public [BDAG].

**21:20** And having-heard they-glorified$^a$ God and said to-him, "You-see, brother, how-many thousands$^b$ there-are among the Jews of-those having-believed and all are zealots$^c$ for-the law.

LEXICON—a. imperf. act. indic. of δοξάζω (LN 33.357) (BDAG 1. p. 258): 'to glorify' [Bar, BECNT, LN; ESV, KJV, NASB], 'to praise' [AB,

BDAG, LN; CEV, GW, NCV, NET, NIV, NLT, NRSV, TEV], 'to give praise' [CBC; REB], 'to honor, to extol' [BDAG]. This verb means to speak of something as being unusually fine and deserving honor [LN]. It means to influence one's opinion about another so as to enhance the latter's reputation [BDAG].
   b. μυριάς (LN 60.8) (BDAG 2. p. 661): 'thousands' [BECNT, CBC; all versions except CEV], 'tens of thousands' [AB, Bar; CEV], 'countless, innumerable, many many' [LN], 'myriads (in the plural)' [BDAG]. This noun denotes a very large indefinite number [LN]. It is a very large number, not precisely defined [BDAG].
   c. ζηλωτής (LN 25.77) (BDAG 1.a.β. p. 427): 'zealous person' [LN], 'staunch upholders' [CBC; REB], 'ardent observer' [BDAG; NET], 'adherent, loyalist' [BDAG], 'enthusiast' [BDAG, LN]. This noun is also translated as an adjective: 'zealous' [Bar, BECNT; ESV, KJV, NASB, NIV, NRSV], 'devoted' [AB]. It is also translated as a phrase: 'eager to obey' [CEV], 'deeply committed to' [GW], 'devoted to' [TEV], '(they think it's) very important to obey' [NCV], 'follow…very seriously' [NLT]. This noun denotes one who is deeply committed to something and therefore zealous [LN]. It is one who is earnestly committed to a side or cause [BDAG].

QUESTION—Should μυριάς 'thousands' be taken in its literal sense of 'tens of thousands' or simply as hyperbole, but representing actual thousands?

The population of Jerusalem at that time has been estimated as being between 25,000 and 55,000 [AB, BECNT, NICNT, PNTC], so perhaps this should be taken to be hyperbole, meaning 'thousands' [AB, BECNT, NICNT, PNTC]. It might also be that the large number would include visitors to Jerusalem for the festival [PNTC].

QUESTION—What law is referred to here?

It is the law of Moses [TH, TRT; CEV, GW, NCV, NLT].

**21:21** And they-have-been-informed[a] about you that you-teach all those Jews among the Gentiles abandonment[b] from Moses telling them not to-circumcise (their) children nor to-walk-according-to[c] (our) customs.[d]

LEXICON—a. aorist pass. indic. of κατηχέω (LN 33.190) (BDAG 1. p. 534): 'to be informed' [Bar, BDAG, LN; KJV, NET, NIV], 'to be told' [AB, BECNT, LN; CEV, ESV, GW, NASB, NLT, NRSV, TEV], 'to be given information' [CBC; REB], 'to have reported (to)' [BDAG, LN]. This passive verb is also translated as active: 'to hear' [NCV]. This verb means to report in a relatively detailed manner [LN]. It means to share a communication that one receives [BDAG].
   b. ἀποστασία (LN 39.34) (BDAG p. 120): 'abandonment' [BDAG], 'defection' [Bar], 'rebellion' [BDAG, LN], 'breach of faith' [BDAG]. This noun is also translated as a verb: 'to forsake' [BECNT; ESV, KJV, NASB, NRSV], 'to abandon' [GW, NET, TEV], 'to renounce' [AB], 'to give up' [CBC], 'to disobey' [CEV], 'to leave' [NCV], 'to turn away'

[NIV], 'to turn one's back on' [NLT, REB]. This noun denotes a rising up in open defiance of authority, with the presumed intention to overthrow it or to act in complete opposition to its demands [LN]. It is defiance of an established system or authority [BDAG].

c. pres. act. indic. of περιπατέω (LN 41.11) (BDAG 2.a.β. p. 803): 'to walk according to' [ESV, NASB], 'to walk in accordance with' [Bar], 'to walk after' [KJV], 'to live according to' [AB; NET, NIV], 'to live' [BDAG, LN], 'to follow' [BECNT, CBC; CEV, GW, NLT, REB, TEV], 'to observe' [NRSV], 'to obey' [NCV], 'to behave' [BDAG, LN], 'to go about doing' [LN], 'to comport oneself' [BDAG]. This verb means to live or behave in a customary manner, with possible focus upon continuity of action [LN]. It means to conduct one's life [BDAG].

d. ἔθος (LN 41.25) (BDAG 2. p. 277): 'custom' [BDAG, LN; all translations except CBC; REB], 'way of life' [BDAG, CBC; REB], 'habit' [LN]. This noun denotes a pattern of behavior more or less fixed by tradition and generally sanctioned by the society [LN]. It is long-established usage or practice common to a group [BDAG].

QUESTION—To what does 'Moses' refer in this verse?

It refers to the Law of Moses [Bar; CEV, NCV, NLT, TEV].

**21:22** What<sup>a</sup> then is-to be (done)? They-will- certainly<sup>b</sup> -hear that you-have-come. **21:23** Therefore do this that we-tell you; we-have four men having (a)-vow<sup>c</sup> upon<sup>d</sup> them.

TEXT—Some manuscripts add δεῖ συνελθεῖν πλῆθος 'the multitude must come together' and omit πάντως 'certainly'. GNT rejects this variant reading with a B rating to indicate that it was regarded as almost certain not to be original. Only KJV follows these variants.

LEXICON—a. τίς (LN 92.14): 'what?' [LN], 'who?' [LN]. The phrase 'What then is to be done?' [BECNT; ESV, NASB, NRSV, REB], is also translated 'What then should we do?' [NET], 'What shall we do?' [NIV], 'What should we do?' [NCV, NLT], 'What should we do now?' [CEV], 'What should we do about this' [GW], 'What should be done, then?' [TEV], 'What now?' [AB], 'What then?' [Bar], 'What is the position then?' [CBC], 'What is it therefore?' [KJV]. This pronoun is an interrogative reference to someone or something [LN].

b. πάντως (LN 71.16) (BDAG 1. p. 755): 'certainly' [AB, Bar, BDAG, BECNT, LN; ESV, GW, NASB, NIV, NLT, NRSV], 'doubtless' [BDAG, LN], 'no doubt' [LN; NET], 'sure (to hear)' [CBC; REB, TEV], 'by all means, probably' [BDAG], 'really' [LN], not explicit [CEV, KJV, NCV]. This adverb describes being in every respect certain [LN]. It describes strong assumption [BDAG].

c. εὐχή (LN 33.469) (BDAG 2. p. 416): 'vow' [BDAG, LN; all translations except AB; CEV, GW, NCV], 'vow to God' [GW], 'Nazirite vow' [AB], 'a promise to God' [NCV], 'special promises to God' [CEV]. This noun denotes a promise to God that one will do something, with the implication

that failure to act accordingly will result in divine sanctions against the person in question [LN]. It is a solemn promise with the understanding that one is subject to penalty for failure to discharge the obligation [BDAG].
  d. ἐπί with genitive object (LN 90.23) (BDAG 1.a. p. 363): 'upon' [BDAG], 'on' [Bar, BDAG; KJV], 'concerning, with respect to, with reference to, about, in' [LN]. The phrase 'upon them' is also translated 'who are under' [AB, BECNT, CBC; ESV, NASB, NRSV, REB], 'who have taken' [NET, TEV], 'who have made' [CEV, GW, NCV, NIV], 'who have completed' [NLT]. This preposition marks content as a means of specifying a particular referent [LN]. It marks location or surface, answering the question 'where?' [BDAG].

QUESTION—What was the nature of the vow that these four men had taken upon themselves?
  It would have been a Nazirite vow [AB, CBC, EBC, NAC, NICNT, TH, TNTC], often taken for a period of thirty days, involving abstention from wine and contact with corpses, and after which the hair of the person under the vow would be cut and burnt sacrifices would be offered, which would include the hair that had been cut [NICNT, TH]. These men may have contracted a ritual uncleanness requiring purification which they would be undergoing at this point [AB, Bar, NICNT, TH], or possibly were coming to the end of their period of consecration and were ready to offer the sacrifices marking the fulfillment of their vows [NAC, PNTC]. Other persons not under the Nazirite vow could also associate with those involved in the vow by paying their expenses for the sacrifices [NAC, NICNT, PNTC]. Paul was probably contributing to the cost of their sacrifices [CBC, NAC, PNTC].

**21:24** Having-taken these-(men) purify-yourself[a] with them and pay-expenses[b] for them so-that they-will-shave their heads, and all will-know that there-is nothing of-what they-have-been-told[c] about you but you-yourself also live-in-accordance-with[d] and are-keeping[e] the law.

LEXICON—a. aorist pass. impera. of ἁγνίζω (LN 53.30) (BDAG 1.b. p. 12): 'to purify oneself' [AB, BECNT; ESV, KJV, NASB, NET], 'to purify' [BDAG, LN], 'to be purified' [Bar], 'to go through the ritual/rite of purification' [CBC; NRSV, REB], 'to go through the purification ceremony' [GW], 'to join in purification rites' [NIV], 'to join in the purification ceremony' [NLT], 'to join in the ceremony of purification' [TEV], 'to share in a cleansing ceremony' [NCV], 'to prepare for a ceremony (that goes with the promises)' [CEV]. This verb means to purify and cleanse ritually and thus acquire a state of ritual acceptability [LN]. It means to purify or cleanse and so make acceptable for cultic use [BDAG].
  b. aorist act. impera. of δαπανάω (LN 57.146) (BDAG 1. p. 212): 'to pay expenses' [Bar, BECNT, CBC, LN; ESV, GW, NASB, NCV, NET, NIV, REB, TEV], 'to pay costs' [CEV], 'to pay' [AB; NLT, NRSV], 'to be at

charges with' [KJV], 'to spend' [BDAG, LN], 'to pay out' [LN]. This verb means to pay out money (or other assets) as a means of obtaining benefits or in payment for benefits [LN]. It means to use up or pay out material or physical resources [BDAG].

c. perf. pass. indic. of κατηχέω (LN 33.190) (BDAG 1. p. 534): 'to be told' [Bar, CBC, LN; ESV, GW, NASB, NET, NRSV, TEV], 'to be informed' [BDAG, LN; KJV], 'to be taught' [BECNT], 'to have reported (to)' [BDAG, LN]. This passive verb is also translated as active: 'to hear' [AB; NCV, REB]. The phrase 'what they have been told' is also translated 'the/these reports' [CEV, NIV], 'the rumors' [NLT]. This verb means to report in a relatively detailed manner [LN]. It means to share a communication that one receives [BDAG].

d. pres. act. indic. of στοιχέω (LN 41.12) (BDAG p. 946): 'to live in accordance with' [LN], 'to live (keeping)' [BECNT], 'to observe' [NRSV], 'to maintain' [AB], 'to conform' [Bar], 'to be (a) practicing (Jew)' [CBC; REB], 'to walk orderly' [KJV, NASB], 'to hold to, to agree with, to follow' [BDAG], 'to behave in accordance with' [LN]. The phrase 'live in accordance with and are keeping the law' is also conflated and translated 'observe the Jewish laws' [NLT], 'live in observance of the law' [ESV], 'living in obedience to the law' [NIV], 'live in conformity with the law' [NET], 'live in accordance with the Law of Moses' [TEV], 'obey the law' [CEV], 'you follow the law of Moses' [NCV], 'you carefully follow Moses' teachings' [GW]. This verb means to live in conformity with some presumed standard or set of customs [LN]. It means to be in line with a person or thing considered as standard for one's conduct [BDAG].

e. pres. act. participle of φυλάσσω (LN 36.19) (BDAG 5.a. p. 1068): 'to keep' [BECNT, CBC; KJV, NASB], 'to observe' [AB, Bar, BDAG; REB], 'to follow' [BDAG], 'to guard' [NRSV], 'to obey' [LN], 'to keep commandments' [LN]. See entry d. for CEV, ESV, GW, NCV, NET, NIV, NLT, TEV. This verb means to continue to obey orders or commandments [LN]. It means to continue to keep a law or commandment from being broken [BDAG].

QUESTION—In what sense would Paul need to be purified?

Having recently returned from travel in Gentile areas, he would be viewed as having contracted ritual uncleanness in those places [Bar, BECNT, EBC, NICNT, PNTC, TNTC, TRT], particularly with respect to entering the temple precincts [Bar] or participating in temple worship [PNTC].

QUESTION—What was involved in paying their expenses?

It meant to pay for the sacrifices involved in completing the days of purification [Bar, PNTC, TH, TRT], which could be quite costly [Bar, PNTC, TH]. A person could contribute toward the cost of the offerings of another person who was under a vow [EBC, NICNT].

QUESTION—What relationship is indicated by 'and' in the phrase 'and all will know'?

It shows a logical relationship; paying their expenses will prove to everyone that the rumors were false and that you live according to the law [Bar, TH].

**21:25** But concerning[a] the Gentiles who-have-believed we wrote-(a-letter) having-decided[b] (that) they keep-from[c] both meat-offered-to-idols[d] as-well-as blood[e] and what-has-been-strangled[f] and sexual-immorality.[g]"

TEXT—Some manuscripts add μηδὲν τοιοῦτο τηρεῖν 'that they observe no such thing.' Manuscripts that omit this reading are given a B rating by GNT to indicate that it was regarded to be almost certain not to be original. Only KJV follows this variant reading.

LEXICON—a. περί with genitive object (LN 89.6): 'concerning' [Bar, LN; NASB], 'as for' [AB, BECNT, CBC; ESV, NIV, NLT, NRSV, REB, TEV], 'as touching' [KJV], 'regarding' [NET], 'in relation to, with regard to' [LN], not explicit [CEV, GW, NCV]. This preposition indicates a relation, usually involving content or topic [LN].

  b. aorist act. participle of κρίνω (LN 30.75) (BDAG 4. p. 568): 'to decide' [BDAG, LN; NASB, NET, TEV], 'to reach a decision' [AB, BDAG], 'to conclude' [KJV], 'to come to a conclusion, to make up one's mind' [LN], 'to propose, to intend' [BDAG], not explicit [NCV, NLT]. The phrase 'having decided' is also translated 'with the/our decision' [Bar; GW], 'our decision' [CBC; NIV, REB], 'with our judgment' [ESV, NRSV], 'judging what they are to keep' [BECNT], 'what we think they should do' [CEV]. This verb means to come to a conclusion in the process of thinking and thus to be in a position to make a decision [LN]. It means to come to a conclusion after a cognitive process [BDAG].

  c. pres. mid. infin. of φυλάσσω (LN 13.154) (BDAG 3. p. 1068): 'to keep from' [LN; KJV], 'to abstain from' [BECNT, CBC; ESV, NASB, NIV, NLT, NRSV, REB], 'to avoid' [AB, BDAG; NET], 'to be on one's guard against' [Bar], 'not to (eat…commit)' [CEV], 'do not (eat…take part in)' [NCV], 'they should not (eat…commit)' [GW], 'must not (eat)' [TEV], 'to be careful not to, to make an effort not to, to seriously avoid' [LN], 'look out for' [BDAG]. This verb means to make a distinct effort to keep oneself from doing something [LN]. It means to be on one's guard against [BDAG].

  d. εἰδωλόθυτον (LN 5.15) (BDAG p. 280): 'meat/food that has been offered to idols' [AB, BECNT; NCV, NRSV, TEV], 'food sacrificed to idols/false gods' [Bar, BDAG; GW], 'food offered to idols' [NLT], 'meat sacrificed to idols' [NASB, NET], 'what has been sacrificed to idols' [BECNT; ESV, NRSV], 'things/food offered to idols' [KJV, NLT], 'anything offered to idols' [CEV], 'sacrificial meat, meat of animals sacrificed to an idol' [LN], 'something offered to a cultic image or idol' [BDAG]. This noun denotes the meat of animals which have been sacrificed to idols [LN].

e. αἷμα (LN 8.64) (BDAG 1.b. p. 26): 'blood' [BDAG, LN; all translations except CEV, GW, NLT], 'bloody meat' [GW], 'meat with blood still in it' [CEV], 'consuming blood' [NLT]. This noun denotes blood as the basic component of an organism [BDAG].

f. πνικτός (LN 19.54) (BDAG p. 838): 'what has been/is strangled' [AB, BECNT; ESV, NASB, NET, NRSV], 'anything that has been strangled' [CBC; REB], 'strangled meat' [Bar], 'meat of strangled animals' [GW, NIV, NLT], 'meat of an animal that has been strangled' [CEV], 'animal/s that has/have been strangled' [NCV, TEV], 'strangled' [BDAG, LN; KJV], 'choked' [LN], 'choked to death' [BDAG]. This adjective describes what is choked or strangled [LN].

g. πορνεία (LN 88.271) (BDAG p. 854): 'sexual immorality' [LN; ESV, NET, NIV, NLT, TEV], 'sexual impurity' [AB], 'fornication' [Bar, BDAG, CBC, LN; KJV, NASB, NRSV, REB], 'unchastity' [BDAG, BECNT], 'sexual sin/s' [GW, NCV], 'terrible sexual sins' [CEV], 'prostitution' [BDAG, LN]. This noun denotes the act of engaging in sexual immorality of any kind, often with the implication of prostitution [LN]. It is unlawful sexual intercourse [BDAG].

QUESTION—What is the function of the conjunction 'but' that begins this sentence?

It shifts the focus from Jewish believers to Gentile believers [TH].

QUESTION—Why did they restate what was decided at the earlier council, since Paul was fully aware of that ruling?

It served as a reminder to everyone that they were not going back to revisit that issue, and that their decision about Gentile believers still stands [BECNT, CBC, EBC, NAC, NICNT, PNTC].

QUESTION—What is shown by the use of the first person plural pronoun 'we', which would not normally be required grammatically, since it is included in the first person plural form of the verb?

It is emphatic, meaning 'we ourselves', and indicating that James and Paul were involved in the sending of that directive [Bar].

**DISCOURSE UNIT—21:26–36** [NLT]. The topic is Paul is arrested.

**21:26** Then Paul having-taken[a] the men, the next day purified-himself[b] with them, (and) he-went into the temple giving-notice-of[c] the completion[d] of-the days of-purification when the offering which would-be-offered for each one of-them.

LEXICON—a. aorist act. participle of παραλαμβάνω (LN 15.168) (BDAG 1. p. 767): 'to take' [BECNT, CBC; all versions except CEV, NLT], 'to take with' [AB, Bar, BDAG; CEV], 'to go with' [NLT], 'to take along' [BDAG, LN], 'to bring along' [LN], 'to take (to oneself)' [BDAG]. This verb means to take or bring someone along with [LN]. It means to take into close association [BDAG].

b. aorist pass. participle of ἁγνίζω (LN 53.30) (BDAG 1.a. p. 12): 'to purify oneself' [AB, BECNT; ESV, KJV, NASB, NET, NIV, NRSV], 'to be purified' [Bar, BDAG, LN], 'to go through the ritual/ceremony of purification' [CBC; GW, REB], 'to perform the ceremony of purification' [TEV], 'to start the purification ritual' [NLT], 'to share in the cleansing ceremony' [NCV], 'to get ready' [CEV]. This verb means to purify and cleanse ritually and thus acquire a state of ritual acceptability [LN]. It means to purify or cleanse and so make acceptable for cultic use [BDAG].

c. pres. act. participle of διαγγέλλω (LN 33.203) (BDAG 2. p. 227): 'to give notice' [AB, BECNT, CBC, LN; ESV, NASB, NET, NIV, REB], 'to notify' [Bar, LN], 'to tell when' [CEV], 'to announce' [BDAG; GW, NCV], 'to publicly announce' [NLT], 'to make public' [NRSV], 'to signify' [KJV], 'to report' [BDAG]. This verb means to provide specific information (especially with regard to some future contingency) [LN]. It means to make a report [BDAG].

d. ἐκπλήρωσις (LN 67.69) (BDAG p. 308): 'completion' [BDAG, LN; NASB, NET, NRSV], 'end' [AB, LN; TEV], 'fulfillment' [Bar], 'accomplishment' [KJV]. This noun is also translated as a verb: 'to be fulfilled' [BECNT; ESV, NCV], 'to take place' [CEV], 'to be over' [GW], 'to end' [CBC; NIV, NLT, REB]. This noun denotes the totality of a period of time, with the implication of proper completion [LN]. It is a process viewed in its entirety with focus on its being brought to a proper conclusion [BDAG].

QUESTION—To whom does 'each one of them' refer?

It refers to the four men, but does not include Paul [TH].

**DISCOURSE UNIT—21:27–40** [AB; NASB]. The topic is Paul arrested by the Romans [AB], Paul seized in the temple [NASB].

**DISCOURSE UNIT—21:27–39** [CBC]. The topic is from Jerusalem to Rome.

**DISCOURSE UNIT—21:27–36** [BECNT, EBC, NAC; CEV, ESV, NIV, NRSV, TEV]. The topic is the riot and the arrest at the temple [BECNT], arrest in the temple [EBC], the riot in the temple area [NAC], Paul arrested in the temple [ESV, NRSV], Paul is arrested in the temple [TEV], Paul is arrested [CEV], Paul arrested [NIV].

**DISCOURSE UNIT—21:27–32** [PNTC]. The topic is misrepresented and attacked.

**DISCOURSE UNIT—21:27–30** [NICNT]. The topic is riot in the temple.

**21:27** **And as the seven days were-about[a] to-be-completed,[b] the Jews from Asia having-seen him in the temple stirred-up[c] the whole crowd[d] and laid[e] hands on him**

LEXICON—a. imperf. act. indic. of μέλλω (LN 67.62) (BDAG 1.c.α. p. 627): 'to be about to' [BDAG, LN; TEV]. This verb is also translated as an adverb: 'nearly' [AB; NIV], 'almost' [Bar, BECNT; CEV, ESV, GW, KJV, NASB, NCV, NET, NLT, NRSV], 'just before' [CBC; REB]. This verb means to occur at a point of time in the future which is subsequent to

another event and closely related to it [LN]. It means to take place at a future point of time and so to be subsequent to another event [BDAG].
b. pre. pass. infin. of συντελέω (LN 67.67) (BDAG 4. p. 975): 'to be completed' [Bar, BECNT; ESV, NRSV], 'to be ended' [AB, LN; KJV, NLT], 'to be over' [BDAG; CEV, GW, NASB, NCV, NET, NIV], 'to be up' [CBC; REB], 'to come to an end' [BDAG, LN; TEV]. This verb means to occur or happen at the end of a duration [LN]. It means to come to the end of a duration [BDAG].
c. imperf. act. indic. of συγχέω (LN 25.221) (BDAG p. 953): 'to stir up' [BDAG; all translations except CEV, NCV, NLT], 'to rouse' [NLT], 'to get (a crowd) together' [CEV], 'to cause (people) to be upset' [NCV], 'to confuse, to trouble' [BDAG], 'to cause consternation' [LN], 'to confound' [BDAG, LN]. This verb means to cause such astonishment as to bewilder and to dismay [LN]. It means to cause dismay [BDAG].
d. ὄχλον (LN 11.1) (BDAG 1.a. p. 745): 'crowd' [BDAG, LN; all translations except KJV, NCV, NLT], 'people' [KJV, NCV], 'mob' [NLT], 'multitude' [LN]. This noun denotes a casual non-membership group of people, fairly large in size and assembled for whatever purpose [LN]. It is a relatively large number of people gathered together [BDAG].
e. aorist act. indic. of ἐπιβάλλω (LN 37.110) (BDAG 1.b. p. 367): 'to lay on, to put on' [BDAG]. The idiom ἐπιβάλλω τὰς χεῖρας 'to lay hands on' [AB, Bar, BECNT; ESV, KJV, NASB] means to seize, to arrest [LN]. It is also translated 'to seize' [CBC; NET, NIV, NRSV, REB], 'to grab' [GW, NCV, NLT, TEV], 'to start attacking' [CEV]. It means to take a person into custody for alleged illegal activity [LN].

**21:28** crying-out, "Men of-Israel, help; this is the man (who) teaches everyone everywhere[a] against the people and the law and this place, and what-is-more even brought Greeks[b] into the temple and has-defiled[c] this holy place."

LEXICON—a. πανταχῇ (LN 83.8) (BDAG p. 754): 'everywhere' [BDAG, LN; all translations except CBC; REB], 'all over' [CBC], 'the whole world over' [REB], 'anywhere, all over' [LN]. This adverb describes all possible positions [LN].
b. Ἕλλην (LN 11.40) (BDAG 2.a. p. 318): 'Greek' [LN; all translations except CEV, NLT, REB, TEV], 'Gentile' [BDAG, LN; CEV, NLT, REB, TEV], 'non-Jew' [LN], 'polytheist, Greco-Roman' [BDAG]. This noun denotes a person who is a Gentile in view of being a Greek [LN]. It describes all persons who came under the influence of Greek culture, as distinguished from Israel's culture [BDAG].
c. perf. act. indic. of κοινόω (LN 53.33) (BDAG 2.b. p. 552): 'to defile' [AB, BDAG, BECNT, LN; ESV, NASB, NIV, NLT, NRSV, TEV], 'to profane' [Bar, BDAG, CBC, LN; REB], 'to make unclean' [LN; GW, NCV], 'to make ritually unclean' [NET], 'to bring shame to' [CEV], 'to pollute' [KJV], 'to desecrate, to make impure, to defile' [BDAG]. This

verb means to cause something to become unclean, profane, or ritually unacceptable [LN].

QUESTION—To whom does 'everyone everywhere' refer?
It refers to all Gentiles [Bar]. It refers to Paul's teaching all over the world [NICNT].

QUESTION—What is ironic about this accusation?
There is irony in the fact that they would accuse him of desecrating the temple at a time when he is in the act of purifying himself ritually so as to avoid desecrating the temple [EBC, NAC, PNTC, TNTC]. The irony is that Paul was accused of not caring about his Jewish identity and roots when he was involved in an action that clearly support and express those roots [BECNT].

**21:29** For they-had previously-seen[a] Trophimus the Ephesian in the city with him, whom they-supposed[b] Paul had-brought into the temple.

LEXICON—a. perf. act. participle of προοράω (LN 24.5) (BDAG 2. p. 873): 'to have seen previously' [BDAG, LN], 'to see beforehand' [BDAG, LN]. This perfect tense verb is also translated 'they had seen' [CEV, GW, NCV, NET, NLT, TEV]. The prefix προ- attached to this verb indicates an action that has already occurred: 'had previously seen' [Bar, BECNT, CBC; ESV, NASB, NIV, NRSV, REB], 'had seen earlier' [AB], 'had seen before' [KJV]. This verb means to have seen something or someone beforehand or prior to an event in question [LN]. It means to see at a time prior to the present [BDAG].

b. imperf. act. indic. of νομίζω (LN 31.29) (BDAG p. 675): 'to suppose' [Bar, BECNT, LN; ESV, KJV, NASB, NRSV], 'to assume' [CBC, LN; NET, NIV, NLT, REB], 'to think' [AB, BDAG, LN; CEV, GW, NCV, TEV], 'to presume, to imagine' [LN], 'to believe' [BDAG, LN]. This verb means to regard something as presumably true, but without particular certainty [LN]. It means to form an idea about something but with some suggestion of tentativeness or refraining from a definitive statement [BDAG].

QUESTION—What part or parts of the temple would have been off-limits to Gentiles?
The temple consisted of four courts. All Israelites, both men and women, could go into the court known as the court of women. After that was the court into which only Israelite men could go, then another court into which only priests could go, and then in the innermost court, the holy of holies, only the high priest could go once a year [BECNT, NAC]. Gentiles could only go into the area outside the court of women [BECNT, NAC, TNTC]. Between the outermost court and the court of women there were stone markers with warnings engraved on them that no Gentile could pass beyond them on pain of death [BECNT, EBC, NAC, NICNT, PNTC, TNTC].

**21:30** And the whole city was-stirred-up[a] and there-was (a)-running-together[b] of-the people, and having-seized[c] Paul they-were-dragging[d] him out-of the temple and immediately the gates were-shut.

LEXICON—a. aorist pass. indic. of κινέω (LN 39.44) (BDAG 2.b. p. 545): 'to be stirred up' [ESV, NET], 'to be aroused' [BDAG, BECNT; NIV, NRSV], 'to be roused' [AB], 'to be excited' [Bar], 'to be in an uproar' [CEV], 'to be in a turmoil' [CBC; REB], 'to be in chaos' [GW], 'to be provoked' [NASB], 'to be rocked' [NLT], 'to become upset' [NCV], 'to be moved' [KJV], 'to be stirred up against' [LN], 'to be caused to start a riot' [LN], 'to be caused to start an uproar' [LN]. The phrase 'the whole city was stirred up' is also translated 'confusion spread through the whole city' [TEV]. This verb means to cause people to riot against [LN]. It means to cause to be in turmoil [BDAG].

b. συνδρομή (LN 15.133) (BDAG p. 967): 'a running together' [BDAG, LN], 'mob' [CEV, GW], 'crowd' [AB], 'tumultuous concourse' [Bar], 'a great riot' [NLT], 'a rushing together, an assembling quickly' [LN]. This noun is also translated as a verb: 'to run together' [BECNT; ESV, KJV, NCV, TEV], 'to rush together' [NASB, NET, NRSV], 'to come running from all directions' [CBC; NIV, REB]. This noun denotes an event of people coming together quickly to form a crowd [LN]. It is a formation of a mob by persons running together [BDAG].

c. aorist mid. (deponent = act.) participle of ἐπιλαμβάνομαι (LN 18.2) (BDAG 1. p. 374): 'to seize' [AB, BECNT, CBC; ESV, NET, NIV, NRSV, REB], 'to grab' [CEV, GW, TEV], 'to lay hands on' [Bar], 'to take hold of' [BDAG, LN; NASB], 'to take' [KJV, NCV], 'to grasp' [BDAG, LN], 'to catch' [BDAG]. This active verb is also translated as passive: 'to be grabbed' [NLT]. This verb means to take hold of or grasp, with focus upon the goal of the motion [LN]. It means to make the motion of grasping or taking hold of something [BDAG].

d. imperf. act. indic. of ἕλκω (LN 15.178) (BDAG 1. p. 318): 'to drag' [BDAG, LN; all translations except KJV, NLT], 'to lead by force' [LN], 'to draw' [BDAG; KJV]. This active verb is also translated as passive: 'to be dragged' [NLT]. This verb means to drag or pull by physical force, often implying resistance [LN]. It means to move an object from one area to another in a pulling motion [BDAG].

QUESTION—Why were the temple gates shut?

They were shut to prevent any further desecration [EBC, NAC, PNTC], and to prevent any mob action that was beginning in the large outer precincts open to the Gentiles from coming into the inner courts [NAC]. If they were to kill Paul in the temple it would defile it [Bar, EBC, NICNT, TH, TRT]. They dragged him out and closed the door so he could not run back in and find sanctuary in a place where they would not be willing to kill him [TH]. This would refer to the gates separating the area where Gentiles could gather from the more restricted courts [Bar, EBC, NAC, NICNT, PNTC, TNTC, TRT].

**DISCOURSE UNIT—21:31-36** [NICNT]. The topic is Paul rescued by the Romans.

**21:31** And as-they-were-seeking[a] to-kill him (a)-report[b] went-up[c] to-the tribune[d] of-the cohort[e] that all Jerusalem was-in-(an)-uproar.[f]

LEXICON—a. pres. act. participle of ζητέω (LN 68.60): 'to seek' [Bar; ESV, NASB], 'to try' [AB, BECNT, LN; GW, NCV, NET, NIV, NLT, NRSV, TEV], 'to seek to do' [LN], 'to be about to' [CEV], 'to go about to' [KJV], 'to clamor for (his death)' [CBC], 'to be bent on' [REB]. This verb means to seek to do something, but without success [LN].
  b. φάσις (LN 33.211) (BDAG p. 1050): 'report' [AB, BDAG, CBC, LN; GW, NASB, NET, TEV], 'news' [BDAG, LN; NIV], 'word' [Bar, BECNT, LN; ESV, NLT, NRSV, REB], 'tidings' [KJV], 'information' [LN], 'announcement' [BDAG]. The phrase 'a report went up (to the tribune)' is also translated '(the army commander) heard' [CEV], '(the commander)...learned' [NCV]. This noun denotes information concerning a person or an event [LN]. It is information concerning a person or event [BDAG].
  c. aorist act. indic. of ἀναβαίνω (LN 15.101) (BDAG 1.b. p. 58): 'to go up' [Bar, BDAG, LN], 'to come up' [LN; NASB], 'to come' [BECNT; ESV, KJV, NRSV, REB], 'to reach' [CBC; NIV, NLT], 'to be made' [AB], not explicit [CEV, NCV]. This active verb is also translated as passive; 'to be sent up' [NET, TEV]. The phrase 'a report went up' is also translated 'received a report' [GW]. This verb means to move up [LN]. It means to be in motion upward [BDAG].
  d. χιλίαρχος (LN 55.15) (BDAG p. 1084): 'tribune' [AB, Bar, BECNT; ESV, NRSV], 'military tribune' [BDAG], 'commander' [CEV, NASB, NCV, NIV, NLT, TEV], 'commanding officer' [LN; NET], 'officer commanding' [CBC; REB], 'officer in charge' [GW], 'chief captain' [KJV], 'general, chiliarch' [LN]. This noun denotes a military officer, normally in command of a thousand soldiers [LN]. It is the commander of a cohort, of about 600 men [BDAG].
  e. σπεῖρα (LN 55.9) (BDAG p. 936): 'cohort' [AB, Bar, BDAG, BECNT, CBC, LN; ESV, NET, NRSV, REB], 'Roman cohort' [NASB], 'Roman soldiers' [GW], 'Roman troops' [NIV, TEV], 'Roman army' [NCV], 'army' [CEV], 'band of soldiers' [LN], 'band' [KJV], not explicit [CEV]. This noun denotes a Roman military unit of about six hundred soldiers, though only a part of such a cohort was often referred to as a cohort [LN]. A cohort is the tenth part of a legion [BDAG].
  f. pres. pass. indic. of συγχέω (LN 25.221) (BDAG p. 953): 'to be in an uproar' [AB, Bar, CBC; KJV, NIV, NLT, NRSV, REB], 'to be stirred up' [BDAG], 'to riot' [GW, TEV], 'to start to riot' [CEV], 'to be in confusion' [BECNT; ESV, NASB, NET], 'to be confused, to be troubled' [BDAG], 'to be confounded' [BDAG, LN], 'to be caused consternation' [LN]. The phrase 'all Jerusalem was in an uproar' is also translated as

'there was trouble in the whole city' [NCV]. This verb means to cause such astonishment as to bewilder and dismay [LN]. It means to cause dismay [BDAG].

QUESTION—What does it mean that a report 'went up'?
The Antonia fortress tower overlooked the temple area [Bar, BECNT, CBC, EBC, NAC, NICNT, PNTC, TNTC, TH]. One of the fortress towers was one hundred feet high, giving a good view of all that happened in the temple precincts [BECNT], such that a constant watch for disturbances was always possible [TNTC].

QUESTION—What is meant by 'all Jerusalem'?
This is hyperbole, meaning that the disruption was widespread [BECNT]. Since the outer area of the temple courts, the one where Gentiles were allowed, was quite large and it functioned more or less as a town square, a considerable number of people could congregate there [NAC].

**21:32** He ran-down[a] to them at-once[b] taking soldiers and centurions,[c] and seeing the tribune and the soldiers they-stopped beating[d] Paul.

LEXICON—a. aorist act. indic. of κατατρέχω (LN 15.233) (BDAG p. 528): 'to run down' [AB, Bar, BDAG, BECNT; ESV, KJV, NASB, NET, NIV, NLT, NRSV], 'to run' [CEV, NCV], 'to come down' [CBC; REB], 'to rush down' [TEV], 'to charge' [GW], 'to run down to' [LN].

b. ἐξαυτῆς (LN 67.113) (BDAG p. 346): 'at once' [AB, BDAG, BECNT, LN; ESV, NASB, NIV, TEV], 'immediately' [Bar, BDAG, LN; GW, KJV, NCV, NET, NLT, NRSV], 'immediately...at the double' [CBC; REB], 'quickly' [CEV], 'suddenly' [LN], 'soon thereafter' [LN]. This adverb describes an extremely short period of time between a previous state or event and a subsequent state or event [LN].

c. ἑκατοντάρχης (LN 55.16) (BDAG p. 299): 'centurion' [AB, Bar, BDAG, BECNT, CBC, LN; ESV, KJV, NASB, NET, NRSV, REB], 'officer' [CEV, GW, NCV, NIV, NLT, TEV], 'captain' [BDAG, LN]. This noun denotes a Roman officer in command of about one hundred men [LN]. It is a Roman officer commanding about a hundred men (subordinate to a tribune) [BDAG].

d. pres. act. participle of τύπτω (LN 19.1) (BDAG a. p. 1020): 'to beat' [BDAG, LN; all translations], 'to hit' [LN], 'to strike' [BDAG, LN]. This verb means to strike or hit an object, one or more times [LN]. It means to inflict a blow [BDAG].

**DISCOURSE UNIT—21:33–40** [PNTC]. The topic is arrested and questioned.

**21:33** Then the tribune coming-near arrested[a] him and ordered-(him) to-be-bound[b] with-two chains,[c] and was-inquiring[d] who he-was and what he-had done.

LEXICON—a. aorist mid. indic. of ἐπιλαμβάνομαι (LN 37.110) (BDAG 1. p. 374): 'to arrest' [BECNT, CBC, LN; CEV, ESV, NCV, NET, NIV, NLT, NRSV, REB, TEV], 'to seize' [AB, LN], 'to get hold of' [Bar], 'to

grab' [GW], 'to take' [KJV], 'to take hold of' [BDAG; NASB], 'to grasp, to catch' [BDAG]. This verb means to take a person into custody for alleged illegal activity [LN]. It means to make the motion of grasping or taking hold of something [BDAG].
  b. aorist pass. infin. of δέω (LN 18.13) (BDAG 1. p. 221): 'to be bound' [AB, Bar, BECNT, LN; CEV, ESV, KJV, NASB, NIV, NLT, NRSV, TEV], 'to be tied' [BDAG, LN], 'to be shackled' [CBC; REB], 'to be tied together' [LN], 'to be tied up' [LN; GW, NET]. This passive verb is also translated as active: 'to tie' [NCV]. This verb means to tie objects together [LN]. This verb means to confine a person or thing by various kinds of restraints [BDAG].
  c. ἅλυσις (LN 6.16) (BDAG 1. p. 48): 'chain' [BDAG, LN; all translations]. This noun denotes a linked, metal instrument for binding [LN].
  d. imperf. mid. or pass. (deponent = act.) indic. of πυνθάνομαι (LN 33.181) (BDAG 1. p. 897): 'to inquire' [AB, Bar, BDAG, BECNT, LN; ESV, NRSV, REB], 'to make an inquiry' [LN], 'to ask' [BDAG, CBC, LN; GW, NASB, NCV, NET, NIV, NLT, TEV], 'to try to find out' [CEV], 'to demand' [KJV]. This verb means to inquire about something [LN]. It means to seek to learn by inquiry [BDAG].

QUESTION—Why was he bound with two chains?
  He probably would have been chained to a soldier on each side [Bar, NICNT, PNTC, TH, TNTC, TRT].

QUESTION—Whom did the tribune ask about Paul?
  The tribune was asking the crowd about Paul [EBC, TH, TRT; NLT, TEV].

**21:34** And some in the crowd were-shouting[a] one-thing (or) another. He not being-able to-find-out[b] the certain-truth[c] because-of the uproar[d] ordered him to-be-led into the barracks.[e]

LEXICON—a. imperf. act. indic. of ἐπιφωνέω (LN 33.77) (BDAG p. 386): 'to shout' [LN; all translations except Bar; KJV, NCV], 'to call out' [Bar, LN], 'to yell' [NCV], 'to cry' [KJV], 'to cry out' [BDAG, LN], 'cry out loudly' [BDAG], 'to speak loudly' [LN]. This verb means to speak with considerable volume or loudness [LN].
  b. aorist act. infin. of γινώσκω (LN 27.2) (BDAG 2.a. p. 200): 'to find out' [BDAG, LN; CEV, NASB, NET, NLT, TEV], 'to learn' [BDAG, BECNT, LN; ESV, NCV, NRSV], 'to gain (information)' [AB], 'to get (information/facts)' [Bar; GW], 'to get at (the truth)' [CBC; NIV, REB], 'to know' [KJV], 'to ascertain' [BDAG]. This verb means to acquire information by whatever means, but often with the implication of personal involvement or experience [LN]. It means to acquire information through some means [BDAG].
  c. ἀσφαλής (LN 31.42) (BDAG 2. p. 147): 'truth' [CBC; NET, NIV, NLT, REB], 'facts' [BECNT; ESV, GW, NASB, NRSV], 'clear information' [AB], 'trustworthy information' [Bar], 'certainty' [KJV], 'what had happened' [NCV], 'exactly what had happened' [TEV], '(what is) certain'

[BDAG], 'worthy of being believed, certainly true, completely believable' [LN], not explicit [CEV]. This adjective is used pronominally to denote something that is certain and thus completely believable [LN]. It describes certainty about something [BDAG].

d. θόρυβος (LN 14.79) (BDAG 1. p. 458): 'uproar' [AB, BECNT; ESV, NASB, NIV, NRSV], 'uproar and confusion' [NLT], 'noise and confusion' [GW], 'noise' [BDAG, LN; CEV], 'confusion' [TEV], 'confusion and shouting' [NCV], 'clamor' [BDAG, LN], 'tumult' [Bar; KJV], 'hubbub' [CBC; REB], 'disturbance' [NET]. This noun denotes noise or clamor marked by confusion [LN]. It is a raising of voices that contributes to lack of understanding [BDAG].

e. παρεμβολή (LN 7.22) (BDAG 2. p. 775): 'barracks' [AB, Bar, BDAG, BECNT, CBC, LN; ESV, GW, NASB, NET, NIV, NRSV, REB], 'fortress' [CEV, NLT], 'fort' [TEV], 'army building' [NCV], 'castle' [KJV], 'soldiers' quarters' [LN]. This noun denotes a camp or barracks for soldiers [LN]. It is the headquarters of the Roman troops in Jerusalem [BDAG].

QUESTION—Where were they taking Paul?

They were taking him into the fortress Antonia [Bar, BECNT, EBC, NICNT, PNTC, TH, TNTC, TRT], which was adjacent to and overlooking the temple precincts on the northwest side, and was connected by two flights of steps [BECNT, NICNT, PNTC, TH, TRT].

**21:35** And when he-was on the steps, it-happened he was-carried by the soldiers because-of the violence[a] of-the crowd,[b] **21:36** for the multitude[c] of-the people followed shouting, "Do-away-with[d] him!"

LEXICON—a. βία (LN 20.1) (BDAG b. p. 175): 'violence' [AB, Bar, BECNT, CBC, LN; ESV, KJV, NASB, NET, NIV, NRSV, REB], 'force' [BDAG, LN]. This noun is also translated as a phrase: 'was so violent' [GW], 'grew so violent' [NLT], 'was so wild' [TEV], 'became so wild' [CEV], 'were ready to hurt him' [NCV]. This noun denotes a strong, destructive force [LN]. It is strength or energy brought to bear in varying degrees on things or persons [BDAG].

b. ὄχλος (LN 11.1) (BDAG 1.a. p. 745): 'crowd' [AB, Bar, BDAG, BECNT, LN; CEV, ESV, GW], 'mob' [CBC; NASB, NET, NIV, NLT, NRSV, REB, TEV], 'multitude' [LN], 'people' [KJV, NCV]. This noun denotes a casual non-membership group of people, fairly large in size and assembled for whatever purpose [LN]. It is a relatively large number of people gathered together [BDAG].

c. πλῆθος (LN 59.9) (BDAG 2.b.a. p. 825): 'multitude' [Bar, BECNT, LN; KJV, NASB], 'crowd' [NET], 'large number of' [BDAG, LN], 'mob' [ESV], not explicit [TEV]. The phrase 'throng of the people' is also translated 'crowd' [CEV, NIV, NLT, NRSV], 'whole crowd' [CBC; REB], 'whole mob' [NCV], 'mob' [AB; GW]. This noun denotes a large number of countable objects or events, with the probable implication of some type of grouping [LN]. It is a large amount [BDAG].

d. pres. act. impera. of αἴρω (LN 20.65) (BDAG 3. p. 28): 'to kill' [CBC, LN; CEV, GW, NCV, NLT, REB, TEV], 'to execute' [LN], 'take away, remove' [BDAG]. The phrase 'Do away with him!' is also translated 'Away with him!' [AB, Bar, BECNT; ESV, KJV, NASB, NET, NRSV], 'Get rid of him!' [NIV]. This verb means to deprive a person of life, with the implication of this being the result of condemnation by legal or quasi-legal procedures [LN]. It means to take away, remove, or seize control without suggestion of lifting up [BDAG].

QUESTION—What does 'do away with him' mean?

It is a call for Paul to be executed [AB, CBC, EBC, PNTC, TH, TNTC, TRT; CEV, GW, NCV, NLT, REB, TEV]. It is the same thing that was said in that same place about Jesus years earlier [AB, Bar, BECNT, EBC, NAC, NICNT, TNTC]. It indicates that the Jews themselves wanted to kill him [TH]. It means for him to be taken away and judged [BECNT].

**DISCOURSE UNIT—21:37–22:29** [BECNT, TNTC]. The topic is Paul defends himself [BECNT], Paul's defense before the crowd [TNTC].

**DISCOURSE UNIT—21:37–22:22** [EBC]. The topic is Paul's defense before the people.

**DISCOURSE UNIT—21:37–40** [NAC, NICNT; CEV, ESV, GW, NIV, NLT, NRSV, TEV]. The topic is Paul's request to address the crowd [NAC], Paul obtains leave to address the crowd [NICNT], Paul speaks to the people [ESV], Paul speaks to the crowd [CEV, NIV, NLT], Paul speaks in his own defense [GW], Paul defends himself [NRSV, TEV].

**21:37** And as Paul was-about to-be-brought into the barracks he-says to-the tribune, "Would-it-be-allowed[a] for-me to-say something to you?" and he-said, "You-know[b] Greek? **21:38** Then you are not the Egyptian before these days having-caused-(a)-revolt[c] and having-led four thousand men of-the assassins[d] into the desert[e]?"

LEXICON—a. pres. act. indic. of ἔξεστι (LN 71.1) (BDAG 1.b. p. 348): 'to be allowed' [AB], 'to be permitted' [BDAG], 'to be proper' [BECNT], 'to be authorized, to be right' [BDAG], 'to be possible' [LN]. The phrase 'would it be allowed for me' is also translated 'May I' [Bar, CBC; all versions except CEV], 'Can I' [CEV]. This verb means to mark an event as being possible in a highly generic sense [LN]. It means to be authorized for the doing of something [BDAG].

b. pres. act. indic. of γινώσκω (LN 32.16) (BDAG 6.e. p. 200): 'to know' [BDAG, BECNT; CEV, ESV, NASB, NET, NLT, NRSV], 'to know how to speak' [Bar], 'to speak' [AB, CBC; GW, KJV, NCV, NIV, REB, TEV], 'to have come to know' [BDAG], 'to come to understand, to perceive, to comprehend' [LN]. This verb means to come to an understanding as the result of ability to experience and learn [LN]. It means to have come to the knowledge of [BDAG].

c. aorist act. participle of ἀναστατόω (LN 39.41) (BDAG p. 72): 'to start a revolt' [CBC; NIV, REB], 'to rise up in revolt' [BECNT], 'to stir up a revolt' [ESV, NASB, NRSV], 'to lead a rebellion' [NLT], 'to start a rebellion' [NET], 'to start a riot' [CEV], 'to start a revolution' [GW, TEV], 'to stir up trouble' [AB], 'to start trouble against the government' [NCV], 'to make an uproar' [KJV], 'to raise' [Bar], 'to incite to revolt, to cause to rebel' [LN], 'to disturb, to trouble, to upset' [BDAG]. This verb means to cause people to rebel against or to reject authority [LN]. It means to upset the stability of a person or group [BDAG].

d. σικάριος (LN 20.86) (BDAG p. 923): 'assassin' [BDAG, BECNT, LN; ESV, NASB, NET, NLT, NRSV], 'extremist' [AB], 'terrorist' [BDAG, CBC, LN; CEV, GW, NIV, REB], 'armed terrorist' [TEV], 'sicarii' [Bar], 'murderer' [KJV], 'killer' [NCV], 'dagger man' [BDAG]. This noun denotes one who kills someone with intent and as a part of a plot [LN]. It is one who is intent on killing someone as part of an organized subversive political program [BDAG].

e. ἔρημος (LN 1.86) (BDAG 2. p. 392): 'desert' [AB, Bar, BDAG, LN; CEV, GW, KJV, NLT, REB, TEV], 'wilderness' [BDAG, BECNT, LN; ESV, KJV, NASB, NET, NIV, NRSV], 'wilds' [CBC], 'lonely place' [LN], 'grassland' [BDAG]. This noun denotes a largely uninhabited region, normally with sparse vegetation (in contrast with πόλις 'a population center') [LN]. It is an uninhabited region or locality (in contrast to cultivated and inhabited country) [BDAG].

QUESTION—Did the tribune expect a 'yes' answer or a 'no' answer to his question 'are you not the Egyptian'?

1. His question shows that the tribune was surprised that Paul could speak Greek, which then led him to suspect that he might be the Egyptian [Bar, BECNT, EBC, TNTC, TRT], or confirmed his suspicion that he was that Egyptian [PNTC], since Greek was known and spoken in Egypt [Bar, BECNT, PNTC, TNTC].
2. His question shows that the tribune was surprised that Paul could speak Greek, which then led him to suspect that he was probably not the Egyptian [AB, CBC, NAC, NICNT; NCV, NET, NRSV, REB, TEV].

QUESTION—Who were these assassins?

They were men who carried small, hidden daggers [Bar, BECNT, TH], and who killed many people in the time prior to the Jewish wars with Rome [Bar, TH], especially in crowds at festival times [NICNT, PNTC, TH]. They were extremists and enemies of Rome as well as of anyone who sympathized with Rome [NICNT, PNTC, TH].

**21:39** And Paul said, "I am (a)-Jew, (a)-citizen[a] of-Tarsus of-Cilicia, not an-insignificant[b] city; and I-ask you, permit[c] me to-speak to the people."

LEXICON—a. πολίτης (LN 11.68) (BDAG 1. p. 846): 'citizen' [BDAG, LN; all translations except CEV], not explicit [CEV]. This noun denotes a

person having full status as a member of a socio-political unit of people [LN]. It is one who lives in or comes from a city or country [BDAG].
b. ἄσημος (LN 87.59) (BDAG 1. p. 142): 'insignificant' [BDAG, LN; NASB], 'mean' [Bar, BECNT, CBC; KJV, REB], 'obscure' [ESV], 'ordinary' [NIV], 'unimportant' [BDAG], 'low, inferior' [LN]. The phrase 'not…insignificant' is also translated 'important' [CEV, NCV, NET, NLT, NRSV, TEV], 'well-known' [GW], 'considerable' [AB]. This adjective describes being obscure or insignificant, with the possible implication of lacking in noble descent [LN]. It describes something as unmarked [BDAG].
c. aorist act. impera. of ἐπιτρέπω (LN 13.138) (BDAG 1. p. 385): 'to permit' [Bar, BDAG, BECNT, LN; ESV], 'to allow' [BDAG, LN; NASB, NET], 'to let' [AB, LN; CEV, GW, NCV, NIV, NLT, NRSV, TEV], 'to suffer' [KJV]. This verb is also translated as a noun: '(ask/have) permission' [CBC; REB]. This verb means to allow someone to do something [BDAG, LN].

QUESTION—Why does Paul use the litotes 'not insignificant' to describe Tarsus?

The litotes means that it was an important city [TRT]. Tarsus was important politically, as well as intellectually and culturally [BECNT, TH]. It was also a commercial city, with a population of several hundred thousand people [BECNT]. The litotes is a way of expressing something positive, which is Paul's status as a citizen from a city of importance politically, economically, and intellectually, and that the tribune should recognize and respect that status [BECNT, PNTC]. Paul was proud to belong to such a self-governing city [TNTC]. In describing Tarsus this way, Paul is stating his credentials [CBC]. This phrase was used by various cities to describe their own significance [BECNT, EBC, NAC].

**21:40** And he having-given-(him)-permission,[a] Paul, standing on the steps motioned[b] with-the hand to-the people. And (a)-great quiet[c] having-occurred, he-addressed[d] (them) in-the Hebrew[e] language saying,

LEXICON—a. aorist act. participle of ἐπιτρέπω aorist act. impera. of ἐπιτρέπω (LN 13.138) (BDAG 1. p. 385): 'to give permission' [AB, Bar; ESV, GW, NASB, NCV, NET, NRSV, TEV], 'to permit' [BDAG, LN], 'to give leave' [BECNT], 'to give license' [KJV], 'to allow' [BDAG, LN], 'to let' [LN]. The phrase 'having given him permission' is also translated 'when permission had been given' [CBC], 'when this was given' [REB], 'receiving…permission' [NIV], '(he) told him he could (speak)' [CEV], 'the commander agreed' [NLT]. This verb means to allow someone to do something [BDAG, LN].
b. aorist act. indic. of κατασείω (LN 33.478) (BDAG 2. p. 526): 'to motion' [BDAG, BECNT; CEV, ESV, GW, NASB, NIV, NLT, NRSV, TEV], 'to gesture' [AB, Bar; NET], 'to beckon' [KJV], 'to wave' [NCV], 'to make a sign' [BDAG, LN], 'to give a signal' [LN], 'to raise the hand to call for

attention' [REB]. This verb is also translated as a phrase: 'with a gesture' [CBC]. This verb means to communicate by means of a sign or signal [LN]. It means to signal by a gesture [BDAG].

c. σιγή (LN 33.120) (BDAG p. 922): 'quiet' [BDAG, CBC; CEV, REB], 'silence' [AB, Bar, BDAG, LN; KJV, NCV, NLT], 'hush' [BECNT; ESV, NASB, NRSV]. This noun is also translated as an adjective: '(be/became) silent' [GW, NET, NIV, TEV]. This noun denotes the absence of noise [LN]. It is the absence of all noise, whether made by speaking or by anything else [BDAG].

d. aorist act. indic. of προσφωνέω (LN 33.27) (BDAG 1. p. 887): 'to address' [BDAG, CBC, LN; ESV, NET, NLT, NRSV, REB], 'to speak' [AB, BECNT; CEV, GW, KJV, NASB, NCV, TEV], 'to call out' [Bar, BDAG], 'to say' [NIV], 'to speak out to' [LN]. This verb means to address an audience, with possible emphasis upon loudness [LN]. It means to call out or speak to [BDAG].

e. Ἑβραΐς (LN 93.104) (BDAG p. 270): 'Hebrew' [AB, Bar, LN; ESV, GW, KJV, NASB, NCV, NLT, NRSV, TEV], 'the language used by the Hebrews' [BECNT], 'Aramaic' [CEV, NET, NIV], 'Jewish (language)' [CBC; REB]. This adjective describes what pertains to the Hebrews [LN]. It describes the Hebrew language, more specifically, the Aramaic spoken at that time in Palestine [BDAG].

QUESTION—What language would Paul have used to address the people?

He was using Aramaic, which was the language used by the Jews of that day [Bar, BECNT, CBC, EBC, NAC, NICNT, PNTC, TH; CEV, NET, NIV].

**DISCOURSE UNIT—22:1–30** [NASB]. The topic is Paul's defense before the Jews.

**DISCOURSE UNIT—22:1–29** [Bar; NCV]. The topic is Paul speaks to the people [NCV], Paul's temple speech and the sequel [Bar].

**DISCOURSE UNIT—22:1–21** [AB, NAC, NICNT, PNTC; NET]. The topic is Paul's speech before the temple mob [NAC], Paul's defense [NET], Paul's defense to the people of Jerusalem [NICNT], defending his mission and his gospel [PNTC], Paul's speech from the steps of the fortress [AB].

**DISCOURSE UNIT—22:1–16** [AB]. The topic is Paul's speech from the steps of the fortress.

**DISCOURSE UNIT—22:1** [NICNT]. The topic is Paul's early days.

**22:1** "Brothers and fathers,[a] listen- now -to[b] my defense[c] to you."

LEXICON—a. πατήρ (LN 11.26) (BDAG 4. p. 787): 'father' [AB, Bar, BECNT, BDAG, CBC, LN; all versions except CEV, NLT, TEV], 'esteemed father' [NLT], 'leader(s) of our nation' [CEV]. The phrase 'brothers and fathers' is also translated 'my fellow Jews' [TEV]. This noun means a member of a well-defined socio-religious entity and

ACTS 22:1

representing an older age group than the so-called reference person [LN]. It is a title of respectful address [BDAG].
- b. aorist act. impera. of ἀκούω (LN 31.56): 'to listen to' [AB, Bar; CEV, GW, NCV, NET, NIV, NLT, NRSV], 'to hear' [BECNT; ESV, KJV, NASB, TEV], 'to give (me) a hearing' [CBC; REB], 'to accept, to listen and respond, to pay attention and respond, to heed' [LN]. This verb means to believe something and to respond to it on the basis of having heard [LN].
- c. ἀπολογία (LN 33.436) (BDAG 1. p. 117): 'defense' [AB, Bar, BECNT, BDAG, CBC, LN; all versions except CEV, GW, REB]. The phrase 'listen to my defense' is also translated 'listen as I explain what happened' [CEV], 'listen as I now present my case to you' [GW], 'give me a hearing while I put my case to you' [REB]. This noun denotes the content of what is said in defense [LN]. It is a speech of defense [BDAG].

QUESTION—What may be implied by his calling them 'brothers and fathers'?

'Fathers' may reflect the fact that at least some of the Jewish leaders would have been in the crowd [BECNT]. It expresses respect [Bar, NAC, TRT]. It expresses respect to a crowd that would include men older than himself as well as men younger than himself [PNTC]. 'Brothers' would refer to men of his own age, and 'fathers' would refer to men older than Paul [TH]. It is a formal Jewish address similar to Stephen's in Acts 7:2, and the use of 'fathers' need not imply that members of the Sanhedrin were in the crowd [EBC]. 'Fathers' probably refers to priests or members of the Sanhedrin [TNTC].

QUESTION—What is an ἀπολογία 'defense'?

It means to speak in one's own defense [BECNT, EBC], to explain and justify what one is doing or believing [BECNT]. Several of these occur in the later portions of Acts [BECNT]. It is not a defense about the issue in question of having desecrated the temple [EBC, NAC, PNTC], but was meant to show his faithfulness to Judaism [NAC, PNTC], and that he was not an apostate [EBC]. The ἀπολογία was also a witness to Jesus [PNTC, TNTC]. 'Defense' is a theme for much of the rest of the book of Acts [Bar, TNTC].

**22:2** And hearing that he-was-addressing[a] them in-the Hebrew[b] language, they-became quiet.[c] And he-said:

LEXICON—a. imperf. act. indic. of προσφωνέω (LN 33.27) (BDAG 1. p. 887): 'to address' [Bar, BDAG, BECNT, LN; ESV, NASB, NET, NRSV], 'to speak to' [AB, CBC; CEV, GW, NIV, REB, TEV], 'to speak out to' [LN], 'to speak' [KJV, NCV, NLT], 'to call out to' [BDAG]. This verb means to address an audience, with possible emphasis upon loudness [LN]. It means to call out or speak to [BDAG].
- b. Ἑβραΐς (LN 93.104) (BDAG p. 270): 'Hebrew' [AB, Bar, BECNT, LN; ESV, GW, KJV, NASB, NCV, NRSV, TEV], 'the Hebrew language' [BDAG], 'Aramaic' [CEV, NET, NIV]. The phrase 'the Hebrew

language' is also translated 'their own language' [CBC; NLT, REB]. This adjective describes something as pertaining to the Hebrews [LN].
  c. ἡσυχία (LN 33.119) (BDAG 2. p. 440): 'quiet' [BECNT, LN; ESV, GW, NASB, NCV, NIV, NRSV], '(more) quietly' [CBC; REB], '(even) quieter' [CEV, NET, TEV], '(even greater) silence' [Bar; NLT], '(more) silence' [BDAG; KJV]. 'They became quiet' is also translated 'they calmed down (still more)' [AB]. This noun denotes a state of silence, with a possible focus upon the attitude involved [LN]. It denotes a state of saying nothing or very little [BDAG].

QUESTION—What language was Paul speaking here?
  1. He was speaking Aramaic [Bar, BDAG, BECNT, CBC, EBC, NAC, NICNT, PNTC, TH; CEV, NET, NIV].
  2. He was speaking Hebrew [AB].

**DISCOURSE UNIT—22:3–5** [PNTC]. The topic is Paul's former life in Judaism.

**22:3** "I am (a)-Jew, born in Tarsus in Cilicia but brought-up$^a$ in this city, at the feet of-Gamaliel educated$^b$ strictly$^c$ according-to the law of-(our)-fathers, having zeal$^d$ for-God just-as all (of) you are today;

LEXICON—a. perf. pass. participle of ἀνατρέφω (LN 33.232) (BDAG b. p. 74): 'to be brought up' [all translations except CEV, GW, NCV], 'to be raised' [CEV, GW]. This passive participle is also translated as an active verb: 'I grew up' [NCV]. This verb means to be given extensive and formal instruction by someone [LN]. It means to be brought up, reared, trained [BDAG].
  b. perf. pass. participle of παιδεύω (LN 33.226) (BDAG 1. p. 749): 'to be educated' [Bar, BECNT; ESV, NASB, NET, NRSV], 'to receive one's education' [GW], 'to receive instruction' [TEV], 'to be instructed' [AB, BDAG], 'to be trained' [BDAG, CBC; REB], 'to be taught' [KJV]. The phrase 'educated at the feet of Gamaliel' is also translated 'I studied under Gamaliel' [NIV], 'I was a student of Gamaliel' [CEV, NCV], 'as a pupil of Gamaliel' [REB]. This verb means to provide instruction, with the intent of forming proper habits of behavior [LN]. It means to provide instruction for informed and responsible living [BDAG].
  c. ἀκρίβεια (LN 72.20) (BDAG p. 39): 'strictness, strict conformance to, accurateness' [LN], 'exactness, precision' [BDAG]. The phrase 'strictly according to the law' [NASB, NRSV] is also translated 'strictly in the…law' [Bar], 'in the strict laws' [GW], 'with strictness according to the law' [NET], 'strict instruction in the law' [TEV], 'carefully instructed/trained in the law' [AB; NLT], 'according to the strict manner' [BECNT; ESV], 'according to the perfect manner' [KJV], 'thoroughly trained in every point of our (ancestral) law' [CBC; REB], 'thoroughly trained in the law of our ancestors' [NIV], 'I was taught to follow every single law' [CEV], '(who) carefully taught me everything' [NCV]. This noun denotes strict conformity to a norm or standard, involving both

detail and completeness [LN]. It means strict conformity to a norm or standard [BDAG].

d. ζηλωτής (LN 25.77) (BDAG 1.a.α. p. 427): 'enthusiast' [BDAG, LN], 'zealous person' [LN], 'adherent, loyalist' [BDAG]. The phrase 'having zeal' is also translated 'zealous' [AB, Bar; ESV, KJV, NASB, NET, NIV, NLT, NRSV], 'a zealot' [BECNT], 'ardent' [CBC; REB], 'I was eager' [CEV], 'I was devoted' [GW], 'I was dedicated' [TEV], 'I was very serious' [NCV]. This noun denotes one who is deeply committed to something and therefore zealous [LN]. It means one who is earnestly committed to a side or cause [BDAG].

QUESTION—Was Paul brought up in Tarsus or Jerusalem?

1. He was brought up in Jerusalem [AB, Bar, BECNT, CBC, NAC, NICNT, PNTC, TH, TNTC, TRT; ESV, KJV, NASB, NCV, NET, NIV, NLT, NRSV, REB, TEV].
2. He was brought up in Tarsus [CEV, GW].

QUESTION—Which of the participles in this sentence are linked to 'at the feet of Gamliel'?

The clause having the participle 'brought up' is punctuated as being separate from the next clause, which has the participle 'educated', indicating a possible distinction in association, and meaning that his upbringing may or may not have any relation to his education under Gamaliel [Bar, CBC; ESV, NASB, NCV, NET, NIV, REB].

1. 'Educated' refers only to his being educated at the feet of Gamaliel, but not to his having been 'brought up' [AB, NAC, NICNT, PNTC, TNTC, TRT].
2. Both verbs refer to the action of Gamaliel: Paul was brought up *and* educated under Gamaliel [BECNT, CBC, EBC, LN (33.232); CEV, GW, KJV, NLT, NRSV, TEV]. Each participle stands at the head of its respective clause, and since the phrase 'at the feet of Gamaliel' occurs before 'educated strictly' it should be seen as completing the thought of the previous participle, 'brought up', meaning that he was brought up at the feet of Gamaliel, and instructed strictly according to the laws of the fathers [EBC].

QUESTION—Who was Gamaliel?

He was one of the most respected Pharisaic rabbis of his day [Bar, BECNT, NICNT, PNTC, TRT].

QUESTION—Does 'strictly' modify 'educated' or 'the law of our fathers'?

1. It modifies the manner of instruction [AB, Bar, CBC; CEV, NASB, NCV, NET, NIV, NLT, NRSV, REB, TEV]: strictly instructed in the law.
2. It modifies the manner of observing the law [BECNT, EBC, NICNT, PNTC; ESV, GW, KJV]: instructed in the strict manner of the law.

**22:4** I persecuted[a] this way[b] to-the-death binding[c] and handing-over[d] to prison both men and women,

LEXICON—a. aorist act. indic. of διώκω (LN 39.45) (BDAG 2. p. 254): 'to persecute' [BDAG, LN; all translations except CEV], 'to harass' [LN], 'to make trouble (for everyone)' [CEV]. This verb means to systematically organize a program to oppress and harass people [LN]. It means to harass someone, especially because of beliefs [BDAG].

b. ὁδός (LN 41.35) (BDAG 3.c. p. 691): 'way' [AB, Bar, BDAG, BECNT; ESV, KJV, NASB, NET, NRSV], 'movement' [CBC; REB], 'religion, teaching' [BDAG], 'Christian way of life' [LN]. The phrase 'this way' is also translated 'the followers of this way' [NIV, NLT], 'everyone who followed the Lord's way' [CEV], 'the people who followed this way' [TEV], 'people who followed the way of Christ/Jesus' [GW, NCV]. This noun denotes behavior in accordance with Christian principles and practices [LN]. It denotes the whole way of life from a moral and spiritual viewpoint in the most comprehensive sense [BDAG].

c. pres. act. participle of δεσμεύω (LN 18.15) (BDAG 1. p. 219): 'to bind' [AB, Bar, BDAG, BECNT, LN; ESV, KJV, NASB, NRSV], 'to tie up' [GW, NET], 'to tie' [LN], 'to arrest' [CBC; NCV, NIV, NLT, REB, TEV], 'to have arrested' [CEV]. This verb means to bind or tie on [LN].

d. pres. act. participle of παραδίδωμι (LN 57.77) (BDAG 1.b. p. 762): 'to deliver to/into (prison)' [AB, Bar, BECNT; ESV, KJV], 'to put in/into (jail/prison)' [CEV, GW, NASB, NCV, NET, NRSV], 'to throw into (prison)' [NIV, NLT, TEV], 'to commit to (prison)' [REB], 'to put in (chains)' [CBC], 'to give over' [LN], 'to hand over' [BDAG, LN], 'to turn over, give up a person' [BDAG]. This verb means to hand over to or to convey something to someone [LN].

QUESTION—Why does Paul refer to the church and the Christian faith as 'this way'?

It is how early Christians in Jerusalem had described themselves in Acts 9:2 [BECNT, EBC, NAC, NICNT]. It may reflect an idea held by early Jewish Christians that they followed the true way within the broader context of Judaism [NAC], that they followed the way of life or the way of salvation [BECNT, NICNT].

QUESTION—In what sense did Paul persecute Christians to the death?

He was involved with and cooperated with the efforts of others who put Christians to death [BECNT, PNTC]. He had taken an active part in persecuting the church [AB]. He may have actually caused the death of some people [TH].

**22:5** As also the high-priest and the whole council-of-elders[a] (may) testify of-me. Having-received letters from them to the brothers[b] I-was-going to Damascus to-bring also those who-were there in-bonds to Jerusalem to-be-punished.[c]

LEXICON—a. πρεσβυτέριον (LN 11.83) (BDAG a. p. 861): 'council of elders' [BDAG, BECNT, CBC, LN; ESV, NASB, NCV, NET, NET, NLT, NRSV, REB], 'council' [NIV, TEV], 'council of leaders' [GW], '(the) council members' [CEV], 'estate of elders' [KJV], 'presbytery' [AB], 'company of elders' [Bar], 'Sanhedrin, high council of the Jews' [LN]. This noun denotes the highest council of the Jews but with the

implication of the maturity and relative advanced age of those constituting the membership of such a council [LN]. It denotes the highest Judean council in Jerusalem, usually called the Sanhedrin [BDAG].
   b. ἀδελφός (LN 11.25): 'brother' [AB, LN; ESV, KJV, NASB, NCV, NET, NRSV], 'Jewish brother' [BECNT, Bar; NLT], 'fellow Jew' [CBC, LN; REB, TEV], 'Jewish leader' [CEV], 'Jewish community' [GW]. This word is also translated as describing the Jewish leaders in Damascus relative to the Jewish leaders in Jerusalem: 'their associates' [LN; NIV]. This noun denotes a person belonging to the same socio-religious entity and being of the same age group as the so-called reference person [LN].
   c. aorist pass. subj. of τιμωρέω (LN 38.6) (BDAG p. 1006): 'to be punished' [BDAG, BECNT, LN; all versions except GW, NRSV, REB]. This infinitive is also translated 'for punishment' [AB, Bar, CBC; NRSV, REB], 'to punish them' [GW]. This verb means to punish, with the implication of causing people to suffer what they deserve [LN].
QUESTION—Who was the high priest at this time?
   When Paul received letters to the Jewish community in Damascus, the high priest had been Caiaphas [BECNT, TNTC], but now at the time of this event it was Ananias [AB, BECNT, CBC, TNTC]. Ananias was appointed high priest by Herod Agrippa in AD 48, but after ten years was deposed and was later murdered when the Jewish war began [CBC].
QUESTION—Who are 'the brothers' he refers to here?
   They were the Jews in Damascus [BECNT, CBC, TH; GW, REB, TEV], specifically the Jewish leaders there [PNTC, TRT; CEV, NIV].
QUESTION—How could the high priest give Paul authority to take Jewish people prisoner in another country?
   An earlier Roman edict had granted the Jewish state power to extradite people who had fled from Judea to neighboring states [NICNT].

**DISCOURSE UNIT—22:6–16** [NRSV, TEV]. The topic is Paul tells of his conversion.

**DISCOURSE UNIT—22:6–11** [NICNT, PNTC]. The topic is Paul's encounter with the risen Jesus [PNTC], the Damascus Road [NICNT].

**22:6** It-happened as I-was-going and drawing-near[a] to-Damascus about midday[b] suddenly from heaven[c] (a)-very-bright[d] light shone[e] around me,
LEXICON—a. pres. act. participle of ἐγγίζω (LN 15.75) (BDAG 1.b.α. p. 270): 'to draw near' [Bar, BDAG, BECNT, LN; ESV], 'to come near' [BDAG, LN; NCV, NIV, TEV], 'to near' [CBC; REB], 'to be near' [NET], 'to come nigh' [KJV], 'to approach' [AB, BDAG, LN; GW, NASB, NLT, NRSV], 'to get close to' [CEV]. This verb means to move nearer to a reference point [LN]. It means to move in space and so draw closer to a reference point [BDAG].
   b. μεσημβρία (LN 67.74) (BDAG 1. p. 634): 'midday' [Bar, BDAG, CBC, LN; REB, TEV], 'noon' [AB, BDAG, BECNT, LN; CEV, ESV, GW,

KJV, NCV, NET, NIV, NLT, NRSV], 'noontime' [NASB]. This noun denotes the midpoint of a day [LN].
- c. οὐρανός (LN 1.5) (BDAG 2.b. p. 739): 'heaven' [BDAG; all translations except CBC; REB, TEV], 'sky' [CBC, LN; REB, TEV]. This noun denotes the space above the earth, including the vault arching high over the earth from one horizon to another, as well as the sun, moon, and stars [LN]. It is the transcendent abode, heaven [BDAG].
- d. ἱκανός (LN 78.14) (BDAG 3.b. p. 472): 'very bright' [AB, BDAG; NASB, NET, NLT], 'bright' [LN; CEV, GW, NCV, NIV, TEV], 'great' [Bar, BECNT, CBC, LN; ESV, KJV, NRSV, REB], 'intense' [LN]. This adjective describes a relatively high point on a scale of extent [LN]. It describes something as being large in extent or degree [BDAG].
- e. aorist act. infin. of περιαστράπτω (LN 14.45) (BDAG 1. p. 799): 'to shine around' [AB, Bar, BDAG; ESV, KJV], 'to shine down around' [NLT], 'to shine about' [BECNT; NRSV], 'to shine brightly around' [LN], 'to flash around' [CBC, LN; CEV, GW, NET, NIV, TEV], 'to flash all around' [NASB, NCV, REB]. This verb means to shine very brightly on an area surrounding an object [LN] or that is all around a person [BDAG].

**22:7** and I-fell[a] to the ground and I-heard (a)-voice saying[b] to-me, 'Saul, Saul, why do-you-persecute[c] me?' **22:8** And I answered, 'Who are-you, Lord[d]?' And he-said to me, 'I am Jesus the Nazarene, whom you are-persecuting.'

LEXICON—a. aorist act. indic. of πίπτω (LN 15.118) (BDAG 1.b.α.ℵ. p. 815): 'to fall' [LN; all translations], 'to fall to the ground, to fall down violently' [BDAG]. This verb means to fall from one level to another [LN], to move rapidly in a downward direction [BDAG].
- b. pres. act. participle of λέγω (LN 33.69): 'to say' [LN; all translations except CEV, GW], 'to ask' [CEV, GW], 'to talk, to tell, to speak' [LN]. This verb means to speak or talk, with apparent focus upon the content of what is said' [LN].
- c. pres. act. indic. of διώκω (LN 39.45) (BDAG 2. p. 254): 'to persecute' [BDAG, LN; all translations except CEV], 'to be cruel to' [CEV], 'to harass' [LN]. This verb means to systematically organize a program to oppress and harass people [LN]. It means harass someone, especially because of beliefs [BDAG].
- d. κύριος (LN 12.9): 'Lord' [LN, all translations except GW], 'Sir' [GW], 'Ruler' [LN]. This noun, which is a title for God and for Christ, denotes one who exercises supernatural authority over mankind [LN].

**22:9** Now those who-were with me saw[a] (the) light but did- not -hear[b] the voice[c] of the one-speaking to-me.

TEXT—Some manuscripts include καὶ ἔμφοβοι ἐγένοντο 'and were afraid'. Manuscripts omitting this variant are given a B rating by GNT to indicate that the text is almost certain. Only KJV accepts this reading.

LEXICON—a. aorist mid. (deponent = act.) indic. of θεάομαι (LN 24.14) (BDAG 1.a. p. 445): 'to see' [BDAG; all translations], 'to look at' [BDAG, LN], 'to behold' [BDAG], 'to observe' [LN]. This verb means to observe something with continuity and attention, often with the implication that what is observed is something unusual [LN]. It means to have an intent look at something, to take something in with one's eyes, with the implication that one is especially impressed [LN].
   b. aorist act. indic. of ἀκούω (LN 24.52) (BDAG 1.b.α. p. 37): 'to hear' [AB, Bar, BDAG, BECNT, CBC, LN; CEV, KJV, NRSV, REB, TEV], 'understand' [ESV, GW, NASB, NCV, NET, NIV, NLT]. This verb means to have or exercise the faculty of hearing [BDAG].
   c. φωνή (LN 33.103) (BDAG 2.d. p. 1072): 'voice' [BDAG, LN; all translations except GW]. The phrase 'the voice of the one speaking to me' is also translated 'what the person who was speaking to me said' [GW]. This noun denotes the human voice as an instrument of communication [LN]. It denotes the faculty of utterance [BDAG].

QUESTION—Did they not hear the voice, or not understand what was said?

They heard the voice, but did not understand what was being said [BECNT, NAC, PNTC, TNTC]. They shared with Paul certain aspects of the experience, seeing the light and hearing sound, but not the revelatory aspects of actually seeing Jesus and hearing what he had to say [PNTC]. They did not see or hear the person Paul was speaking to [NICNT].

**22:10** And I-said, 'What shall-I-do,[a] Lord?' And the Lord said to me, 'Arise,[b] go into Damascus and-there it-will-be-told[c] you concerning all that-is appointed[d] for-you to-do.'

LEXICON—a. aorist act. subj. of ποιέω (LN 90.45): 'to do' [LN; all translations].
   b. aorist act. participle of ἀνίστημι (LN 17.7): 'to arise' [KJV], 'to get up' [all translations except ESV, KJV], 'to rise' [ESV], 'to cause to stand, to raise up' [LN]. This verb means to cause someone to stand up [LN].
   c. future pass. indic. of λαλέω (LN 33.70) (BDAG 2.a.γ. p. 582): 'to be told' [LN; all translations], 'to be spoken, to be said' [BDAG, LN]. This verb means to speak or talk, with the possible implication of more informal usage [LN]. It means to utter words [BDAG].
   d. perf. pass. indic. of τάσσω (LN 37.96) (BDAG 2.a. p. 991): 'to be appointed' [Bar, BDAG, LN; ESV, KJV, NASB], 'to be assigned' [LN; NRSV], 'to stand appointed' [BECNT], 'to be decided' [AB], 'to be determined' [BDAG], 'to be given a task' [LN]. The phrase 'all that is appointed for you to do' is also translated 'everything that you have been designated to do' [NET], 'all that you have been assigned to do' [NIV], 'all that you are appointed to do' [REB], 'what I've arranged for you to do' [GW], 'all the things I have planned for you to do' [NCV], 'everything you are to do' [NLT], 'all the tasks that are laid upon you' [CBC], 'what to do' [CEV]. This verb means to assign someone to a

particular task, function, or role [LN]. It means to give instructions as to what must be done [BDAG]. The TEV is missing.

QUESTION—What does Paul mean when he addresses Jesus as 'Lord'?

As Paul used it in the first instance, it was a customary way of recognizing a person as being of superior status, but does not necessarily mean that Paul would have been acknowledging Jesus' deity [BECNT, NAC, TNTC], but in the second instance it was a confession of Jesus' lordship [NAC, TNTC]. In the first instance it was a polite address, 'Sir', but in the second instance Paul addressed him as 'Lord' [GW].

QUESTION—Is there any significance in the use of the perfect tense of the verb τάσσω 'appointed'?

It implies that what Paul was being sent to do was a part of God's eternal plan [Bar, BECNT]. It shows that Paul's task had already been determined, and all that remained was for him to learn of it and carry it out [PNTC].

QUESTION—What is implied by the use of the verb 'appointed'?

What Paul was being instructed to do is part of God's larger plan [BECNT].

**22:11** And since I-was- not -seeing<sup>a</sup> because-of the brightness<sup>b</sup> of-that light, being-led-by-(the)-hand<sup>c</sup> by those who-were-with me I-came into Damascus.

LEXICON—a. imperf. act. indic. of ἐμβλέπω (LN 24.9) (BDAG 1. p. 321): 'to see' [AB, Bar, BECNT; ESV], 'to look at, gaze on' [BDAG], 'to look straight at, to look directly at' [LN]. The phrase 'I was not seeing' is also translated 'I could not see' [CEV, KJV, NASB, NCV, NET, NRSV], 'I was blinded' [CBC; NLT], 'I was blind' [GW, TEV], '(the brilliance of the light) blinded me' [NIV], 'I had been blinded' [REB]. This verb means to direct one's vision and attention to a particular object [LN]. It means to look at something directly and therefore intently [BDAG].

b. δόξα (LN 14.49) (BDAG 1.a. p. 257): 'brightness' [AB, BDAG, BECNT, LN; ESV, NASB, NRSV], 'brilliance' [CBC; NET, NIV, REB], 'glory' [Bar; KJV], 'shining' [LN], 'radiance' [BDAG, LN], 'splendor' [BDAG]. The phrase 'the brightness of that light' is also translated 'the light had been so bright' [CEV, GW], 'the bright light' [NCV, TEV], 'the intense light' [NLT]. This noun denotes the state of brightness or shining [LN]. It denotes the condition of being bright or shining [BDAG].

c. aorist pass. participle of χειραγωγέω (LN 15.184) (BDAG p. 1083): 'to be led by the hand' [AB, Bar, BDAG, BECNT, LN; ESV, KJV, NASB, NET, NLT], 'to be taken by the hand' [BDAG, LN]. This passive verb is also translated as active: 'lead/led me by the hand' [CBC; CEV, GW, NIV, REB], 'took me by the hand' [NRSV, TEV], 'led me' [NCV]. This verb means to lead or guide by taking by the hand [LN].

**DISCOURSE UNIT—22:12–16** [NICNT, PNTC; TEV]. The topic is Paul's call to preach to the Gentiles [TEV], Ananias and the redirection of Paul's life [PNTC], Ananias of Damascus [NICNT].

**22:12** And a-certain Ananias, (a)-devout[a] man according-to[b] the law[c] well-spoken-(of)[d] by all the Jews dwelling-(there),

LEXICON—a. εὐλαβής (LN 53.8) (BDAG p. 407): 'devout' [AB, BDAG, CBC; ESV, GW, KJV, NASB, NET, NIV, NRSV, REB], 'pious' [Bar, BECNT, LN], 'religious' [NCV, TEV], 'godly' [NLT], 'God-fearing' [BDAG], 'reverent' [LN], not explicit [CEV]. This adjective describes being reverent toward God [LN]. It describes religious attitudes [BDAG].
  b. κατά with accusative object (LN 89.4): 'according to' [AB, Bar, BECNT; ESV, KJV, NET, NRSV], 'by the standard of' [NASB], 'in relation to, with regard to' [LN]. The phrase 'devout according to the law' is also translated 'devout observer of the law' [CBC; NIV, REB], 'who followed Moses' teachings' [GW], 'he obeyed the law of Moses' [NCV], 'who faithfully obeyed the law' [CEV], 'who obeyed our law' [TEV], 'deeply devoted to the law' [NLT]. This preposition marks a specific element bearing a relation to something else [LN].
  c. νόμος (LN 33.55) (BDAG 2.b. p. 677): 'the Law/law' [BDAG, LN; all translations except CEV, GW, NCV], 'the Law of Moses' [CEV, NCV], 'Moses' teachings' [GW]. This noun denotes the first five books of the OT called the Torah (often better rendered as 'instruction') [LN]. It denotes a constitution or statutory legal system, and specifically of the law that Moses received from God and is the standard according to which membership in the people of Israel is determined [BDAG].
  d. pres. pass. participle of μαρτυρέω (LN 33.263) (BDAG 2.b. p. 618): 'to be well spoken of' [BDAG, LN; ESV, NASB, NET, NRSV, REB], 'to be highly respected' [NIV, TEV], 'to be well-regarded' [NLT], 'to be testified to' [BECNT], 'to be approved of' [BDAG, CBC, LN], 'to be well-liked' [CEV], 'to have a good report' [KJV]. The phrase 'well-spoken of' is also translated '(the Jews) spoke highly of him' [GW], 'the Jews) respected him' [NCV], 'of good reputation' [AB], 'had a good reputation' [Bar]. This verb means to speak well of a person on the basis of personal experience [LN]. It means to affirm in a supportive manner [BDAG].

QUESTION—What does εὐλαβὴς κατὰ τὸν νόμον 'a devout man according to the law' mean?

He was devout, living as a careful observer of the law [CBC, NAC, TH; CEV, GW, NCV, NIV, NLT, TEV]. He was devout according to the standards of the law [BECNT, NICNT; NASB].

**22:13** having-come to me and standing-beside me said to-me, 'Brother[a] Saul, receive-your-sight.'[b] And at- that-same -hour[c] I-saw[d] him.

LEXICON—a. ἀδελφός (LN 11.25): 'brother' [LN; all translations except CEV], 'friend' [CEV], 'fellow countryman, fellow Jew, associate' [LN]. This noun denotes a person belonging to the same socio-religious entity and being of the same age group as the so-called reference person [LN].

b. aorist act. impera. of ἀναβλέπω (LN 24.42) (BDAG 1. p. 59): 'to receive one's sight' [BECNT; ESV, GW, KJV, NASB, NIV], 'to receive one's sight again' [REB], 'to regain one's sight' [Bar, LN; NET, NLT, NRSV], 'to see again' [CEV, NCV, TEV], 'to recover one's sight' [CBC], 'to open one's eyes' [AB], 'to gain sight, to be able to see' [LN], 'to look up' [BDAG]. This verb means to become able to see, whether for the first time or again [LN]. It means to direct one's vision upward [BDAG].

c. ὥρα (LN 67.199) (BDAG 2.c. p. 1103): 'hour' [Bar, BDAG, BECNT, LN; ESV, KJV, NRSV], 'moment' [AB; GW, NET, NIV, NLT, TEV], 'time' [NASB], not explicit [CBC; CEV, NCV, REB]. The phrase 'at that same hour' is also translated 'instantly' [CBC; REB], 'at once' [CEV], 'immediately' [NCV]. This noun denotes the twelfth part of a day, measured from sunrise to sunset (in any one day the hours would be of equal length, but would vary somewhat depending on the time of the year) [LN]. It is a period of time as a division of a day, a temporal indicator, reckoned from the beginning of the day (6 hours or 6 a.m., our time) or the night [BDAG].

d. aorist act. indic. of ἀναβλέπω (LN 24.42) (BDAG 2.a.α. p. 59). In this second occurrence of this verb the phrase 'I saw him' is also translated 'I looked up' [AB; NASB], 'I looked up and saw' [NET], 'I looked upon' [Bar], 'I looked up upon' [KJV], 'I received my sight and saw' [BECNT; ESV], 'I recovered my sight and saw' [CBC; REB], 'I regained my sight and saw' [NRSV], 'I was able to see' [NIV], 'I could see' [CEV, NLT], 'my sight came back and I could see' [GW], 'I was able to see' [NCV], 'I saw again and looked' [TEV].

QUESTION—Is Ananias' use of 'brother' a reference to Paul being a fellow Jew, or a fellow Christian?

It means that Ananias considers Paul to be a fellow Christian [Bar, EBC, PNTC], one whom Jesus had already accepted [EBC].

**22:14** And he-said, 'The God of our fathers[a] appointed[b] you to-know[c] his will[d] and to-see the righteous-one[e] and to-hear (a)-voice[f] from his mouth,[g]

LEXICON—a. πατήρ (LN 10.20): 'father' [AB, Bar, BECNT, CBC; ESV, KJV, NASB, REB], 'ancestor' [CEV, GW, NCV, NET, NIV, NLT, NRSV, TEV], 'forefather' [LN]. The phrase 'the God of our fathers' is also translated 'the God that our ancestors worshiped' [CEV]. This noun denotes a person several preceding generations removed from the reference person [LN].

b. aorist mid. (deponent = act.) indic. of προχειρίζομαι (LN 30.89) (BDAG p. 891): 'to appoint' [Bar, BDAG, BECNT, CBC; ESV, NASB, REB], 'to choose' [AB; CEV, GW, KJV, NET, NIV, NLT, NRSV, TEV], 'to choose for oneself, select [BDAG], 'to choose long ago' [NCV], 'to choose in advance, to select beforehand, to designate in advance' [LN]. This verb means to choose for a particular purpose in advance [LN]. It means to express preference of someone for a task [BDAG].

c. aorist act. infin. of γινώσκω (LN 28.1): 'to know' [LN; all translations except AB], 'to learn' [AB], 'to know about, to have knowledge of, to be acquainted with' [LN]. This verb means to possess information about [LN].

d. θέλημα (LN 25.2) (BDAG 1.c.γ. p. 447): 'will' [all translations except CEV, NCV], 'plan' [NCV], 'wish, desire' [LN], 'what is willed' [BDAG]. The phrase 'his will' is also translated 'what he wants done' [CEV]. This noun denotes that which is desired or wished for [LN]. It denotes what one wishes to happen [BDAG].

e. δίκαιος (LN 88.12) (BDAG 1.b.β. p. 246): 'righteous' [AB, Bar, CBC, LN; ESV, NASB, NCV, NET, NIV, NLT, NRSV, REB], 'just' [BDAG, BECNT, LN; KJV], 'upright' [BDAG]. The title 'the righteous one' is also translated 'righteous Servant' [TEV], 'the One Who Obeys God' [CEV], 'the one who has God's approval' [GW]. This adjective describes being in accordance with what God requires [LN]. It describes being in accordance with high standards of rectitude [BDAG].

f. φωνή (LN 33.103): 'voice' [AB, Bar, CBC, LN; CEV, ESV, KJV, NRSV], 'utterance' [BECNT; NASB], 'command' [NET], 'words' [NCV, NIV]. The phrase 'to hear a voice from his mouth' is also translated 'to hear him speak' [GW, NLT, REB], 'to hear him speaking with his own voice' [TEV]. This noun denotes the human voice as an instrument of communication [LN].

g. στόμα (LN 8.19) (BDAG 1.a. p. 947): 'mouth' [Bar, BDAG, BECNT, LN; ESV, KJV, NASB, NET, NIV], 'lips' [AB], not explicit [CBC; CEV, GW, NCV, NLT, NRSV, REB, TEV].

QUESTION—What is meant by 'to know his will'?

It means he has been chosen to see the risen Christ and to hear him actually speak to Paul [PNTC]. God's will for Paul is spelled out in vv. 15–16, which is to live in intimate fellowship with God and to be his servant as a witness for Christ [Bar]. It refers to God's will for Paul's life [TRT], what he wants Paul to do [CEV].

QUESTION—What is meant by 'the righteous one'?

It is a messianic title [CBC, EBC, NAC, NICNT, PNTC, TNTC, TRT]. It shows that Jesus had been exalted [BECNT], that his innocence had been vindicated [BECNT, PNTC].

**22:15** for you-will-be (a)-witness[a] for-him[b] to all men[c] about-what you-have-seen and have-heard.

LEXICON—a. μάρτυς (LN 33.270) (BDAG 2.c. p. 620): 'witness' [BDAG, LN; all translations except CEV], 'one who testifies' [LN], 'testifier' [BDAG]. The phrase 'witness…to all men' is also translated 'you must tell everyone what you have seen and heard' [CEV]. This noun denotes a person who witnesses [LN]. It denotes one who affirms or attests [BDAG].

b. αὐτός (LN 92.11): 'he, him, she, her, it, they, them' [LN]. In the phrase μάρτυς αὐτῷ 'witness for him' the relation of αὐτῷ 'for him' to the noun 'witness' is also translated 'witness for him' [Bar, BECNT; ESV, NASB, TEV], 'his witness' [AB, CBC; GW, KJV, NCV, NET, NIV, NLT, NRSV, REB], not explicit [CEV]. This pronoun refers to a definite person or persons spoken or written about (with an added feature of emphasis in the nominative forms) [LN].

c. ἄνθρωπος (LN 9.1) (BDAG 4.a.ζ. p. 82). In the plural: 'people' [LN], 'mankind' [LN]. The phrase 'all men' [Bar, BECNT; KJV, NASB] is also translated 'all people' [NCV, NET, NIV], 'everyone' [CEV, ESV, GW, NLT, TEV], 'all the world' [NRSV], 'the world' [CBC; REB], 'all mankind' [AB]. This noun denotes human beings [BDAG, LN].

QUESTION—To whom does 'all men' refer?

It refers to Gentiles, as mentioned in v. 21 [EBC, NAC, PNTC, TNTC]. At this point the crowd did not fully understand that 'all men' referred to the Gentiles, but they did understand when Paul reported in v. 22 that Jesus was sending him to the Gentiles [Bar, NAC, PNTC].

**22:16** And now why delay[a]? Get-up,[b] be-baptized and wash-away[c] your sins calling-on[d] his name.'

LEXICON—a. pres. act. indic. of μέλλω (LN 67.121) (BDAG 4. p. 628): 'to delay' [BDAG, CBC, LN; NASB, NRSV, REB], 'to hesitate' [AB], 'to wait' [BECNT, LN; ESV], 'to wait longer' [NCV, TEV], 'to tarry' [KJV]. The question 'Why delay?' is also translated 'What are you waiting for?' [CEV, GW, NET, NIV, NLT], 'What are you going to do?' [Bar]. This verb means to extend time unduly, with the implication of lack of decision [LN].

b. aorist act. participle of ἀνίστημι (LN 17.7): 'to get up' [all translations except CBC; ESV, KJV, REB], 'to arise' [KJV], 'to rise' [ESV], 'to cause to stand, to raise up' [LN], not explicit [CBC; REB]. This verb means to cause someone to stand up' [LN].

c. aorist mid. impera. of ἀπολούω (LN 88.30) (BDAG p. 117): 'to wash away' [Bar, BECNT, CBC; CEV, ESV, KJV, NASB, NCV, NIV, REB], 'to have (your sins) washed away' [GW, NET, NLT, NRSV, TEV] 'to purify, to cause to be pure' [LN], 'wash oneself' [BDAG]. This middle voice verb is also translated as passive: 'will be washed away' [AB]. This verb means to cause a state of moral purity [LN]. It means to wash something away from oneself [BDAG].

d. aorist mid. participle of ἐπικαλέω (LN 33.131) (BDAG 1. p. 373): 'to call on/upon' [BDAG; all translations except CBC; CEV, NCV, TEV], 'to call' [LN], 'to call out' [BDAG]. The phrase 'calling on his name' is also translated 'with invocation of his name' [CBC], 'by praying to the Lord/to him' [CEV, TEV], 'trusting in him to save you' [NCV]. This verb means to use an attribution in speaking of a person [LN]. This verb means to call upon deity for any purpose [BDAG].

QUESTION—What does the question 'And now why delay' mean?
It is a rhetorical question meaning that Paul should not delay to follow through with what Ananias is about to tell him to do [NAC, TRT]. Ananias is urging Paul to take action [TNTC].

QUESTION—What relationship is indicated by the middle voice of the aorist imperatives 'be baptized' and 'wash away'?
It is causative, meaning that he should take action to have himself baptized [Bar, NAC, NICNT, PNTC, TH]. Normally the middle voice indicates an action taken by a person with reference to himself, but in this case it would not mean baptizing oneself or taking one's own sins away, but a permissive action allowing him to be baptized and have his sins washed away [BECNT].

QUESTION—What is meant by 'calling on his name'?
It means to profess faith in Jesus [Bar, BECNT, NAC, PNTC, TNTC] and give obedience to him [Bar]. It is to profess Jesus as Lord by being baptized in his name [Bar, CBC, NICNT, TNTC].

**DISCOURSE UNIT—22:17–21** [NICNT, PNTC; NRSV]. The topic is Paul sent to the Gentiles [NRSV], Paul's subsequent vision in the temple [PNTC], Paul's vision in the temple [NICNT].

**22:17** And it-happened-that when- I -returned to Jerusalem and I-was-praying in the temple I-fell into (a)-trance<sup>a</sup> **22:18** and I-saw him saying to-me, 'Make-haste<sup>b</sup> and leave Jerusalem quickly because they-will- not -accept<sup>c</sup> your testimony<sup>d</sup> about me.'

LEXICON—a. ἔκστασις (LN 33.489) (BDAG 2. p. 309): 'trance' [BDAG, BECNT, CBC; all versions except CEV, NCV, TEV], 'state of ecstasy' [AB], 'ecstasy' [Bar, BDAG], 'ecstatic vision' [LN]. The phrase 'I fell into a trance' is also translated 'I had/saw a vision' [CEV, NCV, TEV]. This noun denotes a vision accompanied by an ecstatic psychological state [LN]. It is a state of being in which consciousness is wholly or partially suspended, frequently associated with divine action [BDAG].

b. aorist act. impera. of σπεύδω (LN 68.79) (BDAG 1.a. p. 937): 'to make haste' [AB, Bar, BDAG, BECNT, CBC; ESV, KJV, NASB, REB], 'to hurry' [LN; CEV, GW, NCV, NET, NLT, NRSV, TEV], 'to hasten to' [BDAG, LN], 'to do quickly' [LN]. This imperative is also translated 'Quick!' [NIV]. This verb means to do something hurriedly, with the implication of associated energy [LN]. It means to be in a hurry [BDAG].

c. fut. mid. (deponent = act.) indic. of παραδέχομαι (LN 31.52) (BDAG 1. p. 761): 'to accept' [BDAG, LN; all translations except Bar; CEV, KJV], 'to receive' [Bar, LN; KJV], 'to listen to' [CEV]. This verb means to come to believe something to be true and to respond accordingly, with some emphasis upon the source [LN]. It means to acknowledge something to be correct [BDAG].

d. μαρτυρία (LN 33.264) (BDAG 1.b.β.ℵ. p. 618): 'testimony' [BDAG, LN; all translations except CEV, NCV, TEV], 'witness' [LN; TEV]. The phrase 'your testimony about me' is also translated 'what you say about me' [CEV], 'the truth about me' [NCV]. This noun denotes the content of what is witnessed or said [LN]. It denotes a confirmation or attestation on the basis of personal knowledge or belief [BDAG].

QUESTION—When did this event occur?

This occurred three years after his conversion [EBC, NAC, PNTC]. It was the visit referred to in Acts 9:26–30 [EBC, NAC, NICNT, TNTC], and in Galatians 1:18–19 [NAC].

**22:19** And I-said, 'Lord, they-know that in[a] the synagogues I was imprisoning[b] and beating[c] those who-believed in you,

LEXICON—a. κατά with accusative object (LN 89.90) (BDAG B. 1.d. p. 512): 'throughout, from… to, … after…' [LN]. The phrase 'in the synagogues' [AB; TEV] is also translated 'in every synagogue' [CBC; KJV, NCV, NLT, NRSV, REB], 'in one synagogue after another' [BECNT; ESV, NASB], 'from synagogue to synagogue' [Bar; GW], 'from one synagogue to another' [NIV], 'in the various synagogues' [NET], 'in many of our meeting places' [CEV]. This preposition marks distributive relations, whether of place, time, or number [LN]. It marks spatial aspects, here of places viewed serially [BDAG].

  b. pres. act. participle of φυλακίζω (LN 37.114) (BDAG p. 1068): 'to imprison' [BDAG, LN; all translations except CEV, NCV, TEV], 'to arrest' [CEV, TEV], 'to put in jail' [LN; NCV], 'to take into custody' [BDAG]. This verb means to confine someone in prison [LN].

  c. pres. act. participle of δέρω (LN 19.2) (BDAG p. 218): 'to beat' [BDAG, LN; all translations except CBC; GW, REB], 'to flog' [CBC; REB], 'to strike' [LN], 'to whip' [BDAG, LN; GW]. This verb means to strike or beat repeatedly [LN].

QUESTION—Does 'Lord' refer to God the Father or to Jesus Christ?

It refers to Jesus Christ [AB, BECNT, EBC, NAC, NICNT, PNTC]. It is ambiguous, but in the context the flow of the story would indicate that it is the exalted Christ who is speaking; the ambiguity serves to emphasize that either God or Christ can speak with divine authority [BECNT]. It is best to retain this ambiguity in this passage by not identifying 'the Lord' specifically as Jesus, since the ambiguity served a purpose in Paul's address [TH].

**DISCOURSE UNIT—22:20–23:22** [NCV]. The topic is Paul speaks to leaders.

**22:20** and when the blood of your witness[a] Stephen was-being-shed[b] I-was standing-(by)[c] and approving[d] and guarding[e] the clothing[f] of-those who-were-killing[g] him.'

LEXICON—a. μάρτυς (LN 20.67, 33.270) (BDAG 3. p. 620): 'witness' [Bar, CBC, BECNT, LN (33.270); ESV, NASB, NCV, NET, NLT, NRSV, REB, TEV], 'one who testifies' [LN (33.270)], 'martyr' [AB, BDAG, LN (20.67); KJV, NIV]. The phrase 'your witness Stephen' is also translated

'Stephen...spoke for you' [CEV], 'Stephen...witnessed about you' [GW]. This noun denotes a person who witnesses [LN (33.270)], or it may denote a person who has been deprived of life as the result of bearing witness to his beliefs [LN (20.67)], one who witnesses at the cost of life [BDAG].

b. imperf. act. indic. of ἐκχέω (LN 20.84) (BDAG 1.a. p. 312): 'to be shed' [AB, Bar, BECNT, CBC; ESV, KJV, NASB, NET, NIV, NRSV, REB], 'to be poured out' [BDAG]. The phrase 'the blood...was being shed' is also translated 'was killed/was being killed' [CEV, GW, NCV, NLT], 'was put to death' [TEV]. This verb means cause to be emitted in quantity [BDAG]. When used with the noun 'blood' it means to cause the death of someone by violent means [LN], 'to commit murder' [BDAG], 'to murder, to kill' [LN].

c. perf. act. participle of ἐφίστημι (LN 85.13) (BDAG 1. p. 418): 'to stand by' [Bar, BECNT, CBC; ESV, KJV, NASB, NLT, NRSV, REB], 'to stand near/nearby' [BDAG; NET], 'to stand there' [CEV, GW, NIV], 'to stand at' [BDAG], 'to be near, to be at, to be nearby' [LN]. The phrase 'I was standing by' is also translated 'I was there' [AB; NCV, TEV]. This verb means to be in proximity to something [LN]. It means to stand at or near a specific place [BDAG].

d. perf. act. participle of συνευδοκέω (LN 31.17) (BDAG p. 970): 'to approve/approve of' [Bar, BDAG, BECNT, CBC; ESV, GW, NASB, NET, NRSV, REB], 'to give approval' [NIV], 'to approve of the murder' [TEV], 'to agree to' [AB, LN; NCV], 'to cheer on' [CEV], 'to consent to' [BDAG, LN; KJV], 'to be in complete agreement' [NLT], 'to agree with, sympathize with' [BDAG]. This verb means to decide with someone else that something is preferable or good [LN]. It means to join in approval [BDAG].

e. pres. act. participle of φυλάσσω (LN 37.120) (BDAG 2.b. p. 1068): 'to guard' [BDAG; CEV, GW, NET, NIV], 'to look after' [AB, CBC; REB], 'to watch over' [ESV], 'to watch out for' [NASB], 'to keep' [Bar, BECNT; KJV, NLT, NRSV], 'to hold' [NCV], 'to take care of' [TEV], 'to guard closely' [LN], 'to protect' [BDAG]. This verb means to hold someone in close custody [LN]. It means to protect by taking careful measures [BDAG].

f. ἱμάτιον (LN 6.172) (BDAG 2. p. 475): 'clothes' [AB, Bar, CBC; CEV, NIV, REB], 'garment' [BECNT; ESV], 'coat' [LN; GW, NASB, NCV, NLT, NRSV], 'cloak' [BDAG, LN; NET, TEV], 'raiment' [KJV], 'robe' [BDAG, LN]. This noun denotes any type of outer garment [LN]. It is the outer clothing, which would be laid off in order to leave the arms free [BDAG].

g. pres. act. participle of ἀναιρέω (LN 20.71) (BDAG 2. p. 64): 'to kill' [AB, Bar, BECNT, CBC, LN; ESV, NCV, NET, NIV, NRSV, REB], 'to murder' [CEV, GW], 'to slay' [KJV, NASB], 'to stone' [NLT], 'to execute' [LN], 'do away with, destroy' [BDAG]. The phrase 'those who were killing him' is also translated 'his murderers' [TEV]. This verb means to get rid of someone by execution, often with legal or quasi-legal procedures [LN]. It means to get rid of by execution [BDAG].

QUESTION—What does Paul imply by the use of the noun 'witness'?

In this context it means that the witness becomes a martyr, that his testimony costs him his life [AB, BDAG, LN (20.67), NAC, TH; KJV, NIV]. The transition in the meaning of μάρτυς from 'witness' to 'martyr' probably has its beginning with its use in this passage [NAC, NICNT, PNTC, TNTC]. This is the first place in the New Testament where this word is used in the sense of dying for faith in Christ [NAC].

**22:21** And he-said to me, 'Go,[a] for I am-sending[b] you far-away[c] to (the)-Gentiles.[d]'"

LEXICON—a. pres. mid. or pass. (deponent = act.) impera. of πορεύομαι (LN 15.10): 'to go' [LN; all translations except AB, BECNT, KJV, NET], 'depart' [AB, BECNT, KJV], 'to leave' [NET], 'to move' [LN]. This verb means to move from one place to another, with the possible implication of continuity and distance [LN].

b. future act. indic. of ἐξαποστέλλω (LN 15.68) (BDAG 1.b. p. 346): 'to send' [LN; all translations except GW], 'to send away' [BDAG], 'to send out' [BDAG, LN], 'to send forth' [LN], 'to send off' [BDAG]. The phrase 'I am sending you far away' is also translated 'I'll send you on a mission. You'll go far away' [GW]. This verb means to send out or away from, presumably for some purpose [LN]. It means to send someone off to a locality or on a mission to fulfill a mission in another place [BDAG].

c. μακράν (LN 83.30) (BDAG 1.a.α. p. 612): 'far away' [BDAG, LN; all translations except Bar; KJV], 'far from here' [Bar], 'far hence' [KJV], 'far' [BDAG, LN], 'at a distance, some distance away' [LN]. This adverb describes a position at a relatively great distance from another position [LN]. It describes being at a relatively great distance from some position [BDAG].

d. ἔθνη (plural of ἔθνος) (LN 11.37): 'Gentiles' [all translations except GW, NCV], 'people who aren't Jewish' [GW], 'other nations' [NCV], 'heathen, pagans' [LN]. This noun denotes those who do not belong to the Jewish or Christian faith [LN].

**DISCOURSE UNIT—22:22–30** [PNTC]. The topic is claiming his right as a Roman citizen.

**DISCOURSE UNIT—22:22–29** [AB, CBC, NAC, NICNT; ESV, NET, NIV, NRSV]. The topic is the result [CBC], Paul before the council [ESV], the Roman commander questions Paul [NET], Paul the Roman citizen [NIV], Paul reveals his Roman citizenship [NICNT], the attempted examination by the tribune [NAC], Paul and the Roman tribune [AB; NRSV].

**22:22** Up-to this word[a] they-listened[b] to-him and (then) they-raised[c] their voice saying, "Away[d] with such-a-person[e] from the earth, for it-is- not - fitting[f] for-him to-live."

LEXICON—a. λόγος (LN 33.98) (BDAG 1.a.γ. p. 600): 'word' [Bar, BDAG, BECNT, LN; ESV, KJV], 'statement' [LN; NASB], 'assertion' [AB, BDAG], 'point' [CBC; GW, NRSV, REB]. The phrase 'up to this word' is also translated 'until Paul/he said this' [CEV, NCV, NET, NIV, NLT, TEV]. This noun denotes that which has been stated or said, with primary focus upon the content of the communication [LN]. It denotes a communication whereby the mind finds expression, an individual declaration or remark [BDAG].
  b. imperf. act. indic. of ἀκούω (LN 31.56): 'to listen/listen to' [LN; all translations except CBC; KJV, REB], 'to give a hearing' [CBC; REB], 'to give audience' [KJV], 'to accept, to listen and respond, to pay attention and respond, to heed' [LN]. This verb means to believe something and to respond to it on the basis of having heard [LN].
  c. aorist act. indic. of ἐπαίρω (LN 33.78) (BDAG 1. p. 357): 'to raise the voice' [AB, BDAG, LN; ESV, NASB, NET, NIV], 'to lift up the voice' [Bar, BECNT; KJV], 'to shout' [CBC; CEV, GW, NCV, NLT, NRSV, REB], 'to shout at the top of the voice' [TEV], 'to cry out, to speak loudly' [LN]. This verb means to increase the volume with which one speaks, so as to overcome existing noise or the speech of someone else [LN].
  d. pres. act. impera. of αἴρω (LN 20.43) (BDAG 3. p. 28): 'to get rid of' [CEV, NCV], 'to rid the earth of' [NIV], 'to kill' [GW], 'to take away, remove' [BDAG], 'to destroy, to do away with' [LN]. This imperative verb is also translated 'Away with...!' [AB, Bar, BECNT; ESV, KJV, NASB, NET, NLT, NRSV], 'Away with him! Kill him!' [TEV], 'Down with…!' [CBC; REB]. This verb means to destroy, with the implication of removal and doing away with [LN]. It means to take away, remove, or seize control [BDAG].
  e. τοιοῦτος (LN 64.2) (BDAG c.α.ℵ. p. 1010): 'such a person' [BDAG], 'such a man' [AB, Bar], 'such a fellow' [BECNT; ESV, KJV, NASB, NLT, NRSV], 'the scoundrel' [REB], 'a scoundrel like that' [CBC], 'a man like this' [GW], 'this man' [CEV, NET], 'such, like such, like that' [LN], not explicit [NCV, NIV, TEV]. This adjective describes being like some identified entity or event [LN].
  f. imperf. act. indic. of καθήκω (LN 66.1) (BDAG p. 491): 'to be fitting/fit' [Bar, BDAG, LN; KJV, NIV, NLT, REB, TEV], 'to be right' [AB, BDAG, LN], 'to be allowed' [ESV, GW, NASB, NET, NRSV], 'to deserve' [CEV, NCV]. The phrase 'it is not fitting for him to live' is also translated 'he ought not to live' [BECNT], '(he) is better dead' [CBC]. This verb means to be fitting or right, with the implication of possible moral judgment involved [LN]. It means to be appropriate [BDAG].

**DISCOURSE UNIT—22:23-29** [EBC]. The topic is Paul claims his Roman citizenship.

**22:23** **And as- they -were-shouting[a] and throwing-off[b] (their) cloaks[c] and throwing[d] dust[e] into the air,**

LEXICON—a. pres. act. participle of κραυγάζω (LN 33.83) (BDAG p. 565): 'to shout' [AB, Bar, LN; CEV, ESV, NCV, NIV, NRSV], 'to cry out' [BDAG, BECNT; KJV, NASB], 'to yell' [CBC; GW, NLT, REB], 'to scream' [LN; NET, TEV], 'to scream excitedly' [BDAG]. This verb means to shout or cry out, with the possible implication of the unpleasant nature of the sound [LN]. It means to utter a loud sound, ordinarily of harsh texture [BDAG].

b. pres. act. participle of ῥίπτω (LN 16.10) (BDAG 1. p. 906): 'to throw off' [BECNT; ESV, NASB, NCV, NET, NIV, NLT, NRSV], 'to cast off' [KJV], 'to take off' [GW], 'to throw' [AB, BDAG], 'to fling' [Bar], 'to wave' [CBC, LN; REB, TEV], 'to wave around' [CEV], 'to throw into the air' [LN]. This verb means to wave or possibly to throw something into the air [LN]. It means to propel something with a forceful motion, possibly as a statement of protest [BDAG].

c. ἱμάτιον (LN 6.172) (BDAG 2. p. 475): 'cloak' [BDAG, CBC, LN; ESV, NASB, NET, NIV, NRSV, REB], 'clothes' [AB, Bar; CEV, KJV, TEV], 'garments' [BECNT], 'coat' [LN; GW, NCV, NLT], 'robe' [BDAG, LN]. This noun denotes any type of outer garment [LN]. It is the outer clothing, which would be laid off in order to leave the arms free [BDAG].

d. pres. act. participle of βάλλω (LN 15.215) (BDAG 1.b. p. 163): 'to throw' [Bar, BDAG, BECNT, LN; CEV, GW, KJV, NCV, TEV], 'to hurl' [AB], 'to fling' [CBC; ESV, NIV, REB], 'to toss' [NASB, NET, NLT, NRSV]. This verb means to cause to move from one location to another through use of forceful motion [BDAG].

e. κονιορτός (LN 2.15) (BDAG p. 558): 'dust' [BDAG, LN; all translations except GW, NLT], 'handfuls of dust' [NLT], 'dirt' [GW], 'soil' [LN].

QUESTION—What is meant by the gestures of casting off their cloaks and throwing dust into the air?

Throwing dust expresses horror or grief at hearing something considered to be blasphemous [BECNT, TH, TNTC]. The exact meaning is not fully known for either of these actions, though they do express outrage [NAC, PNTC, TNTC]. These actions express their complete rejection of Paul [AB]. They threw dust because it was the first thing they could lay hold of to throw [Bar].

**DISCOURSE UNIT—22:24-29** [CEV, NLT]. The topic is Paul and the Roman army commander [CEV], Paul reveals his Roman citizenship [NLT].

**22:24** the commander[a] ordered him to-be-brought into the barracks,[b] saying (that) he-should-be-examined[c] by-flogging[d] in-order-to know (the) reason[e] they-were-shouting against-him this-way.

LEXICON—a. χιλίαρχος (LN 55.15) (BDAG p. 1084): 'commander' [CEV, NASB, NCV, NIV, NLT], 'tribune' [AB, Bar, BECNT; ESV, NRSV], 'military tribune' [BDAG], 'captain' [KJV], 'commandant' [CBC; REB], 'Roman commander' [TEV], 'officer' [GW], 'commanding officer' [LN; NET], 'general, chiliarch' [LN]. This noun denotes a military officer, normally in command of a thousand soldiers [LN]. It denotes the commander of a cohort, usually about 600 men [BDAG].

b. παρεμβολή (LN 7.22) (BDAG 2. p. 775): 'barracks' [AB, Bar, BDAG, BECNT, CBC, LN; ESV, GW, NASB, NET, NIV, NRSV, REB], 'fortress' [CEV], 'fort' [TEV], 'castle' [KJV], 'army building' [NCV], 'soldiers' quarters' [LN], 'headquarters' [BDAG], not explicit [NLT]. This noun denotes a camp or barracks for soldiers [LN].

c. pre. pass. infin. of ἀνετάζω (LN 56.16) (BDAG p. 78): 'to be examined' [Bar, BECNT, LN; ESV, KJV, NASB, NRSV, REB], 'to examine (him)' [CBC], 'to be questioned' [AB], 'to question (Paul)' [GW], 'to interrogate' [NET], 'to be interrogated' [LN; NIV], 'to be given a hearing' [BDAG]. The phrase 'examined by flogging' is also translated 'beaten with a whip' [CEV], 'beat him…to make Paul tell' [NCV], '(lashed with whips) to make him confess' [NLT], 'whip him in order to find out' [TEV]. This verb means to interrogate a defendant during a judicial hearing, often by means of torture or lashing [LN]. It means to give a hearing, and use torture (in the form of a lashing) in connection with it [BDAG].

d. μάστιξ (LN 19.9) (BDAG 1. p. 620): 'flogging' [CBC, LN; ESV, NRSV], 'be flogged' [NIV], 'scourging' [BDAG, BECNT; KJV, NASB], '(with the) scourge' [Bar], 'under the lash' [AB; REB], 'by beating him with a lash' [NET], 'beat him' [NCV], 'lashed with whips' [NLT], 'with the whip' [BDAG; CEV], 'as they whipped him' [GW], 'whip him' [TEV], 'whipping' [LN], 'lash' [BDAG]. This noun denotes a whipping or flogging [LN]. It is the act of scourging [BDAG].

e. αἰτία (LN 89.15) (BDAG 1. p. 31): 'reason' [BDAG, CBC, LN; NET, NRSV, REB], 'why' [AB, Bar, BECNT; CEV, ESV, GW, NCV, NIV, NLT, TEV], 'reason why' [NASB], 'wherefore' [KJV], 'cause' [BDAG, LN]. This noun denotes reason or cause for an event or state [LN]. It is that which is responsible for a condition [BDAG].

QUESTION—What was the nature of the flogging mentioned here?

It was much more severe than the beating that Paul and Silas experienced at Philippi [EBC, NAC, TNTC]. This kind of beating could cause permanent physical damage or even death [Bar, EBC, NAC, NICNT, PNTC]. Only slaves and non-Romans were subjected to this kind of torture, as it was illegal to do this to a Roman citizen [AB, EBC, NAC, PNTC, TH, TNTC].

QUESTION—Why did the commander not understand why the Jews were shouting against Paul in this way?

The conversation would have been in Aramaic, so he would not have followed what Paul had been saying very well [BECNT, EBC, NAC, NICNT, PNTC, TNTC].

**22:25** And as they-stretched- him -out[a] for the whip,[b] Paul said to the centurion[c] standing-nearby, "Is-it-lawful[d] for-you(pl) to-flog (a)-man (who is) a-Roman-citizen and (is) not-(yet)-found-guilty[e]?"

LEXICON—a. aorist act. indic. of προτείνω (LN 16.21) (BDAG p. 888): 'to stretch out' [Bar, BDAG, BECNT, LN; ESV, NASB, NET, NIV], 'to tie up' [AB, CBC; CEV, NCV, NRSV, REB, TEV], 'to tie down' [NLT], 'to stretch out to tie up' [GW], 'to bind' [KJV], 'to spread out' [BDAG]. This verb means to stretch out or to spread out an object [LN]. It means to stretch out the hands of a criminal who is to be flogged [BDAG].

b. ἱμάς (LN 6.20) (BDAG p. 475): 'whip' [ESV], 'lash' [Bar, CBC; NET], 'thong' [BDAG, BECNT, LN; KJV, NASB, NRSV], 'strap' [BDAG]. The phrase 'for the whip' is also translated 'to lash him' [NLT], 'to flog him' [NIV], 'to be flogged' [AB], 'for the flogging' [REB], 'to be whipped' [TEV], 'to be beaten' [CEV], 'preparing to beat him' [NCV], 'to the whipping post with the straps' [GW]. The dative case of this noun is translated as indicating purpose: *for* the whip/to be whipped: [AB, Bar, BECNT, CBC; CEV, ESV, NCV, NET, NIV, NLT, REB, TEV]. It is also translated as indicating the means of tying: '*with* straps/thongs' [GW, KJV, NASB, NRSV]. This noun denotes a leather strap or thong used in binding sandals or shoes, and as thongs in a whip [LN]. Note that since the whip consisted of multiple leather straps or thongs, the plural τοῖς ἱμᾶσιν may be translated as singular: 'for the whip'.

c. ἑκατοντάρχης (LN 55.16) (BDAG p. 299): 'centurion' [AB, Bar, BDAG, BECNT, CBC, LN; ESV, KJV, NASB, NET, NIV, NRSV, REB], 'officer' [CEV, NCV, NLT, TEV], 'sergeant' [GW], 'captain' [BDAG, LN]. This noun denotes a Roman officer in command of about one hundred men [BDAG, LN], and who is subordinate to a tribune [BDAG].

d. pres. act. indic. of ἔξεστι (LN 71.1) (BDAG 1.b. p. 348): 'to be lawful' [Bar, BECNT; ESV, KJV, NASB, TEV], 'to be legal' [CEV, GW, NET, NIV, NLT, NRSV], 'to be allowed' [AB], 'to have the right' [NCV], 'to be permitted' [BDAG], 'to be authorized' [BDAG], 'to be proper' [BDAG], 'to be possible' [LN]. The phrase 'is it lawful' is also translated 'can you legally (flog)' [CBC], 'does the law allow' [REB]. This verb marks an event as being possible in a highly generic sense [LN]. It means to be authorized for the doing of something [BDAG].

e. ἀκατάκριτος (LN 56.19) (BDAG p. 35): 'uncondemned' [BDAG, BECNT; ESV, KJV, NASB, NRSV], 'unconvicted' [REB], 'without trial/a proper trial' [AB, LN; NET], 'not (even) tried' [Bar; NLT], 'not found guilty' [CBC; NIV], 'not been proven guilty' [NCV], 'before being tried in court' [CEV], '(who) hasn't had a trial' [GW], 'who hasn't even been tried for any crime' [TEV], 'without due process' [BDAG]. This adjective describes not having gone through a judicial hearing, with the implication of not having been condemned [LN]. It describes not undergoing a proper legal process [BDAG].

QUESTION—Does τοῖς ἱμᾶσιν mean 'for the whip' or 'with the thongs'?
1. They were stretching him out for the whip, which was made with leather thongs or strips [AB, Bar, BECNT, CBC, NICNT; CEV, ESV, NCV, NET, NIV, NLT, REB, TEV].
2. Paul was being tied to the whipping post with leather thongs [BECNT; GW, KJV, NASB, NRSV].

**22:26** And the centurion having-heard-(this) and having-gone to-the commander said, "What are-you-about[a] to-do? For this man is (a)-Roman-citizen.[b]" **22:27** And the commander having-come said to-him, "Tell me, are you (a)-Roman-citizen?" And he-said, "Yes."

LEXICON—a. pres. act. indic. of μέλλω (LN 67.62) (BDAG 1.c.α. p. 627): 'to be about to' [AB, BDAG, BECNT, LN; ESV, NASB, NET, NRSV, REB], 'to be going to' [Bar; NIV], 'to mean to' [CBC]. The phrase 'what are you about to do' is also translated 'what are you doing?' [CEV, GW, NCV, NLT, TEV], 'take heed what thou doest' [KJV]. This verb means to occur at a point of time in the future which is subsequent to another event and closely related to it [LN]. It means to take place at a future point of time and so to be subsequent to another event [BDAG].
b. Ῥωμαῖος (LN 93.562) (BDAG p. 908): 'Roman citizen' [BECNT, CBC; all versions except ESV, KJV, NASB ], 'a Roman' [AB, Bar, LN; ESV, KJV, NASB], 'Roman' [BDAG]. As a noun this word denotes a person who lives in or is a native of Rome or a citizen of the Roman Empire [LN]. As an adjective it describes the city of Rome or the Roman Empire [BDAG].

**22:28** And the commander answered, "I bought[a] this citizenship[b] with (a)-great sum-of-money.[c]" And Paul said, "But I was-born[d] (a citizen)."

LEXICON—a. aorist mid. (deponent = act.) indic. of κτάομαι (LN 57.58) (BDAG 1. p. 572): 'to buy' [AB, BECNT; ESV], 'to acquire' [Bar, BDAG, LN; NASB, NET], 'to pay' [CEV, ESV, NCV, NIV, TEV], 'to obtain' [KJV], 'to get' [BDAG, LN], 'to gain' [LN], 'to procure for oneself' [BDAG]. 'I bought' is also translated 'it cost me' [CBC; NLT, NRSV, REB]. This verb means to acquire possession of something [LN]. It means to gain possession of [BDAG].
b. πολιτεία (LN 11.70) (BDAG 1. p. 845): 'citizenship' [AB, Bar, BDAG, BECNT, CBC, LN; ESV, NASB, NET, NIV, NRSV, REB], 'freedom' [KJV], not explicit [NLT, TEV]. The phrase '(bought) this citizenship' is also translated 'to become a Roman citizen' [CEV, GW, NCV]. This noun denotes the right to be a citizen of a particular socio-political entity [BDAG, LN].

c. κεφάλαιον (LN 57.162) (BDAG 2. p. 541): 'sum of money' [AB, BDAG; NASB, NET, NRSV, REB], 'amount of money' [TEV], 'sum' [BECNT, CBC; ESV, KJV], 'money' [CEV, GW, NCV, NIV], 'some money' [LN], 'price' [Bar, LN], not explicit [NLT].

d. perf. pass. indic. of γεννάω (LN 23.52) (BDAG 2. p. 194): 'to be born' [Bar, BDAG, BECNT, LN; CEV, GW, NASB, NCV, NET, NIV, NRSV], 'to be freeborn' [KJV], 'to be begotten' [BDAG]. The phrase 'born a citizen' is also translated 'citizen by birth' [AB; ESV, NLT, TEV], 'mine by birth' [CBC; REB]. This verb means to give birth to a child [LN]. It means to be born [BDAG].

QUESTION—What might be implied by the commander's statement that he paid a high price for his citizenship?

He may be sarcastically implying that since the time he obtained citizenship it had become so easy that just about anyone could afford it [Bar, EBC, NAC, NICNT, PNTC, TNTC]. The 'price' paid was most likely in the form of a bribe, which by that time under the emperor Claudius had become a common practice [BECNT, EBC, NICNT, PNTC, TNTC, TRT]. Paul's status of having been born a citizen shows that in one sense he actually outranked the commander [AB, Bar, PNTC, TRT].

**22:29** So those about-to examine[a] him withdrew[b] from him immediately, and the commander also was-afraid[c] when-he-realized that he-is (a)-Roman-citizen and that he had-bound[d] him.

LEXICON—a. pres. act. infin. of ἀνετάζω (LN 56.16) (BDAG p. 78): 'to examine' [Bar, CBC, LN; ESV, KJV, NASB, NRSV, REB], 'to question' [AB; GW, NCV, TEV], 'to beat and question' [CEV], 'to interrogate' [BECNT, LN; NET, NIV, NLT]. This verb means to interrogate a defendant during a judicial hearing, often by means of torture or lashing [LN]. It means to give a hearing, and use torture (in the form of a lashing) in connection with it [BDAG].

b. aorist act. indic. of ἀφίστημι (LN 34.26) (BDAG 2.b. p. 158): 'to withdraw' [BECNT, CBC; ESV, NIV, NLT, REB], 'to draw back' [AB; NRSV, TEV], 'to stand back' [Bar], 'to back off' [CEV], 'to step away' [GW], 'to move away' [NCV], 'to stay away' [NET], 'to depart' [KJV], 'to let go (of him)' [NASB], 'to turn away' [LN], 'to keep away' [BDAG]. This verb means to abandon a former relationship or association, or to dissociate (a type of reversal of beginning to associate) [LN]. It means distance oneself from some person or thing [BDAG].

c. aorist pass. (deponent = act.) indic. of φοβέομαι (LN 25.252): 'to be afraid' [AB, Bar, BECNT, LN; ESV, GW, KJV, NASB, NRSV], 'to be alarmed' [CBC; NIV, REB], 'to be frightened' [CEV, NCV, NET, NLT, TEV], 'to fear' [LN]. This verb means to be in a state of fearing [LN].

d. perf. act. participle of δέω (LN 18.13) (BDAG 1.b. p. 221): 'to bind' [Bar, BDAG, BECNT; ESV, KJV, NRSV], 'to put in chains' [AB; CEV, NASB, NIV, TEV], 'to put in irons' [CBC; REB], 'to tie up' [LN; GW,

NET], 'to tie' [BDAG, LN; NCV], 'to order to be bound and whipped' [NLT]. This verb means to tie objects together [LN]. It means to confine a person or thing by various kinds of restraints [BDAG].

**DISCOURSE UNIT—22:30–26:32** [REB]. The topic is Paul's trials.

**DISCOURSE UNIT—22:30–23:11** [Bar, BECNT, EBC, NAC; CEV, GW, NET, NIV, NLT, NRSV, TEV]. The topic is Paul before the Jewish council [BECNT], Paul in front of the Jewish council [GW], Paul before the high council [NLT], Paul before the council [Bar; CEV, NRSV], Paul before the Sanhedrin [NAC; NET, NIV], Paul's defense before the Sanhedrin [EBC], the plot against Paul's life [TEV].

**DISCOURSE UNIT—22:30–23:10** [AB, CBC, TNTC]. The topic is Paul appears before the Sanhedrin [TNTC], before the Sanhedrin [CBC], Paul's examination before the Sanhedrin [AB].

**DISCOURSE UNIT—22:30** [NICNT]. The topic is Paul brought before the Sanhedrin.

**22:30** And on-the next-day desiring[a] to-know the real-reason[b] why he-was-being-accused[c] by the Jews, he-unbound[d] him and ordered[e] the chief priests and all the Sanhedrin[f] to assemble, and having-brought- Paul -down set[g] (him) before them.

LEXICON—a. pres. mid. or pass. (deponent = act.) participle of βούλομαι (LN 25.3) (BDAG 2.a.β. p. 182): 'to desire' [BECNT, LN; ESV], 'to wish' [AB, Bar, CBC; NASB, REB], 'to want' [LN; CEV, GW, NET, NIV, NLT, NRSV, TEV], 'to decide' [NCV], 'intend, plan, will' [BDAG]. The phrase 'desiring to know' is also translated 'he would have known' [KJV]. This verb means to desire to have or experience something, with the implication of some reasoned planning or will to accomplish the goal [LN]. It means to plan on a course of action [BDAG].

b. ἀσφαλής (LN 31.42) (BDAG 2. p. 147): 'real reason' [BECNT; CEV, ESV], 'true reason' [NET], 'exactly' [AB; GW, NIV], 'the truth' [Bar], 'quite sure' [CBC; REB], 'for sure' [TEV], 'certainty' [KJV], 'for certain' [NASB], 'certain' [BDAG], not explicit [NCV, NLT, NRSV]. This adjective describes being certain and thus completely believable [LN]. It describes a verbal statement that ensures certainty about something [BDAG].

c. pres. pass. indic. of κατηγορέω (LN 33.427) (BDAG 1.a. p. 533): 'to be accused' [AB, BECNT, LN; ESV, KJV, NASB, NET, NIV, NRSV], 'to have charges brought' [BDAG, LN]. This passive verb is also translated as active: 'to bring charges' [BDAG, CBC, LN; CEV, REB]. The phrase 'why he was being accused' is also translated 'what accusation was being brought' [Bar], 'what accusation (they) had' [GW], 'why they were accusing' [NCV], 'what they were accusing him of' [TEV], 'what the trouble was about' [NLT]. It means to bring serious charges or accusations against someone [BDAG, LN], with the possible connotation of a legal or court context [LN].

d. aorist act. indic. of λύω (LN 18.18) (BDAG 2.a. p. 607): 'to unbind' [BECNT; ESV], 'to untie' [BDAG, LN], 'to loose' [BDAG], 'to loosen' [LN], 'to take off bonds' [Bar], 'to loose from bonds' [KJV], 'to have chains removed' [CEV], 'to take chains off' [NCV], 'to have chains taken off' [TEV], 'to let (him) out' [AB], 'to release' [CBC; GW, NASB, NET, NIV, NLT, NRSV, REB], 'to set free' [BDAG]. This verb means to reverse the result of tying by untying [LN]. It means to set free a person, animal, or thing that is bound or tied or similarly constrained [BDAG].
   e. aorist act. indic. of κελεύω (LN 33.323) (BDAG p. 538): 'to order' [BDAG, LN; all translations except AB, BECNT; ESV, KJV], 'to command' [BDAG, BECNT, LN; ESV, KJV], 'to give orders' [AB]. This verb means to state with force and/or authority what others must do [LN]. It means to give a command, ordinarily of an official nature [BDAG].
   f. συνέδριον (LN 11.80) (BDAG 1.c. p. 967): 'Sanhedrin' [AB, Bar, BDAG, BECNT, LN; NIV], 'council' [CBC; CEV, ESV, KJV, NASB, NCV, NET, NRSV, REB, TEV], 'Jewish council' [GW], 'the council of the Jews' [LN], 'Jewish high council' [NLT]. This noun denotes the highest Jewish council, exercising jurisdiction in civil and religious matters, but having no power over life and death or over military actions or taxation [LN]. It is the high council in Jerusalem [BDAG].
   g. aorist act. indic. of ἵστημι (LN 85.40) (BDAG A.1. p. 482): 'to set before' [AB, BECNT; ESV, KJV, NASB], 'to stand (him) before' [CBC; NCV], 'to cause/make to stand before' [Bar, LN; CEV, TEV], 'to bring to stand before' [REB], 'to have (him) stand in front of/before' [GW, NET, NIV, NLT, NRSV], 'to place, to set' [BDAG, LN]. This verb means to cause to be in a place, with or without the accompanying feature of standing position [LN]. It means to cause to be in a place or position [BDAG].

QUESTION—What does it mean that the commander 'unbound' him?

He released Paul from his chains [Bar, BECNT, EBC, PNTC; CEV, ESV, KJV, NCV, TEV]. He probably released Paul from confinement [AB, CBC, NICNT, TNTC; GW, NASB, NET, NIV, NLT, NRSV, REB].

QUESTION—Did the commander have the authority to command the Sanhedrin to meet with him?

He did have the authority to convene the Sanhedrin for this matter [EBC, NICNT]. This was a fact-finding inquiry [Bar, BECNT, PNTC, TNTC], to which the Sanhedrin would have been happy to respond so that they could present their case against Paul [Bar, BECNT, PNTC]. The commander was authorized to act for the procurator when the procurator was absent, so his actions expressed the authority of Rome in Jerusalem [NICNT]. Because the commander was responsible for keeping the peace in Jerusalem, he could order the Sanhedrin to meet to find out the cause of the riot, though he would not have been able to take part in their deliberations [EBC]. He may have convened the meeting in the Antonia fortress, which is where the Roman garrison was [NAC].

**DISCOURSE UNIT—23:1-11** [PNTC; NASB]. The topic is Paul before the council [NASB], appearing before the Sanhedrin [PNTC].

**DISCOURSE UNIT—23:1-10** [NICNT]. The topic is Paul before the Sanhedrin.

**DISCOURSE UNIT—23:1-5** [NICNT]. The topic is interchange with the high priest.

**23:1** And looking-intently[a] at-the Sanhedrin Paul said, "Brothers, I have-lived-(my)-life[b] in-all good conscience[c] (before)-God to this day." **23:2** And the high-priest[d] Ananias ordered those standing-beside him to-strike[e] (him) on-the mouth.

LEXICON—a. aorist act. participle of ἀτενίζω (LN 24.49) (BDAG p. 148): 'to look intently at' [BDAG; ESV, NASB, NRSV], 'to gaze intently at' [NLT], 'to fix one's eyes on' [Bar], 'to keep one's eyes fixed on' [LN], 'to look steadily at' [AB], 'to earnestly behold' [KJV], 'to look at' [NCV], 'to look directly at' [NET], 'to look straight at' [LN; CEV, NIV, TEV], 'stare at' [BDAG, LN; GW], 'to fix one's eyes on' [CBC]. This participial phrase is also translated 'with his eyes steadily fixed on (the Council)' [REB]. This verb means to fix one's eyes on some object continually and intensely [LN].

b. perf. (deponent = mid. or pass.) indic. of πολιτεύομαι (LN 41.34) (BDAG 3. p. 846): 'to live one's life' [CBC; ESV, NASB, NCV, NET, NRSV, REB], 'to live' [AB, BDAG, LN; KJV, NLT, TEV], 'to conduct one's life' [BDAG, LN], 'to conduct oneself' [Bar, BECNT], 'to lead one's life' [BDAG], 'to serve (God)' [CEV], 'to fulfil one's duty' [NIV], 'to live in relation to others' [LN]. The phrase 'I have lived my life in all good conscience before God' is also translated 'my relationship with God has always given me a perfectly clear conscience' [GW]. This verb means to conduct oneself with proper reference to one's obligations in relationship to others, as part of some community [LN]. It means to conduct one's life [BDAG].

c. συνείδησις (LN 26.13) (BDAG p. 968): 'conscience' [BDAG, LN; all translations except NCV], 'moral consciousness' [BDAG], 'moral sensitivity' [LN]. The phrase 'in all good conscience' is also translated 'without guilt feelings' [NCV]. This noun denotes the psychological faculty which can distinguish between right and wrong [LN]. It is the inward faculty of distinguishing right and wrong [BDAG].

d. ἀρχιερεύς (LN 53.89): 'high priest' [LN; all translations except GW], 'chief priest' [GW], 'most important priest' [LN]. This noun denotes the principal member among the chief priests [LN].

e. pres. act. infin. of τύπτω (LN 19.1) (BDAG p. 1020): 'to strike' [BDAG, LN; all translations except CEV, KJV, NCV, NLT], 'to hit' [LN; CEV, NCV, NLT], 'to smite' [KJV], 'to beat' [BDAG, LN]. This verb means to strike or hit an object, one or more times [LN]. It means to inflict a blow [BDAG].

QUESTION—What is implied by Paul's addressing the council as 'brothers'?
It shows that he regards them as equals [Bar, PNTC]. This was a common formal address when Jews were assembled [EBC]. It is deferential, and intended to show his loyalty to Judaism [NAC]. He is trying to identify with his audience [BECNT].

QUESTION—Did Paul's claim to have lived with a good conscience refer only to his life after conversion, or even before that, when he was a persecutor?
1. It is a reference to how he has lived as a Christian [NAC, PNTC, TNTC]. It is not a claim to sinlessness [PNTC]. It is a reference to the more recent past, not to the distant past [TNTC].
2. It refers to his entire life, including his pre-conversion days [Bar, NICNT], in which even his persecution of Christians was done in the belief that it was the right thing to do [NICNT].

QUESTION—Who was Ananias?
Ananias served as high priest from about A.D. 47 to about A.D. 58 [BECNT, EBC, NAC, NICNT]. He was the son of Nedebaeus, and was appointed to the high priesthood in A.D. 47 by Herod of Chalcis (grandson of Herod the Great); Josephus describes Ananias as one of the worst of the high priests [NAC], and as being insolent and of a bad temper [BECNT, TNTC]. He advanced his own interests through violence and assassination [NICNT]. He was known for his cruelty, bribery, and greed, and was eventually assassinated by Jewish Zealots at the beginning of the second Jewish war in A.D. 66 [EBC, NAC, NICNT, PNTC], which was less than ten years after this incident in the Sanhedrin [NAC]. At the end of his life he was hunted and had to live in hiding until he was assassinated by Jewish revolutionaries [EBC].

**23:3** Then Paul said to him, "God is-going to-strike you, (you) whitewashed[a] wall! And do- you -sit to-judge[b] me according-to the law and acting-contrary-to-the-law[c] you-order me to-be-struck?"

LEXICON—a. perf. pass. participle of κονιάω (LN 88.234) (BDAG p. 558): 'whitewashed' [Bar, BDAG, BECNT, CBC, LN; CEV, ESV, NASB, NET, NIV, NRSV, REB, TEV], 'whited' [AB; KJV], '(a wall) that has been painted white' [NCV]. The idiom 'whitewashed wall' is also translated 'hypocrite' [LN; GW], 'corrupt hypocrite' [NLT], 'impostor' [LN]. It denotes one who pretends to be one thing, while in reality he is something quite different [LN].

b. pres. act. participle of κρίνω (LN 56.20) (BDAG 5.a.α. p. 568): 'to judge' [BDAG, LN; all translations except AB; NASB, NLT], 'to try' [NASB], 'to decide a legal question, to act as a judge, making a legal decision, to arrive at a verdict, to try a case' [LN], 'to decide, to hale before a court' [BDAG]. The phrase 'sit to judge' is also translated 'to sit in judgment' [AB], 'what kind of judge are you' [NLT]. This verb means to decide a question of legal right or wrong, and thus determine the innocence or guilt of the accused and assign appropriate punishment or retribution [LN]. It means to engage in a judicial process [BDAG].

c. pres. act. participle of παρανομέω (LN 36.28) (BDAG p. 769): 'to act contrary to the law' [BDAG], 'to break the law' [BDAG, LN], 'to disobey, to transgress' [LN]. The participle 'acting contrary to the law' is also translated 'contrary to the law' [AB, Bar, BECNT; ESV, KJV], 'in defiance of the law' [CBC; REB], 'in violation of the law' [NASB, NET, NRSV], 'you violate the law' [NIV], 'you break the law' [NLT, TEV], 'you order men to break the law' [CEV], 'you break those teachings' [GW], 'that is against the law' [NCV]. This verb means to act contrary to established custom or law, with the implication of intent [LN].

QUESTION—What would Paul have meant when he called Ananias a 'whitewashed wall'?

He is calling Ananias a hypocrite [BECNT, CBC, NAC, NICNT, PNTC, TNTC, TRT; GW, NLT]. For all his finery in his high priestly robes, he did not fulfill his office in terms of intercession for the people and he violated the very law he was supposed to be upholding in his function as judge [NAC]. His behavior was out of character with his fine appearance, and such a person was bound to come to a bad end [NICNT].

QUESTION—How would it have been contrary to Jewish law to have Paul struck?

Such striking of a defendant was against the Jewish legal code, which presumed a defendant innocent until proven guilty [BECNT, EBC, NICNT]. It was contrary to Jewish law to punish someone who had not been found guilty, and in this case Paul had not yet even had a trial [NAC, NICNT]. Lev 19:15 requires fairness and justice in court cases [Bar].

**23:4** Then those standing-(by) said, "Do-you-insult[a] God's high-priest?"
**23:5** And Paul said, "I did- not -know,[b] brothers, that he-is (the)-high-priest; for it-is-written 'You-will- not -speak evil[c] (of) (a)-leader[d] of- your -people.'"

LEXICON—a. pres. act. indic. of λοιδορέω (LN 33.393) (BDAG p. 602): 'to insult' [all translations except BECNT, ESV, KJV, NASB], 'to revile' [BDAG, BECNT; ESV, KJV, NASB], 'to abuse' [BDAG], 'to slander, to insult strongly' [LN]. This verb means to speak in a highly insulting manner [LN].

b. pluperf. act. indic. of οἶδα (LN 28.1): 'to know' [AB, Bar, BECNT, LN; CEV, ESV, GW, NCV, TEV], 'to realize' [NET, NIV, NLT, NRSV], 'to be aware' [NASB], 'to know about, to have knowledge of' [LN]. The phrase 'I did not know' is also translated 'I had no idea' [CBC; REB], 'I wist not' [KJV]. This verb means to possess information about [LN].

c. κακῶς (LN 88.106) (BDAG 2. p. 502): 'evil' [BDAG; all translations except AB, CBC; NCV, REB], 'insultingly' [AB], 'in an evil manner' [LN], 'wrongly, wickedly' [BDAG], 'harshly' [LN]. The phrase 'you will not speak evil of' is also translated 'you must/shall not abuse' [CBC; REB], 'you must not curse' [NCV]. This word describes being bad, with the implication of harmful and damaging [LN]. It describes being bad in a moral sense [BDAG].

d. ἄρχων (LN 37.56) (BDAG 2.a. p. 140): 'leader' [BDAG; CEV, NCV] 'ruler' [LN; all translations except CEV, NCV], 'official' [BDAG], 'governor' [LN]. This noun denotes one who rules or governs [LN]. It is one who has administrative authority [BDAG].

QUESTION—Should verse 4 be punctuated as a question or a statement?

It is a rhetorical question: Do you dare to insult the high priest? [AB, Bar, BECNT, CBC, TH; CEV, ESV, KJV, NASB, NET, NLT, NRSV, REB]. It is translated as a statement: You are insulting the high priest! [GW, NCV, NIV, TEV].

QUESTION—What did Paul mean when he said he was unaware that the man who ordered him to be struck was the high priest?

Because this was not a regular meeting of the Sanhedrin, the high priest may not have been wearing his official robes or sitting in his customary place, so Paul may not have known he was the high priest [EBC, PNTC]. Since Paul had been absent from Jerusalem for several years, he may not have even known who the high priest was at that time [EBC] or did not recognize him by sight [NICNT, PNTC]. Perhaps Paul spoke without stopping to think about the fact that Ananias was the high priest, because Ananias certainly did not conduct himself like a high priest should [NAC]. He said this with irony or sarcasm, communicating that it is hard to see how a man doing something like this could be high priest [CBC, TNTC].

**DISCOURSE UNIT—23:6–10** [NICNT]. The topic is the resurrection hope.

**23:6** **And Paul, perceiving<sup>a</sup> that part<sup>b</sup> (of the Sanhedrin) was Sadducees and the other was Pharisees cried-out in the Sanhedrin, "Brothers, I am (a)-Pharisee, (the)-son of-Pharisees; concerning<sup>c</sup> (the)-hope<sup>d</sup> and resurrection<sup>e</sup> of-(the)-dead I am-on-trial.<sup>f</sup>"**

LEXICON—a. aorist act. participle of γινώσκω (LN 32.16) (BDAG 4.c. p. 200): 'to perceive' [BDAG, BECNT, LN; ESV, KJV, NASB], 'to know' [AB; NCV, NIV], 'to notice' [Bar, BDAG; NET, NRSV], 'to see' [CEV, GW, TEV], 'to be well aware' [CBC; REB], 'to realize' [BDAG; NLT], 'to come to understand, to comprehend' [LN]. This verb means to come to an understanding as the result of ability to experience and learn [LN]. It means to be aware of something [BDAG].

b. μέρος (LN 63.14) (BDAG 1.b.ζ. p. 633): 'part' [Bar, BECNT, LN; ESV, KJV, NET], 'some' [CEV, GW, NCV, NIV, NLT, NRSV, TEV], 'party' [AB, BDAG], 'section' [CBC; REB], 'group' [NASB]. This noun denotes a part in contrast with a whole [BDAG, LN].

c. περί with genitive object (LN 89.6): 'concerning' [BECNT, LN; NET, NRSV], 'because' [CEV, GW, NCV, NLT], 'because of' [AB; NIV, TEV], 'for' [Bar; NASB], 'with respect to' [ESV], 'of' [KJV], 'the issue

is' [CBC; REB], 'in relation to, with regard to' [LN]. This preposition marks a relation, usually involving content or topic [LN].
  d. ἐλπίς (LN 25.59) (BDAG 1.b.α. p. 320): 'hope' [BDAG, LN; all translations except CEV, GW, NCV]. This noun is also translated as a verb: 'I believe' [CEV, NCV], 'I expect' [GW]. This noun denotes a looking forward with confidence to that which is good and beneficial [LN]. This speaks especially of Israel's messianic hope [BDAG].
  e. ἀνάστασις (LN 23.93) (BDAG 2.b. p. 71): 'resurrection' [BDAG, LN; all translations except CEV, GW, NCV, TEV]. This noun is also translated as a verb phrase: 'will be raised to life' [CEV], 'will come back to life' [GW, NCV], 'will rise to life' [TEV]. This noun denotes coming back to life after having once died [LN]. It means the future resurrection from the dead [BDAG].
  f. pres. pass. indic. of κρίνω (LN 30.108) (BDAG 5.a.α. p. 568): 'to be on trial' [Bar, BECNT; all versions except KJV, NIV, REB], 'to stand on trial' [NIV], 'to be tried' [AB], 'to be called in question' [KJV], 'to be judged' [BDAG, LN], 'to be haled before a court, to be handed over for judicial punishment' [BDAG], 'to be evaluated' [LN]. The phrase 'concerning…I am on trial' is also translated 'the issue in this trial' [CBC; REB]. This verb means to make a judgment based upon the correctness or value of something [LN]. It means to engage in a judicial process [BDAG].

QUESTION—Should ἐλπίδος καὶ ἀναστάσεως '(the) hope and resurrection' be understood as two related beliefs or as a hendiadys describing the resurrection?
  1. It is a hendiadys in which the second of the two nouns indicates more specifically what the first noun refers to more generally: the hope *of* the resurrection [Bar, BECNT, CBC, NICNT, PNTC, TRT; CEV, GW, NCV, NET, NIV, NLT, NRSV, REB, TEV]. Israel's hope is rooted in the concept of the resurrection [BECNT], and fulfilled in the resurrection of Christ [PNTC].
  2. There are two separate but related ideas: the hope *and* the resurrection of the dead [AB, NAC; ESV, KJV, NASB]. The resurrection of the dead is a part of Israel's hope, but not the entirety of it [NAC].

QUESTION—What was Paul's intent in asking this question?
  Paul saw the resurrection as the real issue for which he was opposed by Jews, as his subsequent defense speeches in Acts emphasizing the resurrection show [NAC, PNTC]. The resurrection of the dead, and Jesus' own resurrection as the central factor in the general resurrection, was of central importance to Paul [EBC, NICNT, PNTC]. In appealing to this issue he hoped to find support among some of the Pharisees, even though they were a minority in the Sanhedrin [NAC, NICNT]. For those who believe in a resurrection, the ancestral hope of Israel was closely tied to the resurrection of the dead, and in particular, the resurrection of Christ [NICNT].

**23:7** When- he -said this (a)-dissension$^a$ arose (between) the Pharisees and the Sadducees and the assembly was-divided.$^b$ **23:8** For (the) Sadducees say there-is no resurrection nor angel(s), nor spirit(s), but (the) Pharisees acknowledge$^c$ them all.$^d$

LEXICON—a. στάσις (LN 33.448) (BDAG 3. p. 940): 'dissension' [AB, BECNT; ESV, KJV, NASB, NRSV], 'heated quarrel' [LN], 'conflict' [Bar], 'big argument' [CEV, NCV, NET], 'dispute' [NIV], 'strife, discord' [BDAG], not explicit [NLT]. The phrase 'a dissension arose' is also translated 'began/started to quarrel' [GW, TEV], 'fell out among themselves' [CBC; REB]. This noun denotes intense and emotional expressions of different opinions [LN]. It denotes a lack of agreement respecting policy [BDAG].

   b. aorist pass. indic. of σχίζω (LN 63.26) (BDAG 2.b. p. 981): 'to be divided' [BDAG, LN; all translations except CEV, NLT], 'to be split' [LN], 'to be torn in two' [LN], 'to become disunited' [BDAG]. This passive verb is also translated as active: 'this divided (the council)' [NLT], '(the council members) started taking sides' [CEV]. This verb means to split or divide into two parts [LN]. It means to be torn apart through conflicting aims or objectives [BDAG].

   c. pres. act. indic. of ὁμολογέω (LN 33.275) (BDAG 2. p. 708): 'to acknowledge' [BECNT; ESV, NASB, NET, NRSV], 'to believe in' [CEV, GW, NCV, NLT, REB, TEV], 'to believe' [NIV], 'to accept' [AB, CBC], 'to confess' [LN; KJV], 'to confess belief' [Bar], 'to agree' [BDAG], 'to admit' [LN]. This verb means to acknowledge a fact publicly, often in reference to previous bad behavior [LN]. It means to share a common view or be of common mind about a matter [BDAG].

   d. ἀμφότεροι (LN 59.26) (BDAG 2. p. 55): 'all' [BDAG, BECNT, LN; ESV, NASB, NCV, NET], 'all of these' [CEV, NLT], 'all these things' [GW, NIV], 'all three' [NRSV, REB, TEV], 'them' [AB, CBC], 'both' [Bar; KJV]. This adjective describes all of a few (three or more) [LN]. It describes all, even when more than two are involved [BDAG].

QUESTION—What was the nature of the Sadducees' belief?

They only acknowledged the five books of Moses as inspired Scripture [NAC, PNTC] and saw no substantiation for the resurrection in the books of Moses [NAC]. They denied any spiritual world [CBC]. They did not believe in a spiritual realm with a hierarchy of angels and demons [NICNT]. It is not known exactly what it was that they rejected about spirits and angels, though they may have rejected the Pharisees' notions of a hierarchy of spirits and angels [NAC], or possibly that people lived as spirits or angels either in a resurrected afterlife [BECNT, NAC, TNTC] or in an intermediate state [Bar, BECNT, PNTC], or that angels or spirits would speak through human beings [NAC, NICNT]. Because of their strong emphasis on free will they may have rejected the notion that angels or spirits were involved in the outworking of God's sovereign will in the affairs of men [BECNT]. Most of the scribes, who were the scholars of the law, were not Sadducees [NICNT].

**23:9** And (a)-great uproar[a] arose, and some of-the scribes[b] of-the Pharisees' rising-up contended-sharply[c] saying, "We-find nothing wrong[d] in this man; (what)-if (a)-spirit or angel spoke to-him?"

LEXICON—a. κραυγή (LN 33.84) (BDAG 1.a. p. 565): 'uproar' [CBC; NASB, NCV, NIV, NLT, REB], 'clamor' [BECNT; ESV, NRSV], 'outcry' [AB, Bar], 'cry' [LN; KJV], 'commotion' [NET], 'shouting' [BDAG; CEV, GW], 'shout' [BDAG, LN], 'scream' [LN]. The phrase 'a great uproar arose' is also translated 'the shouting became louder' [TEV]. This noun denotes the sound of a loud scream or shout [LN]. It is a clamor of excited persons [BDAG].

b. γραμματεύς (LN 53.94): 'scribe' [AB, Bar, BECNT; ESV, KJV, NASB, NRSV, REB], 'doctor of the law' [CBC], 'teacher of the law' [CEV, NCV, NIV, TEV], 'teacher of religious law' [NLT], 'expert in Moses' teaching' [GW], 'expert in the Law' [LN; NET]. This noun denotes a recognized expert in Jewish law (including both canonical and traditional laws and regulations) [LN].

c. imperf. mid. or pass. (deponent = act.) indic. of διαμάχομαι (LN 39.27) (BDAG p. 233): 'to contend sharply' [BDAG; ESV], 'to contend' [Bar, BECNT; NRSV], 'to contend with' [LN], 'to fight hotly' [AB], 'to argue forcefully' [GW, NLT], 'to protest strongly' [LN; NET, TEV], 'to argue heatedly' [NASB], 'to argue vigorously' [NIV], 'to argue' [NCV], 'to openly take sides' [CBC; REB], 'to strive' [KJV]. The phrase 'contended sharply saying' is also translated 'became angry and said' [CEV]. This verb means to fight or contend with, involving severity and thoroughness [LN].

d. κακός (LN 72.22) (BDAG 1.c. p. 501): 'wrong' [BECNT, LN; all versions except KJV, REB], 'evil' [AB, Bar, BDAG; KJV], 'fault' [CBC; REB], 'incorrect' [LN], 'bad' [BDAG]. This adjective describes being incorrect or inaccurate, with the possible implication of also being reprehensible [LN]. It describes being socially or morally reprehensible [BDAG].

QUESTION—What is meant by κραυγὴ μεγάλη 'great uproar'?

The proceedings had turned into a near riot [Bar, PNTC]. It was a violent argument [NAC, TH].

**23:10** And (when) a-great dissension arose, the commander, fearing lest Paul be-torn-apart[a] ordered (that) the soldiers go-down[b] to-take- him -away–by-force[c] from their midst and bring (him) into the barracks.

LEXICON—a. aorist pass. subj. of διασπάω (LN 19.29) (BDAG p. 236): 'to be torn apart' [BDAG, LN], 'to be torn to/in pieces' [AB, Bar, CBC; ESV, NASB, NIV, REB, TEV], 'to be pulled apart' [LN; CEV], 'to be pulled in pieces' [KJV]. This passive verb is also translated as active: 'they would tear (Paul) in/to pieces' [BECNT; GW, NCV, NET, NRSV], 'tear Paul apart' [NLT]. This verb means to pull or tear an object apart [LN].

b. aorist act. participle of καταβαίνω (LN 15.107) (BDAG 1.a.α. p. 514): 'to go down' [BDAG, BECNT, CBC, LN; ESV, KJV, NASB, NCV, NET, NIV, NRSV, REB], 'to go down into (the group)' [TEV], 'to come down' [Bar, BDAG, LN], 'to move down' [AB, LN], 'to go in' [CEV], 'to go' [NLT], not explicit [GW]. This verb means to move down, irrespective of the gradient [LN]. It means to move downward [BDAG].

c. aorist act. infin. of ἁρπάζω (LN 18.4) (BDAG 2.a. p. 134): 'to take away by force' [NASB, NET, NIV], 'to take by force' [BECNT; KJV, NRSV], 'to take away' [LN; ESV, NCV], 'to take' [TEV], 'to rescue' [AB; CEV], 'to rescue by force' [NLT], 'to seize' [Bar, LN], 'to pull out' [CBC; REB], 'to snatch away' [BDAG, LN]. The phrase 'to take him by force…and bring him into the barracks' is conflated and translated 'to drag Paul back to the barracks' [GW]. This verb means to grab or seize by force, with the purpose of removing and/or controlling [LN]. It means to grab or seize suddenly so as to remove or gain control [BDAG].

QUESTION—What does it mean that the commander ordered the soldiers to 'go down' to rescue Paul?

The meeting chamber of the Sanhedrin was at the eastern end of a bridge crossing over the Tyropoean valley immediately to the west of the temple mount, and was at a lower level than the Antonia fortress where the garrison was housed [EBC, NICNT].

**DISCOURSE UNIT—23:11–35** [AB, TNTC]. The topic is Paul taken into safety in Caesarea [AB], Paul is transferred to Caesarea [TNTC].

**DISCOURSE UNIT—23:11–22** [CBC]. The topic is the plot to kill Paul.

**DISCOURSE UNIT—23:11** [NICNT]. The topic is the Lord appears to Paul in the night.

**23:11** And on-the-next[a] night the Lord standing-(by) him said, "Take-courage,[b] for as you-(have)-testified[c] of the-things concerning me in Jerusalem, so you must testify[d] in Rome."

LEXICON—a. pres. act. participle of ἔπειμι (LN 67.208) (BDAG p. 361): 'the next day/night' [BDAG, LN], 'on the next day' [LN]. The phrase 'and on the next night' is also translated 'the following night' [AB, Bar, BECNT, CBC; ESV, NET, NIV, REB], 'the night following' [KJV], 'the night immediately following' [NASB], 'the next night' [GW, NCV], 'that night' [CEV, NLT, NRSV, TEV]. This participle form denotes a day immediately following a previous day [LN].

b. pres. act. impera. of θαρσέω (LN 25.156) (BDAG p. 444): 'to take courage' [BECNT; ESV, NASB, NIV], 'to be of good courage' [AB, Bar], 'be of good cheer' [KJV], 'to keep up one's courage' [CBC; NRSV, REB], 'to have courage' [LN; NET], 'to be brave' [NCV], 'to be encouraged' [NLT], 'to be enheartened' [BDAG], 'to be courageous' [BDAG, LN], 'to be bold' [LN]. 'Take courage' is also translated 'don't worry' [CEV], 'don't be afraid' [TEV], 'don't lose your courage' [GW].

This verb means to have confidence and firmness of purpose in the face of danger or testing [LN]. It means to be firm or resolute in the face of danger or adverse circumstances [BDAG].
  c. aorist mid. (deponent = act.) indic. of διαμαρτύρομαι (LN 33.223) (BDAG 1. p. 233): 'to testify' [Bar, BDAG, BECNT, LN; ESV, KJV, NET, NIV, NRSV], 'to bear witness' [AB, BDAG], 'to solemnly witness' [NASB], 'to be a witness' [NLT], 'to give witness' [TEV], 'to affirm the truth' [CBC; REB], 'to tell the truth' [GW], 'to tell (about me)' [CEV, NCV], 'to declare, to assert' [LN]. This verb means to make a serious declaration on the basis of presumed personal knowledge [LN]. It means to make a solemn declaration about the truth of something [BDAG].
  d. aorist act. Infin. Of μαρτυρέω (LN 33.262) (BDAG 1.b. p. 618): 'to testify' [ESV, NET, NIV], 'to bear witness' [AB, Bar, BDAG, BECNT; KJV, NRSV], 'to witness' [LN; NASB], 'be a witness' [BDAG], 'to tell the truth' [GW], 'to tell about (me)' [CEV], 'to preach the Good news' [NLT], not explicit [CBC; NCV, REB, TEV]. This verb means to provide information about a person or an event concerning which the speaker has direct knowledge [LN]. It means to confirm or attest something on the basis of personal knowledge or belief [BDAG].

QUESTION—What is significant about Jesus' encouragement of Paul?
  The only other uses of the verb θαρσέω 'take courage' in the New Testament are in statements by Jesus (see Mt 9:2, 22; 14:27; Mark 6:50; 10:49; John 16:33) [NAC]. Jesus appeared to Paul to encourage him at other critical moments in his life as well, and this encouragement no doubt helped Paul endure the difficulties and rigors of all that happened to him over the next several years [EBC, NICNT]. The present imperative indicates the ongoing need for Paul to keep up his courage [PNTC].

QUESTION—Was this on the evening of the following day, or the evening of the day of the hearing?
  1. It was that night, on the same day as the hearing [BECNT, NICNT, TH, TNTC, TRT; CEV, NASB, NLT, NRSV, TEV].
  2. It was the night of the next day, the day after the hearing [EBC].

QUESTION—What does ὡς...οὕτω 'as...so' mean with regard to Paul's testimony in Rome?
  He would give testimony in Rome just as he had done in Jerusalem [Bar, BECNT, NAC, NICNT, TNTC]. His primary purpose in court in Rome, just as it was before the Sanhedrin, will be for giving witness, not for defending himself [TNTC]. It means that Paul would testify before a high official in Rome, just as he had testified before high officials in Jerusalem [AB]. In Jerusalem he has given the testimony the Lord intended him to give, with Jesus' protecting him in persecution; so also he will suffer in Rome while testifying, and Jesus will protect him there as well [PNTC].

**DISCOURSE UNIT—23:12–35** [NET]. The topic is the plot to kill Paul.

**DISCOURSE UNIT—23:12–25** [PNTC; GW]. The topic is rescued from death again [PNTC], some Jews plot to kill Paul [GW].

**DISCOURSE UNIT—23:12–22** [BECNT, EBC, NAC; CEV, ESV, NASB, NIV, NLT, NRSV]. The topic is a plot to kill Paul [EBC; CEV, ESV], the plot to kill Paul [NIV, NRSV], a conspiracy to kill Paul [NASB], the plan to kill Paul [NLT], the plot to ambush Paul [NAC], the plot against Paul uncovered [BECNT].

**DISCOURSE UNIT—23:12–15** [NICNT, PNTC]. The topic is the plot against Paul's life [NICNT], hatching the plot [PNTC].

**23:12** And when it-was day, the Jews forming (a)-conspiracy[a] bound-themselves -by-an-oath[b] saying neither to-eat nor to-drink until they-killed[c] Paul. **23:13** And there-were more-than forty who formed this plot.[d]

LEXICON—a. συστροφή (LN 30.72) (BDAG 2. p. 979): 'conspiracy' [AB, BDAG, LN; GW, NASB, NET, NIV, NRSV], 'plot' [Bar, BDAG, BECNT, LN; ESV], 'plan' [NCV], 'scheme' [LN]. The phrase 'forming a conspiracy' is also translated 'banded together' [CBC; KJV, REB], 'got together' [CEV, NLT], 'met together and made a plan' [TEV]. This noun denotes a plan devised by a number of persons who agree to act against someone or some institution [LN]. It is the product of a clandestine gathering [BDAG].
  b. aorist act. indic. of ἀναθεματίζω (LN 33.472) (BDAG a. p. 63): 'to bind oneself by/with an oath' [Bar, BECNT; ESV, NET, NIV, NLT, NRSV], 'to bind oneself under an oath' [NASB], 'to take an oath' [CBC; NCV, REB], 'to bind oneself under a curse' [KJV], 'to bind oneself under pain of a curse' [AB], 'to vow' [CEV], 'to take a vow' [TEV], 'to ask God to curse' [GW], 'to curse' [LN], 'to put under a curse' [BDAG]. This verb means to invoke divine harm if what is said is not true or if one does not carry out what has been promised [LN].
  c. aorist act. subj. of ἀποκτείνω (LN 20.61): 'to kill' [LN; all translations]. This verb means to cause someone's death, normally by violent means, with or without intent and with or without legal justification [LN].
  d. συνωμοσία (LN 30.73) (BDAG p. 978): 'plot' [AB, BDAG, LN; GW, NASB, NIV], 'conspiracy' [Bar, BDAG, BECNT, CBC, LN; ESV, KJV, NLT, NRSV, REB], 'plan' [NCV, NET], not explicit [CEV]. The phrase 'who formed this plot' is also translated 'who planned this together' [TEV]. This noun denotes a plan for taking secret action against someone or some institution, with the implication of an oath binding the conspirators [LN].

QUESTION—To whom does the term 'the Jews' refer?
  It is vague, referring to some, but not all, Jews [BECNT, TRT]. It refers specifically to the forty who were involved in the plot [AB, NAC]. Many of them were probably the Asian Jews who were involved in the earlier unrest in chapter 21 [EBC]. 'The Jews' implies that their plot was a reflection of

the attitude of Jews more generally; also, when this plot is being reported to the commander, it makes sense to refer to them as Jews, by contrast with him as a Roman [TNTC].

QUESTION—What would have become of these men, since they were not able to kill Paul?

Jewish law made allowances for vows that could not be fulfilled because of things beyond the control of the one who made the vow [BECNT, EBC, NAC, NICNT, TH]. There were ways to escape the implications of vows that were not fulfilled [TNTC]. The vow would have meant that they would accept being banned from the synagogue if they failed to achieve their purpose [Bar].

**23:14** They going to-the chief-priests and to-the elders said, "We-have-strictly[a] -bound ourselves by-an-oath to-taste[b] nothing until we-(have)-killed Paul.

LEXICON—a. ἀνάθεμα (LN 33.473) (BDAG 3. p. 63): 'curse' [BDAG, LN]. The dative form of this noun is also translated 'strictly' [BECNT; ESV, NRSV], 'solemnly' [AB], '(by a) solemn (oath)' [CBC; NASB, NET, NIV, REB], 'solemn vow' [TEV], 'great (curse)' [KJV], not explicit [Bar; CEV, GW, NCV, NLT]. This noun denotes the content of what is expressed in a curse [BDAG, LN].

b. aorist mid. indic. of γεύομαι (LN 23.3) (BDAG 1. p. 195): 'to taste' [NASB], 'to taste food' [BECNT, CBC; ESV, GW, NRSV, REB], 'to eat' [Bar, LN; CEV, KJV, NIV, NLT, TEV], 'to eat or drink' [AB; NCV], 'to partake' [NET]. This verb means to consume solid food [LN]. It means to partake of something by mouth [BDAG].

QUESTION—Was this plan presented to the whole Sanhedrin or only to a few members?

It was probably only the Sadducean high priestly aristocracy that were involved [EBC, NAC, NICNT, PNTC, TNTC], not the Pharisees, who would have been more open to Paul [NAC, NICNT, PNTC].

**23:15** So you now with[a] the Sanhedrin notify[b] the commander that he-bring- him -down[c] to you as-though[d] (you) were-going to-determine[e] more-closely[f] his case;[g] and we before he comes-near are prepared to-kill[h] him."

LEXICON—a. σύν with dative object (LN 89.107) (BDAG 3.a.β. p. 962): 'with' [Bar, BDAG, LN; KJV], 'together with' [AB, BDAG, LN], 'along with' [BECNT; ESV], 'acting with' [CBC]. '(you) and (the council/Sanhedrin)' [CEV, GW, NASB, NET, NIV, NLT, NRSV, REB, TEV], not explicit [NCV]. This preposition marks an associative relation, often involving joint participation in some activity [LN].

b. aorist act. impera. of ἐμφανίζω (LN 56.8) (BDAG 2. p. 326): 'to notify' [NASB, NRSV], 'to give notice' [BECNT; ESV], 'to request' [AB; NET], 'to apply to' [CBC; REB], 'to ask' [CEV, NLT], 'to petition' [NIV], 'to signify' [KJV], 'to send word' [TEV], 'to send a message' [NCV], 'to make a representation' [Bar], 'make clear, explain, inform, make a report'

[BDAG], 'to bring charges, to accuse formally' [LN], not explicit [GW]. This verb means to make a formal report before authorities on a judicial matter [LN]. It means to provide information [BDAG].

c. aorist act. subj. of κατάγω (LN 15.175) (BDAG p. 516): 'to bring down' [AB, Bar, BDAG, BECNT, CBC, LN; ESV, KJV, NASB, NET, NRSV, TEV], 'to have brought down' [REB], 'to bring before' [CEV, NIV], 'to bring back' [NLT], 'to bring out' [NCV], 'to lead down' [BDAG, LN], not explicit [GW]. This verb means to lead or to bring down [LN].

d. ὡς (LN 64.12) (BDAG 3.b. p. 1105): 'as though' [AB, Bar, BECNT; ESV, KJV, NASB, NCV], 'as if' [NET], 'on the pretext of/that' [CBC; NIV, NRSV, REB], 'pretend (that)' [CEV, NLT, TEV], 'make it look as though' [GW], 'as' [BDAG, LN], 'like' [LN]. This conjunction is a relatively weak marker of a relationship between events or states [LN]. It introduces the perspective from which a person, thing, or activity is viewed or understood as to character, function, or role, with a focus based solely on someone's assertion or existing only in someone's imagination [BDAG].

e. pres. act. infin. of διαγινώσκω (LN 27.3) (BDAG 1. p. 227): 'to determine' [BDAG, BECNT; ESV, NASB, NET], 'to make (further) inquiry' [Bar], 'to enquire' [KJV], 'to find out (more)' [CEV], 'to get...information' [GW, TEV], 'to want...information' [NIV], 'to ask...questions' [NCV], 'to make...examination' [NRSV], 'to examine' [NLT], 'to end (his case)' [AB], 'to learn about accurately, to get detailed information, to examine thoroughly' [LN], 'to make a thorough examination' [BDAG]. The infinitive 'to determine' is also translated as a noun: 'investigation' [CBC; REB]. This verb means to obtain accurate and thorough information about [LN]. It means to give careful attention (to facts or a subject) as a basis for forming a judgment [BDAG].

f. ἀκριβῶς (LN 72.19) (BDAG p. 39): 'more closely' [ESV], 'more exactly' [BECNT], 'more fully' [NLT], 'more perfectly' [KJV], 'more accurate' [GW, NIV, TEV], 'more thorough examination/investigation/ inquiry' [AB; NASB, NET, NRSV], 'accurately' [BDAG, LN], 'closer' [CBC; REB], 'more' [CEV, NCV], 'further...with a view toward reaching a decision' [Bar], 'carefully, well' [BDAG], 'strictly' [LN]. This adverb describes strict conformity to a norm or standard [BDAG, LN], involving both detail and completeness [LN] and with focus on careful attention [BDAG].

g. περί with genitive object (LN 89.6) (BDAG 1.i. p. 798): 'in relation to, regarding, concerning' [LN], 'what concerns someone or something, his or its circumstances, situation, condition' [BDAG]. The phrase τὰ περὶ αὐτοῦ literally, 'the things concerning him', is also translated 'his case' [AB, Bar, BECNT, CBC; ESV, NASB, NET, NIV, NLT, NRSV, REB], 'something concerning him' [KJV], 'information about him' [GW, TEV], 'the charges against (Paul)' [CEV], not explicit [NCV]. This preposition marks a relation, usually involving content or topic [LN].

h. aorist act. infin. of ἀναιρέω (LN 20.71) (BDAG 2. p. 64): 'to kill' [LN; all translations except CBC; NASB, NRSV, REB], 'to do away with' [BDAG, CBC; NRSV], 'to make away with' [REB], 'to slay' [NASB], 'to destroy' [BDAG], 'to execute' [LN]. This verb means to get rid of someone by execution [BDAG, LN], often with legal or quasi-legal procedures [LN].

**DISCOURSE UNIT—23:16–22** [NICNT, PNTC]. The topic is the plot revealed [NICNT], exposing the plot [PNTC].

**23:16** But the son of Paul's sister hearing-about[a] the ambush[b], going and entering the barracks told[c] Paul. **23:17** And calling one of-the centurions Paul said, "Take this young-man[d] to the commander, for he-has something to-report[e] to-him."

LEXICON—a. aorist act. participle of ἀκούω (LN 33.212) (BDAG 3.b. p. 38): 'to hear' [LN; all translations except REB], 'to learn of' [REB], 'to receive news' [LN], 'to learn about' [BDAG]. This verb means to receive news or information about something [LN, BDAG], normally by word of mouth [LN].
- b. ἐνέδρα (LN 39.51) (BDAG p. 334): 'ambush' [AB, Bar, BECNT, CBC, LN; ESV, GW, NASB, NET, NRSV], 'plot' [CEV, NIV, REB, TEV], 'lying in wait' [KJV], 'plan' [NCV, NLT], 'secret attack' [LN], 'surprise attack' [BDAG]. This noun denotes concealing oneself or proceeding secretly, while waiting for an appropriate opportunity to attack [LN]. It denotes concealment for a surprise attack [BDAG].
- c. aorist act. indic. of ἀπαγγέλλω (LN 33.198) (BDAG 1. p. 95): 'to tell' [BDAG, LN; all translations except Bar, CBC; REB], 'to report' [Bar, CBC; REB], 'to inform' [LN], 'to report back, to announce' [BDAG]. This verb means to announce or inform, with possible focus upon the source of information [LN]. It means to give an account of something [BDAG].
- d. νεανίας (LN 9.32) (BDAG p. 667): 'young man' [BDAG, LN; all translations], 'youth' [BDAG]. This noun denotes a young man beyond the age of puberty, but normally before marriage [LN].
- e. aorist act. infin. of ἀπαγγέλλω (see entry c. above). The second instance of this verb in this verse is also translated 'to tell' [AB, Bar, BECNT; CEV, ESV, GW, KJV, NIV, NLT, TEV], 'to report' [CBC; NASB, NET, NRSV, REB]. The phrase ἀπαγγεῖλαί τι αὐτῷ 'something to report to him' is also translated 'a message for him' [NCV].

QUESTION—What else do we know of Paul's family in Jerusalem?
Almost nothing else is known of his family other than what is reported here [Bar, EBC, NAC, NICNT]. There is a good possibility that Paul had been disowned by his extended family for being a Christian [AB, CBC, EBC, NICNT], though now because of these troubles they may have become reconciled to him [CBC]. Paul and his sister were probably brought up in Jerusalem, and she stayed on there [PNTC].

QUESTION—Approximately how old would Paul's nephew have been?
    He was probably in his late teens [BECNT, NAC] or early twenties [BECNT].

**23:18** So<sup>a</sup> taking him he-brought-(him) to the commander and said, "The prisoner Paul called me (and) asked-(me) to-bring this young-man to you, (as) he-has something to-say to-you." **23:19** And the commander taking (him) by-his hand and going-aside<sup>b</sup> privately<sup>c</sup> asked "What is-it that you-have to-report to-me?"

LEXICON—a. μὲν οὖν (LN 89.50): 'so' [AB, Bar, BECNT, LN; ESV, KJV, NASB, NCV, NET, NIV, NLT, NRSV], 'therefore, consequently, accordingly, then, so then' [LN], not explicit [CBC; CEV, GW, REB, TEV]. This idiomatic phrase marks result, often implying the conclusion of a process of reasoning [LN].
  b. aorist act. participle of ἀναχωρέω (LN 15.53) (BDAG p. 75): 'to go aside' [BECNT; ESV, KJV], 'to lead aside' [AB; NLT], 'to draw aside' [CBC; NRSV, REB], 'to take aside' [CEV], 'to step aside' [NASB], 'to draw aside' [NIV], 'to withdraw' [Bar, BDAG, LN; NET], 'to go' [GW], 'to lead off' [TEV], 'to lead to a place' [NCV], 'to retire' [BDAG, LN], 'to go off, to go away' [LN]. This verb means to move away from a location, implying a considerable distance [LN]. It means to depart from a location [BDAG].
  c. ἴδιος (LN 28.67) (BDAG 5. p. 467). The idiomatic phrase κατ' ἰδίαν is also translated 'privately' [Bar, BDAG, LN; ESV, KJV, NASB, NET, NRSV], 'in private' [CEV], 'where they could be alone' [GW, NCV], 'by himself' [TEV]. It is conflated with 'go aside' and not translated explicitly [AB, BECNT, CBC; NIV, NLT, REB]. It describes what occurs in a private context or setting, in the sense of not being made known publicly [LN].

QUESTION—What is the function of μὲν οὖν 'so' (which also occurs in vv. 22, 31)?
    Luke uses it often in Acts (nineteen times), as well as in the Gospel of Luke, as a connective or to indicate transition [EBC].

**23:20** And he-said "The Jews (have)-agreed<sup>a</sup> to-ask you to-bring Paul to the Sanhedrin tomorrow as-though (they-were)-going to-inquire<sup>b</sup> more-closely about his-(case).

LEXICON—a. aorist mid. indic. of συντίθημι (LN 31.18) (BDAG 3. p. 975): 'to agree' [BECNT; ESV, KJV, NASB, NET, NIV, NRSV, TEV], 'to agree on a plan' [REB], 'to agree on, to arrange together' [LN], 'to decide' [AB; NCV], 'to plan' [Bar; CEV, GW], 'to make a plan' [CBC], 'to decide through agreement' [BDAG], not explicit [NLT]. This verb means to work out a joint arrangement [LN]. It means to reach a decision in group discussion [BDAG].
  b. pres. mid. or pass. (deponent = act.) infin. of πυνθάνομαι (LN 27.11) (BDAG 1. p. 897): 'to inquire' [BDAG, BECNT; ESV, KJV, NASB, NET, NRSV], 'to make inquiry' [Bar], 'to make (an) examination' [AB],

'to obtain information' [CBC; REB], 'to get information' [NLT, TEV], 'to want information' [GW, NIV], 'to find out about' [CEV], 'to ask questions' [NCV], 'to learn about, to find out about by inquiry' [LN], 'to ask' [BDAG]. This verb means to acquire information by questioning [LN]. It means to seek to learn by inquiry [BDAG].

QUESTION—What noun would be the antecedent and implied agent of the participle μέλλον in the phrase ὡς μέλλον 'as though they were going...'?

The antecedent of the neuter accusative plural of the participle μέλλον is the neuter accusative plural noun συνέδριον 'Sanhedrin', with which it is in grammatical agreement [EBC, NICNT, PNTC]. It is the Sanhedrin, not the commander, who would make further inquiry [Bar, BECNT, CBC; CEV, ESV, GW, KJV, NASB, NCV, NET, NLT, NRSV, TEV].

**23:21** But do- not -be-persuaded[a] by-them; for more-than forty of-their men are-lying-in-ambush[b] for him, who have-bound- themselves -by-oath not to-eat or drink until they-have-killed him, and now they-are ready, awaiting your consent.[c]"

LEXICON—a. aorist pass. subj. of πείθω (LN 33.301) (BDAG 3.c. p. 792): 'to be persuaded' [Bar, BDAG, LN; ESV, NRSV], 'to let someone persuade' [GW, NET], 'to agree' [AB], 'to yield' [BECNT; KJV], 'to give in' [NIV], 'to listen' [CBC; NASB, REB, TEV], 'to do what someone says' [CEV], 'to believe' [NCV], 'to be convinced' [LN]. The phrase 'do not be persuaded by them' is also translated 'don't do it' [NLT]. This verb means to convince someone to believe something and to act on the basis of what is recommended [LN]. It means to be won over as the result of persuasion [BDAG].

b. pres. act. indic. of ἐνεδρεύω (LN 39.51) (BDAG 1. p. 334): 'to lie in ambush' [BECNT; ESV, NET, NRSV], 'to wait in ambush' [NIV], 'to lie in wait' [AB, Bar, BDAG, CBC; KJV, NASB, REB], 'to plan to ambush' [GW], 'to be going to attack' [CEV], 'to hide ready to ambush' [NLT], 'to hide and wait to kill' [NCV], 'to hide and wait' [TEV], 'to be in an ambush, to make plans for a secret attack' [LN]. This verb means to conceal oneself or to proceed secretly, while waiting for an appropriate opportunity to attack [LN]. It means to conceal oneself in a suitable position for surprise attack [BDAG].

c. ἐπαγγελία (LN 33.280) (BDAG 2. p. 356): 'consent' [BECNT, CBC; ESV, NLT, NRSV, REB], 'promise' [Bar; KJV, NASB], 'decision' [TEV], 'what you decide' [CEV], 'agreement, approval' [LN], 'assurance of agreement' [BDAG]. This noun is also translated as a verb: 'to agree' [AB; NCV], 'to agree to a request' [NET], 'to consent to a request' [NIV], 'to promise' [GW]. It denotes the content of one's agreement or approval [LN]. It means the entertainment of a request and approval of it [BDAG].

QUESTION—What is the function or purpose of Luke's repeating the information about the plot, since it does not introduce anything new?

The repetition increases the dramatic tension in the narrative [NAC, PNTC].

**23:22** So the commander dismissed[a] the young-man charging[b] (him) "Tell[c] no-one that you-(have)-informed[d] me (about) these-(things)."

LEXICON—a. aorist act. indic. of ἀπολύω (LN 15.43): 'to dismiss' [Bar, BECNT, CBC, LN; ESV, GW, NIV, NRSV, REB], 'to let go' [AB; NASB], 'to send away' [CEV, NCV, NET, TEV], 'to let depart' [KJV], 'to let go away' [LN], not explicit [NLT]. This verb means to cause (or permit) a person or persons to leave a particular location [LN].
    b. aorist act. participle of παραγγέλλω (LN 33.327) (BDAG p. 760): 'to charge' [ESV, KJV], 'to order' [LN; GW, NCV, NRSV], 'to warn' [AB; NLT], 'to instruct' [BDAG; NASB], 'to direct' [BDAG; NET], 'to say' [CEV, TEV], 'to give orders' [BDAG], 'to command' [BDAG, BECNT, LN]. This verb is also translated as a noun phrase: 'with orders' [CBC; REB], 'with the command' [Bar], 'with this warning' [NIV]. It means to announce what must be done [LN]. It means to make an announcement about something that must be done [BDAG].
    c. aorist act. infin. of ἐκλαλέω (LN 33.73) (BDAG p. 305): 'to tell' [LN; all translations except CBC; CEV, NLT, REB], 'to let (someone) know' [CBC; CEV, NLT, REB], 'to inform, to report on' [LN]. This verb means to speak out about or publicize something [LN].
    d. aorist act. indic. of ἐμφανίζω (LN 33.208) (BDAG 2. p. 326): 'to inform' [BDAG, BECNT, LN; ESV, NRSV], 'to tell' [LN; CEV, NCV, NLT], 'to report' [LN; NET, NIV, TEV], 'to give information' [Bar, CBC; REB], 'to come with information about' [AB], 'to notify' [NASB], 'to show' [KJV], 'to make a report' [BDAG], 'to make clear, to explain' [BDAG]. The phrase 'that you have informed me about these things' is also translated 'this information' [GW]. This verb means to reveal something which is not generally known [LN]. It means to provide information [BDAG].

**DISCOURSE UNIT—23:23–35** [BECNT, CBC, EBC, NAC, PNTC; CEV, ESV, NASB, NCV, NIV, NLT, NRSV]. The topic is Paul is sent to Felix the governor [CEV, ESV, NRSV], Paul is sent to Caesarea and to Felix [BECNT], Paul is sent to Caesarea [NAC; NCV, NLT], Paul transferred to Caesarea [NIV], Paul moved to Caesarea [NASB], imprisonment at Caesarea [EBC], to Caesarea [CBC], preventing the plot [PNTC].

**DISCOURSE UNIT—23:23–24** [NICNT]. The topic is the tribune prepares to send Paul to Caesarea.

**23:23** And calling two of-the centurions he-said, "Get- two-hundred soldiers[a] -ready[b] to go[c] as-far-as Caesarea, plus seventy horsemen[d] and two-hundred spearmen[e] at[f] (the)-third hour[g] of-the night,

LEXICON—a. στρατιώτης (LN 55.17): 'soldier' [LN; all translations except CBC; GW, NIV, REB], 'infantry' [CBC; REB], 'infantryman' [GW]. The phrase 'two hundred soldiers' is also translated 'a detachment of two hundred soldiers' [NIV]. This noun denotes a person of ordinary rank in an army [LN].

b. aorist act. impera. of ἑτοιμάζω (LN 77.3) (BDAG b. p. 400): 'to get ready' [Bar, BECNT, CBC; ESV, NASB, NCV, NIV, NLT, NRSV, TEV], 'to have ready' [CEV, GW, REB], 'to make ready' [KJV, NET], 'to be ready' [AB], 'to prepare' [BDAG, LN], 'to make ready' [LN], 'to put or keep in readiness' [BDAG]. This verb means to cause to be ready [BDAG, LN].
c. aorist pass. (deponent = act.) subj. of πορεύομαι (LN 15.18) (BDAG 1. p. 853): 'to go' [AB, Bar, BDAG, BECNT; CEV, ESV, GW, KJV, NCV, NET, NIV], 'to proceed' [BDAG; NASB], 'to leave' [NLT, NRSV], 'to travel' [BDAG, LN], 'to journey, to be on one's way' [LN]. The phrase 'get ready…to go' is also translated 'get ready to go…to leave' [TEV], 'get ready to proceed…parade' [CBC; REB]. This verb means to move a considerable distance, either with a single destination or from one destination to another in a series [LN]. It means to move over an area, generally with a point of departure or destination specified [BDAG].
d. ἱππεύς (LN 55.21) (BDAG p. 480): 'horseman' [AB, BECNT, LN; ESV, KJV, NASB, NCV, NET, NIV, NRSV, TEV], 'cavalryman' [BDAG, CBC, LN; REB], 'cavalry' [Bar], 'man on horseback' [CEV], 'soldier on horseback' [GW], 'mounted troop(s)' [NLT], 'horse rider' [BDAG]. This noun denotes a soldier who fights on horseback [LN].
e. δεξιολάβος (LN 55.22) (BDAG p. 217): 'spearman' [BECNT, LN; ESV, KJV, NASB, NET, NIV, NLT, NRSV, TEV], 'lancer' [Bar], 'lightly armed troop(s)' [AB, CBC; REB], 'soldier with a spear' [GW], 'foot soldier with a spear' [CEV], 'man with a spear' [NCV], 'bowman, slinger' [BDAG]. This noun denotes a soldier armed with a spear [LN].
f. ἀπό with genitive object (LN 67.131) (BDAG 2.b.α. p. 105): 'at' [AB, BECNT; ESV, GW, KJV, NCV, NIV, NLT], 'from' [Bar, BDAG, LN], 'by' [CEV, NASB, NET, NRSV, TEV], not explicit [CBC; REB]. This preposition marks the extent of time from a point in the past [LN].
g. ὥρα (LN 67.199) (BDAG 2.c. p. 1102): 'hour' [AB, Bar, BDAG, BECNT, LN; ESV, KJV, NASB]. The phrase 'the third hour of the night' is also translated 'three hours after sunset' [CBC; REB], 'nine o'clock tonight' [CEV, GW, NCV, NET, NLT, NRSV, TEV], 'nine tonight' [NIV]. This noun denotes the twelfth part of a day, measured from sunrise to sunset (in any one day the hours would be of equal length, but would vary somewhat depending on the time of the year) [LN]. It means a period of time as division of a day [BDAG].

QUESTION—Why did Lysias decide to send Paul to the governor in Caesarea?
The immediate reason was the danger posed by more than forty men plotting to kill Paul [NAC, NICNT, PNTC], but Lysias would have had to send him to the procurator (governor) anyway since only the procurator had jurisdiction in cases of capital punishment [NAC]. The commander did not have legal authority to try someone from one of the provinces [TNTC], nor did he want to be held responsible for the death of a Roman citizen in his custody, so he sent him to Caesarea where the procurator would be

responsible for him [EBC, NICNT]. The commander realized that, since Paul's nephew knew of it, that rumor of the plot was beginning to spread, and he needed to act quickly to insure Paul's safety, but also to keep the peace by removing Paul as a cause of public unrest [PNTC]. The governor would have been responsible to try a case involving a serious disturbance of the peace [BECNT].

QUESTION—How far was Caesarea from Jerusalem?

It was about sixty miles from Jerusalem, but Antipatris, the first stop, was only about thirty five miles [BECNT, EBC, NAC, NICNT, PNTC], which would have necessitated a forced march for the infantry in order to arrive sometime the next day [BECNT, NICNT]. Luke had probably traveled this road while coming from Caesarea to Jerusalem some two weeks earlier with Paul [NICNT]. This departure by night marks the last time in Acts that Paul is in Jerusalem [BECNT].

QUESTION—What is a δεξιολάβος 'spearman'?

Other than its occurrence here, this word is unknown in any Greek literature until five or six centuries after this was written [NAC, NICNT]. It was translated as 'spearman' in the Latin version [Bar, TNTC]. Its literal meaning is 'holding with the right hand' [Bar, BECNT, NAC], and probably refers to spearmen [BECNT]. It refers to some form of light-armed troops [NICNT]. This rare word may actually have referred to additional horses being led for riding or for carrying baggage [EBC].

QUESTION—How many Roman troops total were there in Jerusalem at that time?

The garrison would have been about twice the size of this contingent, so he is sending out about half the garrison [Bar, BECNT, NAC, NICNT, TNTC]. The garrison may have only been about 600 men, but even if the δεξιολάβοι were horses, not spearmen, a contingent of 270 men would still have been about half the garrison [EBC]. If the garrison there was a normal Roman cohort with a single commander, the total force would not be much more than 400 soldiers, so this contingent was more than half the available personnel [PNTC].

**23:24** and provide[a] mounts[b] (for)-Paul to-ride to-bring-(him)-safely[c] to Felix the governor."

LEXICON—a. aorist act. infin. of παρίστημι (LN 57.81) (BDAG 1.a. p. 778): 'to provide' [LN; all translations except CEV, NCV], 'to get ready' [CEV], 'to get' [NCV], 'to make available' [LN], 'to put at someone's disposal' [BDAG]. This verb means to make something available to someone without necessarily involving actual change of ownership [LN]. It means to cause to be present in any way [BDAG].

b. κτῆνος (LN 4.6) (BDAG p. 572): 'mount' [AB, BECNT, CBC; ESV, NASB, NET, NRSV, REB], 'horse' [CEV, NCV, NIV, NLT, TEV], 'animal' [GW], 'beast' [Bar; KJV], 'beast of burden, riding animal' [LN], 'pack-animal, animal used for riding' [BDAG]. This noun denotes a larger

type of domesticated animal, primarily one used for riding or carrying loads [LN]. It denotes a domestic animal capable of carrying loads [BDAG].
c. aorist act. subj. of διασῴζω (LN 21.19) (BDAG p. 237): 'to bring safely' [AB, Bar, BECNT; ESV, NASB], 'to bring safe' [KJV], 'to take safely' [GW, NRSV], 'to get safely' [NLT], 'to get safely through' [CEV, TEV], 'to bring safely through' [BDAG]. This active verb is also translated as passive: 'to be brought safely' [NET], 'to be taken safely' [NCV, NIV], 'to be conducted under safe escort' [REB]. The phrase 'for Paul to ride to bring him safely' is also translated 'so that he may ride through under safe escort' [CBC]. This verb means to rescue completely from danger [LN]. It means to rescue or deliver from a hazard or danger [BDAG].

QUESTION—Why is κτήνη 'mounts' plural?
They may have provided two mounts so Paul could change animals and continue to move rapidly [EBC, PNTC, TH, TNTC, TRT], or the second one could have been used to carry baggage [EBC, TH, TRT]. Another possibility is that additional mounts could have been for traveling companions for Paul [PNTC, TRT], or possibly for carrying baggage for the soldiers [TNTC]. The mounts could have been horses, mules or donkeys [BECNT, TH].

**DISCOURSE UNIT—23:25–30** [NICNT]. The topic is letter from the tribune to Felix.

**23:25** (And) he-wrote a-letter having this pattern:ᵃ **23:26** "Claudius Lysias to- (his) -excellencyᵇ Governor Felix, greeting.

LEXICON—a. τύπος (LN 90.28, 58.25) (BDAG 4.,5. p. 1020): 'pattern' [BDAG], 'form' [BDAG 4; NASB], 'figure' [BDAG 4]. 'content' [BDAG 5, LN (90.28)], 'kind, class, type' [LN (58.25)]. The phrase 'having this pattern' is also translated 'to this effect' [AB, CBC; ESV, NRSV, REB], 'as follows' [Bar; NIV], 'that went like this' [BECNT; NET, TEV], 'that said' [CEV, NCV], 'with the following message' [GW], 'after this manner' [KJV], 'this (letter)' [NLT]. This noun denotes the content of a discourse or a document [LN (90.28)], or a kind or class, implying a relationship to some model or pattern [LN (58.25)]. It is a kind, class, or thing that suggests a model or pattern [BDAG].
b. κράτιστος (LN 87.55) (BDAG p. 565): 'excellency' [Bar, BECNT, CBC, LN; ESV, GW, NET, NIV, NLT, NRSV, REB, TEV], 'most excellent' [BDAG, LN; KJV, NASB, NCV], 'honorable' [AB; CEV], 'most noble' [BDAG, LN], 'your honor' [LN]. This adjective describes having noble status, with the implication of power and authority, often employed as a title [LN]. It is a strongly affirmative honorary form of address [BDAG].

QUESTION—Does ἔχουσαν τὸν τύπον τοῦτον 'having this pattern' mean that this is the actual text of the letter, or that this is more or less a summary of it?
1. It means that it gives the gist of what was written [Bar, CBC, EBC, NICNT, TNTC], as the contents would only have become known from

Paul who would have surmised its contents from when the governor questioned him [EBC]. However, it follows the pattern of style of similar documents of that time and is probably accurate in reflecting what would have been written [TH, TNTC].

2. This is probably a Greek translation of the actual Latin text of the letter, not just a summary [BECNT]. The letter may well have been read aloud to the governor in Paul's presence, so he would have been able to report the substance of it to Luke; on the other hand, Luke may have actually seen a transcript of this letter [PNTC]. While it could mean that this only gives the gist of what was written, it is possible that Luke actually had access to the letter in court records [NAC].

QUESTION—What do we know about Claudius Lysias?

The name Lysias would be his original Greek name and indicates that he was a Gentile by birth [EBC, NICNT, TNTC]. Claudius would have been the Roman name that he adopted upon becoming a citizen [BECNT, PNTC, TNTC], taken from the Caesar of that name who was reigning at the time [EBC, TNTC]. He may have received his citizenship from Emperor Claudius [PNTC]. He probably came from a Greek-speaking area either from coastal Syria or from Samaria [TNTC].

QUESTION—What does the title κράτιστος '(his) excellency' communicate?

It was an honorific title, usually only addressed to someone of the Roman equestrian class [EBC, NAC, NICNT, TNTC], that is, those who were knights [Bar]. Felix, as a former slave, would not have belonged to the equestrian class but was accorded this title by virtue of being the governor [Bar, EBC, NICNT, TNTC].

QUESTION—Who was Felix?

He was a freed slave who owed his position as governor to the influence of his brother Pallas, a position that was normally only possible for upper class nobility [EBC, NAC, NICNT, PNTC]. According to the Roman historian Tacitus, Felix wielded royal power with the mentality of a slave [BECNT, EBC, NAC, NICNT, PNTC, TH, TNTC], and seems not to have outgrown his low-class origins [TNTC]. Tacitus described him as a master of cruelty [EBC, PNTC]. He seemed to lack any understanding of the Jews he governed, and dealt brutally with political and religious unrest until he was finally removed from his office for incompetence [NAC]. His ruthlessness in suppressing Jewish uprisings only provoked more uprisings [BECNT, NICNT]. Felix governed from A.D. 52 to 59 [EBC]. His first wife was the granddaughter of Antony and Cleopatra, and his third wife was the daughter of Agrippa 1 [BECNT, EBC]. All three of his wives were of royal birth [EBC, NICNT].

**23:27** This man was-seized[a] by the Jews and was-about to-be-killed by them, (when) I-came-upon them with the soldiers (and) rescued[b] (him), having-learned[c] that he-was (a)-Roman (citizen). **23:28** And wishing to-know the charge[d] for which they-were-accusing him I-brought-(him) to their Sanhedrin.

LEXICON—a. aorist pass. participle of συλλαμβάνω (LN 37.109) (BDAG 1.a. p. 955): 'to be seized' [AB, BDAG, BECNT, CBC, LN; ESV, NET, NIV, NLT, NRSV, REB], 'to be arrested' [BDAG, LN; NASB], 'to be taken' [Bar, LN; KJV], 'to be apprehended' [BDAG], 'to be caught' [LN]. This passive verb is also translated as active: 'to seize' [GW, TEV], 'to take' [NCV], 'to grab' [CEV]. It means to seize and to take along with [LN]. It means to take into custody [BDAG].

b. aorist mid. indic. of ἐξαιρέω (LN 85.43) (BDAG 2. p. 344): 'to rescue' [Bar, BDAG, BECNT; all versions except NCV, NLT, REB], 'to intervene and remove to safety' [REB], 'to intervene and remove' [CBC], 'to remove to safety' [NLT], 'to save' [NCV], 'to set free, to deliver' [BDAG], 'to take out, to remove' [LN]. This active verb is also translated as passive: 'to be rescued' [AB]. This verb means to take something out of its place [LN]. It means to deliver someone from peril or confining circumstance [BDAG].

c. aorist act. participle of μανθάνω (LN 27.15) (BDAG 2.b. p. 615): 'to learn' [AB, Bar, BDAG, BECNT, LN; ESV, NASB, NCV, NET, NIV, NLT, NRSV, TEV], 'to discover' [CBC; REB], 'to find out' [BDAG; CEV, GW], 'to understand' [KJV], 'to ascertain' [BDAG], 'to come to realize' [LN]. This verb means to learn from experience, often with the implication of reflection [LN]. It means to make the acquaintance of something [BDAG].

d. αἰτία (LN 89.15) (BDAG 3.a. p. 31): 'charge' [BDAG, BECNT, CBC; ESV, NASB, NET, NRSV], 'why' [NCV, NIV], 'what' [TEV], 'ground' [Bar; REB], 'reason' [AB, LN], 'ground for complaint' [BDAG], 'basis' [NLT], 'cause' [LN; KJV]. The phrase 'the charge for which they were accusing him' is also translated 'what they had against him' [CEV, GW]. This noun denotes reason or cause for an event or state [LN]. It is a legal technical term for a basis for legal action [BDAG].

QUESTION—Was Claudius Lysias claiming to have rescued Paul because he knew that Paul was a Roman?

1. Claudius Lysias described the order of events in such a way that it appears that he rescued Paul because he learned that he was a Roman citizen [BECNT, CBC, EBC, NAC, NICNT, PNTC, TH, TNTC; CEV, ESV, GW, KJV, NASB, NCV, NET, NIV, NLT, NRSV, REB, TEV]. This was to make himself look better than he would look if he told the story as it actually happened [EBC, NAC, NICNT, PNTC, TNTC].

2. The verbal form used here could be understood to mean that he learned of Paul's citizenship after he rescued him [AB].

**23:29** I-found (that) he was-being-accused over questions[a] about their law,[b] but being-charged-with nothing worthy[c] of-death or imprisonment.

LEXICON—a. ζήτημα (LN 33.440) (BDAG p. 428): 'question' [ESV, KJV, NASB, NIV, NRSV, TEV], 'dispute' [AB, Bar, BECNT, LN; GW], 'controversial matter' [CBC; REB], 'controversial question' [BDAG; NET], 'issue, argument' [BDAG]. The phrase 'over questions about their law' is also translated '(the charges) concern only their religious laws' [CEV], 'some things that were wrong by their own laws' [NCV], 'something regarding their religious law' [NLT]. This noun denotes the forceful expression of differences of opinion without necessarily having a presumed goal of seeking a solution [LN].

b. νόμος (LN 33.55) (BDAG 2.b. p. 677): 'law' [BDAG; all translations except CEV, NLT], 'religious law' [CEV, NLT], 'the Law' [LN]. This noun denotes the first five books of the OT called the Torah (often better rendered as 'instruction') [LN]. It refers to a constitutional or statutory legal system, in this case the law that Moses received from God and is the standard according to which membership in the people of Israel is determined [BDAG].

c. ἄξιος (LN 65.17) (BDAG 1.b. p. 93): 'worthy' [BDAG, LN; KJV, NCV, NLT], 'deserving' [BECNT; ESV, NASB, NRSV], 'meriting' [CBC], 'calling for' [Bar], 'that might lead to' [AB], 'that deserved' [NET, NIV], 'for which he deserved' [GW, TEV], 'which merited' [REB], 'for which he should (die)' [CEV]. This adjective describes having a relatively high degree of comparable worth [BDAG, LN], value [BDAG], or merit [LN].

QUESTION—What is the nature of 'their law' that Claudius Lysias refers to?

He saw that this was a theological or religious issue, not something that would be a concern to Roman law [Bar, NICNT, TNTC; CEV, NLT]. He recognized that there was no infraction of Roman law that warranted Paul being tried [NAC]. The issue of bringing Gentiles into the temple is not mentioned [Bar, NICNT].

**23:30** And (when) it-was-disclosed[a] to-me (that) there-was (a)-plot[b] against the man, immediately[c] I-sent-(him) to you, and ordering (his) accusers to-state before you what-(charges) (they)-have against him."

LEXICON—a. aorist pass. of μηνύω (LN 33.209) (BDAG p. 648): 'to be disclosed' [BECNT; ESV], 'to be informed' [AB, BDAG, CBC, LN; GW, NASB, NET, NIV, NLT, NRSV, TEV], 'to be told' [KJV, NCV], 'to be made known' [Bar, BDAG], '(information) to be brought to someone's notice' [REB], 'to be revealed' [BDAG, LN]. This passive verb is also translated as active: 'I learned' [CEV]. This verb means to provide information concerning something, with emphasis upon the fact that such information is secret or known only to a select few [LN]. It means to offer information presumed to be of special interest [BDAG].

b. ἐπιβουλή (LN 30.71) (BDAG p. 368): 'plot' [AB, Bar, BDAG, BECNT, LN; CEV, ESV, GW, NASB, NET, NIV, NRSV, TEV], 'plan, scheme'

[LN]. The phrase 'a plot against the man' is also translated 'a plot to kill him' [NLT], 'an attempt to be made on the man's life' [CBC; REB], '(the Jews) laid wait for the man' [KJV], 'some were planning to kill Paul' [NCV]. This noun denotes a plan for treacherous activity against someone [LN]. It is a secret plan to do something evil or to cause harm [BDAG].
   c. ἐξαυτῆς (LN 67.113) (BDAG p. 346): 'immediately' [Bar, BDAG, LN; GW, NLT], 'at once' [AB, BDAG, BECNT, CBC, LN; ESV, NASB, NCV, NET, NIV, NRSV, TEV], 'without delay' [REB], 'straightway' [KJV], 'soon thereafter' [BDAG], 'suddenly' [LN], not explicit [CEV]. This adverb describes an extremely short period of time between a previous state or event and a subsequent state or event [LN].

QUESTION—How should we understand the aorist tense of the verb 'sent' and of the participle 'ordering' in this letter?

By the time Felix read the letter they were actions that would have occurred in the past, though they had not yet occurred when Lysias wrote it [AB, NAC, TNTC].

**DISCOURSE UNIT—23:31–26:32** [NICNT]. The topic is Paul at Caesarea.

**DISCOURSE UNIT—23:31–35** [CBC, NICNT]. The topic is Paul taken to Caesarea [NICNT], to Caesarea [CBC].

**23:31** So the soldiers according-to their instructions[a] taking Paul brought (him) by night to Antipatris. **23:32** And the next-day leaving the horsemen to-go with him they-returned to the barracks. **23:33** Having-come to Caesarea and delivering the letter to-the governor they-presented[b] Paul to-him.

LEXICON—a. aorist pass. participle of διατάσσω (LN 33.325) (BDAG 2. p. 238): 'instructions' [Bar, BECNT, LN; ESV, NRSV], 'orders' [BDAG, CBC, LN; CEV, NASB, NET, NIV, REB, TEV], 'what is commanded' [LN]. The phrase 'according to their instructions' is also translated 'as ordered' [NLT], 'as they had been ordered' [AB; GW], 'as it was commanded them' [KJV], 'what they had been told' [NCV]. This verb means to give detailed instructions as to what must be done [BDAG, LN].
   b. aorist act. indic. of παρίστημι (LN 37.111) (BDAG 1.b.α. p. 778): 'to present' [Bar, BDAG, BECNT; ESV, KJV, NASB, NET, NLT, NRSV], 'to hand over' [CBC, LN; CEV, GW, NIV, REB], 'to turn over to' [LN; NCV, TEV], 'to set before' [AB]. This verb means to deliver a person into the control of someone else, involving either the handing over of a presumably guilty person for punishment by authorities or the handing over of an individual to an enemy who will presumably take undue advantage of the victim [LN].

**23:34** And on-reading (it), asking which province[a] he-was from, and having-learned that-(he-was) from Cilicia **23:35** he-said, "I-will-give- you - (a)-hearing[b] whenever those-accusing you arrive," and he-ordered him to-be-held in Herod's praetorium.[c]

LEXICON—a. ἐπαρχεία (LN 1.84) (BDAG p. 359): 'province' [BDAG, LN; all translations except CEV, NCV], 'area' [NCV], 'region' [LN], not explicit [CEV]. This noun denotes a part of the Roman Empire (usually acquired by conquest) and constituting an administrative unit ruled over by an εἴπαρχος selected by the Roman Senate [LN]. It is a Roman administrative area ruled by an εἴπαρχος or prefect [BDAG].

b. fut. mid. indic. of διακούω (LN 56.13) (BDAG p. 231): 'to give a hearing' [BDAG; ESV, NASB, NET, NRSV], 'to hear a case' [CBC, LN; GW, NCV, NIV, NLT, REB], 'to schedule a hearing' [BECNT], 'to hear someone' [Bar; KJV, TEV], 'to question someone' [AB], 'to listen to a case' [CEV], 'to provide a legal hearing, to hear a case in court' [LN]. This verb means to give a judicial hearing in a legal matter [LN]. It means to give someone an opportunity to be heard in court [BDAG].

c. πραιτώριον (LN 7.7) (BDAG p. 859): 'praetorium' [Bar, BDAG, BECNT; ESV, NASB], 'palace' [AB, LN; CEV, GW, NCV, NET, NIV], 'headquarters' [NLT, NRSV, TEV], 'headquarters in Herod's palace' [CBC; REB], 'judgment hall' [KJV], 'fortress' [LN]. This noun denotes a governor's official residence [LN].

QUESTION—Why did Felix ask what province Paul was from?

He needed to know if Paul's case came under his jurisdiction [NAC, NICNT]. If Paul had come from one of the client kingdoms in Syria or Asia Minor it would have been necessary to consult the ruler of that state before beginning legal proceedings with a citizen of that area [Bar, NICNT, PNTC]. He may have been seeking an easy way to pass the matter on to some other ruler [PNTC].

QUESTION—Does giving a hearing mean having a trial, or something preliminary to a trial?

It would be a trial, not just a pre-trial hearing [BECNT, TNTC, TH].

QUESTION—Was the praetorium more like a royal palace or a military fortress?

It had originally been built by Herod the Great as his royal residence, or palace, but by this time was used as the headquarters of the Roman government [AB, CBC, NAC, NICNT, TH, TNTC].

**DISCOURSE UNIT—24:1–26:32** [NAC]. The topic is witness before Gentiles and the Jewish king.

**DISCOURSE UNIT—24:1–27** [AB, BECNT, CBC, EBC, PNTC, TNTC; GW, NASB, NLT, NIV]. The topic is Paul with Felix [AB], Paul's trial before Felix [NIV], the trial before Felix [CBC], Paul's defense before Felix [EBC], Paul appears before Felix [TNTC; NLT], appearing before Felix [PNTC], Paul before

Felix [NASB], Paul presents his case to Felix [GW], Paul's first defense and custody before Felix [BECNT].

**DISCOURSE UNIT—24:1-23** [NAC; ESV, NCV]. The topic is Paul before Felix at Caesarea [ESV], Paul is accused [NCV], the trial in Caesarea [NAC].

**DISCOURSE UNIT—24:1-9** [CBC, NICNT, PNTC; CEV, NET, NRSV, TEV]. The topic is Paul accused before Felix [NICNT], the accusation [CBC], the accusation of the Jews [PNTC], the accusations against Paul [NET], the case against Paul [TEV], Paul before Felix at Caesarea [NRSV], Paul is accused in the court of Felix [CEV].

**24:1** After five days the high-priest Ananias came-down[a] with some (of the) elders[b] and a-certain lawyer[c] Tertullus, who presented-(their)-case[d] against Paul to-the governor.

LEXICON—a. aorist act. indic. of καταβαίνω (LN 15.107) (BDAG 1.a.β. p. 514): 'to come down' [AB, Bar, BDAG, BECNT, CBC, LN; ESV, NASB, NET, NRSV, REB], 'to go down' [BDAG, LN; NIV], 'to go' [CEV, GW, NCV, TEV], 'to arrive' [NLT], 'to descend' [KJV], 'to move down, to descend' [LN]. This verb means to move down, irrespective of the gradient [LN]. It means to move downward, and is used of going away from Jerusalem [BDAG].

b. πρεσβύτερος (LN 53.77) (BDAG 2.a.b. p. 862): 'elder' [BDAG; all translations except CEV, GW], 'leader' [CEV], 'leader of the people' [GW]. This noun denotes a person of responsibility and authority in matters of socio-religious concerns, both in Jewish and Christian societies [LN]. It denotes an official [BDAG].

c. ῥήτωρ (LN 56.36) (BDAG p. 905): 'lawyer' [LN; CEV, NCV, NIV, NLT, TEV], 'attorney' [BDAG, LN; GW, NASB, NET, NRSV], 'advocate' [AB, BDAG, CBC, LN; REB], 'legal advocate' [BECNT], 'barrister' [Bar], 'spokesman' [ESV], 'orator' [KJV]. This noun denotes one who speaks in court as an attorney or advocate (either for the prosecution or for the defense) [LN]. It denotes a speaker in court [BDAG].

d. aorist act. indic. of ἐμφανίζω (LN 56.8) (BDAG 3. p. 326): 'to present a case' [CEV, NLT], 'to bring charges' [BDAG, LN; NASB, NIV], 'to bring formal charges' [NET], 'to make charges' [NCV, TEV], 'to report charges' [GW], 'to report a case' [NRSV], 'to lay accusations' [AB], 'to lay charges' [REB], 'to lay a case' [BECNT; ESV], 'to lay an information' [CBC], 'to inform (against)' [Bar; KJV], 'to accuse formally' [LN], 'present evidence' [BDAG]. This verb means to make a formal report before authorities on a judicial matter [LN]. It means to convey a formal report about a judicial matter [BDAG].

QUESTION—What period of time does 'after five days' describe?
  1. 'After five days' means that it had been five days since Paul's arrival in Caesarea [Bar, BECNT, NAC, NICNT, PNTC, TH, TNTC]. 'After five

days' is also translated 'five days later', which would reasonably be taken to mean after his arrival in Caesarea [AB, CBC; CEV, GW, NCV, NIV, NLT, NRSV, REB, TEV]. It had been five days from the time of Paul's first conversation with Felix [TH].

2. It had probably been five days since Paul's arrest in the temple [EBC].

QUESTION—Who was Tertullus and what was his role or function?

He was a legal advocate hired to present the case [Bar, BECNT]. He was a legal consultant for the Sanhedrin [AB], and a specialist in Roman law [TH]. His presence as a legal advocate indicates the importance of the case [Bar]. It is not clear if he was Jewish or not [BECNT, NAC, PNTC]; sometimes he seems to be speaking as a Jew, and at other times as a Gentile [AB, Bar]. He was probably a Hellenistic Jew [EBC, NICNT].

QUESTION—Why did the high priest himself go to Caesarea?

The Jewish delegation may have hoped that their social standing and rank would influence the trial in their favor, though this probably did not actually hold much weight with Felix [PNTC]. The presence of the high priest would show the seriousness of the case [CBC].

**24:2** (Paul) having-been-summoned[a] Tertullus began to-accuse[b] (Paul) saying, "We-have-experienced much peace[c] through you and reforms[d] are-happening for this nation through your foresight,[e]

LEXICON—a. aorist pass. participle of καλέω (LN 33.131) (BDAG 3.c. p. 503): 'to be summoned' [AB, BDAG; ESV, GW, NASB, NET, NRSV], 'to be called' [Bar, BECNT, CBC, LN; REB], 'to be called in' [CEV, NIV, NLT, TEV], 'to be called into (the) meeting' [NCV], 'to be called forth' [KJV]. This verb means to use an attribution in speaking of a person [LN]. It means to use authority to have a person or group appear [BDAG].

b. pres. act. infin. of κατηγορέω (LN 33.427) (BDAG 1.a. p. 533): 'to accuse' [BECNT, LN; ESV, GW, KJV, NASB, NCV, NET, NRSV], 'to bring charges' [BDAG, LN], 'to present the charges' [NLT], 'to present a case' [NIV], 'to start a case' [AB], 'to open a case' [CBC; REB], 'to state a case' [CEV], 'to make an accusation' [TEV], '(begin) an accusation' [Bar]. This verb means to bring serious charges or accusations against someone, with the possible connotation of a legal or court context [LN]. It is nearly always used as a legal technical term [BDAG].

c. εἰρήνη (LN 22.42) (BDAG 1.a. p. 287): 'peace' [BDAG, LN; all translations except KJV], 'quietness' [KJV], 'tranquility' [LN], 'harmony' [BDAG]. This noun denotes a set of favorable circumstances involving peace and tranquility [LN]. It denotes a state of concord [BDAG].

d. διόρθωμα (LN 72.17) (BDAG p. 251): 'reform' [AB, Bar, BDAG, BECNT, LN; ESV, GW, NASB, NET, NIV, NLT, NRSV, TEV], 'improvement' [BDAG, CBC; REB], 'very worthy deed' [KJV]. The phrase 'reforms are happening' is also translated 'many wrong things are being made right' [NCV], '(our nation) is much better off' [CEV]. This

noun denotes the result of having corrected a wrong or bad situation [LN]. It denotes that which results from correcting a wrong or undesirable situation [BDAG].
   e. πρόνοια (LN 30.47) (BDAG p. 872): 'foresight' [BDAG, LN; ESV, NET, NIV, NLT, NRSV], 'provident foresight' [Bar], 'provident care' [CBC; REB], 'providence' [KJV, NASB], 'provision' [BECNT], 'planning' [AB], 'concern' [CEV], 'wise leadership' [GW, TEV], 'wise help' [NCV], 'forethought' [BDAG]. This noun denotes thinking about something ahead of time, with the implication that one can then respond appropriately [LN]. It denotes thoughtful planning to meet a need [BDAG].
QUESTION—Who was summoned?
   1. Paul was called in [CBC, NAC, NICNT, PNTC; CEV, GW, NASB, NCV, NET, NIV, NLT, NRSV, REB, TEV]. The Greek construction is somewhat ambiguous [TH]. The phrase 'having been summoned is a genitive absolute, which would have a different subject from the subject of the main clause 'Tertullus began to accuse' [PNTC].
   2. Tertullus was called in [BECNT].

**24:3** in-every-way$^a$ and everywhere we-acknowledge-(this)$^b$ with all$^c$ gratitude,$^d$ most-excellent$^e$ Felix.
LEXICON—a. πάντῃ (LN 83.8) (BDAG p. 755): 'in every way' [AB, BDAG, BECNT; ESV, GW, NASB, NET, NIV, NRSV], 'in all ways' [Bar], 'in all kinds of ways' [CBC; REB], 'always' [KJV, NCV], 'everywhere' [LN; TEV], 'anywhere, all over' [LN]. The phrase 'in every way and everywhere' is also translated 'for all of this' [NLT], 'all of us' [CEV]. This adverb describes all possible positions or locations, though some scholars interpret it in Ac 24:3 as 'at all times,' which would be a rare example of this meaning in Greek [LN]. It describes pertaining to all possible considerations or positions [BDAG].
   b. pres. mid. or pass. (deponent = act.) indic. of ἀποδέχομαι (LN 31.26) (BDAG 3. p. 109): 'to acknowledge' [AB, BDAG, LN; NASB, NET, NIV], 'to welcome' [Bar, CBC; NRSV, TEV], 'to accept' [BECNT; ESV, KJV, NCV], 'to appreciate' [GW, REB], 'to recognize' [BDAG, LN], 'to praise' [BDAG], 'to think about favorably' [LN], not explicit [CEV, NLT]. This verb means to recognize or acknowledge the truth of something, normally implying something good [LN]. It means to approve or commend as praiseworthy [BDAG].
   c. πᾶς (LN 59.23) (BDAG 3.a. p. 783): 'all' [Bar, BDAG, BECNT, LN; ESV, KJV, NASB, NET], 'great' [AB], 'profound' [NIV], 'utmost' [NRSV], 'always' [CEV], 'most (gratefully)' [CBC], 'most (grateful)' [REB], 'deeply (grateful)' [TEV], 'very (grateful)' [NLT], '(thank you) very much' [GW], not explicit [NCV]. This adjective describes the totality of any object, mass, collective, or extension [LN]. It describes the highest degree of something [BDAG].

d. εὐχαριστία (LN 33.349) (BDAG p. 416): 'gratitude' [AB, Bar, BDAG, BECNT; ESV, NET, NIV, NRSV], 'thankfulness' [BDAG, LN; KJV, NASB], 'thanksgiving' [LN]. The phrase 'with…gratitude' is also translated 'gratefully' [CBC], 'we are grateful' [CEV, NCV, NLT, REB, TEV], 'we want to thank you' [GW]. This noun denotes the expression of gratitude for benefits or blessings [LN]. It denotes the quality of being grateful, with implication of appropriate attitude [BDAG].

e. κράτιστος (LN 87.55) (BDAG p. 565): 'most excellent' [Bar, BDAG, BECNT, LN; ESV, NASB, NCV, NET, NIV], 'your excellency' [CBC; GW, NLT, NRSV, REB, TEV], 'excellency' [LN], 'most noble' [AB, BDAG; KJV], 'honorable' [CEV]. This adjective describes having noble status, with the implication of power and authority, often employed as a title [LN]. It is a strongly affirmative honorary form of address [BDAG].

QUESTION—Does the phrase 'in every way and everywhere' refer to the Jews' acceptance of Felix's work with gratitude, or to improvements and reforms he is said to have brought about everywhere and in every way?

1. It goes with the action of acknowledging with all gratitude [AB, Bar, BECNT, PNTC; CEV, ESV, GW, KJV, NASB, NCV, NET, NIV, NLT, NRSV, TEV].
2. It refers to improvements made in all kinds of ways and places [CBC; REB]

QUESTION—Were any of these compliments actually true of Felix?

It was customary to praise a ruler at the beginning of a legal proceeding [BECNT, CBC, NAC, NICNT, PNTC, TH, TNTC]. This was flattery [AB, EBC, NAC, NICNT, TNTC, TH, TRT], calculated to appeal to Felix's vanity [EBC]. Tertullus hoped to make Felix disposed to grant whatever was being asked [BECNT, NAC, TRT]. The Jewish leaders had a very dim view of Felix [Bar, BECNT, EBC, NAC], so there is a lack of sincerity here [BECNT]. Felix had suppressed terrorism [BECNT, CBC], though civil disorder actually became worse over the time of Felix's tenure as governor [BECNT, EBC, NAC, TNTC]. Felix had suppressed violent robbers, but there was not a lot of peace during his rule [Bar]. This was exaggeration, as there was considerable political and social agitation during Felix's rule [EBC, NAC, PNTC, TNTC]. Not only had Felix not brought about improvements, he had often angered the Jews, resulting in an increase in uprisings [NAC]. Although Tertullus describes Felix in terms of 'kindness' Felix was known more for his harshness [NICNT]. Felix had previously quelled a rebellion by an Egyptian prophet and restored order, so Tertullus is trying to present Paul's case in a similar light, asking Felix to rule against Paul to restore civil order [PNTC].

**24:4** But in-order-that I- not -trouble[a] you further,[b] I-urge you by- your -kindness[c] to-hear us briefly.[d]

LEXICON—a. pres. act. subj. of ἐγκόπτω (LN 25.185) (BDAG p. 274): 'to trouble' [LN], 'to weary' [AB, Bar; NASB, NIV], 'to detain' [BECNT;

ESV, NRSV], 'to take up/take time' [CBC; NCV, REB, TEV], 'to delay' [NET], 'to bother' [CEV], 'to keep (someone)' [GW], 'to be tedious' [KJV], 'to bore' [NLT], 'to offend, to irritate' [LN], 'to hinder, to thwart' [BDAG]. This verb means to cause an offense to someone [LN]. It means to make progress slow or difficult [BDAG].

b. πολύς (LN 67.89) (BDAG 2.b.β. p. 849): 'further' [Bar, BECNT; ESV, KJV, NASB, NET, NIV, NRSV], 'too long' [AB, BDAG; GW], 'too much' [CBC; REB, TEV], 'any more' [NCV], 'any longer' [BDAG], 'long, long time' [LN], 'much, extensive' [BDAG], not explicit [CEV, NLT]. This adverb describes a relatively long duration of time [LN]. It describes being relatively large in quantity or measure [BDAG].

c. ἐπιείκεια (LN 88.62) (BDAG p. 371): 'kindness' [AB, BECNT; ESV, NASB], 'indulgence' [BDAG, CBC; REB], 'forbearance' [Bar, LN], 'clemency' [KJV], 'courtesy' [BDAG], 'graciousness' [BDAG, LN; NET, NRSV], '(be) patient' [CEV], '(be) kind' [NCV, NIV, TEV], 'gentleness' [BDAG, LN], not explicit [GW, NLT]. This noun denotes the quality of gracious forbearing [LN]. It denotes the quality of making allowances despite facts that might suggest reason for a different reaction [BDAG].

d. συντόμως (LN 67.108) (BDAG p. 976): 'briefly' [Bar, BDAG, BECNT, LN; ESV, NET, NIV, NRSV], 'brief' [CBC; GW, NASB, REB, TEV], 'for a short time' [AB], 'for just a few minutes' [CEV], 'for only a moment' [NLT], 'in a short time' [LN], 'few words' [KJV, NCV], 'concisely' [BDAG]. This adverb describes a relatively brief period of time, implying some measure of reduction or shortening [LN]. It describes making something short [BDAG].

QUESTION—What did Tertullus mean when he asked Felix to hear them briefly?

It was normal to begin a presentation this way [BECNT, EBC, NICNT, TNTC, TH]. It could be mostly a formality, as whatever followed might or might not be brief [EBC, NICNT]. Tertullus is aware that there is no solid evidence to offer, so he is asking that Felix pay close attention to the charges [BECNT], since preserving the peace is something for which Felix is responsible [BECNT, TNTC].

**24:5** For having-found this man (a)-pest[a] and stirring-up[b] riots[c] (among)-all the Jews throughout the world, and (is) (a)-ringleader[d] of-the Nazarene sect,[e]

LEXICON—a. λοιμός (LN 22.6) (BDAG 2. p. 602): 'pest' [Bar, CBC, LN; CEV, NASB, REB], 'troublemaker' [LN; GW, NCV, NET, NIV, NLT], 'pestilent fellow' [KJV, NRSV], 'pestilence' [AB], 'plague' [BECNT; ESV], 'dangerous nuisance' [TEV], 'public menace/enemy' [BDAG]. This noun denotes one who causes all sorts of trouble [LN].

b. pres. act. participle of κινέω (LN 90.53) (BDAG 4.a. p. 545): 'to stir up' [AB, Bar; ESV, NASB, NCV, NET, NIV, NLT], 'to start' [GW, TEV], 'to cause' [BDAG, LN], 'to bring about' [BDAG]. This participle is also

translated as a noun: 'agitator' [BECNT; NRSV], 'fomenter' [CBC; REB], 'troublemaker' [CEV], 'mover' [KJV]. This verb indicates a causative relation, with the implication of significant activity [LN]. It means to cause something to happen [BDAG].
- c. στάσις (LN 39.34) (BDAG 3. p. 940): 'riot' [Bar; ESV, NET, NIV, NLT, TEV], 'trouble' [AB], 'discord' [BDAG, CBC; REB], 'sedition' [KJV], 'quarrel' [GW], 'dissension' [BDAG; NASB], 'insurrection, rebellion' [LN], 'strife' [BDAG], not explicit [BECNT; CEV, NCV, NRSV]. This noun denotes open defiance of authority, with the presumed intention to overthrow it or to act in complete opposition to its demands [LN]. It denotes a lack of agreement respecting policy [BDAG].
- d. πρωτοστάτης (LN 87.52) (BDAG p. 894): 'ringleader' [BDAG, LN; all translations except AB; CEV, NCV, TEV], 'leader' [AB, BDAG, LN; CEV, NCV, TEV]. This noun denotes a person of top rank in view of leadership [LN]. It denotes a person who is at the head of a group [BDAG].
- e. αἵρεσις (LN 11.50) (BDAG 1.a. p. 28): 'sect' [BDAG, LN; all translations except CEV, NCV, NLT, TEV], 'group' [CEV, NCV], 'cult' [NLT], 'party' [BDAG; TEV], 'religious party' [LN], 'faction' [BDAG]. This noun denotes a division or group based upon different doctrinal opinions and/or loyalties and hence by implication in certain contexts an unjustified party or group (applicable in the NT to religious parties) [LN]. It denotes a group that holds tenets distinctive to it [BDAG].

QUESTION—What is meant or implied by the term 'sect'?

In Acts the term 'sect' is used of the Pharisees and the Sadducees [Bar, BECNT, NAC, NICNT, PNTC], as well as of Christians [BECNT, NICNT], so it may mean no more than 'party' [Bar, NAC]. A sect is a recognizable group with distinctive beliefs [BECNT]. However, Tertullus implies that this group is different, and more dangerous [PNTC]. Tertullus wanted to depict Christians in terms of political sedition, hoping that Felix would deal with Paul with the severity he typically employed when putting down uprisings [EBC]. Although the word originally referred to a party, here it seems to be used in a negative sense, describing a group whose beliefs are not right [TH]. Tertullus is attempting to depict Christians as something other than Judaism and therefore as an unauthorized religion, which under Roman law was punishable by death [TRT].

**24:6** who even[a] tried to-desecrate[b] the temple and we-arrested[c] him,

LEXICON—a. καί (LN 89.93): 'even' [AB, BECNT, CBC, LN; ESV, NASB, NET, NIV, NRSV], 'also' [Bar, LN; GW, KJV, NCV, TEV], 'furthermore' [NLT], 'and also' [LN], 'and' [LN], not explicit [CEV, REB]. This conjunction marks an additive relation which is not coordinate [LN].
- b. aorist act. infin. of βεβηλόω (LN 53.33) (BDAG p. 173): 'to desecrate' [AB, BDAG; NASB, NET, NIV, NLT], 'to profane' [Bar, BDAG,

BECNT, CBC, LN; ESV, KJV, NRSV, REB], 'to disgrace' [CEV], 'to defile' [LN; TEV], 'to make unclean' [LN; NCV], 'to violate tradition' [GW], 'to violate sanctity' [BDAG]. This verb means to cause something to become unclean, profane, or ritually unacceptable [LN]. It means to cause something highly revered to become identified with the commonplace [BDAG].

c. aorist act. indic. of κρατέω (LN 37.110) (BDAG 3. p. 564): 'to arrest' [BDAG, CBC, LN; CEV, GW, NASB, NET, NLT, REB, TEV], 'to seize' [AB, Bar, BDAG, BECNT, LN; ESV, NIV, NRSV], 'to stop' [NCV], 'to take' [KJV]. This verb means to take a person into custody for alleged illegal activity [LN]. It means to take control of someone or something, to take into custody [BDAG].

**24:7** [We wanted to judge him according to our own Law. 7 But Lysias the commander came, and with much force took him out of our hands, 8 ordering his accusers to come before you.]

TEXT—Manuscripts omitting this verse are given a B rating by GNT, indicating that it was almost certain that the original text did not include it. This verse is omitted by CEV, ESV, GW, NET, NIV, NLT, NRSV, REB, TEV. It is included by KJV, and is included in brackets by NASB, NCV.

**24:8** by-examining-(him)[a] yourself you-will-be-able to-find-out[b] from him about all these-things of-which we are-accusing him." **24:9** And the Jews also joined-in[c] asserting[d] these-things to-be so.

LEXICON—a. aorist act. participle of ἀνακρίνω (LN 56.12) (BDAG 2. p. 66): 'to examine' [Bar, BECNT, CBC; ESV, KJV, NASB, NET, NIV, NLT, NRSV, REB], 'to cross-examine' [GW], 'to make inquiry' [AB], 'to question' [BDAG, LN; CEV, TEV], 'to ask questions' [NCV], 'to hear a case' [BDAG, LN], 'to interrogate' [LN], 'to investigate in court' [BDAG]. This verb means to conduct a judicial inquiry [LN] or a judicial hearing [BDAG].

b. aorist act. infin. of ἐπιγινώσκω (LN 27.8) (BDAG 2.c. p. 369): 'to find out about' [Bar, LN; ESV], 'to find out' [CEV, GW, NLT], 'to learn about' [BECNT, LN; NET, NIV], 'to learn concerning' [NRSV], 'to learn' [TEV], 'to obtain information' [AB], 'to ascertain' [CBC; NASB, REB], 'to decide' [NCV], 'to take knowledge' [KJV]. This verb means to acquire information, probably in a somewhat more exact or detailed form and perhaps with focus upon what is learned [LN].

c. aorist mid. indic. of συνεπιτίθημι (LN 39.50) (BDAG p. 969): 'to join in an attack' [Bar, BDAG, LN; NASB], 'to join in a verbal attack' [NET], 'to join in an accusation' [NIV, TEV], 'to join in a charge' [BECNT; ESV, NRSV], 'to support an attack' [CBC], 'to support a charge' [REB], 'to support accusations' [GW], 'to accuse' [AB], 'to agree' [CEV, NCV], 'to assent' [KJV], 'to chime in' [NLT]. This verb means to join in attacking [LN]. It means to join with others in attacking [BDAG].

d. aorist act. participle of φάσκω (LN 33.218) (BDAG p. 1050): 'to assert' [BDAG, LN; GW, NASB, NIV, NRSV], 'to affirm' [Bar, BECNT; ESV], 'to say' [AB; KJV, NCV, TEV], 'to allege' [CBC; REB], 'to claim' [BDAG; NET], 'to speak up' [CEV], 'to declare' [LN; NLT]. This verb means to speak about something with certainty [LN]. It means to state something with confidence [BDAG].

**DISCOURSE UNIT—24:10–27** [CEV]. The topic is Paul is kept under guard.

**DISCOURSE UNIT—24:10–23** [PNTC; CEV, NET, NRSV, TEV]. The topic is Paul defends himself [CEV], Paul's defense before Felix [NET, NRSV, TEV], Paul's defense [PNTC].

**DISCOURSE UNIT—24:10–21** [CBC, NICNT]. The topic is Paul's defense before Felix [NICNT], the defense [CBC].

**24:10** And the governor having-motioned[a] to-him to-speak, Paul answered, "Knowing you have-been (a)-judge over-this nation for many years I-cheerfully[b] -make-a-defense[c] concerning myself,

LEXICON—a. aorist act. participle of νεύω (LN 33.485) (BDAG p. 670): 'to motion' [Bar, BECNT, CBC, LN; CEV, GW, NIV, NLT, NRSV, REB, TEV], 'to nod' [AB, LN; ESV, NASB], 'nod to someone as a signal' [BDAG], 'to make a sign' [NCV], 'to beckon' [LN; KJV], 'to gesture' [LN; NET]. This verb means to signal to someone by means of part of the body, especially by means of the head or hands [LN], possibly by inclination of the head [BDAG].

b. εὐθύμως (LN 25.147) (BDAG p. 406): 'cheerfully' [Bar, BDAG, BECNT; ESV, KJV, NASB, NRSV], 'confidently' [NET], 'with confidence' [AB, CBC; REB], 'gladly' [NIV, NLT], 'to be glad' [CEV], 'to be happy' [NCV, TEV], 'to be pleased' [GW]. This adverb describes a state of being encouraged [LN].

c. pres. mid. indic. of ἀπολογέομαι (LN 33.435) (BDAG p. 117): 'to make a defense' [Bar, BDAG, BECNT, CBC; ESV, NASB, NET, NIV, NRSV, REB], 'to defend oneself' [BDAG, LN; CEV, NCV, TEV], 'to present a defense' [NLT], 'to present a case' [GW], 'to set forth a case' [AB], 'to answer for oneself' [KJV]. This verb means to speak on behalf of oneself or of others against accusations presumed to be false [BDAG, LN].

QUESTION—What is the essence of Paul's argument in the following statements? He is asserting that he did not cause a disturbance, that his beliefs are consistent with Judaism, he did not desecrate the temple, and that the charges against him have not been supported by any evidence presented [BECNT]. Paul's main point is to show his respect for the temple by his intent to worship there, not to desecrate it [PNTC]. He is saying that since he had only come to Jerusalem twelve days earlier, there had not been enough time to foment rebellion, nor could they cite a time that he stirred up anything in the city, and finally that the charge of desecrating the temple was not provable because there was no basis for it to begin with [EBC].

**24:11** you are-able to-verify[a] that it-is not more-than twelve days since I-went-up to Jerusalem to-worship,[b]

LEXICON—a. aorist act. indic. of ἐπιγινώσκω (LN 27.8) (BDAG 2.c. p. 369): 'to verify' [ESV, GW, NET, NIV], 'to ascertain' [BDAG, BECNT, CBC; REB], 'to obtain confirmation' [AB], 'to find out' [Bar; CEV, NRSV, TEV], 'to find out about' [LN], 'to learn' [NCV], 'to discover' [NLT], 'to take note' [NASB], 'to understand' [KJV], 'to learn of/about' [BDAG, LN]. This verb means to acquire information, probably in a somewhat more exact or detailed form and perhaps with focus upon what is learned [LN]. It means to ascertain or gain information about something [BDAG].

b. fut. act. participle of προσκυνέω (LN 53.56) (BDAG b.α. p. 883): 'to worship' [BDAG, LN; all translations except CBC; REB], 'to prostrate oneself in worship, to bow down and worship' [LN], 'to do obeisance to, to prostrate oneself before, to do reverence to' [BDAG]. The phrase 'to worship' is also translated as 'on a pilgrimage' [CBC; REB]. This verb means to express by attitude and possibly by position one's allegiance to and regard for deity [LN]. It means to express in attitude or gesture one's complete dependence on or submission to a high authority figure [BDAG].

QUESTION—From what point are the twelve days to be reckoned?

It had been twelve days from the time he arrived in Jerusalem until the time he was arrested [NAC, TNTC]. It was twelve days from the time of his arrival in Jerusalem until the time he was taken by night to Caesarea [NICNT]. It had been twelve days between the time he arrived in Jerusalem and his appearance before Felix [AB, CBC, EBC]. The point was that there had hardly been time for Paul to have done the things of which he was being accused [Bar, EBC, NAC, NICNT, TNTC], and since the incident was so recent it should not have been difficult to find witnesses to speak about it [PNTC, TNTC].

**24:12** and they-did- not -find me arguing[a] with anyone in the temple nor stirring-up[b] (a)-crowd either in the synagogues or throughout[c] the city, **24:13** nor are-they-able to-prove[d] to-you concerning (the-things)-of which they- now -accuse me.

LEXICON—a. pres. mid. participle of διαλέγομαι (LN 33.446) (BDAG 1. p. 232): 'to argue' [AB, Bar, BDAG, CBC, LN; CEV, NCV, NET, NIV, NLT, REB, TEV], 'to dispute' [BECNT, LN; ESV, KJV, NRSV], 'to have a discussion' [GW], 'to carry on a discussion' [NASB], 'to discuss' [BDAG]. This verb means to argue about differences of opinion [LN]. It means to engage in speech interchange [BDAG].

b. pres. act. participle of ποιέω (LN 13.9) (BDAG 2.c. p. 839): 'to stir up' [BECNT; ESV, GW, NCV, NET, NIV, NRSV, TEV], 'to raise up' [KJV], 'to collect' [CBC; REB], 'to cause (a mob) to collect' [AB], 'to cause the onset' [Bar], 'to cause (a riot)' [NASB], 'to cause to be' [LN], 'to cause' [BDAG], 'to bring about' [BDAG, LN]. The phrase 'stirring up a crowd'

is also translated 'stirring up a riot' [NLT], 'cause trouble' [CEV]. This verb means to cause a state to be [LN]. It means to undertake or do something that brings about an event, state, or condition [BDAG].
   c. κατά with accusative object (LN 84.31) (BDAG B.1.a. p. 511): 'throughout' [LN; GW, NET, NRSV], 'in' [AB, BECNT; CEV, ESV, KJV, NASB, NCV], 'anywhere in' [Bar], 'anywhere else in' [NIV, REB, TEV], 'up and down' [CBC], 'on the streets of' [NLT], 'through' [BDAG]. This preposition describes extension in every direction throughout an area [LN]. It marks spatial aspect, and describes extension in space [BDAG].
   d. aorist act. infin. of παρίστημι (LN 72.4) (BDAG 1.f. p. 778): 'to prove' [Bar, BDAG, BECNT, LN; all versions except REB, TEV], 'to give proof' [TEV], 'to have proof to give' [AB], 'to make good (a charge)' [CBC; REB], 'to demonstrate' [BDAG], 'to show to be true, to present evidence of truth' [LN]. This verb means to establish evidence to show that something is true [LN]. It means to cause to be present in any way [BDAG].

QUESTION—Do the two verbs 'arguing' and 'stirring-up a crowd' refer to different actions done in different places, or to the same actions in all three places?
   1. It refers to two different actions in the three different places: arguing in the temple, and also causing trouble in the synagogues and city [CEV, GW, KJV, NCV, NIV, NLT, NRSV, TEV]. He is describing arguing in the temple or stirring up crowds in synagogues *throughout* the city [GW].
   2. It refers to both actions in all three places: arguing and stirring up crowds in the temple as well as in synagogues and throughout the city [ESV, NASB, NET, REB].

**24:14** But I-admit[a] to-you that according-to the way[b] which they-call (a)-sect,[c] I-worship[d] the God of-(our)-fathers, believing everything according-to[e] the law and the-things written in the prophets,

LEXICON—a. pres. act. indic. of ὁμολογέω (LN 33.221) (BDAG 3.b. p. 708): 'to admit' [AB, BDAG, BECNT, CBC; CEV, GW, NASB, NIV, NLT, NRSV, REB, TEV], 'to confess' [Bar, BDAG; ESV, KJV, NET], 'to tell' [NCV], 'to grant' [BDAG], 'to declare, to assert' [LN]. This verb means to make an emphatic declaration, often public, and at times in response to pressure or an accusation [LN]. It means to concede that something is factual or true [BDAG].
   b. ὁδός (LN 41.16) (BDAG 3.c. p. 692): 'way' [AB, Bar, BDAG, BECNT; ESV, KJV, NASB, NET, NIV, NLT, NRSV, TEV], 'new way' [CBC; REB], 'the Lord's way' [CEV], 'the way of Christ' [GW], 'the way of Jesus' [NCV], 'way of life' [BDAG, LN], 'way to live' [LN], 'teaching' [BDAG]. This noun denotes a customary manner of life or behavior, probably with some implication of goal or purpose [LN]. It denotes a

course of behavior, a whole way of life from a moral and spiritual viewpoint [BDAG].
c. αἵρεσις (LN 11.50) (BDAG 1.a. p. 28): 'sect' [Bar, BDAG, BECNT, CBC, LN; ESV, GW, NASB, NET, NIV, NRSV, REB], 'sectarian' [AB], 'cult' [NLT], 'heresy' [KJV], 'religious party' [LN], 'party, faction' [BDAG]. The phrase 'which they call a sect' is also translated 'which their leaders think is based on wrong beliefs' [CEV], 'the others say…is not the right way' [NCV], 'which they say is false' [TEV]. This noun denotes a division or group based upon different doctrinal opinions and/or loyalties and hence by implication in certain contexts an unjustified party or group (applicable in the NT to religious parties) [LN]. It denotes a group that holds tenets distinctive to it [BDAG].
d. pres. act. indic. of λατρεύω (LN 53.14) (BDAG p. 587): 'to worship' [LN; all translations except Bar; GW, NASB], 'to serve' [Bar, BDAG; GW, NASB], 'to perform religious rites, to venerate' [LN]. This verb means to perform religious rites as a part of worship [LN]. It means to carry out religious duties, especially of a cultic nature [BDAG].
e. κατά with accusative object (LN 89.8) (BDAG B.1.a. p. 511): 'according to' [Bar; NET], 'in accordance with' [LN; NASB, NIV], 'laid down according to' [NRSV], 'laid down by' [BECNT; ESV], 'that is taught in' [NCV], 'throughout' [BDAG], 'in relation to' [LN], 'in' [BDAG]. The phrase 'everything according to the law and the things written in the prophets' is also translated 'all that is written in the Law and the Prophets' [AB, CBC; KJV, REB, similarly CEV, TEV], 'everything written in Moses' Teachings and the Prophets' [GW], '(firmly believe) the Jewish law and everything written in the prophets' [NLT]. This preposition marks a relation involving similarity of process [LN]. It marks spatial aspect, and describes extension in space, which in this case means throughout the law [BDAG].

QUESTION—In what sense was Paul's Christian faith a 'way'?

It was the way to God, as well as the way to salvation [BECNT, TNTC]. The Christian way was the way in which Paul worshipped God as a true Jew [CBC, PNTC, NICNT, TNTC]. Here Paul contrasts 'sect' with 'way', as he views the Christian way as more than just a sect within Israel [Bar, NAC, NICNT, TNTC], and that it in fact is *the* way for all Israel [Bar, NAC, TNTC].

**24:15** having (the) hope[a] in God which these-men themselves also accept,[b] (that) there- will -be (a)-resurrection both of-(the)-righteous[c] and of-(the)-unrighteous.[d]

LEXICON—a. ἐλπίς (LN 25.59) (BDAG 1.b.β. p. 320): 'hope' [Bar, BDAG, BECNT, LN; all versions except CEV, GW, REB], 'expectation' [BDAG]. The participial phrase 'having the hope in God' is also translated 'trusting in God' [AB], 'in reliance on God I hold the hope' [CBC; REB], 'I'm…sure' [CEV], 'I hope' [GW]. This noun denotes

looking forward with confidence to that which is good and beneficial [LN]. It denotes looking forward to something with some reason for confidence respecting fulfillment [BDAG].
   b. pres. mid. indic. of προσδέχομαι (LN 31.53) (BDAG 2.b. p. 877): 'to accept' [Bar, BECNT, CBC, LN; ESV, NET, NRSV, REB], 'to have' [NCV, NIV, NLT, TEV], 'to allow' [KJV], 'to cherish' [NASB], 'to receive, to hold' [LN], 'to wait for' [BDAG], not explicit [AB; CEV, GW]. This verb means to accept a message for oneself and to act accordingly [LN]. It means to look forward to [BDAG].
   c. δίκαιος (LN 88.12) (BDAG 1.a.α. p. 246): 'righteous' [AB, Bar, LN; NASB, NET, NIV, NLT, NRSV], 'just' [BDAG, BECNT, LN; ESV, KJV], 'good' [CBC; CEV, NCV, REB, TEV], 'people with God's approval' [GW], 'upright' [BDAG]. This adjective describes being in accordance with what God requires [LN]. It describes being in accordance with high standards of rectitude [BDAG].
   d. ἄδικος (LN 88.20) (BDAG 1. p. 21): 'unrighteous' [AB, Bar, BECNT, LN; NET, NLT, NRSV], 'unjust' [BDAG, LN; ESV, KJV], 'wicked' [CBC; NASB, NIV, REB], 'evil' [CEV], 'bad' [NCV, TEV], 'those without (God's approval)' [GW], 'crooked' [BDAG]. This adjective describes not being right or just [LN]. It describes acting in a way that is contrary to what is right [BDAG].
QUESTION—In what sense will the unrighteous experience the resurrection from the dead?
   Paul believed what many Jews believed, which is that all will be raised from the dead for the great judgment at the end of time [Bar, BECNT, CBC, EBC, NAC, PNTC, TNTC], as is described in Daniel 12:2 [CBC, EBC, TNTC].

**24:16** Therefore[a] I-myself always strive[b] to-have (a)-clear[c] conscience[d] toward[e] God and-also (toward) men.
LEXICON—a. οὗτος (LN 92.29) (BDAG 1.b.α. p. 741): 'this' [BDAG, LN]. This idiomatic phrase ἐν τούτῳ καί, literally 'and in this' is also translated 'therefore' [AB; NRSV], 'so' [BECNT; ESV, NIV], 'and so' [Bar; TEV], 'accordingly' [CBC; REB], 'in view of this' [NASB], 'because of this' [NLT], 'with this belief' [GW], 'this is why' [NCV], 'this is the reason' [NET], 'and herein' [KJV], 'and because I am sure' [CEV]. This pronoun is a reference to an entity regarded as a part of the discourse setting, with pejorative meaning in certain contexts [LN]. It refers to the person or thing comparatively near at hand in the discourse material [BDAG].
   b. pres. act. indic. of ἀσκέω (LN 68.72) (BDAG p. 143): 'to strive' [AB; NIV], 'to do one's best' [BDAG, LN; GW, NASB, NET, NRSV, TEV], 'to try' [NCV, NLT], 'to try one's best' [CEV], 'to exercise oneself' [Bar; KJV], 'to train oneself' [CBC; REB], 'to take pains' [BECNT; ESV], 'to endeavor' [LN]. This verb means to engage in some activity, with both

continuity and effort [LN]. It means to apply oneself with a commitment to some activity [BDAG].
c. ἀπρόσκοπος (LN 88.318) (BDAG 1. p. 125): 'clear' [all translations except Bar; KJV, NASB, NCV], 'blameless' [Bar, BDAG, LN; NASB], 'void of offense' [KJV], 'without blame' [LN], 'undamaged' [BDAG], not explicit [NCV]. This adjective describes being blameless in view of not having given offense [LN]. It describes being without fault because of not giving offense [BDAG].
d. συνείδησις (LN 26.13) (BDAG 2. p. 968): 'conscience' [BDAG, LN; all translations except NCV], 'moral sensitivity' [LN], 'moral consciousness' [BDAG]. The phrase 'I always endeavor to have a clear conscience' is also translated 'I always try to do what I believe is right' [NCV]. This noun denotes the psychological faculty which can distinguish between right and wrong [LN]. It denotes the inward faculty of distinguishing right and wrong [BDAG].
e. πρός with accusative object (LN 90.20) (BDAG 3.e.α. p. 875): 'toward/s' [AB, Bar, BECNT; ESV, KJV, NET, NRSV], 'before' [CBC; NASB, NCV, NIV, NLT, REB, TEV], 'for' [CEV], 'in the sight of' [LN; GW], 'with respect to, with regard to' [BDAG], 'in the opinion of, in the judgment of' [LN]. This preposition marks a participant whose viewpoint is relevant to an event [LN]. It marks movement or orientation toward someone or something [BDAG].

QUESTION—What does the verb ἀσκέω 'strive' mean in this context?
This word does not occur elsewhere in the New Testament, but in Greek literature it describes physical or athletic training [Bar, PNTC, TH], and could easily be applied to training in the spiritual and moral sphere as well [Bar, PNTC].

**24:17** Now after several[a] years I-came to-bring alms[b] to my nation[c] and (to-present) offerings,[d]

LEXICON—a. comparative form of πολύς (LN 59.1) (BDAG 1.b.a. p. 848): 'several' [CBC; CEV, ESV, NASB, NCV, NET, NIV, NLT, REB, TEV], 'many' [AB, Bar, BDAG, LN; GW, KJV], 'some' [BECNT; NRSV], 'a great number of' [BDAG, LN]. This adjective describes a relatively large quantity of objects or events [LN]. It describes a large number [BDAG].
b. ἐλεημοσύνη (LN 57.112) (BDAG 1. p. 316): 'alms' [AB, Bar, BDAG, BECNT; ESV, KJV, NASB, NRSV], 'gifts for the poor/poor people' [CEV, GW, NET, NIV], 'charitable gift' [CBC; REB], 'money' [NCV, TEV], 'money to aid (my people)' [NLT], 'gift, money given to the needy, charity donation' [LN], 'charitable giving' [BDAG]. This noun denotes that which is given to help the needy [LN]. It denotes the exercise of benevolent goodwill [BDAG].
c. ἔθνος (LN 11.55): 'nation' [Bar, BECNT, CBC, LN; CEV, ESV, KJV, NASB, NRSV, REB], 'people' [AB, LN; GW, NCV, NET, NIV, NLT, TEV]. This noun denotes the largest unit into which the people of the

world are divided on the basis of their constituting a socio-political community [LN].

d. προσφορά (LN 53.16) (BDAG 1. p. 887): 'offering' [AB, Bar, BDAG, BECNT, LN; ESV, KJV, NASB, NET, NIV], 'offering for God' [GW], 'sacrifice' [CBC, LN; CEV, NCV, NLT, NRSV, REB, TEV], 'sacrificing' [BDAG]. This noun denotes that which is offered to God in religious activity [LN]. It denotes the act of bringing an offering as a voluntary expression [BDAG].

QUESTION—How long had Paul been away from Jerusalem?

Paul had not been in Jerusalem since the Jerusalem council described in chapter 15, though a brief visit seems to be implied in 18:22, which would have been three to five years earlier [AB, Bar, NICNT, PNTC, TRT]. It had been nine years since the Jerusalem council, though he had also visited briefly six years earlier to complete a Nazirite vow as described in 18:22 [EBC]. His absence of 'several years' means that he had not often been in the capital [PNTC]. What he means here is that he had been away for an extended time, which was around five years [BECNT]. He means that it had been many years since his break with the people of Jerusalem after his conversion [Bar]. The description of how long he had been away is variously described as 'several' [CBC, NICNT, PNTC. TNTC; CEV, ESV, NASB, NCV, NET, NIV, NLT, REB, TEV], or as 'many' [AB, Bar; GW, KJV].

QUESTION—What is Paul's main point here?

He is showing that he is actually supportive of the people of Israel and the beliefs that they hold, and the fact that he is on trial despite this support is ironic [BECNT].

**24:18** in which they-found me in the temple having-been-purified[a] not with (a)-crowd nor with (any)-disturbance,[b] **24:19** but certain Jews from Asia, who ought to-be-present[c] before you and make-(an)-accusation[d] if they-have anything against me.

LEXICON—a. perf. pass. participle of ἁγνίζω (LN 53.30) (BDAG 1.b. p. 12): 'to be purified' [BDAG, LN; ESV, KJV, NASB], 'to be ritually purified' [CBC; NET, REB], 'to purify oneself' [AB], 'to be in a state of purity' [Bar], 'to engage in a rite of purification' [BECNT], 'to go through a ceremony' [CEV], 'to go through/complete the purification ceremony' [GW, NLT, NRSV, TEV], 'to have finished the cleansing ceremony' [NCV], 'to be ceremonially clean' [NIV]. This verb means to purify and cleanse ritually and thus acquire a state of ritual acceptability [LN]. It means to purify or cleanse and so make acceptable for cultic use [BDAG].

b. θόρυβος (LN 14.79) (BDAG 3.b. p. 458): 'disturbance' [AB, CBC; NET, NIV, NRSV, REB], 'tumult' [Bar, BECNT; ESV, KJV], 'uproar' [BDAG; CEV, NASB], 'noisy mob' [GW], 'people gathered around' [NCV], 'rioting' [NLT], 'disorder' [TEV], 'clamor, noise' [LN], 'turmoil, excitement' [BDAG]. This noun denotes noise or clamor marked by confusion [LN]. It denotes a state or condition of varying degrees of

commotion, particularly the noise or confusion of excited crowds [BDAG].
c. pres. act. infin. of πάρειμι (LN 85.23) (BDAG 1.a. p. 773): 'to be present' [Bar, BDAG, LN; NASB], 'to be here' [AB, BECNT, LN; all versions except NASB, REB, TEV], 'to be at hand' [LN]. The phrase 'ought to be present before you' is also translated 'who ought to come before you' [TEV], 'who ought to have been in court' [CBC; REB]. This verb means to be present at a particular time and place [LN].
d. pres. act. infin. of κατηγορέω (LN 33.427) (BDAG 1.a. p. 533): 'to accuse' [AB, LN; GW, NCV], 'to make an accusation' [BECNT; ESV, NASB, NRSV, TEV], 'to bring an accusation' [Bar], 'to state a charge' [CBC; REB], 'to bring charges' [BDAG, LN; NET, NIV, NLT], 'to object' [KJV], not explicit [CEV]. This verb means to bring serious charges or accusations against someone, with the possible connotation of a legal or court context [LN]. It is nearly always a legal technical term meaning to bring charges in court [BDAG].

QUESTION—What is the unstated proposition in the incomplete clause beginning with 'but certain Jews from Asia'?

The unstated proposition is that it was the Jews from Asia who actually instigated the disturbance in the temple that brought about his arrest [BECNT]. The unstated proposition is that certain Jews from Asia had alleged that he caused a disturbance [Bar]. Paul is so upset by the fact that these Asian Jews were not present to make an accusation that he breaks off in mid-sentence [NAC]. It is worth noting that the Romans looked very unfavorably on people who press a legal charge and then abandon it [BECNT, EBC, PNTC, TNTC], and their absence at this hearing indicates that their charges were unprovable [EBC, NAC, PNTC]. The proposition is expressed in such a way as to show that they actually did not have anything of substance against Paul [TH].

**24:20** or let- these-men themselves -say what crime[a] they-found (as)-I was-standing before the council, **24:21** other-than this one statement[b] which I-shouted-out[c] while-standing among them that 'Concerning[d] (the)-resurrection of-(the)-dead I am-on-trial before you today.'"

LEXICON—a. ἀδίκημα (LN 88.23) (BDAG 1. p. 20): 'crime' [AB, Bar, BDAG, CBC; NET, NIV, NLT, NRSV, REB, TEV], 'wrongdoing' [BECNT; ESV], 'wrong' [BDAG; NCV], 'evil doing' [KJV], 'misdeed' [BDAG; NASB], 'unrighteous act, crime' [LN]. The phrase 'what wrongdoing they found' is also translated 'find me guilty of anything' [CEV], 'what I was charged with' [GW]. This noun denotes what is done in an unrighteous or unjust manner [LN]. It denotes a violation of norms of justice [BDAG].
b. φωνή (LN 33.80) (BDAG 2.c. p. 1071): 'statement' [AB; NASB], 'declaration' [REB], 'open assertion' [CBC], 'sentence' [NRSV], 'voice' [KJV], 'cry' [BDAG, LN], 'outcry' [BDAG], 'shout' [LN], 'loud or

288  ACTS 24:20-21

solemn declaration' [BDAG], not explicit [Bar, BECNT; CEV, ESV, GW, NCV, NET, NIV, NLT TEV]. This noun denotes the sound of a cry or shout [LN]. This verb means to communicate something in a loud voice [BDAG].
  c. aorist act. indic. of κράζω (LN 33.83) (BDAG 2.a. p. 563): 'to shout out' [CEV, NASB, NET, NLT], 'to shout' [AB, LN; GW, NCV, NIV], 'to cry out' [Bar, BECNT; ESV], 'to call out' [BDAG; NRSV, TEV], 'to call' [BDAG], 'to cry' [BDAG; KJV], 'to scream' [LN], not explicit [CBC; REB]. This verb means to shout or cry out, with the possible implication of the unpleasant nature of the sound [LN]. It means to communicate something in a loud voice [BDAG].
  d. περί with genitive object (LN 89.6): 'concerning' [Bar, BECNT, LN; NET, NIV], 'with respect to' [ESV], 'about' [NRSV], 'because of' [AB], 'because (I believe)' [CEV, GW, NCV, NLT], 'touching' [KJV], 'for' [NASB], 'for (believing)' [TEV], 'the true issue/issue is' [CBC; REB], 'in relation to, with regard to' [LN]. This preposition marks a relation, usually involving content or topic [LN].
QUESTION—What is the summation of Paul's legal defense?
  Paul has shown that he was in a purified state in the temple, and that he holds orthodox Jewish beliefs [BECNT, EBC, NAC], which neither Jews nor Romans consider to be a legal or civil infraction; thus Paul is no threat to Rome [BECNT, NAC]. Paul emphasizes his clear conscience and personal discipline in his life before God and service to God, his piety in Jewish worship, and his theological orthodoxy [PNTC].

**DISCOURSE UNIT—24:22–27** [CBC; ESV]. The topic is the adjournment [CBC], Paul kept in custody [ESV].

**DISCOURSE UNIT—24:22–23** [NICNT]. The topic is Felix adjourns proceedings.

**24:22** But Felix, knowing more-accurately[a] about the Way, put- them -off,[b] saying, "Whenever Lysias the commander[c] comes-down, I-will-decide-on[d] your case;"
LEXICON—a. comparative of ἀκριβής (LN 72.19) (BDAG p. 39): 'more accurately' [NET], 'accurately' [LN], 'rather accurate' [BECNT; ESV], 'accurate' [Bar, LN], 'fairly detailed' [AB], 'more perfect' [KJV], 'more exact' [NASB], 'rather well' [GW], 'well (informed/acquainted)' [CBC; NIV, NRSV, REB, TEV], 'quite (familiar)' [NLT], '(knew) a lot' [CEV], '(understood) much' [NCV]. This adverb describes strict conformity to a norm or standard [BDAG, LN], and involving both detail and completeness [LN], with a focus on careful attention [BDAG].
  b. aorist mid. indic. of ἀναβάλλω (LN 56.18) (BDAG p. 59): 'to put off' [BECNT; ESV, NASB], 'to defer' [KJV], 'to announce a deferment' [AB], 'to adjourn a hearing' [Bar, CBC, LN; NET, NLT, NRSV, REB], 'to adjourn a trial' [BDAG; GW], 'to adjourn a proceeding' [NIV], 'to

bring a trial to an end' [CEV], 'to bring a hearing to a close' [TEV], 'to stop a trial' [NCV], 'to stop a hearing and put it off until later' [LN]. This verb means to adjourn a court proceeding until a later time [LN].
c. χιλίαρχος (LN 55.15) (BDAG p. 1084): 'commander' [CEV, NASB, NCV, NIV, TEV], 'commanding officer' [CBC, LN; NET, REB], 'garrison commander' [NLT], 'tribune' [AB, Bar, BECNT; ESV, NRSV], 'officer' [GW], 'chief captain' [KJV], 'military tribune' [BDAG], 'general, chiliarch' [LN]. This noun denotes a military officer, normally in command of a thousand soldiers [LN]. It denotes the commander of a cohort, usually about six hundred men [BDAG].
d. fut. mid. (deponent = act.) indic. of διαγινώσκω (LN 56.21) (BDAG 2. p. 227): 'to decide a case' [BDAG, BECNT, LN; all versions except CEV, KJV], 'to make a decision' [CEV], 'to reach a decision' [Bar], 'to hear a case' [BDAG], 'to conclude a case' [AB], 'to go into a case' [CBC], 'to know the uttermost of a matter' [KJV], 'to arrive at a verdict after examination' [LN]. This verb means to make a judgment on legal matters, with the implication of thorough examination [LN]. It means to make a judicial decision [BDAG].

QUESTION—Why did Felix want Lysias' input in the matter?

He probably felt that Lysias would be a valuable witness who could bring more information [BECNT, NICNT, TNTC]. Lysias was probably the only independent witness [PNTC]. Felix also was unwilling to rule on a case that, so far, was apparently a theological dispute [Bar, PNTC]. Felix realized that the problem was religious, not political, so he hoped that by promising, untruthfully, to rule when he received testimony from Lysias, he could bring about an indefinite delay in the procedure [EBC]. Felix had no intention of consulting Lysias as Lysias had already stated what he knew in his letter; rather, Felix knew that Paul was innocent but simply did not want to issue a ruling that would be unpopular with the Jews [NAC].

QUESTION—To whom does the plural pronominal adjective 'your' refer?

Since it is plural, it refers to the Jews' case, that is, the case they had presented [PNTC, TRT].

**24:23** having-given-orders to-the centurion (that) he be-kept-in-custody,[a] but to-have-(some) freedom[b] and to-prevent none-of his-own-(friends) to-care-for[c] him.

LEXICON—a. pre. pass. infin. of τηρέω (LN 37.122) (BDAG 1. p. 1002): 'to be kept in custody' [BECNT; ESV, NASB], 'to be kept under guard' [AB; CEV, NIV, TEV], 'to be guarded' [BDAG, LN], 'to keep guarded' [NCV], 'to guard' [GW, NET], 'to keep' [KJV], 'to keep in custody' [NLT, NRSV], 'to be kept safe' [Bar], 'to be kept watch over' [BDAG, LN]. The phrase 'be kept in custody but to have some freedom' is also translated 'keep under open arrest' [CBC; REB]. This verb means to continue to hold in custody [LN]. It means to retain in custody [BDAG].

b. ἄνεσις (LN 37.137) (BDAG 1. p. 77): 'some freedom' [AB, BDAG; GW, NASB, NCV, NET, NIV, NLT, TEV], 'some liberty' [BDAG, BECNT, LN; ESV, NRSV], 'liberty' [KJV], 'relief from prison regimen' [Bar], not explicit [CBC; REB]. The phrase 'to have some freedom' is also translated 'not to lock him up' [CEV]. This noun denotes a partial degree of liberty or freedom [LN]. It denotes a relaxation of custodial control [BDAG].

c. pres. act. infin. of ὑπηρετέω (LN 35.32) (BDAG p. 1035): 'to take care of needs' [GW, NIV, NLT, NRSV], 'to provide for needs' [TEV], 'to attend to wants' [AB], 'to attend to needs' [BECNT; ESV], 'to meet needs' [NET], 'to provide for' [LN], 'to do service for someone' [Bar], 'to make oneself useful to someone' [CBC; REB], 'to help' [CEV], 'to minister to' [NASB], 'to minister or come to' [KJV], 'to bring what someone needs' [NCV], 'to support' [LN], 'to serve, to be helpful' [BDAG]. This verb means to provide continuous and possibly prolonged assistance and help by supplying the needs of someone [LN]. It means to render service [BDAG].

QUESTION—Why did Felix give Paul the freedom that he did?

Felix recognized that Paul was innocent [CBC]. Paul's Roman citizenship was also a consideration [EBC, NAC, NICNT].

**DISCOURSE UNIT—24:24–27** [NAC, PNTC; NCV, NET, NRSV, TEV]. The topic is Paul speaks to Felix and his wife [NCV], Paul speaks repeatedly to Felix [NET], Paul held in custody [NRSV], Paul before Felix and Drusilla [TEV], Paul and Felix in private [NAC], challenging Felix and Drusilla personally [PNTC].

**DISCOURSE UNIT—24:24–26** [NICNT]. The topic is Paul's interviews with Felix.

**24:24** And after some[a] days Felix, having-come with Drusilla his wife, who-was (a)-Jewess, sent-for Paul and listened[b] to-him (speak) about faith in Jesus Christ.

LEXICON—a. τὶς (LN 92.12): 'some' [all translations except CEV, NIV, NLT, KJV], 'several' [CEV, NIV], 'a few' [NLT], 'certain' [KJV], 'someone, something' [LN]. This adjective describes someone or something indefinite, spoken or written about [LN].

b. aorist act. indic. of ἀκούω (LN 24.52) (BDAG 1.c. p. 38): 'to listen/listen to' [BDAG; CEV, GW, NCV, NIV, NLT, TEV], 'to hear' [AB, Bar, BDAG, BECNT, LN; ESV, KJV, NASB, NET, NRSV], 'to let someone talk' [CBC; REB]. This verb means to have or exercise the faculty of hearing [BDAG].

QUESTION—Who was Drusilla?

She was the daughter of Herod Agrippa I and sister to Herod Agrippa II [AB, BECNT, CBC, EBC, NAC, NICNT, PNTC, TH], and also the sister of Berenice [AB, CBC, TH]. She had left her first husband for Felix [BECNT,

NAC, NICNT, TH, TNTC], and was less than twenty years old at this point [BECNT, NICNT, TH]. It is ironic that Herod Agrippa I opposed the new Christian movement as much as he did, but then his daughter, Drusilla, and his son Agrippa II (in Acts 26) actually engaged Paul in conversation about the gospel of Christ [PNTC].

**24:25** As- he -reasoned[a] about righteousness[b] and self-control[c] and the coming judgment Felix becoming afraid,[d] answered "Go-away (for)-now, (and) when-I-have (an)-opportunity[e] I-will-summon[f] you,"

LEXICON—a. pres. mid. or pass. (deponent = act.) participle of διαλέγομαι (LN 33.26) (BDAG 1. p. 232): 'to reason' [ESV, KJV, NLT], 'to discuss' [BDAG; GW, NASB, NET, NRSV, TEV], 'to discourse' [Bar], 'to speak' [AB; NCV], 'to argue' [BDAG, BECNT], 'to talk' [CEV, NIV], 'to converse' [BDAG], 'to address, to make a speech' [LN]. This verb is also translated as a noun: 'the discourse' [CBC; REB]. This verb means to speak in a somewhat formal setting and probably implying a more formal use of language [LN]. It means to engage in speech interchange [BDAG].
b. δικαιοσύνη (LN 88.13) (BDAG 3.1. p. 248): 'righteousness' [AB, Bar, BDAG, BECNT, LN; ESV, KJV, NASB, NET, NIV, NLT], 'morals' [CBC; REB], 'justice' [NRSV], 'God's approval' [GW], 'goodness' [TEV], 'living right' [NCV], 'doing right' [CEV], 'doing what God requires, doing what is right' [LN], 'uprightness' [BDAG]. This noun denotes the act of doing what God requires [LN]. It denotes the quality or characteristic of upright behavior [BDAG].
c. ἐγκράτεια (LN 88.83) (BDAG p. 274): 'self-control' [BDAG, LN; all translations except AB, KJV], 'temperance' [AB; KJV]. This noun denotes the exercise of complete control over one's desires and actions [LN]. It denotes the restraint of one's emotions, impulses, or desires [BDAG].
d. ἔμφοβος (LN 25.256) (BDAG p. 326): 'afraid' [Bar, BDAG; GW, NCV, NIV, TEV], 'frightened' [CEV, NASB, NET, NLT, NRSV], 'alarmed' [BECNT, CBC; ESV, REB], 'conscience-smitten' [AB], 'very frightened, very much afraid' [LN], 'terrified' [BDAG, LN]. The phrase 'became frightened' is also translated 'trembled' [KJV]. This adjective describes being extremely afraid [LN]. It describes being in a state of fear [BDAG].
e. καιρός (LN 22.45) (BDAG 1.b. p. 497): 'opportunity' [Bar, BECNT, BDAG, LN; ESV, NET, NRSV], 'time' [AB, BDAG; CEV, GW, NASB, NCV], 'good occasion' [LN]. The phrase 'have an opportunity' is also translated 'find it convenient' [CBC; NIV, REB], 'have a convenient season' [KJV], 'it is more convenient' [NLT], 'get the chance' [TEV]. This noun denotes a favorable opportunity or occasion in view of propitious circumstances [LN]. It denotes a moment or period as especially appropriate [BDAG].
f. fut. mid. indic. of μετακαλέω (LN 33.311) (BDAG p. 639): 'to summon' [BDAG, BECNT, LN; ESV, NASB], 'to send for' [Bar, CBC; CEV, GW,

NET, NIV, NRSV, REB], 'to call for' [KJV, NCV, NLT], 'to call' [AB; TEV], 'to tell to come' [LN], 'to call to oneself' [BDAG]. This verb means to summon someone, with considerable insistence and authority [LN].

QUESTION—What was it about Paul's message that frightened Felix?

Because Felix had enticed Drusilla to leave her first husband for him, they realized that their lifestyle was in conflict with what Paul preached [Bar, BECNT, EBC, NAC, NICNT, TNTC]. Felix's conscience was disturbed, though not deeply enough to bring repentance [NAC, TNTC].

**24:26** **and at-(the)-same-time hoping that money[a] would-be-given to-him by Paul; and so sending-for him often[b] he-conversed[c] with-him.**

LEXICON—a. χρῆμα (LN 6.68) (BDAG 2.a. p. 1089): 'money' [AB, Bar, BECNT, BDAG, LN; ESV, GW, KJV, NASB, NCV, NET, NRSV, TEV], 'bribe' [CBC; CEV, NIV, REB]. The phrase 'that money would be given to him by Paul' is also translated 'that Paul would bribe him' [NLT]. This noun denotes a generic term for currency, occurring mostly in the plural [LN]. It denotes any kind of currency [BDAG].

b. comparative of πυκνός (LN 67.13) (BDAG p. 897): 'often' [BDAG, BECNT; CEV, ESV, NCV, TEV], 'very often' [AB, CBC; NRSV], 'quite often' [NASB, NLT], 'pretty often' [Bar], 'rather often' [GW], 'as often as possible' [NET], 'oftener' [KJV], 'frequently' [BDAG; NIV, REB], 'very often, as often as possible' [LN]. This adverb describes a number of related points of time occurring with short intervals [LN]. It means occurring frequently at intervals [BDAG].

c. imperf. act. indic. of ὁμιλέω (LN 33.156) (BDAG p. 705): 'to converse with' [Bar, BECNT; ESV, NASB, NRSV], 'to talk (with)' [AB, CBC, LN; CEV, NCV, NET, NIV, NLT, REB, TEV], 'to speak (with)' [LN], 'to have friendly conversation with' [GW], 'to commune with' [KJV], 'to speak, to converse, to address' [BDAG]. This verb means to speak with someone, with the implication of a reversal of roles in communication [LN]. It means to be in a group and speak [BDAG].

QUESTION—Is Luke's depiction of Felix positive or negative?

Luke's description of Felix is not very flattering [BECNT]. Luke shows Felix in a positive light in that he did not wrongly convict Paul, but also in a negative light in that he hoped for a bribe and did not release him [Bar]. Felix is shown to be a conflicted and divided man with mixed motives [NAC, PNTC].

**DISCOURSE UNIT—24:27** [NICNT]. The topic is Felix replaced by Festus: Paul left in custody.

**24:27** But two-years having-elapsed[a] Felix took Porcius Festus (as) successor,[b] and wishing to-do (a)-favor[c] for-the Jews, Felix left Paul imprisoned.[d]

LEXICON—a. aorist pass. participle of πληρόω (LN 59.33) (BDAG 2. p. 828): 'to elapse' [BECNT; ESV], 'to pass' [AB, BDAG, CBC; GW, NASB, NET, NIV, NRSV, REB, TEV], 'to be up' [Bar], 'to be completed' [BDAG], 'to be made complete' [LN]. The phrase 'two years having elapsed' is also translated 'after two years' [CEV, KJV, NCV], 'two years went by' [NLT]. This verb means to make something total or complete [LN]. It means for a period of time to be completed [BDAG].
  b. διάδοχος (LN 61.11) (BDAG p. 228): 'successor' [BDAG, LN]. The idiomatic expression 'took as successor' is also translated 'was succeeded by' [AB, Bar, BECNT, CBC; ESV, NASB, NIV, NLT, NRSV, REB], 'was replaced by' [NCV], 'became governor in place of' [CEV], 'took (Felix's) place' [GW], 'succeeded (Felix)' [NET, TEV], 'came into (Felix's room)' [KJV]. This noun denotes one who succeeds another in a position or responsibility [LN]. It denotes one who comes next in a series, especially of a political figure [BDAG].
  c. χάρις (LN 57.103) (BDAG p. 3.a. p. 1079): 'favor' [AB, BECNT; CEV, ESV, GW, NASB, NET, NIV, NRSV], 'gift' [LN], 'gracious gift' [BDAG, LN], '(a sign of) favor, gracious deed, benefaction' [LN]. The phrase 'to do a favor for' is also translated 'to curry favor with' [Bar, CBC; REB], 'to gain favor with' [NLT, TEV], 'to please' [NCV], 'to show…a pleasure' [KJV]. This noun denotes that which is given freely and generously [LN]. It denotes a practical application of goodwill [BDAG].
  d. perf. pass. participle of δέω (LN 37.114) (BDAG 1.b. p. 221): '(to be) imprisoned' [LN; NASB], 'in prison' [AB, Bar, BECNT; ESV, GW, NCV, NET, NIV, NLT, NRSV, TEV], 'in jail' [CEV], 'in custody' [CBC; REB], '(to be) bound' [BDAG; KJV]. This verb means to confine someone in prison [LN]. It means to confine a person or thing by various kinds of restraints [BDAG].

QUESTION—To what does the lapse of two years refer?
  1. It refers to Paul's time in prison in Caesarea [AB, BECNT, CBC, NAC, NICNT, PNTC, TH, TNTC, TRT].
  2. It probably refers to Felix's tenure as governor [Bar].

QUESTION—Was he wanting to grant a favor to the Jews, or to gain favor with the Jews?
  1. He wanted to do a favor *for* the Jews [AB, BECNT, PNTC; CEV, ESV, GW, KJV, NASB, NCV, NET, NIV, NRSV].
  2. He wanted to gain favor *with* the Jews [Bar, CBC, NICNT, TH; NLT, REB, TEV], though unfortunately this did not come about [Bar].

QUESTION—Who is being referred to here as 'the Jews'?
  1. It is the Jewish people [AB, EBC, TNTC; NLT].
  2. It is the Jewish leaders [BECNT, PNTC; CEV].

**DISCOURSE UNIT—25:1–22** [PNTC; NASB, NLT]. The topic is Paul before Festus [NASB], Paul appears before Festus [NLT], appearing before Festus [PNTC].

**DISCOURSE UNIT—25:1–12** [AB, BECNT, CBC, EBC, NAC, TNTC; CEV, ESV, GW, NCV, NET, NIV, NRSV]. The topic is Paul asks to be tried by the Roman emperor [CEV], Paul appeals to Caesar [ESV, NET], Paul asks to see Caesar [NCV], Paul makes an appeal [GW], Paul appeals to the emperor [NRSV, TEV], Paul before Festus [AB], Paul appears before Festus [TNTC], Paul's trial before Festus [NIV], Festus takes up the case [CBC], Paul's defense before Festus [EBC], Paul's appeal to Caesar before Festus [BECNT].

**DISCOURSE UNIT—25:1–5** [NAC, NICNT, PNTC]. The topic is Festus pressured by the Jews [NAC], Festus visits Jerusalem [NICNT], Festus meets Paul's accusers [PNTC].

**25:1** Now[a] three days after having-arrived in-the province[b] Festus went-up from Caesarea to Jerusalem,

LEXICON—a. οὖν (LN 89.50) (BDAG 2.b. p. 737): 'now' [BDAG, BECNT; ESV, KJV, NET], 'so' [Bar, BDAG, LN], 'then' [BDAG, LN; NASB], 'so then' [LN], 'therefore, consequently, accordingly' [LN], not explicit [AB, CBC; CEV, GW, NCV, NIV, NLT, NRSV, REB, TEV]. This conjunction indicates result, often implying the conclusion of a process of reasoning [LN]. It marks the continuation of a narrative [BDAG].

b. ἐπαρχεία (LN 1.84) (BDAG p. 359): 'province' [AB, Bar, BDAG, BECNT, LN; ESV, KJV, NASB, NET, NIV, NRSV, TEV], 'region' [LN]. The phrase 'after having arrived in the province' is also translated 'after taking up his appointment' [CBC; REB], 'after (Festus) had become/became governor' [CEV, NCV], 'after (Festus) took over his duties in the province' [GW], 'after (Festus) arrived (in Caesarea) to take over his new responsibilities' [NLT]. This noun denotes a part of the Roman Empire (usually acquired by conquest) and constituting an administrative unit ruled over by an ἔπαρχος selected by the Roman Senate [LN]. It is a Roman administrative area ruled by an ἔπαρχος or prefect [BDAG].

QUESTION—Was this three days after arrival or after taking up his appointment?

1. It describes three days after his arrival in the province [AB, Bar, BECNT, NAC, NICNT; ESV, KJV, NASB, NET, NIV, NRSV, TEV].
2. It describes three days after taking up his administrative duties [CBC, TNTC; CEV, GW, NCV, REB].
3. It can describe both [Bar, TH; NLT].

**25:2** and the chief-priests[a] and leading-men[b] of-the Jews brought-charges[c] to-him against Paul and were-urging[d] him

LEXICON—a. ἀρχιερεύς (LN 53.88): 'chief priest' [LN; all translations except KJV, NCV, NLT], 'leading priest' [NCV, NLT], 'high priest' [KJV]. This

noun denotes a principal priest, in view of belonging to one of the high priestly families [LN].
b. πρῶτος (LN 87.45) (BDAG 2.a.β. p. 894): 'leading men' [Bar; NASB], 'leader' [AB, CBC; CEV, NIV, NLT, NRSV, REB, TEV], 'important leader' [GW, NCV], 'principal men' [BECNT; ESV], 'chief' [KJV], 'most prominent men' [NET], 'most prominent, most important' [BDAG], 'great, prominent, important' [LN], 'first' [BDAG], 'foremost' [BDAG, LN]. This adjective describes being of high rank, with the implication of special prominence and status [LN]. It describes prominence [BDAG].
c. aorist act. indic. of ἐμφανίζω (LN 56.8) (BDAG 3. p. 326): 'to bring charges' [BDAG, LN; NASB, TEV], 'to bring formal charges' [NET], 'to make charges' [AB; NCV], 'to present charges' [NIV], 'to tell about charges' [CEV], 'to bring a case' [CBC], 'to lay out a case' [ESV], 'to lay a charge' [REB], 'to make accusations' [NLT], 'to inform' [Bar, BECNT; KJV], 'to inform about charges' [GW], 'to make a report' [NRSV], 'to accuse formally' [LN], 'to present evidence' [BDAG]. This verb means to make a formal report before authorities on a judicial matter [LN]. It means to convey a formal report about a judicial matter [BDAG].
d. imperf. act. indic. of παρακαλέω (LN 33.168) (BDAG 3. p. 765): 'to request' [BDAG, LN], 'to ask for (earnestly), to plead for, to appeal to' [LN], 'to implore, to entreat' [BDAG]. The phrase 'they were urging him, asking a favor' [BECNT], is also translated 'they were urging him, requesting a concession' [NASB], 'begged him, asking a favor' [Bar], 'they urged him, asking as a favor' [ESV], 'besought him, and desired favor' [KJV]. The two verbs are conflated and translated 'they asked as a favor' [CBC], 'they asked/begged Festus to do them a/the favor' [NCV, TEV], 'urging/requesting him to do them the/a favor' [GW, NET], 'they requested/asked...as a favor' [NIV, NLT, NRSV], 'they begged him that as a favor' [AB], 'they urged' [REB], 'they asked' [CEV]. This verb means to ask for something earnestly and with propriety [LN]. It means to make a strong request for something [BDAG].

QUESTION—What is the sense given by the imperfect tense of 'urging'?
It shows that this has been an ongoing request, and may imply an element of pressure being put on Festus [BECNT]. It indicates ongoing action [TH].

**25:3** asking (a)-favor[a] against[b] (Paul) that he-summon[c] him to Jerusalem, planning[d] (an)-ambush[e] to-kill[f] him on the way.

LEXICON—a. χάρις (LN 57.103) (BDAG 3. p. 1079): 'favor' [all translations except CBC; CEV, NASB, REB], 'concession' [NASB], 'sign of favor' [BDAG], 'gift' [LN], 'gracious gift' [BDAG, LN], 'gracious deed' [BDAG], not explicit [CEV]. This noun is also translated as a verb: 'to favor (them)' [CBC], 'to support them (in their case)' [REB]. This noun denotes that which is given freely and generously [LN]. It is the practical application of goodwill [BDAG].

b. κατά with genitive object (LN 90.31) (BDAG 2.b.β. p. 511): 'against' [Bar, BDAG, CBC, LN; ESV, KJV, NASB, NET, NRSV], 'to injure' [AB], 'in opposition to' [LN], not explicit [BECNT; CEV, GW, NCV, NIV, NLT, REB, TEV]. This preposition marks opposition, with the possible implication of antagonism [LN]. It is used after words and expressions that designate hostile speech, especially an accusation [BDAG].

c. aorist mid. (deponent = act.) subj. of μεταπέμπομαι (LN 15.73) (BDAG p. 641): 'to summon' [BDAG, LN; ESV, NET], 'to bring' [CEV], '(for him) to be brought' [CBC], 'to have (him/Paul) brought' [AB; ESV, NASB], 'to have (Paul/him) transferred' [NIV, NRSV], 'to have (Paul) come' [TEV], 'to transfer' [NLT], 'to have (the man/him) sent' [BECNT; REB], 'to send' [Bar], 'to send back' [NCV], 'to send for' [BDAG, LN; KJV]. This verb means to send someone to obtain something or someone [LN].

d. pres. act. participle of ποιέω (LN 13.9) (BDAG 2.d. p. 839): 'to plan' [BECNT, CBC; CEV, ESV, NET, NLT, NRSV], 'to make' [Bar], 'to plot' [REB], 'to set' [NASB], 'to prepare' [BDAG; NIV], 'to cause' [BDAG], 'to bring about' [BDAG, LN], 'to cause to be, to make to be, to make, to result in, to bring upon' [LN], not explicit [AB; KJV]. This verb is also translated as a noun: 'a plan' [GW, NCV], 'a plot' [TEV]. This verb means to cause a state to be [LN]. It means to undertake or do something that brings about an event, state, or condition [BDAG].

e. ἐνέδρα (LN 39.51) (BDAG p. 334): 'ambush' [Bar, BDAG, BECNT, CBC, LN; ESV, NASB, NET, NIV, NLT, NRSV], 'attack' [CEV], 'secret attack' [LN], not explicit [NCV, REB, TEV]. This noun is also translated as a verb: 'to ambush' [GW]. The phrase 'planning an ambush' is also translated 'laying wait in the way to kill him' [KJV], 'they would lie in wait to kill him' [AB]. This noun denotes the act of concealing oneself or proceeding secretly, while waiting for an appropriate opportunity to attack [LN]. It is the act of concealment for surprise attack [BDAG].

f. aorist act. infin. of ἀναιρέω (LN 20.71) (BDAG 2. p. 64): 'to kill' [LN; all translations], 'to execute' [LN], 'do away with, destroy' [BDAG]. This verb means to get rid of someone by execution [BDAG, LN], often with legal or quasi-legal procedures [LN].

**25:4** Then[a] Festus answered (that) Paul was-being-held[b] in Caesarea, and he-himself was-about-to go-(there) shortly; **25:5** he said, "So,[c] the men-of-authority[d] among you, let-them-go-down-with-(me) (and) if there-is anything wrong[e] against the man let-them-accuse[f] him."

LEXICON—a. οὖν (LN 89.50) (BDAG 2.a. p. 736): 'then' [BDAG, LN; NASB, NET], 'now' [BECNT], 'but' [CEV, KJV, NCV, NLT], 'however' [CBC; REB], 'so' [BDAG, LN], 'so then' [LN], 'therefore, consequently, accordingly' [LN], not explicit [AB, Bar; ESV, GW, NIV, NRSV, TEV]. This conjunction indicates result, often implying the

conclusion of a process of reasoning [LN]. It serves to resume a subject once more after an interruption [BDAG].
b. pre. pass. infin. of τηρέω (LN 13.32) (BDAG 1. p. 1002): 'to be held' [NIV], 'to be kept' [Bar, BECNT, LN; CEV, ESV, KJV, NCV, NET, NRSV], 'to be kept a prisoner' [TEV], 'to be kept in custody' [NASB], 'to keep' [GW], 'to be in safe custody' [CBC; REB], 'to be under guard' [AB], 'to be guarded' [BDAG], 'to be at' [NLT], 'to be kept watch over' [BDAG], 'to be retained' [LN], 'to be caused to continue' [LN]. This verb means to cause a state to continue [LN]. It means to retain in custody [BDAG].
c. οὖν (LN 89.50): 'so' [Bar, BECNT, CBC, LN; ESV, NET, NLT, NRSV, REB], 'therefore' [LN; KJV, NASB], 'consequently, accordingly, then, so then' [LN], not explicit [AB; CEV, GW, NCV, NIV, TEV]. This conjunction indicates result, often implying the conclusion of a process of reasoning [LN].
d. δυνατός (LN 87.43) (BDAG 1.a.β. p. 264): '(men) of authority' [BECNT; ESV], 'in authority' [NLT], 'who have authority' [NRSV], 'authorities' [GW], 'competent' [AB], 'eminent' [Bar], 'leading' [CBC; REB], 'leaders' [CEV, NCV, NET, NIV, TEV], 'important' [LN], 'influential' [LN; NASB], 'able' [BDAG; KJV], 'capable, powerful' [BDAG]. This adjective describes important persons, based upon their power or influence [LN]. It describes people as being capable or competent [BDAG].
e. ἄτοπος (LN 88.111) (BDAG 2. p. 149): 'wrong' [BDAG; all translations except KJV, REB], 'wickedness' [KJV], '(at) fault' [REB], 'evil, improper' [BDAG], 'not fitting, what should not be done, bad' [LN]. This adjective describes not being in accordance with what is right, appropriate, or fitting [LN]. It describes being behaviorally out of place [BDAG].
f. pres. act. impera. of κατηγορέω (LN 33.427) (BDAG 1.a. p. 533): 'to accuse' [Bar, BECNT, LN; GW, KJV, NCV, NRSV, TEV], 'to bring charges' [LN; CEV, ESV, NET], 'to press charges' [NIV], 'to charge' [AB], 'to make accusations' [NLT], 'prosecute' [CBC; NASB, REB]. This verb means to bring serious charges or accusations against someone, with the possible connotation of a legal or court context [LN]. It means to bring charges against someone in court [BDAG].

QUESTION—What is the function of μὲν οὖν 'then'?
Luke uses μὲν οὖν frequently to tie parts of his narrative together [EBC].
QUESTION—Who are the 'men of authority'?
They are the same as 'the leading men' mentioned in v.2 [BECNT]. They were men who were competent in matters of law [AB], a delegation of responsible people [TNTC].

**DISCOURSE UNIT—25:6–12** [NAC, NICNT, PNTC]. Paul's appeal to Caesar [NAC], Paul appeals to Caesar [NICNT, PNTC].

**25:6** And having-stayed not more-than eight or ten days, he-went-down to Caesarea, (and) the-next-day taking-(his)-seat[a] on the tribunal[b] ordered Paul to-be-brought.[c]

LEXICON—a. aorist act. participle of καθίζω (LN 17.12) (BDAG 3. p. 492): 'to take one's seat' [BECNT, CBC; ESV, NASB, NLT, NRSV, REB], 'to sit' [AB, LN], 'to sit on' [KJV, NET], 'to sit down' [Bar, BDAG, LN; TEV], 'to take one's place (as judge/in court)' [CEV, GW], 'to be seated' [LN; NCV], not explicit [NIV]. This verb means to be in a seated position or to take such a position [LN]. It means to take a seated position [BDAG].

b. βῆμα (LN 7.63) (BDAG 3. p. 175): 'tribunal' [AB, BDAG, BECNT; ESV, NASB, NRSV], 'place of judgment' [Bar], 'judgment place' [LN], 'judgment court' [TEV], 'judgment seat' [LN; KJV, NET], 'judge's seat' [NCV]. The phrase 'on the tribunal' is also translated 'in court' [CBC; GW, NLT, REB], 'as judge' [CEV]. The phrase 'seating himself on the tribunal' is also translated 'he convened the court' [NIV]. This noun denotes a raised platform mounted by steps and usually furnished with a seat, used by officials in addressing an assembly, often on judicial matters [LN]. It is a dais or platform that required steps to ascend [BDAG].

c. aorist pass. infin. of ἄγω (LN 15.165) (BDAG 2. p. 16): 'to be brought' [Bar, BECNT, LN; ESV, KJV, NASB, NET, NIV, NRSV, REB], 'to be brought in/into' [AB; CEV, NLT, TEV], 'to be brought up' [CBC], 'to be led' [LN], 'to be led away, to be arrested' [BDAG]. The phrase 'ordered Paul to be brought' is also translated 'summoned Paul' [GW], 'told the soldiers to bring Paul' [NCV]. This verb means to direct or guide the movement of an object, without special regard to point of departure or goal [LN]. It means to take into custody [BDAG].

**25:7** And when-he-had-arrived[a] the-Jews who-had-come-down from Jerusalem stood-around[b] him bringing[c] many serious[d] charges[e] which they-were- not -able to-prove.[f]

LEXICON—a. aorist mid. (deponent = act.) participle of παραγίνομαι (LN 85.7) (BDAG 1.a. p. 760): 'to arrive' [Bar, BDAG; ESV, NASB, NET, NLT, NRSV, TEV], 'to appear' [AB, CBC; REB], 'to come' [BDAG, BECNT; KJV], 'to come in' [CEV, NIV], 'to come into the room' [NCV], 'to enter the room' [GW], 'to be present, to draw near' [BDAG], 'to come to be, to appear, to be in a place' [LN]. This verb means to come to be in a place [LN]. It means to be in movement so as to be present at a particular place [BDAG].

b. aorist act. indic. of περιΐστημι (LN 17.4) (BDAG 1.a. p. 801): 'to stand around/round' [BDAG, CBC, LN; ESV, NASB, NCV, NET, NIV, REB, TEV], 'to stand round about' [KJV], 'to crowd around' [CEV], 'to stand about' [BECNT], 'to gather round' [AB; NLT], 'to surround' [Bar; GW, NRSV], 'to be around' [LN]. This verb means to stand around someone or

to encircle [LN]. It means to encircle by standing around some entity [BDAG].
c. pres. act. participle of καταφέρω (LN 13.133) (BDAG 2. p. 529): 'to bring' [Bar, CBC; ESV, NASB, NET, NIV, NRSV, REB], 'to bring against' [BECNT, LN], 'to make' [AB; GW, NCV, NLT, TEV], 'to lay (complaints)' [KJV], 'to cause to happen to, to bring about' [LN], 'to cast against' [BDAG], not explicit [CEV]. This verb means to cause something adverse to happen to someone, usually in connection with accusations or condemnations [LN]. It means to cause something to happen that is opposed to another's interest [BDAG].
d. βαρύς (LN 86.1) (BDAG 3. p. 167): 'serious' [all translations except Bar, CBC; KJV, REB], 'weighty' [Bar, BDAG], 'grave' [CBC; REB], 'grievous' [KJV], 'heavy, burdensome' [LN]. This adjective describes something as being relatively heavy [LN]. It describes something as being important because of unusual significance particularly with regard to certain legal directives [BDAG].
e. αἰτίωμα (LN 56.5) (BDAG p. 31): 'charge' [BDAG, LN; all translations except CEV, GW, KJV, NLT], 'accusation' [LN; GW, NLT], 'complaint' [BDAG, LN; KJV]. The phrase 'bringing many serious charges' is also translated 'said he was guilty of many serious crimes' [CEV]. This noun denotes the content of legal charges brought against someone [LN].
f. aorist act. indic. of ἀποδείκνυμι (LN 72.5) (BDAG 3. p. 108): 'to prove' [LN; all translations except AB, BECNT], 'to give proof' [AB], 'to demonstrate' [BECNT], 'to show to be true' [LN]. This verb means to demonstrate that something is true [LN]. It means to demonstrate that something is true [BDAG].

QUESTION—Do the pronouns 'he' and 'him' refer to Paul or to Festus?
They refer to Paul, whom they surrounded when he arrived [Bar, NICNT, TH; CEV, GW, NASB, NCV, NIV, NLT, TEV].
QUESTION—What is implied by the use of the imperfect verb ἴσχυον 'were not able'?
It represents repeated or continued action that was unsuccessful [PNTC].

**25:8** Paul argued-in-(his)-defense,[a] "Neither against the law of-the Jews nor against the temple nor against Caesar have-I-committed- any - offense.[b]"

LEXICON—a. pres. mid. or pass. (deponent = act.) participle of ἀπολογέομαι (LN 33.435) (BDAG p. 117): 'to argue in one's (own) defense' [ESV, NRSV], 'to say/speak in one's (own) defense' [Bar, BECNT; CEV, NASB, NET], 'to declare in one's (own) defense' [AB], 'to defend oneself' [BDAG, LN; GW, TEV], 'to say to defend oneself' [NCV], 'to make a defense' [NIV], 'to answer for oneself' [KJV]. The clause 'Paul argued in his own defense' is also translated 'Paul's plea was' [CBC], 'Paul denied the charges' [NLT], 'Paul protested' [REB]. This verb means to speak on behalf of oneself or of others against accusations presumed to

be false [LN]. It means to speak in one's own defense against charges presumed to be false [BDAG].
  b. aorist act. indic. of ἁμαρτάνω (LN 88.289) (BDAG d.β. p. 150): 'to commit an offense' [AB, CBC; ESV, NASB, NET, NRSV, REB], 'to do something wrong' [Bar; NCV, NIV, TEV], 'to break...law or do something (against)' [CEV, GW], 'to sin' [BDAG, BECNT, LN], 'to be guilty of crime' [NLT], 'to offend' [KJV], 'to engage in wrongdoing' [LN]. This verb means to act contrary to the will and law of God [LN]. It means to commit a wrong [BDAG].

**25:9** But Festus, wishing to-do<sup>a</sup> (a)-favor<sup>b</sup> for-the Jews answering Paul said, "Are-you-willing<sup>c</sup> to-go-up to Jerusalem to-be-tried<sup>d</sup> before<sup>e</sup> me there?"

LEXICON—a. aorist mid. infin. of κατατίθημι (LN 90.62) (BDAG 2. p. 528): 'to do' [AB, BECNT; ESV, GW, KJV, NASB, NET, NIV, NRSV], 'to grant, to give' [BDAG], 'to gain, to obtain, to experience' [LN]. The phrase 'do a favor for' is also translated 'gain favor with' [TEV], 'curry favor with' [Bar], 'to ingratiate himself with' [CBC; REB], 'to please' [CEV, NCV, NLT]. This verb means to experience, with the implication of something having been bestowed upon [LN].
  b. χάρις (LN 88.66) (BDAG 3. p. 1079): 'a favor' [AB, BECNT; ESV, GW, KJV, NASB, NET, NIV, NRSV], 'favor' [Bar; TEV], '(a sign of) favor, gracious deed/gift, benefaction' [BDAG], 'kindness, graciousness, grace' [LN], not explicit [CBC; CEV, NCV, NLT, REB]. This noun denotes showing kindness to someone, with the implication of graciousness on the part of the one showing such kindness [LN]. It is the practical application of goodwill [BDAG].
  c. pres. act. indic. of θέλω (LN 25.1) (BDAG 1. p. 447): 'to be willing' [all translations except BECNT; ESV, NCV, NRSV], 'to wish' [BECNT, LN; ESV, NRSV], 'to want' [BDAG, LN; NCV], 'to desire' [BDAG, LN]. This verb means to desire to have or experience something [LN].
  d. aorist pass. infin. of κρίνω (LN 30.108) (BDAG 5.a.α. p. 568): 'to be tried' [Bar, BECNT; CEV, ESV, GW, NET, NRSV, TEV], 'to stand trial' [AB, CBC; NASB, NIV, NLT, REB], 'to be judged' [BDAG, LN; KJV]. This passive verb is also translated as active: '(for me) to judge (you)' [NCV]. This verb means to make a judgment based upon the correctness or value of something [LN]. It means to engage in a judicial process [BDAG].
  e. ἐπί with accusative object (LN 90.5): 'before' [all translations except CEV, GW, NCV], 'by' [LN; CEV]. 'Before me' is also translated 'with me as your judge' [GW], 'for me to judge you' [NCV]. This preposition marks the agent, with the added implication of effect upon the agent [LN].

QUESTION—What is meant by 'before me'?
  It means that Paul's case would be judged by Festus himself [AB, CBC, NAC, NICNT, PNTC, TH, TNTC; CEV, GW, NCV].

**25:10** And Paul said, "I-am standing[a] at Caesar's tribunal,[b] where I ought to-be-tried. I-have-done- no -wrong[c] (to-the) Jews as you yourself also know very-well.[d]

LEXICON—a. perf. act. participle of ἵστημι (LN 85.40) (BDAG C.2.b. p. 528): 'to be standing' [Bar, BECNT, CBC; ESV, GW, NASB, NCV, NET, NIV, REB, TEV], 'to stand' [KJV], 'to make stand, to be there' [LN], 'to stand (there), be (there)' [BDAG]. The phrase 'I am standing at Caesar's tribunal' is also translated 'I am on trial in the Emperor's court' [CEV], 'this is the official Roman court' [NLT], 'I am appealing to the court of Caesar/the emperor's tribunal' [AB; NRSV]. This verb means to cause to be in a place, with or without the accompanying feature of standing position [LN]. This verb means to be at a place, with the emphasis on being rather than standing [LN]. This perfect tense verb is also translated as present tense: 'I am standing' [Bar, BECNT; ESV, GW, NASB, NCV, NET. TEV], 'I am now standing' [CBC; NIV, REB], 'I stand' [KJV]. The perfect tense of this verb is often translated as a present tense. (Daniel B. Wallace, p. 579)

b. βῆμα (LN 7.63) (BDAG 3. p. 175): 'tribunal' [BDAG, BECNT, CBC; ESV, NASB, NRSV, REB], 'court' [AB, Bar; CEV, GW, NIV], 'judgment seat' [LN; KJV, NCV, NET], 'official court' [NLT], 'judgment court' [TEV], 'judgment place' [LN]. This noun denotes a raised platform mounted by steps and usually furnished with a seat, used by officials in addressing an assembly, often on judicial matters [LN]. It is a dais or platform that required steps to ascend [BDAG].

c. aorist act. indic. of ἀδικέω (LN 88.22) (BDAG 1.c. p. 20): 'to do wrong' [Bar, BDAG, BECNT; all versions except CEV, NLT, REB], 'to commit an offense' [AB, CBC; REB], 'to do something to harm someone' [CEV], 'to be guilty of harming someone' [NLT], 'to do what is wrong, to act unjustly' [LN]. This verb means to do that which is unjust or unrighteous [LN]. It means to act in an unjust manner [BDAG].

d. comparative of καλός (LN 78.21) (BDAG 7. p. 506): 'very well' [BDAG, LN; all translations except Bar; NCV, TEV], 'well' [Bar; TEV], 'certainly' [LN]. The phrase 'you know very well' is also translated 'you know this is true' [NCV]. This adverb describes a positive degree (and even more emphatic in the comparative form) with an implication of correctness [LN].

QUESTION—Why was Paul unwilling to go to Jerusalem to stand trial?

He reasoned that if Festus were willing to concede to the Jews the issue of moving the trial to Jerusalem, he might make other concessions as well [NAC, NICNT]. Paul also feared that powerful influences in Jerusalem would adversely affect the process of Roman justice [BECNT, EBC, NAC, NICNT]. Paul was eager to present the gospel in Rome, the seat of imperial power, and also hoped for Christian churches to be legally recognized and allowed to practice their religion [NICNT, PNTC].

QUESTION—Did Paul's statement 'I am standing at Caesar's tribunal' refer to his hearing before Festus, or was it an appeal to be tried before Caesar?
1. He was referring to the current hearing before Festus, which was already in progress [Bar, BECNT, CBC, NICNT, PNTC, TRT; CEV, ESV, GW, NASB, NCV, NET, NIV, NLT, REB, TEV]. This is indicated by the translation of this perfect participle as being a present, ongoing action; 'I am standing' [Bar, BECNT, CBC; ESV, GW, NASB, NCV, NET, NIV, REB, TEV], and also by the use of the word 'now' [CBC; NIV, REB].
2. He was appealing to the court of Caesar, to which he wanted to be sent [AB, TH; NRSV].

**25:11** If then[a] I-have-done-wrong[b] and have-committed anything worthy[c] of-death, I-do- not -refuse[d] to-die; but if there-is nothing[e] to-what these (men) are-accusing[f] me, no-one can hand- me -over[g] to-them. I-appeal-to[h] Caesar."

LEXICON—a. οὖν (LN 89.50): 'then' [Bar, BECNT; ESV, NASB, NET], 'now' [AB; NRSV], 'for' [KJV], 'so, therefore, consequently, accordingly, then, so then' [LN], not explicit [CBC; CEV, GW, NCV, NIV, NLT, REB, TEV]. This conjunction marks result, often implying the conclusion of a process of reasoning [LN].
   b. pres. act. indic. of ἀδικέω (LN 88.22) (BDAG 1.b. p. 20): 'to do wrong' [BDAG; NCV], 'to be a wrongdoer' [Bar; ESV, NASB], 'to be in the wrong' [NET, NRSV], 'to be guilty' [BECNT; GW], 'to commit an offence' [AB], 'to be an offender' [KJV], 'to break the law' [TEV], 'to do what is wrong' [LN], 'to act unjustly' [LN]. The phrases 'if I have done wrong' and '(I) have committed anything worthy of death' are conflated and translated 'if I am guilty of any crime' [CBC; REB], 'if I have done something deserving/worthy of death' [CEV, NLT], 'if I am guilty of doing anything deserving death' [NIV]. This verb means to do that which is unjust or unrighteous [LN]. It means to act in an unjust manner [BDAG].
   c. ἄξιος (LN 65.17) (BDAG 1.b. p. 93): 'worthy' [Bar, BDAG, LN; KJV, NASB, NLT], 'deserving' [AB; CEV, NIV], 'that deserves' [NET]. The phrase 'worthy of death' is also translated 'for which I deserve to die' [BECNT; ESV, NRSV], 'for which I deserve the death penalty' [GW, TEV], 'capital (crime)' [CBC; REB], 'the law says I must die' [NCV]. This adjective describes having a relatively high degree of comparable worth [BDAG, LN], value [BDAG], or merit [LN].
   d. pres. mid. or pass. (deponent = act.) indic. of παραιτέομαι (LN 34.35) (BDAG 2.b.β. p. 764): 'to refuse' [Bar; KJV, NASB, NIV, NLT], 'to try/seek/ask to escape' [AB, BECNT, CBC; CEV, ESV, NET, NRSV, REB, TEV], 'to ask to be saved' [NCV], 'to reject the idea' [GW], 'to reject, to refuse to accept' [LN]. This verb means to refuse to accept one into a particular association [LN].
   e. οὐδέν (LN 92.23) (BDAG 2.b.β. p. 735): 'nothing' [Bar, BDAG, BECNT, LN; ESV, NRSV], 'no substance' [CBC; REB], 'no truth'

[TEV], 'none (of these things)' [KJV], 'no one, none' [LN], 'meaningless, invalid' [BDAG]. The phrase 'if there is nothing to what these men are accusing me' is also translated 'if none of those things is true' [NASB], 'if these charges are not true' [NCV, NIV], 'if not one of their charges against me is true' [NET], 'since none of the charges they make against me is true' [AB], 'if their accusations are untrue' [GW], 'I am not guilty of any of these crimes' [CEV], 'if I am innocent' [NLT]. This noun is a negative reference to an entity, event, or state [LN].
f. pres. act. indic. of κατηγορέω (LN 33.427) (BDAG 1.a. p. 533): 'to accuse' [Bar, LN; KJV, NASB], 'to bring charges' [BDAG, LN], not explicit [CEV]. This verb is also translated as a noun: 'charges' [AB, BECNT, CBC; ESV, NCV, NET, NIV, NRSV, REB, TEV], 'accusations' [GW], not explicit [NLT]. This verb means to bring serious charges or accusations against someone, with the possible connotation of a legal or court context [LN]. It means to bring charges against someone in court [BDAG].
g. aorist mid. (deponent = act.) infin. of χαρίζομαι (LN 37.30) (BDAG 1. p. 1078): 'to hand someone over' [AB, LN; CEV, GW, NASB, NET, NIV, REB, TEV], 'to hand someone over as a sop' [CBC], 'to give someone up' [BECNT; ESV, NCV], 'to turn someone over' [NLT, NRSV], 'to make a present of' [Bar], 'to deliver someone unto' [KJV], 'to put into the control of someone [LN], 'to give graciously' [BDAG]. This verb means to hand someone over into the control of another person, without some reasonable cause [LN]. It means the giving of a man to those who wish him ill results in harm to him [BDAG].
h. pres. mid. indic. of ἐπικαλέω (LN 33.176) (BDAG 3. p. 373): 'to appeal to' [BDAG, LN; all translations except CEV, GW, NCV], 'to appeal a case' [GW], 'to call upon, to ask for help' [LN]. The phrase 'I appeal to Caesar' is also translated 'I want Caesar to hear my case' [NCV], 'I ask to be tried by the Emperor himself' [CEV]. This verb means to call upon someone to do something, normally implying an appeal for aid [LN]. It is a request put to a higher judicial authority for review of a decision in a lower court [BDAG].

QUESTION—What did it mean for Paul to 'appeal to' Caesar?

Only a Roman citizen could appeal for his case to be tried by Caesar, and then only in a capital case in which the penalty would be death [EBC, TH]. It was not the appeal of a verdict, but an appeal to be tried by Caesar himself as opposed to being tried in a provincial court [Bar, BECNT, EBC, NICNT, PNTC].

**25:12** Then Festus after-conferring[a] with the council[b] answered, "To Caesar you-have-appealed, to Caesar you-will-go."

LEXICON—a. aorist act. participle of συλλαλέω (LN 33.157) (BDAG p. 955): 'to confer' [all translations except Bar; CEV, GW, NCV], 'to speak with' [Bar], 'to talk over' [CEV], 'to talk about' [NCV], 'to discuss with' [BDAG;

GW], 'to talk with, to converse' [BDAG, LN], 'to discuss' [BDAG]. This verb means to converse with someone, including a clear implication as to reciprocal response [LN]. It means to exchange thoughts with [BDAG].
b. συμβούλιον (LN 11.86) (BDAG 4. P. 957): 'council' [AB, Bar, BDAG, BECNT, LN; ESV, KJV, NASB, NET, NIV, NRSV], 'members of (his) council' [CEV], 'advisers' [CBC; GW, NCV, NLT, REB, TEV]. This noun denotes an advisory council [LN]. It is an official deliberative assembly as a body [BDAG].

QUESTION—With what council did Festus discuss the case?

This was an advisory council of high officials that assisted the governor in his administrative duties [NAC, NICNT]. The decision was his alone, but he would ask their advice and opinion [Bar, NAC]. He consulted with them to determine if this case was *extra ordinem,* outside the normal provincial jurisdiction, a situation in which such an appeal would be legitimate [EBC]. This case was in fact *extra ordinem,* outside the normal guidelines of clear and established law [BECNT, EBC, NAC]. He sought their advice about how to report this unusual case to Caesar [PNTC].

QUESTION—Did Festus have the option of denying Paul's appeal to be tried by the emperor?

A Roman citizen had the right to request a trial by the emperor himself, and a local provincial governor such as Felix could not refuse it [EBC, NAC, NICNT, TNTC], at least in an *extra ordinem* case such as this where the charge being brought did not fit clearly within the boundaries of established law [NAC].

**DISCOURSE UNIT—25:13–26:32** [BECNT, TNTC; GW]. The topic is King Agrippa meets Paul [GW], Paul appears before Festus and Agrippa [TNTC], before Agrippa and Bernice [BECNT].

**DISCOURSE UNIT—25:13–27** [AB, CBC; CEV, ESV, NCV, TEV]. The topic is Paul before King Agrippa [NCV], Paul speaks to Agrippa and Bernice [CEV], Paul before Agrippa and Bernice [ESV, TEV], King Agrippa's visit to Festus [AB], the state visit of Herod Agrippa II and Bernice [CBC].

**DISCOURSE UNIT—25:13–22** [EBC, NAC, NICNT, PNTC; NET, NIV, NRSV]. The topic is Festus asks King Agrippa for advice [NET], Festus consults Agrippa [PNTC], Festus consults King Agrippa [NIV, NRSV], Festus consults with Herod Agrippa II [EBC], Festus' conversation with Agrippa [NAC], Agrippa II and Bernice visit Festus [NICNT].

**25:13** Now when- some days -passed Agrippa the king[a] and Bernice arrived at Caesarea to-greet[b] Festus.

LEXICON—a. βασιλεύς (LN 37.67) (BDAG 1. p. 169): 'king' [BDAG, LN; all translations]. This noun denotes one who has absolute authority within a particular area and is able to convey this power and authority to a successor (though in NT times, certain kings ruled only with the approval of Roman authorities and had no power to pass on their prerogatives)

[LN]. It denotes one who rules as possessor of the highest office in a political realm [BDAG].
b. aorist mid. (deponent = act.) participle of ἀσπάζομαι (LN 34.55) (BDAG 1.b. p. 144): 'to greet' [Bar, BDAG; ESV], 'to visit' [AB; CEV, NCV], 'to welcome' [BDAG, BECNT, LN; GW, NRSV], 'to pay respects' [NASB, NET, NIV, NLT], 'to pay a visit of welcome' [TEV], 'to salute' [KJV], 'to accept gladly' [LN]. This participle is also translated 'on a courtesy visit' [CBC; REB]. This verb means to welcome something or someone, with focus upon the initial greeting [LN]. It means to engage in hospitable recognition of another [BDAG].

QUESTION—Over what area was Agrippa the king?
During the years of his reign he ruled over various regions to the north and east of Judea [AB, CBC, BECNT, NICNT, PNTC, TH, TNTC]. He also was authorized to appoint the high priest in Jerusalem [BECNT, CBC, NAC, NICNT, PNTC, TH, TNTC], and had recently deposed the previous high priest, Ananias [CBC].

QUESTION—Who were Agrippa and Bernice?
Herod Agrippa II and Bernice were the son and daughter of Herod Agrippa I [AB, BECNT, EBC, NAC, NICNT, PNTC], and great-grandchildren of Herod the Great [AB, BECNT, EBC, NAC]. Agrippa was brought up in the court of Claudius Caesar, as was his father Agrippa I before him, and was a favorite of Claudius. He was also considered by Rome to be an expert on the Jewish religion [EBC]. Bernice had been married to her uncle Herod of Chalcis [AB, BECNT, EBC, NAC, NICNT, PNTC, TH, TNTC], and at his death her brother Herod Agrippa II was appointed king in his uncle's place [Bar, CBC, EBC, NAC, NICNT]. Bernice and Agrippa then lived together [AB, NICNT, PNTC, TNTC], and it was believed by many that their relationship was incestuous [BECNT, EBC, NAC, PNTC, TNTC]. Their sister Drusilla had been the wife of Felix, who was the governor prior to Festus [AB, BECNT, CBC, NICNT, PNTC]. Herod Agrippa II was the last of the Herod dynasty [EBC, PNTC].

**25:14** And as they-passed many days there, Festus placed[a] the-case against Paul to-the king, saying "There-is a-certain man left (a)-prisoner[b] by Felix, **25:15** about whom, when I-was in Jerusalem, the chief-priests and the elders of-the Jews were-seeking (a)-sentence-of-condemnation[c] against him.

LEXICON—a. aorist mid. indic. of ἀνατίθημι (LN 33.151) (BDAG 2. p. 74): 'to lay (a case)' [AB, BECNT, CBC; ESV, NASB, NRSV], 'to refer (a case)' [Bar], 'to declare (a case)' [BDAG; KJV], 'to explain (a case)' [LN; NET], 'to discuss (a case)' [NIV, NLT], 'to tell about (a case)' [GW, NCV], 'to raise (a case)' [REB], 'to tell about (charges)' [CEV], 'to explain (a situation)' [TEV], 'to make clear' [LN], 'to communicate, to refer' [BDAG]. This verb means to explain something, presumably by putting forward additional or different information [LN]. It means to lay something before someone for consideration [BDAG].

b. δέσμιος (LN 37.117) (BDAG p. 219): 'prisoner' [AB, Bar, BDAG, BECNT, LN; ESV, NASB, NET, NIV, NLT, TEV]. This noun is also translated as a phrase: 'in prison' [GW, NCV, NRSV], 'in custody' [CBC; REB], 'in jail' [CEV], 'in bonds' [KJV]. This noun denotes a person who is under custody in prison [LN].

c. καταδίκη (LN 56.31) (BDAG p. 516): 'sentence of condemnation' [BDAG; ESV, NASB, NET], 'condemnation' [BDAG, CBC, LN; REB], 'sentence' [Bar; NRSV], 'judgment' [BECNT; KJV], 'conviction, guilty verdict' [BDAG]. This noun is also translated as a verb phrase: 'that he might be sentenced' [AB], 'that he be condemned' [NIV], '(asked me) to find him guilty' [CEV], '(asked me) to condemn him' [GW, NLT, TEV], 'to sentence him to death' [NCV]. This noun denotes the action of judging someone as definitely guilty and thus subject to punishment [LN].

**25:16** I-answered them that it-is not (the) Roman custom[a] to-hand-over[b] any man before the accused meets the accusers face-to-face and has opportunity[c] for-defense[d] concerning the accusation.[e]

LEXICON—a. ἔθος (LN 41.25) (BDAG p. 277): 'custom' [Bar, BECNT, LN; CEV, ESV, NASB, NET, NIV, NRSV], 'practice' [CBC; REB], 'way of doing things' [GW], 'manner' [KJV], 'habit' [BDAG, LN; TEV], 'usage' [BDAG], not explicit [NCV, NLT]. The phrase 'it is not the Roman custom' is also translated 'it is not customary for Romans' [AB]. This noun denotes a pattern of behavior more or less fixed by tradition and generally sanctioned by the society [LN]. It denotes a usual or customary manner of behavior [BDAG].

b. pres. mid. or pass. (deponent = act.) infin. of χαρίζομαι (LN 37.30) (BDAG 1. p. 1078): 'to hand over' [AB, Bar, CBC, LN; CEV, NASB, NCV, NET, NIV, NRSV, REB, TEV], 'to give (someone) up' [BECNT; ESV], 'to be sentenced as a favor' [GW], 'to deliver someone to die' [KJV], 'to convict someone without a trial' [NLT], 'to put into the control of someone' [LN]. This verb means to hand someone over into the control of another person, without some reasonable cause [LN].

c. τόπος (LN 71.6) (BDAG 4. p. 1012): 'opportunity' [AB, Bar, BDAG, BECNT, CBC, LN; ESV, NASB, NET, NIV, NLT, NRSV, REB], 'chance' [BDAG, LN; CEV, GW, TEV], 'license' [KJV], 'possibility' [BDAG, LN]. The phrase 'has opportunity' is also translated 'he has been allowed' [NCV]. This noun denotes the possibility of some occasion or opportunity [LN]. It denotes a favorable circumstance for doing something [BDAG].

d. ἀπολογία (LN 33.435) (BDAG 2.a. p. 117): 'defense' [Bar, BDAG, BECNT; ESV, NASB, NET, NRSV], 'defending oneself' [LN]. This noun is also translated as a verb: 'to defend (himself)' [AB; CEV, GW, NCV, NIV, NLT, REB], 'to answer for himself' [KJV], 'to answer the charge' [CBC; REB]. This noun denotes the action of speaking on behalf

of oneself or of others against accusations presumed to be false [LN]. It is the act of making a defense [BDAG].
e. ἔγκλημα (LN 56.6) (BDAG 1. p. 274): 'accusation' [BDAG, LN; GW, NET, TEV], 'charge' [AB, Bar, BDAG, BECNT, CBC; CEV, ESV, NASB, NCV, NIV, NRSV, REB], 'crime laid against someone' [KJV], 'case, indictment' [LN], not explicit [NLT]. This noun denotes a formal indictment or accusation brought against someone [LN]. It denotes an indictment or charge brought against someone through judicial proceedings [BDAG].

**25:17** So when-they-came-together here I-made no delay<sup>a</sup> taking-a-seat the next-(day) at the tribunal, I-ordered the man to-be-brought; **25:18** about whom when-(his)-accusers<sup>b</sup> stood-up<sup>c</sup> they-brought no charge<sup>d</sup> of-(such)-evils<sup>e</sup> as-I expected,<sup>f</sup>

TEXT—Manuscripts reading πονηρῶν 'evils' are given a C rating by GNT to indicate that choosing it over variant texts was difficult. Only KJV omits this word.

LEXICON—a. ἀναβολή (LN 67.127) (BDAG p. 59): 'delay' [AB, Bar, BECNT; ESV, KJV, NASB], 'postponement' [BDAG, LN]. The phrase 'I made no delay' is also translated 'I did not delay' [NIV, NLT], 'I lost no time' [CBC; NRSV, REB, TEV], 'I wasted no time' [CEV], 'I did not waste time' [NCV], 'I did not postpone' [NET], 'immediately' [GW]. This noun denotes the act of extending a period of time by postponing or putting off an event [LN].
b. κατήγορος (LN 33.429) (BDAG p. 533): 'accuser' [BDAG, LN; all translations except CEV, NCV, NLT, TEV], 'opponents' [TEV], not explicit [CEV, NCV, NLT]. This noun denotes one who brings an accusation [LN].
c. aorist pass. participle of ἵστημι (LN 85.40): 'to stand up' [BECNT; ESV, GW, KJV, NASB, NCV, NET, NRSV, TEV], 'to stand' [Bar], 'to stand there' [AB], 'to rise to speak' [CBC; REB], 'to get up to speak' [NIV], 'to stand up to make a charge' [CEV], 'to be made to stand, to be there' [LN], not explicit [NLT]. This verb means to cause to be in a place, with or without the accompanying feature of standing position [LN].
d. αἰτία (LN 56.4) (BDAG 3.β. p. 31): 'charge' [AB, Bar, BECNT, CBC; ESV, NASB, REB], 'accusation' [BDAG; KJV, NLT], 'case, basis for an accusation' [LN]. The phrase 'they brought no charge' is also translated 'they did not charge him' [NET, NIV, NRSV], 'they did not accuse him' [CEV, GW, TEV], 'they accused him, but not (of any serious crime)' [NCV]. This noun denotes the basis of or grounds for an accusation in court [LN]. It denotes the charges against someone [BDAG].
e. πονηρός (LN 88.110) (BDAG 1.a.β. p. 851): 'evil' [BDAG, BECNT, LN; ESV], 'evil thing' [Bar], 'evil deed' [NET], 'evil crime' [TEV], 'crime' [AB; CEV, GW, NASB, NIV, NLT, NRSV], 'serious crime' [NCV], 'immoral' [LN], 'wicked' [BDAG, LN], 'thing' [KJV], not

explicit [CBC; REB]. This adjective describes being morally corrupt and evil [LN]. It describes being morally or socially worthless [BDAG].
  f. imperf. act. indic. of ὑπονοέω (LN 31.32) (BDAG p. 1040): 'to expect' [AB, CBC; GW, NASB, NIV, NLT, NRSV, REB], 'to suppose' [BDAG, BECNT; ESV, KJV], 'to suspect' [Bar, BDAG, LN; NET], 'to think' [CEV, NCV, TEV], 'to imagine, to conjecture' [LN]. This verb means to have an opinion based on scant evidence, often with the implication of regarding a false opinion as true [LN]. It means to form an opinion or conjecture on the basis of slight evidence [BDAG].

QUESTION—Does 'no charge…as I expected' mean that Festus was expecting that they would bring charges against Paul of a serious nature, but did not, or that he expected that they would not bring serious charges?

His expectation was that they would bring charges of a serious nature, which however did not happen [AB, Bar, BECNT, CBC, EBC, NAC, NICNT, TH, TRT; all versions].

**25:19** **but they-had certain disputes<sup>a</sup> with him about their-own religion<sup>b</sup> and about a-certain dead-man Jesus whom Paul asserted<sup>c</sup> to-be-alive.**

LEXICON—a. ζήτημα (LN 33.440) (BDAG p. 428): 'dispute' [AB, Bar, LN], 'point of dispute' [BECNT; ESV, NIV], 'point of disagreement' [CBC; NASB, NET, NRSV, REB], 'argument' [BDAG; TEV], 'question' [KJV], 'controversial question, issue' [BDAG], not explicit [NLT]. The phrase 'they had certain disputes' is also translated 'they were disputing' [GW], 'they argued' [CEV], 'the things they said' [NCV]. This noun denotes the forceful expression of differences of opinion without necessarily having a presumed goal of seeking a solution [LN].
  b. δεισιδαιμονία (LN 53.2) (BDAG 2. p. 216): 'religion' [BDAG, LN; all translations except BECNT, CEV, KJV], 'religious belief' [BECNT], 'beliefs' [CEV], ''superstition' [KJV]. This noun denotes a set of beliefs concerning deity, with the implication of corresponding behavior [LN]. It denotes a system of cultic belief or practice [BDAG].
  c. imperf. act. indic. of φάσκω (LN 33.218) (BDAG p. 1050): 'to assert' [AB, BDAG, BECNT, LN; ESV, NASB, NRSV], 'to allege' [Bar, CBC; REB], 'to claim' [BDAG; GW, NET, NIV, TEV], 'to say' [BDAG; CEV, NCV], 'to affirm' [KJV], 'to insist' [NLT], 'to declare' [LN]. This verb means to speak about something with certainty [LN]. It means to state something with confidence [BDAG].

QUESTION—Does δεισιδαιμονία mean 'religion' or 'superstition'?

It means 'religion' [BECNT, NICNT, PNTC, TH]. Since Festus is speaking to a man of Jewish background, he would not use a term that would be considered derogatory [BDAG, PNTC, TH]. It is translated 'superstition' by KJV; however, this may have had a different connotation at the time the KJV was translated four centuries ago.

**25:20** And I being-perplexed[a] about (the)-investigation[b] of-these-things I-asked if he-were-willing[c] to-go to Jerusalem and be-tried[d] there regarding these-things.

LEXICON—a. pres. mid. participle of ἀπορέω (LN 32.9) (BDAG p. 119): 'to be at a loss' [AB, Bar, BDAG, BECNT, LN; ESV, NASB, NET, NIV, NLT, NRSV], 'to be out of one's depth' [CBC; REB], 'to be undecided' [TEV], 'to be uncertain' [BDAG, LN], 'to doubt' [KJV], 'to be in doubt' [BDAG, LN]. The phrase 'being perplexed' is also translated 'I did not know how' [CEV], 'not knowing how' [NCV], 'left me puzzled' [GW]. This verb means to be in perplexity, with the implication of serious anxiety [LN]. It means to be in a confused state of mind [BDAG].

b. ζήτησις (LN 27.34) (BDAG p. 428): 'investigation' [BDAG], 'inquiry' [Bar], 'discussion' [CBC; REB], 'debate' [GW], 'question' [KJV], 'to try to learn, to search, to try to find out, to seek information' [LN]. The phrase 'about the investigation' is also translated 'how to investigate' [AB, BECNT; ESV, NASB, NIV, NLT, NRSV], 'how I could investigate' [NET], 'how I could get information' [TEV], 'how to find out about' [NCV], 'how to find out the truth' [CEV]. This noun denotes the attempt to learn something by careful investigation or searching [LN]. It denotes a search for information [BDAG].

c. pres. mid. or pass. (deponent = act.) opt. of βούλομαι (LN 25.3) (BDAG 2.a.γ. p. 182): 'to be willing' [Bar, CBC; CEV, NASB, NET, NIV, NLT, REB, TEV], 'to will' [BDAG, LN], 'to wish' [BECNT; NRSV], 'to want' [LN; ESV, NCV], 'to desire' [LN], 'to intend, to plan' [BDAG]. The phrase 'if he were willing to go' is also translated 'if/whether he would go' [AB; KJV], 'if he would like to go' [GW]. This verb means to desire to have or experience something, with the implication of some reasoned planning or will to accomplish the goal [LN]. It means to plan on a course of action [BDAG].

d. pres. pass. indic. of κρίνω (LN 30.108) (BDAG 5.a.α. p. 568): 'to be tried' [Bar, BECNT; ESV, NET, NRSV, TEV], 'to be judged' [BDAG, LN; KJV, NCV], 'to stand trial' [AB, CBC; NASB, NIV, NLT, REB], 'to be put on trial' [CEV], 'to have one's case heard' [GW], 'to be evaluated' [LN]. This verb means to make a judgment based upon the correctness or value of something [LN]. It means to engage in a judicial process [BDAG].

**25:21** But Paul appealed[a] to-be-kept-in-custody[b] for the decision[c] of-the emperor,[d] I-ordered him to-be-held[e] until I-send[f] him to Caesar." **25:22** And Agrippa (said) to Festus, "I- myself -would-like[g] to-hear the man." "Tomorrow," he-said, "you-will-hear him."

LEXICON—a. aorist mid. participle of ἐπικαλέω (LN 33.176) (BDAG 3. p. 373): 'to appeal' [Bar, BDAG, BECNT, CBC, LN; ESV, KJV, NASB, NET, NRSV, REB, TEV], 'to appeal one's case' [GW], 'to appeal to have one's case decided' [NLT], 'to appeal to' [LN], 'to make an appeal'

[NIV], 'to demand' [AB], 'to ask' [CEV, NLT], 'to call upon, to ask for help' [LN]. This verb means to call upon someone to do something, normally implying an appeal for aid [LN]. It is a request put to a higher judicial authority for review of a decision in a lower court [BDAG].

b. aorist pass. inf. of τηρέω (LN 13.32) (BDAG 2.a. p. 1002): 'to be kept in custody' [AB, BECNT; ESV, NET, NRSV], 'to be kept in jail' [CEV], 'to be kept under guard' [TEV], 'to be kept in Caesarea' [NCV], 'to be held in custody' [NASB], 'to be held in prison' [GW], 'to be held over' [NIV], 'to be held' [BDAG], 'to be kept' [Bar, BDAG, LN], 'to be remanded in custody' [CBC; REB], 'to be reserved' [KJV], 'to be retained' [LN], not explicit [NLT]. This verb means to cause a state to continue [LN]. This verb means to cause a state, condition, or activity to continue [BDAG].

c. διάγνωσις (LN 56.21) (BDAG p. 227): 'decision' [Bar, BDAG, BECNT, CBC; ESV, NASB, NCV, NET, NIV, NRSV, REB], 'verdict' [AB, LN], 'hearing' [KJV]. This noun is also translated as a verb: 'to decide (his case)' [CEV, GW, TEV], 'to (have his case) be decided' [NLT]. This noun denotes a judgment made on legal matters, a verdict arrived at after thorough examination [LN]. It is a judicial inquiry or investigation that culminates in a decision [BDAG].

d. σεβαστός (LN 37.75) (BDAG p. 917): 'the Emperor/emperor' [AB, Bar, BECNT, LN; CEV, ESV, NASB, NCV, NIV, NIV, TEV], 'His Imperial Majesty' [CBC; NRSV, REB], 'His Majesty the Emperor' [BDAG; GW, NET], 'Augustus' [KJV]. This noun is a title for the Roman Emperor and denoting his semi-divine status [LN]. It is a translation of the Latin Augustus and is a designation of the Roman emperor [BDAG].

e. pres. pass. infin. of τηρέω (see item b. above): 'to be kept in custody' [AB; NASB], 'to be held in custody' [NLT], 'to be kept under guard' [NET, TEV], 'to be held' [BECNT; ESV, NCV, NIV, NRSV], 'to be held in prison' [GW], 'to be kept' [Bar; CEV, KJV], 'to be detained' [CBC; REB].

f. aorist act. subj. of ἀναπέμπω (LN 15.71) (BDAG 2. p. 70): 'to send' [BDAG; all translations except Bar], 'to send up' [Bar, LN], 'to send on' [LN]. This verb means to send on or up to some higher or appropriate authority [LN]. It means to send on to someone in authority [BDAG].

g. imperf. mid. or pass. (deponent = act.) indic. of βούλομαι (LN 25.3) (BDAG 1. p. 182): 'to desire, to want' [BDAG, LN], 'to wish' [BDAG], 'to will' [LN]. This imperfect form is also translated 'I would like' [AB; all versions except KJV, REB], 'I should like' [BECNT], 'I should rather like' [CBC; REB], 'I could wish' [Bar], 'I would' [KJV]. This verb means to desire to have or experience something, with the implication of some reasoned planning or will to accomplish the goal [LN]. It means to desire to have or experience something, with the implication of planning accordingly [BDAG].

QUESTION—What does the title ὁ σεβαστός 'emperor' mean?
It is the equivalent of the Latin title Augustus and refers to the Roman emperor [BDAG, BECNT, CBC, EBC, PNTC]. It is a title of majesty [PNTC] and denotes one who is exalted above other humans [EBC], one who is august or worthy of reverence [BECNT].

**DISCOURSE UNIT—25:23–26:32** [EBC, PNTC; NIV, NLT]. The topic is Paul before Agrippa [NIV], Paul speaks to Agrippa [NLT], appearing before Agrippa [PNTC], Paul's defense before Herod Agrippa [EBC].

**DISCOURSE UNIT—25:23–27** [NAC, NICNT, PNTC; NASB, NET, NRSV]. The topic is Paul before King Agrippa and Bernice [NET], Paul before Agrippa [NASB], Paul appears before Agrippa [NICNT], Paul brought before Agrippa [NRSV], Paul's address before Agrippa: the setting [NAC], Festus initiates the proceedings [PNTC].

**25:23** So the next-day Agrippa and Bernice came with much pomp[a] and came-into the audience-hall[b] with the commanders[c] and men of prominence[d] of-the city and when- Festus -commanded Paul was-brought.
- LEXICON—a. φαντασία (LN 87.57) (BDAG p. 1049): 'pomp' [Bar, BDAG, BECNT; ESV, KJV, NASB, NET, NIV, NLT, NRSV], 'show' [NCV], 'pageantry' [BDAG], 'pomp and ceremony' [LN; TEV], 'pompous display' [LN]. The phrase 'with much pomp' is also translated 'with pomp and ceremony' [AB], 'with a lot of fanfare' [GW], 'in full state' [CBC; REB], 'made a big show' [CEV]. This noun denotes a pompous ceremony, implying a cheap display of high status [LN].
- b. ἀκροατήριον (LN 7.13) (BDAG p. 39): 'audience hall' [BDAG, BECNT, LN; ESV, NET, NRSV, TEV], 'audience chamber' [AB, Bar, CBC; REB], 'audience room' [NIV], 'auditorium' [LN; GW, NASB, NLT], 'meeting room' [CEV], 'judgment room' [NCV], 'place of hearing' [KJV]. This noun denotes a relatively large building normally used for legal hearings, though possibly also employed for more general purposes [LN]. It is the audience hall of the procurator, in which hearings were held and justice was privately dispensed [BDAG].
- c. χιλίαρχος (LN 55.15) (BDAG p. 1084): 'commander' [NASB], 'commanding officer' [LN], 'military tribune' [BDAG, BECNT; ESV, NRSV], 'tribune' [AB, Bar], 'high ranking officer' [CBC; REB], 'high ranking army/military officer' [CEV, NIV], 'military officer' [NET, NLT], 'Roman army officer' [GW], 'army leader' [NCV], 'military chief' [TEV], 'chief captain' [KJV], 'general, chiliarch' [LN]. This noun denotes a military officer, normally in command of a thousand soldiers [LN]. It is the commander of a cohort, usually about 600 men, and roughly equivalent to a major or colonel [BDAG].
- d. ἐξοχή (LN 87.19) (BDAG p. 354): 'prominence' [BDAG, LN], 'high position, high rank' [LN]. The phrase 'men of prominence' is also translated 'prominent men' [BECNT; ESV, NASB, NET, NIV, NLT,

NRSV], 'prominent citizens' [CBC; REB], 'leading men' [AB, Bar; TEV], 'leading citizens' [CEV], 'important men' [NCV], 'most important men' [GW], 'principal men' [KJV]. This adjective describes a position of high status [LN]. It describes having special status [BDAG].

QUESTION—Who were these commanders?

There were five military tribunes in Caesarea, each commanding a cohort of up to 1,000 men [BECNT, NAC, NICNT, PNTC].

**25:24** **And Festus said, "King Agrippa and all men present with-us, you-see this-man about whom the-whole[a] people[b] of-the Jews petitioned[c] me in Jerusalem and here shouting[d] (that) he ought[e] not live any-longer.**

LEXICON—a. ἅπας (LN 59.23) (BDAG 1. p. 98): 'whole' [AB, Bar, BDAG, BECNT, CBC, LN; ESV, NIV, NRSV, REB], 'all' [BDAG, LN; GW, KJV, NASB, NCV, NLT, TEV], 'entire' [NET], 'every, each' [LN]. The phrase 'the whole people of the Jews' is also translated 'every Jew' [CEV]. This noun denotes the totality of any object, mass, collective, or extension [LN]. It is the totality of a mass or object [BDAG].

b. πλῆθος (LN 59.9) (BDAG 2.b.γ. p. 825): 'people' [Bar; ESV, NASB, NCV, TEV], 'crowd' [AB], 'multitude' [BECNT; KJV], 'body (of the Jews)' [CBC; REB], 'population' [NET], 'community' [NIV, NRSV], 'large number of, a multitude of' [BDAG, LN], not explicit [CEV, GW, NLT]. This noun denotes a large number of countable objects or events, with the probable implication of some type of grouping [LN]. It denotes a large amount [BDAG].

c. aorist act. indic. of ἐντυγχάνω (LN 33.169) (BDAG 1.a. p. 341): 'to petition' [Bar, BECNT, LN; ESV, NET, NIV, NRSV], 'to talk to' [GW], 'to deal with' [KJV], 'to appeal to' [BDAG, LN; NASB], 'to complain' [NCV], 'to bring complaints' [TEV], 'to plead, to beg' [LN], 'to approach someone' [BDAG]. The phrase 'petitioned me...shouting' is also translated 'came to me...crying' [AB], 'has come to me, demanding' [CEV], 'approached me...insisting' [CBC; REB], 'demanded' [NLT]. This verb means to ask for something with urgency and intensity [LN]. It means to make an earnest request through contact with the person approached [BDAG].

d. pres. act. participle of βοάω (LN 33.81) (BDAG 1.a. p. 180): 'to shout' [BDAG, BECNT, LN; ESV, GW, NCV, NET, NIV, NRSV], 'to shout out' [Bar], 'to declare loudly' [NASB], 'to insist loudly' [CBC; REB], 'to scream' [LN; TEV], 'to cry' [AB, LN; KJV], 'to cry out' [BDAG, LN], 'to call' [BDAG], not explicit [CEV, NLT]. This verb means to cry or shout with unusually loud volume [LN]. This verb means to use one's voice at high volume [BDAG].

e. pres. act. infin. of δεῖ (LN 71.21): 'ought' [AB, Bar, BECNT, LN; ESV, KJV, NASB, NET, NIV, NRSV], 'must (not) be allowed' [GW], 'to have (no) right' [CBC; REB], 'should' [LN; NCV, TEV]. The phrase 'he ought not to live any longer' is also translated 'for him to be put to death'

[CEV], 'whose death is demanded' [NLT]. This verb speaks of something which should be done as the result of compulsion, whether internal (as a matter of duty) or external (law, custom, and circumstances) [LN].

QUESTION—Is θεωρεῖτε an indicative verb, 'you see', or an imperative 'behold'?

1. It is indicative: 'you see' [AB, Bar, BECNT, CBC, EBC, NICNT; ESV, GW, KJV, NASB, NCV, NET, NIV, NRSV, REB, TEV].
2. It is imperative: 'see' [CEV].

QUESTION—What is meant or implied by 'the whole people of the Jews'?
Festus assumes that the Sanhedrin speaks for all the nation [EBC, TNTC]. It is not the Jewish leaders only who are accusing Paul, but all the Jews [TH].

**25:25** But I found[a] him to-have-done nothing worthy[b] of-death,[c] and when-he himself -appealed-to[d] the emperor I-decided to-send-(him).

LEXICON—a. aorist mid. indic. of καταλαμβάνω (LN 27.10) (BDAG 4.a. p. 520): 'to find' [BDAG, BECNT, LN; CEV, ESV, KJV, NASB, NET, NIV, NRSV, TEV], 'to see' [Bar], 'to think' [GW], 'to judge' [NCV], 'to learn about, to find out about, to discover' [LN], 'understand, grasp' [BDAG]. The phrase 'I found him' is also translated 'it became clear to me that he' [AB, CBC], 'it was clear to me that he' [REB], 'in my opinion he' [NLT]. This verb means to acquire definite information, with the possible implication of effort [LN]. It means to process information, to learn about something through a process of inquiry [BDAG].

b. ἄξιος (LN 65.17) (BDAG 1.b. p. 93): 'worthy' [Bar, BDAG, LN; KJV, NASB], 'deserving' [BDAG, BECNT; CEV, ESV, NIV, NLT, NRSV]. The phrase 'worthy of' is also translate 'that deserved' [AB; NET], 'to deserve' [GW], 'for which he deserved' [TEV], not explicit [CBC; CEV, REB]. This adjective describes having a relatively high degree of comparable merit or worth [LN]. It describes having a relatively high degree of comparable worth or value [BDAG].

c. θάνατος (LN 23.99) (BDAG 1.b.α. p. 443): 'death' [Bar, BDAG, BECNT, LN; CEV, ESV, KJV, NASB, NET, NIV, NLT, NRSV], 'the death sentence' [AB; TEV], 'the death penalty' [GW]. The phrase 'to have done nothing worthy of death' is also translated 'he had committed no capital crime' [CBC; REB], 'no reason to order his death' [NCV]. This noun denotes the process of dying [LN]. It means the termination of physical life [BDAG].

d. aorist mid. participle of ἐπικαλέω (LN 33.176) (BDAG 3. p. 373): 'to appeal to' [AB, Bar, BDAG, BECNT, CBC, LN; ESV, KJV, NASB, NET, NRSV, REB], 'to make an appeal' [GW, NIV, TEV], 'to appeal one's case' [NLT], 'to ask to be judged by' [CEV, NCV], 'to call upon, to ask for help' [LN]. This verb means to call upon someone to do something, normally implying an appeal for aid [LN]. It is a request put to a higher judicial authority for review of a decision in a lower court [BDAG].

**25:26** About him I-do- not -have anything-definite[a] to-write to (my) lord,[b] so I-brought him before you and especially[c] to you, King Agrippa, so-that (after) the inquiry[d] has-happened I-would-have[e] something to-write;

LEXICON—a. ἀσφαλής (LN 31.42) (BDAG 2. p.147): 'definite' [Bar, BDAG, BECNT, CBC; ESV, NASB, NCV, NET, NIV, NRSV, REB, TEV], 'certain' [AB, BDAG; KJV], 'reliable' [GW], 'worthy of being believed, certainly true, completely believable' [LN], not explicit [CEV]. The phrase 'I do not have anything definite to write' is also translated 'but what shall I write?' [NLT]. This adjective describes something as being certain and thus completely believable [LN]. It describes expression that ensures certainty about something [BDAG].

  b. κύριος (LN 37.51) (BDAG 2.b.β. p. 578): 'lord' [AB, BDAG, BECNT, LN; ESV, KJV, NASB, NET], 'emperor' [Bar; CEV, GW, NCV, NLT, TEV], 'his majesty' [NIV], 'sovereign' [CBC; NRSV, REB], 'ruler' [LN], 'master' [BDAG, LN]. This noun denotes one who rules or exercises authority over others [LN]. It is someone who is in a position of authority [BDAG].

  c. μάλιστα (LN 78.7) (BDAG 1. p. 613): 'especially' [BDAG, LN; all translations except CBC; KJV, REB], 'specially' [KJV], 'particularly' [BDAG, CBC, LN; REB], 'most of all, above all' [BDAG], 'very much, exceptionally' [LN]. This adverb describes a very high point on a scale of extent [LN]. It describes an unusual degree [BDAG].

  d. ἀνάκρισις (LN 56.12) (BDAG p. 66): 'preliminary inquiry' [AB, CBC; REB], 'preliminary hearing' [BDAG; NET], 'investigation' [BDAG; NASB, NIV], 'examination' [Bar; KJV], 'hearing' [BDAG], 'investigation in court, hearing of a case, interrogation, questioning' [LN]. The phrase 'after the inquiry has happened' is also translated 'after we have examined him' [BECNT; ESV, NLT, NRSV], 'after he is cross-examined' [GW], 'after we have talked about his case' [CEV], 'after investigating his case' [TEV], 'I hope you can question him' [NCV]. This noun denotes a judicial inquiry [LN]. It is a judicial hearing [BDAG].

  e. aorist act. subj. of ἔχω (LN 57.1) (BDAG 5. p. 421): 'to have' [BDAG, LN; all translations except Bar; NCV], 'to get' [Bar], 'to possess' [LN], 'can, be able' [BDAG]. The phrase 'I would have something' is also translated 'you can…give me something' [NCV]. This verb means to have or possess objects or property (in the technical sense of having control over the use of such objects) [LN]. It means to be in a position to do something [BDAG].

QUESTION—What, if anything, is implied by the use of κύριος 'lord' to describe Caesar?

  There was at least some implication of divinity in the use of the title [EBC, NAC, NICNT, TRT], particularly in the eastern empire and in the reigns of Nero and Domitian [EBC, NAC]. Conflicts between Christians and Rome would eventually arise out of the fact that Christians would say that Jesus is Lord [TH]. It conveys the idea of majesty [EBC]. Here it appears in its normal secular use [BECNT].

**25:27** for it-seems[a] unreasonable[b] to-me in-sending (a)-prisoner not to-indicate[c] also (the) charges against him."
LEXICON—a. pres. act. indic. of δοκέω (LN 31.29) (BDAG 2.b.β. p. 255): 'to seem' [AB, Bar, BDAG, BECNT, CBC; ESV, KJV, NASB, NET, NRSV, REB, TEV], 'to be recognized as' [BDAG], 'to suppose, to presume, to assume, to imagine, to believe, to think' [LN], not explicit [CEV, NLT]. The phrase 'it seems to me' is also translated 'I find it' [GW], 'I think it' [NCV, NIV]. This verb means to regard something as presumably true, but without particular certainty [LN]. It means to appear to one's understanding [BDAG].
- b. ἄλογος (LN 89.19) (BDAG 2. p. 48): 'unreasonable' [BECNT, LN; ESV, KJV, NET, NIV, NRSV, TEV], 'pointless' [AB], 'nonsense' [Bar], '(there is/it makes) no sense' [CBC; CEV, NLT, REB], 'ridiculous' [GW], 'absurd' [LN; NASB], 'foolish' [NCV], 'without basis' [LN], 'contrary to reason' [BDAG]. This adjective describes not providing a reason or cause, in view of something being contrary to reason [LN]. It describes the lack of a basis or cause [BDAG].
- c. aorist act. infin. of σημαίνω (LN 33.153) (BDAG 1. p. 920): 'to indicate' [BECNT, CBC; ESV, NASB, NRSV, REB], 'to indicate clearly' [LN; NET, TEV], 'to state' [AB; CEV], 'to signify' [Bar], 'to specify' [GW, KJV, NIV, NLT], 'to tell' [NCV], 'to make clear' [LN], 'to report, to communicate' [BDAG]. This verb means to cause something to be both specific and clear [LN]. It means to make known [BDAG].

**DISCOURSE UNIT—26:1–32** [CEV, NET]. The topic is Paul's defense before Agrippa [CEV], Paul offers his defense [NET].

**DISCOURSE UNIT—26:1–23** [AB, CBC, NAC, PNTC; NCV]. The topic is Paul defends himself [NCV], Paul's address before Agrippa: the speech [NAC], Paul's speech before Agrippa [AB], before Agrippa [CBC], Paul's defense [PNTC].

**DISCOURSE UNIT—26:1–11** [PNTC; ESV, NRSV, TEV]. The topic is Paul's defense before Agrippa [ESV], Paul defends himself before Agrippa [NRSV, TEV], his Jewish credentials [PNTC].

**DISCOURSE UNIT—26:1** [NICNT]. The topic is Paul accepts Agrippa's invitation to speak.

**26:1** And Agrippa said to Paul, "Permission-is-given[a] to-you to-speak for yourself." Then Paul, stretching-out[b] (his) hand, made-his-defense.[c]
LEXICON—a. pres. pass. indic. of ἐπιτρέπω (LN 13.138) (BDAG 1. p. 385): 'to be permitted' [AB, Bar, BDAG, LN; KJV, NASB], 'to have permission' [BECNT, CBC; CEV, NET, NIV, NRSV, REB, TEV], 'to be allowed' [BDAG, LN], 'to be free (to speak)' [GW], 'you may (speak)' [CEV, NCV, NLT]. This verb means to be allowed to do something [BDAG, LN].

b. aorist act. participle of ἐκτείνω (LN 16.19) (BDAG 1. p. 310): 'to stretch out' [Bar, BDAG, BECNT, CBC, LN; CEV, ESV, NASB, NRSV, REB, TEV], 'to stretch forth' [KJV], 'to gesture with' [AB; NLT], 'to motion with' [NIV], 'to raise' [NCV], 'to hold out' [NET], 'to extend, to reach out' [LN]. The phrase 'Paul, stretching out his hand' is also translated 'Paul acknowledged Agrippa' [GW]. This verb means to cause an object to extend in space (for example, by becoming straight, unfolded, or uncoiled) [LN]. It means to cause an object to extend to its full length in space. To stretch out the hand is the gesture of a speaker [BDAG].

c. imperf. mid. or pass. (deponent = act.) indic. of ἀπολογέομαι (LN 33.435) (BDAG p. 116): 'to make a defense' [BECNT; ESV, NASB], 'to begin a defense' [Bar, CBC; GW, NET, NIV, REB], 'to start a defense' [NLT], 'to defend oneself' [BDAG, LN; NCV, TEV], 'to begin to defend' [NRSV], 'to answer for oneself' [KJV], 'to make a speech in defense' [AB], 'to say' [CEV]. This verb means to speak on behalf of oneself or of others against accusations presumed to be false [LN]. It means to speak in one's own defense against charges presumed to be false [BDAG].

QUESTION—What was Paul signaling when he extended his hand?

It was the traditional gesture of an orator about to begin speaking [AB, NAC, PNTC, TNTC]. It was Paul's way of greeting the king [BECNT, NICNT]. It was used to get attention from the audience [EBC].

QUESTION—What kind of 'defense' is Paul making?

This is not a formal trial, but was an opportunity for the governor Festus to prepare a proper evaluation of Paul's case to send to Caesar [PNTC]. Since Paul has already been recognized as being innocent, and this hearing is being held so that Festus can find a credible charge to send to the emperor, Paul now takes this opportunity to explain his life and ministry [BECNT, NAC]. Because Paul had already been declared innocent by Festus of any capital crime, he now defends himself against the accusation that he had committed any offense against Judaism [EBC].

**DISCOURSE UNIT—26:2–23** [NICNT]. The topic is Paul's 'Apologia pro vita sua'.

**DISCOURSE UNIT—26:2–3** [NICNT]. The topic is exordium.

**26:2** "I-consider myself fortunate,[a] King Agrippa, (that) (it is) before you I-am-going to-make-my-defense today concerning all of-which I-am-accused[b] by (the)-Jews,

LEXICON—a. μακάριος (LN 25.119) (BDAG 1.a. p. 610): 'fortunate' [BDAG; all translations except AB; CEV, KJV, NCV], 'most fortunate' [AB], 'happy' [BDAG, LN; KJV], 'blessed' [NCV]. The phrase 'I consider myself fortunate' is also translated 'I am glad' [CEV]. This adjective describes being happy, with the implication of enjoying favorable circumstances [LN]. It describes being fortunate or happy because of circumstances [BDAG].

b. pres. pass. indic. of ἐγκαλέω (LN 33.427) (BDAG p. 273): 'to be accused' [Bar, BDAG, LN; KJV, NASB, NET], 'to have charges brought against oneself' [LN]. The phrase 'all of which I am accused' is also translated 'all the accusations' [BECNT; ESV, NIV, NLT, NRSV], 'all the charges made/brought against me' [AB, CBC; CEV, NCV, REB], 'every charge brought against me' [GW], 'all the things (these Jews) accuse me of' [TEV]. This verb means to bring serious charges or accusations against someone, with the possible connotation of a legal or court context [LN]. It means to bring charges against [BDAG].

QUESTION—Why would Paul consider himself fortunate that Agrippa was hearing his case?

Because of Agrippa's understanding of Jewish matters he is equipped to understand the situation Paul is about to describe [BECNT, NAC, NICNT]. Agrippa lived a Roman lifestyle, so he was in a position to understand both Jewish and Roman legal concerns [NAC].

**26:3** especially-because[a] you are familiar-with[b] all (the) customs[c] and controversies[d] of (the)-Jews, therefore I-ask-(you) to-listen to-me patiently.[e]

LEXICON—a. μάλιστα (LN 78.7) (BDAG 1. p. 613): 'especially because' [ESV, KJV, NASB, NIV], 'because' [AB, BECNT; NET, NRSV], 'especially' [BDAG, LN], 'especially since' [Bar], 'since' [GW], 'particularly since' [TEV], 'particularly as' [CBC; REB], 'particularly' [BDAG, LN], 'for' [NLT], 'most of all, above all' [BDAG], not explicit [CEV, NCV ]. This adverb describes a very high point on a scale of extent [LN]. It means to an unusual degree [BDAG].

b. γνώστης (LN 28.11) (BDAG p. 204): 'familiar with' [Bar; ESV], 'especially familiar with' [BECNT; GW, NET, NRSV], 'one who knows' [LN], 'expert' [BDAG, CBC, LN; KJV, NASB, NLT, REB], 'great expert' [AB], 'well acquainted with' [NIV], 'one acquainted with' [BDAG]. The phrase 'especially because you are knowledgeable is also translated 'you know a lot' [CEV], 'you know so much' [NCV], 'you know so well' [TEV]. This noun denotes one who knows, with the usual implication of to know well [LN]. It is one who is knowledgeable about something [BDAG].

c. ἔθος (LN 41.25) (BDAG 2. p. 277): 'custom' [BDAG, LN; all translations], 'habit' [LN]. This noun denotes a pattern of behavior more or less fixed by tradition and generally sanctioned by the society [LN]. It is long-established usage or practice common to a group [BDAG].

d. ζήτημα (LN 33.440) (BDAG p. 428): 'controversy' [AB; ESV, GW, NIV, NLT, NRSV, REB], 'controversial issue' [NET], 'dispute' [Bar, BECNT, CBC, LN; TEV], 'question' [KJV, NASB], 'beliefs that divide' [CEV], 'things (they) argue about' [NCV], 'controversial question, issue, argument' [BDAG]. This noun denotes the forceful expression of differences of opinion without necessarily having a presumed goal of seeking a solution [LN].

e. μακροθύμως (LN 25.169) (BDAG p. 613): 'patiently' [BDAG, LN; all translations except CBC; REB, TEV], 'with patience' [BDAG; TEV]. The phrase 'to listen to me patiently' is also translated 'to give me a patient hearing' [CBC; REB]. This adverb describes being patient [LN].

QUESTION—Does μάλιστα 'especially' modify Paul's reason to consider himself fortunate or Agrippa's knowledge of Jewish customs and controversies?
    1. It indicates that Paul considers himself especially fortunate to have Agrippa hear his case [Bar, CBC, NICNT, TRT; ESV, KJV, NASB, NIV, REB, TEV].
    2. It indicates that Paul recognizes that Agrippa is especially knowledgeable about Jewish issues [AB, BECNT, TNTC; GW, NCV, NET, NRSV].

**DISCOURSE UNIT—26:4-8** [NICNT]. The topic is the resurrection hope.

**26:4** All the Jews know my way-of-life[a] from-(my) youth from (the)-beginning being among my own nation[b] and in Jerusalem.

LEXICON—a. βίωσις (LN 41.18) (BDAG p. 177): 'way of life' [AB; NRSV], 'manner of life' [Bar, BDAG, BECNT; ESV, KJV, NASB], 'life' [CBC, LN; REB], '(my) whole life' [NCV], 'kind of life' [CEV], 'daily life, existence' [LN]. The phrase 'my way of life' is also translated 'how I lived' [GW], 'the way I lived' [NET, NIV], 'how I have lived...my whole life' [TEV], 'a thorough Jewish training' [NLT]. This noun denotes how one conducts oneself, with focus upon everyday activity [LN].
    b. ἔθνος (LN 11.55): 'nation' [Bar, BECNT, LN; ESV, KJV, NASB, REB], 'people' [AB, CBC, LN; GW, NET, NLT, NRSV], 'country' [CEV, NCV, NIV, TEV]. This noun denotes the largest unit into which the people of the world are divided on the basis of their constituting a socio-political community [LN].

QUESTION—What is the function of μὲν οὖν (not translated) in this sentence?
It indicates that this is the beginning point of Paul's speech in his own defense [PNTC, TH, TRT]. Luke uses μὲν οὖν throughout Acts to tie sections of narrative together; here it has the rhetorical function of introducing the fact that it was because of his Jewish and Pharisaical background that he held his Christian commitment [EBC].

QUESTION—What nation is Paul referring to as his own nation?
    1. He is referring to his early life in Jerusalem, where he grew up [BECNT, NAC, NICNT, PNTC, TNTC].
    2. He is referring to his early upbringing in Cilicia, his birthplace [TH; CEV, TEV].

**26:5** They-have-known for-(a)-long-time,[a] if they-would-be-willing to-testify,[b] that according-to the strictest[c] party[d] of-our religion[e] I-have-lived-(as) (a)-Pharisee.

LEXICON—a. ἄνωθεν (LN 67.90) (BDAG 2. p. 92): 'for a long time' [AB, BECNT, LN; ESV, GW, NASB, NCV, NIV, NLT], 'from of old' [Bar],

'from the beginning' [KJV], 'from time past' [NET], 'long enough' [CBC; REB], 'always' [TEV], 'from the beginning' [BDAG], not explicit [CEV, NLT]. This adverb describes the duration of time for a relatively long period in the past [LN]. It describes a time from another point of time marking the beginning of something [BDAG].
  b. pres. act. infin. of μαρτυρέω (LN 33.262) (BDAG 1. p. 617): 'to testify' [all translations except AB; CEV, NCV, NLT], 'to admit' [AB; NLT], 'to tell' [CEV, NCV], 'to bear witness, to be a witness' [BDAG], 'to witness' [LN]. This verb means to provide information about a person or an event concerning which the speaker has direct knowledge [LN]. It means to confirm or attest something on the basis of personal knowledge or belief [BDAG].
  c. superlative of ἀκριβής (LN 72.19) (BDAG p. 39): 'strict' [BDAG, LN; all translations except KJV, NCV], 'strait' [KJV], 'carefully' [NCV], 'exact' [BDAG], 'accurate' [LN]. This adjective describes strict conformity to a norm or standard, involving both detail and completeness [LN].
  d. αἵρεσις (LN 11.50) (BDAG 1. p. 29): 'party' [Bar, BDAG, BECNT; ESV, GW, NET, TEV], 'religious party' [LN], 'sect' [AB, BDAG, LN; KJV, NASB, NIV, NLT, NRSV], 'group' [CBC; CEV, NCV, REB], 'school, faction' [BDAG]. This noun denotes a division or group based upon different doctrinal opinions and/or loyalties and hence by implication in certain contexts an unjustified party or group (applicable in the NT to religious parties) [LN]. It is a group that holds tenets distinctive to it [BDAG].
  e. θρησκεία (LN 53.1) (BDAG p. 459): 'religion' [LN; all translations except CEV, NCV], 'tradition' [NCV], 'piety' [LN], 'worship' [BDAG], not explicit [CEV]. This noun denotes appropriate beliefs and devout practice of obligations relating to supernatural persons and powers [LN]. It is the expression of devotion to transcendent beings, especially as it expresses itself in cultic rites [BDAG].

QUESTION—Does 'for a long time' modify the Jews' knowledge of Paul or how long Paul lived as a Pharisee?
  It indicates how long the Jews have known about Paul [AB, Bar, BECNT, CBC, NICNT, TRT; ESV, GW, KJV, NASB, NCV, NET, NIV, NRSV, REB, TEV]. It describes how long he had a good reputation among his own people [PNTC].

QUESTION—What is meant by the term αἵρεσις 'party'?
  It describes a sub-group within a larger group, and does not have the same meaning as it did in 24:14 where it describes a group holding false beliefs [TH]. Here it has a positive connotation [PNTC].

QUESTION—What is meant by the term θρησκεία 'religion'?
  It describes the entire mode of worship of a particular group of people, and is not the same word Festus used to describe Jewish belief in 25:19 [TH]. It is a more neutral term than δεισιδαιμονία, which Festus used to describe Judaism in 25:19 [PNTC]. It describes religious practice [BECNT].

**26:6** And now for (the)-hope[a] of-the promise[b] made by God to our fathers I-stand being-tried,[c]

LEXICON—a. ἐλπίς (LN 25.59) (BDAG 1.b.α., β. p. 320): 'hope' [BDAG, LN; all translations except AB; CEV, GW, NCV], 'expectation' [BDAG]. This noun denotes the act of looking forward with confidence to that which is good and beneficial [LN]. This noun is also translated as a verb: 'I hope' [AB; NCV], 'I believe' [CEV], 'I expect' [GW]. It is the looking forward to something with some reason for confidence respecting fulfillment, especially in matters spoken of in God's promises [BDAG].

b. ἐπαγγελία (LN 33.288) (BDAG 1.b.α. p. 356): 'promise' [BDAG, LN; all translations except NIV], 'pledge, offer' [BDAG]. This noun is also translated as a verb phrase: 'what God has promised' [NIV]. This noun denotes the content of what is promised [LN]. It is a declaration to do something with implication of obligation to carry out what is stated [BDAG].

c. pres. pass. participle of κρίνω (LN 30.108) (BDAG 5.a.α. p. 568): 'to stand trial' [Bar; NASB], 'to stand here on trial' [ESV, NET, NRSV], 'to be on trial' [CEV, GW, NIV, NLT, REB], 'to stand in the dock' [CBC], 'to be judged' [BDAG, BECNT, LN; KJV, NCV], 'to be tried' [TEV], 'to be haled before a court' [BDAG], 'to be evaluated' [LN]. This participle is also translated as a phrase: 'on trial' [AB]. This verb means to make a judgment based upon the correctness or value of something [LN]. It means to be engaged in a judicial process [BDAG].

QUESTION—What hope is he referring to?

It is the hope of the resurrection [BECNT, CBC, NAC, NICNT, PNTC, TH, TNTC]. Israel's hope in God's promises are fulfilled in the resurrection [NAC].

QUESTION—Was Paul actually on trial?

The purpose of his hearing was not to determine guilt, but was an occasion for governor Festus to prepare an evaluation of Paul's case to send to Rome [BECNT, PNTC]. Paul was not technically on trial, though to him it may have felt like it [Bar, PNTC].

**26:7** to which (promise) our twelve-tribes in earnestness[a] worshiping[b] night and day hope to-attain,[c] about which hope I-am-accused[d] by (the)-Jews, O king.

LEXICON—a. ἐκτένεια (LN 25.70) (BDAG p. 310): 'earnestness' [BDAG, LN], 'perseverance' [BDAG], 'eager perseverance' [LN]. The phrase 'in earnestness' is also translated 'earnestly' [BECNT; CEV, ESV, NASB, NET, NIV, NRSV], 'constantly' [AB], 'zealously' [Bar; NLT], 'instantly' [KJV], 'with intense devotion' [CBC; GW, REB], not explicit [NCV, TEV]. This noun denotes a state of eagerness involving perseverance over a period of time [LN]. It is a state of persistence in an undertaking or enterprise, with implication of exceptional interest or devotion [BDAG].

b. pres. act. participle of λατρεύω (LN 53.14) (BDAG p. 587): 'to worship' [AB, Bar, BECNT, CBC, LN; ESV, GW, NLT, NRSV, REB, TEV], 'to

serve' [BDAG; CEV, KJV, NASB, NCV, NET, NIV], 'to perform religious rites, to venerate' [LN]. This verb means to perform religious rites as a part of worship [LN]. It means to carry out religious duties, especially of a cultic nature [BDAG]. This verb is translated as having 'God' as the direct object, though it is not in the Greek text [AB, Bar; CEV, KJV, NASB, NCV, NET, NIV, NLT, TEV].
c. aorist act. infin. of καταντάω (LN 13.121) (BDAG 2.a. p. 523): 'to attain' [Bar, BDAG, BECNT; ESV, NASB, NET, NRSV], 'to share' [AB], 'to see the fulfillment of' [CBC; REB], 'to see fulfilled' [NIV], 'to expect to be kept' [GW], 'to arrive at, meet' [BDAG], 'to come upon' [LN]. The phrase 'hope to attain' is also translated 'wait for' [CEV], 'hope to come' [KJV], 'hope to receive' [NCV, TEV], not explicit [NLT]. This verb means to happen to, with the implication of something definitive and final [LN]. It means to reach a condition or goal [BDAG].
d. pres. pass. indic. of ἐγκαλέω (LN 33.427) (BDAG p. 273): 'to be accused' [AB, Bar, BDAG, BECNT, LN; ESV, KJV, NASB, NRSV, REB, TEV], 'to be impeached' [CBC], 'to have charges brought against oneself' [LN; CEV]. The phrase 'I am accused by the Jews' is also translated 'the Jews are making accusations against me' [GW], 'the Jews are accusing me' [NET, NIV], 'they accuse me' [NLT], 'they have accused me' [NCV]. This verb means to bring serious charges or accusations against someone, with the possible connotation of a legal or court context [LN]. It means to bring charges against someone [BDAG].

QUESTION—What is meant by 'our twelve tribes'?

The people of Israel still saw themselves as a nation composed of twelve tribes [NAC]. It describes all of Israel [BECNT, NAC], Israel in its totality [NICNT, TNTC]. It probably represents an idealized Israel, meaning all true Israelites throughout time and wherever they may be in the world [PNTC].

QUESTION—What is it that the twelve tribes hope to attain?

They hope to experience the fulfillment of the promise Paul has referred to in the previous verse, which is to experience the resurrection of the dead [Bar, NICNT, PNTC, TH, TNTC]. Paul is saying that because the resurrection of the dead is at the heart of the hopes of Judaism it is surprising that they should be the ones to oppose his message [EBC].

QUESTION—What may be implied by the phrase 'by the Jews' at the end of this sentence?

There may be a note of irony here; this is a central hope that Jews have, yet here Paul is being tried *by the Jews themselves* for believing this hope [Bar, BECNT, NAC, PNTC]. By its position at the end of the sentence the phrase 'by the Jews' shows emphasis, indicating that their resistance is somewhat surprising [EBC, TH].

**26:8** Why is-it-thought[a] incredible[b] by you(pl) that[c] God raises (the)-dead?

LEXICON—a. pres. pass. indic. of κρίνω (LN 56.20) (BDAG 3. p. 568): 'to be thought' [BDAG, BECNT; ESV, KJV, NRSV], 'to be judged' [Bar,

BDAG], 'to be considered' [AB, BDAG, CBC; NASB], 'to decide a legal question, to act as a judge, making a legal decision, to arrive at a verdict, to try a case' [LN], not explicit [CEV, GW]. This passive verb is also translated as active: 'to think' [NCV, NET], 'to consider' [NIV], 'to find (it)' [REB, TEV], 'to seem' [NLT]. This verb means to decide a question of legal right or wrong, and thus determine the innocence or guilt of the accused and assign appropriate punishment or retribution [LN]. It means to make a judgment based on taking various factors into account [BDAG].
  b. ἄπιστος (LN 31.40) (BDAG 1. p. 103): 'incredible' [AB, Bar, BDAG, CBC; ESV, KJV, NASB, NIV, NLT, NRSV, REB], 'unbelievable' [BDAG, BECNT, LN; NET], 'impossible' [NCV], 'impossible to believe' [TEV], 'impossible to be believed' [LN]. The phrase 'why is it deemed incredible' is also translated 'why should any of you doubt' [CEV], 'why do all of you refuse to believe' [GW]. This adjective describes not being believable [LN].
  c. εἰ (LN 90.26): 'that' [LN; all translations except NASB, NCV], 'if' [LN; NASB], 'for (God to raise people from the dead)' [NCV], 'whether' [LN]. This particle marks an indirect question as content [LN].
QUESTION—To whom is Paul addressing this question?
  The plural pronoun 'you' is translated 'any of you' [BECNT; CEV, ESV, NCV, NIV, NLT, NRSV], 'all of you' [GW].
  1. It is addressed to all present, both Jew and Gentile [BECNT, EBC, NAC, PNTC; CEV, ESV, GW, NCV, NIV, NLT, NRSV, TEV].
  2. It is addressed to the Jews who are present [Bar, TH, TRT], although this may have also included Agrippa [Bar]. 'You' refers to any Jews who don't believe in the resurrection [REB].

**DISCOURSE UNIT—26:9–11** [NICNT]. The topic is Paul's persecuting zeal.

**26:9** **So I-myself was-convinced**ᵃ **(that I) must do many-things**ᵇ **in-opposition**ᶜ **to the name of-Jesus of Nazareth,**
LEXICON—a. aorist act. indic. of δοκέω (LN 31.29) (BDAG 2.a.α. p. 255): 'to be convinced' [BECNT; CEV, NET, NIV, NRSV], 'to be sure' [AB], 'to think' [Bar, CBC, LN; CEV, GW, KJV, NCV, REB, TEV], 'to think to oneself' [NASB], 'to believe' [LN; NLT], 'to suppose, to presume, to assume, to imagine' [LN], 'to seem, to be recognized as' [BDAG]. This verb means to regard something as presumably true, but without particular certainty [LN]. It means to appear to one's understanding [BDAG].
  b. πολύς (LN 59.1): 'many' [AB, Bar, BECNT, LN; CEV, KJV, NASB, NCV, NET, NRSV], 'a lot' [GW], 'everything (I could)' [CEV, NLT, TEV], 'all (that was possible)' [NIV], 'a great deal of, a great number of' [LN], not explicit [CBC; REB]. This adjective describes a relatively large quantity of objects or events [LN].
  c. ἐναντίος (LN 39.6) (BDAG 2. p. 331): 'in opposing' [BECNT; ESV], 'to oppose' [CEV, GW, NIV, NLT], 'opposed to' [BDAG], 'against' [AB, CBC; NCV, NRSV, REB, TEV], 'contrary to' [Bar, BDAG; KJV],

ACTS 26:9   323

'hostile' [LN; NASB, NET]. This adjective describes being hostile toward [LN]. It describes being in opposition [LN].

QUESTION—What is the function of μὲν οὖν 'so' here?

It resumes his discourse about his past life and why he opposed Christ [Bar, EBC, PNTC, TRT]. It indicates a transition to a new section with new content [TH].

QUESTION—What does it mean to do things in opposition to the *name* of Jesus of Nazareth?

It means to oppose his cause [TEV]. It means to oppose Jesus himself [TH; CEV, NCV], that is, the one named Jesus of Nazareth [GW]. Paul opposed what was claimed about Jesus [PNTC, TNTC], as well as those who followed him [PNTC]. The 'name' of Christ represents his power and presence among his people [NAC]. Paul describes him here by the name Jesus of Nazareth', which is how he would have referred to him when he was persecuting Christians, leaving out 'Lord' or 'Christ', [BECNT].

**26:10** which also I-did in Jerusalem, and I-myself locked-up[a] in prison[b] many of-the saints,[c] having-received authority[d] from the chief-priests,[e] and cast- (my)-vote -against[f] (them) as-they-were-being-killed.[g]

LEXICON—a. aorist act. indic. of κατακλείω (LN 37.125) (BDAG p. 518): 'to lock up' [BDAG; ESV, NASB, NET, NRSV], 'to lock in' [GW], 'to shut up' [AB, Bar, BDAG, BECNT; KJV], 'to put (in jail)' [CEV, NCV], 'to put (in prison)' [NIV, TEV], 'to send (to prison)' [REB], 'to cause to be sent (to prison)' [NLT], 'to put into prison, to cause to be put in prison' [LN]. The phrase 'I locked up in prison' is also translated 'I imprisoned' [CBC]. This verb means to cause a person to be consigned to prison [LN].

b. φυλακή (LN 7.24) (BDAG 3. p. 1067): 'prison' [BDAG, LN; all translations except CBC; CEV, NCV], 'jail' [LN; CEV, NCV], not explicit [CBC]. This noun denotes a place of detention [LN]. It is the place where guarding is done [BDAG].

c. ἅγιος (LN 11.27): 'saint' [AB, Bar, BECNT; ESV, KJV, NASB, NET, NRSV], 'God's people' [CBC, LN; CEV, NCV, REB, TEV], 'the Lord's people' [NIV], 'Christian' [GW], 'believer' [NLT]. This noun denotes persons who belong to God, and as such constitute a religious entity [LN].

d. ἐξουσία (LN 37.36) (BDAG 3. p. 353): 'authority' [BDAG; all translations except NCV, NLT], 'power' [NCV], 'absolute power' [BDAG], 'warrant' [BDAG], 'jurisdiction' [LN]. The phrase 'having received authority' is also translated 'authorized' [NLT]. This noun denotes the domain or sphere over which one has authority to control or rule [LN]. It is the right to control or command [BDAG].

e. ἀρχιερεύς (LN 53.88): 'chief priest' [LN; all translations except NCV, NLT], 'leading priest' [NCV, NLT]. This noun denotes a principal priest, in view of belonging to one of the high-priestly families [LN].

f. aorist act. indic. of καταφέρω (LN 30.103) (BDAG 2. p. 529): 'cast (one's vote) against' [Bar, BDAG, BECNT; ESV, NASB, NET, NIV,

NLT, NRSV], 'cast one's vote (in favor of their being killed)' [AB], 'to vote (to have them killed)' [GW], 'to vote (for them to be killed)' [CEV], 'to vote against' [LN; TEV], 'to give voice against' [KJV]. The phrase 'I...cast my vote against them' is also translated 'my vote was cast against them' [CBC; REB], 'I agreed it was a good thing' [NCV]. The phrase καταφέρω ψῆφον (an idiom, literally 'to bring a pebble against someone', a reference to a white or black pebble used in voting for or against someone), means to make known one's choice against someone [LN]. It means to cause something to happen that is opposed to another's interest [BDAG].

g. pres. pass. participle of ἀναιρέω (LN 20.71) (BDAG 2. p. 64): 'to be killed' [AB, Bar, LN; CEV, NCV], 'to be put to death' [BECNT; ESV, KJV, NASB, NIV], 'to be condemned to death' [BDAG, CBC; NLT, NRSV, REB], 'to be sentenced to death' [NET, TEV], 'to be executed' [LN]. This passive verb form is also translated as active: 'to have them killed' [GW]. This verb means to get rid of someone by execution [BDAG, LN], often with legal or quasi-legal procedures [LN].

QUESTION—Was Paul a member of the Sanhedrin such that he would actually have a vote when Christians were being tried?

He was probably not a member of the Sanhedrin such that he had a formal vote, but was giving approval in a less formal way [BECNT, NAC, PNTC, TRT]. He is simply saying that he expressed his approval of their being executed [EBC, NAC].

QUESTION—How many Christians were actually put to death during the time Paul was persecuting Christians?

Paul may simply be generalizing here based on his involvement in the death of Stephen [NAC, NICNT, TNTC]. There were probably many Christians who suffered this fate, and Paul seems to be suggesting that he and the Jewish leadership were violating the Roman prohibition against the Jews executing anyone [BECNT]. The Jews did not have permission to execute Christians, but illegal assassinations may have happened [AB].

**DISCOURSE UNIT—26:11–32** [NASB]. The topic is Paul's defense before Agrippa.

**26:11** And often punishing[a] them in all the synagogues I-was-trying-to-make[b] (them) blaspheme[c] and being- furiously[d] -enraged[e] persecuted[f] them even to foreign cities.

LEXICON—a. pres. pass. participle of τιμωρέω (LN 38.6) (BDAG p. 1006): 'to punish' [Bar, BDAG, BECNT, LN; ESV, GW, KJV, NASB, NCV, NET, NRSV], 'to have someone punished' [CEV, NIV, NLT, TEV]. The phrase 'punishing them' is also translated 'by threat of punishment' [AB], 'by repeated punishment' [CBC; REB]. This verb means to punish, with the implication of causing people to suffer what they deserve [LN].

b. imperf. act. indic. of ἀναγκάζω (LN 37.33) (BDAG 1. p. 60): 'to make' [Bar, CBC; CEV, ESV, NCV, REB, TEV], 'to force' [AB, BDAG, BECNT, LN; GW, NASB, NET, NIV, NRSV], 'to compel' [BDAG, LN;

KJV], 'to get (them to curse)' [NLT]. The imperfect tense of this verb is translated as indicating an attempt to force or make someone do something: 'I tried' [AB, Bar, BECNT, CBC; ESV, NASB, NCV, NET, NIV, NRSV, REB, TEV]. This verb means to compel someone to act in a particular manner [BDAG, LN].

c. pres. act. infin. of βλασφημέω (LN 33.400) (BDAG b.β. p. 178): 'to blaspheme' [AB, Bar, BECNT, LN; ESV, KJV, NASB, NET, NIV, NRSV], 'to commit blasphemy' [REB], 'to renounce one's faith' [CBC], 'to deny one's faith' [TEV], 'to give up one's faith' [CEV], 'to curse the name of Jesus' [GW], 'to curse Jesus' [NLT], 'to speak against Jesus' [NCV], 'to revile, to defame' [BDAG, LN], 'to speak irreverently, impiously, or disrespectfully of or about' [BDAG]. This verb means to speak against someone in such a way as to harm or injure his or her reputation (occurring in relation to persons as well as to divine beings) [LN]. It means to speak in relation to transcendent or associated entities in a disrespectful way that demeans, denigrates, or maligns [BDAG].

d. περισσῶς (LN 78.31) (BDAG p. 806): 'furiously' [NASB, NET, NRSV], 'exceedingly' [Bar, BDAG; KJV], 'so violently' [NLT], 'beyond measure, very' [BDAG], 'so (angry/obsessed/furious)' [CEV, NCV, NIV, TEV], 'very great, excessive, extremely, emphatic, surpassing, all the more, much greater' [LN]. The phrase 'furiously enraged' is also translated 'in furious rage' [GW], 'in raging fury' [AB, BECNT; ESV], 'my fury rose to such a pitch' [CBC; REB]. This adverb describes a degree which is considerably in excess of some point on an implied or explicit scale of extent [LN]. It describes an exceptionally high degree on a scale of intensity [BDAG].

e. pres. mid. or pass. (deponent = act.) participle of ἐμμαίνομαι (LN 88.182) (BDAG p. 322): 'to be enraged' [BDAG, LN; NASB, NET, NRSV], 'to be furious' [TEV], 'to be mad' [Bar; KJV], 'to be angry' [NCV], 'to be obsessed' [NIV], 'to be opposed' [NLT], 'to be infuriated, to be insanely angry' [LN], not explicit [AB, BECNT, CBC; CEV, ESV, GW, NCV (see entry d.)]. This verb means to be so furiously angry with someone as to be almost out of one's mind [LN]. It means to be filled with such anger that one appears to be mad [BDAG].

f. imperf. act. indic. of διώκω (LN 39.45) (BDAG 2. p. 254): 'to persecute' [AB, Bar, BDAG, BECNT, LN; ESV, KJV, NET, TEV], 'to extend persecution' [CBC; REB], 'to pursue' [NASB, NRSV], 'to go looking for' [CEV], 'to hunt down' [GW, NIV], 'to chase down' [NLT], 'to find and punish' [NCV], 'to harass' [LN]. This verb means to systematically organize a program to oppress and harass people [LN]. It means to harass someone, especially because of beliefs [BDAG].

QUESTION—What is implied by the use of the imperfect tense of ἠνάγκαζον 'tried to make them blaspheme'?

It is conative, indicating what he intended or attempted to do [AB, Bar, BECNT, CBC, NAC, NICNT, PNTC, TH, TNTC, TRT; ESV, NASB, NCV,

NET, NIV, NRSV, REB, TEV]. He was probably not successful [BECNT, NAC, PNTC]. He probably succeeded with some, but not with others [TH, TRT].

QUESTION—What was Paul trying to make them do?
He tried to make them renounce their faith in Christ [CBC, NICNT, TH, TNTC, TRT; CEV, TEV], to renounce or even curse Jesus [AB, BECNT, NICNT, TNTC, TRT; GW, NCV, NLT], to deny Christ [PNTC], to deny who Jesus really is [BECNT]. He may have tried to get them to say things that Jewish people would have considered blasphemous enough to punish [PNTC].

**DISCOURSE UNIT—26:12–32** [ESV]. The topic is Paul tells of his conversion.

**DISCOURSE UNIT—26:12–18** [NICNT; NRSV, TEV]. The topic is Paul tells of his conversion [NRSV, TEV], the heavenly vision [NICNT].

**DISCOURSE UNIT—26:12–23** [PNTC]. The topic is his calling and mission.

**26:12** **In which-things<sup>a</sup> I-was-journeying to Damascus with authorization<sup>b</sup> and commission<sup>c</sup> of-the chief-priests.**

LEXICON—a. ὅς (LN 92.27): 'who, which, what, that which' [LN]. The phrase 'in which things' is also translated 'in this connection' [ESV], 'in the course of this' [AB], 'while so engaged' [NASB], 'while doing this very thing' [NET], 'I was carrying out these activities' [GW], 'on one such occasion' [CBC; REB], 'on one of these journeys' [NIV], 'one time' [NCV], 'one day' [NLT], 'whereupon' [KJV], 'with this in mind' [NRSV], 'it was for this purpose' [TEV], 'as (I was traveling)' [Bar], 'thus (I was journeying)' [BECNT], 'one day (I was on my way)' [CEV]. This relative pronoun refers to an entity, event, or state, either occurring overtly in the immediate context or clearly implied in the discourse or setting [LN].

b. ἐξουσία (LN 37.35) (BDAG 3. p. 353): 'authority' [BDAG; all translations except GW, NCV], 'power' [GW], 'permission' [NCV], 'absolute power, warrant' [BDAG], 'authority to rule, right to control' [LN]. This noun denotes the right to control or govern over [LN]. It means the right to control or command [BDAG].

c. ἐπιτροπή (LN 37.40) (BDAG p. 385): 'commission' [Bar, BDAG, BECNT, CBC; ESV, KJV, NASB, NIV, NLT, NRSV, REB], 'permission' [AB, BDAG; CEV], 'orders' [TEV], 'authority' [LN; GW], 'power' [NCV], 'complete power' [LN; NET], 'full power' [BDAG]. This noun denotes the full authority to carry out an assignment or commission [LN]. It is the authorization to carry out an assignment [BDAG].

QUESTION—To what does Ἐν οἷς refer?
It indicates this event took place when he was on one such journey [Bar, BECNT, CBC, PNTC, TRT; CEV, KJV, NCV, NIV, NLT, REB]. It indicates the circumstances, or Paul's intention when he was involved in this pursuit [AB, NICNT, TH; ESV, GW, NET, NRSV, TEV].

QUESTION—What was the ἐπιτροπή 'commission'?
It was a document that showed he had authority to do this [TH]. It was authorization in the form of letters written by the leading priests [TNTC].

**26:13** (At the) middle[a] of-(the)-day (while) on the way[b] I-saw, O king, (a)-light beyond the brightness[c] of-the sun shining-around[d] me and those traveling with me.

LEXICON—a. μέσος (LN 83.10) (BDAG 1.a. p. 634): 'at the middle' [AB], 'in the middle' [BDAG, CBC, LN], 'middle' [BDAG]. The phrase 'at the middle of the day' is also translated 'at midday' [Bar, BECNT; ESV, KJV, NASB, NRSV, REB, TEV], 'at noon' [GW, NCV], 'about noon' [CEV, NET, NIV, NLT]. This adjective describes a position in the middle of an area (either an object in the midst of other objects or an area in the middle of a larger area) [LN]. It describes a middle position spatially or temporally [BDAG].

b. ὁδός (LN 15.19) (BDAG 2. p. 691): 'way' [BDAG, BECNT, CBC; ESV, KJV, NASB, NCV, REB], 'road' [Bar; NET, NIV, NLT, NRSV, TEV], 'journey' [AB, BDAG, LN], 'trip' [BDAG], not explicit [CEV]. The phrase 'while on the way' is also translated 'while I was traveling' [GW]. This noun denotes the process of travelling, presumably for some distance [LN]. It is the action of traveling [BDAG].

c. λαμπρότης (LN 14.49) (BDAG p. 585): 'brightness' [Bar, LN; KJV], 'shining' [BDAG, LN], 'radiance' [LN]. The phrase 'beyond the brightness' is also translated 'brighter than' [AB, BECNT; all versions except KJV, REB, TEV], 'much brighter than' [TEV], 'more brilliant than' [CBC; REB]. This noun denotes the state of brightness or shining [LN]. It is the state of being splendid [BDAG].

d. aorist act. participle of περιλάμπω (LN 14.44) (BDAG p. 802): 'to shine around' [Bar, BDAG, LN; ESV, GW, NRSV, TEV], 'to shine all around' [CBC; NASB, REB], 'to shine everywhere around' [NET], 'to shine round' [AB, BECNT; KJV], 'to shine down on' [NLT], 'to blaze around' [NIV], 'to flash on' [CEV], 'to flash all around' [NCV]. This verb means to illuminate an area surrounding an object [LN].

**26:14** And all of-us having-fallen to the ground, I-heard (a)-voice saying to me in-the Hebrew[a] language, 'Saul, Saul, why do-you-persecute[b] me? (It is)-hard[c] for-you to-kick against (the)-goads.[d] **26:15** And I said, 'Who are-you, Lord[e]?' And the Lord said, 'I am Jesus whom you are-persecuting.

LEXICON—a. Ἑβραΐς (LN 93.104) (BDAG p. 270): 'Hebrew' [LN], 'Hebrew language' [BDAG]. The phrase 'in the Hebrew language' [Bar, BECNT; ESV, NCV, NRSV] is also translated 'in Hebrew' [AB; GW, TEV], 'in the Hebrew tongue' [KJV], 'in the Hebrew dialect' [NASB], 'in Aramaic' [CEV, NET, NIV, NLT], 'in the Jewish language' [CBC; REB]. This adjective describes something as pertaining to the Hebrews [LN].

b. διώκω (LN 39.45) (BDAG 2. p. 254): 'to persecute' [BDAG, LN; all translations except CEV], 'to be cruel to' [CEV], 'to harass' [LN]. This verb means to systematically organize a program to oppress and harass people [LN]. It means to harass someone, especially because of beliefs [BDAG].

c. σκληρός (LN 88.136) (BDAG 3. p. 930): 'hard' [Bar, BDAG, CBC, LN; ESV, GW, KJV, NASB, NIV], 'severe, demanding' [LN]. The phrase 'it is hard for you' is also translated 'it hurts you' [AB, BECNT; NRSV], 'it hurts' [REB], 'you are hurting yourself' [NET, TEV], 'you are only hurting yourself' [NCV], 'it is foolish' [CEV], 'it is useless' [NLT]. This adjective describes something as being hard and demanding in one's behavior [LN]. It describes what is difficult to the point of being impossible [BDAG].

d. κέντρον (LN 39.19) (BDAG 2. p. 539): 'goad' [AB, Bar, BDAG, BECNT, CBC, LN; ESV, NASB, NET, NIV, NRSV, REB], 'prick' [KJV]. The phrase 'to kick against the goads' is also translated 'to fight against me' [CEV], 'to fight against my will' [NLT], 'by fighting me' [NCV], 'for a mortal like you to resist God' [GW], 'by hitting back, like an ox kicking against its owner's stick' [TEV]. This noun denotes a pointed stick that serves the same purpose as a whip [BDAG]. The idiom 'kick against the goad' means to react against authority in such a way as to cause harm or suffering to oneself [LN].

e. κύριος (LN 12.9): 'Lord' [LN; all translations except CEV, GW], 'sir' [GW], 'Ruler' [LN], not explicit [CEV]. This noun denotes one who exercises supernatural authority over mankind, and is used as a title for God and for Christ [LN].

QUESTION—What language is referred to here as 'the Hebrew language'?

It was Aramaic [CBC, EBC, NICNT, PNTC, TNTC; CEV, NET, NIV, NLT].

QUESTION—What does it mean to kick against the goads?

This is a common agricultural image, in which a sharp pointed stick was used to prod an ox in the right direction, and here implies that Paul was being impelled by the Lord into a new direction, different than the one in which he was heading [BECNT, PNTC]. It describes fighting against one's destiny [NAC, TNTC] or against the divine will [Bar, NAC], against God's call to become a believer in Christ [TRT]. He was resisting God's discipline and direction, and fighting against Jesus himself [BECNT]. It does not imply that Paul had a guilty conscience about what he had been doing [Bar, NAC, NICNT, PNTC, TNTC].

**26:16** But arise and stand on your feet; for I-have-appeared[a] to-you for this[b] (purpose), to-appoint[c] you (as) (a)-servant[d] and witness[e] of- (the) - (things in)-which you-have-seen[f] me and of- (the) -things-(in which) I-will-appear[g] to-you,

TEXT—Manuscripts reading με 'me' are given a C rating by GNT to indicate that choosing it over manuscripts that omit it was difficult. It is included by: CEV, ESV, NLT, NRSV, TEV. It is omitted by: GW, NASB, NCV, NET. Inclusion or omission is ambiguous in NIV, REB.

LEXICON—a. aorist pass. indic. of ὁράω (LN 24.1) (BDAG A.1.d. p. 719): 'to appear' [BDAG; all translations except AB; NCV], 'to reveal oneself' [AB], 'to come to' [NCV], 'to be seen' [LN], 'to become visible' [BDAG].

b. τοῦτο (LN 92.29): 'this' [LN]. The phrase 'for this purpose' [BECNT; ESV, KJV, NASB, NRSV] is also translated 'for a purpose' [CBC; REB], 'for this reason' [NET], 'for a reason' [GW], 'this is why' [AB, Bar; NCV], 'because' [CEV], not explicit [NIV, NLT, TEV]. This demonstrative pronoun refers to an entity regarded as a part of the discourse setting [LN].

c. aorist mid. (deponent = act.) infin. of προχειρίζομαι (LN 30.89) (BDAG p. 891): 'to appoint' [BDAG; all translations except CEV, KJV, NCV, NET], 'to choose' [CEV, NCV], 'to designate' [NET], 'to make' [KJV], 'to choose for oneself, to select' [BDAG]. 'to choose in advance, to select beforehand, to designate in advance' [LN]. This verb means to choose for a particular purpose in advance [LN]. It means to express preference of someone for a task [BDAG].

d. ὑπηρέτης (LN 35.20) (BDAG p. 1035): 'servant' [BECNT, CBC, LN; all versions except KJV, NASB, NRSV], 'minister' [Bar; KJV, NASB], 'interpreter' [AB], 'helper, assistant' [BDAG]. This noun is also translated as a verb: 'to serve' [NRSV]. This noun denotes a person who renders service [LN]. This noun denotes one who functions as a helper, frequently in a subordinate capacity [BDAG].

e. μάρτυς (LN 33.270) (BDAG 2.c. p. 620): 'witness' [BDAG, LN; all translations except CEV, NRSV, TEV], 'one who testifies' [LN], 'testifier' [BDAG]. This noun is also translated as a verb: 'to testify' [NRSV]. It is also translated as a phrase: 'you are to tell others' [CEV, TEV]. This noun denotes a person who witnesses [LN]. It is one who affirms or attests [BDAG].

f. aorist act. indic. of εἶδον (LN 24.1): 'to see' [LN; all translations except AB; CEV], 'to know' [AB], 'to learn' [CEV].

g. fut. pass. indic. of ὁράω (LN 24.1) (BDAG 1.b. p. 719): 'to appear' [Bar, BDAG, BECNT; ESV, KJV, NASB, NET, NRSV], 'to be revealed' [AB], 'to be seen' [LN]. The phrase 'the things in which I will appear to you' is also translated 'what you shall yet see of me' [CBC; REB], 'what you will see of me' [NIV], 'the things that I will show you' [NCV], 'what I will show you' [GW], 'what I will show you in the future' [NLT, TEV], 'what I will show you later' [CEV]. This verb means to be perceived by the eye [LN].

QUESTION—What is the relation between the words 'servant' and 'witness'? 'Witness' explains what service Paul is to give [BECNT, NICNT]. 'Servant' or 'steward' describes his relationship to the Lord, and 'witness' describes the activity he will engage in toward people of all ethnicities and of any

330 ACTS 26:16

status [NAC]. 'Witness' and 'messenger' are how the ministries of Jeremiah and Ezekiel were described [NICNT].

QUESTION—To what does 'things in which you have seen me' refer?

It refers to the supernatural vision of Christ on the road to Damascus that he has been relating [PNTC, TNTC]. The next phrase, 'the things in which I will appear to you', refers to future visions of the Lord [Bar, PNTC, TNTC, TRT].

**26:17** delivering[a] you from the people and from the Gentiles to whom I am-sending you

LEXICON—a. pres. mid. participle of ἐξαιρέω (LN 21.17) (BDAG 2. p. 344): 'to deliver' [BDAG, BECNT; ESV, KJV], 'to rescue' [AB, Bar, BDAG, CBC; GW, NASB, NET, NIV, NLT, NRSV, REB, TEV], 'to protect' [CEV], 'to keep safe' [NCV], 'to set free' [BDAG], 'to rescue or set someone free from danger' [LN]. It means to deliver someone from peril or confining circumstance [BDAG].

QUESTION—To whom does 'the people' refer?

It refers to the Jewish people [AB, CBC, PNTC, TH, TNTC, TRT; CEV, GW, NASB, TEV]. Some translate 'the people' as 'your people' [ESV, NRSV], 'your own people' [NCV, NET, NIV, NLT, REB].

QUESTION—Who is referred to by the phrase 'to whom I am sending you'?

His commission is similar to that of Jeremiah and Ezekiel [AB, Bar, BECNT, EBC, NAC, NICNT, PNTC, TH, TNTC], as well as Isaiah [AB, NAC].

1. God is sending Paul to both Jews and Gentiles [CBC, PNTC, TNTC, TRT], though primarily to the Gentiles [TNTC]. His witness, at least, is to everyone everywhere, which includes Jews as well as Gentiles [NAC].
2. God is sending Paul to the Gentiles [AB, Bar, BECNT, NICNT], or at least primarily to the Gentiles [TNTC].

**DISCOURSE UNIT—26:19–32** [TEV]. The topic is Paul tells of his work.

**DISCOURSE UNIT—26:19–23** [NRSV]. The topic is Paul tells of his preaching.

**DISCOURSE UNIT—26:19–20** [NICNT]. The topic is Paul's obedience to the vision.

**26:18** to-open[a] their eyes, to-turn-(them) from darkness to (the)-light and from the power[b] of-Satan to God, (that) they receive forgiveness[c] of-sins and (a)-share[d] among those sanctified[e] by-faith[f] in me.'

LEXICON—a. aorist act. infin. of ἀνοίγω (LN 24.43) (BDAG 5.b. p. 84): 'to open' [BDAG; all translations], 'to open the eyes' [LN], 'to cause to function' [BDAG], 'to cause a blind person to see' [LN]. The idiom 'to open the eyes', means to cause someone to be able to see [LN]. It means to cause bodily parts, particularly the eyes or ears, to function [BDAG].

b. ἐξουσία (LN 37.36) (BDAG 2. p. 352): 'power' [AB, BDAG, BECNT; CEV, ESV, KJV, NCV, NET, NIV, NLT, NRSV, TEV], 'authority' [Bar], 'dominion' [CBC; NASB, REB], 'control' [GW], 'jurisdiction' [LN]. This noun denotes the domain or sphere over which one has authority to control or rule [LN]. It is the potential or resource to command, control, or govern [BDAG].

c. ἄφεσις (LN 40.8) (BDAG 2. p. 155): 'forgiveness' [LN; all translations except CEV, NCV, TEV], 'pardon' [BDAG, LN], 'cancellation' [BDAG]. The phrase 'receive forgiveness of sins' is also translated 'their sins will/can be forgiven' [CEV, NCV], 'they will have their sins forgiven' [TEV]. This noun denotes the removal of guilt resulting from wrongdoing [LN]. It is the act of freeing from an obligation, guilt, or punishment [BDAG].

d. κλῆρος (LN 63.18) (BDAG 2. p. 548): 'share' [BDAG, LN; GW, NET], 'place' [AB, BECNT, CBC; ESV, NCV, NIV, NLT, NRSV, REB, TEV], 'lot' [Bar], 'inheritance' [KJV, NASB], 'part' [LN], 'portion' [BDAG]. The phrase 'receive...a share among those sanctified' is also translated 'become part of God's holy people' [CEV]. This noun denotes a share or portion which has been assigned or granted [LN]. It is that which is assigned by lot or simply given as a portion or share [BDAG].

e. perf. pass. participle of ἁγιάζω (LN 88.26) (BDAG 2. p. 10): 'to be sanctified' [AB, Bar, BDAG, BECNT; ESV, KJV, NASB, NET, NIV, NRSV], 'to be made holy' [LN; NCV], 'to be consecrated' [BDAG]. The phrase 'those who are sanctified' is also translated 'those whom God has made his own' [CBC; REB], 'God's chosen people' [TEV], 'God's holy people' [CEV], 'God's people who are made holy' [GW], 'God's people who are set apart' [NLT]. This verb means to cause someone to have the quality of holiness [LN]. It means to include a person in the inner circle of what is holy, in both cultic and moral associations of the word [BDAG].

f. πίστις (LN 31.85) (BDAG 2.b.β. p. 819): 'faith' [BDAG, LN; all translations except CBC; GW, NCV], 'trust' [BDAG, CBC, LN], 'confidence' [BDAG]. The phrase 'by faith' is also translated 'by believing' [GW, NCV]. This noun denotes belief to the extent of complete trust and reliance [LN]. It is a state of believing on the basis of the reliability of the one trusted [BDAG].

QUESTION—What is the 'share' they are to receive?

In this context it means they will share in the resurrection of the dead [PNTC]. It is to have fellowship with God along with others who also are sanctified [BECNT]. It is to have a place in God's eternal kingdom [NAC], a place among the people of God [TH]. They were to be equal heirs with the Jews in God's blessings [NICNT]. It is their membership in the church both now as well as in the age to come [Bar].

QUESTION—What is meant by the verb 'sanctified'?

It means to be set apart [BECNT]. It is to live a life that is in Christ, one that is characterized by righteousness and is directed by God, as opposed to a self-centered and self-directed life [NAC]. It represents a state given by God, not a process of becoming holy [PNTC].

**26:19** Therefore,[a] O King Agrippa, I-was not disobedient[b] to-the heavenly[c] vision[d]

LEXICON—a. ὅθεν (LN 89.25) (BDAG 2. p. 693): 'therefore' [AB; ESV, NET], 'consequently' [Bar], 'wherefore' [BECNT], 'so' [CBC; NASB, REB], 'and so' [NLT, TEV], 'so then' [NIV], 'at that point' [GW], 'after that' [NRSV], 'after' [NCV], 'whereupon' [KJV], 'for which reason' [BDAG], 'because of' [LN], not explicit [CEV]. This conjunction marks cause or reason, with focus upon the source [LN]. It marks the basis for an action or procedure [BDAG].

b. ἀπειθής (LN 36.24) (BDAG a. p. 99): 'disobedient' [Bar, BDAG, BECNT, LN; ESV, KJV, NASB, NET, NIV, NRSV]. The phrase 'I was not disobedient' is also translated 'I did not disobey' [AB, CBC; GW, REB, TEV], 'I obeyed' [CEV, NCV, NLT]. This adjective describes being continuously disobedient [LN].

c. οὐράνιος (LN 1.12) (BDAG p. 737): 'heavenly' [AB, Bar, BDAG, BECNT, CBC, LN; ESV, KJV, NASB, NET, NRSV, REB], 'in heaven, pertaining to heaven' [LN]. This word is also translated as a phrase: 'from heaven' [CEV, NCV, NIV, NLT, TEV], 'I saw from heaven' [GW]. This adjective describes someone or something as related to or located in heaven [LN]. It describes someone or something as belonging to heaven, coming from or living in heaven [LN].

d. ὀπτασία (LN 33.488) (BDAG 1. p. 717): 'vision' [BDAG, LN; all translations], 'celestial sight' [BDAG]. This noun denotes an event in which something appears vividly and credibly to the mind, although not actually present, but implying the influence of some divine or supernatural power or agency [LN]. It is an event of a transcendent character that impresses itself vividly on the mind [BDAG].

QUESTION—How is the double negative 'was not disobedient' to be understood?

It shows emphasis: he certainly did obey [Bar, PNTC, TH, TRT]. It means he was fully obedient [BECNT], that he obeyed enthusiastically [NICNT].

**26:20** but to-those in Damascus first and (to-those) in-Jerusalem, and all the country of-Judea and to-the Gentiles I-proclaimed[a] (they should) repent[b] and to-turn[c] to God, doing deeds[d] fitting[e] for-repentance.

LEXICON—a. imperf. act. indic. of ἀπαγγέλλω (LN 33.327) (BDAG 2. p. 95): 'to proclaim' [Bar, BDAG], 'to preach' [AB; CEV, NIV, NLT, REB, TEV], 'to declare' [BECNT; ESV, NASB, NET, NRSV], 'to sound the call' [CBC], 'to spread the message' [GW], 'to show' [KJV], 'to tell' [NCV], 'to order, to command' [LN]. This verb means to announce what must be done [LN]. It means to make something known publicly [BDAG].

b. pres. act. infin. of μετανοέω (LN 41.52) (BDAG 2. p. 640): 'to repent' [AB, Bar, BDAG, BECNT, CBC, LN; ESV, KJV, NASB, NET, NIV,

NRSV, REB], 'to repent of one's sins' [NLT, TEV], 'to stop sinning' [CEV], 'to change one's heart and life' [NCV], 'to change the way one thinks' [GW], 'to change one's way' [LN], 'to feel remorse, to be converted' [BDAG]. This verb means to change one's way of life as the result of a complete change of thought and attitude with regard to sin and righteousness [LN].

c. pres. act. infin. of ἐπιστρέφω (LN 31.60) (BDAG 4.a. p. 382): 'to turn to' [BDAG, LN; all translations], 'to return' [BDAG], 'to come to believe, to come to accept' [LN]. This verb means to change one's belief, with focus upon that to which one turns [LN]. It means to change one's mind or course of action, for better or worse [BDAG].

d. ἔργον (LN 42.11) (BDAG 1.c.β. p. 390): 'deed' [BDAG, BECNT, CBC, LN; ESV, NASB, NET, NIV, NRSV, REB], 'action' [BDAG], 'act' [LN], 'work' [AB, Bar; KJV], '(do) things' [GW, NCV, TEV], 'the way you live' [CEV], 'things they do' [NLT]. This noun denotes that which is done, with possible focus on the energy or effort involved [LN]. It is that which displays itself in activity of any kind [BDAG].

e. ἄξιος (LN 66.6) (BDAG 1.b. p. 93): 'fitting' [AB, LN], 'worthy of' [Bar, BDAG, BECNT, LN], 'in keeping with' [BDAG; ESV], 'appropriate to' [NASB], 'consistent with' [NET, NRSV], 'meet with' [KJV], 'corresponding, comparable' [BDAG], 'proper, correspond to' [LN]. The phrase 'doing actions fitting for repentance' is also translated 'prove their repentance by deeds' [CBC; REB], 'demonstrate their repentance by their deeds' [NIV], 'prove what you have done by the way you live' [CEV], 'do things that prove they had changed their lives' [GW], 'do the things that would show they had repented' [TEV], 'prove they have changed by the good things they do' [NLT], 'do things to show they really had changed' [NCV]. This adjective describes something as being fitting or proper in corresponding to what should be expected [LN]. It describes something as having a relatively high degree of comparable worth or value [BDAG].

QUESTION—How should we understand Paul's statement that he preached in all Judea in light of the fact that no mention is made of such preaching in Acts?

The accusative case of πᾶσάν τε τὴν χώραν τῆς Ἰουδαίας 'all the country of Judea' is unusual [BECNT, EBC, NAC, NICNT, TNTC]. Paul's reference to having witnessed in Judea does not necessarily mean that it was carried out before he went to the Gentiles, but covers all witnessing in that region at any point in his ministry [BECNT, PNTC]. Preaching to Jews in Jerusalem would have had an effect on Jews all over Judea [TRT]. One variant text has 'Jews' instead of 'Judea', which could simply mean that he preached to Jews and Gentiles wherever he went [NAC, NICNT, TNTC]. It is possible that 'in all Judea' is a gloss that was incorrectly added to the text because of a misunderstanding of Romans 15:19 [EBC]. (Note that GNT does not discuss any variant texts for this verse.)

QUESTION—What do 'repent' and 'turn to God' mean in Paul's preaching?
To repent means to change one's thinking [BECNT, TRT], and to turn means to change the direction of one's life [BECNT], to turn to God and believe his message [TRT]. The two words describe the same action of completely changing one's direction in life [NAC]. The genuineness of repentance is to be shown in a changed life [Bar].

**DISCOURSE UNIT—26:21** [NICNT]. The topic is Paul's arrest.

**26:21** **On-account-of[a] these-things (the)-Jews having-seized[b] me in the temple tried to-kill[c] (me).**

LEXICON—a. ἕνεκα with genitive object (LN 89.31) (BDAG 1. p. 334): 'on account of' [BDAG, LN], 'because of' [AB, Bar, BDAG, LN], 'for this reason' [BECNT; ESV, GW, NASB, NET, NRSV, TEV], 'for these causes' [KJV], 'that/this is why' [CBC; CEV, NIV, REB], 'this is why' [NCV], 'for (preaching this)' [NLT], 'for the sake of' [BDAG]. This preposition indicates cause or reason [BDAG, LN].

b. aorist mid. participle. of συλλαμβάνω (LN 37.109) (BDAG 1.b. p. 955): 'to seize' [AB, Bar, BDAG, BECNT, CBC, LN; ESV, NASB, NET, NIV, NRSV, REB, TEV], 'to arrest' [BDAG, LN; NLT], 'to take prisoner' [GW], 'to grab' [CEV], 'to catch' [KJV], 'to take' [LN; NCV]. This verb means to seize and to take along with [LN]. It means to take into custody [BDAG].

c. aorist mid. infin. of διαχειρίζω (LN 20.62) (BDAG p. 240): 'to kill' [AB, BDAG, BECNT; all versions except GW, NASB, REB], 'to murder' [BDAG; GW], 'to put to death' [NASB], 'to do away with' [CBC; REB], 'to make away with' [Bar], 'to seize and kill, to arrest and cause the death of' [LN], 'to lay violent hands on' [BDAG]. This verb means to lay hands on someone and kill [LN]. It means to take hold of someone forcibly with malicious intent and frequently ending in the taking of life [BDAG].

QUESTION—To what does 'for this reason' refer?
It refers to Paul's preaching mentioned in v. 20 [Bar, BECNT, CBC, NICNT, PNTC, TH, TNTC; NLT]. The Jews seized Paul because he had been preaching to Gentiles [Bar, EBC]. The Jews seized Paul because the effect of his preaching made Gentiles equal to or on the same level as Jews [BECNT, NICNT, PNTC, TNTC].

**DISCOURSE UNIT—26:22–23** [NICNT]. The topic is peroration.

**26:22** **So having-obtained[a] help[b] from God to this day I-stand testifying[c] to-small[d] and to-great[e] saying nothing except what the prophets and Moses said was-going to-happen,**

LEXICON—a. aorist act. participle of τυγχάνω (LN 90.61) (BDAG 1. p. 1019): 'to obtain' [Bar; KJV, NASB], 'to have' [BECNT, CBC; ESV, NRSV, REB], 'to experience' [BDAG, LN; NET], 'to have happen to' [LN], 'to meet, to attain, to gain, to find' [BDAG]. The phrase 'having obtained help from God' is also translated 'God has helped me' [CEV,

NCV, NIV], 'God has been helping me' [GW], 'God having helped me' [AB], 'I have been helped by God' [TEV], 'God has protected me' [NLT]. This verb means to experience some happening [BDAG, LN], (generally neutral in connotation) [LN].

b. ἐπικουρία (LN 35.7) (BDAG p. 374): 'help' [Bar, BDAG, BECNT, CBC, LN; ESV, KJV, NASB, NET, NRSV, REB]. This noun is also translated as a verb: 'to help' [AB; CEV, GW, NCV, NIV], 'to be helped' [TEV], 'to protect' [NLT]. This noun denotes help, with the possible implication of assistance provided by an ally [LN].

c. pres. mid. or pass. (deponent = act.) participle of μαρτύρομαι (LN 33.223) (BDAG 1. p. 619): 'to testify' [Bar, BDAG, BECNT, CBC, LN; ESV, GW, NASB, NET, NIV, NLT, NRSV], 'to witness' [KJV], 'to be a witness' [AB], 'to give witness' [TEV], 'to bear witness' [BDAG; REB], 'to preach' [CEV], 'to tell' [NCV], 'to declare, to assert' [LN], This verb means to make a serious declaration on the basis of presumed personal knowledge [LN]. It means to affirm something with solemnity [BDAG].

d. μικρός (LN 87.58) (BDAG 1.b. p. 651): 'small' [BDAG; all translations except CEV, NLT, REB], 'poor' [CEV], 'lowly' [REB], 'low' [LN], 'unimportant' [LN; GW], 'least' [NLT], 'short' [BDAG]. This adjective describes someone or something as being of low or unimportant status [LN]. It describes a relatively limited size, measure, or quantity [BDAG].

e. μέγας (LN 87.22) (BDAG 1.d. p. 623): 'great' [BDAG, LN; all translations except CEV, GW, NLT], 'greatest' [NLT], 'rich' [CEV], 'important' [LN; GW], 'large' [BDAG]. This adjective describes someone or something as being great in terms of status [LN], or as exceeding a standard involving related objects [BDAG].

QUESTION—To what action does 'to this day' refer?
1. He is saying that to this day he has been helped by God [TRT; CEV, ESV, GW, NET, NIV, NLT, NRSV, REB, TEV].
2. He is saying that to this day he has been a witness [AB, Bar, BECNT, CBC, NICNT, TNTC; KJV, NASB, NCV]. (Note that the statement that he had been a witness 'to this day' would not exclude the idea that God had helped him up to that time, and in fact would presuppose it.)

QUESTION—What is meant by 'small and great'?
His testimony is offered to a wide social spectrum of people [PNTC], to all kinds of people [BECNT, NAC, TH, TRT]. He spoke to people in the marketplace as well to the governor [Bar]. There were no social boundaries in Paul's preaching of the gospel; he preached the same gospel to all alike [NAC]. He preached to poor and rich, to unimportant people and important people, to young and old [TRT].

**26:23** that (having been) subject-to-suffering[a] the Christ, first of (the)-resurrection[b] of-(the)-dead, would proclaim[c] light to-the people and to-the Gentiles."

LEXICON—a. παθητός (LN 24.85) (BDAG p. 748): 'subject to suffering' [BDAG, LN]. The phrase 'having been subject to suffering' is also translated 'must suffer' [AB, BECNT, CBC; ESV, NRSV, TEV], 'was to suffer' [Bar; NASB, NET], 'would suffer' [CEV, GW, NIV, NLT, REB], 'should suffer' [KJV], 'would die' [NCV]. This adjective describes being subject to suffering [LN].

b. ἀνάστασις (LN 23.93) (BDAG 2.b. p. 71): 'resurrection' [BDAG, LN]. The phrase 'first of the resurrection' is also translated 'the first to rise from the dead' [AB, BECNT, CBC; ESV, NCV, NET, NIV, NLT, NRSV, REB], 'the first that should rise from the dead' [KJV], 'the first one to rise from death' [TEV], 'the first to be raised from death' [CEV], 'the first to come back to life' [GW], 'on the basis of the resurrection of the dead' [Bar], 'by reason of his resurrection from the dead' [NASB]. This noun denotes the act of coming back to life after having once died [LN]. It means resurrection from the dead [BDAG].

c. pres. act. infin. of καταγγέλλω (LN 33.204) (BDAG a. p. 515): 'to proclaim' [Bar, BDAG, BECNT; ESV, NASB, NET, NRSV], 'to bring' [AB; CEV, NCV, NIV], 'to announce' [BDAG, CBC, LN; NLT, REB, TEV], 'to spread' [GW], 'to show' [KJV], 'to proclaim throughout, to speak out about' [LN]. This verb means to announce, with focus upon the extent to which the announcement or proclamation extends [LN]. It means to make known in public, with implication of broad dissemination [BDAG].

QUESTION—What does 'first of the resurrection of the dead' mean?

Jesus was the first to rise from the dead [AB, BECNT, CBC, NICNT, TNTC, TRT; CEV, ESV, GW, KJV, NCV, NET, NIV, NLT, NRSV, REB]. Christ's resurrection is the first of many more to come in the general resurrection [NAC], a kind of first-fruits of the future harvest [NAC, NICNT, PNTC, TNTC].

QUESTION—To whom does 'the people' refer?

It refers to the Jewish people [BECNT, CBC, EBC, NICNT, PNTC, TH, TNTC, TRT; CEV, GW, NASB, NIV, NLT, REB, TEV]. The translation 'our people' implies that it is to the Jewish people [AB; ESV, NET, NRSV].

**DISCOURSE UNIT—26:24–32** [AB, CBC, PNTC; NCV, NRSV]. The topic is Paul tries to persuade Agrippa [NCV], Paul appeals to Agrippa to believe [NRSV], Paul's personal appeal and the outcome [PNTC], Festus and Agrippa state their opinion of Paul's case [AB], the result [CBC].

**DISCOURSE UNIT—26:24–29** [NAC, NICNT]. The topic is Paul's appeal to Agrippa [NAC], interchange between Festus, Paul, and Agrippa [NICNT].

**26:24** And (as) he was-saying- these-things -in-his-defense, Festus said in-(a)-loud voice, "You-are-insane,[a] Paul! (Your) great[b] learning[c] is-turning you to insanity[d]!"

LEXICON—a. pres. mid. or pass. (deponent = act.) indic. of μαίνομαι (LN 30.24) (BDAG p. 610): 'to be insane' [LN; NLT], 'to be out of one's mind' [BDAG, LN; ESV, NASB, NCV, NIV, NRSV], 'to be crazy' [AB, Bar, BDAG, BECNT, LN; CEV, GW], 'to lose one's mind' [NET], 'to be mad' [TEV], 'to be raving' [CBC; REB], 'to be beside oneself' [KJV], 'to not be in one's right mind' [LN]. This verb means to think or reason in a completely irrational manner [LN].

b. πολύς (LN 59.11) (BDAG 2.a.α.ℶ. p. 848): 'great' [AB, Bar, BECNT, LN; ESV, NASB, NET, NIV, TEV], 'much' [BDAG, LN; KJV], 'too much' [CBC; CEV, GW, NCV, NLT, NRSV, REB], 'extensive' [BDAG, LN]. This adjective describes a relatively large quantity [LN]. It describes something as relatively large in quantity or measure [BDAG].

c. γράμμα (LN 27.21) (BDAG 3. p. 206): 'learning' [AB, Bar, BDAG, BECNT, LN; CEV, ESV, KJV, NASB, NET, NIV, NRSV, TEV], 'study' [CBC; NCV, NLT, REB], 'education' [GW], 'knowledge' [BDAG], 'education, scholarship' [LN]. This plural noun denotes the body of information acquired in school or from the study of writings [LN].

d. μανία (LN 30.24) (BDAG p. 615): 'insanity' [LN], 'madness' [Bar, BDAG, LN], 'frenzy, delirium' [BDAG]. The phrase 'turning you to insanity' is also translated 'is driving you insane' [NET, NIV, NRSV], 'is driving you mad' [CBC; NASB, REB, TEV], 'makes you mad' [AB; KJV], 'is turning you mad' [BECNT], 'is driving you crazy' [GW], 'has driven you crazy' [NCV], 'has made you crazy' [NLT], 'has driven you out of your mind' [CEV], 'is driving you out of your mind' [ESV]. This noun denotes the condition of thinking or reasoning in a completely irrational manner [LN].

QUESTION—Why was it at this particular moment that Festus accused Paul of being insane?

Festus thinks that the idea of the resurrection is so preposterous that Paul has become insane to believe in it [Bar, BECNT, EBC, NAC, TRT], and also a king would not become such on the basis of suffering and death [Bar]. The resurrection is something no Roman would find reasonable [BECNT, EBC, NICNT]. Festus is disturbed at the prospect of having to report as evidence in this case the fact that a crucified and risen Jesus had commissioned Paul to bring people from every nation to faith and repentance [PNTC].

**26:25** But Paul (said), "I-am- not -insane, most-excellent[a] Festus, but I-speak words of-truth[b] and reason[c].

LEXICON—a. κράτιστος (LN 87.55) (BDAG p. 565): 'most excellent' [BDAG, BECNT, LN; ESV, NASB, NCV, NET, NIV, NLT, NRSV], 'most noble' [AB, Bar, BDAG; KJV], 'your excellency' [CBC; GW, REB, TEV], 'excellency' [LN], 'honorable' [CEV], 'your honor' [LN].

This adjective describes having noble status, with the implication of power and authority, often employed as a title [LN]. It is used as a strongly affirmative honorary form of address [BDAG].
- b. ἀλήθεια (LN 72.2) (BDAG 2.a. p. 42): 'truth' [AB, Bar, BDAG, BECNT, CBC, LN; KJV, NASB, NLT, NRSV, REB, TEV]. This noun is also translated as an adjective: 'true' [CEV, ESV, GW, NCV, NET, NIV]. This noun denotes the content of that which is true and thus in accordance with what actually happened [LN]. It is the content of what is true [BDAG].
- c. σωφροσύνη (LN 32.34) (BDAG 1. p. 987): 'reasonableness, rationality' [BDAG], 'sober-mindedness' [Bar], 'soberness' [KJV], 'sound judgment' [LN]. This noun is also translated as an adjective: 'sober' [AB, BECNT, CBC; NASB, NLT, NRSV, REB, TEV], 'rational' [ESV, NET], 'reasonable' [NIV], 'sane' [GW], 'sensible' [NCV]. It is also translated as a phrase: 'it makes sense' [CEV]. This noun denotes the condition of having understanding about practical matters and thus to be able to act sensibly [LN]. It is soundness of mind [BDAG].

QUESTION—How do Paul's and Festus' assessments of Paul's state of mind compare?

Paul had used the verb ἐμμαίνομαι to describe his former rage against Christians, whereas Festus uses the same verb here to describe Paul's present condition; Paul says that, in contrast to his past state, his frame of mind now can be described in terms of rationality, not mania [PNTC]. Whereas Festus assumes Paul has lost contact with the real world through speculation, Paul makes his appeal based on events that are public and well-known [BECNT]. Paul points out that he is sober-minded and not engaging in wild speculation because what he is dealing with is a matter of publicly known events [TNTC].

**26:26** For the king knows about these-things, to whom also I-speak freely,[a] for I-am-persuaded[b] (that) none of-these-things has-escaped- his -notice;[c] for this has- not -been-done in (a)-corner.[d]

LEXICON—a. pres. mid. or pass. (deponent = act.) participle of παρρησιάζομαι (LN 33.90) (BDAG 1. p. 782): 'to speak freely' [AB, BDAG, CBC; KJV, NCV, NET, NIV, NRSV, REB], 'to speak with boldness' [Bar], 'to speak with all boldness' [TEV], 'to speak boldly' [LN; ESV, NLT], 'to speak openly' [BDAG, BECNT, LN], 'to speak plainly' [CEV], 'to speak easily' [GW], 'to speak with confidence' [NASB], 'to speak fearlessly' [BDAG]. This verb means to speak openly about something and with complete confidence [LN]. It means to express oneself freely [BDAG].
- b. pres. pass. indic. of πείθω (LN 33.301) (BDAG 3.a. p. 792): 'to be persuaded' [Bar, BDAG, BECNT, LN; ESV, KJV, NASB], 'to be convinced' [AB, LN; NIV], 'to be sure' [CEV, GW, NLT, TEV], 'to be certain' [NRSV], 'to believe' [BDAG, CBC; NET, REB], 'to know' [NCV]. This verb means to convince someone to believe something and

to act on the basis of what is recommended [LN]. It means to be won over as the result of persuasion [BDAG].
c. pres. act. infin. of λανθάνω (LN 28.83) (BDAG p. 586): 'to escape notice' [BDAG, BECNT, LN; ESV, NASB, NET, NIV, NRSV], 'to escape attention' [AB; GW], 'to be unaware' [REB], 'to be hidden' [BDAG; KJV]. The phrase 'has escaped his notice' is also translated 'has escaped him' [Bar], 'that he can be unaware' [CBC], 'King Agrippa knows' [CEV], 'he has heard' [NCV], 'are familiar to him' [NLT], 'you have taken notice' [TEV]. This verb means to cause oneself to not be known, with the implication of concealment and secrecy [LN]. It means to succeed in avoiding attention or awareness [BDAG].
d. γωνία (LN 79.107) (BDAG p. 209): 'corner' [Bar, BDAG, BECNT, LN; all versions except GW, REB]. The phrase 'done in a corner' is also translated 'done secretly' [GW], 'a hole-and-corner affair/business' [AB, CBC; REB]. This noun denotes the corner of an area or construction, either an inside corner or an outside corner [LN].

QUESTION—To what does 'these things' refer?

It refers to Jesus' death and resurrection [AB, EBC, PNTC], and Jesus' bringing light both to Jews and to all nations [PNTC]. It refers to Jewish hope in the resurrection of the dead and its basis in scripture, and the belief of Christians that Christ had been raised from the dead [NAC]. It is the events which showed the fulfillment of the promises of long ago [NICNT].

QUESTION—Why does Paul feel free to speak so openly in this issue?

Paul, who now addresses his remarks to Agrippa, knew that Agrippa would have been well aware of the origins and history of the Christian movement [PNTC]. Agrippa would have known of the life, ministry, and resurrection of Jesus, events that had actually been quite public [AB, EBC, BECNT]. These events were well known and public, such that most anyone paying attention would have been aware of them [BECNT, NICNT]. Christians, and the faith they held, were not insignificant and unknown, and Paul's ministry had been very public and widespread [NAC].

**26:27** King Agrippa, do-you-believe the prophets? I-know that you-believe." **26:28** And Agrippa-(said) to Paul, "In (a)-short-(time)[a] would-you-persuade[b] me to-become[c] (a)-Christian?"

LEXICON—a. ὀλίγος (LN 67.106) (BDAG 2.a.β. p. 703): 'a short time' [LN; CEV, ESV, NASB, NCV, NET, NIV, TEV], 'a little while' [AB, BECNT, LN], '(so) quickly' [NLT, NRSV], 'almost' [KJV], 'quickly' [GW], 'brief, briefly' [LN], 'little, small, short' [BDAG]. The phrase ἐν ὀλίγῳ 'in a short time' is also translated 'with little trouble' [Bar], 'not take much (to win me over)' [CBC], 'with a little more (of your persuasion)' [REB]. It describes a relatively brief extent of time [LN]. This adjective describes being relatively small on a scale of extent [BDAG].
b. pres. act. indic. of πείθω (LN 33.301) (BDAG 1.b. p. 791): 'to persuade' [AB, Bar, BDAG, LN; ESV, GW, KJV, NASB, NCV, NET, NIV, NLT,

NRSV], 'to win someone over' [CBC], 'to talk someone into' [CEV], 'to convince' [LN], 'to appeal to, to cajole, to mislead' [BDAG], not explicit [TEV]. This verb is also translated as a phrase: 'with persuasion' [BECNT; REB]. The present tense of this verb has a conative force, indicating intent: 'to try (to persuade, etc.)' [Bar, BECNT]. This verb means to convince someone to believe something and to act on the basis of what is recommended [LN]. It means to cause to come to a particular point of view or course of action [BDAG].

c. aorist act. infin. of ποιέω (LN 13.9): 'to become' [GW, NASB, NCV, NET, NLT, NRSV], 'to be' [CEV, ESV, KJV, NIV], 'to make (a Christian)' [BECNT, CBC; REB, TEV], 'to turn (Christian)' [AB], 'to play (the Christian)' [Bar], 'to make to be, to cause to be, to make, to result in, to bring about' [LN]. This verb means to cause a state to be [LN].

QUESTION—What is meant by Ἐν ὀλίγῳ 'in a short time'?
1. It refers to a short period of time [AB, BECNT, EBC, NAC, PNTC; CEV, ESV, GW, NASB, NCV, NET, NIV, NLT, NRSV, TEV].
2. It refers to a small degree of difficulty [Bar, CBC; REB].
3. It is a way of summing up in a few words what Agrippa perceived Paul's intent to be: 'in short…you are trying' [NICNT].

QUESTION—What did Agrippa mean by his statement?
It was Agrippa's way of challenging Paul's hope to bring Agrippa to repentance and conversion [CBC, EBC, NAC, PNTC]. It was a courteous way of evading the question by saying that Paul was close to making a Christian of Agrippa, though in fact Agrippa had no intent of doing such a thing [AB]. Since the term 'Christian' had been used in a derisive way in Acts 11:26, Agrippa is probably using the term in the same way, which shows that Agrippa is not really serious here [BECNT].

**26:29** And Paul (said), "I-wish[a] to-God-(that) whether in (a)-short-(time) or in (a)-long-(time)[b] not only you but also all hearing me today would- also -become such-as I am, except-for[c] these chains.[d]"

LEXICON—a. aorist mid. (deponent = act.) optative of εὔχομαι (LN 33.178) (BDAG 1. p. 417): 'to wish' [Bar, CBC; CEV, GW, NASB, REB], 'to pray' [BDAG, LN; NCV, NET, NIV, NLT, NRSV], 'to speak to God, to ask God for' [LN]. The phrase 'I wish to God' is also translated 'I would to God' [AB, BECNT; ESV, KJV], 'my prayer to God is' [TEV]. It means to speak to or to make requests of God [BDAG, LN].

b. μέγας (LN 67.89): 'long time' [LN; CEV, NASB, NCV, NET, TEV], 'long' [BECNT, LN; ESV, NIV]. The phrase 'whether in a short time or in a long time' is also translated 'whether quickly or not' [NLT, NRSV], 'whether in small or great matters' [AB], 'with little trouble or much' [Bar], 'much or little' [CBC], 'little or much' [REB], 'quickly and completely' [GW], 'both almost and altogether' [KJV]. The phrase ἐν μεγάλῳ describes a relatively long duration of time [LN],

c. παρεκτός (LN 58.38) (BDAG 2. p. 774): 'except for' [BDAG, BECNT; all versions except KJV, REB], 'except' [KJV], 'apart from' [AB, Bar, BDAG, CBC; REB], 'besides, additional' [LN]. This adjective describes being different and in addition to something else, with the implication of something being external to central concerns [LN]. It describes something as being left out of other considerations [BDAG].

d. δεσμός (LN 6.14) (BDAG 1.a. p. 219): 'chain' [LN; all translations except Bar; GW, KJV], 'bond' [Bar, BDAG, LN; KJV], 'fetter' [BDAG, LN]. The phrase 'except for these chains' is also translated 'except for being a prisoner' [GW]. This noun denotes any instrument or means of binding or tying [LN]. It is that which serves as a means of restraint by tying or fastening [BDAG].

QUESTION—Does εὔχομαι express a wish or an actual prayer that Paul prays? This word expresses Paul's earnest desire [AB, CBC, EBC, NAC, NICNT, PNTC, TNTC], but also his prayer [NAC, TH]. Paul desires to intercede in prayer for them [BECNT]. The fact that this verb is in the rarely used optative mood expresses extreme politeness [EBC].

QUESTION—Was Paul actually in chains during this hearing? He was actually in chains [EBC, NICNT, PNTC, TNTC]. He may have been in chains, or this statement may have been a metaphorical use of the term to refer to the fact of his imprisonment [NAC].

**DISCOURSE UNIT—26:30–32** [NAC, NICNT]. The topic is Paul's innocence declared by governor and king [NAC], agreement on Paul's innocence [NICNT].

**26:30** The king rose[a] and the governor and Bernice and those sitting-with them, **26:31** and having-withdrawn[b] they-spoke to one-another saying "This man has done nothing worthy[c] of-death or imprisonment.[d]" **26:32** And Agrippa said to-Festus, "This man would-have-been-able to-be-released[e] if he-had- not -appealed[f] to-Caesar."

LEXICON—a. aorist act. indic. of ἀνίστημι (LN 17.7) (BDAG 6. p. 83): 'to rise' [AB, BDAG, CBC; ESV, NIV, REB], 'to rise up' [Bar; KJV], 'to arise' [BECNT], 'to get up' [CEV, GW, NET, NRSV, TEV], 'to stand up' [BDAG; NASB, NCV, NLT], 'to cause to stand, to raise up' [LN]. This verb means to cause someone to stand up [LN]. It means to stand up from a recumbent or sitting position [BDAG].

b. aorist act. participle of ἀναχωρέω (LN 15.53): 'to withdraw' [AB, Bar, BECNT, CBC, LN; ESV, REB], 'to leave' [CEV, GW, NET, NLT, NRSV, TEV], 'to leave the room' [NCV, NIV], 'to go aside' [KJV, NASB], 'to retire, to go off, to go away' [LN]. This verb means to move away from a location, implying a considerable distance [LN].

c. ἄξιος (LN 65.17) (BDAG 1.b. p. 93): 'worthy' [Bar, BDAG, LN; KJV, NASB], 'deserving' [AB; NET], 'of comparable worth' [LN], 'corresponding, comparable' [BDAG]. This adjective is also translated as a verb: 'to deserve' [BECNT, CBC; CEV, ESV, GW, NIV, NLT, NRSV, REB]. The phrase 'this man has done nothing worthy of…(imprisonment)'

is also translated 'this man has not done anything for which he should...(be put in prison)' [TEV], 'there is no reason why this man should be (put in jail)' [NCV]. This adjective describes having a relatively high degree of comparable merit or worth [LN]. It describes having a relatively high degree of comparable worth or value [BDAG].
  d. δεσμός (LN 6.14) (BDAG 1.a. p. 219): 'imprisonment' [Bar, BECNT, CBC; ESV, NASB, NET, NIV, NLT, NRSV, REB], 'chain' [AB, BDAG, LN], 'bond' [BDAG, LN; KJV], 'fetter' [BDAG, LN]. This noun is also translated as a passive verb: 'being put in jail' [CEV, NCV], 'be put in prison' [GW, TEV]. This noun denotes any instrument or means of binding or tying [LN]. It is that which serves as a means of restraint by tying or fastening [BDAG].
  e. perf. pass. infin. of ἀπολύω (LN 37.127) (BDAG 1. p. 117): 'to be released' [AB, Bar, BDAG, LN; NET, TEV], 'to be set free' [BDAG, BECNT, LN; CEV, ESV, GW, NASB, NIV, NLT, NRSV], 'to be set at liberty' [KJV], 'to be discharged' [CBC; REB], 'to let (someone) go free' [NCV], 'to be pardoned' [BDAG]. This verb means to release from control, to set free (highly generic meaning applicable to a wide variety of circumstances, including confinement, political domination, sin, sickness) [LN]. As legal term, it means to grant acquittal [BDAG].
  f. pluperf. mid. indic. of ἐπικαλέω (LN 56.15) (BDAG 3. p. 373): 'to appeal' [BDAG; all translations except CEV, GW, NCV], 'to appeal one's case' [LN; GW], 'to ask to be tried' [CEV], 'to ask (someone else) to hear one's case' [NCV], 'to appeal to a higher court' [LN]. This verb means to claim one's legal right to have a case reviewed by a higher tribunal [LN]. It means to request a higher judicial authority to review a decision in a lower court [BDAG].

**DISCOURSE UNIT—27:1–28:31** [NAC; REB]. The topic is Paul's journey to Rome [REB], Paul's witness to Jews and Gentiles without hindrance [NAC].

**DISCOURSE UNIT—27:1–28:16** [BECNT, NAC, TNTC]. The topic is Paul's journey to Rome [NAC], the long sea journey to Rome [BECNT], the journey to Italy [TNTC].

**DISCOURSE UNIT—27:1–28:15** [CBC, EBC, PNTC]. The topic is journeying to Rome [PNTC], the journey to Rome [EBC], to Rome [CBC].

**DISCOURSE UNIT—27:1–44** [AB, NICNT, PNTC]. The topic is from Caesarea to Malta [PNTC], Paul's voyage and shipwreck [NICNT], the voyage to Rome [AB].

**DISCOURSE UNIT—27:1–26** [GW]. The topic is Paul sails for Rome.

**DISCOURSE UNIT—27:1–20** [PNTC]. The topic is sailing into danger.

**DISCOURSE UNIT—27:1–13** [NASB]. The topic is Paul is sent to Rome.

ACTS 27:1 343

**DISCOURSE UNIT—27:1-12** [CBC, EBC; CEV, ESV, NCV, NIV, NLT, NRSV, TEV]. The topic is Paul sails for Rome [ESV, NCV, NIV, NLT, NRSV, TEV], Paul is taken to Rome [CEV], to Crete [CBC], from Palestine to Crete [EBC].

**DISCOURSE UNIT—27:1-8** [NAC; NET]. The topic is Paul and company sail for Rome [NET], the journey to Fair Havens [NAC].

**DISCOURSE UNIT—27:1-5** [NICNT]. The topic is Caesarea to Myra.

**27:1** **And when it-was-decided[a] (for) us to-sail[b] for Italy, they delivered[c] Paul and some other prisoners to-(a)-centurion[d] of-(the)-Augustan[e] cohort,[f] Julius by-name.**

LEXICON—a. aorist pass. indic. of κρίνω (LN 30.75) (BDAG 4. p. 568): 'to be decided' [BDAG, LN; all translations except CEV, KJV, NLT], 'to be determined' [KJV], 'to be proposed, to be intended' [BDAG]. The phrase 'when it was decided' is also translated 'when it was time' [CEV], 'when the time came' [NLT]. This verb means to come to a conclusion in the process of thinking and thus to be in a position to make a decision [LN]. It means to come to a conclusion after a cognitive process [BDAG].
  b. pres. act. infin. of ἀποπλέω (LN 54.7) (BDAG p. 119): 'to sail' [all translations except AB, Bar; NLT], 'to set sail' [AB, Bar; NLT], 'to sail away' [BDAG, LN], 'to sail from' [LN]. This verb means to sail away from a point [LN].
  c. imperf. act. indic. of παραδίδωμι (LN 57.77) (BDAG 1.b. p. 762): 'to deliver' [BECNT; ESV, KJV, NASB], 'to hand over' [AB, Bar, BDAG, LN; NET, TEV], 'to transfer' [NRSV], 'to turn over, give up a person' [BDAG], 'to give over' [LN]. This active verb is also translated as passive: 'to be handed over' [CBC; NIV, REB], 'to be turned over' [GW], 'to be placed in the custody of' [NLT]. The phrase 'they delivered Paul...to...Julius' is also translated 'Julius...was put in charge of Paul' [CEV], 'Julius...guarded Paul' [NCV]. This verb means to hand over to or to convey something to someone, particularly a right or an authority [LN].
  d. ἑκατοντάρχης (LN 55.16) (BDAG p. 299): 'centurion' [AB, Bar, BECNT, CBC, LN; ESV, KJV, NASB, NET, NIV, NRSV, REB], 'captain' [LN; CEV], 'officer in the Roman army' [TEV], 'army officer' [GW, NCV], 'officer' [NLT]. This noun denotes a Roman officer in command of about one hundred men [LN]. It is a Roman officer commanding about a hundred men (subordinate to a tribune) [BDAG].
  e. σεβαστός (LN 37.76) (BDAG p. 917): 'Augustan' [AB, Bar, BECNT, CBC; ESV, NASB, NET, NRSV, REB], 'Augustus' [KJV], 'imperial' [BDAG, LN; NIV, NLT], 'the Emperor's' [GW, NCV, TEV], 'the Emperor's special (troops)' [CEV]. This adjective describes something as pertaining to the Emperor [LN]. This was an honorary title frequently given to auxiliary troops [BDAG].
  f. σπεῖρα (LN 55.9) (BDAG p. 936): 'cohort' [AB, Bar, BDAG, BECNT, CBC, LN; ESV, NASB, NET, NRSV, REB], 'regiment' [NIV, NLT,

TEV], 'troops' [CEV], 'division' [GW], 'army' [NCV], 'band' [KJV], 'band of soldiers' [LN]. This noun denotes a Roman military unit of about six hundred soldiers, though often only a part of such a cohort was referred to as a cohort [LN]. It is the tenth part of a legion, and normally had about 600 men, though the number varied [BDAG].

QUESTION—Who is included in the pronoun 'us'?

It describes everyone traveling on the ship, not just Paul, Luke, and Aristarchus [PNTC]. It describes Paul, Luke, and some other prisoners [TRT].

QUESTION—What was the 'Augustan' cohort?

It would have consisted of recruits from Syria, not Rome [BECNT, PNTC]. The term σεβαστός 'Augustan' or 'imperial' was used to describe auxiliary forces recruited from the local population [NAC, TH].

**27:2** And having-embarked[a] on-a-ship of-Adramyttium (that was) about to-sail to ports[b] along-(the coast of) Asia, Aristarchus (a)-Macedonian of-Thessalonica being with us, we-put-out-to-sea.[c]

LEXICON—a. aorist act. participle of ἐπιβαίνω (LN 15.97) (BDAG 1. p. 367): 'to embark' [Bar, BECNT, CBC, LN; ESV, NASB, NRSV, REB], 'to go onto' [LN], 'to go aboard' [AB; CEV, TEV], 'to go on board' [NET], 'to board' [BDAG; NIV], 'to enter into' [KJV], 'to get on' [NCV], 'to go up, 'to go upon' [BDAG], not explicit [GW, NLT]. This verb means to move up onto some object [LN]. It means to move up onto something [BDAG].
  b. τόπος (LN 80.1) (BDAG 1.a. p. 1011): 'port' [BECNT, CBC; all versions except KJV, NASB, TEV], 'seaport' [TEV], 'place' [AB, Bar, BDAG, LN], 'region' [NASB], 'coast' [KJV]. This noun denotes an area of any size, regarded in certain contexts as a point in space [LN]. It denotes an area of any size, generally specified as a place of habitation, an inhabited geographical area [BDAG].
  c. aorist pass. indic. of ἀνάγω (LN 54.4) (BDAG 4. p. 62): 'to put out to sea' [Bar, BDAG, CBC, LN; NASB, NET, NIV, REB], 'to put to sea' [BECNT; ESV, NRSV], 'to set sail' [AB, LN; GW], 'to sail' [CEV], 'to sail away' [TEV], 'to leave (on a ship)' [NLT], 'to launch' [KJV], not explicit [NCV]. This verb means to begin to go by boat [BDAG, LN].

QUESTION—How is it that Luke and Aristarchus were allowed to accompany Paul on this voyage?

This was probably a privately owned vessel, and any passenger who could pay for passage could go on board [NAC, NICNT, PNTC]. They were paying passengers, and Paul's status as a Roman citizen may have given him a favored status such that he could bring personal attendants [EBC].

**27:3** And on-the next-(day) we-put-in[a] at Sidon, and Julius treating[b] Paul kindly,[c] permitted-(him) to-go to friends to-get care.[d]

LEXICON—a. aorist pass. indic. of κατάγω (LN 54.15) (BDAG p. 516): 'to put in' [AB, Bar, BDAG, BECNT, LN; ESV, NASB, NET, NRSV], 'to land' [CBC; NIV, REB], 'to come to shore' [CEV], 'to come to' [NCV], 'to arrive' [GW, TEV], 'to touch (at)' [KJV], 'to dock' [NLT], 'to arrive at

land' [LN]. As a nautical term this verb means to go by ship toward the shore [LN]. It means to put in at a harbor [BDAG].
  b. aorist mid. (deponent = act.) participle of χράομαι (LN 41.4): 'to treat' [AB, Bar, BECNT, LN; ESV, GW, NASB, NET, NRSV], 'to entreat' [KJV], 'to behave toward' [LN], not explicit [CBC; CEV, NCV, NIV, NLT, REB, TEV]. This verb means to conduct oneself in a particular manner with regard to some person [LN].
  c. φιλανθρώπως (LN 88.72) (BDAG p. 1056): 'kindly' [BDAG, BECNT, LN; ESV, GW, NET, NRSV], 'in a kindly way' [Bar], 'in kindness to' [NIV], 'with kindness' [AB], 'with consideration' [NASB], 'considerately' [CBC], 'very considerately' [REB], 'benevolently' [BDAG], 'courteously' [KJV], 'in a friendly way' [LN]. The phrase 'treating Paul kindly' is also translated 'was kind to' [TEV], 'was very kind to' [CEV, NLT], 'was very good to' [NCV]. This adjective describes friendly concern and kindness toward someone [LN].
  d. ἐπιμέλεια (LN 35.44) (BDAG p. 375): 'care' [Bar, BDAG, LN; NASB], 'attention' [BDAG], 'provision for whatever is needed' [LN]. The phrase 'to get care' is also translated 'to be cared for' [AB, BECNT, CBC; ESV, NRSV, REB], 'to receive any care he needed' [GW], 'who took care of his needs' [NCV], 'to be given what he needed' [TEV], 'so they could give him whatever he needed' [CEV], 'so they could provide him with what he needed' [NET], 'so they might/could provide for his needs' [NIV, NLT], 'to refresh himself' [KJV]. This noun denotes the action of caring for someone with diligent concern [LN]. It is careful attention displayed in discharge of obligation or responsibility [BDAG].
QUESTION—Why would a prisoner such as Paul be allowed to go visit friends?
  Paul was probably accompanied by one or more soldiers [BECNT, EBC, NICNT, PNTC, TNTC], but he was not viewed as a security risk [BECNT, NAC]. The centurion was gracious, but also he trusted Paul [NAC]. He had a higher regard for Paul than for other prisoners [CBC]. The centurion had probably been instructed by Festus to be lenient with Paul, and may have already had a favorable impression of Paul anyway [EBC].
QUESTION—What was the nature of the 'care' that Paul received from friends?
  He probably received supplies and financial support [BECNT, TNTC], plus the comfort of friendship and a meal [TNTC].

**27:4** From-there putting-out-to-sea[a] we-sailed-under-the-lee-of[b] Cyprus, because-of the wind being against[c] (us), **27:5** and having-sailed-across[d] the open-sea[e] along-(the coast of) Cilicia and Pamphylia we-arrived at Myra in Lycia.
LEXICON—a. aorist pass. participle of ἀνάγω (LN 54.4) (BDAG 4. p. 62): 'to put out to sea' [BDAG, LN], 'to set sail' [LN]. This verb means to begin to go by boat [BDAG, LN]. See this verb at v. 2.

b. aorist act. indic. of ὑποπλέω (LN 54.10) (BDAG p. 1040): 'to sail under the lee of' [Bar, BECNT, CBC; ESV, NET, NRSV, REB], 'to keep under the lee of' [AB], 'to pass to the lee of' [NIV], 'to sail close to' [CEV, NCV], 'to sail to the northern side of' [GW], 'to sail to the north of' [NLT], 'to sail under' [KJV], 'to sail under the shelter of' [LN; NASB], 'to sail to the sheltered side of' [TEV], 'to sail on, protected by' [LN]. This verb means to sail or move along beside some object which provides a degree of protection or shelter [LN].

c. ἐναντίος (LN 82.11) (BDAG 1. p. 331): 'against' [BDAG, BECNT, LN; ESV, GW, NET, NIV, NRSV], 'blowing against' [CEV, NCV, TEV], 'contrary' [AB, Bar, BDAG; KJV, NASB], 'opposite' [BDAG]. The phrase 'because of the wind being against us' is also translated 'because of the headwinds' [CBC; REB], 'we encountered strong headwinds' [NLT]. This adjective describes something as being oriented in the direction opposite to a movement [LN]. It describes being opposite in terms of direction [BDAG].

d. aorist act. participle of διαπλέω (LN 54.11) (BDAG p. 235): 'to sail across' [Bar, BECNT, LN; ESV, NET, NIV, NRSV], 'to sail through' [BDAG; NASB], 'to sail' [CEV, GW], 'to sail over' [KJV], 'to cross over' [TEV], 'to go across' [NCV], 'to traverse' [AB]. The phrase 'having sailed through the open sea' is also translated 'then across the open sea' [CBC; REB], 'keeping to the open sea, we passed along' [NLT]. This verb means to sail through an area from one side to the other [LN]. It means to cross an area by ship [BDAG].

e. πέλαγος (LN 1.73) (BDAG 2. p. 794): 'open sea' [Bar, CBC, LN; ESV, NET, NIV, NLT, REB], 'waters' [AB], 'sea' [BDAG, BECNT; KJV, NASB, NCV, NRSV, TEV], 'high sea, the deep, ocean' [LN], not explicit [CEV, GW]. This noun denotes the relatively deep area of the sea or ocean sufficiently far from land as to be beyond the range of any protection from the seacoast [LN]. It is an independent part of a whole body of water [BDAG].

QUESTION—What does it mean that they sailed under the lee of Cyprus?

They sailed on the east side of the island, with the island providing some shelter from winds blowing from the west and northwest [Bar, BECNT, EBC, NAC, NICNT, PNTC, TH, TNTC]. Once they got across the open sea, currents along the coast of Asia Minor moving toward the west would have helped them travel along the coast [Bar, BECNT, NAC, NICNT, TH], especially with the help of winds coming from the nearby shore [EBC, NAC, NICNT].

**DISCOURSE UNIT—27:6–8** [NICNT]. The topic is they trans-ship at Myra and sail to Crete.

**27:6** And-there having-found an-Alexandrian ship sailing-for[a] Italy the centurion put- us -on-board[b] in it. **27:7** And sailing-slowly[c] for many days having-come with-difficulty[d] along-(the coast of) Cnidus, the wind not permitting[e] us we-sailed-under-the-lee-of Crete along (the coast of) Salmone, **27:8** and sailing-past[f] it with-difficulty we-came to a-certain place called Fair Havens near to-which was (the)-city (of) Lasea.

LEXICON—a. pres. act. participle of πλέω (LN 54.1) (BDAG p. 825): 'to sail to/for' [Bar, BDAG, BECNT, LN; ESV, NASB, NET, NIV, TEV], 'to sail into' [KJV], 'to go to' [CEV, NCV], 'to travel by sea' [BDAG]. This participle is also translated 'bound for' [AB, CBC; NLT, NRSV, REB], 'on its way to' [GW]. This verb means the movement of a boat or ship through the water, either rowed or blown by the wind [LN].
- b. aorist act. indic. of ἐμβιβάζω (LN 15.96) (BDAG p. 321): 'to put someone on board [AB, BDAG, BECNT, CBC; ESV, NIV, NLT, NRSV, REB], 'to put someone aboard' [NASB, NET, TEV], 'to put someone on (it)' [GW, NCV], 'to put someone therein' [KJV], 'to embark someone' [Bar], 'to cause someone to board a ship' [CEV], 'to cause to go aboard' [LN], 'to cause someone to embark' [BDAG, LN]. This verb means to cause someone to go into, as in the case of a boat [LN]. It means to put someone into something [BDAG].
- c. pres. act. participle of βραδυπλοέω (LN 54.2) (BDAG p. 183): 'to sail slowly' [AB, Bar, BDAG, BECNT, LN; ESV, GW, KJV, NASB, NCV, NET, NRSV, TEV], 'to sail along slowly' [CEV], 'to make slow headway' [NIV], 'to make little headway' [CBC; REB], 'to have days of slow sailing' [NLT]. This verb means to move slowly by boat [LN].
- d. μόλις (LN 22.33) (BDAG 1. p. 657): 'with difficulty' [BDAG, BECNT, LN; ESV, NASB, NET, NRSV], 'with great difficulty' [AB; NLT, TEV], 'barely' [Bar], 'hardly' [KJV]. This adverb is also translated as a verb phrase: 'we had difficulty' [NIV], 'we had a hard time' [CEV, NCV], 'we were hard put to it' [CBC; REB], 'our difficulties began' [GW]. This word describes that which can be accomplished only with difficulty [LN], being hard to accomplish [BDAG].
- e. pres. act. participle of προσεάω (LN 13.139) (BDAG p. 877): 'to permit to go farther' [BDAG; NASB], 'to allow to go farther' [LN; ESV], 'to allow to hold a course' [NIV], 'to let go further' [GW], 'to allow to go on' [BECNT], 'to permit to approach' [Bar], 'to allow to make headway' [AB], 'to suffer (someone)' [KJV]. The phrase 'the wind not permitting us' is also translated 'the wind prevented us from going any farther' [NET], 'the wind did/would not let us go any farther in that direction' [CEV, TEV], 'the wind was against us' [NRSV], 'the wind was blowing against us, and we could not go any farther' [NCV], 'the wind continued against us' [CBC; REB], 'we struggled along' [NLT]. This verb means to allow to go beyond what is expected [LN].
- f. pres. mid. or pass. (deponent = act.) participle of παραλέγομαι (LN 54.8) (BDAG p. 768): 'to sail past' [AB; NASB, NCV, NRSV], 'to coast along' [Bar, BDAG, BECNT; ESV], 'to hug the coast' [CBC; REB], 'to go slowly along the coast' [CEV], 'to sail along the coast' [LN; GW, NET], 'to move along the coast' [NIV], 'to pass' [KJV], 'to pass by' [TEV], 'to

sail along the shore' [LN], not explicit [NLT]. This verb means to sail along beside some object [LN].

QUESTION—What is the effect of this one very long sentence in vv. 7–8?
It increases the sense of tension in the narrative [PNTC].

**DISCOURSE UNIT—27:9–38** [NET]. The topic is caught in a violent storm.

**DISCOURSE UNIT—27:9–12** [NAC, NICNT]. The topic is Paul's advice rejected [NICNT], the decision to sail on [NAC].

**27:9** And much time having-passed[a] and it- already -being dangerous[b] for-sailing because the Fast[c] having- already -gone-by Paul urged[d] saying **27:10** to-them, "Sirs, I-foresee that the voyage (will be) with damage[e] and much[f] loss[g] not only of-the cargo and of-the ship but also of-our lives."

LEXICON—a. aorist mid. (deponent = act.) participle of διαγίνομαι (LN 67.84) (BDAG p. 227): 'to pass' [AB, BDAG, LN; ESV, NASB, NET], 'to elapse' [Bar, BDAG], 'to have been lost' [BECNT, CBC; NIV, NRSV, REB], 'to have been spent' [KJV]. The phrase 'much time having elapsed' is also translated 'we had lost much/a lot of time' [GW, NCV, NLT], 'we had already lost a lot of time' [CEV], 'we spent much time there' [TEV]. This verb means to mark the passage of time [LN].

b. ἐπισφαλής (LN 21.3) (BDAG p. 383): 'dangerous' [AB, BDAG, BECNT, LN; all versions except CEV], 'risky' [Bar, CBC], 'no longer safe' [CEV], 'unsafe' [BDAG]. This adjective describes that which poses danger [LN]. It describes that which causes mishap [BDAG].

c. νηστεία (LN 51.11) (BDAG 2.a. p. 671): 'Fast/fast' [AB, Bar, BECNT, CBC; ESV, KJV, NASB, NET, NRSV, REB], 'day of fasting' [GW], 'Day of Atonement' [BDAG; NIV, TEV], 'the Great Day of Forgiveness' [CEV], 'Day of Cleansing' [NCV], 'festival of the atonement, day to commemorate the atonement of sin' [LN]. The phrase 'the Fast having already gone by' is also translated 'it was so late in the fall' [NLT]. This noun denotes a Jewish festival celebrating the forgiveness of sins on the Day of Atonement [LN]. It is the act of going without food for a devotional or cultic purpose [BDAG].

d. imperf. act. indic. of παραινέω (LN 33.295) (BDAG p. 764): 'to urge' [BDAG, LN], 'to warn' [AB; NCV, NIV], 'to offer advice' [Bar], 'to give a warning' [REB], 'to give advice' [CBC; TEV], 'to advise' [BECNT; ESV, GW, NET, NRSV], 'to advise strongly' [LN], 'to admonish' [KJV, NASB], 'to recommend' [BDAG]. The phrase 'Paul urged, saying' is also translated 'Paul spoke' [NLT], 'Paul spoke…"Men listen to me!"' [CEV]. This verb means to indicate strongly to someone what he or she should plan to do [LN]. It means to advise strongly [BDAG].

e. ὕβρις (LN 20.19) (BDAG 3. p. 1022): 'damage' [Bar, BDAG, LN; NASB], 'hardship' [AB, BDAG], 'injury' [BECNT; ESV], 'disaster' [BDAG; GW, NET], 'hurt' [KJV], 'trouble' [NCV], 'danger' [NRSV], 'shipwreck' [NLT], 'harm' [LN]. The phrase 'with hardship' is also

translated 'disastrous' [CBC; NIV, REB], '(our ship and its cargo) will be badly damaged' [CEV]. The phrase 'with hardship and much loss' is also translated 'dangerous...great damage...and loss' [TEV]. This noun denotes the condition resulting from violence or mistreatment [LN]. It is the damage caused by use of force [BDAG].
f. πολύς (LN 59.11) (BDAG 3.a.α. p. 849): 'much' [Bar, BDAG, BECNT, LN; ESV, KJV], 'much heavy' [NRSV], 'heavy' [REB], 'great' [AB, BDAG, LN; NASB, NET, NIV, TEV], 'grave' [CBC], 'badly' [CEV], 'a lot' [NCV], 'extensive' [LN], 'severe' [BDAG], not explicit [GW, NLT]. This adjective describes a relatively large quantity [LN]. It describes being high on a scale of extent [BDAG].
g. ζημία (LN 57.69) (BDAG p. 428): 'loss' [BDAG, LN; all translations except CEV, KJV, NCV, NLT], 'loss (of cargo) and danger (to our lives)' [NLT], 'damage' [BDAG; KJV], 'disadvantage' [BDAG], 'forfeit' [BDAG, LN]. The phrase 'much loss' is also translated 'will be lost' [CEV], 'may be lost' [NCV]. This noun denotes the loss of something which one has previously possessed, with the implication that the loss involves considerable hardship or suffering [LN]. It is suffering the loss of something with implication of sustaining hardship or suffering [BDAG].

QUESTION—Why would sailing be dangerous at this time of year?
During this time of year daylight was shorter and nights were longer, cloudy conditions would obscure the sun and stars, making navigation more difficult, and there were also stronger winds and problems from rain and even snow [BECNT]. Sea travel on the Mediterranean stopped altogether from early November until February [CBC, EBC, NAC, NICNT, PNTC, TH, TNTC], but even during late September through October it was difficult [NAC, NICNT, PNTC, TH, TNTC].

QUESTION—To which nouns do 'damage' and 'loss' apply?
1. Both damage and loss will be to the ship, the cargo, and to their lives [AB, Bar, BECNT, CBC; ESV, KJV, NASB, NCV, NET, NIV, NRSV, REB].
2. There will be damage to the cargo and ship, and loss of lives [TH; CEV, GW, NLT, TEV].

QUESTION—Was Paul's warning based on a prophetic insight or on his previous sailing experience?
His comments were based on his own experience in sea travel, not on any divine revelation [BECNT, CBC, NICNT, PNTC].

**27:11** But the centurion was-persuaded[a] by-the pilot[b] and by-the ship-owner[c] more than by the-things being-spoken by Paul.

LEXICON—a. imperf. pass. indic. of πείθω (LN 33.301) (BDAG 3.c. p. 792): 'to be persuaded' [Bar, BDAG, LN; GW, NASB], 'to be convinced' [LN; NET, TEV], 'to take someone's advice' [BDAG]. This passive verb is also translated as active: 'to listen to' [AB; CEV, NLT], 'to pay attention to' [BECNT, CBC; ESV, NRSV, REB], 'to believe' [KJV, NCV], 'to follow the advice of' [NIV]. This verb means to convince someone to believe something and to act on the basis of what is recommended [LN]. It means to be won over as the result of persuasion [BDAG].

b. κυβερνήτης (LN 54.28) (BDAG 1. p. 574): 'pilot' [ESV, GW, NASB, NIV, NRSV], 'captain of a ship' [LN; CEV], 'captain' [Bar, BECNT, CBC; NCV, NET, NLT, REB, TEV], 'master' [AB; KJV], 'shipmaster' [BDAG]. This noun denotes one who commands a ship [LN]. It is one who is responsible for the management of a ship [BDAG].

c. ναύκληρος (LN 54.29) (BDAG p. 667): 'ship owner' [BDAG, LN; NET], 'owner of a ship' [BECNT, CBC; ESV, GW, KJV, NCV, NIV, NRSV, REB, TEV], 'owner' [AB, Bar; CEV, NLT], 'captain of a ship' [NASB], 'captain' [BDAG]. This noun denotes one who owns a ship [LN].

QUESTION—What were the roles of the pilot and the ship-owner?

The pilot was the nautical expert and the ship-owner had the financial interest in the voyage [Bar, TNTC]. The owner would choose the pilot and the pilot would choose the sailors [NICNT].

**27:12** **And the harbor[a] being unfavorably-situated[b] for spending-the-winter[c] the majority made (a)-decision[d] to-set-sail from-there, if somehow once-having-arrived in Phoenix (a)-harbor of-Crete facing southwest and northwest they-might-be-able to-spend-(the)-winter.[e]**

LEXICON—a. λιμήν (LN 1.75) (BDAG p. 596): 'harbor' [BDAG, LN; all translations except AB; KJV], 'port' [AB], 'haven' [KJV]. This noun denotes a relatively small area of the sea which is well protected by land but deep enough for ships to enter and moor [LN].

b. ἀνεύθετος (LN 65.35) (BDAG p. 78): unsuitable' [BDAG, CBC; NIV, REB], 'not suitable' [AB, Bar, BECNT; ESV, NASB, NET, NRSV], 'not commodious' [KJV], 'unusable' [BDAG, LN], 'poor' [BDAG]. The phrase 'was unsuitable' is also translated 'was not a good place' [CEV, GW, NCV], 'was not a good one' [TEV], 'was exposed…a poor place (to spend the winter)' [NLT]. This adjective describes something which should not or cannot be used [LN]. It describes something as being unfavorably situated and therefore unusable [BDAG].

c. παραχειμασία (LN 67.166) (BDAG p. 773): 'spending the winter' [LN; NRSV], 'wintering' [AB, Bar, BDAG, CBC; NASB, REB], 'to be in a place during the winter' [LN]. This noun is also translated as a verb: 'to spend the winter' [CEV, ESV, GW, NET, NLT, TEV], 'to winter (in)' [BECNT; KJV, NIV], '(for the ship) to stay for the winter' [NCV]. This noun denotes the action of experiencing the winter season [LN]. It is the experience of spending winter in a place [BDAG].

d. βουλή (LN 33.296) (BDAG 2.a. p. 182): 'decision' [BDAG; NASB], 'plan' [Bar], 'resolution' [BDAG]. The phrase 'made a decision' means to suggest a plan of action [LN]. It is translated 'decided' [AB; ESV, GW, NCV, NET, NIV], 'advised' [LN; KJV], 'gave counsel' [BECNT], 'wanted' [NLT], 'were in favor of' [CBC; REB], 'was in favor of'

[NRSV, TEV], 'agreed' [CEV]. This noun denotes that which one decides [BDAG].
  e. aorist act. infin. of παραχειμάζω (LN 67.166) (BDAG p. 773): 'to spend the winter' [BDAG, LN; CEV, ESV, GW, NASB, NET, NLT, NRSV, TEV], 'to winter' [AB, Bar, BDAG, BECNT, CBC; KJV, NIV, REB], 'to stay for the winter' [NCV], 'to be in a place during the winter' [LN]. This verb means to experience the winter season [LN].
QUESTION—Why would the harbor be unfavorable for spending the winter? It was open to half the compass, and since it faced east it offered no shelter from easterly winds [NAC, NICNT].

**DISCOURSE UNIT—27:13-44** [EBC]. The topic is storm and shipwreck.

**DISCOURSE UNIT—27:13-38** [CEV, ESV, NCV, NRSV, TEV]. The topic is the storm at sea [CEV, ESV, NRSV, TEV], the storm [NCV].

**DISCOURSE UNIT—27:13-26** [CBC; NIV, NLT]. The topic is to Malta [CBC], the storm [NIV], the storm at sea [NLT].

**DISCOURSE UNIT—27:13-20** [NAC, NICNT]. The topic is the "Northeaster" [NAC], They are caught by the wind Euraquilo [NICNT].

**27:13** And (a)-south-wind having-blown-moderately,[a] thinking they-attained (their) purpose (and) having-raised-(anchor)[b] they-were-sailing-past Crete close-by[c] (the shore).
LEXICON—a. aorist act. participle of ὑποπνέω (LN 14.5) (BDAG p. 1040): 'to blow gently' [BDAG, BECNT, LN; ESV], 'to blow softly' [KJV], 'to begin to blow' [GW, NCV, NIV, NLT, NRSV, TEV], 'to start blowing' [CEV], 'to spring up' [Bar, CBC; NET, REB], 'to come up' [NASB], 'to arise' [AB]. This verb means a gentle blowing of the wind [LN].
  b. aorist act. participle of αἴρω (LN 54.24 See 54.24a in the LN Supplement.) (BDAG 1.a. p. 28): 'to raise anchor' [GW], 'to weigh anchor' [AB, BECNT, CBC; ESV, NASB, NET, NIV, NRSV, REB], 'to pull up the anchor' [CEV, NCV, NLT, TEV], 'to lift anchor, to sail off' [LN], 'to set out' [Bar], 'to loose' [KJV], 'to lift up, take up, pick up' [BDAG]. This verb means to raise the anchor in preparation for departing [LN]. This verb means to raise to a higher place or position [BDAG].
  c. ἆσσον (LN 83.28) (BDAG p. 145): 'close by' [KJV], 'close in' [Bar], 'close to' [ESV, GW, NLT, NRSV], 'close inshore' [BECNT; NASB], 'close along' [NET], 'along the shore' [NIV], 'very close' [NCV], 'hugging (the coast)' [AB], 'hugging (the land)' [CBC; REB], 'along (the coast)' [CEV], 'as close as possible along (the coast)' [TEV], 'as close as possible, very near' [LN], 'nearer' [BDAG]. This adverb describes a position extremely close to another position [LN].

**DISCOURSE UNIT—27:14-44** [NASB]. The topic is shipwreck.

**27:14** But not long afterward (a)-violent[a] wind the-one called Northeaster[b] rushed-down[c] from it. **27:15** And the ship having-been-caught-(in it) and not being-able to-face-directly-into[d] the wind, giving-way[e] (to it) we-were-driven-along.[f]

LEXICON—a. τυφωνικός (LN 14.7) (BDAG p. 1021): 'violent' [NASB, NRSV, REB], 'tempestuous' [Bar, BECNT; ESV, KJV], 'fierce' [CBC], 'powerful' [GW], 'hurricane force' [NET, NIV], 'very strong' [NCV, TEV], 'strong' [CEV], 'typhoon strength' [NLT], 'storm (wind)' [AB], 'of a violent, strong wind' [LN], 'like a whirlwind' [BDAG]. This adjective describes a very strong wind [LN]. It describes a typhoon or a hurricane [BDAG].

b. Εὐρακύλων (LN 14.9) (BDAG p. 411): 'northeaster' [BDAG, LN; all translations except AB, Bar; KJV, NASB]. This noun is transliterated as 'Euraquilo' [Bar; NASB], 'Euroclydon' [AB, KJV]. This noun denotes a strong storm wind blowing from the northeast [LN]. It is the northeast wind, Euraquilo [BDAG].

c. aorist act. indic. of βάλλω (LN 15.112) (BDAG p. 164): 'to rush down' [BDAG, LN; NASB, NRSV], 'to sweep down' [LN; NIV, REB], 'to strike down' [BECNT; ESV], 'to strike' [AB], 'to tear down' [CBC], 'to fling (itself) down' [Bar], 'to blow down' [GW, NET, TEV], 'to blow against' [CEV], 'to burst against' [NLT], 'to arise against' [KJV], 'to come' [NCV]. This verb means to move down suddenly and quickly [LN]. It means to move down suddenly and rapidly [BDAG].

d. pres. act. infin. of ἀντοφθαλμέω (LN 82.9) (BDAG p. 91): 'to face into' [LN], 'to face' [BDAG, BECNT; ESV, NASB], 'to head into' [Bar; NET, NIV], 'to be turned head-on into' [NRSV], 'to keep head to (wind)' [CBC; REB], 'to keep headed into' [TEV], 'to sail against' [CEV, GW, NCV], 'to turn into' [NLT], 'to be turned up against' [AB], 'to bear up into' [KJV], 'to look directly at' [BDAG]. This verb means to face straight ahead [LN].

e. aorist act. participle of ἐπιδίδωμι (LN 39.21) (BDAG 2. p. 371): 'to give way' [AB, Bar, BECNT, CBC; ESV, NASB, NET, NIV, NRSV, REB], 'to give up' [NLT], 'to give in to, to yield' [LN], 'to give up trying' [TEV], 'to stop trying' [NCV], 'to be caught' [KJV], 'to surrender' [BDAG, LN], 'to give up, to give over' [BDAG]. The phrase 'giving way to it' is also translated 'we couldn't do anything' [GW]. The phrase 'giving way (to it) we were driven along' is also translated 'we let the wind carry (the ship)' [CEV]. This verb means to give in to a superior power or force [LN]. It means to yield control of something [BDAG].

f. imperf. pass. indic. of φέρω (LN 15.160) (BDAG 3.a. p. 1051): 'to be driven along' [LN; ESV, NET, NIV], 'to be driven' [BDAG, BECNT; NRSV], 'to let (oneself) be driven' [NASB], 'to be carried along' [GW, TEV], 'to run before' [Bar, CBC; NLT, REB], 'to let oneself be moved' [BDAG], 'to let (her) drive' [KJV], 'to be moved' [BDAG], 'to be carried along' [LN]. The phrase 'we were driven along' is also translated 'we...let ourselves drift' [AB]. '(we let the wind) carry the ship/us' [CEV, NCV]. This verb means to cause an object to move by means of a force [LN]. It means to cause to follow a certain course in direction or conduct [BDAG].

QUESTION—What is the 'northeaster'?

The name 'Euraquilo' is a composite of 'Euro,' which is Greek for 'east', and 'Aquilo', which is Latin for 'north' [Bar, EBC, NAC, NICNT, TNTC]. It is a wind that comes from the northeast [Bar, NAC, TNTC]. It comes down from Mt. Ida on Crete [BECNT, EBC, NAC, NICNT, PNTC]. The violent wind known as τυφωνικός was formed by opposing air currents that created a whirling motion of air, clouds, and sea [NICNT, PNTC].

**27:16** And running-under-the-lee[a] (of) a-certain small-island called Cauda we-were-able with-difficulty to-get the ship's-boat[b] under-control, **27:17** which having-hoisted-up[c] they-were-using supports[d] running-(them)-underneath[e] the ship, and fearing lest they-might-run-aground into the Syrtis, having-let-down the gear,[f] thus they-were-being-driven-along.

LEXICON—a. aorist act. participle of ὑποτρέχω (LN 54.10) (BDAG p. 1040): 'to run under the lee of' [AB, Bar, BECNT, CBC; ESV, NET, NRSV], 'to run under the shelter of' [NASB], 'to pass under the lee of' [REB], 'to pass to the lee of' [NIV], 'sail under the lee of' [BDAG], 'to sail under the shelter of' [LN], 'to get shelter' [TEV], 'to run under' [KJV], 'to go below' [NCV], 'to sail along the sheltered side of' [NLT], 'to go along on the side that is protected from the wind' [CEV], 'to sail on, protected by' [LN], 'to drift to the sheltered side' [GW]. This verb means to sail or move along beside some object which provides a degree of protection or shelter [LN].

b. σκάφη (LN 6.45) (BDAG 2. p. 927): 'ship's boat' [AB, CBC; ESV, NASB, NET, NRSV, REB, TEV], 'ship's lifeboat' [GW], 'lifeboat' [CEV, NCV, NIV, NLT], 'boat' [BECNT; KJV], 'small boat, skiff' [LN], 'dinghy' [Bar]. This noun denotes a small boat which was normally kept aboard a larger ship and used by sailors in placing anchors, repairing the ship, or saving lives in the case of storms [LN].

c. aorist act. participle of αἴρω (LN 15.203) (BDAG 1.a. p. 28): 'to hoist up' [BECNT; ESV, NASB, NRSV, REB], 'to hoist aboard' [CBC; NET, NIV, NLT], 'to haul aboard' [AB], 'to haul up' [Bar], 'to take up' [BDAG; KJV], 'to pull up on deck' [GW], 'to take in' [NCV], 'to make secure' [TEV], 'to get it where it belonged' [CEV], 'to lift up, to pick up' [BDAG], 'to carry (away), to carry off, to remove, to take (away)' [LN]. This verb means to lift up and carry (away) [LN]. It means to raise to a higher place or position [BDAG].

d. βοήθεια (LN 35.10) (BDAG p. 180): 'support' [LN; ESV, NET], 'supporting cables' [NASB], 'ropes' [CEV, GW, NCV, NIV, NLT, TEV], 'protective measures' [AB], 'measures' [BECNT; NRSV], 'auxiliary devices' [Bar], 'helps' [BDAG; KJV], 'tackle' [CBC; REB], 'aid'

[BDAG]. This noun denotes an object which provides help or support, ropes being the most likely means of support in this verse [LN]. It denotes material things that help, possibly cables in this verse [BDAG].

e. pres. act. participle of ὑποζώννυμι (LN 54.25) (BDAG p. 1037): 'to undergird' [AB, BDAG, BECNT, CBC; ESV, KJV, NASB, NET, NRSV], 'to reinforce' [GW], 'to frap' [Bar], 'to pass ropes under a ship to hold it together' [NIV], 'to bind ropes around the hull of the ship to strengthen it' [NLT], 'to tie ropes around to hold something together' [NCV], 'to fasten ropes around' [LN; TEV], 'to hold something together' [CEV], 'to use tackle to brace' [REB], 'to brace' [BDAG, LN]. This verb is a technical, nautical term meaning to brace a ship [LN]. It means to provide a ship with cables that go around the outside of the hull, and in the case of merchantmen, under it to give the ship greater firmness in a heavy sea [BDAG].

f. σκεῦος (LN 6.1) (BDAG p. 927): 'gear' [BECNT; ESV], 'sea anchor' [Bar; NASB, NET, NIV, NLT, NRSV, REB], 'drag anchor' [AB], 'sail' [CEV, GW, KJV, NCV, TEV], 'mainsail' [CBC], 'object' [LN], 'thing' [BDAG, LN]. This noun denotes any kind of instrument, tool, weapon, equipment, container, or property. In this verse, it is probably the mainsail [LN]. It is a material object used to meet some need in an occupation or other responsibility. In this verse it is possibly a kedge or driving-anchor [BDAG].

QUESTION—Who is referred to by the pronoun 'we' in this verse?

Luke is referring to the sailors, but describes it from the perspective of everyone one on the ship as being affected by it [PNTC, TNTC]. Perhaps some of the passengers had to assist because the boat would have been full of water and very heavy [NAC, NICNT].

QUESTION—Why was it difficult to get the ship's boat under control?

It was probably full of water by this point [BECNT, EBC, NAC, NICNT]. This boat would normally have been towed from the stern [PNTC, TNTC, TRT].

QUESTION—What are the supports described here?

They were probably cables or ropes passed under the hull to help hold the ship together [CBC, NAC, PNTC, TH]. This could have been in the form of frapping, which involves using ropes going underneath the ship from one side to the other [Bar, BECNT, NAC, PNTC]. They could have been tied from the front of the ship to the back of it [BECNT, EBC], or possibly across the deck from one side to the other [BECNT, PNTC].

QUESTION—What is the 'gear' referred to here?

1. It is a sea anchor [AB, Bar, NICNT, TNTC; NASB, NET, NIV, NLT, NRSV, REB], also known as a drag anchor [AB]. It may be a kedge or driving-anchor [BDAG].
2. It is a sail [TH; CEV, GW, KJV, NCV, TEV], probably the mainsail [CBC, LN].

QUESTION—Where is Syrtis?
It is on the north coast of Africa, about 400 miles from Cauda [BECNT, NAC, PNTC, TNTC], which gives an indication of the power of the storm and how far they were being blown off course [NAC, PNTC]. Syrtis had a reputation as being very dangerous for sailing ships [AB, Bar, NAC, PNTC, TNTC].

**27:18** And the-next-(day) we being- violently[a] -storm-tossed[b] they-were-taking-(the)-action (of)-throwing-cargo-overboard,[c] **27:19** and on-the third-(day) they-threw-overboard[d] the ship's tackle[e] with-their-own-hands.

LEXICON—a. σφοδρῶς (LN 78.19) (BDAG p. 980): 'violently' [BDAG, BECNT, LN; ESV, GW, NASB, NET, NRSV], 'severely' [Bar], 'hard (pressed)' [AB], 'so hard' [NCV], 'very' [CBC; REB], 'very much' [BDAG], 'greatly' [BDAG, LN], 'exceedingly' [LN; KJV], 'terrible' [LN], not explicit [NLT]. This adverb is also translated as an adjective: 'violent' [NIV, TEV], 'fierce' [CEV]. This adverb describes a very high point on a scale of extent and in many contexts implying vehemence or violence [LN].

b. pres. pass. participle of χειμάζω (LN 14.3) (BDAG 1. p. 1081): 'to be storm-tossed' [Bar, BECNT; ESV, NASB], 'to be tossed in/by a storm' [BDAG; GW], 'to be pounded by a storm' [NRSV], 'to be battered' [NET], 'to be tossed with a tempest' [KJV], 'to be (hard) pressed' [AB], 'to make heavy weather' [CBC; REB], 'to take a battering from a storm' [NIV], 'to undergo bad weather, to be in a storm' [LN]. The phrase 'we were being...storm-tossed' is also translated 'the storm was blowing us' [NCV], 'gale-force winds...battered the ship' [NLT], 'the storm was so fierce' [CEV], 'the violent storm continued' [TEV]. This verb means to be overtaken by or to experience stormy weather [LN]. It means to be exposed to bad weather [BDAG].

c. ἐκβολή (LN 15.220) (BDAG p. 300): 'what is thrown out, what is jettisoned' [LN], 'jettisoning' [BDAG]. The phrase 'they were taking action throwing cargo overboard' is also translated 'they began to throw/throwing cargo overboard' [BECNT; GW, NET, NIV, NLT, NRSV], 'they started/began to jettison the cargo' [AB; ESV, NASB], 'they jettisoned some of the cargo' [Bar], 'they threw out some of the cargo' [NCV], 'they threw/began to throw some of the ship's cargo overboard' [CEV, TEV], 'they began to lighten the ship' [CBC; REB], 'they lightened the ship' [KJV]. This noun denotes what is thrown out of an area or object [LN]. It is what is thrown out of a ship's cargo to save the vessel in a storm [BDAG].

d. aorist act. indic. of ῥίπτω (LN 15.217) (BDAG 1. p. 906): 'to throw overboard' [AB; all versions except KJV, NCV, REB], 'to jettison' [CBC; REB], 'to throw out' [Bar; NCV], 'to cast out' [BECNT; KJV], 'to throw' [BDAG, LN], 'to hurl' [LN]. This verb means to throw with considerable force [LN]. It means to propel something with a forceful motion [BDAG].

e. σκευή (LN 6.2) (BDAG p. 927): 'ship's tackle' [ESV, NASB, NIV, NRSV], 'tackle' [BECNT], 'tackling of the ship' [KJV], 'ship's gear' [AB, Bar, BDAG, CBC; CEV, NET, NLT, REB], 'ship's equipment' [GW, NCV, TEV], 'things' [LN], 'equipment' [BDAG, LN]. This noun is a collective for any kind of artifact which may be referred to by σκεῦος 'object, thing' (see LN 6.1 in v.17). It is a collective for a variety of items that fall in the category of σκεῦος, equipment [BDAG].

QUESTION—What is the 'ship's tackle' they were throwing overboard?
It would be any spare gear [BECNT, TNTC, TRT], but possibly also the main sail and the main yardarm that holds the sail [BECNT, NAC, NICNT]. This is done to make the ship lighter and float higher in the water [BECNT, NAC, TNTC], which may have become necessary because the ship would have begun to develop leaks [NAC, TNTC].

QUESTION—What is implied by the phrase 'with their own hands'?
If it was the yardarm and mainsail that they threw overboard with their own hands, it may have been due to the fact that the ship did not have lifting equipment large enough to lift the large beam used for the yardarm [BECNT, NAC]. That they threw the ship's tackle overboard 'with their own hands' shows how desperate the situation was; that is, it was not washed overboard but they actually discarded it themselves [PNTC].

**27:20** And-when neither sun nor stars appeared[a] over many days, and no small[b] storm[c] was-raging,[d] finally all hope of our being-saved was-abandoned.[e]

LEXICON—a. pres. act. participle of ἐπιφαίνω (LN 24.21) (BDAG 3. p. 385): 'to appear' [AB, BECNT, LN; ESV, KJV, NASB, NET, NIV, NRSV], 'to be seen' [Bar], 'to become apparent' [BDAG]. The verb is also translated as 'we could not see' [CEV, GW, NCV, TEV], 'there was no sign of' [CBC; REB], 'blotting out' [NLT]. This verb means to appear to someone or at some place [LN]. It means to make one's presence known [BDAG].

b. ὀλίγος (LN 59.13) (BDAG 3. p. 703): 'little' [BDAG, LN], 'small amount' [LN], 'slight' [BDAG]. This adjective describes a relatively small quantity [LN]. It describes what is relatively low on a scale of extent or existing only to a small degree [BDAG]. The litotes 'no small' [Bar, BECNT; ESV, KJV, NASB, NRSV], is also translated 'great' [CBC], 'violent' [AB; NET], 'very bad' [NCV], 'very hard' [TEV], 'terrible' [NLT], 'severe' [GW], 'strong' [CEV], 'unabated' [REB], not explicit [NIV].

c. χειμών (LN 14.2) (BDAG 1. p. 1082): 'storm' [AB, Bar, BDAG, CBC; GW, NASB, NCV, NET, NIV, NLT, REB], 'tempest' [BECNT; ESV, KJV, NRSV], 'strong wind' [CEV], 'wind' [TEV], 'bad weather' [BDAG, LN], 'stormy weather' [LN]. This noun denotes stormy weather involving strong wind, overcast sky, and often cold temperature; thunder and lightning may also be present [LN]. It is stormy weather [BDAG].

d. pres. mid. or pass. (deponent = act.) participle of ἐπίκειμαι (LN 19.43) (BDAG 2.a. p. 373): 'to rage' [AB, CBC; NIV, NLT, NRSV, REB], 'to be upon' [Bar], 'to assail' [NASB], 'to lie upon' [BDAG; ESV, KJV], 'to batter' [NET], 'to press upon' [BDAG, BECNT], 'to keep blowing' [CEV, TEV], 'to not let up' [GW], 'to press against, to push against' [LN], 'to press around, to be urgent [BDAG], not explicit [NCV]. This verb means to press or push against [LN]. It means to act upon through force or pressure [BDAG].

e. imperf. pass. indic. of περιαιρέω (LN 68.43) (BDAG 2. p. 799): 'to be abandoned' [AB, BECNT; ESV, NASB, NRSV], 'to be taken away' [BDAG; KJV], 'to be given up, to be stopped, to be quit' [LN], 'to be removed' [BDAG]. This passive verb is also translated as active: 'we abandoned (all hope)' [NET], '(hope)...was disappearing' [Bar], '(hope) began to fade' [CBC; REB], 'we gave up (all hope)' [CEV, NIV, TEV], 'we began to lose (hope)' [GW], 'we lost (all hope)' [NCV], '(all hope) was gone' [NLT]. This verb means to stop doing something, with the implication of complete cessation [LN]. It means to do away with something [BDAG].

QUESTION—Is there any particular significance to the use of the word 'saved' in this passage, along with similar language in vv. 31, 34, 43, 44, and 28:1, 4?

There may be a veiled symbolism here, in which a Christian reader might recognize that the God who saved Paul and his fellow-travelers from the sea is also the one who provides salvation and eternal life [NAC]. Deliverance is the key to the entire passage, as indicated by that vocabulary; this episode is used to symbolize how Paul's message and Paul's God save [BECNT].

**DISCOURSE UNIT—27:21–28** [PNTC]. The topic is trusting God's word.

**DISCOURSE UNIT—27:21–26** [NAC, NICNT]. The topic is Paul's word of assurance [NAC], Paul's encouragement [NICNT].

**27:21** And (they) having no-appetite[a] for-a-long-time, then Paul standing in (the)-midst of-them said, "Men (you) should have-listened to-me not to-set-sail from Crete to-avoid[b] this damage[c] and loss.[d] **27:22** Yet now I-urge[e] you(pl) to-take-heart,[f] for among you there-will-be no loss of-life but (loss) of-the ship.

LEXICON—a. ἀσιτία (LN 23.32) (BDAG p. 143): 'lack of appetite' [BDAG], '(going/being) without food' [Bar, BECNT, CBC, LN; ESV, NASB, NCV, NIV, NRSV, REB, TEV], 'without desiring food' [LN], 'abstinence' [KJV]. The phrase 'having no appetite for a long time' is also translated 'since hardly anyone wanted to eat' [GW], 'many had no desire to eat' [NET], 'none of us had eaten anything for a long time' [CEV], 'no one had eaten for a long time' [NLT], 'as little had been eaten' [AB]. This noun denotes a state of having been without food, frequently with the implication of being caused by a lack of appetite [LN].

b. aorist act. infin. of κερδαίνω (LN 13.137) (BDAG 2. p. 541): 'to avoid' [BDAG, CBC, LN; GW, NET, NLT, NRSV, REB, TEV], 'to not incur' [Bar, BECNT; ESV, NASB], 'to not have' [CEV, NCV], 'to spare oneself' [BDAG; NIV], 'to not suffer' [AB], 'to not gain' [KJV], 'to cause not to occur' [LN]. This verb means to cause a loss not to happen [LN]. Since the avoidance of loss is a gain, this verb can also mean to spare oneself something [BDAG].

c. ὕβρις (LN 20.19): 'damage' [Bar, CBC, LN; CEV, NASB, NET, NIV, NLT, NRSV, REB, TEV], 'hardship' [AB], 'injury' [BECNT, LN; ESV], 'disaster' [GW], 'harm' [LN; KJV], 'trouble' [NCV]. This noun denotes the condition resulting from violence or mistreatment [LN].

d. ζημία (LN 57.69) (BDAG p. 428): 'loss' [BDAG, LN; all translations], 'damage, disadvantage' [BDAG], 'forfeit' [BDAG, LN]. This noun denotes the loss of something which one has previously possessed, with the implication that the loss involves considerable hardship or suffering [LN]. It is suffering the loss of something with the implication of sustaining hardship or suffering [BDAG].

e. pres. act. indic. of παραινέω (LN 33.295) BDAG p. 764): 'to urge' [AB, BDAG, CBC, LN; ESV, NASB, NIV, NRSV, REB], 'to advise' [Bar; GW, NET], 'to beg (someone)' [CEV, TEV], 'to bid (someone)' [BECNT], 'to exhort' [KJV], 'to tell' [NCV], 'to advise strongly' [LN], 'to recommend' [BDAG], not explicit [NLT]. This verb means to indicate strongly to someone what he or she should plan to do [LN]. It means to advise strongly [BDAG].

f. pres. act. infin. of εὐθυμέω (LN 25.146) (BDAG p. 406): 'to take heart' [Bar, BECNT; ESV], 'to not lose heart' [CBC; REB], 'to keep up one's courage' [AB; NASB, NET, NIV, NRSV], 'to take courage' [LN; NLT, TEV], 'to have courage' [GW], 'to be/become encouraged' [LN], 'to cheer up' [CEV, NCV], 'to be of good cheer' [KJV], 'to be cheerful' [BDAG]. This verb means to be or to become encouraged and hence cheerful [LN].

QUESTION—Why had they gone so long without food?

No one had any appetite because of seasickness due to the tossing of the ship in the storm [Bar, BECNT, NAC, NICNT, PNTC, TNTC], and possibly also from sheer anxiety [Bar, BECNT, PNTC, TNTC]. It also would have been difficult to prepare meals under such circumstances [NICNT, PNTC].

QUESTION—What is the function of τὰ νῦν 'yet now' in this sentence?

It is emphatic [PNTC], and introduces a shift in tone of what is being said [BECNT, PNTC].

**27:23** For last night an angel of-the God whose I am and whom I-worship[a] stood[b] before-me **27:24** saying, 'Fear not, Paul, it-is-necessary-for you to-stand-before[c] Caesar, and behold God has-granted[d] to-you all those sailing with you.'

LEXICON—a. pres. act. indic. of λατρεύω (LN 53.14) (BDAG p. 587): 'to worship' [AB, BECNT, CBC, LN; CEV, ESV, NCV, NRSV, REB, TEV], 'serve' [Bar, BDAG; GW, KJV, NASB, NET, NIV, NLT], 'to perform religious rites, to venerate' [LN]. This verb means to perform religious rites as a part of worship [LN].

b. aorist act. indic. of παρίστημ (LN 85.14) (BDAG 2.a.α. p. 778): 'to stand' [Bar, BECNT, CBC; ESV, GW, KJV, NASB, NIV, NLT, NRSV, REB], 'to come to' [NCV, NET, TEV], 'to appear' [AB], 'to be present' [BDAG], 'to approach, to come to someone' [BDAG]. The phrase 'an angel of...God...stood before me' is also translated 'God...sent an angel' [CEV]. This verb means to cause to be in a place—'to present (oneself), to cause to be' [LN]. It means to be present in any way [BDAG].

c. aorist act. infin. of παρίστημι (LN 85.18) (BDAG 2.a.α. p. 778): 'to stand before' [Bar, BECNT, LN; ESV, NASB, NCV, NET, NRSV, TEV], 'to stand trial before' [CEV, NIV, NLT], 'to appear before' [AB, BDAG, CBC; REB], 'to present one's case to' [GW], 'to be brought before' [KJV], 'to be in front of' [LN], 'to be present' [BDAG]. This verb means to be in front of something, presumably facing it [LN]. It means to be present in any way [BDAG].

d. perf. mid./pass. (deponent = act.) indic. of χαρίζομαι (LN 57.102) (BDAG 1. p. 1078): 'to grant' [Bar, BECNT, CBC, LN; ESV, NASB, REB], 'to grant as a favor' [AB], 'to graciously grant' [NET], 'to give' [BDAG, LN; KJV], 'to give graciously' [BDAG; NIV], 'to bestow generously' [LN]. The phrase 'God has granted to you all those sailing with you' is also translated 'because of you God will save the lives of everyone on the ship' [CEV], 'God has promised you that he will save the lives of everyone sailing with you' [NCV], 'God...has granted safety to everyone/all those sailing with you' [GW, NLT, NRSV], 'God...has spared the lives of all those who are sailing with you' [TEV]. This verb means to give or grant graciously and generously, with the implication of good will on the part of the giver [LN]. It means to give freely as a favor [BDAG].

QUESTION—What is the function in the narrative of Paul's vision and the message from the angel?

It is the center of the narrative and the dramatic turning point of the story, providing the interpretive key for the whole account of the storm at sea [NAC]. Note that the unusual word order in the sentence, gives prominence to the phrase 'whose I am and whom I serve' [PNTC].

**27:25** So[a] take-heart,[b] men; for I-believe[c] God that it-will-be so just-as it-has-been-told to-me. **27:26** But it-is-necessary to-run-aground[d] on some island."

LEXICON—a. διό (LN 89.47) (BDAG p. 250): 'so' [Bar, BECNT, CBC; ESV, GW, NCV, NIV, NLT, NRSV, REB, TEV], 'therefore' [AB, BDAG, LN; NASB, NET], 'wherefore' [KJV], 'for this reason' [BDAG, LN], 'for this very reason, so then' [LN], not explicit [CEV]. This conjunction is a relatively emphatic marker of result, usually denoting the fact that the inference is self-evident [LN]. It is an inferential conjunction [BDAG].

b. pres. act. impera. of εὐθυμέω (LN 25.146) (BDAG p. 406): 'to be/become encouraged' [LN], 'to take courage' [LN], 'to be cheerful'

[BDAG]. This verb means to be or to become encouraged and hence cheerful [LN]. See this verb at v. 22.
- c. pres. act. indic. of πιστεύω (LN 31.85) (BDAG 1.c. p. 817): 'to believe' [Bar, BDAG; KJV, NASB, NLT], 'to have faith in' [AB, BECNT, LN; ESV, NRSV, NIV, NRSV], 'to trust in' [CBC; NCV, TEV], 'to trust' [LN; GW, REB], 'to be sure' [CEV], 'to believe in, to have confidence in' [LN]. This verb means to believe to the extent of complete trust and reliance [LN]. It means to consider something to be true and therefore worthy of one's trust [BDAG].
- d. aorist act. infin. of ἐκπίπτω (LN 54.19) (BDAG 2. p. 308): 'to run aground' [BDAG, BECNT, LN; ESV, GW, NASB, NET, NIV, NRSV], 'to be driven ashore' [AB; TEV], 'to be cast ashore' [CBC; REB], 'to be shipwrecked' [CEV, NLT], 'to be cast on/upon' [Bar; KJV], 'to crash' [NCV], 'to be blown off course and run aground' [LN], 'to drift off course' [BDAG]. This verb is a nautical term meaning to drift off or be blown off one's course and hence run aground [LN]. It means to drift or be blown off course and run aground [BDAG].

QUESTION—How likely is it that they would have come to land apart from divine intervention?

It was amazing that they came to the only island in that part of the Mediterranean, which is Malta [BECNT]. To arrive at Malta was a slender hope at best [PNTC].

**DISCOURSE UNIT—27:27–44** [CBC; GW, NIV, NLT]. The topic is the shipwreck [GW, NIV, NLT], the wreck [CBC].

**DISCOURSE UNIT—27:27–32** [NAC]. The topic is the prospect of landing.

**DISCOURSE UNIT—27:27–29** [NICNT]. The topic is they approach land.

**27:27** And as (the)-fourteenth night came, (as)-we were-drifting[a] in the Adriatic-sea, about (the)-middle of-the night the sailors were-suspecting[b] they were-nearing land. **27:28** And having-taken-soundings[c] they-found twenty fathoms,[d] and having-sailed (a)-little-(more) and again having-taken-soundings they-found fifteen.

LEXICON—a. pres. act. participle of διαφέρω (LN 15.163) (BDAG 2. p. 239): 'to drift' [AB, BDAG, BECNT, CBC; GW, NRSV, REB], 'to be tossed about' [Bar], 'to be blown about' [CEV], 'to be driven' [ESV, NASB, NET, NIV, NLT, TEV], 'to be driven up and down' [KJV], 'to be carried around' [NCV], 'to be driven about, to be carried about' [BDAG, LN], 'to carry hither and yon' [BDAG]. This verb means to cause to move in various directions by means of a force [LN]. It means to cause to move from one locality to another [BDAG].
- b. imperf. act. indic. of ὑπονοέω (LN 31.32) (BDAG p. 1040): 'to suspect' [BDAG, BECNT, LN; ESV, GW, NET, NRSV, TEV], 'to suppose' [BDAG], 'to think' [Bar; NCV], 'to feel' [AB, CBC; REB], 'to realize' [CEV], 'to deem' [KJV], 'to surmise' [NASB], 'to sense' [NIV, NLT], 'to

imagine, to conjecture' [LN]. This verb means to have an opinion based on scant evidence, often with the implication of regarding a false opinion as true [LN]. It means to form an opinion or conjecture on the basis of slight evidence [BDAG].

c. aorist act. participle of βολίζω (LN 54.23) (BDAG p. 180): 'to take soundings' [AB, Bar, BDAG, BECNT, LN; ESV, NASB, NET, NIV, NRSV, REB], 'to sound' [CBC; KJV], 'to measure' [CEV], 'to drop a plummet' [LN], 'to heave the lead' [BDAG, LN]. The phrase 'having taken soundings' is also translated 'they threw a line with a weight on it into the water' [GW], 'they lowered a rope with a weight on the end of it into the water' [NCV], 'they dropped a line with a weight tied to it' [TEV], 'they dropped a weighted line' [NLT]. This verb means to use a rope with a lead weight attached to it in order to measure the depth of water [LN]. It means to use a weighted line to determine depth [BDAG].

d. ὀργυιά (LN 81.26) (BDAG p. 721): 'fathom' [AB, Bar, BDAG, BECNT, CBC, LN; ESV, KJV, NASB, NET, NRSV, REB]. The phrase 'twenty fathoms' is also translated 'one hundred and twenty feet' [CEV, GW, NCV, NIV, NLT, TEV]. This noun is a unit of measure, traditionally the measurement of a man's arms stretched out horizontally, reckoned at approximately six feet or almost two meters and used as a technical, nautical term to measure the depth of water [LN]. It is the distance measured by a person's arms stretched out horizontally [BDAG].

QUESTION—To what does 'the fourteenth night' refer?

It had been two weeks since leaving Crete [BECNT, EBC, TNTC]. It had been two weeks since the storm began [NAC, TH, TRT], and during which the ship had been adrift at sea [NAC].

QUESTION—Why does Luke refer to this region of the Mediterranean Sea so far south of the Adriatic Sea as the Adriatic?

In ancient times 'Adria' or 'Adriatic' referred to a much larger region of the sea than today [Bar, BECNT, NAC, NICNT, PNTC, TH, TNTC]. It could cover the entire area from North Africa to Venice [Bar].

QUESTION—How might the sailors have known, or suspected, that they were nearing land?

They may have heard breakers from the shore [Bar, BECNT, CBC, EBC, NAC, NICNT, PNTC, TNTC]. They may have been near Point Koura [BECNT, NAC, NICNT, PNTC], near the northeast projection of Malta, and the breakers there can be heard for some distance [NAC].

QUESTION—What is a fathom?

It is approximately six feet [BECNT, TH, TRT], which is the distance between a person's hands when their arms are stretched out at full length [TH, TRT].

**27:29** And fearing lest we-run-aground against rocky[a] places, having-cast four anchors from (the)-stern[b] they-were-praying-(for)[c] day[d] to-come.

LEXICON—a. τραχύς (LN 79.84) (BDAG p. 1014): 'rocky' [Bar; NET], 'rugged' [CBC; REB], 'rough' [BDAG, LN], 'uneven' [BDAG]. The phrase 'rocky places' is also translated 'on the rocks' [AB, BECNT; ESV, NASB, NRSV, TEV], 'rocks' [CEV, GW, KJV, NCV, NIV, NLT]. This adjective describes something as being uneven and rough, as of terrain [LN].

b. πρύμνα (LN 6.47) (BDAG p. 892): 'stern' [AB, Bar, BDAG, BECNT, CBC, LN; ESV, KJV, NASB, NET, NIV, NRSV, REB], 'back of the ship' [CEV, GW, NLT, TEV]. The phrase 'from the stern' is also translated 'into the water' [NCV]. This noun denotes the back part of a boat [LN]. It is the after part of a boat [BDAG].

c. imperf. mid./pass. (deponent = act.) indic. of εὔχομαι (LN 25.6) (BDAG p. 417): 'to pray' [all translations except Bar; KJV, NASB, NET], 'to wish' [Bar, BDAG, LN; KJV, NASB, NET], 'to desire' [LN]. This verb means to desire something, with the implication of a pious wish [LN].

d. ἡμέρα (LN 14.40) (BDAG 1.a. p. 436): 'day' [Bar, BDAG, BECNT; ESV, KJV, NET, NRSV], 'daylight' [CBC, LN; CEV, NCV, NIV, NLT, REB, TEV], 'daybreak' [NASB], 'dawn' [AB], 'morning' [GW]. This noun denotes the light of the day in contrast with the darkness of night [LN]. It is the period between sunrise and sunset [BDAG].

QUESTION—Why did they cast anchors from the stern, instead of from the bow as would normally have been done?

The ship had not been facing toward the direction of the land, so anchors put out from the stern would have enabled the bow of the ship to point in the direction of the shore [BECNT, NAC, NICNT, PNTC]. They wanted to slow down the ship [Bar, PNTC] and anchoring from the stern was the best way to do that [Bar].

QUESTION—Were they wishing for daylight to come or were they praying for it to come?

1. They were praying for daylight to come [AB, BECNT, CBC, NAC, PNTC, TH; CEV, ESV, GW, NCV, NIV, NLT, NRSV, REB, TEV].
2. They were wishing for it to come [Bar, NICNT; KJV, NASB, NET].

**DISCOURSE UNIT—27:30–32** [NICNT]. The topic is the sailors' attempt to escape frustrated.

**27:30** And (as) the sailors were-seeking to-escape[a] from the ship and having-lowered the ship's-boat[b] into the sea in-pretense[c] as-though being-about-to cast-out anchors from (the)-bow, **27:31** Paul said to-the centurion and to-the soldiers, "Unless these-men remain in the ship, you are- not -able to-be-saved.[d]" **27:32** Then the soldiers cut-away the ropes of-the ship's-boat and let it fall-away.[e]

LEXICON—a. aorist act. infin. of φεύγω (LN 15.61) (BDAG 1. p. 1052): 'to escape' [AB, Bar, BECNT; CEV, ESV, GW, NASB, NET, NIV, NRSV, TEV], 'to abandon (ship)' [CBC; NLT, REB], 'to flee' [BDAG, LN; KJV], 'to leave' [NCV], 'to run away' [LN]. This verb means to move quickly from a point or area in order to avoid presumed danger or difficulty [LN]. It means to seek safety in flight [BDAG].

b. σκάφη (LN 6.45) (BDAG 2. p. 927): 'ship's boat' [AB, CBC; ESV, NASB, NET, REB], 'boat' [BECNT; KJV, NRSV, TEV], 'lifeboat' [CEV, GW, NCV, NIV, NLT], 'small boat' [BDAG, LN], 'skiff' [BDAG, LN], 'dinghy' [Bar]. This noun denotes a small boat which was normally kept aboard a larger ship and used by sailors in placing anchors, repairing the ship, or saving lives in the case of storms [LN].

c. πρόφασις (LN 88.230) (BDAG 2. p. 889): 'pretense' [Bar, BECNT, LN; ESV, NASB], 'as though' [AB; KJV, NLT], 'pretext' [BDAG; NRSV], 'ostensible reason, excuse' [BDAG]. The phrase 'in pretense' is also translated as a participle: 'pretending' [CBC; CEV, NCV, NET, NIV, REB]; as a finite verb: 'pretended' [GW, TEV]. This noun denotes the pretense of being engaged in a particular activity [LN]. It is a falsely alleged motive [BDAG].

d. aorist pass. infin. of σῴζω (LN 21.18) (BDAG 1. p. 982): 'to be saved' [AB, Bar, BDAG, BECNT; ESV, KJV, NASB, NCV, NET, NIV, NRSV, TEV], 'to come off safely' [CBC], 'to save one's life' [CEV], 'to stay alive' [GW], 'to reach safety' [REB], 'to be saved from death' [BDAG], 'to be delivered, to be made safe' [LN], 'to be rescued' [BDAG, LN], 'to be kept from harm, to be preserved' [BDAG]. The phrase 'you are not able to be saved' is also translated 'you will all die' [NLT]. This verb means to rescue from danger and to restore to a former state of safety and well-being [LN]. It means to preserve or rescue from natural dangers and afflictions [BDAG].

e. aorist act. infin. of ἐκπίπτω (LN 15.120) (BDAG 1. p. 308): 'to fall away' [Bar; NASB], 'to drop away' [CBC; REB], 'to fall' [BDAG, LN], 'to fall into the sea' [CEV], 'to fall into the water' [NCV], 'to fall off' [LN; KJV], 'to drift away' [AB; GW, NET, NIV, NLT], 'to go' [BECNT; ESV, TEV], 'to fall from' [LN]. The phrase 'let it fall away' is also translated 'set it adrift' [NRSV]. This verb means to fall from a particular point or location [LN]. It means to fall from some point [BDAG].

QUESTION—Why would anyone need to get into a boat to put out anchors from the bow?

They would put them as far from the bow as possible so as to stabilize the ship [NAC]. Putting anchors out from in front of the bow would help prevent the ship from being hit broadside by the waves [Bar, PNTC].

**DISCOURSE UNIT—27:33–38** [NAC, NICNT]. The topic is the meal on board [NICNT], Paul's further encouragement [NAC].

**27:33** And when day[a] was-about to-come, Paul was-urging[b] everyone to-take food saying, "Today (is the)-fourteenth day you-are-continuing waiting[c] without-eating[d] having-taken nothing. **27:34** Therefore I-urge you to take food; for this is for your preservation,[e] for not- (a)-hair of-the head - of-any of-you will-be-lost."

LEXICON—a. ἡμέρα (LN 14.40): 'day' [BECNT; ESV, KJV, NASB, NET, NLT] 'daybreak' [NRSV, REB], 'daylight' [LN], 'dawn' [AB; NCV,

NIV, TEV]. The phrase 'daybreak was about to come' is also translated 'shortly before daybreak' [CBC], 'just before daybreak' [GW], 'just before daylight' [CEV], 'it was nearly day' [Bar]. This noun denotes the light of the day in contrast with the darkness of night [LN].

b. imperf. act. indic. of παρακαλέω (LN 33.168) (BDAG 2. p. 765): 'to urge' [AB, BDAG, BECNT, CBC; ESV, NET, NIV, NLT, NRSV, REB], 'to encourage' [BDAG; GW, NASB], 'to exhort' [Bar, BDAG], 'to beg' [CEV, TEV], 'to persuade' [NCV], 'to beseech' [KJV], 'to ask for (earnestly), to request, to plead for' [LN], 'to appeal to' [BDAG, LN]. This verb means to ask for something earnestly and with propriety [LN]. It means to urge strongly [BDAG].

c. pres. act. participle of προσδοκάω (LN 25.228) (BDAG c. p. 877): 'to wait' [AB; GW, NCV, TEV], 'to tarry' [KJV], 'to wait for, to look for, to expect' [BDAG], 'to wait with apprehension, to wait with anxiety' [LN], not explicit [CEV]. The phrase 'you are continuing waiting' is also translated 'you have continued in suspense' [BECNT; ESV], 'you have lived in suspense' [CBC; REB], 'you have been in suspense/constant suspense' [NET, NIV], 'you have been in suspense and remaining (without food)' [NRSV], 'you have been constantly watching' [NASB], 'you are looking to (the fourteenth day) and continuing (without food)' [Bar], 'you have been so worried (that you haven't touched food)' [NLT]. This verb means to await with apprehension concerning impending danger or trouble [LN]. This verb means to give thought to something that is viewed as lying in the future [BDAG].

d. ἄσιτος (LN 23.32) (BDAG p. 143): 'without eating' [BDAG], 'going without eating' [NASB], 'not eating' [NCV], 'without food' [AB, Bar, BECNT, LN; ESV, NIV], 'without desiring food' [LN], 'fasting' [BDAG; KJV], 'gone hungry' [CBC; REB], 'haven't eaten a thing' [CEV, TEV], 'haven't touched food' [NLT], 'have had nothing to eat' [GW], 'you have eaten nothing' [NET]. This noun denotes a state of having been without food, frequently with the implication of being caused by a lack of appetite [LN].

e. σωτηρία (LN 21.18) (BDAG 1. p. 986): 'preservation' [BDAG; NASB], 'welfare' [Bar], 'health' [KJV], 'for your own good' [NLT], 'deliverance' [BDAG, LN]. The phrase 'this is for your preservation' is also translated 'it will strengthen you' [AB], 'it will give you strength' [BECNT; ESV], 'your lives depend on it' [CBC; CEV, REB], 'will help you survive' [GW, NRSV], 'you need it to survive' [NIV, TEV], 'this is important for your survival' [NET], 'you need it to stay alive' [NCV]. This noun denotes rescue from danger and restoration to a former state of safety and well-being [LN].

QUESTION—Was it true that they had eaten literally nothing at all for fourteen days?

This may have been a bit of hyperbole, but they probably had not had any real meal during that time [BECNT, NAC, TNTC, TRT].

QUESTION—What does the idiom 'not a hair of the head…will be lost' mean? This idiom means that they will not be harmed at all [BECNT, TH]. This is a biblical maxim, found also in 1 and 2 Samuel and 1 Kings [Bar, BECNT, PNTC].

**27:35** And having-said this and having-taken bread he-gave-thanks to-God before[a] all-of-them and breaking[b] (it) he-began to-eat. **27:36** And all-of-them becoming encouraged[c] they took food also.

LEXICON—a. ἐνώπιον with genitive object (LN 83.33) (BDAG 2.a. p. 342): 'before' [Bar, LN; NCV, NLT, TEV], 'in the presence of' [BECNT; ESV, KJV, NASB, NRSV], 'in front of' [CBC, LN; CEV, GW, NET, NIV, REB], 'in the sight of' [AB, BDAG], 'in the presence of, among' [BDAG]. This preposition denotes a position in front of an object, whether animate or inanimate, which is regarded as having a spatial orientation of front and back [LN]. It denotes being present or in view [BDAG].

b. aorist act. participle of κλάω (LN 19.34) (BDAG p. 546): 'to break' [BDAG, LN; all translations except NCV, NLT], 'to break off (a piece)' [NCV, NLT], 'to break bread' [LN]. This verb means to break an object into two or more parts [LN]. In the NT this verb is used only of breaking bread [BDAG, LN].

c. εὔθυμος (LN 25.147) (BDAG p. 406): 'encouraged' [BDAG, BECNT, LN; CEV, ESV, GW, NASB, NET, NIV, NLT, NRSV], 'of good cheer' [KJV], 'cheerful, in good spirits' [BDAG]. The phrase 'becoming encouraged' is also translated 'took courage' [AB; TEV], 'took heart' [Bar], 'plucked up courage' [CBC; REB], 'felt better' [NCV]. This adjective describes being encouraged [LN].

QUESTION—Should this breaking of bread be seen as possibly being or suggesting a Eucharistic meal?

It is not a Eucharistic meal [Bar, BECNT, CBC, NAC, PNTC, TNTC, TRT], although the moment is sacred in the sense that God will deliver them [BECNT]. Blessing God for the food and breaking the bread were a normal Jewish practice [Bar, NAC, PNTC, TNTC]. This might have been a Eucharistic meal of sorts in the minds of the Christians on board, but certainly not for the pagans [NICNT]. In the gospel of Luke Jesus is often depicted as sharing meals with disciples, which the believers present here would have remembered, though the pagans would not have known [NAC].

**27:37** And all-of-us in the ship were two-hundred seventy six persons.[a]
**27:38** And having-eaten-enough[b] food they-lightened[c] the ship (by)-throwing- the wheat -overboard[d] into the sea.

LEXICON—a. ψυχή (LN 9.20) (BDAG 3. p. 1099): 'person' [BDAG, BECNT, LN; ESV, NASB, NET, NRSV], 'soul' [AB, Bar; KJV], 'people' [LN; CEV, NCV], not explicit [CBC; GW, NIV, NLT, REB, TEV]. This noun denotes a person as a living being [LN]. It denotes an entity with personhood [BDAG].

b. aorist pass. participle of κορέννυμι (LN 57.22) (BDAG a. p. 559): 'to eat enough' [BDAG, BECNT; ESV, KJV, NASB, TEV], 'to eat enough to be satisfied' [NET], 'to eat one's fill' [AB], 'to eat as much as one wants' [CBC; NIV, REB], 'to eat all one wants' [GW, NCV], 'to be satisfied' [Bar], 'to satisfy one's hunger' [NRSV], 'to eat' [CEV, NLT], 'to have enough' [BDAG, LN], 'to be satiated' [BDAG, LN], 'to be filled' [BDAG]. This verb means to have enough, often with the implication of even more than enough [LN].

c. imperf. act. indic. of κουφίζω (LN 86.3) (BDAG p. 563): 'to lighten' [BDAG, LN; all translations except CEV, NCV], 'to make lighter' [CEV, NCV], 'to make light' [BDAG], 'to make less heavy' [LN]. This verb means to cause something to weigh less [LN]. It means to make something less heavy [BDAG].

d. pres. mid. participle of ἐκβάλλω (LN 15.220) (BDAG 1. p. 299): 'to throw overboard' [BDAG; NLT], 'to throw out' [BECNT, LN; ESV, NASB], 'to throw' [AB; CEV, NCV, NET, NIV, NRSV, TEV], 'to cast' [Bar], 'to cast out' [KJV], 'to dump' [CBC; GW, REB], 'to jettison (from a boat)' [LN]. This verb means to throw out of an area or object [LN].

QUESTION—Why did they throw the wheat into the sea?

Lightening the ship would allow it to ride higher in the water so it could come closer to the shore or up on to the shore [BECNT, CBC, NAC, NICNT, PNTC, TH, TNTC].

**DISCOURSE UNIT—27:39-44** [NAC, PNTC; CEV, ESV, NCV, NET, NRSV, TEV]. The topic is the shipwreck [CEV, ESV, NRSV, TEV], the ship is destroyed [NCV], Paul is shipwrecked [NET], the deliverance of all [NAC], experiencing God's deliverance [PNTC].

**DISCOURSE UNIT—27:39-41** [NICNT]. The topic is the shipwreck.

**27:39** And when daybreak[a] came, they were- not -recognizing[b] the land, but they-were-noticing a-certain bay[c] having (a)-beach[d] into which they-were-planning if possible to-run- the boat –aground.[e]

LEXICON—a. ἡμέρα (LN 14.40) (BDAG 1.a. p. 436): 'day' [AB, Bar, BDAG, BECNT, CBC; ESV, KJV, NASB, NET, REB, TEV], 'daylight' [LN; NCV, NIV], 'morning' [CEV, GW, NLT, NRSV]. This noun denotes the light of the day in contrast with the darkness of night [LN]. It is the period between sunrise and sunset [BDAG].

b. imperf. act. indic. of ἐπιγινώσκω (LN 28.2) (BDAG 1.b. p. 369): 'to recognize' [all translations except KJV, NCV], 'to know' [BDAG; KJV, NCV], 'to know about, to know definitely about' [LN]. This verb means to possess more or less definite information about, possibly with a degree of thoroughness or competence [LN]. It means to have knowledge of something or someone [BDAG].

c. κόλπος (LN 1.74) (BDAG 3. p. 557): 'bay' [BDAG, LN; all translations except CEV, KJV], 'cove' [CEV], 'creek' [KJV], 'gulf' [LN]. This noun

denotes a part of the sea which is partially enclosed by land [LN]. It is a part of the sea that indents a shoreline [BDAG].
d. αἰγιαλός (LN 1.63) (BDAG p. 25): 'beach' [BDAG, LN; all translations except CBC; KJV, REB], 'sandy beach' [CBC; REB], 'shore' [BDAG, LN; KJV]. This noun denotes a strip of land immediately bordering the edge of a body of water and gradually sloping down into the water [LN].
e. aorist act. infin. of ἐξωθέω (LN 54.17) (BDAG p. 355): 'to run aground' [LN; NET, NIV, NLT, TEV], 'to run aground on a beach' [CEV], 'to ground' [AB], 'to run ashore' [BDAG, CBC; ESV, GW, NRSV, REB], 'to bring ashore' [BECNT], 'to run' [Bar], 'to run a ship onto a beach' [LN], 'to drive onto' [NASB], 'to beach' [BDAG], 'to sail to a beach' [NCV], 'to thrust in' [KJV]. This verb means the movement of a ship being driven ashore [LN]. It means to run or drive ashore [BDAG].

**27:40** And having-cast-away[a] the anchors leaving (them) in the sea, at-(the)-same-time having-loosened[b] the ropes of-the rudders[c] and having-raised the foresail[d] to-the wind they-were-heading[e] toward the beach.

LEXICON—a. aorist act. participle of περιαιρέω (LN 15.204) (BDAG 1. p. 799): 'to cast off' [AB, BDAG, BECNT; ESV, NASB, NRSV], 'to remove' [BDAG, LN], 'to detach' [Bar], 'to cut free' [GW], 'to cut loose' [CEV, NIV], 'to cut off' [NLT, TEV], 'to cut the ropes to' [NCV], 'to slip' [CBC; NET, REB], 'to take away' [BDAG], 'to take up' [KJV], 'to take from around' [LN]. This verb means to remove something which is around something else [LN]. It means take away from around something [BDAG].

b. aorist act. participle of ἀνίημι (LN 18.19) (BDAG 1. p. 82): 'to loosen' [Bar, BDAG, BECNT, CBC, LN; ESV, NASB, NET, NRSV, REB], 'to loose' [KJV], 'to untie' [CEV, GW, NCV, NIV, TEV], 'to unlash' [AB], 'to lower' [NLT], 'to unfasten' [BDAG, NLT]. This verb means to cause something to become loose [LN].

c. πηδάλιον (LN 6.50) (BDAG p. 811): 'rudder' [Bar, BDAG, BECNT, LN; CEV, ESV, KJV, NASB, NCV, NIV, NLT], 'steering oar' [AB; GW, NET, NRSV, TEV], 'steering paddle' [BDAG, CBC; REB]. This noun denotes a large plank at the stern of a ship used to direct its course [LN].

d. ἀρτέμων (LN 6.49) (BDAG p. 135): 'foresail' [AB, Bar, BDAG, BECNT, CBC; ESV, NASB, NET, NIV, NLT, NRSV, REB], 'front sail' [NCV], 'sail at the front of the ship' [CEV, TEV], 'top sail' [GW], 'mainsail' [KJV], 'sail' [LN]. This noun denotes a cloth attached above a boat in such a way as to catch the wind and thus propel the boat through the water [LN].

e. κατέχω (LN 54.22) (BDAG 7. p. 533): 'to head for' [BDAG, LN; NASB, TEV], 'to head toward' [NLT], 'to make for' [AB, BECNT; ESV, NIV, NRSV], 'to make toward' [KJV], 'to sail toward' [NCV], 'to steer to/toward' [LN; GW, NET], 'to let (her) drive' [CBC; REB], 'to (let the wind) carry (the ship)' [CEV], 'to hold on' [Bar], 'to hold course'

[BDAG]. This verb is a nautical term meaning to control the movement of a ship to a particular point [LN].

QUESTION—Why would they loosen the rudder ropes or hoist the foresail?
Loosening the ropes allowed them to use the rudders for steering [AB, BECNT], and raising the foresail would enable them to steer by that sail [AB, BECNT, NICNT, TNTC]. Hoisting the foresail would increase their forward speed [PNTC, TH].

**27:41** But having-struck[a] (a)-place between-two-seas[b] they-ran- the vessel -aground[c] and the bow[d] having-stuck[e] remained unmovable,[f] but the stern[g] was-broken-up[h] by the force[i] of-the waves.[j]

TEXT—Manuscripts reading ὑπὸ τῆς βίας τῶν κυμάτων 'by the force of the waves' are given a C rating by GNT to indicate that choosing it over variant texts was difficult. Manuscripts that omit 'by the force' are followed by ESV, REB. Some manuscripts omit 'by the waves', NASB includes 'by the waves' in italics.

LEXICON—a. aorist act. participle of περιπίπτω (LN 15.85) (BDAG 1. p. 804): 'strike' [AB, BDAG, BECNT, LN; ESV, GW, NASB, NIV, NRSV], 'to hit' [NCV, NLT, TEV], 'to fall into' [KJV], 'to encounter' [NET], 'to run upon' [Bar], 'to be caught' [CBC; REB], 'to run into, to hit against' [LN], not explicit [CEV]. This verb means to move to and strike against, involving both movement and impact [LN]. It means to move toward something and hit against it [BDAG].

b. διθάλασσος (LN 1.68) (BDAG p. 245): 'shoal' [Bar, BECNT; NLT], 'sandbank' [CEV, NCV, TEV], 'sandbar' [LN; GW, NIV], 'reef' [LN; ESV, NRSV]. The phrase τόπος διθάλασσος 'a place between two seas' is also translated 'a place where two seas met' [KJV], 'a place where two currents met' [AB], 'a reef where two seas met' [NASB], 'a patch of crosscurrents' [NET], 'between cross-currents' [CBC; REB]. This phrase denotes a bar or reef produced in an area where two currents meet [LN]. The phrase is a semantic unit signifying a point of land jutting out with water on both sides [BDAG].

c. aorist act. indic. of ἐπικέλλω (LN 54.18) (BDAG p. 374): 'to run aground' [BDAG, LN; all translations except NCV, TEV], 'to go aground' [TEV], not explicit [NCV]. This verb is a nautical term meaning to cause a ship to run up onto or against a shore [LN].

d. πρῷρα (LN 6.46) (BDAG p. 892): 'bow' [AB, Bar, BDAG, BECNT, CBC, LN; ESV, NET, NIV, NLT, NRSV, REB], 'front of the ship' [CEV, GW, NCV], 'front part of the ship' [TEV], 'forepart' [KJV], 'prow' [BDAG; NASB]. This noun denotes the forepart of a boat [BDAG, LN].

e. aorist act. participle of ἐρείδω (LN 15.5) (BDAG p. 391): 'to stick' [ESV, GW, NCV, NRSV], 'to stick fast' [CBC; KJV, NASB, NET, NIV, NLT, REB], 'to become stuck' [BECNT], 'to get stuck' [TEV], 'to become fixed' [Bar], 'to become fixed and remain, to jam fast' [BDAG, LN], 'to stick firmly' [CEV], 'to bore (itself) in and stick' [AB]. This verb means to become not able to be moved [LN]. It means to stick in something [BDAG].

f. ἀσάλευτος (LN 15.4) (BDAG p. 141): 'immovable' [BDAG, BECNT, CBC, LN; ESV, NASB, NRSV, REB], 'unmovable' [KJV], 'immovably fast' [AB], 'firm' [Bar], 'would not move' [NIV], 'could not move' [NCV, TEV], 'could not be moved' [GW, NET], 'not able to move' [LN], not explicit [CEV, NLT]. This adjective describes that which cannot be moved [LN]. It describes not being subject to movement [BDAG].

g. πρύμνα (LN 6.47): 'stern' [AB, Bar, BECNT, CBC, LN; ESV, NASB, NET, NIV, NLT, NRSV, REB], 'rear' [CEV], 'back of the ship' [GW, NCV], 'back part' [TEV], 'hinder part' [KJV]. This noun denotes the back part of a boat [LN].

h. imperf. pass. indic. of λύω (LN 20.53) (BDAG 3. p. 607): 'to be broken up' [BECNT; ESV, NASB, NET, NRSV], 'to break up' [AB, Bar; NCV], 'to be broken to pieces' [LN; GW, NIV, TEV], 'to be broken' [KJV], 'to be pounded to pieces' [CBC; REB], 'to be smashed' [CEV], 'to be repeatedly smashed' [NLT], 'to be torn down' [LN], 'to be destroyed' [BDAG, LN]. The imperfect tense of this verb is translated as indicating ongoing action: 'was being broken/smashed, etc.' [BECNT, CBC; CEV, ESV, NCV, NET, NRSV, REB, TEV]. It is also translated as indicating inceptive action: 'began to be broken/smashed, etc.' [AB, Bar; NASB, NCV, NLT]. This verb means to destroy or reduce something to ruin by tearing down or breaking to pieces [LN]. It means to reduce something by violence into its components [BDAG].

i. βία (LN 20.1) (BDAG a. p. 175): 'force' [AB, BDAG, LN; CEV, GW, NASB, NET, NLT, NRSV], 'violence' [Bar, LN; KJV, TEV], 'pounding' [NIV], 'big (waves)' [NCV], not explicit [BECNT, CBC; ESV, REB]. This noun denotes a strong, destructive force [LN]. It is strength or energy brought to bear in varying degrees on things or persons [BDAG].

j. κῦμα (LN 14.25) (BDAG p. 575): 'wave' [AB, Bar, BDAG, LN; all versions except ESV, NIV, REB], 'surf' [BECNT; ESV, NIV], 'breakers' [CBC; REB], 'billow, surge' [LN]. This noun denotes a moving ridge or succession of swells on the surface of a body of water [LN].

QUESTION—What is meant by διθάλασσος 'between two seas'?

It is a sandbar or shoal [Bar, BECNT, EBC, PNTC; CEV, GW, NCV, NIV, NLT, TEV]. It is a reef [ESV, NRSV]. It is a place where two currents meet [AB, CBC; KJV, NASB, NET, REB], which produces a bar or reef [LN]. It is a point of land jutting out with water on both sides [BDAG], or a sandbar with deeper water on both sides [EBC].

**DISCOURSE UNIT—27:42–44** [NICNT]. The topic is safe ashore.

**27:42** And (the)-plan[a] of-the soldiers was that they-would-kill the prisoners, lest swimming-away any should-escape. **27:43** But the centurion, wanting to-save[b] Paul, kept[c] them-(from carrying out) the plan, and he-ordered[d] the-ones being-able to-swim having-jumped-(overboard)[e] first to-go to the land 27:44 and the rest on planks^f or on pieces of-the ship. And thus it-was (that) all were-brought-safely^g to the land.

LEXICON—a. βουλή (LN 30.57) (BDAG 2.a. p. 182): 'plan' [Bar, BECNT, LN; ESV, GW, NASB, NET, NRSV], 'to make a plan' [TEV], 'counsel' [KJV], 'intention, purpose' [LN], 'resolution, decision' [BDAG]. The phrase 'the plan of the soldiers' is also translated 'the soldiers planned' [NIV], 'the soldiers decided' [AB; CEV, NCV], 'the soldiers wanted' [NLT], 'the soldiers thought they had better (kill the prisoners)' [CBC; REB]. This noun denotes that which has been purposed and planned [LN]. It is that which one decides [BDAG].

b. aorist act. infin. of διασῴζω (LN 21.19) (BDAG p. 237): 'to save' [AB, BDAG, BECNT, LN; ESV, GW, KJV, NRSV, TEV], 'to save (Paul's) life' [CEV, NET], 'to spare' [NLT], 'to spare (Paul's) life' [NIV], 'to get safely through' [Bar], 'to bring safely through' [BDAG, CBC; NASB, REB], 'to let live' [NCV], 'to rescue' [BDAG, LN]. This verb means to rescue completely from danger [LN]. It means to rescue or deliver from a hazard or danger [BDAG].

c. aorist act. indic. of κωλύω (LN 13.146) (BDAG 1.a. p. 580): 'to keep (someone) from' [BECNT; ESV, KJV, NASB, NIV, NRSV], 'to prevent' [AB, BDAG, CBC, LN; NET, REB], 'to stop (someone)' [GW, TEV], 'to put a stop to' [Bar], 'to not allow' [NCV], 'to not let' [CEV, NLT], 'to hinder' [BDAG, LN], 'to forbid' [BDAG]. This verb means to cause something not to happen [LN]. It means to keep something from happening [BDAG].

d. aorist act. indic. of κελεύω (LN 33.323) (BDAG p. 538): 'to order' [AB, BDAG, BECNT, LN; CEV, ESV, GW, NCV, NET, NIV, NLT, NRSV, TEV], 'to command' [Bar, BDAG, LN; KJV, NASB], 'to give orders' [CBC; REB], 'to urge' [BDAG]. This verb means to state with force and/or authority what others must do [LN]. It means to give a command, ordinarily of an official nature [BDAG].

e. aorist act. participle of ἀπορίπτω (LN 15.242) (BDAG 3. p. 119): 'to jump overboard' [AB, CBC; ESV, GW, NASB, NET, NIV, NLT, NRSV, REB, TEV], 'to throw oneself overboard' [Bar, BECNT], 'to jump into the water' [NCV], 'to dive into the water' [CEV], to cast oneself into the sea' [KJV], 'to jump off, to leap overboard' [LN], 'to throw oneself down, to jump' [BDAG]. This verb means to throw oneself off from some object (as from a ship) [LN]. It means to propel oneself downward [BDAG].

f. σανίς (LN 7.79) (BDAG p. 913): 'plank' [BDAG, LN; all translations except KJV, NCV], 'board' [BDAG; KJV, NCV]. This noun denotes a large board or plank of wood [LN].

g. aorist pass. infin. of διασῴζω (LN 21.19) (BDAG p. 237): 'to be brought safely' [ESV, NASB, NET, NRSV], 'to be brought safely through' [BDAG], 'to come safely' [AB, CBC; REB], 'to get safely' [Bar; GW, TEV], 'to reach (shore/land) safely' [CEV, NIV], 'to make it safely' [NCV], 'to escape' [BECNT], 'to escape safe/safely' [KJV, NLT], 'to be saved' [BDAG, LN], 'to be rescued' [BDAG, LN]. This verb means to rescue completely from danger [LN]. It means to rescue or deliver from a hazard or danger [BDAG].

QUESTION—Why would the soldiers want to kill the prisoners to keep them from escaping?

The soldiers might be punished if any prisoners escaped [BECNT, NAC, PNTC]. Under Roman law they could be executed if prisoners escaped [AB, NAC, TRT]. They would be subject to the same penalty as a prisoner whom they allowed to escape [EBC].

QUESTION—What might be Luke's purpose in narrating this rather long account of the sea voyage and shipwreck?

Luke wants to show how Paul's getting to Rome was actually the will of God, who protected him despite all the difficulty encountered in getting there [BECNT, NICNT, TNTC]. It also shows how Paul became a means of salvation for others through God's grace [NAC, PNTC]. It also shows Paul's character and leadership as he encourages the crew and other passengers [NAC, PNTC, TNTC].

**DISCOURSE UNIT—28:1–16** [AB]. The topic is Paul travels from Malta to Rome.

**DISCOURSE UNIT—28:1–15** [PNTC]. The topic is from Malta to Rome.

**DISCOURSE UNIT—28:1-10** [CBC, EBC, NICNT, PNTC; CEV, ESV, GW, NASB, NCV, NET, NIV, NLT, NRSV, TEV]. The topic is Paul on the island of Malta [GW, NCV, NLT, NRSV], Paul ashore on Malta [NIV], ashore at Malta [EBC], Paul on Malta [ESV, NET], on the island of Malta [CEV], in Malta [CBC; TEV], winter in Malta [NICNT], safe at Malta [NASB], hospitality from pagans [PNTC].

**DISCOURSE UNIT—28:1–6** [NAC, NICNT]. The topic is welcome to Malta! [NICNT], deliverance from the viper [NAC].

**28:1** And having-been-brought-safely-through[a] then we-learned that the island is-called Malta. **28:2** And the natives[b] were-showing unusual[c] kindness[d] to-us, for having-kindled[e] (a)-fire they-welcomed[f] us all, because-of the rain having-set-in[g] and because-of the cold.

LEXICON—a. aorist pass. participle of διασῴζω (LN 21.19): 'to be brought safely through' [ESV, NASB], 'to get safely through' [Bar], 'to make one's way to safety' [CBC; REB], 'to reach safety' [NRSV], 'to escape' [AB, BECNT], 'to be escaped' [KJV], 'to be safe on land/shore' [NCV, NLT], 'to be safely on shore/ashore' [GW, NIV, TEV], 'to safely reach shore' [NET], 'to come ashore' [CEV], 'to be saved, to be rescued' [LN]. This verb means to rescue completely from danger [LN].

b. βάρβαρος (LN 11.94) (BDAG 2.b. p. 166): 'native' [BECNT; NASB, NRSV, REB, TEV], 'native people' [LN; ESV], 'local people' [CEV], 'local inhabitants' [NET], 'inhabitants' [AB, Bar], 'people who lived there' [NCV], 'people of the island' [NLT], 'people who lived on the island' [GW], 'islanders' [NIV], 'rough islanders' [CBC], 'barbarous people' [KJV], 'a non-Hellene' [BDAG], 'foreigner' [BDAG, LN], 'uncivilized' [LN]. This noun denotes the native people of an area in which a language other than Greek or Latin was spoken (such persons would be regarded as being outside the civilized world of NT times) [LN]. It describes those who do not speak Greek or who do not participate in Greek culture [BDAG].

c. aorist act. participle of τυγχάνω (LN 90.61) (BDAG 2.d. p. 1019): 'to happen, to turn out' [BDAG], 'to experience, to have happen to' [LN]. The phrase οὐ τὴν τυχοῦσαν 'unusual' [BECNT; ESV, NIV, NRSV] is also translated 'uncommon' [AB, CBC; REB], 'extraordinary' [NASB, NET], 'no ordinary' [Bar], 'no little' [KJV], 'unusually (friendly)' [GW], 'very (friendly)' [CEV, TEV], 'very kind' [NLT], 'very (good)' [NCV]. This verb means to experience some happening (generally neutral in connotation) [LN]. It means to prove to be in the result [BDAG].

d. φιλανθρωπία (LN 88.71) (BDAG p. 1056): 'kindness' [AB, Bar, BECNT, CBC, LN; ESV, KJV, NASB, NET, NIV, NRSV, REB], '(loving) kindness' [BDAG], 'friendliness' [LN]. The phrase 'were showing...kindness' is also translated 'were...friendly' [CEV, TEV], 'were...kind' [GW, NLT], 'were...good' [NCV]. This noun denotes the expression of friendly concern for someone [LN]. It is affectionate concern for and interest in humanity [BDAG].

e. aorist act. participle of ἅπτω (LN 14.65) (BDAG 1. p. 126): 'to kindle' [BDAG, BECNT, LN; ESV, KJV, NASB, NRSV], 'to light' [AB, Bar, BDAG, CBC; REB], 'to build (a fire)' [CEV, NET, NIV, NLT, TEV], 'to make (a fire)' [GW, NCV], 'to ignite, to set ablaze, to start a fire, to light a lamp' [LN]. This verb means to cause the process of burning to begin [LN]. It means to cause illumination or burning to take place [BDAG].

f. aorist mid. indic. of προσλαμβάνομαι (LN 34.53) (BDAG 4. p. 883): 'to welcome' [BECNT, LN; CEV, ESV, NCV, NET, NIV, NLT], 'to welcome (us) around it' [GW, NRSV], 'to make welcome' [CBC; REB, TEV], 'to look after' [AB], 'to receive' [LN; KJV, NASB], 'to accept, to have as a guest' [LN], 'to receive in(to) one's home or circle of acquaintances' [BDAG]. This verb is translated as referring to the action of bringing the survivors to the fire: 'they...brought us to it' [Bar]. This verb means to accept the presence of a person with friendliness [LN]. It means to extend a welcome [BDAG].

g. pres. act. participle of ἐφίστημι (LN 68.7) (BDAG 4. p. 418): 'to set in' [NASB], 'to begin' [AB, BDAG, BECNT, LN; ESV, NRSV], 'to start' [CBC; NET, REB, TEV], 'to commence' [LN], 'to come on' [Bar, BDAG]. The phrase 'the rain having set in' is also translated 'it was raining [NCV, NIV], 'it was rainy' [CEV, NLT], 'because of the rain' [GW], 'because of the present rain' [KJV]. This verb means to begin, with the focus upon the initial stages of an activity [LN]. It means to be present to begin something [BDAG].

QUESTION—Where and what is Malta?

It is an island that is 18 miles long and 8 miles wide, 58 miles south of Sicily and 180 miles from Africa [BECNT, PNTC]. It is about 150 miles southwest of the tip of Italy [TH]. The people there were of Phoenician ancestry and spoke a variant of the Punic language [BECNT, NAC, NICNT, TNTC].

QUESTION—What does the term βάρβαρος mean?

The term βάρβαρος refers to people who do not speak Greek [Bar, BECNT, EBC, NAC, NICNT, TH, TNTC] or Latin [BECNT, EBC, NICNT]. It means that Greek was not their first language and they did not have a Greco-Roman cultural background [PNTC].

**28:3** And Paul having-gathered[a] a-bundle of-sticks and having-placed-(them) on the fire, (a)-viper[b] having-come-out from the heat fastened-onto[c] his hand.

LEXICON—a. aorist act. participle of συστρέφω (LN 15.125) (BDAG 1. p. 979): 'to gather' [Bar, BECNT; all versions except REB, TEV], 'to gather up' [TEV], 'to get together' [CBC; REB], 'to gather together, to call together' [LN], 'to collect' [AB]. This verb means to cause to come together [BDAG, LN], whether of animate or inanimate objects [LN].

b. ἔχιδνα (LN 4.53) (BDAG p. 419): 'viper' [AB, Bar, BECNT, CBC, LN; ESV, KJV, NASB, NET, NIV, NRSV, REB], 'snake' [BDAG; CEV, TEV], 'poisonous snake' [GW, NCV, NLT], 'asp, cobra' [LN]. This noun denotes a species of poisonous snakes [BDAG].

c. aorist act. indic. of καθάπτω (LN 18.7) (BDAG p. 488): 'to fasten on/onto/to' [LN; all translations except CEV, GW, NCV, NLT], 'to bite' [CEV, NCV, NLT], 'to bite and not let go' [GW], 'to seize' [BDAG, LN], 'to take hold of' [BDAG]. This verb means to seize and fasten onto [LN].

QUESTION—Was this snake poisonous or non-poisonous?

The term ἔχιδνα normally refers to a poisonous snake [Bar, BDAG, BECNT, LN, NAC, NICNT, TNTC], but sometimes can be used with less precision, meaning that the snake could have been non-poisonous [NAC]. Although there are no poisonous snakes on Malta today, this does not mean that there were none in the first century [EBC, NAC, NICNT, PNTC, TNTC]. The people of the island would have known if there were poisonous snakes there or not [PNTC, TNTC], but it may be that the Maltese islanders mistakenly thought this snake was poisonous [NICNT, PNTC].

**28:4** And when the natives saw the creature[a] hanging[b] from his hand, they said to each-other, "No-doubt[c] this man is (a)-murderer whom having-been-saved from the sea Justice[d] did- not -allow to-live."

LEXICON—a. θηρίον (LN 4.3) (BDAG 1.a.β.ℸ. p. 456): 'creature' [AB, Bar, BECNT; ESV, NASB, NET, NRSV], 'snake' [CBC; CEV, GW, NCV, NIV, REB, TEV], 'animal' [BDAG, LN], 'beast' [BDAG; KJV], not

explicit [NLT]. This noun denotes any living creature, not including man [LN]. It denotes any living creature, excluding humans [BDAG].
- b. pres. mid. participle of κρεμάννυμι (LN 18.22) (BDAG 2.a. p. 566): 'to hang (from)' [BDAG; all translations except CBC; KJV, REB, TEV], 'to hang down from' [LN], 'to hang (on/on to)' [CBC; KJV, REB, TEV]. This verb means to hang down from some point [BDAG, LN].
- c. πάντως (LN 71.16): 'no doubt' [AB, Bar, BECNT, LN; ESV, KJV, NET, NLT], 'undoubtedly' [NASB], 'must be' [CBC; CEV, GW, NCV, NIV, NRSV, REB, TEV], 'certainly, really, doubtless' [LN]. This adverb describes being in every respect certain [LN].
- d. δίκη (LN 12.27) (BDAG 2. p. 250): 'Justice' [Bar, BDAG, LN; NCV], 'justice' [AB, BECNT; GW, NASB, NLT, NRSV], 'Justice herself' [NET], 'divine justice' [CBC; REB], 'the goddess Justice' [LN; ESV, NIV], 'the goddess of justice' [CEV], 'Fate' [TEV], 'vengeance' [KJV]. This noun denotes a goddess who personifies justice in seeking out and punishing the guilty [LN]. It is Justice personified as a deity [BDAG].

QUESTION—Does ἡ δίκη 'justice' represent the idea of justice as an abstraction, or as a god or goddess, personifying justice?

It is a god or goddess [AB, Bar, BDAG, BECNT, EBC, LN, NAC, NICNT, PNTC, TH, TNTC, TRT; CEV, ESV, NCV, NET, NIV, TEV].

**28:5** Having-shaken-off[a] the creature into the fire he-suffered[b] no harm.[c]

LEXICON—a. aorist act. participle of ἀποτινάσσω (LN 16.8) (BDAG p. 124): 'to shake off' [BDAG, LN; all translations except GW], 'to shake' [GW], 'to shake out, to shake from' [LN]. This verb means to shake something out or off, in order to get rid of an object or a substance [LN].
- b. aorist act. indic. of πάσχω (LN 24.78) (BDAG 3.b. p. 785): 'to suffer' [Bar, BDAG, BECNT, LN; ESV, NASB, NET, NIV, NRSV], 'to feel' [KJV], 'to be in pain' [LN], 'to endure' [BDAG]. The phrase 'he suffered no harm' is also translated 'he was not harmed' [AB; CEV, GW], 'he was unharmed' [NLT], 'without being harmed' [TEV], 'was not hurt' [NCV], 'he was none the worse' [CBC; REB]. This verb means to suffer pain [LN].
- c. κακός (LN 20.18) (BDAG 2. p. 501): 'harm' [Bar, BDAG, BECNT, LN; ESV, KJV, NASB, NET, NRSV], 'ill effect' [NIV], 'evil' [BDAG, LN], 'injurious, dangerous, pernicious' [BDAG], not explicit [AB, CBC; CEV, GW, NCV, NLT, REB, TEV]. This noun denotes the experience of harm [LN]. It is what is harmful or injurious [BDAG].

**28:6** And they-were-expecting[a] him to-begin to-swell-up[b] or to-fall-down[c] dead suddenly. But (after) waiting[d] for (a)-long-time and having-observed nothing unusual[e] happening to him having-changed-their-minds[f] they-said he was (a)-god.

LEXICON—a. imperf. act. indic. of προσδοκάω (LN 30.55) (BDAG d. p. 877): 'to expect' [AB, Bar, BDAG, CBC, LN; NASB, NET, NIV, NRSV, REB], 'to think' [CEV, NCV], 'to wait for' [BDAG; ESV, GW, NLT,

TEV], 'to wait, expecting' [BECNT], 'to look' [KJV], 'to look for' [BDAG], 'to anticipate' [LN]. The imperfect tense of this verb is translated as indicating ongoing action: 'they waited, expecting' [BECNT], 'were expecting/waiting' [Bar; ESV], 'they kept thinking' [CEV], 'they still expected' [CBC]. This verb means to expect something to happen, whether good or bad [LN]. It means to give thought to something that is viewed as lying in the future [BDAG].
- b. pre. pass. infin. of πίμπρημι (LN 23.163) (BDAG 2. p. 814): 'to swell up' [all translations except AB; KJV], 'to swell' [AB; KJV], 'to become distended' [BDAG].
- c. pres. act. infin. of καταπίπτω (LN 15.119) (BDAG p. 524): 'to fall down (dead)' [AB, Bar, BDAG, BECNT; ESV, KJV, NASB, NCV, TEV], 'to drop down (dead)' [CBC; REB], 'to drop (dead)' [CEV, GW, NET, NLT, NRSV], 'to fall (dead)' [NIV], 'to fall down' [LN], 'to fall' [LN]. This verb means to fall from a standing or upright position down to the ground or surface [LN].
- d. pres. act. participle of προσδοκάω (LN 30.55) (BDAG c. p. 877): 'to wait' [all translations except CEV, NCV, KJV], 'to watch' [CEV], 'to wait and watch' [NCV], 'to wait for, to look for' [BDAG], 'to look' [KJV], 'to expect' [BDAG, LN], 'to anticipate' [LN]. The present participle form of this verb is translated as indicating ongoing action: 'they went on waiting' [Bar]. This verb means to expect something to happen, whether good or bad [LN]. It means to give thought to something that is viewed as lying in the future [BDAG].
- e. ἄτοπος (LN 58.54) (BDAG p. 149): 'unusual' [BDAG, LN; GW, NASB, NET, NIV, NRSV, TEV], 'amiss' [Bar], 'out of the way' [REB], 'misfortune' [BECNT; ESV], 'harm' [KJV], 'bad' [NCV], 'unusual and bad' [LN], 'extraordinary' [CBC], 'surprising' [BDAG], not explicit [AB; CEV]. The phrase 'nothing unusual happening' is also translated 'he wasn't harmed' [NLT]. This adjective describes that which is unusual, and generally with the implication of harmful or dangerous [LN]. It describes something as being out of the ordinary [BDAG].
- f. aorist mid. participle of μεταβάλλω (LN 31.58) (BDAG p. 638): 'to change one's mind' [LN; all translations], 'to alter an opinion' [LN], 'to change' [BDAG]. This verb means to change one's thinking about something [LN]. It means to change one's way of thinking [BDAG].

QUESTION—What is conveyed by the imperfect tense of the verb 'expecting' and the present tense of the infinitives in this verse?

It gives a sense of drama in the situation [PNTC]. Luke's vivid account emphasizes that Paul had a God-given mission and was protected by God [EBC].

**DISCOURSE UNIT—28:7–10** [NAC, NICNT]. The topic is the hospitality of Publius [NAC], works of healing in Malta [NICNT].

**28:7** And in the-(area) around[a] that place were lands[b] (belonging to) the chief-man[c] of-the island, Publius by-name, who having-received[d] us entertained[e] (us) hospitably[f] (for) three days.

LEXICON—a. περί with accusative object (LN 83.18) (BDAG 2.a.γ. p. 798): 'around' [LN; GW, NCV], 'region around' [NET], 'about' [BDAG; CEV], 'near' [AB], 'nearby' [NIV], 'neighborhood' [Bar, BECNT, CBC; ESV, NASB, NRSV, REB], 'quarters' [KJV], 'not far from' [TEV]. The phrase 'in the area around that place' is also translated 'near the shore where we landed' [NLT]. This preposition indicates a position or a series of positions around an area, but not necessarily involving complete encirclement [LN]. It describes a region around a place [BDAG].

b. χωρίον (LN 1.95) (BDAG 1. p. 1095): 'land' [BECNT, CBC, LN; CEV, ESV, NASB, NRSV, REB], 'field' [BDAG, LN; NCV, NET, TEV], 'estate' [AB; NIV, NLT], 'domain' [Bar], 'property' [GW], 'possession' [KJV], 'piece of land' [BDAG], 'place' [BDAG]. This noun denotes land under cultivation or used for pasture [LN]. It is a piece of land other than a populated area [BDAG].

c. πρῶτος (LN 87.45): 'chief man' [Bar, BECNT; ESV, KJV], 'chief magistrate' [AB, CBC; REB], 'chief official' [NET, NIV, NLT], 'chief' [TEV], 'leading man' [NASB, NRSV], 'governor' [CEV, GW], 'important man' [NCV], 'great, prominent, important, foremost' [LN]. This adjective describes being of high rank, with the implication of special prominence and status [LN].

d. aorist mid. participle of ἀναδέχομαι (LN 34.53) (BDAG 2. p. 62): 'to receive' [Bar, BDAG, BECNT, LN; ESV, KJV, NRSV], 'to receive as a guest' [AB], 'to welcome' [BDAG, LN; GW, NASB, NET, NIV, NLT, TEV], 'to welcome into one's house' [NCV], 'to take in' [CBC; REB], 'to be (very) friendly' [CEV], 'to accept, to have as a guest' [LN]. This verb means to accept the presence of a person with friendliness [LN]. It means to extend hospitality to [BDAG].

e. aorist act. indic. of ξενίζω (LN 34.57) (BDAG 1. p. 673): 'entertain' [Bar, BDAG, BECNT, CBC; ESV, NASB, NET, NRSV, REB], 'to treat' [AB; GW, NLT], 'to lodge (someone)' [KJV], 'to show hospitality, to receive a stranger as a guest, hospitality' [LN], 'to receive as a guest' [BDAG]. The phrase 'entertained us hospitably' is also translated 'welcomed us into his home' [CEV], 'was very good to us' [NCV], 'showed us generous hospitality' [NIV], 'we were his guests' [TEV]. This verb means to receive and show hospitality to a stranger, that is, someone who is not regarded as a member of the extended family or a close friend [LN]. It means to show hospitality [BDAG].

f. φιλοφρόνως (LN 88.72) (BDAG p. 1060): 'hospitably' [BDAG, BECNT, CBC; ESV, NET, NRSV, REB], 'kindly' [AB, LN; GW, NLT, TEV], 'with kindly hospitality' [Bar], 'courteously' [KJV, NASB], 'in a friendly way' [LN], 'in a friendly manner' [BDAG]. See entry e. for CEV,

NCV, NIV. This adverb describes friendly concern and kindness toward someone [LN].

QUESTION—What does it mean that Publius was the chief man of the island?
He may have been the governor appointed by Rome [BECNT, EBC; CEV, GW]. 'Chief man' designated him as an official [NICNT, TH]. He could have been a governor, or the chief local official functioning under the authority of a regional governor, or he may have just been wealthy and well-known [PNTC]. He was the main governing official [NAC].

QUESTION—Does the first person plural pronoun 'us' refer to the entire ship's company, or only to Paul, Luke, and Aristarchus?
It is unclear [NAC, PNTC, TH, TNTC]. He may be referring to all of them [PNTC], or he may be referring only to Paul, Luke, and Aristarchus [NAC, TH]. He is referring to the whole ship's company [EBC].

**28:8** And it-happened-(that) the father of-Publius was-lying-in-bed[a] suffering[b] with-fevers and with-dysentery,[c] Paul having-come and having-prayed for him having-laid hands-(on) him healed[d] him.

LEXICON—a. pres. mid. or pass. (deponent = act.) infin. of κατάκειμαι (LN 17.27) (BDAG 1.b. p. 518): 'to lie in bed' [NASB], 'to be in bed' [AB, CBC; CEV, REB], 'to be sick in bed' [GW, NIV], 'to be in bed sick' [TEV], 'to lie sick in bed' [NET, NRSV], 'to lie sick' [BECNT; ESV, KJV], 'to be confined to bed' [Bar], 'to lie down [BDAG], 'to lie' [LN], 'to be lying down' [LN], not explicit [NCV, NLT]. This verb means to lie down, often with the implication of some degree of incapacity [LN]. It means to be in a recumbent position free from any activity [BDAG].

b. pre. pass. participle of συνέχω (LN 90.65) (BDAG 5. p. 571): 'to be suffering' [CBC; GW, NET, REB], 'to be ill' [AB; NLT], 'to be sick' [Bar; CEV, NCV], 'to be afflicted' [NASB], 'to be seized, to be attacked, to be distressed, to be tormented' [BDAG], 'to experience, to have' [LN], not explicit [BECNT; ESV, NET, NIV, NRSV, TEV]. This verb means to experience a state or condition, generally involving duration [LN]. It means to cause distress by force of circumstances [BDAG].

c. δυσεντέριον (LN 23.160) (BDAG p. 265): 'dysentery' [BDAG, LN; all translations except CEV, KJV], 'stomach trouble' [CEV], 'bloody flux' [KJV]. This noun denotes an infectious disease of the intestinal tract, usually involving severe pain and diarrhea [LN].

d. aorist mid. (deponent = act.) indic. of ἰάομαι (LN 23.136) (BDAG 1. p. 465): 'to heal' [BDAG, BECNT, CBC, LN; all versions except GW, NRSV], 'to cure' [AB, Bar, BDAG, LN; NRSV], 'to make well' [LN; GW], 'healing' [LN]. This verb means to cause someone to become well again after having been sick [LN]. It means to restore someone to health after a physical malady [BDAG].

QUESTION—Why is 'fevers' plural?
There were recurring bouts of fever [EBC, NICNT, PNTC, TH].

QUESTION—What is the illness that Publius' father had?
This appears to be the condition known as Malta fever [EBC, NAC, NICNT, PNTC, TNTC], which is endemic to Malta [TNTC]. Malta fever is caused by a microbe in goats' milk [BECNT, EBC, NAC, NICNT, PNTC], and is a condition that may last for months or even for several years [BECNT]. Dysentery is acute diarrhea with severe abdominal pain [TRT].

**28:9** And this having-happened the rest (of the people) in the island having diseases[a] were-coming and were-being-healed,[b] **28:10** and they-honored[c] us with many honors[d] and when-we-were-putting-out-to-sea[e] supplied[f] the-things for (our)-needs.[g]

LEXICON—a. ἀσθένεια (LN 23.143) (BDAG 1. p. 142): 'disease' [BDAG, BECNT; ESV, KJV, NASB, NRSV], 'sickness' [BDAG], 'illness' [Bar, LN], 'disability, weakness' [LN]. The phrase 'having diseases' is also translated 'who were ill' [AB], 'who were sick' [NET], 'the sick' [NIV], 'sick (people)' [CBC; CEV, GW, NCV, NLT, REB, TEV]. This noun denotes the state of being ill and thus incapacitated in some manner [LN]. It is a state of debilitating illness [BDAG].

b. imperf. pass. indic. of θεραπεύω (LN 23.139) (BDAG 2. p. 453): 'to be healed' [Bar, BDAG, LN; CEV, KJV, NET, NLT, TEV], 'to be cured' [AB, BECNT, CBC; ESV, NASB, NIV, NRSV, REB], 'to be made well' [GW], 'to be restored' [BDAG], 'to be taken care of' [LN]. This passive verb is also translated as active, with Paul as the subject: 'he healed them' [NCV]. This verb means to cause someone to recover health, often with the implication of having taken care of such a person [LN].

c. aorist act. indic. of τιμάω (LN 87.8) (BDAG 1. p. 1004): 'to honor' [AB, BDAG, BECNT, CBC, LN; KJV, NASB, REB], 'to respect' [LN], 'to revere' [BDAG]. The phrase 'honored us with many honors' is also translated 'honored us greatly' [ESV], 'honored us in many ways' [NIV], 'gave us many honors' [NCV], 'gave us many gifts' [TEV], 'bestowed many honors' [NET, NRSV], 'bestowed upon us many honors' [Bar], 'we were showered with honors' [NLT], 'were very respectful toward us' [CEV], 'showed respect for us in many ways' [GW]. This verb means to attribute high status to someone by honoring [LN]. It means to show high regard for [BDAG].

d. τιμή (LN 87.4) (BDAG 2.a. p. 1005): 'honor' [Bar, BDAG, LN; KJV, NCV, NET, NLT, NRSV], 'token of esteem' [AB], 'mark of respect' [CBC; NASB, REB], 'gift' [BECNT; TEV], 'respect, status' [LN], 'reverence' [BDAG], not explicit [CEV, ESV, GW, NIV]. This noun denotes honor as an element in the assignment of status to a person [LN]. It denotes a manifestation of esteem [BDAG].

e. pres. pass. participle of ἀνάγω (LN 54.4) (BDAG 4. p. 62): 'to put out to sea' [LN], 'to set sail' [AB, LN; GW, NASB], 'to sail' [BECNT; CEV, ESV, NLT, NRSV, TEV], 'to prepare to sail' [NET], 'to be ready to sail' [NIV], 'to leave' [Bar, CBC; NCV, REB], 'to depart' [KJV]. This verb means to begin to go by boat [BDAG, LN].

f. aorist mid. indic. of ἐπιτίθημι (LN 57.78) (BDAG 1.b. p. 384): 'to supply' [NASB, NLT], 'to give' [AB, BDAG, LN; CEV, NCV, NET], 'to furnish' [NIV], 'to put on board' [Bar, BECNT, CBC; ESV, GW, NRSV, REB, TEV], 'to lade' [KJV], 'to provide, to grant' [LN]. This verb means to place something at the disposal of someone else [LN]. It means to place something on or transfer to a place or object, to give something to someone [BDAG].

g. χρεία (LN 57.40): 'need' [LN], 'lack, what is needed' [LN]. The phrase 'the things for our needs' is also translated 'all we needed' [NASB], 'what was needed' [AB], 'what/whatever we needed' [BECNT; ESV, GW, TEV], 'everything we needed' [CEV], 'everything we would need' [NLT], 'the things that we needed' [Bar; NCV], 'the supplies we needed' [NIV, REB], 'all the supplies we needed' [NET], 'such things as were necessary' [KJV], 'provision for our needs' [CBC], 'all the provisions we needed' [NRSV]. This noun denotes that which is lacking and particularly needed [LN].

QUESTION—Does the difference between the two verbs for 'heal' indicate that Paul healed the father of Publius but Luke cured the other people through medicine?

Both verbs are describing incidents of miraculous healing [EBC, TH, TNTC]. These terms are general and do not indicate specifically that Luke used his medical skills to treat the sick [BECNT]. Whether or not Luke used any of his skills as a medical doctor, here he is describing only what Paul did [TNTC].

QUESTION—What are the honors that were given to them?

The islanders gave them gifts [NICNT, PNTC, TH, TNTC, TRT], probably of clothes and food [TRT], of provisions for their journey [NAC, PNTC].

**DISCOURSE UNIT—28:11–31** [NICNT; NASB]. The topic is Rome at last [NICNT], Paul arrives in Rome [NASB].

**DISCOURSE UNIT—28:11–16** [EBC, NAC; ESV, GW, NET, NIV, NLT, NRSV]. The topic is Paul sails from Malta to Rome [GW], Paul's arrival at Rome [NIV], Paul arrives in Rome [ESV, NRSV], Paul arrives at Rome [NLT], arrival at Rome [EBC], Paul finally reaches Rome [NET], the final leg to Rome [NAC].

**DISCOURSE UNIT—28:11–15** [CBC, NICNT, PNTC; CEV, NCV, TEV]. The topic is from Malta to Rome [CEV, TEV], to Rome [CBC], Paul goes to Rome [NCV], hospitality from Christians [PNTC], the last lap: 'And so we came to Rome' [NICNT].

**28:11** **And after three months we-set-sail**[a] **in an-Alexandrian-(ship) wintering**[b] **in the island, with-the-figurehead-(of)**[c] **(the)-Twin-Gods.**[d] **28:12 And having-put-into-port**[e] **at Syracuse we-stayed three days,**

LEXICON—a. aorist pass. indic. of ἀνάγω (LN 54.4) (BDAG 4. p. 62): 'to set sail' [AB, Bar, BECNT, CBC, LN; ESV, NASB, NLT, NRSV], 'to sail'

[CEV, GW], 'to sail away' [TEV], 'to depart' [KJV], 'to get on a ship' [NCV], 'to put out to sea' [BDAG, LN; NET, NIV], 'to put to sea' [REB]. This verb means to begin to go by boat [BDAG, LN].

b. pres. act. participle of παραχειμάζω (LN 67.166) (BDAG p. 773): 'to winter' [BDAG, LN; all translations except CEV, GW, NCV, TEV], 'to spend the winter' [BDAG, LN; GW, TEV], 'to be docked for the winter' [CEV], 'to stay during the winter' [NCV], 'to be in a place during the winter' [LN]. This verb means to experience the winter season [LN].

c. παράσημος (LN 6.51) (BDAG 2. p. 771): 'figurehead' [AB, BECNT, LN; ESV, NASB, NET, NIV, NLT, NRSV], 'ship's sign' [Bar], 'sign' [KJV, NCV], 'emblem' [LN], 'marked' [BDAG], not explicit [CBC; CEV, REB, TEV]. The phrase 'with the figurehead of the Twin Gods' is also translated 'the ship had the gods Castor and Pollux carved on its front' [GW]. This noun denotes an identifying emblem, possibly a carved figurehead at the prow of a ship [LN]. It describes something as being marked (on the side) so as to be distinguished [BDAG].

d. Διόσκουροι (LN 93.98) (BDAG p. 251): 'Twin Gods' [CEV, ESV, NCV, NLT, TEV], 'the twin gods Castor and Pollux' [NIV], 'Twin Brothers' [BECNT; NASB, NRSV], 'heavenly twins' [LN; NET], 'Sign of the Twins' [AB], 'Castor and Pollux' [CBC; GW, KJV, REB], 'Dioscuri' [Bar, BDAG, LN]. This noun is a joint name for Castor and Pollux, pagan deities of an Alexandrian ship [LN].

e. aorist pass. participle of κατάγω (LN 54.16) (BDAG p. 516): 'to put in at' [AB, BECNT, CBC, LN; ESV, NASB, NET, NIV, NRSV], 'to land' [Bar, LN; KJV, REB], 'to stop at' [GW, NCV], 'to arrive' [CEV, TEV], 'to bring to shore' [LN], 'to put in at a harbor' [BDAG]. The phrase 'having put into port' is also translated 'our first stop was' [NLT]. This verb means to cause a boat to put in at a shore or to land [LN].

QUESTION—Who were the twin gods?

Castor and Pollux were believed to come to the aid of sailors [AB, Bar, BECNT, NAC]. They were the patron gods of seafarers [NICNT, PNTC, TH, TNTC]. Sailors considered it a sign of good fortune to see their constellation, Gemini (Latin for 'twins'), in a storm [EBC, NAC, NICNT, PNTC, TNTC]. Ships usually had the same names as their figureheads [Bar, NICNT].

**28:13** (and) from-there having-weighed-anchor[a] we-arrived at Rhegium. And after one day (a-)south-wind having-come-up, on-(the)-second-day we-came to Puteoli, **28:14** where, having-found[b] brothers[c] we-were-invited[d] to-stay with them seven days. And so[e] we-came to Rome.

TEXT—Manuscripts reading περιελόντες 'having weighed anchor' (meaning to cast loose from mooring, to weigh anchor, or to set sail) are given a C rating by GNT to indicate that choosing it over variant texts that read περιελθόντες 'having gone around' was difficult. Manuscripts that read περιελόντες 'having weighed anchor' are followed by CEV, GW, NCV,

NET, NIV, NRSV, and TEV. Manuscripts that read περιελθόντες 'having gone around' are followed by ESV, KJV, NASB, REB.
LEXICON—a. aorist act. participle of περιαιρέω (LN 54.24) (BDAG 1. p. 799): 'to weigh anchor' [BECNT; NRSV], 'to cast off' [Bar; NET], 'to take away (the anchor), remove (the anchor)' [BDAG], 'to lift anchor, to sail off' [LN], 'to sail' [CEV, GW, NCV], 'to sail on' [AB; TEV], 'to sail across' [NLT], 'to set sail' [NIV], 'to sail round/around' [CBC; NASB], 'to make a circuit' [ESV], 'to fetch a compass' [KJV], 'to sail up the coast' [REB]. This verb is a technical, nautical term meaning to raise the anchor in preparation for departing [LN]. It means take something away from around something [BDAG].
b. aorist act. participle of εὑρίσκω (LN 27.27) (BDAG 1.b. p. 411): 'to find' [BDAG, LN; all translations except AB; GW], 'to meet' [AB], 'to discover' [GW], 'to happen to find' [LN], 'to come upon someone' [BDAG], 'to come upon' [LN], 'to learn the whereabouts of something, to discover' [LN]. This verb means to learn the location of something, either by intentional searching or by unexpected discovery [LN]. It means to come upon something either through purposeful search or accidentally, without seeking [BDAG].
c. ἀδελφός (LN 11.23): 'brother' [AB, Bar, BECNT; ESV, KJV, NASB, NET], 'fellow Christian' [CBC; REB], 'believer' [GW, NCV, NLT, NRSV, TEV], 'fellow believer, (Christian) brother' [LN], 'the Lord's follower' [CEV]. This plural noun is also translated 'brothers and sisters' [NIV]. This noun denotes a close associate of a group of persons having a well-defined membership (in the NT it refers specifically to fellow believers in Christ) [LN].
d. aorist indic. of παρακαλέω (LN 33.315) (BDAG 3. p. 765): 'to be invited' [Bar, CBC, LN; ESV, NASB, NET, NRSV, REB], 'to be asked' [AB; NCV], 'to be prevailed upon' [BECNT], 'to be desired (to tarry)' [KJV], 'to be requested, to be implored, to be entreated' [BDAG]. The passive verb phrase 'we were invited' is also translated as active: 'who invited us' [NIV, NLT], 'who asked us' [TEV], 'they begged us' [CEV, GW]. This verb means to ask a person to accept offered hospitality [LN]. It means to make a strong request for something [BDAG].
e. οὕτως (LN 61.9): 'so' [BECNT, CBC, LN; ESV, GW, KJV, NIV, NLT, NRSV, REB, TEV], 'thus' [AB, LN; NASB], 'in this way' [Bar, LN; NET], 'finally' [NCV], not explicit [CEV]. This adverb refers to that which precedes [LN].
QUESTION—What is the text saying had occurred prior to arriving at Rhegium?
1. It describes the process of removing or 'weighing' the anchor in order to set off [Bar, BECNT, EBC, NICNT, TNTC; NET, NIV, NRSV]. To 'set sail' probably means that they loosed the mooring ropes from around dock posts [TNTC].

2. It describes the track they sailed, which was in a circuit [CBC; ESV, KJV, NASB, REB]. This may mean that they had to tack, or take an indirect route because of contrary winds [NAC].

QUESTION—To whom did the Christians in Puteoli give hospitality?

It was probably just to Paul and his traveling companions [AB, CBC, EBC, NAC, NICNT, PNTC, TNTC].

QUESTION—Why did they go overland from Puteoli to Rome?

Although Puteoli was about 125 miles from Rome, it was the only port city for Rome at that time [TRT]. It was the main port for importing wheat [BECNT, NAC, TNTC].

QUESTION—What does Luke mean that they 'came to Rome' when they arrived in Puteoli?

In this verse he focuses on the arrival in Rome, but in the following verse he goes back in time to talk about something that happened before their arrival in Rome [EBC, NAC, NICNT]. The focus is on how they were able to start the last leg of their trip to Rome, despite all the difficulties they had experienced at sea [TNTC]. Here he is saying that, upon their arrival in Puteoli, their intended goal of getting to Rome was as good as done [NAC]. This was the last stage in their journey to Rome [Bar].

**28:15** And- the brothers -there having-heard[a] the-things about us came to (a)-meeting[b] with-us as-far-as[c] (the) Appian Forum and Three Taverns, (and) Paul, having-seen them gave-thanks[d] to-God and took courage.[e]

LEXICON—a. aorist act. participle of ἀκούω (LN 24.52): 'to hear' [LN; all translations except CBC], 'to have news' [CBC].

b. ἀπάντησις (LN 15.78) (BDAG p. 97): 'meeting' [BDAG], 'drawing near, meeting, meeting up with' [LN]. This noun is also translated as a verb: 'to meet (us)' [all translations]. This noun denotes the action of coming near to, of meeting, either in a friendly or hostile sense [LN]. In the formula εἰς ἀπάντησιν it means 'meeting' [BDAG].

c. ἄχρι (LN 84.19) (BDAG 2. p. 161): 'as far as' [BDAG, LN; all translations except AB; CEV, NLT], 'at' [AB; CEV, NLT], 'to, up to' [LN]. This adverb describes extension up to or as far as a goal [LN]. It is a marker of extension up to a certain point [BDAG].

d. aorist act. participle of εὐχαριστέω (LN 33.349) (BDAG 2. p. 415): 'to give thanks' [Bar, BDAG, CBC; REB], 'to express thanks, to render or return thanks' [BDAG], 'to thank (God)' [AB, BECNT, LN; all translations except REB]. This verb means to express gratitude for benefits or blessings [LN]. It means to express appreciation for benefits or blessings [BDAG].

e. θάρσος (LN 25.157) (BDAG p. 444): 'courage' [BDAG]. The idiom λαμβάνω θάρσος means to become confident or courageous in the face of real or possible danger [LN]. It means 'to take courage' [BECNT, CBC, LN, BDAG; ESV, KJV, NASB, NET, NRSV, REB], 'to be encouraged' [AB; CEV, NCV, NIV, NLT], 'to be greatly encouraged'

[TEV], 'to take heart' [Bar], 'to feel encouraged' [GW], 'to become confident' [LN].

QUESTION—What was it that the believers heard about them?

They heard the news that they were coming [BECNT, NICNT, PNTC, TH; GW, NCV, NIV, NLT]. They heard their story [AB, Bar].

QUESTION—What is meant by 'there'?

It refers to believers in Rome [AB, CBC, NAC, NICNT, PNTC, TH, TNTC; NCV]. It refers to believers at the Appian Forum and Three Taverns [BECNT].

QUESTION—What does it mean that they came 'as far as'?

1. Some of the Roman Christians went as far as Three Taverns, but others went as far as The Forum of Appius [AB, CBC, EBC, NAC, NICNT, PNTC, TH]. They would have escorted Paul back to Rome [NICNT, PNTC]. The Forum of Appius was 43 miles from Rome on the highway called the Appian Way, and the Three Taverns was on the same highway but only 33 miles from Rome [NAC, NICNT, PNTC, TH, TNTC, TRT]. Two different groups of believers made the trip from Rome to the Forum of Appius and Three Taverns [NAC, PNTC, TH].

2. They came *from* the Forum of Appius or Three Taverns to meet him (presumably at Puteoli) [BECNT].

**DISCOURSE UNIT—28:16–31** [CBC, PNTC; CEV, NCV, TEV]. The topic is Paul in Rome [CEV, NCV], in Rome [CBC; TEV], Paul's ministry in the imperial capital [PNTC].

**DISCOURSE UNIT—28:16–22** [PNTC]. The topic is reporting to the Jewish leaders.

**DISCOURSE UNIT—28:16** [NICNT]. The topic is Paul handed over to be kept under guard.

**28:16** And when we-entered[a] Rome, it-was-allowed[b] for-Paul to-live[c] by-himself[d] with the soldier guarding him.

TEXT—Some manuscripts add 'the centurion delivered the prisoners to the captain of the guard'. Manuscripts that omit this are given an A rating by GNT to indicate the omission was regarded to be certain. Only KJV includes this reading.

LEXICON—a. aorist act. indic. of εἰσέρχομαι (LN 15.93): 'to enter' [Bar, CBC, LN; NASB, NET, REB], 'to arrive in' [AB; CEV, NLT, TEV], 'to arrive at' [NCV], 'to come into' [BECNT; ESV, NRSV], 'to come to' [KJV], 'to get to' [NIV], 'to move into, to go into' [LN]. The phrase 'when we entered Rome' is also translated 'after our arrival' [GW]. This verb means to move into a space, either two-dimensional or three-dimensional [LN].

b. aorist pass. indic. of ἐπιτρέπω (LN 13.138) (BDAG 1. p. 385): 'to be allowed' [BDAG, BECNT, CBC; all versions except KJV, NLT], 'to be

permitted' [AB, Bar, BDAG, BECNT, LN; NLT], 'to be suffered' [KJV]. This verb means to allow someone to do something [BDAG, LN].
  c. pres. act. infin. of μένω (LN 85.55) (BDAG 1.a.α. p. 631): 'to live' [CEV, GW, NCV, NET, NIV, NRSV, TEV], 'to stay' [Bar, BDAG, BECNT, LN; ESV, NASB], 'to lodge' [AB, CBC; REB], 'to dwell' [KJV], 'to have (private) lodging' [NLT], 'to remain' [BDAG, LN]. This verb means to remain in the same place over a period of time [LN].
  d. ἑαυτοῦ (LN 92.25) (BDAG 1.a.ζ. p. 269): 'himself' [BDAG, LN]. The phrase καθ' ἑαυτόν is translated 'by himself' [BECNT, CBC; all versions except NCV, NLT, REB], 'on his own' [Bar], 'privately' [AB; REB], 'alone' [NCV], 'private (lodging)' [NLT].
QUESTION—What is the function of v. 16 in the larger narrative?
  It is transitional, bringing the extended narrative about the journey to a close and turning to the topic of Paul's witness in Rome [NAC]. It is also the last place in Acts where the pronoun 'we' occurs, though judging from Col 4: 10–14 and Philemon 23–24 Luke had remained in Rome while Paul was in custody there [EBC, NICNT, PNTC].

**DISCOURSE UNIT—28:17–31** [BECNT, NAC, TNTC; GW, ESV, NET, NIV, NLT, NRSV]. The topic is Paul in Rome [GW, ESV], Paul preaches in Rome [NRSV], Paul preaches at Rome under guard [NIV, NLT], Paul's witness in Rome [NAC], Paul addresses the Jewish community in Rome [NET], Paul and the Jews in Rome [TNTC], visitor in Rome: the gospel preached [BECNT].

**DISCOURSE UNIT—28:17–28** [AB, EBC, NICNT]. The topic is Paul and the Roman Jews [NICNT], Paul and the Jews in Rome [AB], meetings with the Jewish leaders [EBC].

**DISCOURSE UNIT—28:17–22** [NAC, NICNT; NRSV]. The topic is Paul and Jewish leaders in Rome [NRSV], first meeting with the Jews [NAC], the first interview [NICNT].

**28:17** **And it-happened (that) after three days he called-together[a] the-ones being prominent[b] of-(the)-Jews; and they having-come-together[c] he-began-saying to them,**
LEXICON—a. aorist mid. infin. of συγκαλέω (LN 33.309) (BDAG p. 951): 'to call together' [LN; all translations except AB; GW, NCV, TEV], 'to call to a meeting' [TEV], 'to invite' [AB; GW], 'to send for' [NCV], 'to summon' [BDAG]. This verb means to call persons together, presumably at the reference point of the one who calls [LN]. It means to call to one's side [BDAG].
  b. πρῶτος (LN 87.45) (BDAG 2.a.β. p. 894): 'prominent' [LN], 'most prominent' [BDAG], 'most influential' [GW], 'chief' [KJV], 'important, most important, great' [LN], 'foremost' [BDAG, LN]. The phrase 'the ones being prominent' is also translated 'the local leaders' [BECNT, CBC; ESV, NET, NIV, NLT, NRSV, REB, TEV], 'the leaders' [AB; CEV, NCV], 'the leading men' [Bar; NASB]. This adjective describes

being of high rank, with the implication of special prominence and status [LN]. It describes prominence [BDAG].
c. aorist act. participle of συνέρχομαι (LN 15.123) (BDAG 1. p. 969): 'to come together' [LN; KJV, NASB, NCV], 'to come' [AB], 'to assemble' [Bar, BDAG, LN; GW, NET, NIV, NRSV], 'to be assembled' [CBC; REB], 'to gather' [BDAG, BECNT; ESV, TEV], 'to gather together, to go together, to meet' [LN], not explicit [CEV, NLT]. This verb describes the movement of two or more objects to the same location [LN]. It means to come together with others as a group [BDAG].

**"Men (and) brothers,[a] I having-done nothing against[b] the people or to-the ancestral[c] customs[d] I-was-handed-over[e] (as) (a)-prisoner[f] from Jerusalem into the hands of-the Romans,**
LEXICON—a. ἀδελφός (LN 11.25): 'brother' [LN], 'fellow countryman, fellow Jew, associate' [LN]. The phrase 'men and brothers' [KJV] is also translated 'brothers' [all translations except CEV, KJV, TEV], 'friends' [CEV], 'fellow Israelites' [TEV]. This noun denotes a person belonging to the same socio-religious entity and being of the same age group as the so-called reference person [LN].
b. ἐναντίος (LN 82.11) (BDAG 2. p. 331): 'against' [LN; all translations], 'opposed to, contrary to' [BDAG]. This adjective describes being oriented in the direction opposite to a movement [LN]. It describes being in opposition [BDAG].
c. πατρῷος (LN 10.21) (BDAG p. 789): 'ancestral' [Bar], 'of/by (our) ancestors' [LN; CEV, NCV, NET, NIV, NLT, NRSV], 'handed down by our ancestors' [GW], 'that we received from our ancestors' [TEV], 'of (our) fathers' [AB, BECNT; ESV, KJV, NASB], 'of (our) forefathers' [CBC, LN; REB], 'paternal, belonging to one's father, inherited or coming from one's father/ancestors' [BDAG]. This adjective describes what pertains to one's ancestors [LN].
d. ἔθος (LN 41.25) (BDAG 2. p. 277): 'custom' [BDAG, LN; all translations], 'habit' [LN]. This noun denotes a pattern of behavior more or less fixed by tradition and generally sanctioned by the society [LN]. It is long-established usage or practice common to a group [BDAG].
e. aorist pass. indic. of παραδίδωμι (LN 57.77) (BDAG 1.b. p. 762): 'to be handed over' [AB, Bar, BDAG, CBC, LN; CEV, GW, NET, NIV, NLT, NRSV, REB, TEV], 'to be delivered' [BDAG, BECNT; ESV, KJV, NASB], 'to be given to' [NCV], 'to be given over' [BDAG, LN]. This verb means to hand over to or to convey something to someone, particularly a right or an authority [LN]. It means to convey something in which one has a relatively strong personal interest [BDAG].
f. δέσμιος (LN 37.117) (BDAG p. 219): 'prisoner' [AB, Bar, BDAG, BECNT, CBC, LN; CEV, ESV, GW, KJV, NASB, NET, TEV]. The phrase 'as a prisoner' is also translated 'I was arrested' [NCV, NIV, NLT,

NRSV, REB]. This noun denotes a person who is under custody in prison [LN].

QUESTION—What may be indicated by the use of the pronoun Ἐγώ 'I', which comes first in this sentence?

It shows emphasis [NAC, PNTC, TH]. It shows that Paul is now going to present an apologetic defense of himself [EBC]. It helps emphasize what follows about his innocence and the fact that he was not accusing his nation of anything [TH].

QUESTION—What may be being communicated by the passive verb 'was handed over'?

In using the passive Paul is saying as little as possible about the responsibility of the Jewish authorities in handing him over [NICNT]. This word always expresses some degree of wrongdoing on the part of those who handed the person over [TH]. It also parallels what happened to Jesus when he was handed over to the Gentiles (Luke 18:32, 24:7) [NAC].

**28:18** who, having-examined[a] me were-wanting[b] to-release-(me) because[c] there-was no reason[d] (for) death against me;

LEXICON—a. aorist act. participle of ἀνακρίνω (LN 56.12) (BDAG 2. p. 66): 'to examine' [AB, Bar, BECNT, CBC; ESV, KJV, NASB, NIV, NRSV, REB], 'to cross-examine' [GW], 'to look into charges' [CEV], 'to question' [LN; TEV], 'to ask many questions' [NCV], 'to hear a case' [BDAG, LN; NET], 'to try' [NLT], 'to investigate in court, to interrogate' [LN], 'to hear a question' [BDAG]. This verb means to conduct a judicial inquiry [LN]. It means to conduct a judicial hearing [BDAG].

b. imperf. mid. indic. of βούλομαι (LN 30.56) (BDAG 2.a.β. p. 182): 'to want' [CEV, GW, NCV, NET, NIV, NLT, NRSV, TEV], 'to wish' [Bar, BECNT; ESV], 'to purpose' [LN], 'to plan, to intend' [BDAG, LN], 'to will' [BDAG]. The phrase 'they…were wanting to' is also translated 'they were going to' [AB], 'they were willing to' [NASB], 'they would have liked' [CBC; REB], 'they would have (let me go)' [KJV]. This verb means to think, with the purpose of planning or deciding on a course of action [LN]. It means to plan on a course of action [BDAG].

c. διά with accusative object (LN 89.26): 'because' [all translations except CEV, NCV], 'because of, on account of, by reason of' [LN], not explicit [CEV, NCV]. This preposition indicates cause or reason, with focus upon instrumentality, either of objects or events [LN].

d. αἰτία (LN 56.4) (BDAG 3.a. p. 31) 'reason' [BECNT; ESV, NCV, NRSV], 'charge' [BDAG, CBC], 'cause' [LN; KJV, NLT], 'ground' [NASB], 'ground for complaint' [BDAG], 'basis' [NET], 'case, basis for an accusation' [LN]. The phrase 'because there was no reason' is also translated 'because I had done nothing' [AB; TEV], 'I had not done anything' [CEV], 'they found in me no charge' [Bar], 'there was no (capital) charge' [REB], 'I was not guilty' [NIV], 'I was accused of nothing (for which I deserved to die)' [GW]. As a legal term this noun denotes the basis of or grounds for an accusation in court [LN]. In law it is a technical term for a basis for legal action [BDAG].

**28:19** but the Jews having-objected<sup>a</sup> I-was-compelled<sup>b</sup> to-appeal<sup>c</sup> to-Caesar, (though) not as having anything (of which) to-accuse-(me)<sup>d</sup> my nation.<sup>e</sup>

LEXICON—a. pres. act. participle of ἀντιλέγω (LN 33.455) (BDAG 1. p. 89): 'to object' [AB, BECNT, CBC; ESV, GW, NASB, NET, NIV, NRSV, REB], 'to contradict' [Bar], 'to protest a decision' [NLT], 'to disagree' [CEV], 'to oppose' [LN; TEV], 'to speak in opposition to' [LN], 'to speak against' [BDAG; KJV], 'to argue against' [NCV], 'to contradict someone or something' [BDAG]. This verb means to speak against something or someone [LN].

b. aorist pass. indic. of ἀναγκάζω (LN 37.33) (BDAG 1. p. 60): 'to be compelled' [Bar, BDAG, BECNT, LN; ESV, NIV, NRSV], 'to be forced' [AB, BDAG, LN; GW, NASB, NET, TEV], 'to be constrained' [KJV], 'to have no option but (to appeal)' [CBC; REB], 'to have to' [NCV], 'to feel it necessary to' [NLT], not explicit [CEV]. This verb means to compel someone to act in a particular manner [LN]. It means to compel someone to act in a particular manner [BDAG].

c. aorist mid. infin. of ἐπικαλέω (LN 33.176) (BDAG 3. p. 273): 'to appeal' [BDAG, LN; all translations except CEV, GW, NCV, NIV], 'to make an appeal' [NIV], 'to appeal one's case' [GW], 'to ask to be tried (by the Emperor)' [CEV], 'to ask to have a trial (before Caesar)' [NCV], 'to call upon, to ask for help' [LN]. This verb means to call upon someone to do something, normally implying an appeal for aid [LN]. It means to make a request put to a higher judicial authority for review of a decision in a lower court [BDAG].

d. pres. act. infin. of κατηγορέω (LN 33.427) (BDAG 1.a. p. 533): 'to accuse' [Bar, LN; KJV], 'to have a charge to make/bring against' [AB, BECNT; ESV, NCV, NET, NRSV], 'to have charges to bring against' [GW], 'to press charges against' [NLT], 'to bring a charge against' [NIV], 'to have an accusation to bring/make against' [CBC; REB, TEV], 'to have an accusation against' [NASB], 'to have (anything) to say against' [CEV], 'to bring charges' [BDAG, LN]. This verb means to bring serious charges or accusations against someone, with the possible connotation of a legal or court context [LN].

e. (LN 11.55) (BDAG 1. p. 276): 'nation' [Bar, BDAG, BECNT, LN; CEV, ESV, KJV, NASB, NRSV], 'people' [AB, BDAG, CBC, LN; GW, NCV, NET, NIV, NLT, REB, TEV]. This noun denotes the largest unit into which the people of the world are divided on the basis of their constituting a socio-political community [LN]. It is a body of persons united by kinship, culture, and common traditions [BDAG].

QUESTION—What was the objection of the Jewish leaders?
They objected to the prospect of Paul being released instead of being punished [EBC, PNTC, TH]. They objected to King Agrippa's claim that Paul was innocent [BECNT].

**28:20** So for this reason[a] I-have-called- you -together[b] to-see[c] (you) and to-speak-to-(you), for on-account-of[d] the hope[e] of-Israel I-wear[f] this chain.[g]"

LEXICON—a. αἰτία (LN 89.15) (BDAG 1. p. 31): 'reason' [AB, Bar, BDAG, BECNT, LN; ESV, NASB, NET, NIV, NRSV], 'cause' [BDAG, LN; KJV], 'source' [LN]. The phrase 'for this reason' is also translated 'this/that is why' [CBC; CEV, GW, NCV, REB, TEV], 'so' [NLT]. This noun denotes the reason or cause for an event or state [LN]. It is that which is responsible for a condition [BDAG].

b. aorist act. indic. of παρακαλέω (LN 33.310) (BDAG 1.a. p. 764): 'to call together' [LN], 'to call (someone)' [CEV], 'to call for' [KJV], 'to invite' [AB], 'to ask (to see)' [Bar, BECNT, CBC; ESV, GW, NET, NIV, NRSV, REB, TEV], 'to request (to see)' [NASB], 'to ask (to come)' [NLT], 'to want to see' [NCV], 'to call to one's side' [BDAG]. This verb means to call to come to where the speaker is [LN]. It means to ask to come and be present where the speaker is [BDAG].

c. aorist act. infin. of εἶδον (LN 24.1) (BDAG 5. p. 280): 'to see' [LN; all translations except CEV, NLT], 'to look after, to visit' [BDAG], not explicit [CEV]. The phrase 'to see you' is also translated 'so we could get acquainted' [NLT]. This verb means to show an interest in [BDAG].

d. ἕνεκα with genitive object (LN 90.43) (BDAG 1. p. 334): 'on account of' [BDAG], 'because of' [BDAG, BECNT, LN; CEV, ESV, GW, NET, NIV], 'because (I believe)' [NCV, NLT], 'because that' [KJV], 'for the sake of' [AB, BDAG, CBC, LN; NASB, NRSV, TEV], 'for loyalty to' [REB], 'for' [Bar]. This preposition indicates a participant constituting the reason for an event [LN]. It indicates cause of or reason for something [BDAG].

e. ἐλπίς (LN 25.59) (BDAG 1.b.α. p. 320): 'hope' [BDAG, LN; all translations except CEV, GW, NLT, TEV], 'expectation' [BDAG]. The phrase 'the hope of Israel' is also translated 'the hope of Israel – the Messiah' [NLT], 'what we people of Israel hope for' [CEV], 'what Israel hopes for' [GW], 'him for whom the people of Israel hope' [TEV]. This verb means to look forward with confidence to that which is good and beneficial [LN]. It is the looking forward to something with some reason for confidence respecting fulfillment [BDAG].

f. pres. pass. indic. of περίκειμαι (LN 49.4) (BDAG 2.a. p. 802): 'to wear' [Bar, BDAG, LN; ESV, GW, NASB], 'to be in (chains)' [AB, CBC; REB], 'to be bound with (this chain)' [BECNT; CEV, KJV, NCV, NET, NIV, NLT, NRSV], 'to be bound in (chains)' [TEV], 'to have something on' [BDAG], 'to have around' [LN]. This verb means to have in a position around oneself [LN]. It means to put something around [BDAG].

g. ἅλυσις (LN 6.16) (BDAG 1. p. 48): 'chain' [BDAG, LN; all translations], 'handcuffs' [BDAG]. This noun denotes a linked, metal instrument for binding [LN].

QUESTION—To what does 'for this reason' refer?

It refers to what has just been said about his reason for being in Rome [TH]. It refers to what is about to be said, which is that Paul wants them to understand that he is in chains for the sake of the hope of Israel [BECNT]. Paul is saying that the reason for his calling them together is that he wants to make clear to them the facts of his case, that although he must defend himself from the attacks by Jewish leadership, he still wants to preserve all that is best in Judaism [Bar].

QUESTION—What relationship is indicated by γάρ 'for' in the phrase 'for on account of the hope…'?

In addition to his wanting to explain why he has come to Rome as a prisoner, γάρ 'for' introduces another reason for wanting to see them, which is to present the gospel to them [PNTC]. It indicates that he is in chains for the sake of Christ, who is the hope of Israel [TH].

QUESTION—What does Paul mean by 'the hope of Israel'?

It is Israel's hope of the Messiah [AB, Bar, CBC, EBC, NAC, TH, TNTC, TRT; NLT, TEV], and the resurrection of the dead [AB, CBC, NAC, NICNT, TNTC]. Israel's resurrection hope is fulfilled in the Messiah [PNTC]. The hope of the resurrection was a natural part of the messianic hope [CBC]. Although at 23:6 and possibly 24:15 the hope he refers to has to do with the resurrection, here the meaning is probably broader, referring to the hope of Israel as being the promise of Messianic salvation [Bar].

**28:21** And they-said to him, "We have- neither -received letters[a] about you from Judea nor (has)-anyone of-the brothers having-arrived reported[b] or said anything bad[c] about[d] you,

LEXICON—a. γράμμα (LN 6.63) (BDAG 2.a. p. 205): 'letter' [BDAG, LN; all translations except CBC; REB], 'communication' [CBC; REB], 'epistle' [BDAG], 'a document, piece of writing' [BDAG]. This noun denotes an object containing writing addressed to one or more persons [LN]. It is a set of written characters forming a document or piece of writing [BDAG].

b. aorist act. indic. of ἀπαγγέλλω (LN 33.198) (BDAG 1. p. 95): 'to report' [AB, Bar, BECNT; CEV, ESV, GW, NASB, NET, NIV, NRSV], 'to arrive with a report' [CBC; REB], 'to show' [KJV], 'to bring news' [NCV], 'to come with news' [TEV], 'to tell' [BDAG, LN], 'to inform' [LN], 'to report (back), to announce' [BDAG]. The phrase 'nor has anyone…reported' is also translated 'we have had no…reports' [NLT]. This verb means to announce or inform, with possible focus upon the source of information [LN]. It means to give an account of something [BDAG].

c. πονηρός (LN 88.110) (BDAG 1.b.γ. p. 852): 'bad' [BDAG; GW, NASB, NCV, NET, NIV, TEV], 'evil' [BDAG, BECNT, LN; ESV, NRSV], 'ill'

[AB, Bar], '(to) your discredit' [CBC; REB], 'harm' [KJV], 'immoral' [LN], 'wicked' [BDAG, LN], 'base, worthless, vicious, degenerate' [BDAG], not explicit [CEV, NLT]. This adjective describes what is morally corrupt and evil [LN]. It describes being morally or socially worthless [BDAG].

d. περί with genitive object (LN 90.24): 'about' [BECNT, LN; ESV, GW, NASB, NCV, NET, NIV, NRSV, TEV], 'of' [AB, Bar, LN; KJV], 'against (you)' [CEV, NLT], 'concerning' [LN], not explicit [CBC; REB]. This preposition indicates general content, whether of a discourse or mental activity [LN].

QUESTION—Is there any difference in meaning between 'reported' and 'said'? 'Reported' would describe an official communication, and 'said' would refer to an unofficial or private communication [NICNT, TH].

**28:22** but we-desire[a] to-hear from you what you-think,[b] for about this sect[c] it-is known to-us that everywhere[d] it-is-spoken-against.[e]"

LEXICON—a. pres. act. indic. of ἀξιόω (LN 25.5) (BDAG 2.a. p. 94): 'to desire' [BECNT, LN; ESV, KJV, NASB], 'to want' [LN; NCV, NIV, NLT], 'to like' [LN], 'to deem, to hold an opinion' [BDAG]. The phrase 'we desire to hear' is also translated 'we should/would like to hear' [Bar, CBC; CEV, GW, NET, NRSV, REB, TEV], 'we ought to hear' [AB]. This verb means to desire something on the basis of its evident worth or value [LN]. It means to make an evaluation concerning the suitability of something, especially an activity [BDAG].

b. pres. act. indic. of φρονέω (LN 31.1) (BDAG 1. p. 1065): 'to think' [BDAG, BECNT; GW, KJV, NET, NRSV], 'to believe' [NLT], 'to form/hold an opinion, to judge' [BDAG], 'to hold views' [BDAG, LN], 'to have an opinion, to consider, to regard' [LN]. The phrase 'what you think' is also translated 'what your opinions are' [AB], 'what your views are' [CBC; ESV, NASB, NIV, REB], 'what is in your mind' [Bar], 'what you have to say' [CEV], 'your ideas' [NCV, TEV]. This verb means to hold a view [LN], or have an opinion with regard to something [BDAG, LN].

c. αἵρεσις (LN 11.50) (BDAG 1.a. p. 28): 'sect' [BDAG, LN; all translations except CEV, NCV, NLT, TEV], 'new group' [CEV], 'religious group' [NCV], 'party' [BDAG; TEV], 'movement' [NLT], 'religious party' [LN], 'school, faction' [BDAG]. This noun denotes a division or group based upon different doctrinal opinions and/or loyalties and hence by implication in certain contexts an unjustified party or group (applicable in the NT to religious parties) [LN]. It is a group that holds tenets distinctive to it [BDAG].

d. πανταχοῦ (LN 83.8) (BDAG p. 754): 'everywhere' [BDAG, LN; all translations except CBC; REB], 'anywhere, all over' [LN], not explicit [CBC; REB]. This adverb describes all possible positions [LN]. It describes positions in any direction [BDAG].

e. pres. pass. indic. of ἀντιλέγω (LN 33.455) (BDAG 1. p. 89): 'to be spoken against' [AB, Bar, BDAG, BECNT; ESV, KJV, NASB, NRSV], 'to be denounced' [NLT], 'to be opposed, to be spoken of in opposition to' [LN], 'to be contradicted' [BDAG]. This passive verb is also translated as active: '(people) speak against' [NCV, NET, TEV], '(people) talk against' [GW, NIV], '(people) are against' [CEV]. The phrase 'everywhere it is spoken against' is also translated 'no one has a good word to say for it' [CBC; REB]. This verb means to speak against something or someone [BDAG].

**DISCOURSE UNIT—28:23-28** [NAC, NICNT, PNTC]. The topic is separation from the Jews [NAC], responding to Jewish rejection [PNTC], the second interview [NICNT].

**28:23** **And having-appointed[a] for-him (a)-day many (of them) came to him at (his) lodging[b] to-whom he-was-explaining[c] giving-testimony-about[d] the kingdom of-God, and persuading[e] them about Jesus both from the Law of-Moses and the prophets, from morning until evening.**

LEXICON—a. aorist mid. participle of τάσσω (LN 33.346) (BDAG 2.b. p. 991): 'to appoint' [Bar, BDAG, BECNT; ESV, KJV], 'to fix' [AB, BDAG, CBC; REB], 'to set' [BDAG; NASB, NET, NRSV, TEV], 'to be set' [NLT], 'to choose' [NCV], 'to agree on' [CEV], 'to arrange' [NIV], 'to order, to determine' [BDAG], 'to propose, to suggest' [LN]. The phrase 'having appointed...a day' is also translated 'on a designated day' [GW]. This verb means to propose something to someone [LN]. It means to give instructions as to what must be done [BDAG].

b. ξενία (LN 7.31) (BDAG p. 683): 'lodging' [AB, Bar, BECNT; ESV, KJV, NASB, NLT, NRSV, REB], 'lodging for guests, place to stay in' [LN], 'house' [CEV], 'guest room' [BDAG, LN]. The phrase 'at his lodging' is also translated 'the place where Paul/he was staying' [GW, NCV, NIV, TEV], 'where he was staying' [NET], 'as his guests' [CBC]. This noun denotes a place of temporary lodging for a person away from home [LN]. It is a place where a guest is lodged [BDAG].

c. imperf. mid. indic. of ἐκτίθημι (LN 33.151) (BDAG 2. p. 310): 'to explain' [AB, BDAG, LN; GW, NASB, NCV, NET, NIV, NLT, NRSV, TEV], 'to give an exposition' [Bar], 'to expound' [BDAG, BECNT; ESV, KJV], 'to deal at length (with the whole matter)' [CBC], 'to put a case to someone' [REB], 'to make clear' [LN]. The phrase 'explaining and giving testimony' is also translated 'he talked to them about' [CEV]. This verb means to explain something, presumably by putting forward additional or different information [LN]. It means to convey information by careful elaboration [BDAG].

d. pres. mid. participle of διαμαρτύρομαι (LN 33.223) (BDAG 1. p. 233): 'to testify' [Bar, BDAG, BECNT, LN; ESV, KJV, NET, NLT, NRSV], 'to solemnly testify' [NASB], 'to bear witness to' [AB, BDAG], 'to witness' [NIV], 'to speak urgently' [CBC; REB], 'to declare, to assert'

[LN], not explicit [CEV, GW, NCV, TEV]. This verb means to make a serious declaration on the basis of presumed personal knowledge [LN]. It means to make a solemn declaration about the truth of something [BDAG].

- e. pres. act. participle of πείθω (LN 33.301) (BDAG 1.a. p. 792): 'to persuade' [Bar, BDAG, LN; KJV, NASB, NIV, NLT], 'to persuade to believe' [NCV], 'to convince' [AB, BECNT, CBC, LN; ESV, GW, NET, NRSV, REB, TEV], 'to win over' [CEV]. The present tense of this verb is translated as indicating a conative sense: 'to try (to persuade, etc.)' [BECNT, CBC; CEV, ESV, GW, NASB, NCV, NET, NIV, NLT, REB, TEV], 'to seek (to convince)' [CBC; REB]. This verb means to convince someone to believe something and to act on the basis of what is recommended [LN]. It means to cause to come to a particular point of view or course of action [BDAG].

QUESTION—What is the relationship between the finite verb ἐξετίθετο 'he was explaining' and the present participles διαμαρτυρόμενος 'giving testimony' and πείθων 'persuading' that follow?

The two participles amplify what is meant by 'explained' [TH]. The first participle tells the content of what he was explaining, and the second one gives his intention for doing so, which was to persuade them to believe [PNTC].

QUESTION—What is communicated by the fact that 'from morning until evening' comes last in the sentence?

Its place at the end of the sentence gives emphasis to how long Paul was talking to them [TH]. It shows how there was a whole day of intensive discussion [PNTC]. It is a phrase found in the Old Testament in Ex 18:13, 1 Kings 22:35 [NAC].

**28:24** And some were-being-persuaded[a] by-the-things being-said, but others did-not-believe.[b]

LEXICON—a. imperf. pass. indic. of πείθω (LN 33.301) (BDAG 3.a. p. 791): 'to be persuaded' [LN; NASB, NLT], 'to be convinced' [AB, BDAG, BECNT, LN; ESV, GW, NET, NIV, NRSV, TEV], 'to be won over' [CBC; REB], 'to believe' [Bar; KJV, NCV], 'to agree with' [CEV]. This verb means to convince someone to believe something and to act on the basis of what is recommended [LN]. It means to be won over as the result of persuasion [BDAG].

- b. imperf. act. indic. of ἀπιστέω (LN 31.97) (BDAG 1.a. p. 103): 'to not believe' [Bar, LN; KJV, NASB, NIV, NLT, TEV], 'to disbelieve' [AB, BDAG, BECNT; ESV], 'to refuse to believe' [BDAG, LN; NET, NRSV], 'to continue to disbelieve' [GW], 'to be skeptical' [CBC], 'to be unconvinced' [REB], 'to not agree with' [CEV], 'to not trust in' [LN]. The phrase 'some were being persuaded...but others did not believe' is also translated 'some believed...but others did not' [NCV]. The ongoing nature of the action of unbelief expressed in the imperfect tense of this verb is also translated as 'would not (believe)' [NASB, NIV, TEV], 'continued to disbelieve' [GW], 'remained (skeptical/unconvinced)' [CBC; REB]. This verb means to refuse to put one's trust or reliance in something or someone [LN].

QUESTION—What is the meaning of the imperfect tense of the verbs 'being persuaded' and 'did not believe'?

Some were in the process of being persuaded, but others continued not to believe [PNTC]. The οἱ μὲν...οἱ δέ 'some...but others' emphasizes this contrast between the two groups [BECNT, PNTC].

QUESTION—What is meant here by 'the kingdom of God'?

Luke uses this term as a summary of the Christian message [Bar]. The rule of God is the rule of his agent, the Messiah, who is Jesus [TNTC]. Jesus the Messiah is central to the restoration of God's rule [NAC]. The rule of God arrives in Jesus [BECNT]. Paul's message of the kingdom focused on Jesus [EBC].

**28:25** But being in-disagreement[a] with one-another they-left,[b] Paul having-said one-(more) statement,[c] that "Rightly[d] the Holy Spirit spoke through Isaiah the prophet to your fathers

TEXT—Manuscripts reading ὑμῶν 'your' are given a B rating by GNT to indicate it was regarded to be almost certain. Manuscripts reading ἡμῶν 'our' are followed by CEV and KJV only.

LEXICON—a. ἀσύμφωνος (LN 31.24) (BDAG p. 146): 'in disagreement with' [BDAG, LN], 'without agreement' [AB, Bar], 'without reaching any agreement' [CBC; REB], 'to not agree with' [LN], 'to be unable to agree' [LN; GW, NET]. The phrase 'being in disagreement' is also translated 'disagreeing' [ESV, TEV], 'they were disagreeing' [BECNT], 'they disagreed' [NIV, NRSV], 'they agreed not' [KJV], 'they could/did not agree' [CEV, NASB], 'they argued' [NCV, NLT]. This adjective describes not being able to come to some agreement [LN].
  b. imperf. mid. indic. of ἀπολύω (LN 15.38) (BDAG 6. p. 117): 'to leave' [LN; CEV, GW, NASB, NCV, NET, NIV, NLT, NRSV, TEV], 'to depart' [BECNT, LN; ESV, KJV], 'to go away' [BDAG, LN], 'to disperse' [CBC; REB], 'to part' [AB]. This verb is also translated as a phrase: 'the gathering broke up' [Bar]. The imperfect tense of this verb is translated as indicating inceptive action: 'they started/began to leave/disperse' [CBC; CEV, NCV, NET, NIV, REB], 'as they were leaving' [NRSV]. This verb means to depart from a place or set of circumstances, with perhaps an implication of finality or significant separation or rupture being involved [LN]. It means to make a departure from a locality [BDAG].
  c. ῥῆμα (LN 33.9) (BDAG 1. p. 905): 'statement' [AB, BECNT; ESV, NET, NIV, NRSV], 'word' [BDAG, LN; KJV, NASB, NLT, REB], 'thing' [Bar, CBC; NCV, TEV], 'saying' [BDAG, LN], 'expression, or statement of any kind' [BDAG], not explicit [CEV]. The phrase 'having said one

more statement' is also translated 'quoted this passage to them' [GW]. This noun denotes a minimal unit of discourse, often a single word [LN]. It is that which is said [BDAG].

d. καλῶς (LN 72.12) (BDAG 4.b. p. 506): 'rightly' [AB, BDAG, LN; NASB, NET], 'well' [Bar; KJV], 'how well' [CBC; GW, REB, TEV], 'correctly' [BDAG, BECNT, LN], 'accurate, right' [BDAG], 'was right' [ESV, NLT, NRSV], 'the right thing' [CEV], 'the truth' [NCV, NIV]. This adverb describes being accurate and right, with a possible implication of being commendable [LN]. It describes being in accord with a standard [BDAG].

QUESTION—What is conveyed by the genitive absolute construction with the aorist participle 'Paul having said one more statement'?

This shows that Paul is giving a final challenge as they are leaving [Bar, PNTC]. Paul gets in the last word [NAC, TH].

**28:26** saying, 'Go to this people and say, "With-hearing you-will-hear[a] but never[b] understand,[c] and seeing you-will-see[d] and by-no-means perceive.[e]

LEXICON—a. fut. act. indic. of ἀκούω (LN 24.63) (BDAG 1.a. p. 37): 'to hear' [AB, Bar, BDAG, BECNT, CBC; ESV, GW, KJV, NASB, NET, NIV, NLT], 'to listen' [CEV, NCV, NRSV, REB, TEV]. The emphatic nature of the verb phrase 'hearing you will hear' is also translated 'hearing you shall hear' [KJV], 'you shall/will indeed hear' [AB, BECNT; ESV], 'you will indeed listen' [NRSV], 'you will hear and hear' [Bar, CBC], 'you will/may listen and listen' [CEV, NCV, REB, TEV], 'you will hear clearly' [GW], 'you will keep on hearing' [NASB, NET], 'you will be ever hearing' [NIV], 'when you hear what I say' [NLT]. This verb means to have or exercise the faculty of hearing [BDAG]. The Semitic idiom Ἀκοῇ ἀκούσετε means to listen intently and with presumed continuity [LN], 'to listen carefully, to listen and listen' [LN].

b. οὐ μή (LN 69.5): 'never' [AB, BECNT, CBC; CEV, ESV, GW, NET, NIV, NRSV, REB], 'not' [Bar; KJV, NASB, NCV, NLT, TEV], 'certainly not, by no means' [LN]. This phrase is a marker of emphatic negation [LN].

c. aorist act. subj. of συνίημι (LN 32.5) (BDAG p. 972): 'to understand' [BDAG, LN; all translations except GW], 'to comprehend' [BDAG, LN; GW], 'to perceive, to have insight into' [LN]. This verb means to employ one's capacity for understanding and thus to arrive at insight [LN]. It means to have an intelligent grasp of something that challenges one's thinking or practice [BDAG].

d. fut. act. indic. of βλέπω (LN 27.58): 'to see' [AB, BECNT; ESV, GW, KJV, NASB, NIV, NLT], 'to look' [Bar, CBC; CEV, NCV, NET, NRSV, REB, TEV], 'to beware of, to watch out for, to pay attention to' [LN]. This verb means to be ready to learn about future dangers or needs, with the implication of preparedness to respond appropriately [LN].

e. aorist act. subj. of εἶδον (LN 32.11): 'to perceive' [BECNT, LN; ESV, KJV, NASB, NET, NIV, NRSV], 'to see' [Bar, CBC; CEV, REB, TEV], 'to grasp' [AB], 'to comprehend' [GW, NLT], 'to learn' [NCV], 'to understand, to see, to recognize' [LN]. This verb means to come to understand as the result of perception [LN].

QUESTION—To whom does 'this people' refer?

It is referring to the Jewish people [Bar, BECNT, EBC, NAC, PNTC, TH].

**28:27** For the heart[a] of-this people has-become-dull[b] and with-the ears they- hardly[c] -hear, and they-have-closed[d] their eyes, lest[e] they-see with-(their) eyes and with-(their) ears they hear and with-the heart understand[f] and turn,[g] and I-would-heal[h] them."'

LEXICON—a. καρδία (LN 26.3) (BDAG 1.b.β. p. 508): 'heart' [AB, Bar, BDAG, BECNT, CBC, LN; CEV, ESV, KJV, NASB, NET, NIV, NLT, NRSV], 'mind' [LN; REB, TEV], 'inner self' [LN]. The phrase 'the heart of this people has become dull' is also translated 'these people have become close-minded' [GW], 'these people have become stubborn' [NCV]. This noun denotes the causative source of a person's psychological life in its various aspects, but with special emphasis upon thoughts [LN]. It is the center and source of the whole inner life, with its thinking, feeling, and volition [BDAG].

b. aorist pass. indic. of παχύνω (LN 32.45) (BDAG 2. p. 790): 'to become dull' [NASB, NET, REB], 'to grow dull' [AB, BECNT; ESV, NRSV], 'to be made dull' [BDAG], 'to be dull' [TEV], 'to be hardened' [Bar; NLT], 'to become calloused' [NIV], 'to wax gross' [KJV], 'to grow gross' [CBC], 'to become stubborn' [NCV], 'to become close-minded' [GW], 'to be mentally dull, to be unable to understand' [LN], 'to be made impervious' [BDAG]. This verb is also translated as an adjective: 'stubborn (hearts)' [CEV]. This verb means to become unable to understand or comprehend as the result of being mentally dull or spiritually insensitive [LN].

c. βαρέως (LN 32.46) (BDAG p. 167): 'hardly' [NIV], 'scarcely' [NASB], 'barely' [ESV], 'with difficulty' [BDAG]. The phrase 'with the ears they hardly hear' is also translated 'their ears were/are hard of hearing' [AB; NET, NRSV], 'these people have become...hard of hearing' [GW], 'their ears are heavy/dull of hearing' [BECNT; KJV], 'their ears were dull' [CBC], 'they have heard dully' [Bar], 'their ears are stopped up' [CEV], 'they have stopped/stopped up their ears' [REB, TEV], 'they don't hear with their ears' [NCV], 'their ears cannot hear' [NLT]. This verb means to be mentally slow or dull in comprehending [LN]. The idiom βαρέως ἀκούω means 'to be slow to understand, to be mentally dull' [LN].

d. aorist act. indic. of καμμύω (LN 27.50) (BDAG p. 506): 'to close (the eyes)' [BDAG; all translations except Bar; CEV, GW, NRSV], 'to shut' [Bar; GW, NRSV]. The phrase 'they have closed their eyes' is also translated 'your eyes are covered' [CEV]. The idiom καμμύω τοὺς ὀφθαλμούς means to be unwilling to learn and to evaluate something fairly, 'to refuse to learn, to refuse to recognize' [LN].

e. μήποτε (LN 89.62) (BDAG 2.b.α. p. 648): 'lest' [AB, Bar, BECNT, LN; ESV, KJV], 'otherwise' [CBC; NASB, NCV, NIV, REB, TEV], 'in order that…not' [BDAG, LN], 'so that…not' [LN; NET, NRSV], 'so…cannot' [NLT], 'you cannot' [CEV], not explicit [GW]. This conjunction indicates negative purpose, often with the implication of apprehension [LN]. It indicates negated purpose, often expression apprehension [BDAG].

f. aorist act. subj. of συνίημι (LN 32.5) (BDAG p. 972): 'to understand' [BDAG, LN; all translations], 'to comprehend' [BDAG, LN], 'to perceive, to have insight into' [LN]. This verb means to employ one's capacity for understanding and thus to arrive at insight [LN]. It means to have an intelligent grasp of something that challenges one's thinking or practice [BDAG].

g. aorist act. subj. of ἐπιστρέφω (LN 15.90) (BDAG 4.a. p. 382): 'to turn' [AB, Bar, BDAG, BECNT; ESV, NET, NIV, NRSV], 'to turn to (me)' [CEV, GW, NLT, TEV], 'to turn again' [CBC; REB], 'to return' [BDAG, LN; NASB], 'to be converted' [KJV], 'to come back to (me)' [NCV], 'to go back to' [LN]. This verb means to return to a point or area where one has been before, with probable emphasis on turning about [LN]. It means to change one's mind or course of action, for better or worse [BDAG].

h. fut. mid. indic. of ἰάομαι (LN 23.136) (BDAG 2.a. p. 465): 'to heal' [BDAG, LN; all translations except NCV, NLT], 'to let (me) heal' [NLT], 'to be healed' [NCV], 'to cure, to make well' [LN], 'to restore' [BDAG]. This verb means to cause someone to become well again after having been sick [LN]. It means to deliver from a variety of ills or conditions that lie beyond physical maladies [BDAG].

QUESTION—What does it mean that their hearts had become 'dull'?

The picture is of something that has grown fat or thick and consequently so full that it has no ability to respond, meaning that they are closed to what God has to say [BECNT]. It means they were calloused in the sense that they could neither comprehend nor take appropriate action [NAC]. They refused to understand what they were hearing and seeing [TH].

**28:28** Therefore<sup>a</sup> let-it-be known<sup>b</sup> to-you that this salvation<sup>c</sup> of God has-been-sent<sup>d</sup> to-the Gentiles; and they will-listen.<sup>e</sup>"

LEXICON—a. οὖν (LN 89.50): 'therefore,' [CBC, LN; ESV, KJV; NASB, NET, NIV, REB], 'so' [Bar, LN; NLT], 'then' [BECNT, LN; NRSV, TEV], 'consequently, accordingly, so then' [LN], not explicit [AB; CEV, GW, NCV]. This conjunction indicates result, often implying the conclusion of a process of reasoning [LN].

b. γνωστός (LN 28.21) (BDAG 1.a. p. 204): 'known' [AB, Bar, BDAG, BECNT; ESV, KJV, NASB, NRSV], 'what is known, information' [LN]. The phrase 'let it be known' is also translated 'I want you to know' [NCV,

NIV, NLT], 'you need to know' [GW], 'you are to know' [TEV], 'you may be sure' [CEV], 'be advised' [NET], 'take notice' [CBC], 'take note' [REB]. This adjective describes that which is known [LN]. It describes something as being familiar or known [BDAG].

c. σωτήριον (LN 21.30) (BDAG b. p. 986): 'salvation' [all translations except CEV, TEV], 'the message of salvation' [LN; TEV], 'the message about being saved' [LN], 'saving, delivering, preserving, bringing salvation' [BDAG]. The phrase 'salvation of God' is also translated 'God-given salvation' [Bar], 'salvation from God' [NET, NLT], 'God's message of salvation' [TEV]. The phrase 'this salvation of God has been sent to the Gentiles' is also translated 'God wants to save the Gentiles' [CEV], 'God has sent his salvation to people who are not Jews' [GW], 'God has sent his salvation to all nations' [NCV]. This noun denotes the message about God saving people [LN]. It refers to that which pertains to salvation [BDAG].

d. aorist pass. indic. of ἀποστέλλω (LN 15.67) (BDAG 2.a. p. 121): 'to be sent' [BDAG; all translations except CEV, NLT], 'to be offered' [NLT], 'to have something done' [BDAG], 'to send a message, to send word' [LN], not explicit [CEV]. This verb means to send a message, presumably by someone [LN]. It means to dispatch a message [BDAG].

e. fut. mid. indic. of ἀκούω (LN 31.56) (BDAG 4. p. 37): 'to listen' [all translations except KJV, NLT], 'to listen to' [BDAG, LN], 'to hear' [KJV], 'to heed' [BDAG, LN], 'to accept' [LN; NLT], 'to listen and respond, to pay attention and respond' [LN]. This verb means to believe something and to respond to it on the basis of having heard [LN]. It means to give careful attention to [BDAG].

QUESTION—What is the function of γνωστὸν οὖν ἔστω 'therefore let it be known'?

It introduces a declaration that is important and one they should listen to [PNTC]. It is a strong and solemn way of saying that this is something that they must know [BECNT, TH].

QUESTION—To what does τοῦτο 'this' refer in the phrase 'this salvation'?

It points back to the healing of Israel referred to back in v. 27 in the citation from Isaiah [PNTC].

QUESTION—What is to be understood by the use of the pronoun αὐτοί 'they'?

It gives emphasis to the fact that the Gentiles will listen [PNTC, TH].

**28:29 And he-having-said these-things, the Jews left, having much discussion among themselves.**

TEXT—Some manuscripts include v. 29, which reads "And he having said these things, the Jews left, having much discussion among themselves." GNT omits this verse with an A rating, to indicate its omission was regarded to be certain. Only KJV, NASB, and NCV include this variant reading. NASB and NCV include it in brackets.

**DISCOURSE UNIT—28:30–31** [AB, NAC, NICNT, PNTC]. The topic is bold witness to all [NAC], welcoming all with the gospel [PNTC], the gospel advances without hindrance in Rome [NICNT], Paul's two-year imprisonment [AB].

**DISCOURSE UNIT—28:30** [EBC]. The topic is continued ministry for two years.

**28:30** And he-stayed[a] two whole years in his-own rented-quarters[b] and welcomed[c] all-those coming to him,

LEXICON—a. aorist act. indic. of ἐμμένω (LN 85.55) (BDAG 1.a. p. 322): 'to stay' [AB, Bar, BDAG, CBC, LN; CEV, NASB, NCV, NIV, REB], 'to live' [BECNT; ESV, NET, NLT, NRSV, TEV], 'to dwell' [KJV], 'to remain' [BDAG, LN], not explicit [GW]. This verb means to remain in the same place over a period of time [BDAG, LN]. It means to stay in the same place over a period of time [BDAG].

  b. μίσθωμα (LN 57.175) (BDAG p. 654): 'rented quarters' [NASB, NET], 'rented house' [BDAG; CEV, NCV, NIV], 'rented' [LN], 'what is rented' [BDAG], 'hired house' [Bar; KJV], 'hired lodging' [AB], 'hired' [LN]. The phrase 'in his own rented quarters' is also translated 'in a place he rented for himself' [TEV], 'Paul rented a place to live' [GW], 'at his own expense' [BECNT, CBC; ESV, NLT, NRSV, REB]. This noun denotes that which has been hired or rented (but in the NT occurring only in reference to a rented dwelling) [LN].

  c. imperf. mid. indic. of ἀποδέχομαι (LN 34.53) (BDAG 1. p. 109): 'to welcome' [BDAG, BECNT, LN; CEV, ESV, GW, NASB, NCV, NET, NIV, NLT, NRSV, TEV], 'to receive' [AB, Bar, LN; KJV], 'to accept, to have as a guest' [LN]. This verb is also translated as a prepositional phrase: 'with a welcome' [CBC; REB]. This verb means to accept the presence of a person with friendliness [LN]. It means to receive someone favorably [BDAG].

QUESTION—Would 'all' in this verse include both Gentiles and Jews, or only Gentiles?

It would include Jews as well as Gentiles [Bar, NAC, PNTC].

**DISCOURSE UNIT—28:31** [EBC]. The topic is a summary statement.

**28:31** proclaiming[a] the kingdom of-God and teaching[b] the-things about the Lord Jesus Christ with all boldness[c] (and) without-hindrance.[d]

LEXICON—a. pres. act. participle of κηρύσσω (LN 33.256) (BDAG 2.b.β. p. 543): 'to proclaim' [CBC; ESV, NET, NIV, NLT, NRSV, REB], 'to preach' [AB, Bar, BECNT, LN; CEV, KJV, NASB, NCV, TEV], 'to spread the message' [GW], 'to proclaim aloud' [BDAG]. This verb means to publicly announce religious truths and principles while urging acceptance and compliance [LN]. It means to make public declarations [BDAG].

b. pres. act. participle of διδάσκω (LN 33.224): 'to teach' [LN; all translations]. This verb means to provide instruction in a formal or informal setting [LN].
c. παρρησία (LN 25.128) (BDAG 2. p. 781): 'boldness' [Bar, LN; ESV, NET, NIV, NRSV, TEV], 'confidence' [KJV], 'courage' [LN], 'openness' [NASB], 'openness to the public' [BDAG]. The phrase 'with all boldness' is also translated 'very boldly' [GW], 'boldly' [NCV, NLT], 'publicly' [AB], 'quite openly' [BECNT, CBC; REB], 'bravely' [CEV]. This noun denotes a state of boldness and confidence, sometimes implying intimidating circumstances [LN].
d. ἀκωλύτως (LN 13.151) (BDAG p. 40): 'without hindrance' [AB, Bar, BDAG, CBC, LN; ESV, NIV, NRSV, REB], 'unhindered' [BECNT; NASB], 'without restriction' [LN; NET], '(with) freedom' [TEV], 'freely' [LN]. This word is also translated as a phrase: 'no one tried to stop him' [CEV, NLT], 'no one stopped him' [GW, NCV], 'no man forbidding him' [KJV]. This adverb describes a condition of not being prevented [LN].

QUESTION—What is the relation between the words 'proclaiming' and 'teaching'?

They are used synonymously here [Bar, PNTC]. He proclaimed the message of the kingdom by teaching the facts about Jesus [CBC]. Preaching and teaching describe the specifics of how he welcomed those who came to him [TH].

QUESTION—What is encompassed by the term 'kingdom of God' as Luke uses it here to describe the content of Paul's message?

It has been used in six previous passages in Acts, and describes God's rule over sin, death, and everything else that hinders his purpose of the salvation of the human race; the rule of God is realized in the fact that Jesus is now enthroned as Messiah at God's right hand [PNTC]. Jesus has the authority and right to rule over God's kingdom [BECNT]. 'Kingdom of God' is a summary of Christian teaching [Bar]. Mention of the kingdom also forms an inclusio (or 'bookend effect') with the beginning of Acts where the kingdom is mentioned [BECNT, NAC, PNTC].

QUESTION—What is implied by the term ἀκωλύτως 'without hindrance'?

Here it means that the Roman authorities did not restrict the preaching of the message in any way [NAC, NICNT, PNTC, TH]. 'Boldness' describes Paul's own attitude, and 'without hindrance' indicates tolerance on the part of the Roman authorities [TH]. The fact that the preaching of the message of the kingdom is without hindrance suggests that entrance into the kingdom is also without hindrance [BECNT]. Even though the human witnesses experience suffering and trial, God's message still triumphs [NAC]. This term is often used in legal contexts [Bar, NAC, NICNT].

QUESTION—What was the outcome of Paul's trial, and why does Luke not tell what happened?

Paul was probably released after coming before the emperor for trial [EBC, NAC, PNTC]. Luke's reason for not mentioning the outcome of the trial was probably because he was not writing Paul's story, but the story of the advance of the gospel [EBC, NAC, PNTC, TNTC], and the preaching of the gospel continues [BECNT, TNTC]. Leaving it in a seemingly unfinished state as he does implies that the proclamation of the gospel is ongoing [EBC, PNTC], and will continue until the kingdom is finally commutated in Christ [EBC].